Starter Guide For Windows® 10 IoT Enterprise 2nd Edition

By

Sean D. Liming and John R. Malin

Annabooks™

Copyright

Published in the United States by

Annabooks, LLC.
69 Bordeaux
Rancho Mirage, CA 92270
www.annabooks.com

ISBN-13: 979-8-9854172-0-3

Dedication

To all of our clients and customers who have purchased books, attended classes, and hired us for consulting services. It continues to be an incredible run since the days of Windows NT Embedded.

Table of Contents

Preface

It is hard to believe my first book, *Windows NT Embedded Step-by-Step*, was published 22 years ago. Back then, developers would laugh at the idea of using Windows NT in an embedded system. 5 Windows Embedded/IoT versions, 7 books, and many white papers later, I am still writing about creating a custom Windows operating system for embedded/IoT systems. The growth of PC technologies has played a big role in the success of Windows and will continue for the foreseeable future.

The journey has had its highs and lows. There have been many great people at Microsoft to work with and a few whose time at Microsoft was not short enough. There have been many products that have come and gone, but Windows Embedded/IoT has remained. With the focus on Azure and billions of IoT devices connecting to the cloud, Windows Embedded/IoT is not going away any time soon, which brings me to this second edition. The first edition of this book was a scramble to get something out for developers to allow them to get started. Microsoft was pushing a new build tool that was dead on arrival. I had to counter this push in forums and with clients with System Image Manager as still the best tool. The first edition was not as completed as I would have liked and reader feedback confirmed this. This second edition is a rewrite that includes the development workflow that I have been evolving since Windows XP Embedded. Subjects like security have a deeper coverage as Microsoft has clarified the terminology and technologies being implemented. I added coverage of writing .NET 6 applications for microcontroller I/O and demonstrate an application connecting a system to Azure IoT Central. Throughout the book, I have added various tips and tricks to address the little things that get lost when putting a system together.

The process of installing Windows on an Embedded System is not a simple task. Designing for the full life cycle of the product is a major focus that is often overlooked by developers and needs to be addressed. The second edition covers many of these life-cycle topics. I hope you find this new edition helpful for your project, and please let me know if you have any feedback.

Sean D. Liming
Rancho Mirage, CA

Acknowledgements

We have been told that authors are nothing but monkeys behind a keyboard. Obviously, the book would not have been possible without the aid of several people and companies. Our apologies if we forgot anyone.

We cannot mention them by name, but there are many Microsoft PMs who have helped over the years. Their responses to inquiries and sharing of product information helped to make books like this one possible.

Special thanks go to Kim Hartman and all of TenAsys for letting us try out and write about their real-time solutions for Windows Embedded. A brief chapter covers these solutions, and you can find out more about INtime in the book *Real-Time Development from Theory to Practice Featuring TenAsys® INtime®*.

WinSystems has been a long-time partner, and we have used several of their PC boards over the years to develop various exercises.

The team at TabletKiosk has provided us with complete mobile solutions that have been helpful in a few exercises and the POS API projects.

Also special thanks to ASUS for getting us their IMX8P-IM-A, which was used to develop some of the microcontroller exercises. We hope to get more coverage for Windows IoT on ARM and present it in another guide.

Finally, we would like to thank our family members who have put up with us as we focus on writing another book.

Annabooks

Annabooks provides a unique approach to embedded system services with multiple support levels. Our different offerings include books, articles, training, and project consulting. Current publications and courses have focused on embedded PC architecture and Windows Embedded, which reach a wide audience from Fortune 500 companies to small organizations. We will continue to expand our future services into new technologies and unique topics as they become available

Books and eBooks

Java and Eclipse for Computer Science

Open Software Stack for the Intel® Atom™ Processor

Professional's Guide to POS for Windows Runtime

Professional's Guide to POS for .NET

Real-Time Development from Theory to Practice

The PC Handbook

Training Courses

Windows® 10 IoT Enterprise Training Course

Please contact us for more information on consultation and availability.

Web: www.annabooks.com

1 Start Here

If you are new to developing with Windows for devices, welcome to Windows 10 IoT Enterprise. If you have been using Windows Embedded, welcome back! Windows 10 IoT Enterprise is really Windows 10 Enterprise LTSC, which is the same Windows OS that is used on desktop and laptop systems everywhere. Taking the desktop operating system and integrating it into a device is nothing new. MS-DOS was put into many embedded systems back in the day. In fact, if you have been following my articles and books since those early days, all I can say is wow, thank you for following my work and continuing to use Windows Embedded/IoT. My first book was on Windows NT Embedded, and I have covered every major Windows Embedded/IoT release since. Although this book is not covering a major release, this second edition dives deeper into the development workflow, clearer coverage of security features, and new features that have been added to Windows 10 Enterprise LTSC 2021.

The chapter title is more relevant than just a cute title. Beyond the discussions about background, requirements, and the book structure, I think it is important to also cover topics that I have covered in my training courses but not covered in my previous books. The chapter will end with a discussion of licensing, activation, and some important considerations to think about before you start designing your system.

1.1 Windows 10: Another New Direction for Microsoft and IoT

Microsoft has been constantly changing direction in the Embedded/IoT space since the days of MS-DOS. The overall company switch to Azure and Cloud focus has severed them well the past few years, but the device operating system strategy has taken a turn. Windows 10 was released in 2015. There were three offerings: Windows IoT 10 Enterprise, Windows 10 IoT Mobile, and Windows 10 IoT Core. Since Windows CE was dropped, Windows 10 IoT Core was supposed to fill the needs of a small operating system. Windows Phone died and along with it the failed concept of the Universal Windows Platform (UWP). Windows 10 IoT Core only supported UWP GUI apps, and the OS build process was cumbersome compared to Windows 10 IoT Enterprise. Windows 10 IoT Core has been dropped and the concepts to support ARM 64 processors and reduced footprint have been merged into Windows 10 Enterprise LTSC 2021.

Note: Only Intel Architecture processors will be covered in this book. Windows on ARM 64 will be covered in a different guide.

Windows 10 IoT Mobile was a private release between Microsoft and mobile device makers. The product has slowly disappeared. Windows 10 IoT Enterprise is the only product that remains. Since Cloud is the focus and billions of devices will be connected to the Cloud, Microsoft needed something to get into the microcontroller space. Microsoft pushed forward with a system-on-chip solution called Azure Sphere, and then acquired Express Logic, which created the ThreadX RTOS. ThreadX is now known as Azure RTOS. Last but not least, the Azure team developed some Azure IoT SDKs to support other MCU devices. Only time will tell if the direction changes again, but Windows has never wavered since the days of Windows NT Embedded, which makes Windows a good bet to be around for some time.

1.2 Windows XP Embedded and Windows Embedded Standard 7

Before Windows 10 IoT Enterprise was released, there were Windows Embedded 8 Standard and Windows Embedded 8.1 Industry releases. For those who stuck with Windows XP Embedded or Windows Embedded Standard 7, you missed out on some big changes and a whole lot of fun development that Windows 8 offered… no, you didn't miss anything. What you avoided was a lot of pain and agony that these releases brought with them. There was a dynamic shift in the build process. WES8 was the last hurrah for the Windows Embedded team. Around the release of WES8, the Windows Embedded team merged with the Windows Desktop team. All the Windows Embedded folks left for greener pastures, and the new team started to apply desktop thinking to Windows Embedded. The biggest desktop issue was activation. Some good things came out of this merger. Windows Embedded/IoT is a major release along with Windows. The Lockdown features are now mainstream and tested along with the rest of Windows. The development tools that this book covers are the same for desktop, as well as, Embedded/IoT. Here is a short list of changes:

- Special OS build tools like Target Designer and Image Configuration Editor (ICE) are gone. System Image Manager (SIM), free from the Windows ADK, is used to create custom images. SIM is used for all versions of Windows desktop and server starting with Windows 7. ICE was based on SIM so those going from WES7 to Windows 10 IoT Enterprise will have a little easier transition.
- No more creating components. Files are placed in a distribution share and the distribution share can exist anywhere in the file system.
- EWF, FBWF, and Registry Filter have been replaced with Unified Write Filter
- Componentization – there are no components like XPE and WES7 offered. You get the full OS and have to strip out or disable the items you don't want
- DISM can be used to capture a full disk drive to a Full Flash Update (FFU) file.
- Improved malware protection. New security features hook into the firmware to create a trusted boot environment. Other new security features protect the running system using hypervisors and security policies.
- Activation is optional. WES8 forced activation, which was a show-stopper. More on this later in the chapter.
- The "Different Shells for Different Users" concept that I wrote about for XP Embedded is now a feature called Shell Launcher.
- The other concept of hotkey blocking that I wrote about for XP Embedded and was turned into the Keyboard Filter feature in WES 7 has been carried through to Windows 10.
- The ability to add your own boot splash screen in XP Embedded is gone. You have to put the splash screen into the firmware and boot UEFI mode.
- Better controls to disable Microsoft branding have been added.

- Booting from a USB flash disk is no longer supported.
- OS installation from a USB flash is supported.
- Hardware devices can be blocked from loading using Group Policies.
- Windows applications can access microcontroller IO like UART, GPIO, SPI, I2C, PWM, and ADC.
- There are different licensing levels available based on the processor used.

Finally, Windows 10 operating system has many new features and improvements over its predecessors. There are probably more changes, but you get the idea that Windows 10 IoT Enterprise is a different beast. Regardless of if you are coming from any of the older Windows Embedded releases, you will have to start development from scratch. The transition from WES7 is a little easier as the tools are similar.

1.3 What about Windows 11?

Sometimes projects sound good in concept but don't quite make it to market. These projects get reborn into something else. For example, Windows CE is born out of canceled WinPad and Pulsar projects back in the early 1990s. Windows 11 comes from the canceled Windows 10X project. When Windows 11 was released, it was a shock to the Windows community. Trying to avoid leaks, Microsoft didn't tell anyone that they were working on Windows 11. Since there was no feedback during its development, the community support is limited and there have been reports of issues or features people don't like. The new Taskbar being one of them. Microsoft, trying to be like Apple, is never a good thing. Windows 11 only brings new GUI interface options to the table. Since there is limited community testing of the product, I strongly suggest waiting for Windows 11 to get more mature. There is no Windows 11 IoT Enterprise release as of this writing so stick with Windows 10 IoT Enterprise.

1.4 About the Book

Windows is a very large topic to cover. The goal of the book is to provide a cohesive narrative around using the System Image Manager (SIM) tool to configure and deploy Windows 10 IoT Enterprise on Intel Architecture platforms. The book is written in a learn-by-doing style with multiple hands-on exercises to get a feel for the tools and features. The first edition was light in content, so this second edition has reworked the original topics to build on the recommended development workflow, the latest information, additional tools, and utilities now available, and lessons learned since the release of the first edition. The book is split into three parts. The first part runs from Chapter 2 through Chapter 9 and covers the Windows operating system custom integration and system architecture:

- Chapter 2 is the foundation, which covers the Windows 10 IoT Enterprise development workflow. The details of using SIM to create a custom image are now in one chapter.
- Chapters 3 and 4 cover performance options.
- Chapter 5 covers the footprint reduction process.
- Chapters 6 through 8 break the concepts of locking down a system into 3 parts. Chapter 6 covers the user experience, Chapter 7 covers UWF and the Keyboard filter, and Chapter 8 covers security.
- Chapter 9 discusses updating the system in the field.

The second part runs from Chapter 10 through Chapter 16 and covers the Windows Runtime API for the microcontroller IO (GPIO, SPI, I2C, UART, ADC, and PWM). Multiple programming examples demonstrate how to use the Windows Runtime API to access these IO from a user mode application.

- Chapter 10 discusses RHPROXY and the firmware requirements that must be met to use the Windows Runtime API. Available development boards that expose the microcontroller IO on pin headers are covered.
- Chapter 11 discusses the GPIO Windows Runtime API.
- Chapter 12 discusses the UART and the differences with the older Serial Port class.
- Chapter 13 discusses the SPI bus, and Chapter 14 covers the I2C bus. Both chapters show examples using breakout boards for temperature, barometric pressure, humidity, and ADC sensors with serial interfaces.
- Chapter 15 and Chapter 16 cover PWM and ADC respectively. Currently, there is no hardware available that supports these IO, but the chapters cover some preliminary details.

The final part, Chapter 17, puts all the chapters together with a weather station project that sends data to Azure IoT Central.

1.5 Development Machine and Software Requirements

To do the hands-on exercises, you will need the following develop environment:

- Development system with Windows 10 Pro or Enterprise (Earlier versions of Windows are not supported).
- Windows 10 IoT Enterprise LTSC 2021 ISO.
- Windows Features on Demand ISOs – these ISOs contain the language packages, .NET Framework 3 runtime, and other support features.
- Windows Assessment and Deployment Kit version 2004 downloaded from Microsoft.com.
- Windows PE add-on for the ADK version 2004 from Microsoft.com.
- Visual Studio 2022 for developing applications.
- Rufus – Rufus is a disk formatting utility that can be downloaded from www.rufus.ie.
- The Shell Launcher, Keyboard, and UWF utilities from Annabooks.com.

There will be other utilities and hardware discussed in various chapters in the book. There are some files that go along with some of the exercises. The exercise files are available on the book's website at www.annabooks.com.

1.6 Target Hardware Requirements: Chose the Correct Target Hardware that Addressed Performance and Security

This is a long section title for a reason. Choosing the right target hardware is extremely important. Overall system performance is directly correlated to the selected CPU, the amount of RAM, and boot media. There are some performance options in Windows, but they have little impact on the system compared to hardware. Also, the new Windows security features are getting hooked into the hardware and firmware. Booting from UEFI firmware is the norm. Right now, SecureBoot and a TPM chip are optional features, but in Windows 11 these items will be a requirement. The following is an overview of hardware considerations:

- A target PC with a 64-bit processor, 1 GHz or faster CPU with Intel VT-x support is recommended. Docs.microsoft.com has a list of processors that support Windows 10.
- 4 GB RAM minimum. 2GB of RAM will not be enough for a Windows 64-bit OS.
- 32 GB Hard drive space available.
- Network connectivity is recommended.
- Two USB flash disks 16 GB or higher.
- UEFI - SecureBoot feature is an option but recommended for security.
- Optional: TPM chip, but recommended for security

If you want a custom boot splash screen image, you will have to work with your hardware vendor to have the boot splash screen put into the UEFI firmware.

1.7 The License and Activation Story

That last thing, but not least item you will need is a Windows run-time key and stickers. Windows 10 IoT Enterprise is a licensed product. For every unit you ship, you have to pay Microsoft a royalty. Since the development tools are free, this is the "Shared Success Model" that has been in place for a couple of decades. The tools are cheap so you can get up and running quickly without a large upfront investment, and Microsoft gets paid on the backend when you ship your product. Your company needs to sign a license agreement with Microsoft, get a runtime activation key, and purchase stickers for every unit you ship. It sounds simple, doesn't it? Now for a little background.

1.7.1 Getting Signed Up with the CLA

Within Microsoft, there are two sales groups. One group covers OEMs that make general-purpose Windows PCs and Servers, Dell, HP, Lenovo, Samsung, Sony, etc., for example. The other group covers OEMs that build Embedded/IoT devices. It's this latter group that oversees direct sales and distribution for Windows 10 IoT. Buried deep in the Windows IoT website is a document that lists all the Windows Embedded/IoT Distributors that are around the world. If you are not purchasing millions of licenses, then you will be going through a distributor for Windows Licenses. There are different types of distributors on the list. Some distributors sell services, some are electronics distributors, and some are PC manufacturers that can only provide licenses on the devices that they sell. For example, Dell can sell Windows 10 Enterprise licenses only for Dell hardware. When you are ready to get licensing information, you should look up the distributor that is in your region or the distributor that best fits your company's use of Windows 10. The licensing steps are simple:

1. Contact a distributor and ask about the licensing process.

2. If your company has not already signed the Microsoft Client License Agreement (CLA), then someone in your company with the appropriate authority will have to sign the CLA. Take care who signs the CLA, as they will be the contact for Microsoft for all future communications that follow.

Signing a Microsoft CLA to license products from Microsoft is only the first step. Ordering software, getting the latest updates, using the right tools, managing license runtime key requests, and purchasing license stickers are also part of the OEM process. Your distributor should be able to help you with the whole process. Just remember to ask for the runtime key. You will only get one key per company! So larger companies with different divisions need to work with the distributor to get multiple keys. The issue with limited keys is the limited number of activations. That will be covered next.

When you are ready to ship a product, license stickers must be placed on each unit that ships with a Windows 10 Enterprise LTSC Operating System. The stickers are ordered through the Microsoft distributor. Each sticker has a unique serial number key. THIS UNIQUE SERIAL KEY IS NOT THE PRODUCT RUNTIME KEY TO BE USED IN THE IMAGE. The unique serial number key should be entered into a spreadsheet or database along with the serial number of the unit and where it was shipped.

1.7.2 Runtime key and Activation

Ah! Windows Activation. I have said it before, and I will say it again: Windows activation for Embedded/IoT systems is as useful as putting screen doors on a submarine. From MS-DOS to Windows Embedded Standard 7 (WES7), Embedded/IoT OEMs didn't have to worry about activating each system before shipping. Starting with Windows Embedded 8 Standard, activation became a requirement. There were some OEMs, like slot machine vendors, who have to do an image CRC check on OS startup. These OEMs couldn't move off of WES7 because activation would break the CRC check. Microsoft compromised with Windows 10. A runtime license key (aka Product Key) is still required to ship a product; but any Windows 10 device that doesn't connect to the Internet, will remain in a "Deferred Activation State". As soon as a system connects to the Internet for the first time, the activation mechanisms kick in, but sometimes it doesn't. This can be trouble for Embedded/IoT OEMs if they are not careful. Here are a couple of scenarios:

Scenario 1: A system gets connected to the Internet at some point and is later disconnected without being activated. If the system doesn't get activated after 30 days, an overlay appears on the screen saying that activation is required. Not good if this happens at a customer site; especially if you are trying to hide that Windows is running on the system.

Scenario 2: If the Unified Write Filter (UWF) is used to protect the system's C drive. The system must be activated before UWF is enabled. Each runtime license key is limited to 50,000 activations, which is enough for most OEMs. If the system fails to be activated, UWF is enabled, and the system is connected to the Internet, each time the system boots, activation is attempted in the background. The activation information gets put into the system, but it will be lost on a reboot because UWF is enabled. All writes to the disk are lost on reboot. So, you can burn through the 50,000 activations for a key pretty quickly in this scenario.

Scenario 3: A large corporation with multiple divisions using the same key. One division gets a message on the system that the full number of activations have been used up. Thinking they are the only ones using the key, they find out that other divisions are also using the same key. I have seen this happen a couple of times already.

The Windows 10 IoT Enterprise OEM Product Kit (OPK) comes with a test key that can be used during development to avoid burning activations. You will put this into the answer files. Once you are ready to ship, you can put the actual runtime key into the Sysprep unattended file. Later chapters will discuss how to do this.

Activation is not fun, but it has to be addressed. If you are doing a CRC check on startup, where the system is on a closed, non-Internet-connected network or your system has no networking connectivity at all, you don't have to activate the system. From the earlier example, slot machines fall into this category. Everybody else will have to activate each system in manufacturing before it ships to the customer. For those in this category, the recommendation is to have each system in production connected to the Internet. When each system boots the first time, the system will be activated. Fielded systems that get a full OS replacement will have to be activated, which throws a wrinkle into the number of activations, as well as, how the system gets activated.

To help check that a system is activated and to activate manually, Windows 10 still includes a VB script tool called SLMGR.VBS that assists with activation. Since PowerShell is replacing VB scripting, you can check the activation status using the following PowerShell script:

```
$activationStatus = Get-WmiObject -query "SELECT * FROM
SoftwareLicensingProduct WHERE PartialProductKey <> null AND
ApplicationId='55c92734-d682-4d71-983e-d6ec3f16059f' AND LicenseIsAddon=False"
#Write-Host $activationStatus.LicenseStatus
switch ($activationStatus.LicenseStatus) {
 0 {$status = "Unlicensed"}
 1 {$status = "Licensed"}
 2 {$status = "Out-Of-Box Grace Period"}
 3 {$status = "Out-Of-Tolerance Grace Period"}
 4 {$status = "Non-Genuine Grace Period"}
 5 {$status = "Notification"}
 6 {$status = "Extended Grace"}
 default {$out.Status = "Unknown value"}
 }
 Write-Host $status
```

You can also activate the image using PowerShell:

```
$mycomputer = gc env:computername
$runtimekey = "XXXXX-XXXXX-XXXXX-XXXXX-XXXXX"  #where this is the alpha-
numeric runtime key
$service = get-wmiObject -query "select * from SoftwareLicensingService" -
computername $mycomputer
$service.InstallProductKey($runtimekey)
$service.RefreshLicenseStatus()
```

The Volume Activation Management Tool (VAMT) is part of the Windows ADK. VAMT can be used to check how many activations are left for a given key. Chapter 2 has an exercise on how to set up and use the tool.

1.8 Three Things to Keep in Mind – Don't Say I Didn't Warn You

With almost 30 years in the market space, I have seen many successful projects, but I have seen some failures as well. Some projects get trapped by misinformed decisions. There will be design suggestions throughout the book, but there are some concepts and ideas that I need to share before you get started to make sure you go down the right path.

1.8.1 Application Development – Go with .NET 6, UWP IS DEAD!

When it comes to developing applications, Microsoft has opened up Visual Studio and acquired Xamarin to target operating systems beyond Windows. The goal is to connect devices to Azure, which makes sense. The support for different operating systems with all the different libraries is forcing Microsoft to bring things together, which has taken some time. The current plan is the movement to .NET (formally .NET Core) and WinUI. .NET Framework is still supported, but .NET 6 is now available in Visual Studio 2022. WinUI is relatively new as of this writing. WPF + .NET 6 applications will be used in the later chapters that cover the microcontroller IO. The application development story is evolving, so stay tuned for more improvements and a clearer direction.

Before the movement toward a single programming paradigm, Microsoft created some application types that seemed like a good idea at the time but have proven to be very difficult. The Universal Windows Platform (UWP) was something introduced with the new Windows 8 interface and store. Again, trying to be like Apple, is never good. A UWP app is a pain to install, difficult to set up as a shell, and makes Sysprep fail. Since Windows Phone died, creating UWP applications has become passé. YOU SHOULD NOT CREATE UWP APPLICATIONS.!!! UWP IS DEAD! It is not sleeping or resting, UWP IS DEAD!

1.8.2 Windows is not for Everyone – Linux versus Windows

There is more than one RTOS or operating system to choose from. Windows provides a rich graphical interface, great application development tools, and the leading technologies get implemented on Windows, first. The problem is that it is big, requires some big hardware resources, and is limited to higher-end processors. Linux has reached into a variety of devices from consumer electronics like smartphones and TVs to big server systems running Cloud applications. Out of curiosity when Microsoft was fumbling with Windows Embedded in 2008, I took some time to dig into Linux. I was impressed. The Linux Foundation was very helpful in my effort to learn what was available, and I discovered the Yocto Project, which was similar to XP Embedded in concept. I wrote a book from the perspective of someone going from Windows to Linux, which helped me when I was having discussions with developers going from Linux to Windows.

There have been a few times when clients came to me wanting to use Windows, but after having a discussion and learning about their personnel and project details, Linux was the better solution. One client chose to use Windows for the wrong reasons. The client created a headless system that took digital data off the Internet and processed it via a Fast Fourier

Transform (FFT) and did some other tasks. Being deeply rooted in Linux, he didn't understand all the services and registry keys in Windows and was complaining about all the running processes that he didn't understand. I told the client that the system really needs to be a Linux system. His explanation was that Intel had created an FFT Performance Primitive for Windows. I had to explain that the reason Intel created these performance primitives is that Visual Studio compilers will not output the best possible performance for an FFT. The FFT Performance Primitive libraries are optimized to take advantage of the most optimal registers and instructions that Intel Architecture can provide. A simple Internet search shows that there are many FFT libraries available for Linux.

Then there are those who take a Linux approach to Windows. One Linux guru was so scared of Windows XP Embedded that he tracked every single component (10,000+) that went into their image and then compounded their development process by linking everything to CVS with Linux commands. The image architecture was so bad they didn't roll back the image and ran into the hit and miss of copying a live image to another system for manufacturing. The end result was an image process that would normally take a few hours took a few days to walk through 100+ manual steps.

There are a few more stories to share, but in short, my biggest suggestion is this:

- If you have Linux developers stick with Linux. You will not be able to convert Linux developers to Windows.
- If you have Windows developers, stick with Windows.
- If you cannot decide try both and the one that gets you to production faster and makes sense for your overall business support model is the one to choose. Or, talk to a consultant who focuses on Windows or Linux to get their perspective on the system.

1.8.3 Microsoft's Manufacturing Guide versus the My Recommended Workflow

For years, I have written about developing custom Windows Embedded/IoT images. My books have gone all over the world, and have helped many developers get their projects moving forward. I apply my experiences with the product, to provide the best practices to get a product to market in the most direct way possible. Okay so I am tooting my horn, but my successful track record speaks for itself.

Microsoft has turned a blind eye to documentation. Microsoft, over the years, has made attempts to write up the development process for Windows CE and Windows Embedded with limited success. In my first learning session with Windows CE, Microsoft took two days just to discuss building the image. This didn't include all the features that needed to be covered. When developing my own Windows CE training course, I took what I learned and minimized the image building to a half-day session, leaving a few days to talk about the import features. The Windows IoT Core build process was complex. They did a decent job with the online documentation, but some important pieces were missing such as the code signing certificate. This brings me to the Windows IoT Enterprise Manufacturing Guide, which went in a direction that has confused more than one developer. I take a practical approach to development, and this development guide goes in a non-intuitive, round-about way to develop an image.

The suggested development process is not sustainable over the lifecycle of the product:

- Injecting device drivers and features on demand into the install.wim is difficult to debug and correct when something goes wrong.
- Transitioning to new hardware requires going through the whole process rather than just switching out device drivers.
- Transitioning from one LTSC version to the next LTSC version forces one to go through the whole process. The workflow in the second chapter makes it easy to transition by re-using the distribution share and recreating the answer file with the new catalog.
- If the install.wim is lost or corrupted, one has to start all over.
- Something that has happened many times is that the original image developer will move on to a new project or company. Building images is not a career-forwarded job, but a boring task that someone wants someone else to perform, eventually. The next person that comes in to build the image will not know if the install.wim is good or not.

The overuse of audit mode and Sysprep creates the most confusion. The designers of the Windows installer and answer files did a great job in addressing the needs of a variety of developers. Audit mode is intended for IT or PC OEMs to create a generic operating system that they can store someplace to later apply to a production system. All the tasks that need to be performed to set up the image can be done without having to go into audit mode.

One still has to create an answer file for the final Sysprep for manufacturing so there is no getting around this.

The Manufacturing Guide appears to have come from someone at Microsoft engaging with a thin client OEM about how to build an image thinking that this was the way to build an image for everyone. The Manufacturing Guide is a good example of the Dunning-Kruger Effect. It is not the way to build an image for a device.

The recommended Workflow discussed in chapter 2 doesn't require injecting items into the install.wim or going into audit mode to add features. The process keeps the Microsoft-provided files separate from the custom files you want to add to the image. When the next LTSC version is available you can easily migrate the distribution share to the next project and transfer the answer file information to a new answer file. The workflow is designed to get you from a starting point to a working image within a few hours. You don't have to take my word for it. Follow chapter 2 and later chapter 17, so you can test the workflow for yourself.

1.9 Summary: Stay on the Right Path

I hope that the last section gave you food for thought. After many years of doing Windows OS development, I need to be direct about the trappings of going down the wrong path. Many copies of my books have been sold to many developers worldwide, I have taught many classes on the subject, and I have consulted on a variety of devices. Even though I try to evangelize a process, developers seem to go off the rails when building custom Windows images. Misinformation and wrong choices can hurt a project. Some developers make Windows image development more complicated than it has to be, and some make Windows image development complicated for job security. As a consultant, I am sometimes called in to fix the mess. Developing custom Windows images can be boring and a chore when there are other job responsibilities to perform, but Windows development should not be treated lightly.

My core belief is that Windows should not be the critical path of a project. The reason for the books, white papers, and training courses is to provide information about the features available. With the right knowledge, one should be able to successfully design a product for the whole product lifecycle. Enough of being on my soapbox. Let's move on to the next chapter and start building custom images.

2 SIM and the Development Workflow for Intel Architecture

The merging of IoT Core and IoT Enterprise means Windows 10 Enterprise LTSC 2021 supports both Intel and ARM64 processors. As it turns out, different processor architectures require different operating system build processes. For Intel® Architecture, nothing much has changed. System Image Manager (SIM), from the ADK, is used to create a customized operating system. ARM64 development is completely different, which will not be covered in this book. This chapter will interweave the development workflow and SIM with hands-on exercises to walk through the building and deployment of a basic image.

2.1.1 High-Level Overview

Developing a Windows image is more than just setting up a few components and settings, the image has to be architected to address functionality, security, and upgradability.

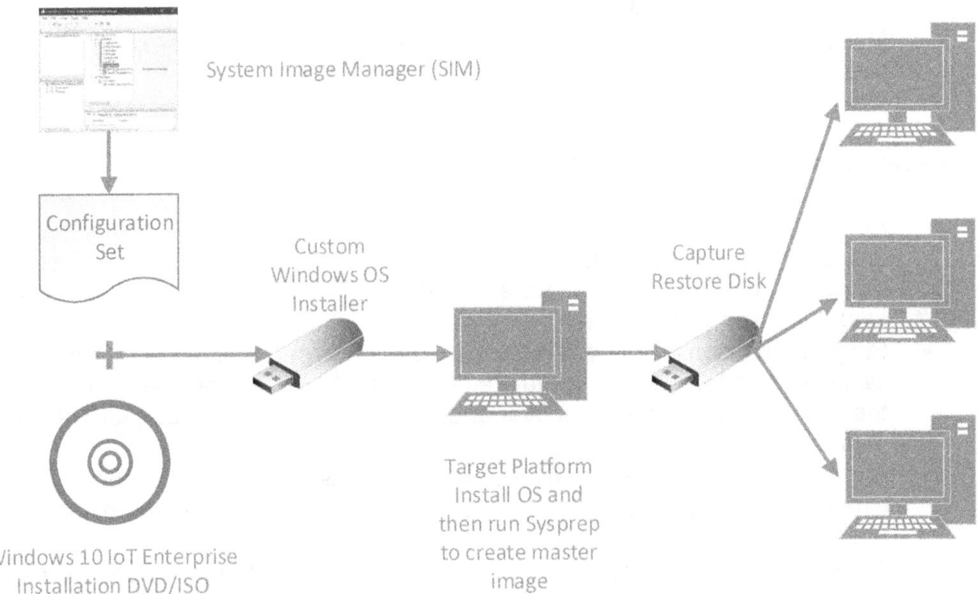

The development workflow goes back to XP Embedded, and to some extent, the NT Embedded approach. As the OS has changed, so have the individual steps. The workflow has the same goal, which is to create an image for production; but it takes a little work.

- The Basics – This step lays the foundation for the rest of the workflow. There are some basic items to gather to set up the project. This chapter breaks this first part of the workflow into 4 parts.
- Building on the start – Once the answer file and distribution share are set up, you can add your custom applications, device drivers, etc. that make your product unique. At this point, determine if the features that are set up are in the master image or each clone image.
- Lockdown – Some of the lockdown features, like Embedded Boot and Embedded Login, can be added in an earlier step; but setting up and testing UWF, Shell Launcher, and the Keyboard filter has to be its own step. We want to make sure that the main application is set up correctly and working before locking down the system. I have some utilities that can help with this.
- Sysprep – Running Sysprep to create the master image is a critical step. You don't want to copy a live system as-is without Sysprep or you could run into problems. Some planning has to go into the Sysprep unattended file to address how each clone boots for the first time in manufacturing.
- Master Image – Sysprep and testing of the master image are really one step, but what mechanism is used to capture and deploy the master image in manufacturing, Q&A, and development needs to be fleshed out.

The goals of this development workflow are as follows:

- Automate the installation of the OS as much as possible. The answer file, distribution share, and synchronous commands should be set up to eliminate as many manual steps as possible to remove human error. Keep in mind not everything can be automated.
- Simplify migration to a new Windows 10 release as much as possible. When a new Windows 10 LTSC version (or future Windows 11 LTSC) is released, you can take the build files and move them over and adapt them to the new project within a few minutes.
- Simplify support for new hardware. Hardware inevitably goes to end-of-life; and when it does, all you have to do is gather the new device drivers and link them to the answer file.
- Provide for sustainability. Anyone picking up the project in the future will be able to modify and update the image with minimal effort.

There is much trial and error to achieve these goals. The development process becomes an iterative process as images are built, tested, and rebuilt until you hit the bullseye with an image for production. There is some work involved to hone the development process, but the end result will make future changes and support easier and remove OS development from the critical task in the project. Most important is that, over the whole product life cycle, you have an answer file and a distribution share that you can go back to over time to make minor changes for new versions or updates. Compare this to Microsoft's design guide process, which requires you to start all over from scratch each time you need to make even the smallest modification to create a new image. Microsoft's design guide process also has a lot of manual steps that are prime places to interject errors into the build.

The basic part of the Workflow is broken down into 4 parts. Before we go over each part, we need to install the tools.

2.2 Exercise 201: Installation of the ADK with SIM Option and Generation of a Catalog File

Before we can cover the details of SIM and the rest of the development workflow, we need to install SIM and other tools from the ADK. In addition, we will create a catalog for the Windows 10 Enterprise LTSC 2021.

2.2.1 ADK Install

1. On your development machine, open a browser and go to the ADK download site: https://docs.microsoft.com/en-us/windows-hardware/get-started/adk-install
2. Done load the last Windows ADK and WinPE-Add-on to the ADK
3. Run the ADKsetup.exe installer.
4. Choose the following items:

    - Deployment Tools (this option Includes SIM)
    - Image and Configuration Designer (ICD)
    - Configuration designer
    - User State Migration Tool (USMT)
    - Volume Activation Management Tool (Which will cover in the last exercise)

5. Click Install.

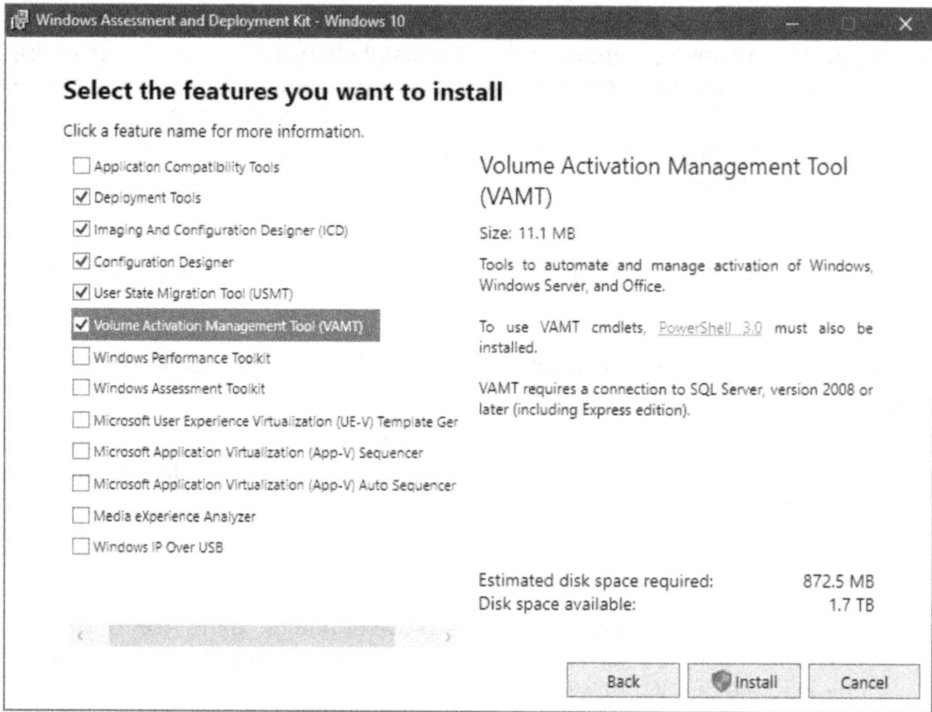

When Installation is finished, System Image Manager will show up under Windows Kit in the start bar.

6. Run the adkwinpesetup.exe to install the WinPE add-ons.
7. There are no options, just click the install button.

2.2.2 Create Catalog

Now, we will create the catalog that contains the components that are used to create the answer file.

1. Create a directory called “WinData” on the C drive.
2. Create two sub-folders in C:\WinData called “Image” and “CS”.
3. Mount the 64-bit Windows 10 Enterprise LTSC 2021 ISO/IMG file.
4. Copy the contents of the mounted disk to the C:\WinData\Image folder.
5. Copy (NOT cut) the intall.wim found in the C:\WinData\Image\Sources folder and Paste it to the C:\WinData folder.
6. Open SIM.
7. From the menu, select Tools->Create Catalog…

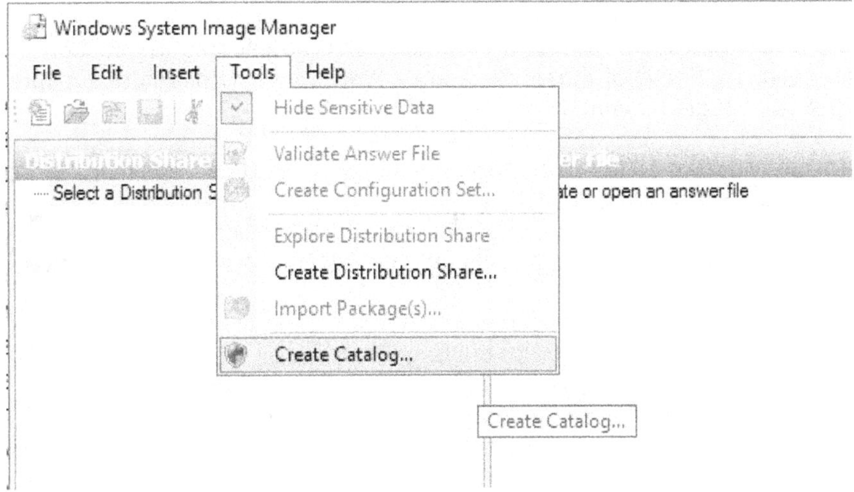

8. Open the install.wim file located in the C:\WinData, and the generation process will start.

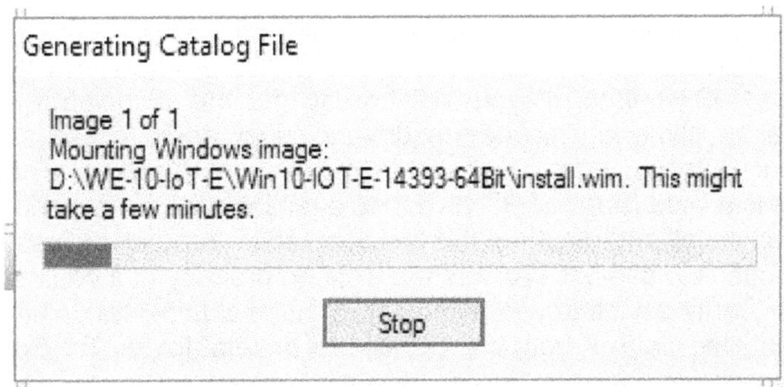

9. The catalog will be generated with a name that matches the Windows OS version. This step only needs to be performed once, and the catalog can be accessed by SIM on any Windows development machine once it is created.

Note: If a new version of Windows 10 LTSC becomes available, you will have to create a new catalog for that version.

install.wim

install_Windows 10 IoT Enterprise LTSC 2021.clg

2.3 *The Basics Part 1: Gather Items from Target Installation*

The first part of the development workflow is to gather the device drivers and other customizations that have been captured from the target system. Let's go over these steps.

Note: This section is only a discussion. Exercise 202 proceeding the section will be the actual lab exercise. Some of these steps are covered in later chapters. Chapter 17 will bring all the steps together with a sample project.

1. Install Windows 10 IoT Enterprise on your target system. This helps to make sure Windows will install successfully.

Note: In some rare cases, you may have to add disk drivers to support SSD drives or RAID drives during installation.

2. Install all the device drivers for the target hardware.
3. Capture the device drivers:
   a. In File Explorer, create a folder in C:\ called "drivers".
   b. Open a command prompt with Administrative privileges.
   c. Run the following command:

```
DISM /online /export-driver /destination:c:\drivers
```

4. Plug in a USB flash disk, and copy the C:\drivers folder to a USB flash disk.

Back in the day of XP Embedded, it could take a couple of days to create all the device driver components. Over time, I figure out how to get this completed in a few hours. Windows 10 makes gathering the device drivers super easy. These steps above are important for four reasons. First, we need to make sure Windows 10 can run on the hardware. There is a wide range of PC platforms available, some new and some very old. If Windows 10 can install and run, then this is a good start. Second, by installing the device drivers, you can check to see if the drivers are working properly or if you need to download the latest drivers. Some device drivers require their installer to be set up properly, but most drivers can be installed via PnP from the "Out-of-box drivers" folder. Third, with the OS and drivers on the system, you can test your application to see how it performs. Forth, you can gather other items needed to customize the image such as a custom security template, custom group policy settings, custom power plan, or custom firewall settings.

5. Create a custom security template to disable password timeout. Chapter 8 covers this process in more detail. Copy the resulting INF file to a USB flash disk.

6. Create custom group policy – Chapter 8 discusses the creation of custom group policy settings. Below are the typical group policy settings that I set:

   <u>Computer Configuration</u>

   - Microsoft OneDrive for Business 2013 – Disabled
   - Microsoft OneDrive for Business 2016 – Disabled
   - Require a password when a computer wakes (on-battery) - Disabled
   - Require a password when a computer wakes (plugged-in) – Disabled
   - Save documents to OneDrive by default – Disabled
   - Set the default behavior for AutoRun – Disabled
   - Turn on Software Notifications – Disabled
   - Disable Windows Error Reporting – Enabled

- Prevent the OneDrive files from syncing over a metered connection – Enabled
- Prevent the usage of OneDrive for file storage – Enabled
- Prevent the usage of OneDrive for file storage on Windows 8.1 – Enabled
- Turn off Autoplay – Enabled
- Turn off reminder balloons - Enabled
- Turn off System Restore - Enabled
- Turn off Windows Error Reporting – Enabled

User Configuration

- Enable screen saver – Disabled
- Microsoft OneDrive for Business 2013 – Disabled
- Microsoft OneDrive for Business 2016 – Disabled
- Password protect the screen saver – Disabled
- Screen saver timeout – Disabled
- Set the default behavior for AutoRun – Disabled
- Desktop Wallpaper – Enabled
    - Wallpaper Name: <path to wallpaper bitmap >
    - Wallpaper Style – <option>
- Disable showing balloon notification toasts – Enabled
- Disable Windows Error Reporting – Enabled
- Load specific theme - Enabled
    - Specific Theme: <path to theme>
- Remove Balloon Tips on Start Menu items – Enabled
- Turn off all balloon notifications – Enabled
- Turn off Autoplay – Enabled
- Turn off feature advertisement balloon notifications – Enabled
- Turn off reminder balloons
- Turn off toast notifications – Enabled
- Turn off toast notifications on the lock screen - Enabled

There are a lot of options that can be set in group policies, and some may require other support files. For example, specific background images, colors, and sounds can be put into a custom theme file, which then can be called by group policy. Some group policy settings shouldn't be set right away. For example, the group policy settings for blocking hardware devices from installing should be set a little later.

7. Custom Power plan – Chapter 3 discusses creating a custom power plan. After you create your custom power plan, copy the resulting .pow file to the USB flash drive.
8. Custom Firewall settings – Custom firewall settings can be configured on the target and then exported to a .wfw file. The settings can be imported using the netsh.exe utility during OS installation. Copy the resulting file to the USB flash drive. Chapter 8 covers the firewall.

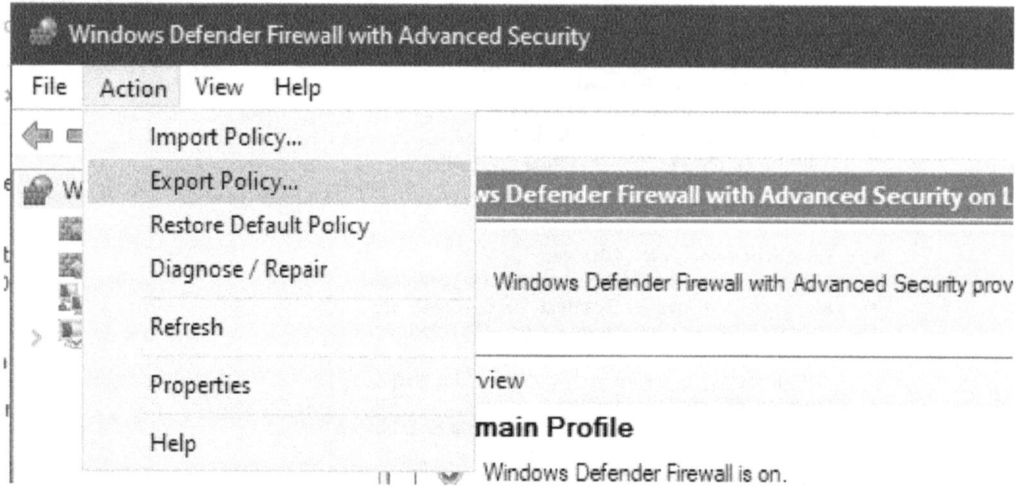

2.3.1 Exercise 202: Capture Drivers and Create a Distribution Share

Now let's capture the device drivers for your target system.

***Note**: The steps to capture the device drivers are for real hardware. If you are using a virtual machine for learning, then you don't have to capture the drivers as these will be installed by the VM.*

1. Install Windows on your target system, if not installed already.
2. Install all the device drivers that came with the board.
3. Run Windows update to download any of the latest drivers available.
4. When all the drivers are installed and appear to be working properly, open File Explorer.
5. Create a folder called "Drivers".
6. Open a Command Window or PowerShell window with elevated privileges.
7. Run the following:

```
DISM.exe /Online /Export-Driver /Destination:c:\Drivers
```

The process goes through all the OEM#.inf and copies the corresponding driver files out of the C:\Windows\System32\DriverStore\FileRepository staging folder and puts them in the C:\drivers folder

8. Plug in a USB flash disk.
9. Copy the C:\Drivers folder to the USB flash disk.
10. Safely eject the USB flash disk.

The next exercise will put the drivers into a distribution share, but before we perform this step we need to discuss SIM.

2.4 SIM Interface Overview

When you install Windows in the last exercise, a wizard appears asking for details like language, accepting the license agreement, partition information, and runtime key. The wizard is known as the Image Build Wizard (IBW). There are questions that appear after Windows has been installed, such as user account name and password, service settings, etc. Having to answer all these questions for every installation is a bit tedious. An answer file is used to automate the process and address all the questions. SIM is a graphical tool that helps create an answer file that automates the installation of a Windows operating system. OS features can be pre-enabled, services can be enabled or disabled and extra applications and drivers can be installed with the OS. As shown in the picture below, SIM's GUI is divided into 5 panes:

- Windows Image – A catalog file must be generated from the Windows OS's image.wim file. This is what we did in the first exercise. The image file can be opened in SIM to present the components and packages available in the OS. The first exercise helps to generate the catalog file.

- Answer File – This pane is where you define what is going into the custom image. Items are added from the Windows Image pane to the answer file. Components are added to different installation passes; and system settings, such as computer name, user accounts, etc., can be preset in the Feature Settings pane. Packages are those OS features that can be enabled for the OS. For example, you can enable the IIS feature.

- Answer File Feature Settings – This pane is used to predefine certain OS feature settings before they get added to the image.

- Messages/Tasks – As you perform actions in the SIM, like Validation, the Messages pane will list all results and present any further action to be taken.

- Distribution Share – Extra applications, drivers, and feature packages can be installed with the operating system. The Distribution share is a staging area for adding applications and drivers to the customized Windows Installer image. A configuration set is created to pull in these extras and create an answer file. This will be covered in the next chapter.

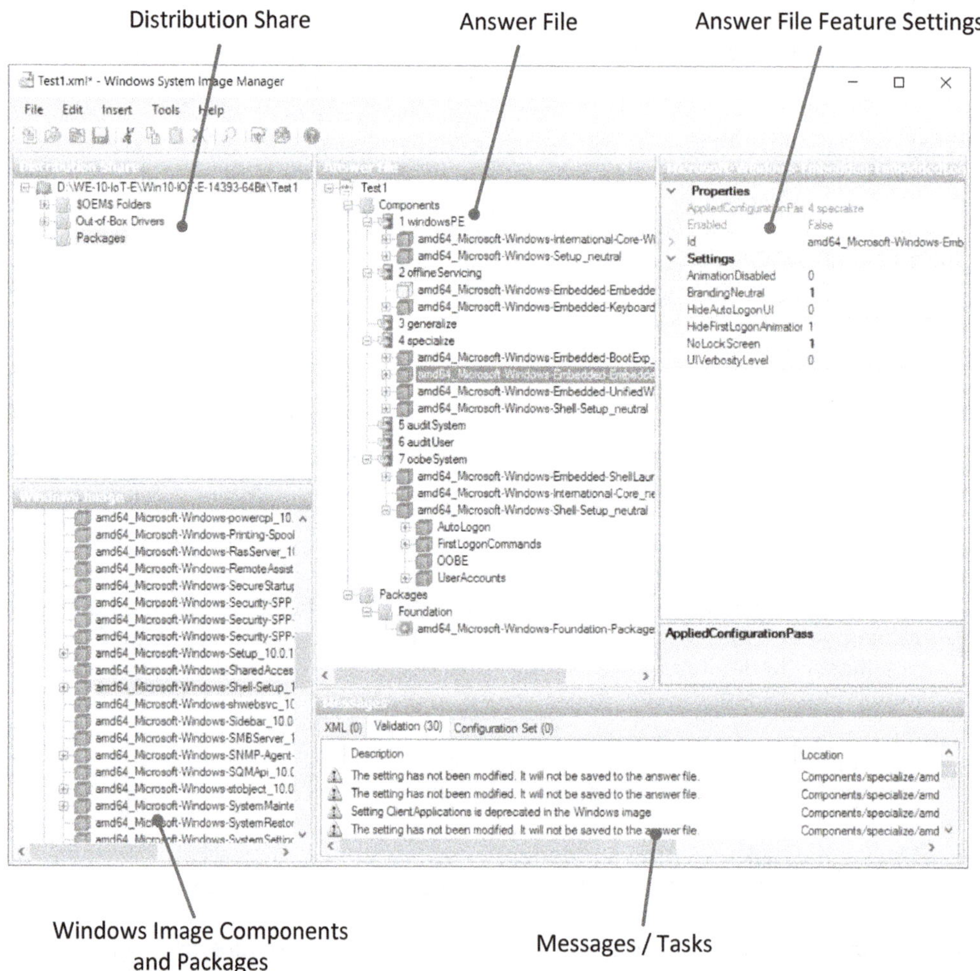

The menu bar contains the basic "file" and "edit" functions and the controls for working with the Answer file. Validation, building configuration sets, and inserting commands will be discussed throughout the book.

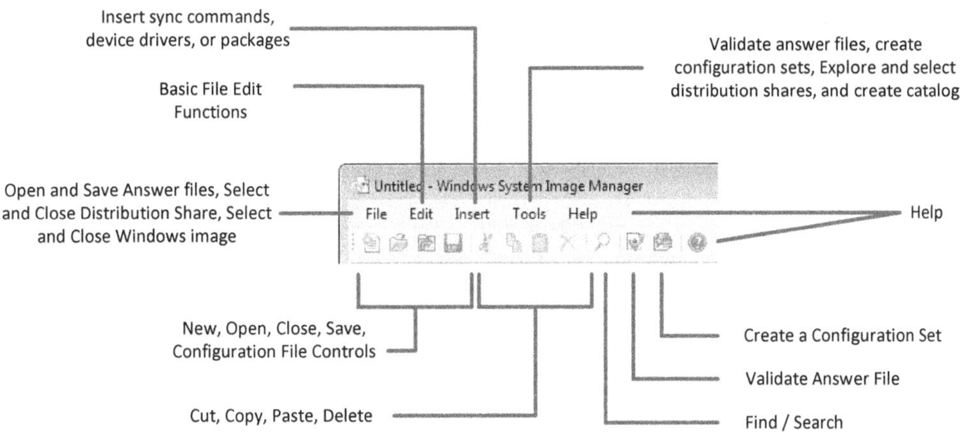

2.5 *Installation Passes and the Answer File*

There are 7 possible passes that Windows goes through during installation. For those familiar with Windows XP Embedded, you will remember the 65,000 phases Windows XP Embedded went through to be installed. Some action was performed at different phases. This all changed to the 7 passes when Windows migrated to Vista and then to Windows 7. In Windows Embedded Standard 7 and 8, the Image Configuration Editor (ICE) tool had the passes as a drop-down to change settings. ICE is a derivative of SIM, but SIM presents the passes in the answer file. The following picture shows the new answer file with nothing added.

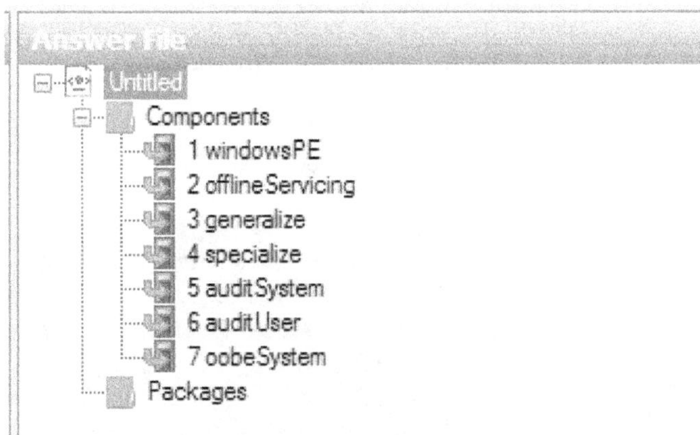

The detailed description of each Pass can be found on the Microsoft Docs site. Here is a brief description of the seven installation passes:

1. WindowsPE - Configures Windows PE (Windows Preinstallation Environment) options and basic Windows Setup options. These options can include setting the product key and configuring a disk. If you require drivers for Windows PE to access the local hard disk drive or a network, use this configuration Pass to add drivers to the Windows PE driver store.

2. OfflineServicing – Copies package contents to build up the Windows image. The Windows image itself is offline or not active since the setup is running in Windows PE. Also, during this Pass, out-of-box drivers are copied to the image's driver store.
3. Generalize - Enables you to minimally configure the Sysprep/Generalize command, as well as, configure other Windows settings that must persist on your reference image. The Sysprep/Generalize command removes system-specific information to create a master image that can be cloned to multiple systems. For example, the unique security ID (SID) and other hardware-specific settings are removed from the image. The Generalize Pass runs only if you run the Sysprep /generalize command. When the image boots the next time, it will go through Passes 4 and 7 again.
4. Specialize - Creates and applies system-specific information. For example, you can configure network settings, computer names, international settings, and domain information.
5. AuditSystem - Processes unattended Setup settings while Windows is running in system context before a user logs onto the computer in Audit mode. Audit mode is enabled if you run Sysprep /Audit command, and reboot the system. An image that has been set up for audit mode can be used as a baseline image to generate different master images.
6. AuditUser - Processes unattended Setup settings after a user logs onto the computer in Audit mode. The AuditUser Pass runs only if you boot to Audit mode.
7. OOBE System - Applies settings to Windows before Windows Welcome starts. Out-of-Box Experience (OOBE) is a wizard that asks for the computer name, user name, security options, etc. before the image comes to the login page.

The catalog contains a list of components and packages that can be added to a specific installation Pass in the answer file. The components allow you to preset features like computer name, user account, enable/disable Windows features, etc.

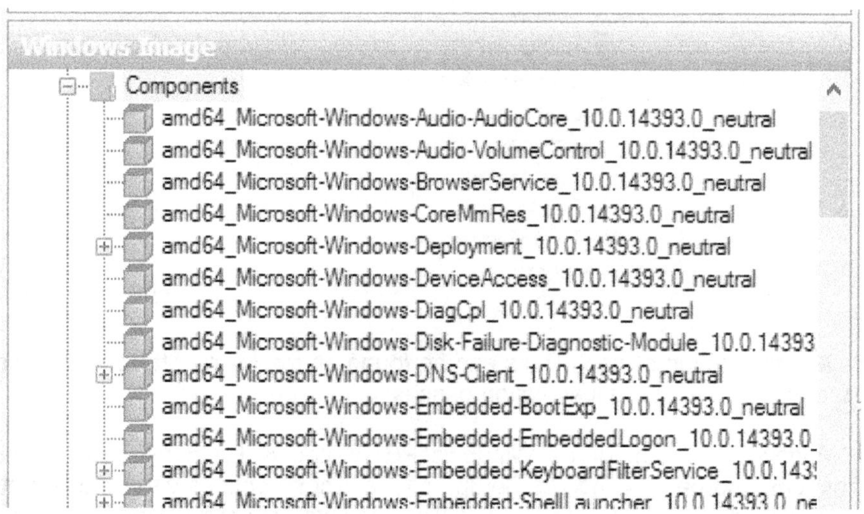

The components are placed into 1 of 7 installation passes. Microsoft creates the components and defines which of the passes they are allowed to go into. Some components can go into multiple passes, and some settings are only available for specific passes. For example, the ComputerName setting is part of the "amd64_Microsoft-Windows-Shell-Setup__neutral" component, which can be placed in passes 2 thru 7, but the ComputerName setting is only available in Pass 4, specialize.

A Windows image doesn't go through all of the passes during installation. Sysprep options will let you either audit the system or package up the image for manufacturing.

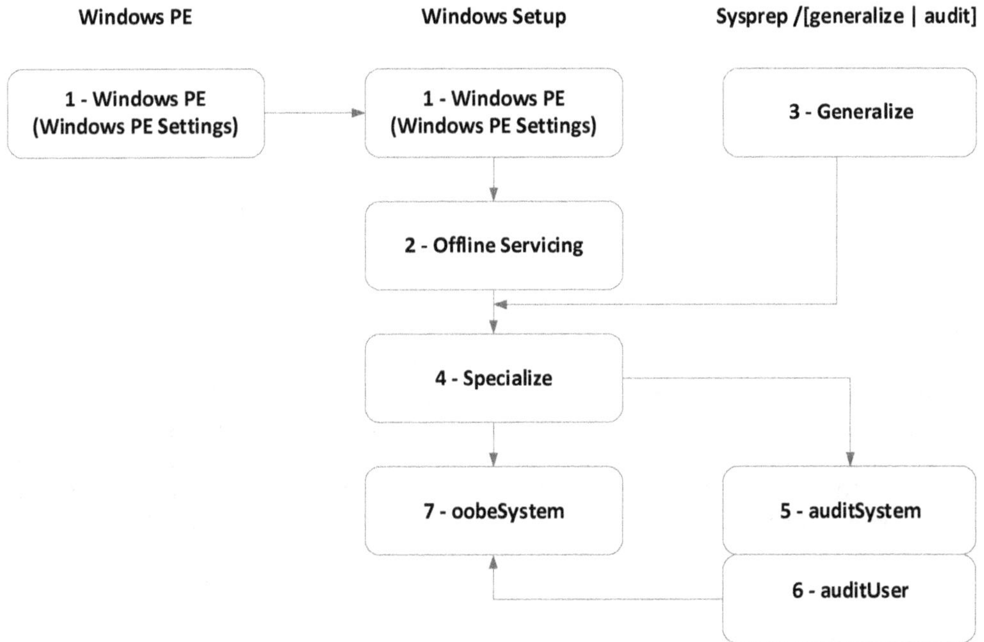

The typical installation process is to go through passes 1, 2, 4, and 7. Once the image is ready for production, Sysprep is run and the image is captured. Each clone of the production image will then go through Passes 3, 4, and 7 when booted for the first time. The fact that the clones go through passes 4 and 7 is important. You don't want to be asked for user and service settings again, so a second answer file is needed to address these items. The benefit is that you can use this Sysprep unattended answer file to run scripts on each clone for further image setup.

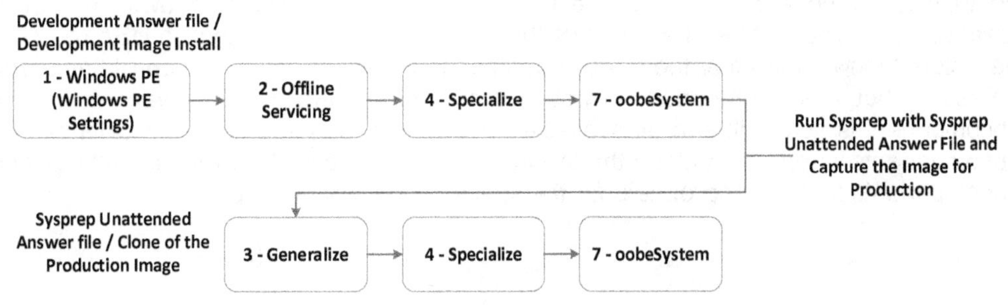

2.6 Components and the Passes: Preset Installation Answers

Now let's look at how components and passes work together in an answer file. The components in a Windows Image file can be placed in different passes. The diagram below shows two components that address language settings. Right-clicking on the component brings up a context menu to select where the component gets placed in the answer file. One covers the installation image and can be placed in either Pass 4 or Pass 7. The other is for WinPE and is only available for Pass 1.

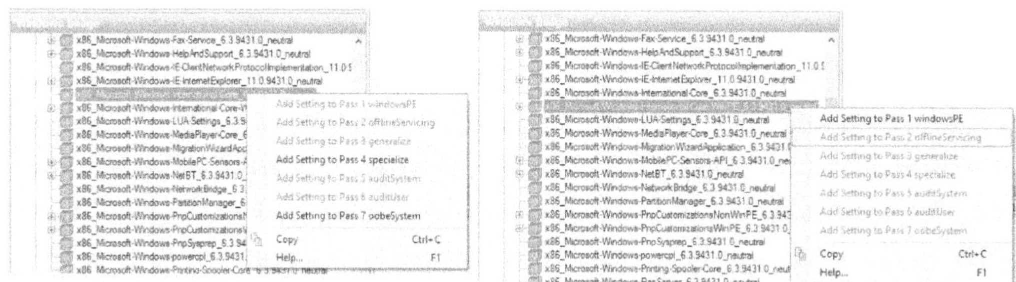

The components get placed into their respective passes in the answer file. The picture below shows the answer file with both components. The choice to place the x86_Microsoft-Windows-Internation-Core_neutral component in Pass 7 versus Pass 4 was arbitrary. You could have the component in Pass 4 and Pass 7, but in this case, the settings are the same. One question that does come up is: "If you have different settings in one Pass versus the other, which one is set?" The basic rule is that the last Pass that the image processes produces the final settings. In general, it is good practice to avoid duplicate settings.

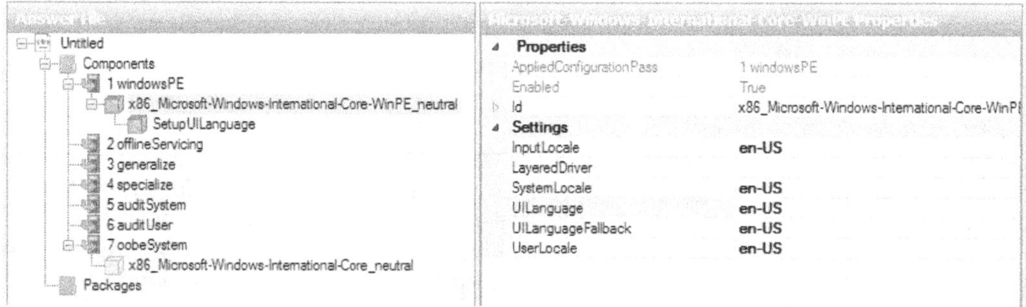

The WinPE component addresses the language settings for the Windows Installation wizard screens. The picture above shows the settings being set for English USA (en-US). The picture below shows that there are subcomponent settings for the Setup UI Language in Pass 1, but a subcomponent is not in the Pass 7 version. Not every setting or subcomponent is accessible to all available passes. You can see all of the settings and subcomponents when you click on the Windows Image pane, but only those settings and subcomponents that are appropriate for the specific Pass will be displayed.

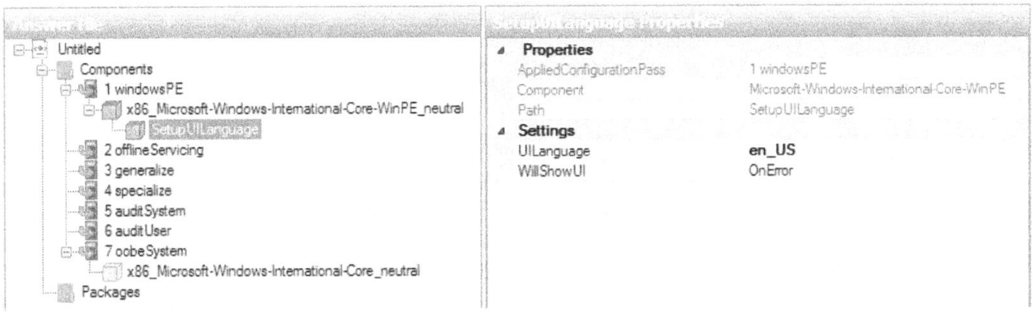

2.7 *The Distribution Share*

The top-right pane in SIM is the distribution share. The distribution share is a file-folder structure that is an organized place for storing applications, drivers, and feature packages that will be installed during Windows installation. You can then select the items and add them to the answer file. The distribution share consists of three basic items: "OEM Folders", "Out-of-Box Drivers", and "Packages".

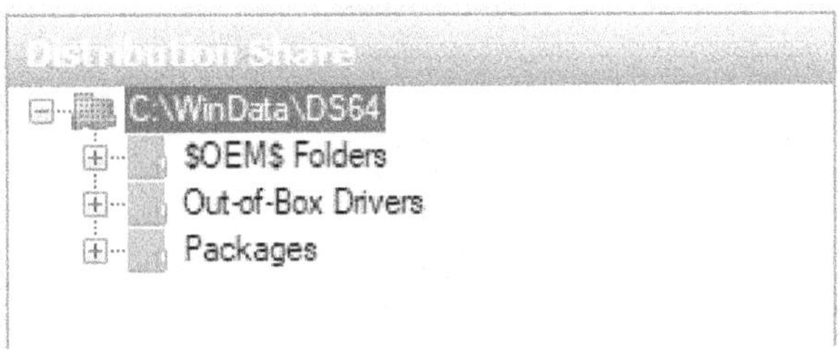

2.7.1 OEM Folders

The "OEM Folders" directory is used to add custom files to an installation image, and "OEM Folders" requires a slightly cryptic path scheme to add files to an image. The non-intuitive folder structure actually maps to the folder structure where the files will be placed during installation on the target system. The table below shows the directory paths and their final resolution when the image is installed.

Path	Definition
OEM Folders	Contains all supplemental folders and files for an automated or customized installation.
\$OEM$ Folders\$$	Contains files that Image Builder copies to the %WINDIR% (for example, C:\Windows) folder during installation.
\$OEM$ Folders\$$\System32	Contains files that Image Builder copies to the %WINDIR%\System32 (e.g., C:\Windows\System32) folder during installation.
\$OEM$ Folders\$1	Represents the root of the target system's drive on which you installed the OS (also known as the boot partition) and contains files that Image Builder copies to the boot partition during installation (e.g., C:\).

\$OEM$ Folders\$Progs	Contains files that Image Builder copies to the %PROGRAM_FILES% folder during installation.
\$OEM$ Folders\$1\Pnpdrivers	Contains new or updated Plug-and-Play drivers. The user specifies the folder name in the Unattend.xml file for unattended installations. For example, this folder might be named \$OEM$ Folders\$1\Pnpdrvs.
\OEM Folders\drive_letter\ subfolder	A subfolder of the drive that contains files that Image Builder copies to the subfolder during installation. Multiple instances of this kind of folder may exist under the \$OEM$ Folders\<drive_letter> folder, for example, \$OEM$ Folders\D\MyFolder would become D:\MyFolder.

For example, if you want to add helloworld.exe to \windows\system32, you create the directory structure, …\$OEM$ Folders\$$\System32 as shown in the picture below. Helloworld.exe is placed in the last (System32) folder.

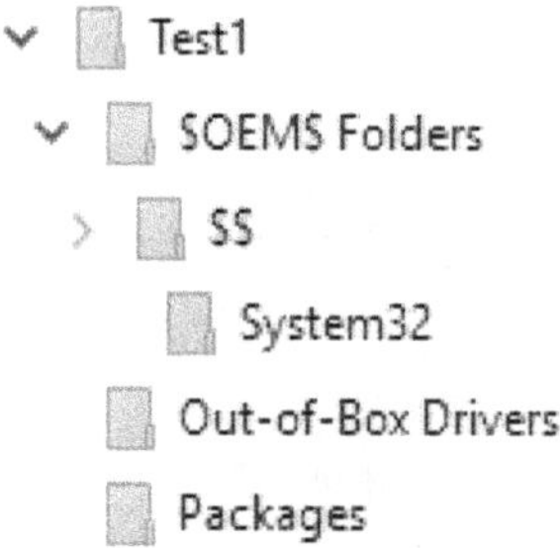

The following picture shows what you see in SIM when you create this directory structure. The file will not be seen. There is no link to the "%OEM% Folders" directory and the answer file, thus interacting with the distribution share is performed in file explorer. When you create the configuration set, you will point to "OEM Folders". The files will be copied to the appropriate target system folders during installation.

2.7.2 Out-of-box Drivers

The "Out-of-Box Drivers" folder is for device drives that can be installed via the PnP manager. Ethernet, video, audio, and chipset drivers can be placed in this folder, but the best-known practice is to place the different drivers under a single folder for your target platform. The following picture shows a folder for the MinnowBoard Max (MBM) and all the separate device driver folders underneath. This allows you to have more than one platform supported in the distribution share.

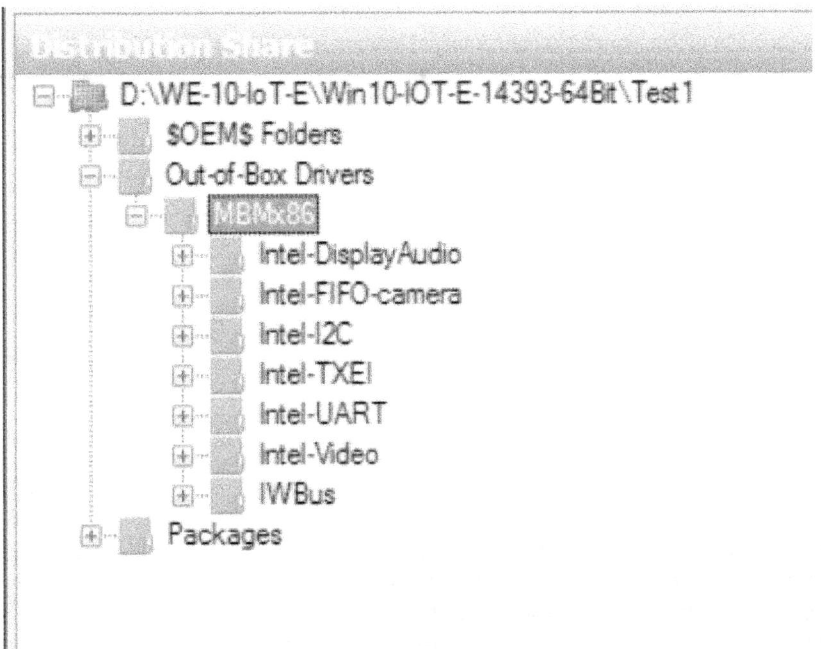

You should copy the driver binaries and any subfolders as they come from the manufacturer directly to this folder. The picture below shows the video device driver files placed in the distribution share folders.

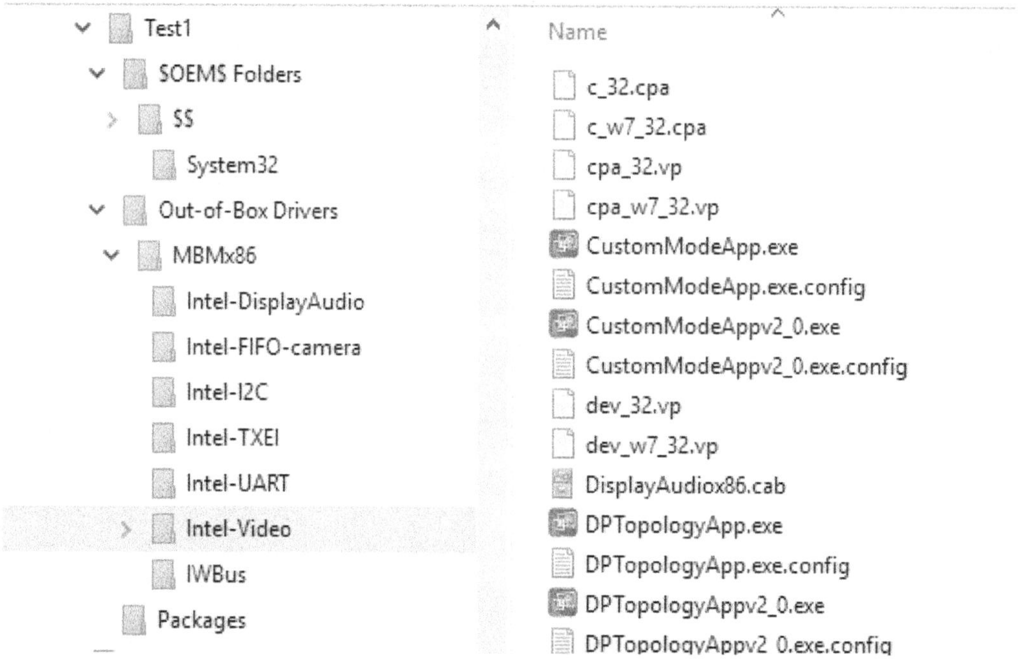

Test1
OEM Folders
$$
System32
Out-of-Box Drivers
MBMx86
Intel-DisplayAudio
Intel-FIFO-camera
Intel-I2C
Intel-TXEI
Intel-UART
Intel-Video
IWBus
Packages

Name
c_32.cpa
c_w7_32.cpa
cpa_32.vp
cpa_w7_32.vp
CustomModeApp.exe
CustomModeApp.exe.config
CustomModeAppv2_0.exe
CustomModeAppv2_0.exe.config
dev_32.vp
dev_w7_32.vp
DisplayAudiox86.cab
DPTopologyApp.exe
DPTopologyApp.exe.config
DPTopologyAppv2_0.exe
DPTopologyAppv2_0.exe.config

If INF files are in one directory and driver files themselves are in a different directory, keep the relative file and folder structure as they are. The INF file will have hard links to the folders containing the drivers. If you place everything in a single flat release folder, the drivers may fail to install properly. Exercise 203 will discuss the development process to extract drivers so you don't have to manually extract them yourself. If the driver cannot be extracted or requires installation, you'll have to set up a folder in "OEM Folders" and place the installer in that folder. A synchronous command can be used to run the installers during installation. Synchronous commands will be covered later in the chapter. Examples of drivers that should be installed include Touch screen drivers and National Instruments drivers. These are drivers that include support applications.

The device drivers are going to be linked to the answer file. In the "Out-of-Box Drivers", you will right-click on the platform or driver that you want to add and select "Insert Driver path to Pass 2 offlineServicing". Pass 2 is used for adding a device driver to the image. The device driver's path will be placed in the amd64_Microsoft-Windows-PnpCustomizationsNonWinPE__neutral component. When the configuration set is created, the path to the device driver is used to pull the files into the configuration set.

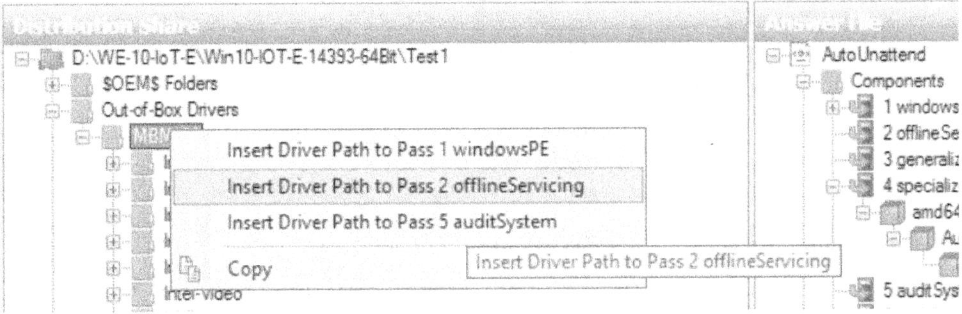

During installation, the system will verify that the drivers in the "Out-of-Box Drivers" folder are signed. All the signed drivers will then be copied (staged) into the C:\Windows\System32\DriverStore\FileRepository. In fact, any driver you install gets placed in this staging folder. The Plug-n-Play manager will then look for drivers as it goes through the plug-n-play hardware IDs to find a match. When a match is found, the INF file is used to place the driver files into the file system, .i.e. *.sys files go to C:\Windows\System32\drivers, and the INF is renamed to OEM#.inf and placed in the C:\Windows\INF directory. The little number scheme helps to unload a bad driver when a boot to last known good start is performed.

2.7.3 Packages

The Windows 10 Enterprise LTSC 2021 ISO/IMG contains the Features on Demand that used to be in a separate DVD image. The MUI packages are still separate. The packages are .MSU files that can be imported into the distribution share and then added to the answer file so that the feature will be installed during Windows installation. Some packages are still separate like language MUI packages.

***Warning**: The only problem is that the package names are long and break the NTFS 256 file path character limit. This results in an error during installation. The workaround is to put the MSU file into an "OEM Folders" directory and use a synchronous command that calls DISM.exe to install the MSU.*

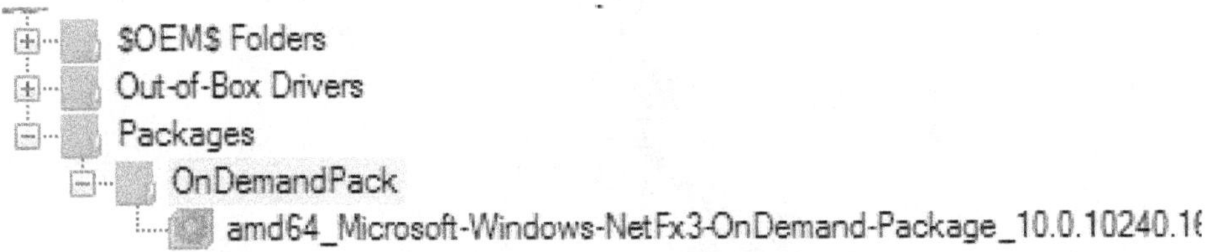

2.8 *The Basics Part 2: Create Distribution Share and Answer File*

Now that we know the basics of SIM, the next step in the development workflow is to set up a distribution share and create an answer file. The next two exercises cover this part.

2.8.1 Exercise 203 Create and Set Up the Distribution Share

In this book's source files under chapter 2, there is a sample application called AB-test-app.exe. The application is a very simple .NET application. We will add the file to the distribution share to demonstrate how the distribution share places files in specific locations during installation. After you have tested the basic image, you can then move on to Build on the Basics to add your own custom files.

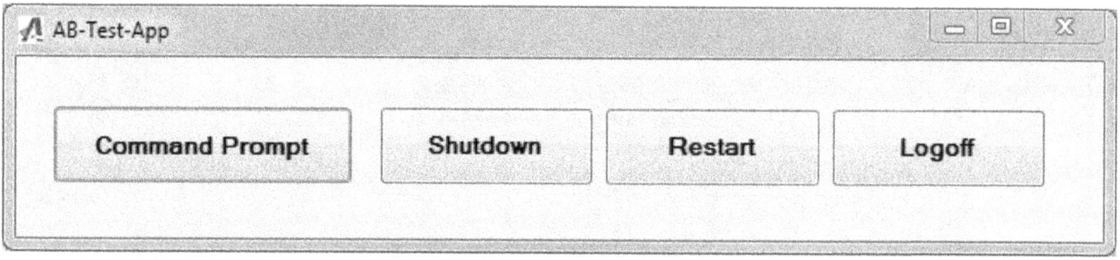

1. Open File Explorer.
2. In C:\WinData create a folder called DS64
3. Open SIM, if it is not opened already.
4. Open the Catalog file, if not already opened.
5. In the bottom left corner, right-click and open the .CLG file generated from Exercise 201. The catalog is open where components can be selected to be added to the answer file.
6. Right-click in the distribution share pane, and select Create Distribution Share from the context menu.
7. Open the C:\WinData\DS64 folder. The 3 folders, "OEM Folders", "Out-of-Box Drivers", and "Packages" will be created. We cannot directly access the files from SIM so we have to go to File Explorer to add files.
8. Open File Explorer and navigate to the DS64 folder location of the distribution share.
9. Under "OEM Folders", create a folder called $1.
10. Under $1, create a folder called "Program Files".
11. Under Program Files, create a folder called Annabooks.
12. Copy the AB-test-app.exe from the book source files to the Annabooks folder.

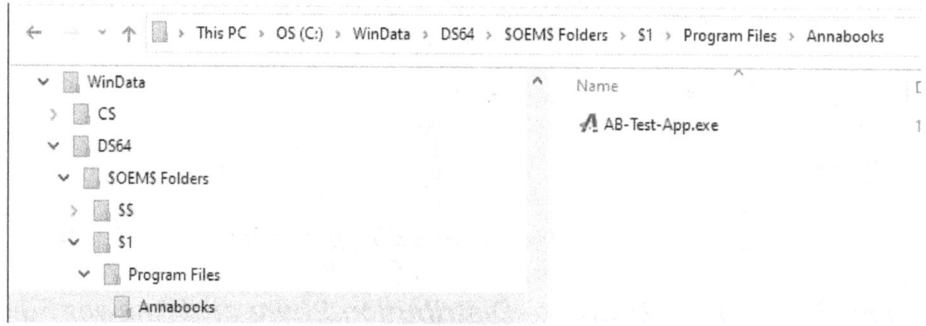

13. Plug in the USB flash disk.
14. Copy the "Drivers" folder from the USB flash disk to "C:\WinData\DS64\Out-of-Box Drivers".
15. Rename the "Drivers" folder to something that matches your board name.

2.8.2 Exercise 204: Create a New Answer File

With the distribution share set up, let's go through the steps to create our first answer file.

1. Open SIM, if not open already.
2. Right-click in the answer file pane, and create a new answer file.
3. Using the table below, add the components to the specific Pass in the answer file and configure the settings. Simply right-click on the component and select the Pass to be put into the answer file.

***Warning**: Do not choose any components with WOW in the name. For 64-bit images, the Windows on Windows (WOW) are for the 32-bit subsystem.*

Note: SIM has a little quirk where not all the optional passes are shown. Just right-click again, and all the passes should be displayed.

Component	Configuration Pass	Component Setting	Possible Value / Notes
amd64_Microsoft-Windows-International-Core-WinPE__neutral	1 WindowsPE	InputLocale	en-US
	1 WindowsPE	SystemLocale	en-US
	1 WindowsPE	UILanguage	en-US
	1 WindowsPE	UILanguageFallback	en-US
	1 WindowsPE	UserLocale	en-US
amd64_Microsoft-Windows-Setup__neutral	1 WindowsPE	UserData: AcceptEULA	True
	1 WindowsPE	UserData : ProductKey : Key	<Enter the license key>
	1 WindowsPE	UserData : ProductKey: WillShowUI	OnError
	1 WindowsPE	ImageInstall: OSImage : InstallFrom: MetaData: Key *(Right-click on InstallFrom to create the MetaData option)*	/IMAGE/NAME
	1 WindowsPE	ImageInstall: OSImage : InstallFrom: MetaData: Value	Windows 10 IoT Enterprise LTSC
amd64_Microsoft-Windows-Shell-Setup__neutral	4 Specialize	ComputerName	ACME
	4 Specialize	TimeZone	Pacific Standard Time
	4 Specialize	AutoLogon: Username	User1
	4 Specialize	AutoLogon: Enabled	True
	4 Specialize	AutoLogon: LogonCount	4294967294
	4 Specialize	AutoLogon: Password: Value	password
amd64_Microsoft-Windows-International-Core__neutral	7 OOBE System	InputLocale	en-US
	7 OOBE System	SystemLocale	en-US
	7 OOBE System	UILanguage	en-US
	7 OOBE System	UserLocale	en-US
amd64_Microsoft-Windows-Shell-Setup__neutral	7 OOBE System	UserAccounts : LocalAccounts : LocalAccount : Name (right-click to insert new local account)	User1

Component	Configuration Pass	Component Setting	Possible Value / Notes
	7 OOBE System	UserAccounts : LocalAccounts : LocalAccount : DisplayName	User1
	7 OOBE System	UserAccounts : LocalAccounts : LocalAccount :Group	Administrators
	7 OOBE System	UserAccounts : LocalAccounts : LocalAccount : Password : Value	password
	7 OOBE System	OOBE : ProtectYourPC	3
	7 OOBE System	OOBE : HideEULAPage	True
	7 OOBE System	OOBE : HideWirelessSetupInOOBE	True
	7 OOBE System	OOBE : HideOEMRegistrationScreen	True
	7 OOBE System	OOBE : HideLocalAccountScreen	True
	7 OOBE System	OOBE : HideOnlineAccountScreen	True

Note: When installing for a single non-English language OS, the SetupUILanugague: UILanguage must be set in Pass 1 to the non-English language that you are using. InputLocale, UILanguage, UserLocale, and SystemLocale settings must also be set to the non-English language. Failure to configure these settings will result in an error in the installer, and you will not be able to install the OS.

Note: The ImageInstall: OSImage : InstallFrom: MetaData: Value has been different for each Windows 10 release. Entering the key and value in the answer file eliminates an OS selection dialog that pops up during installation. A DISM command can be used to find the actual value:

```
Dism /Get-WimInfo /WimFile:e:\Win10-2021\install.wim

Deployment Image Servicing and Management tool
Version: 10.0.19041.844

Details for image : e:\Win10-2021\install.wim

Index : 1
Name : Windows 10 Enterprise LTSC
Description : Windows 10 Enterprise LTSC
Size : 13,557,566,813 bytes

Index : 2
Name : Windows 10 IoT Enterprise LTSC
Description : Windows 10 IoT Enterprise LTSC
Size : 13,560,468,900 bytes

The operation completed successfully.
```

The MetaData Key can be used to select the correct OS from either Index, Name, or Value. In the answer file above, select the value:

- /IMAGE/INDEX - Uses the index number to select the image to install.
- /IMAGE/NAME - Uses the index name to select the image to install.
- /IMAGE/DESCRIPTION - Uses the index description to select the image to install.

Correlating component settings to the passes is important so that you know when something is applied during installation. For example:

- 1 WindowsPE – means when the WinPE OS is booted and running the IBW wizard to install the OS. Most of the Pass 1 settings are for the WinPE OS and not the OS being installed.
- 4 Specialize – means that you are not booted into the custom image and actions are taking place to configure the image.
- 7 OOBE System – the OS is logging in and the OOBE setup screens are running. You can set up commands to run and install target applications and drivers at this time, which brings us to the last section.

If you use the above settings list, the Windows installer will boot to the disk configuration screen. Once you set up the disks and click next, the OS will install. This is a good stopping point as some systems will reboot back into the installation media. The installer will stop at the drive partitioning, so you can reboot the system, remove the USB flash disk, and let the rest of the installation run. You can preset the disk configuration in SIM, which is ideal for a network installation, but there is a real danger if you set this for an OS installation from a USB flash key. If you forget that a USB flash key will bypass all installation wizard screens, you could accidentally wipe out a perfectly good system like your development machine. As a result of this possibility, I am not going to cover pre-setting disk configuration. Please check the sidebar to understand why. You are more than welcome to see how this is done on the Microsoft Docs site.

4. In the distribution share pane, expand the "Out-of-Box Drivers" and then right-click on the name of your platform and select "Insert Driver path to Pass 2 offlineServicing". We don't need to select the driver folders underneath since the root is all that is needed. If you want to add drivers to the platform, just drop them in the folder and they will be included when the configuration set is created.

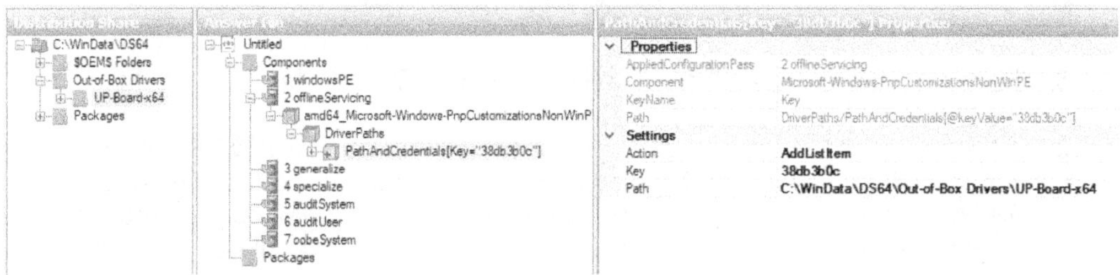

Note: When sharing an answer file and distribution share, the drive paths will change depending on the location of where the answer file and distribution share a placed in the file system.

5. From the menu, select Tools -> Validate Answer File. The following picture shows that the settings not set are ignored and not saved into the answer file. Some settings are considered depreciated.

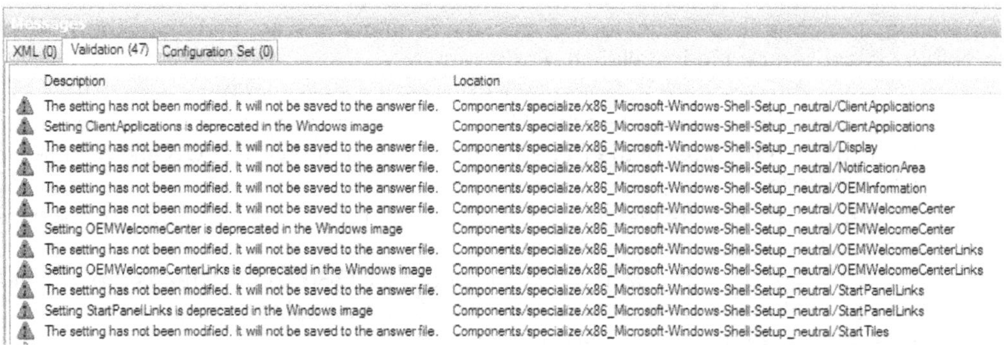

The validation check inspects the answer file for errors. If an error occurs, you can double-click on a message to resolve it. Not all errors are caught in validation; for example, if a setting like Time Zone were misspelled, the misspelling error will not be caught. Once the validation indicates that there are no more errors to resolve, then you are ready to save the answer file.

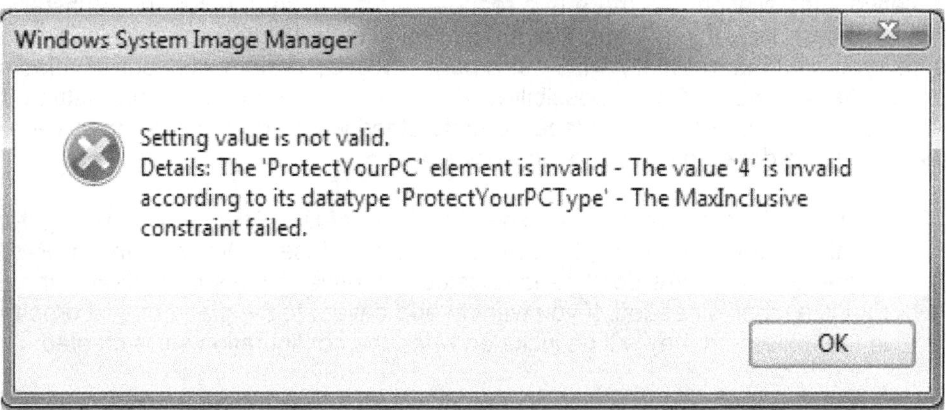

6. Save the answer file as EX202.xml to the C:\WinData folder.

Once the file has been saved, any settings not set will not be shown when you open the answer file again. If you have additional settings, you have to re-add the component to the answer file. Also, since you may enter this information every time you create an answer file, you might want to create a backup answer file with the settings already in place.

2.8.3 Look inside the Answer File

To take the mystery out of the answer files, let's take a look inside an answer file. Open the AutoUnattend.xml in Notepad++ and widen Notepad++ on your screen so that it will not wrap the long lines, and you will be able to pick out the structure.

***Warning**: You can modify the XML file directly if you like, but it is not recommended.*

```
<?xml version="1.0" encoding="utf-8"?>
<unattend xmlns="urn:schemas-microsoft-com:unattend">
  <settings pass="windowsPE">
    <component name="Microsoft-Windows-International-Core-WinPE" processorArchitecture="amd64" publicKeyToken="31bf3856ad364e35" language="neutral" versionScope="nonSxS" xmlns:wcm="http://schemas.microsoft.com/WMIConfig/2002/State" xmlns:xsi="http://www.w3.org/2001/XMLSchema-instance">
      <SetupUILanguage>
        <UILanguage>en-US</UILanguage>
      </SetupUILanguage>
      <InputLocale>en-US</InputLocale>
      <SystemLocale>en-US</SystemLocale>
      <UILanguage>en-US</UILanguage>
      <UILanguageFallback>en-US</UILanguageFallback>
      <UserLocale>en-US</UserLocale>
    </component>
    <component name="Microsoft-Windows-Setup" processorArchitecture="amd64" publicKeyToken="31bf3856ad364e35" language="neutral" versionScope="nonSxS" xmlns:wcm="http://schemas.microsoft.com/WMIConfig/2002/State" xmlns:xsi="http://www.w3.org/2001/XMLSchema-instance">
      <ImageInstall>
        <OSImage>
          <InstallFrom>
            <MetaData wcm:action="add">
              <Key>/IMAGE/NAME</Key>
              <Value>Windows 10 Enterprise 2016 LTSB</Value>
            </MetaData>
          </InstallFrom>
        </OSImage>
      </ImageInstall>
      <UserData>
        <ProductKey>
          <WillShowUI>OnError</WillShowUI>
        </ProductKey>
        <AcceptEula>true</AcceptEula>
      </UserData>
    </component>
  </settings>
  <settings pass="specialize">
    <component name="Microsoft-Windows-Shell-Setup" processorArchitecture="amd64" publicKeyToken="31bf3856ad364e35" language="neutral" versionScope="nonSxS" xmlns:wcm="http://schemas.microsoft.com/WMIConfig/2002/State" xmlns:xsi="http://www.w3.org/2001/XMLSchema-instance">
      <AutoLogon>
        <Password>
          <Value>password=</Value>
          <PlainText>false</PlainText>
        </Password>
        <Enabled>true</Enabled>
        <LogonCount>4294967294</LogonCount>
        <Username>User1</Username>
```

```
        </AutoLogon>
        <ComputerName>ACME</ComputerName>
        <TimeZone>Pacific Standard Time</TimeZone>
      </component>
    </settings>
    <settings pass="oobeSystem">
      <component name="Microsoft-Windows-International-Core" processorArchitecture="amd64"
publicKeyToken="31bf3856ad364e35" language="neutral" versionScope="nonSxS"
xmlns:wcm="http://schemas.microsoft.com/WMIConfig/2002/State"
xmlns:xsi="http://www.w3.org/2001/XMLSchema-instance">
        <InputLocale>en-US</InputLocale>
        <SystemLocale>en-US</SystemLocale>
        <UILanguage>en-US</UILanguage>
        <UILanguageFallback>en-US</UILanguageFallback>
        <UserLocale>en-US</UserLocale>
      </component>
      <component name="Microsoft-Windows-Shell-Setup" processorArchitecture="amd64"
publicKeyToken="31bf3856ad364e35" language="neutral" versionScope="nonSxS"
xmlns:wcm="http://schemas.microsoft.com/WMIConfig/2002/State"
xmlns:xsi="http://www.w3.org/2001/XMLSchema-instance">
        <OOBE>
          <ProtectYourPC>3</ProtectYourPC>
          <HideEULAPage>true</HideEULAPage>
          <HideLocalAccountScreen>true</HideLocalAccountScreen>
          <HideOEMRegistrationScreen>true</HideOEMRegistrationScreen>
          <HideOnlineAccountScreens>true</HideOnlineAccountScreens>
          <HideWirelessSetupInOOBE>true</HideWirelessSetupInOOBE>
        </OOBE>
        <UserAccounts>
          <LocalAccounts>
            <LocalAccount wcm:action="add">
              <Password>
                <Value>password=</Value>
                <PlainText>false</PlainText>
              </Password>
              <Description>User1</Description>
              <DisplayName>User1</DisplayName>
              <Group>Administrators</Group>
              <Name>User1</Name>
            </LocalAccount>
          </LocalAccounts>
        </UserAccounts>
      </component>
    </settings>
    <cpi:offlineImage cpi:source="catalog:d:/we-10-iot-e/win10-iot-e-14393-64bit/install_windows 10 enterprise
2016 ltsb.clg" xmlns:cpi="urn:schemas-microsoft-com:cpi" />
</unattend>
```

The first part is the header information for the XML:

```
<?xml version="1.0" encoding="utf-8"?>
<unattend xmlns="urn:schemas-microsoft-com:unattend">
```

The subtag <oobeSystem> comes next. This is the information for Pass 7 OOBE System. You can see the settings for the different Pass 7 components.

Since the settings are set up via a specific “Pass”, there will be tags for each of the passes. The configuration file above has settings contained in the following tags:

```
<settings pass="specialize">
<settings pass="oobeSystem">
<settings pass="windowsPE">
```

The last tag stores the information about the catalog used to create the answer file:

```
<cpi:offlineImage cpi:source="catalog:d:/we-10-iot-e/win10-iot-e-14393-64bit/install_windows 10 enterprise 2016 ltsb.clg" xmlns:cpi="urn:schemas-microsoft-com:cpi" />
```

If the catalog has changed location or you are opening the configuration file on a different computer, SIM will notify you that the catalog is different and ask if you want to connect to the new catalog.

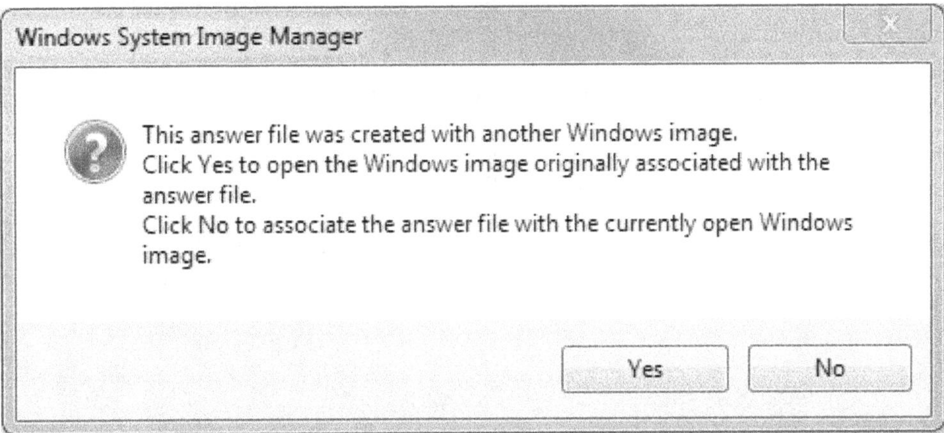

2.9 *The Basics Part 3: Pass 7 Synchronous Commands*

Placing the applications and installers in the appropriate folders of the "OEM Folders" directory structure is only part of the story. The answer file is not only for custom settings, but it acts as a setup script where you can install other applications, device drivers, and other custom settings. If you want something to install during the installation process, you can set up the installer to run during a specific Pass using a "Synchronous Command"; also, answer files don't provide all of the possible operating system options. Synchronous Commands can be used to enable or disable system services using the SC.EXE command, registry keys can be set up with the REG.EXE command, or power settings can be configured using Powercfg.exe.

The picture below shows how to add a Synchronous Command. The context menu lets you specify the specific Pass in which the command will run: windowsPE, specialize, auditUser, or oobeSystem. As soon as you select the configuration Pass, a window opens. This allows you to input the command line for the synchronous command and the order of execution.

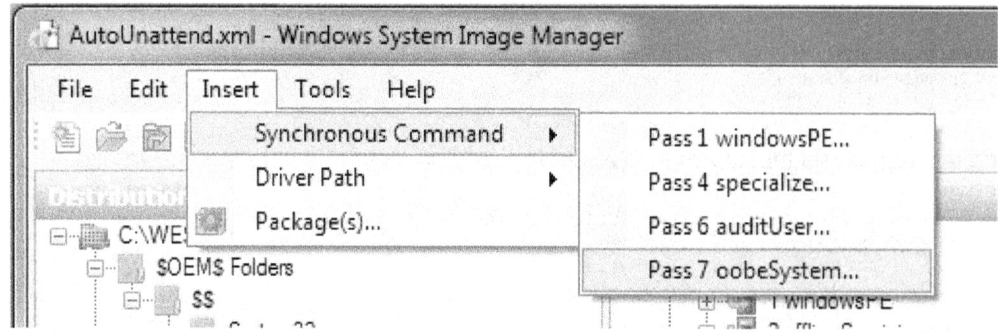

For example, let's say you want to have .NET 6.0 runtime installed during the installation of the OS. If the .NET 6.0 setup utility is placed in the C:\setup directory, you can set up a Synchronous Command for Pass 7, oobeSystem, to run the .NET 6.0 setup utility silently:

```
c:\setup\windowsdesktop-runtime-6.0.4-win-x64.exe /install /quiet /norestart
```

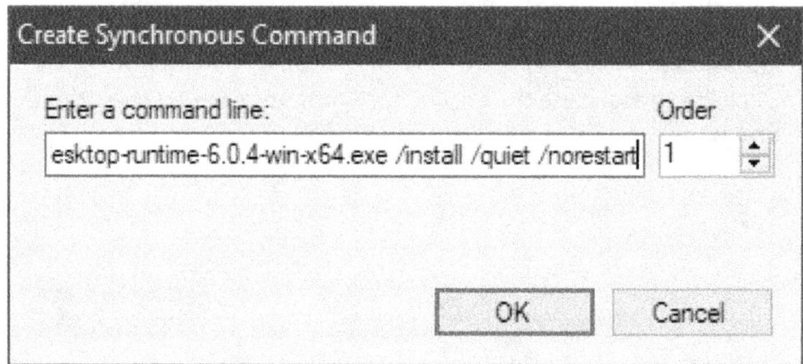

For this example, the command itself gets placed in the answer file under amd64_Microsoft-Windows-Shell-Setup__neutral component FirstLogonCommands setting.

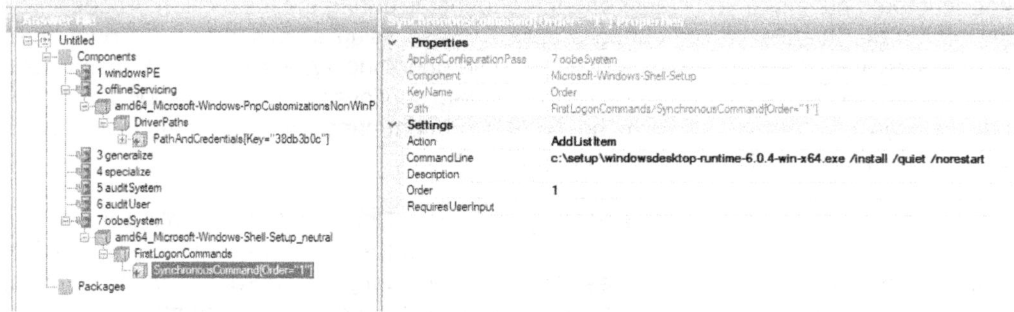

The silent install switches are very helpful when automating the build process. Try to look for silent install switches, but it is perfectly fine to manually walk through an installer during the installation of the OS. Not everything can be automated. There are always some manual steps that must be performed. Keep in mind that, when something is silently installing, it may look like the system hung when it is actually performing an installation. The best practice is to have a PowerShell script run at the end to post a message that it is the last command and possibly wait for a user response.

When adding another Synchronous Command during Pass 7 OOBE, the order value will automatically increment by 1. You can change the order of these custom Synchronous Commands within a specific Pass. Below are the different passes and the locations of the Synchronous Commands in the configuration file.

Synchronous Command Pass	Location in Answer File
1-WinPE	amd64_Microsoft-Windows-Setup__neutral->RunSynchronous-> RunSynchronousCommand
4-Specialize	amd64_Microsoft-Windows-Deployment__neutral-> RunSynchronous-> RunSynchronousCommand
6-AuditUser	amd64_Microsoft-Windows-Deployment__neutral-> RunSynchronous-> RunSynchronousCommand
7-OOBE	amd64_Microsoft-Windows-Shell-Setup__neutral ->FirstLogonCommands-> SynchronousCommand

Pass 4 is good for installing font information and Visual Studio runtimes. Pass 7 is pretty much where you will add sync commands. The other two Passes are rarely used.

Note: It is very important to know that Pass 7 oobeSystem will run the first time an Administrator account runs. If you have your system booting into a Power User account or lower, make sure to log off and log into an Administrator account at least once for the Pass 7 commands to run.

Note: The length of synchronous command lines has a limited number of characters. You may have to place long single-line commands in a batch file and have the synchronous command run the batch file.

Below is a list of the basic Pass 7 synchronous commands for the items gathered from Part 1 of the development workflow. The commands will run during Pass 7 when the system logs into an administrator account for the first time.

- Import the custom power plan and set the GUID

  powercfg.exe /IMPORT c:\setup\custom.pow cd8e9657-ae6f-4c34-8c7b-4023fc8ee91b

- Set the custom power plan as the active plan

  powercfg.exe /S cd8e9657-ae6f-4c34-8c7b-4023fc8ee91b

- Disabled Hibernation

powercfg.exe /H OFF

- Set custom security policies

  secedit.exe /configure /db temp.sdb /cfg c:\setup\Custom-Security.inf

- Import Firewall settings

  netsh advfirewall import c:\setup\Custom-Firewall.wfw

- Delete the copy of the installation disk from ConfigSetRoot

  cmd.exe /C rd /S /Q c:\Windows\ConfigSetRoot

- Set BCD to ignore all errors

  bcdedit /set {current} bootstatuspolicy ignoreallfailures

2.9.1 Other Pass 7 Synchronous Commands for Either Answer File

As mentioned earlier, not all Windows settings can be configured in SIM. Automating the build process to remove manual operations sometimes involves getting creative with some Windows settings. Over the years, I have collected various registry keys, PowerShell scripts, and batch files that help with these tricky items. In the Chapter 2 folder of the exercise are a few of these items.

- Disable-BitLocker.cmd – Some systems will enable BitLocker after OS installation. This command can be used to turn BitLocker off so you can run Sysprep when you are ready to create the production image.

- Extend.txt – Sometimes you want to support different drives that have different sizes. If you create a production image on a small partition, diskpart.exe /s extend.txt can be used to expand the C drive to consume the remaining disk space when the production image goes through mini-setup.

- Hidetaskbar.bat & Hidetaskbar.reg – If you want to use Explorer.exe as the shell, but want to hide the taskbar, the batch file makes a call to set the registry and then restart Explorer.exe.

- Networksetup.ps1 – this PowerShell script demonstrates how to disable a network binding and change the name of a network interface.

- NicPowersave.ps1 – This PowerShell script disables the power-saving mode for network cards.

- Screenbrightness.ps1 – this PowerShell script makes a WMI call to WmiSetBrightness to set the monitor brightness level (0 to 100).

- Scrollwidth.reg – For touch screen systems, increasing the scroll bars can be helpful. The registry key value can be imported using regedit.exe /s scrollwidth.reg.

- Set-audio.ps1 – PowerShell script to set the current audio output volume.

- Set-Path.bat – adding new paths to the Path variable is made possible with this batch file.

- Sticky.reg – Use regedit.exe /s sticky.reg to import the registry keys to disable sticky keys.

- USB-Hub-power.ps1 – PowerShell script to disable power management for all USB Hubs.

- VisualEffects.reg - Use regedit.exe /s VisualEffects.reg to enable/disable visual effects settings to adjust for performance.

Here are the generic calls for the different types of scripts: CMD, PS1, and REG files.

- Cmd.exe /C c:\<path> my.cmd
- Powershell.exe -ExecutionPolicy RemoteSigned -File my.ps1
- Regedit.exe /S <path>my.reg.

There are no exercises for this part, as we will add synchronous commands in the upcoming chapters.

2.10 The Basics Part 4: Test the Basics

With the answer file created, we are ready to build the configuration set and deploy the custom image. We want to test what we have so far to make sure the device drivers are installed correctly, as well as, other items. Lockdown features and other files can be added after the basics have been tested.

2.10.1 Exercise 205: Create the Bootable USB Flash Disk Using Rufus

The simplest solution to deploy the image is to use a USB flash disk. Some USB flash disks are better than others. Cheap USB flash disks typically use an 8051 controller to provide relatively fast reads, but slow writes. The better USB flash disks have high-end controllers that provide full USB 2.0, 3.0, and 3.1 read/write speeds. We have found that USB flash drives from manufacturers such as Memorex, Patriot, Kingston, and PNY have good consistency of manufacture and performance.

As the size of the Install.wim file has increased beyond the size that can be supported by a FAT32 drive, it has become necessary to use an NTFS formatted USB flash disk; however, with more systems supporting UEFI booting, but not always having an NTFS UEFI bootloader, we need to use a flexible USB formatting and partitioning utility to solve this problem. Rufus is a utility that helps format, partition, and create bootable USB flash drives. We will use Rufus to create 2 partitions on the USB drive, one is a small, FAT32 bootable partition and the other is a large NTFS partition that occupies most of the USB drive. The large Windows installation files will be copied to the NTFS partition.

1. You will need to download and install Rufus: https://rufus.ie/ .
2. With Rufus installed, plug in a blank USB flash disk (32GB or larger).
3. Run Rufus.
4. Set the Boot selection to UEFI:NTFS (Note: to get this Boot selection option, you may have to expand the drive properties or show the advanced format option). This option creates the FAT32 and NTFS partitions described above.

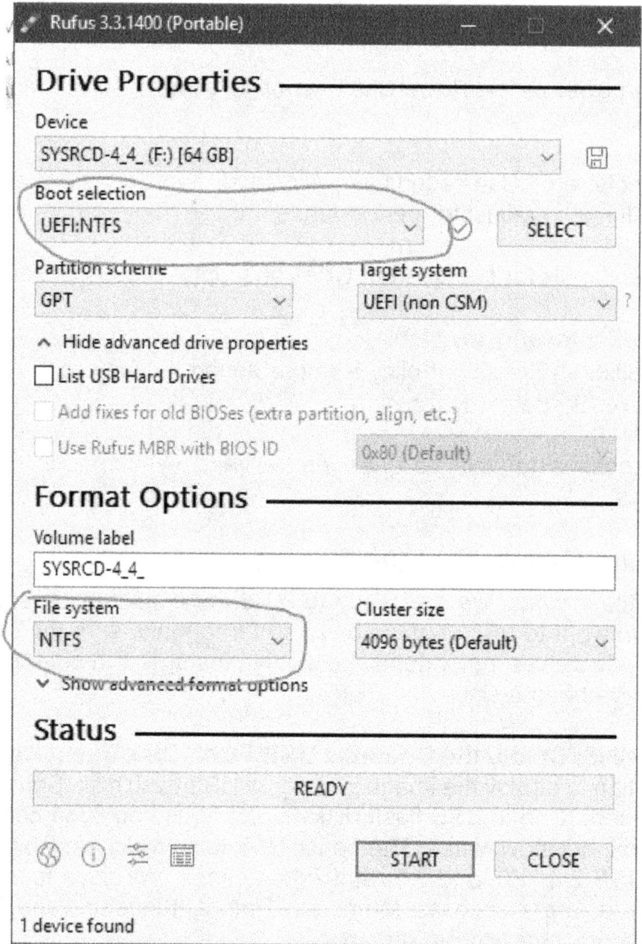

5. The File system should be set to NTFS.
6. Optional: change the volume name to one of your liking.
7. Click Start – The USB flash disk will be split into two partitions. One partition is the small FAT partition with the UEFI boot files. The second is the larger NTFS partition, which will hold the Windows installation files and the configuration set.

8. Copy the contents of the C:\WinDATA\image folder to the USB flash disk's NTFS partition.

2.10.2 Exercise 206: Build the Configuration Set

Now let's create the configuration set:

1. In SIM, from the menu, select Tools-> Create Configuration Set.
2. A dialog box will appear asking for the location for the configuration set to be created and the location of any OEM files. For the location of the configuration set, select C:\WinData\CS. For the OEM folder, point to the "OEM Folders" under the distribution share: C:\WinData\DS64\OEM Folders.

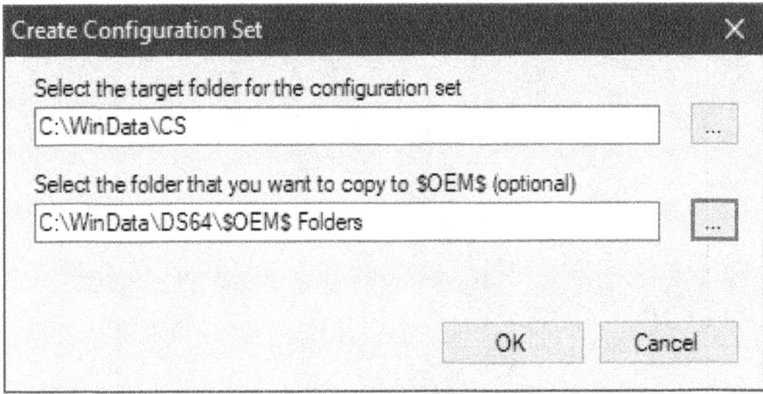

3. Click OK. If you forget to delete the answer file, you will get a notification. Just click yes when asked to overwrite the current answer file.

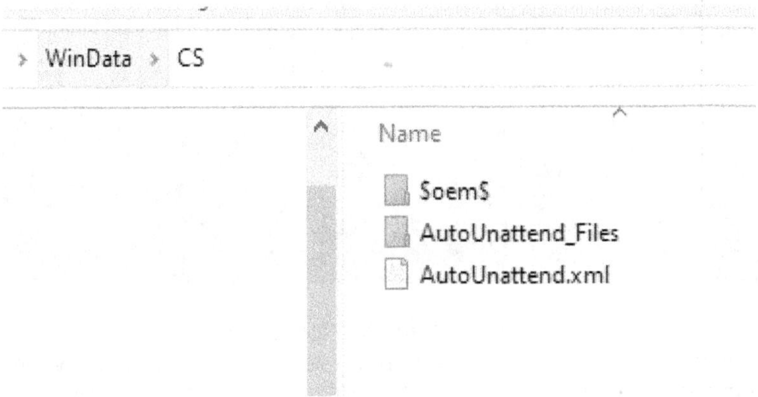

The AutoUnattend.xml file, the "AutoUnattend_files" folder tree that contains the device drivers, and the "OEM folders" directory that contains the application files are generated.

4. Copy the contents of the C:\WinData\CS folder to the USB flash disk that contains the Windows 10 IoT installer files.

Note: If you create a new configuration set in the future, all you need to do is replace these three items on the USB flash disk. The Windows installation files never change.

5. Safely undock the USB flash disk.
6. Plug the USB flash disk into one of the target system's USB ports.
7. Boot the target system to the BIOS configuration menu and set up the BIOS to boot from the USB flash disk.
8. The OS should boot to the disk configuration screen. Select the partition, format the target system's main boot disk, and continue with the rest of the OS installation. When OS installation has been completed, the system will automatically log into the User1 account.

9. At this point, you will want to check the following: that all the device drivers are loaded correctly, the power management has been setup correctly, custom firewall settings are correct, custom security is installed correctly, etc. By building a simple image to test these items provides a launching point to the rest of the development process. For this exercise check to see if the device drviers have been installed and the AB-Test-App.exe is in the image.

2.10.3 DVD/ISO Deployment

To deploy via a DVD, you will need third-party software like PowerISO to create and burn a bootable DVD. The installation DVD must be made bootable, which means the boot information must point to etfsboot.com. The oscdimg.exe utility comes with the ADK, which can be used to create an ISO image file. Here is an example command line using oscdimg.exe to do that:

```
oscdimg.exe" -u2 -h -o -b"c:\WinData\Image\boot\etfsboot.com" "c:\Image" "c:\Image\W10IOT.iso"
```

Note: This information has been left in for completeness as DVD boot is not a practical solution for development.

2.11 Multiple Projects

If you are coming from WES7 to Windows 10, you immediately see that the location of the distribution share is not locked to a specific location. You will also notice that multi-project support is missing or at least not obvious.

Multiple platforms are not an issue. Multiple drivers can be grouped in individual platform folders under the "Out-of-box Drivers" folder just like WES7. In WES7's ICE, the Windows folder can be set up as follows:

```
DSSP1\$OEM$ Folders\<project name>\$OEM$\$$
```

$$ is the shorthand tag for the Windows folder. This folder setup allowed for different projects based on the project name. The OEM was a flag for the installer to install the files under the folder in the specified locations based on the folders and shorthand tags. According to the SIM documentation, the distribution share setup for the Windows directory is as follows:

```
DS\$OEM$ Folders\$$
```

As you can see, there is no facility specified for multiple projects. There are other major differences between ICE and SIM. In ICE, you can point to the project and add it to the answer file so there is a link between the answer file and the "%OEM% Folders" directory. There is no link between the answer file and the "OEM Folders" directory in SIM. Instead, when the build operation to generate the configuration set is started, that is when you point to the "OEM Folders" directory. All the path information shows the absolute path to the "OEM Folders" directory.

Create Configuration Set

Select the target folder for the configuration set

C:\win10MP\CS

Select the folder that you want to copy to OEM (optional)

C:\win10MP\DS64\OEM Folders

OK Cancel

The solution is to first throw out what the SIM documentation says and set up individual project folders under the “OEM Folders” directory. Within the project folders add all the shorthand tags for Windows ($$), drive C: ($1), etc. No extra “$OEM$ Folders” directories were created. Text files were placed in the various subfolders.

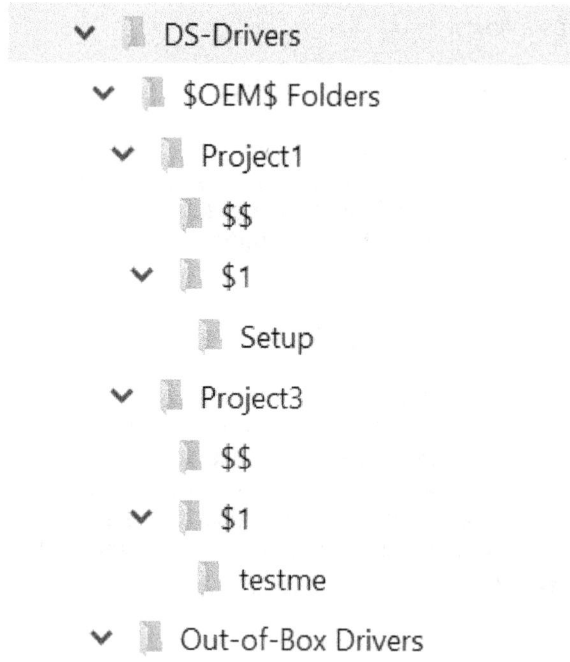

When creating the configuration set, just open the project folder (Project 1) under the *“OEM Folders” directory.*

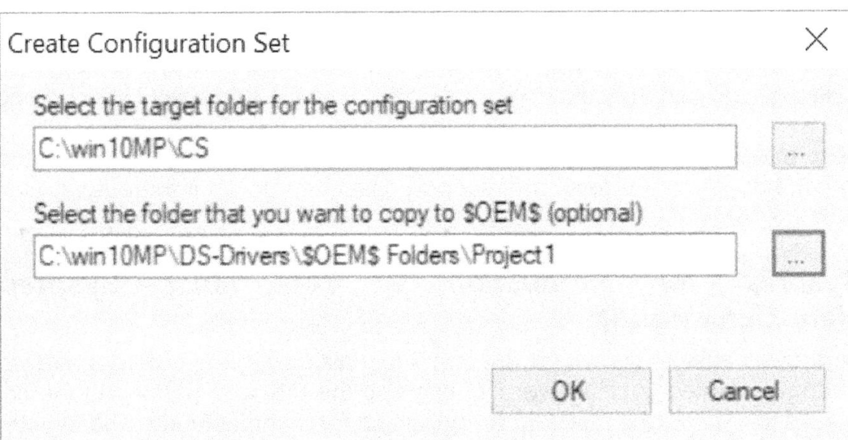

There can be multiple project folders under the "OEM Folders" path, and each project can be independently built by calling that project out (OEM Folders\Project#) in the "Select the folder that you want to copy to OEM" option of the Create Configuration Set dialog.

2.12 Building on the Basics

A lot has been covered, and it is important to point out the importance of what has been covered to this point. The first 4 parts have provided the basic steps for every project. By now the device drivers, group policy settings, power plan, etc. have been set up correctly. The next step is to build on the basics to add your custom application, drivers, and any support runtimes. This will mean adding files to the distribution share and pass 7 synchronous commands to install or configure the Windows OS. The steps can take a few iterations of building and installing images to get everything working correctly.

2.13 Add Lockdown Features: Architect the OS

Once your custom applications and drivers have been added, the next step is to add the lockdown features. The steps address the look and feel of the system, filter implementation, and security. Chapters 6-8 cover these details. Again, there will be several test iterations to verify all the features are set up correctly. Keep in mind, the more you lockdown the system, the more difficult it will be to service in the field, which is a theme that is discussed in Chapter 9. Architecting the system during development is very important, and architecture ideas will be discussed in later chapters. Windows Embedded/IoT projects are more than just picking a few features and building images. Architecting for the whole product life cycle is very important. There are several questions I ask every client before a project:

- What are the hardware features?
- How many user accounts?
- What is the deployment and/or manufacturing process?
- Do you need: UWF, RAM, or DISK-RAM? How do you update a system with these filters in place?
- What security features do you need to implement?

- Is the system networked?
- How does the user interact with the system? Is Shell Launcher used?
- How do you perform field upgrades? Who does the upgrades? What is upgraded?

All of these questions need to be addressed at design time. Once the unit has shipped, anything can happen in the field, and support costs can go up if there is an unforeseen problem.

2.14 Sysprep for Production – You Must Sysprep for Manufacturing!!!!!!

We have a basic answer file with a few items to walk through to create a master image. Once you have created your answer file, installed the OS, and performed the final post-install tweaks to the OS, the last step is duplication for manufacturing. The big step in this process is to run sysprep.exe to create the "Golden" or "Production" master image.

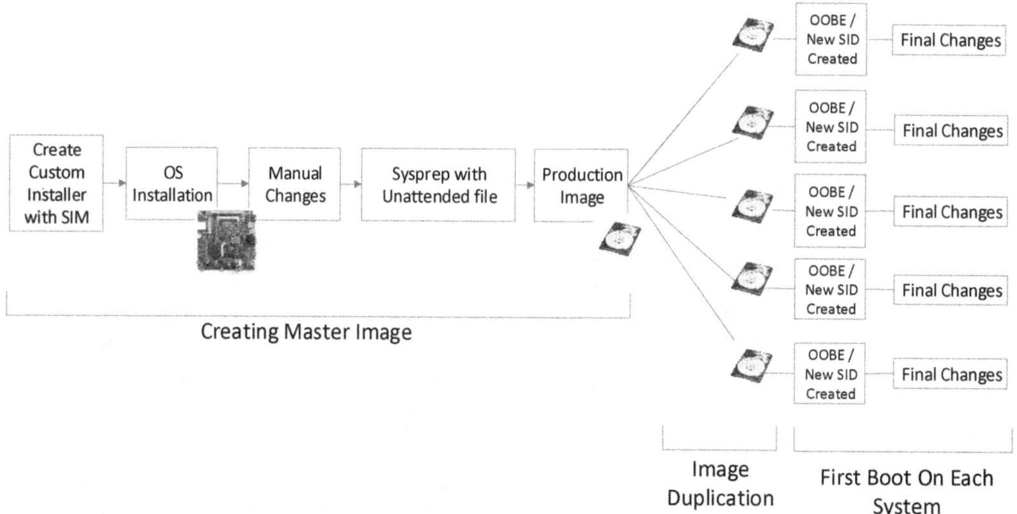

The picture above shows the process of creating a production image that can be deployed to multiple, identical target hardware platforms. Each target platform is guaranteed to have a unique SID. The sequence is as follows:

1. Install the OS on a target.
2. Perform any post-install tweaks to the OS and run Windows Update to add any updates to the image.
3. Run Sysprep – you now have a production image that can be cloned (do not reboot the target after running Sysprep).
4. Copy the cloned image to each production target platform.
5. Boot each clone target platform so that a new SID is generated. You will have to walk through OOBE unless an unattended configuration file is provided.
6. Perform any tests, final post-install tweaks, activate the image and enable any write filters if included in the image.

Once you have tested the application with the lockdown features, you can look to create the master image. Since each clone of the master is going to run through a mini-setup, a Sysprep unattended file is created using SIM. You don't want to re-use the main answer file to install the image as some settings will be different. The answer file will only have components in Pass 3, Pass 4, and Pass 7. Pass 1 and Pass 2 are no longer required as the image is past the installation process.

You can also add synchronous commands to the Sysprep unattended answer file. Here are some examples to consider:

A. Enable Shell Launcher.
B. Enable Keyboard Filter.
C. Enable UWF, which will require a reboot that can be called later in a synchronous command.
D. Disable Windows Update.
E. Enable BitLocker.
F. Delete any setup folders used to create the image.

2.14.1 Sysprep Command

Sysprep is a command line tool that is found in the "\windows\system32\sysprep" directory, and it is part of every Windows image starting with Windows Vista.

Syntax:

> Sysprep.exe [/oobe | /audit] [/generalize] [/reboot | /shutdown | /quit] [/quiet] [/unattend:answerfile]

Note: The Unified Write Filter (UWF) must be disabled to run Sysprep. UWF can be re-enabled once the image has booted on the cloned system. You can set up a sync command in the Sysprep unattended file to enable the filter.

Note: Bitlocker must not be enabled or the drives encrypted before running Sysprep. Bitlocker must be enabled on each clone because the TPM chip is unique on each clone.

Sysprep Options:

/audit - When the system restarts, the OS will be in audit mode where you can add applications and drivers mutually exclusive of the /oobe option.
/generalize - Prepares the image for mass deployment. All unique system information is removed, the security ID (SID) is reset, any system restore points are cleared, and event logs are deleted. When the cloned system first runs, the Specialize configuration Pass runs, and a new security ID (SID) is created.
/oobe - The cloned image will go through the OOBE phase mutually exclusive of the audit option.
/reboot - Restarts the computer when Sysprep is finished.
/shutdown - Shuts down the computer when Sysprep is finished.
/quiet - Runs Sysprep without displaying on-screen information.

/quit - Closes Sysprep after you run the specified commands.
/unattend:configuration_file - Applies settings in a configuration file to the image during unattended installation. configuration_file - specifies the path and file name of the unattend configuration file to use.

Here is an example of running Sysprep with the unattend file:

```
Sysprep /generalize /oobe /shutdown /unattend:c:\sysprep\unattended.xml
```

The basic functions are as follows:

- Removes system-specific data from Windows, like the computer security identifier (SID).
- Unloads device drivers unless PersistAllDevices is set.
- Will enable the Out-of-Box Experience (OOBE) to appear on first boot of the cloned system.

The image will go through Passes 4 and 7 again, thus you can create an unattended answer file that can preset some settings and run synchronous commands that run on each clone.

Note: *Any Pass 7 synchronous commands in the unattended file will only run in an Administrator account on first login to an Administrator account.*

2.14.2 Audit Mode for Baseline Images

I am not a fan of Audit mode, since audit mode is for IT and PC OEMs to create generic images for their general-purpose platforms. Creating IoT devices needs to be direct due to the nature of the lockdown and 3rd party applications installed. When Audit mode is used, one always has to go back to the original development files to make changes. Audit mode images could lead to trouble if changes are made in the audit mode image but not in the core build files. For completeness, here is some information for those who want to use Audit mode to set up their environment.

Audit mode allows you to create a baseline image that can be used to generate different production images with different features. For example, you have a product line skew that consists of model A, model B, and model C. Each model will have different applications and drivers installed. You can create a baseline master image using the following Sysprep command:

```
Sysprep /audit /shutdown
```

Copying the baseline master to each image will allow you to install the applications and drivers for each model. You can then run the Sysprep command again to create the generalized master image for that specific model.

```
Sysprep /generalize /oobe /shutdown
/unattend:c:\windows\system32\sysprep\unattended.xml
```

2.14.3 Yes, You Must Sysprep

I have heard many comments from clients, conference attendees, and forum posts questioning and sometimes arguing about Sysprep. Here are some of the classics:

Comment: *"For Linux, all I have to do is copy the image to the other system. Why do I have to do this Sysprep thing for Windows?"*
My Reply: *"Windows is not Linux. Windows is an operating system with a registry with ties to the hardware. Linux is a kernel. Windows requires Sysprep for the image to be copied.*

Comment: *"I tried using Sysprep with Windows XP Embedded and it didn't work."*
My Reply: *"Yes, I know Sysprep didn't work with XP Embedded since it is so new. You should have been using fbreseal, which I have written about in my book and Microsoft has written about on their website. Sysprep now works and has been working since Windows Vista (a.k.a Windows release that should not be named)."*

Comment: *"I was able to copy my Windows image to identical hardware without using Sysprep."*
My Reply: *"You got lucky. You need to Sysprep."*

Comment: *"There are some performance issues and sometimes the image doesn't boot when I copy the Windows image to another hardware platform without using Sysprep."*
My Reply: *"Yes, performance and failure to boot are what to expect when you don't Sysprep. You need to Sysprep the image before copying the image to other hardware."*

Comment: *"I would like to automate some actions that are unique to each system in manufacturing."*
My Reply: *"Great! When you Sysprep the image, create and use a Sysprep unattend answer file. In the answer file, add the synchronous commands that contain the actions you want to run."*

Comment: *"I thought about manufacturing. Rather than copying the image, I could just install on each system, but I know the process might take a while."*
My Reply: *"Installing the OS on each system in manufacturing is an option. For small production runs, this is fine, but when you get into larger production runs, running Sysprep to create a production image will be faster."*

Unless you are building a slot machine that requires a CRC check on boot, YOU MUST SYSPREP THE IMAGE FOR MANUFACTURING! Sysprep is specifically designed to roll back a system image in preparation for duplication and deployment in manufacturing. One of the operations that Sysprep performs during the roll-back process is to remove the SID. Every Windows operating system is required to have a unique Security ID (SID) used to identify a user or group of users that exist on a particular computer or in a particular domain. SIDs play an important role in Windows networking and NTFS file permissions. There have been some discussions that SIDs don't matter, but SIDs do matter when connecting to domains and running back-office applications. Running Sysprep guarantees that the image can be successfully cloned and deployed to other systems.

2.14.4 Exercise 207: Create a Sysprep Unattended Answer file and Run Sysprep

Each clone goes back through OOBE, which walks back through all of the dialog boxes such as user name, computer name, user password, license key, language, etc. What happens when you run Sysprep /generalize is that the image will go back through Pass 4 Specialize and Pass 7 OOBE. Since these questions were already addressed when the image was installed in the master, why go through them again? For Thin-Client manufacturers, allowing the user to run OOBE makes sense for setting up the system on the network. For embedded device manufacturers, going back through all these questions is not needed. To get past the OOBE screens, you need to create a Sysprep unattended file, which is nothing more than an answer file with Pass 3, 4, and 7 settings.

The Sysprep /unattend option allows a pre-configuration file to address Generalize, Specialize, and OOBE settings. A Sysprep unattend.xml file can be created using SIM.

1. Open SIM.
2. Right-click in the Windows Image pane, and click on Select Windows Image...
3. Create a new answer file.
4. The Windows Embedded Edition core is already added to the image. You don't have to include any packages.
5. Fill in the necessary settings for the computer name, autologon, license key, time zone, etc. The following table lists the possible settings for an unattended file:

Component	Configuration Pass	Component Setting	Possible Value / Notes
amd64_Microsoft-Windows-PnpSysprep__neutral	3 – Generalize	PersistAllDeviceInstalls	true
amd64_Microsoft-Windows-Shell-Setup__neutral	4 Specialize	ComputerName	ACME
	4 Specialize	ProductKey	<5x5 Runtime key> *Don't fill in for now*
	4 Specialize	TimeZone	Pacific Standard Time
	4 Specialize	AutoLogon: Username	User1
	4 Specialize	AutoLogon: Enabled	True
	4 Specialize	AutoLogon: LogonCount	4294967294
	4 Specialize	AutoLogon: Password: Value	password
amd64_Microsoft-Windows-International-Core__neutral	7 OOBE System	InputLocale	en-US
	7 OOBE System	SystemLocale	en-US
	7 OOBE System	UILanguage	en-US
	7 OOBE System	UserLocale	en-US
amd64_Microsoft-Windows-Shell-Setup__neutral	7 OOBE System	UserAccounts : LocalAccounts : LocalAccount : Name	User1
	7 OOBE System	UserAccounts : LocalAccounts : LocalAccount : DisplayName	User1
	7 OOBE System	UserAccounts : LocalAccounts : LocalAccount :Group	Administrators
	7 OOBE System	UserAccounts : LocalAccounts : LocalAccount : Password : Value	password
	7 OOBE System	OOBE : ProtectYourPC	3
	7 OOBE System	OOBE : HideEULAPage	True
	7 OOBE System	OOBE : HideWirelessSetupInOOBE	True
	7 OOBE System	OOBE : HideOEMREgistrationScreen	True

	7 OOBE System	OOBE : HideLocalAccountScreen	True
	7 OOBE System	OOBE : HideOnlineAccountScreen	True
	7 OOBE System	OOBE : SkipMachineOOBE	True
	7 OOBE System	OOBE : SkipUserOOBE	True
	7 OOBE System	OOBE : UnattendEnableRetailDemo	False

You can also add synchronous commands that run on each clone. For example, disabling Windows Update requires several registry key changes, a service disabled, and a task disabled. These items are discussed in chapter 9.

If you do a validation, SIM will warn that SkipUserOOBE and SkipMachineOOBE are depreciated. These warnings can be ignored. SkipMachineOOBE will allow you to preserve the machine name as entered when the OS was installed. SkipUserOOBE will bypass the screen that forces you to enter a new user again. As an added benefit, you can also add Pass 4 and Pass 7 Synchronous Commands for automation of each clone. Maybe you want to enable UWF on each clone before system test. You can use a Synchronous Command in the unattend file to perform that action. Again, the system must boot into an administrator account for the Pass 7 synchronous commands to run.

6. Save the answer file as myUnattended.xml. You will be prompted that the validation didn't pass.
7. Just click yes to continue.
8. Put the unattended XML file into the distribution share under \$$\System32\Sysprep.
9. Build the configuration set, build the installation media, and install the OS on the target system.
10. After the image has been set up on the target, use Sysprep with the unattended file to create the master:

```
Sysprep /generalize /oobe /shutdown
/unattend:c:\windows\system32\sysprep\unattended.xml
```

At this point, the image can be captured using a software or disk duplication utility. When the master has been deployed to a cloned target, the image will boot up and generate a new SID and load device drivers. Any settings addressed in the unattend file will not be asked during OOBE Pass.

11. For simplicity in this exercise, the image doesn't have to be copied. Simply boot the target and watch the system go through the mini-setup.

2.15 Master Image

Once Sysprep has run, you will want to capture the master image for manufacturing.

2.15.1 Exercise 208: Capture, Apply, and FFU

The following steps discus how to create a WinPE disk to capture and deploy the image on the hard drive to a Full Flash Update (.FFU) file.

1. With both the ADK and WinPE add-on installed, from the start menu, go to Windows Kits and open Deployment and Imaging Tool Environment.
2. Run the following command to create a WinPE image and workspace:

   Copype amd64 c:\WinPE64

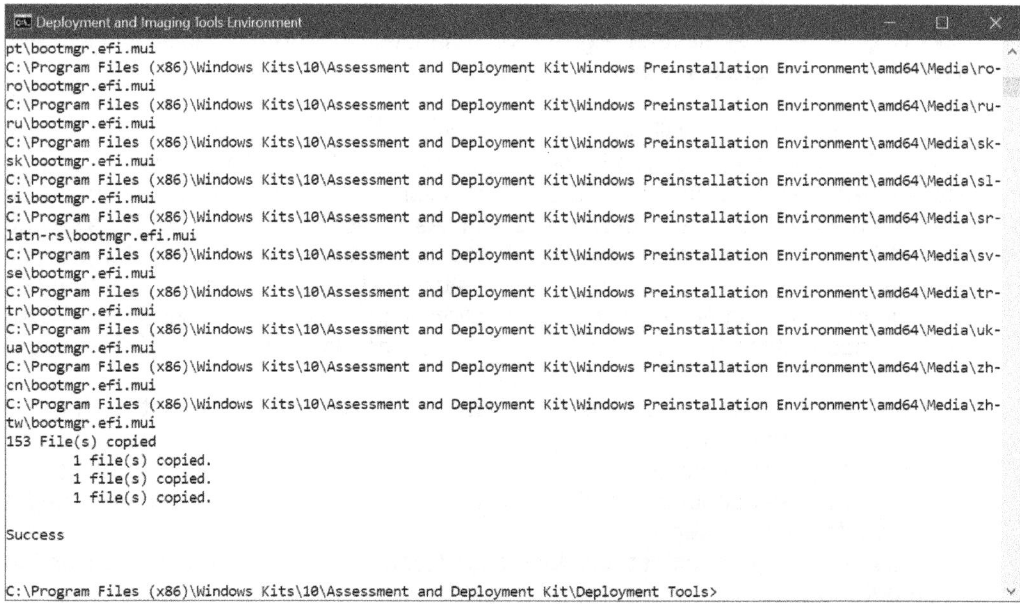

The workspace gets created, and the WinPE image is placed in the C:\WinPE64\media directory. The image, as is, will boot to a command prompt. Some people like to create a shell for their WinPE and have a more user-friendly interface. Chapter 9 covers creating a custom WinPE disk. All we need to capture the image is the basic WinPE disk and a couple of batch files

3. Create the following two batch files and place these files in C:\WinPE64\media

Capture.bat:

```
Dism /Capture-Ffu /ImageFile:d:\My-WIN10-MM-DD-YY.ffu
/CaptureDrive:\\.\PhysicalDrive0 /Name:MYOS /Compress:default
```

Apply.bat:

```
dism.exe /apply-ffu /imagefile:d:\My-WIN10-MM-DD-YY.ffu
/ApplyDrive:\\.\PhysicalDrive0
```

Note: Each batch file is a single line. You may have to change the file path to match the root of the USB flash disk. You can use notepad.exe to make any required changes.

Note: It is best practice to give the .FFU file a name with a date in the name. You will create a few .FFU files during testing.

4. Create another bootable USB flash disk using RUFUS.
5. Copy the contents of the C:\WinPE64\media directory to the NTFS partition of the USB disk.

You can then boot the target with the USB flash disk and run the capture.bat to capture the image. Once captured, run the apply.bat file to make sure the .FFU is good. Shutdown the system by running the following:

Wpeutil shutdown

Then boot the system and verify the clone boots up properly.

2.15.2 Activation and Production Questions

If the clone boots the way you expect, the .FFU is then ready for production...maybe. Per Chapter 1, activation needs to be addressed. It is recommended to activate each clone at start up in manufacturing. This means some lockdown features like UWF are disabled, and it also means the the lockdown features have to be enabled before the unit goes through final Q/A and shipment. Not every production person is well versed with this technology so some steps or a custom interface will have to be created to address final configuration. Every company is different in how they go to production. Keep in mind you will have to test the .FFU deployment and make changes to address these features.

2.16 Exercise 209: Volume Activation Management Tool (VAMT)

Chapter 1 discusses the issues of the runtime key and activations. If you know you're going to ship more than 50,000 units, then you will want to know when to ask for a new key or an extension on the 50,000 units for the current key. If you are curious to see how many activations have been made on your assigned license key, the Volume Activation Management Tool (VAMT), which is part of the Windows Assessment and Deployment Kit (ADK), can provide a report on the remaining activations left for a particular runtime license key.

VAMT requires an SQL server as it will set up a database to record and save license information. SQL Express is sufficient to hold the VAMT database.

1. Download and install SQL Express. Choose the defaults when running the installer.
2. Optional: To help manage all the databases that are in SQL Server, download and install the SQL Server Management Studio (SSMS) tool.

Opening the SSMS tool, you will see all the databases and the tables associated with each database. Columns can be added, the primary key can be set, and data can be modified in the database. It is a good tool to have, but not needed for VAMT to function.

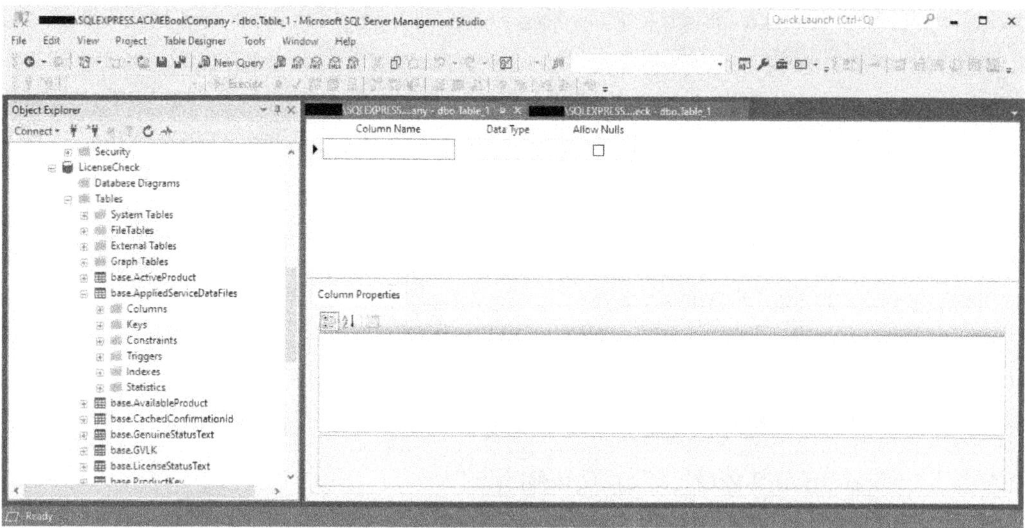

3. If you have already installed the Windows ADK, hopefully, you checked the Volume Activation Management Tool (VAMT) to be installed. If not, re-run the installer and select the Volume Activation Management Tool (VAMT) and click change.

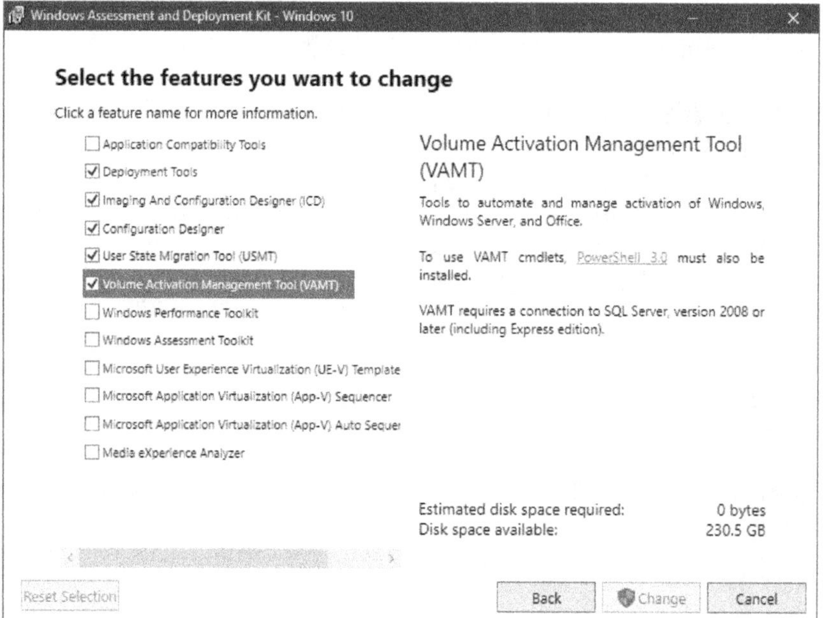

4. Run VAMT
5. When you first run the tool, it will ask for the SQL server location and the database.
   a. Click on the drop-down next to Server, and you should see the instance of the SQL database.

b. Click on the drop-down next to Database and select "<Create new database>".

c. A text box will show up below, enter the name of the database (i.e. LicenseCheck) and click Connect.

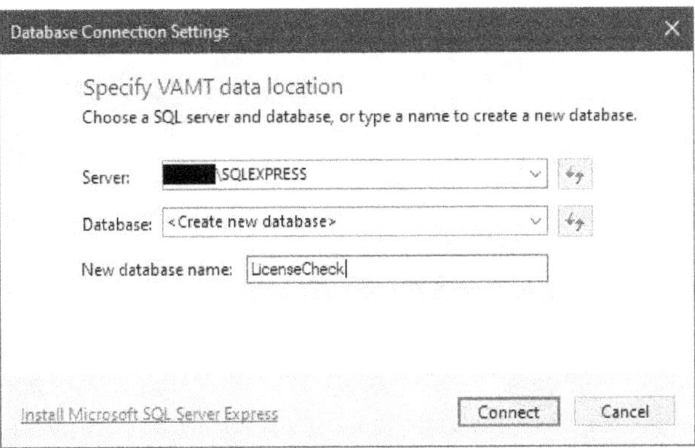

VAMT is an MMC plug-in.

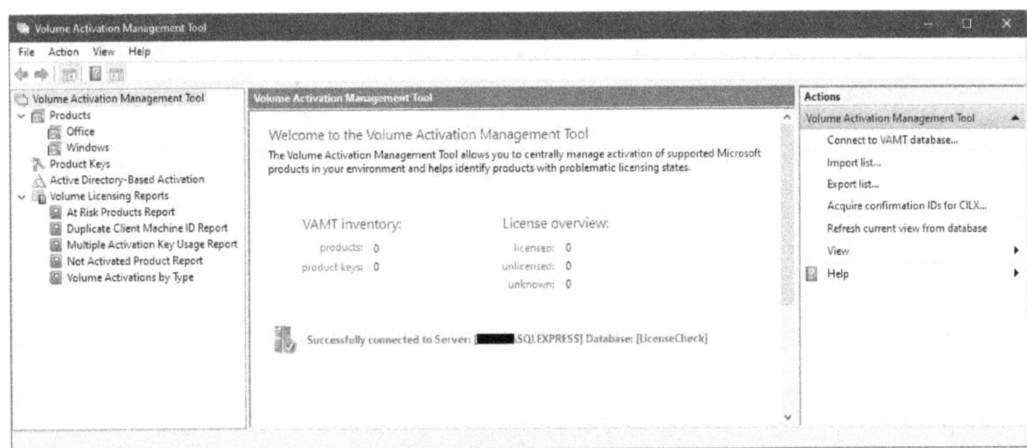

VAMT can be used to get Windows and Office product information for computers on an active directory or local working group, which is perfect for IT departments.

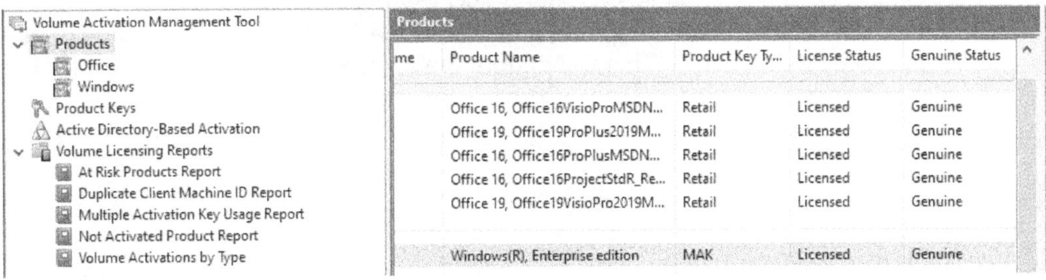

For the Embedded/IoT OEMs, we want to check the license key.

6. Click on the Product Keys on the left pane.

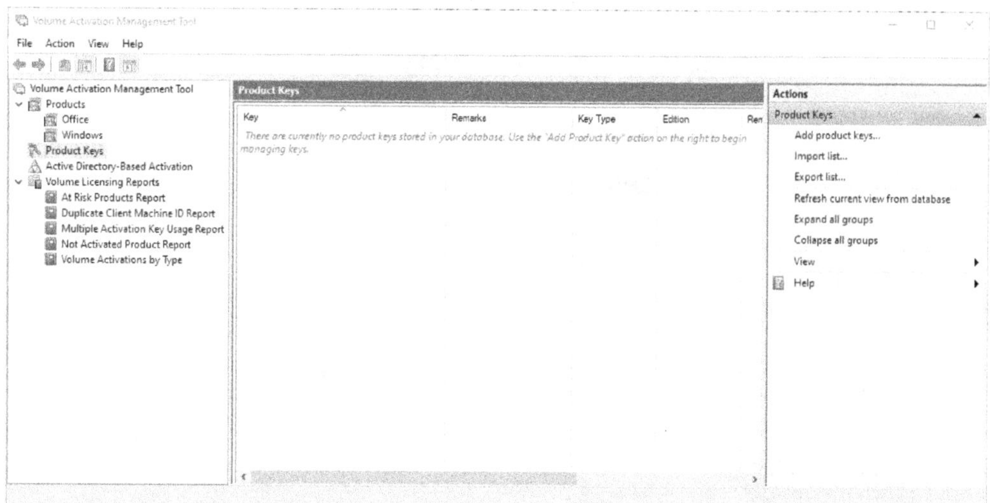

7. In the Actions pane, click on "Add Product keys..."
8. A dialog appears where you can add multiple 5x5 runtime license keys (aka Product keys). Enter your key and click the "Add Key(s)" button.

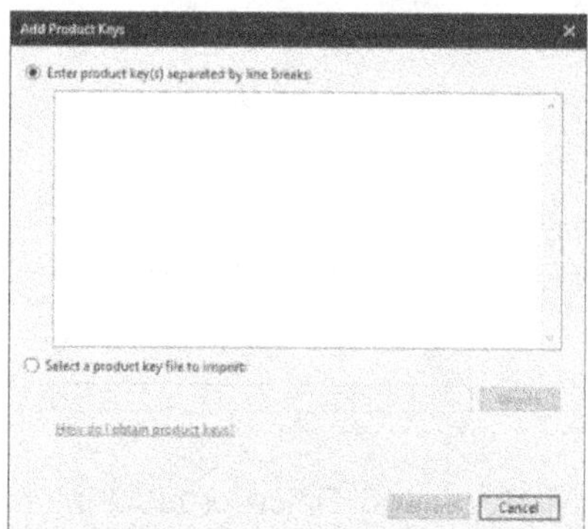

9. Click the "Ok" button on the key-added-success dialog.
10. Click on the key in the center pane, and then in the Actions pane, click on "Refresh product key data online". This will update the Remaining Activation Count for the key in the center pane.

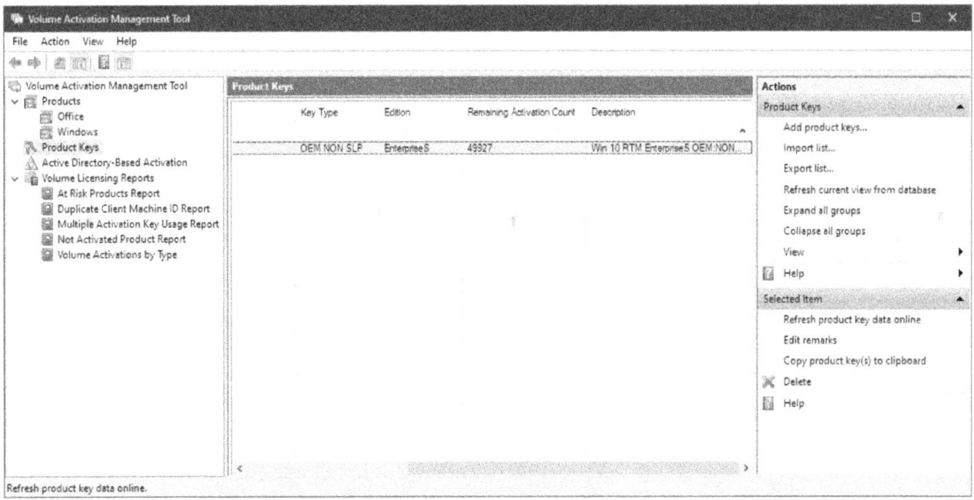

If you are managing multiple keys for multiple devices, you can add remarks to identify which key goes with each product. The VAMT tool provides an important key management solution for monitoring the number of activations per key. If you notice the activations are higher than the number of units shipped, then you need to make sure something like the UWF scenario is not burning through the activations.

2.17 Summary: Horse Meets Water

The chapter interweaved the development workflows with creating the build files and installing a custom image on the target system. The first step in the workflow is The Basics. The four parts of "The Basics" is what I use for every single project. It doesn't matter what the product is, the steps are the same. The goal is to lay a foundation for the rest of the project. The rest of the workflow builds on the foundation to customize the image. Once the Basics are completed, you can build onto the answer file to add the items to lock down the system and address the needs of the product. Chapters 3 through 9 cover additional features to further configure the answer file and add synchronous commands. Once the image has been set up on the target hardware, the final act is to run Sysprep to create the master image. There is a lot of building and rebuilding in the process, but once set up, any future updates will only require some minor changes to the build files. With the workflow now covered, this is the jumping-off point to dive into the next chapters to further customize the image.

3 System Performance

Chapter 1 discussed what features to look for in choosing your hardware and that the choice of hardware plays a big role in system performance. The combination of processor type, system bus speed, the amount of RAM, and boot media are the key factors for system performance. Cost plays a big role in what hardware to choose; and often, choosing a slower-performing system meets the cost goals of a program. There are some features in the Windows OS that can be adjusted to help improve performance on a slower system. This chapter will cover some of these topics.

Warning: No amount of operating system adjustments can address a poor choice of hardware. For example, trying to run Windows 64-bit on a system with 2GB of RAM is not going to give you great performance.

3.1 Choice of Application Type

Over the years, I have seen different application types, .NET, Python, Adobe Air, HTML, etc. The choice of the main application that will run will also affect the system's performance. Writing an application in C/C++ will be a faster application than one written in .NET, but .NET will be faster than a Python application.

3.2 Optimize .NET Apps with NGEN.EXE and Crossgen.exe

Managed code applications, like those built on .NET, have the stigma of being slow. There is an option to tweak the performance by compiling the .NET application to native code using the Native Image Generator (Ngen.exe) for .NET Framework applications or Crossgen.exe for .NET applications. Ngen.exe and Crossgen.exe create processor-specific, native images and place the code into the cache. When the run-time is called the native image in the cache is executed.

The assemblies that come with .NET Framework are also optimized in the background as they are called by the application. Later you will learn about the Unified Write Filter overlay, which can get filled up quickly with these optimizations. Here are two commands that can be added as Pass 7 Synchronous commands to optimize assemblies during OS installation:

```
C:\Windows\Microsoft.NET\Framework64\v4.0.30319\ngen.exe executequeueditems
C:\Windows\Microsoft.NET\Framework\v4.0.30319\ngen.exe executequeueditems
```

3.3 *Exercise 301: Create a Custom Power Plan*

Starting with Windows 7, the power setting options have expanded to support three power setting levels (High Performance, Balanced, and Power Saver) and several different advanced settings for things like USB devices, the power button, and display brightness.

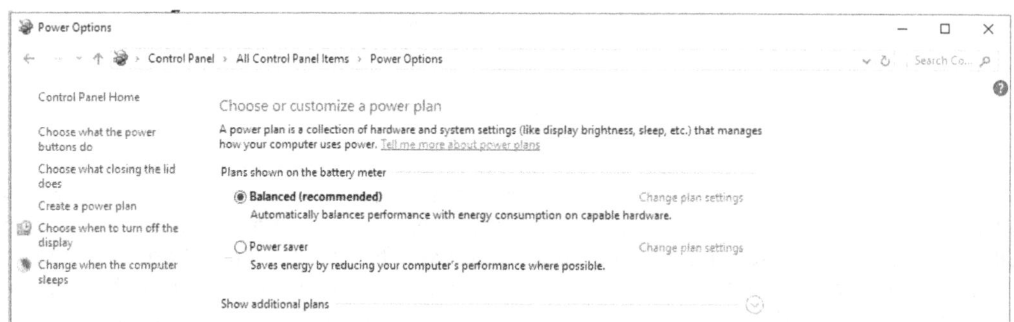

There have been a few customers who have asked me if there is any way to get better performance out of their systems. Typically, these customers are running low-end Intel® Atom™ or AMD G-Series processors. Besides stopping some services, changing the power plan to High Performance can make a difference in how well the system responds. Of course, one needs to take into account thermal cooling and battery life when running a processor at High Performance for extended periods of time. We have had other customers who want specific settings like display timeout disabled, hibernation enabled, and USB selective suspend disabled. SIM doesn't have settings for setting these power options, but you can still set up the power plan during OS installation. The powercfg.exe utility can be used to preset power settings in SIM using synchronous commands. The problem is that the powercfg.exe utility can be a bit cryptic for changing individual settings. GUIDs are used for different setting options, and some settings require multiple GUIDs just to change one setting. With limited space in a synchronous command, some settings might not fit.

The solution is to create the power plan in the target system, and then export the power plan to a single file using the powercfg.exe utility. The file can then be imported and set active via synchronous commands. Here are the basic steps to create a custom power plan and install it along with the operating system:

Note: You should have completed building the answer file and distribution share in chapter 2.

1. If you have not done so already, install the Windows 10 IoT Enterprise LTSC on your target machine and install any missing device drivers.
2. In the target system, open Control Panel.
3. Open the Power Options control panel applet.
4. The best starting point is to choose one of the basic plans first - High Performance, Balanced, or Power Saver. Click on the radio button, so that it becomes the active plan.
5. Next click on the "Change Plan Settings" link that is next to the select plan.

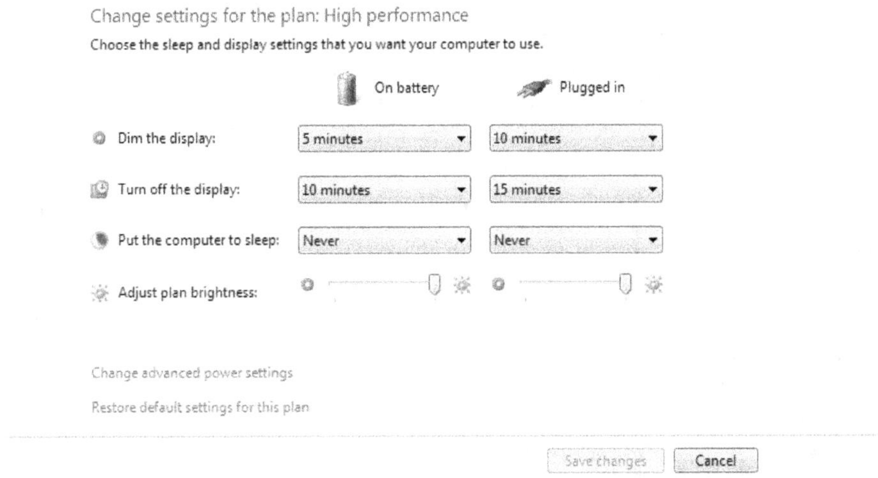

6. The next screen provides the basic settings that can be changed. You can change these settings or click on "Change advanced power settings" to get access to more settings.

Note: The number of available settings in Advanced settings is different from system to system.

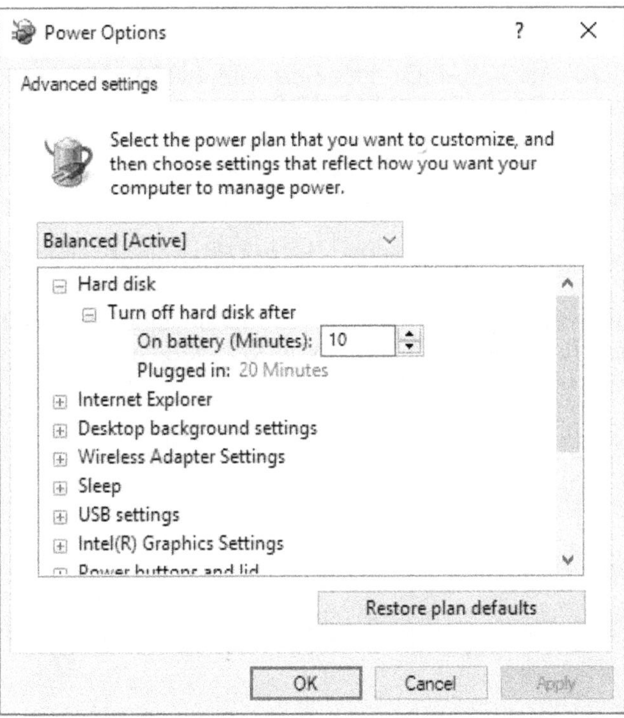

7. A dialog will appear that presents the available power settings for the system. Make the necessary changes and click OK when finished.
8. Click Save Changes on the "Change settings for plan:" page.
9. Open a command window with elevated privileges (run cmd.exe as administrator).
10. Using powercfg.exe, run the following command to list the power settings that are available and active:

C:\>powercfg /L

```
Command Prompt
Microsoft Windows [Version 6.1.7601]
Copyright (c) 2009 Microsoft Corporation.  All rights reserved.

C:\Users\sean>powercfg /l

Existing Power Schemes (* Active)
-----------------------------------
Power Scheme GUID: 381b4222-f694-41f0-9685-ff5bb260df2e  (Balanced)
Power Scheme GUID: 8c5e7fda-e8bf-4a96-9a85-a6e23a8c635c  (High performance) *
Power Scheme GUID: a1841308-3541-4fab-bc81-f71556f20b4a  (Power saver)
Power Scheme GUID: d8bb8260-4900-432c-9404-73b89bb44043  (Samsung Optimized)

C:\Users\sean>
```

11. The * next to the plan indicates the active plan. Make sure this is the plan you made active earlier.
12. Using the GUID associated with the active power plan. You can give your power plan a unique name by running the following:

C:\>powercfg.exe /CHANGENAME 8c5e7fda-e8bf-4a96-9a85-a6e23a8c635c "ACME Power Plan" "Advanced Power Plan for ACME System"

13. Using the GUID associated with the active power plan, run the following command to export the current active plan:

C:\>powercfg.exe /EXPORT mypowerplan.pow 8c5e7fda-e8bf-4a96-9a85-a6e23a8c635c

14. Copy the plan file (mypowerplan.pow) to your development machine and place the plan in the distribution share under \WinData\DS64\$1\Setup.

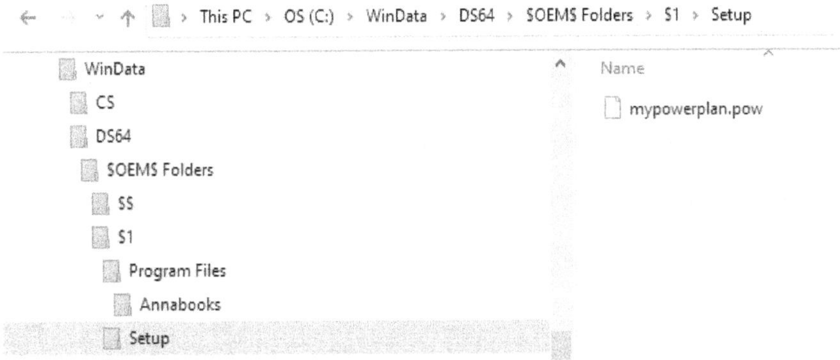

15. Use the GUID generator utility from Visual Studio or the web-based GUID generator found at http://www.guidgenerator.com/ to generate a unique GUID. We will use this new GUID to import the plan and set the plan active.
16. In the EX202 answer file, create a Pass 7 oobeSystem synchronous command to import the power plan:

    powercfg.exe /IMPORT c:\Setup\mypowerplan.pow bbac568e-4b69-4e63-adaa-f34dc3e64313

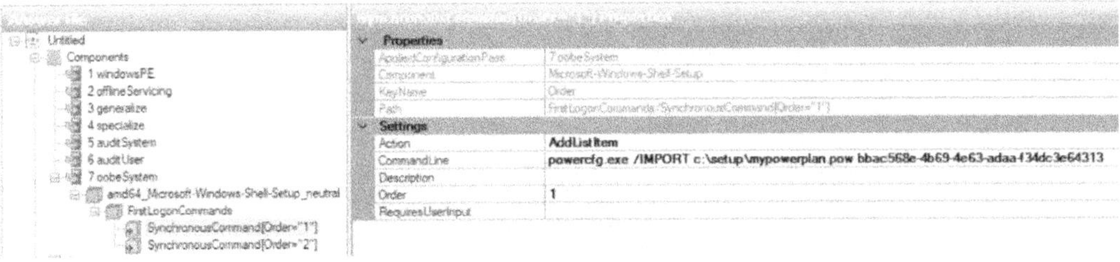

17. Add another Pass 7 oobeSystem synchronous command to set the plan as active:

    powercfg.exe /S bbac568e-4b69-4e63-adaa-f34dc3e64313

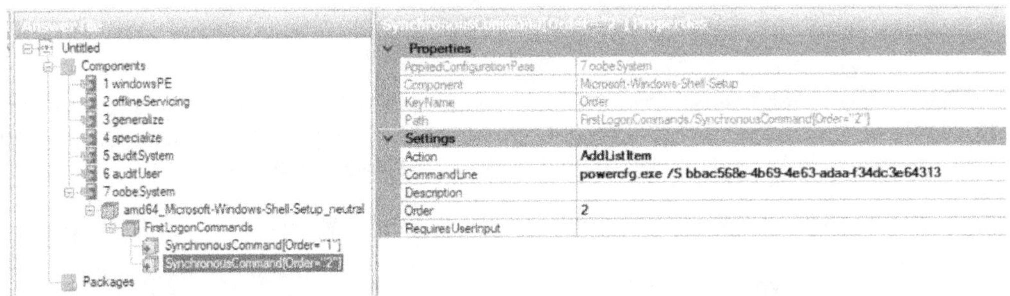

18. Save the answer file.
19. Create the configuration set and the custom USB install disk.

20. Install the OS on the target. If you go to Control Panel->Power Options, you should see the custom power plan set as the main power plan for the system.

3.4 Performance Options and Registry Keys

To help control the performance overhead of the visual effects, you can preset the performance options by importing a registry key. Go to System Control Panel->Advanced System Settings, click on the Advanced Tab, and then click on the settings button under performance.

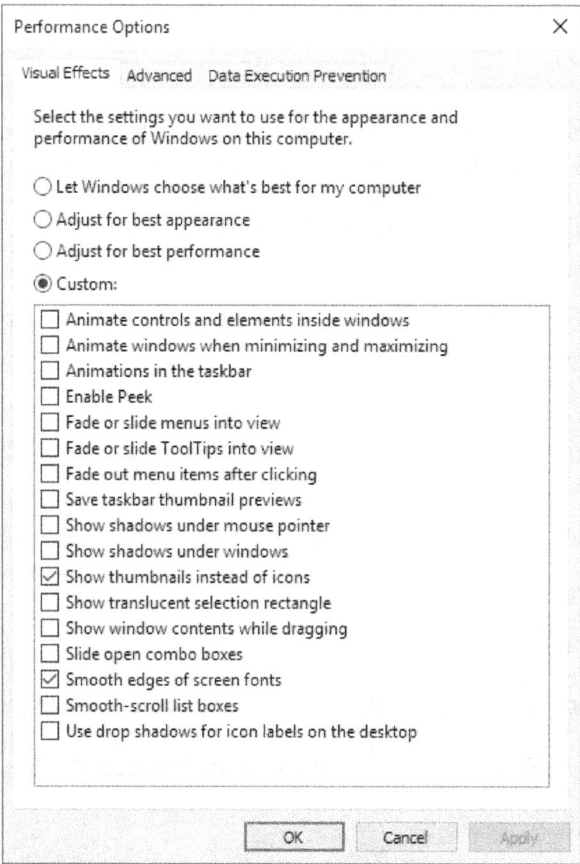

The Visual Effects tab lists all the visual effects available. Make the changes, and select OK. These selections are tied to different registry settings. Open the Registry Editor, and we will export a few keys. The first key handles the top visual effects options.

[HKEY_CURRENT_USER\SOFTWARE\Microsoft\Windows\CurrentVersion\Explorer\VisualEffects]
"VisualFXSetting"=dword:00000003

The values are 0, 1, 2, and 3. The value should be 3, since custom settings are being applied. The rest of the settings are found in different locations.

The following selections are placed in the UserPerenfencesMask under HKEY_CURRENT_USER\Control Panel\Desktop

(A) Smooth-scroll list boxes
(B) Slide open combo boxes
(C) Fade or slide menus into view
(D) Show shadows under mouse pointer
(E) Fade or slide ToolTips into view
(F) Fade out menu items after clicking
(G) Show shadows under windows
(H) Animate controls and elements inside windows

The value is a HEX value, but if we convert the HEX values to binary and identify the user preferences by the corresponding letters in the above list, the visual settings can be written as follows: 1001ABC0 00D1EF10 00000G11 0000100H0

Where: 0=off and 1=on

For example:

(A) Smooth-scroll list boxes: 0
(B) Slide open combo boxes: 0
(C) Fade or slide menus into view: 0
(D) Show shadows under mouse pointer: 0
(E) Fade or slide ToolTips into view: 0
(F) Fade out menu items after clicking: 0
(G) Show shadows under windows: 0
(H) Animate controls and elements inside windows: 0

Plugging in all the zeros for each letter:
1001ABC0 00D1EF10 00000G11 0000100H0

Becomes:
1001**000**0 00**0**1**00**10 00000**0**11 0000100**0**0

Converting this to hex, the UserPreferencesMask becomes:

[HKEY_CURRENT_USER\Control Panel\Desktop]
"UserPreferencesMask"=hex:90,12,03,80,10,00,00,00

The rest of the settings are in HKCU\Software\Microsoft\Windows\CurrentVersion\Explorer\Advanced, HKCU\Control Panel\Desktop, and HKCU\Software\Microsoft\Windows\DWM.

In this book's exercises for Chapter 2, there is a visualeffect.reg file. This contains the following registry keys:

```
Windows Registry Editor Version 5.00

[HKEY_CURRENT_USER\SOFTWARE\Microsoft\Windows\CurrentVersion\Explorer\VisualEffects]
"VisualFXSetting"=dword:00000003

;(A) Smooth-scroll list boxes
;(B) Slide open combo boxes
;(C) Fade or slide menus into view
;(D) Show shadows under mouse pointer
;(E) Fade or slide ToolTips into view
;(F) Fade out menu items after clicking
;(G) Show shadows under windows
;(H) Animate controls and elements inside windows
;1001ABC0 00D1EF10 00000G11 10000000 0000100H0

[HKEY_CURRENT_USER\Control Panel\Desktop]
"UserPreferencesMask"=hex:90,12,03,80,10,00,00,00

;Animate windows when minimizing and maximizing
[HKEY_CURRENT_USER\Control Panel\Desktop\WindowMetrics]
"MinAnimate"="0"

;Animations in the taskbar
[HKEY_CURRENT_USER\Software\Microsoft\Windows\CurrentVersion\Explorer\Advanced]
"TaskbarAnimations"=dword:0

;Enable Peek
[HKEY_CURRENT_USER\Software\Microsoft\Windows\DWM]
"EnableAeroPeek"=dword:0

;Save taskbar thumbnail previews
[HKEY_CURRENT_USER\Software\Microsoft\Windows\DWM]
"AlwaysHibernateThumbnails"=dword:0

;Show thumbnails instead of Icons
[HKEY_CURRENT_USER\Software\Microsoft\Windows\CurrentVersion\Explorer\Advanced]
"IconsOnly"=dword:0
"DisablePreviewDesktop"=dword:0

;Show translucent selection rectangle
[HKEY_CURRENT_USER\Software\Microsoft\Windows\CurrentVersion\Explorer\Advanced]
"ListviewAlphaSelect"=dword:0

;Show window contents while dragging
[HKEY_CURRENT_USER\Control Panel\Desktop]
"DragFullWindows"="0"

;Smooth edges of screen fonts
[HKEY_CURRENT_USER\Control Panel\Desktop]
"FontSmoothing"="2"

;Use drop shadows for icon labels on the desktop
[HKEY_CURRENT_USER\Software\Microsoft\Windows\CurrentVersion\Explorer\Advanced]
"ListviewShadow"=dword:0
```

The file can be imported into the registry using a Pass 7 Synchronous command or set up for each use by running the command in a batch file:

```
Regedit.exe /S c:\setup\VisualEffects.reg
```

3.5 Windows Services

Windows has a hybrid operating system architecture of layers in the kernel with client services that interact with the kernel. As a result, there are over 250 services that are part of Windows. About 81 of these services might be running out of the box. It is common practice to delete some of these services to help improve performance. Below is the typical list of services in Windows. The sc.exe or the PowerShell cmdlets get-service and set-service can be used to manage the state of a service. Some services have dependencies on other services, so you need to address those services before trying to stop a parent service. The table below lists the service name and some of the dependencies that sc.exe or the PowerShell cmdlets will use along with the DisplayName that is shown in the service Control Panel applet.

Name	**DisplayName**	**Dependencies (Not all Dependencies listed)**
AarSvc_b4034	Agent Activation Runtime_b4034	
AJRouter	AllJoyn Router Service	
ALG	Application Layer Gateway Service	
AppIDSvc	Application Identity	applockerfltr
Appinfo	Application Information	
AppMgmt	Application Management	
AppReadiness	App Readiness	
AppVClient	Microsoft App-V Client	
AppXSvc	AppX Deployment Service (AppXSVC)	
AssignedAccessM...	AssignedAccessManager Service	
AudioEndpointBuilder	Windows Audio Endpoint Builder	AarSvc_b4034, AarSvc, Audiosrv
Audiosrv	Windows Audio	AarSvc_b4034, AarSvc
autotimesvc	Cellular Time	
AxInstSV	ActiveX Installer (AxInstSV)	
BcastDVRUserService_21760a5	GameDVR and Broadcast User Service_...	
BDESVC	BitLocker Drive Encryption Service	
BFE	Base Filtering Engine	XboxNetApiSvc, WdNisSvc, WdNisDrv, SharedAccess
BITS	Background Intelligent Transfer Ser...	
BluetoothUserService_21760a5	Bluetooth User Support Service_b4034	
BrokerInfrastructure	Background Tasks Infrastructure Ser...	workfolderssvc, WMPNetworkSvc, WSearch, CDPSvc

Name	DisplayName	Dependencies (Not all Dependencies listed)
BTAGService	Bluetooth Audio Gateway Service	
BthAvctpSvc	AVCTP service	
bthserv	Bluetooth Support Service	BluetoothUserService_b4034, BluetoothUserService
camsvc	Capability Access Manager Service	
CaptureService_21760a5	CaptureService_b4034	
cbdhsvc_b4034	Clipboard User Service_b4034	
CDPSvc	Connected Devices Platform Service	
CDPUserSvc_b4034	Connected Devices Platform User Ser...	
CertPropSvc	Certificate Propagation	
ClipSVC	Client License Service (ClipSVC)	
COMSysApp	COM+ System Application	
ConsentUxUserSvc_21760a5	ConsentUX_b4034	
CoreMessagingRegistrar	CoreMessaging	
cphs	Intel(R) Content Protection HECI Se...	
CredentialEnrol...	CredentialEnrollmentManagerUserSvc_ ...	
CryptSvc	Cryptographic Services	applockerfltr, AppIDSvc
CscService	Offline Files	
DcomLaunch	DCOM Server Process Launcher	PrintWorkflowUserSvc_b4034, DevicesFlowUserSvc_b4034, DevicePickerUserSvc_b4034, DeviceAssociationBrokerSvc_ b4034
defragsvc	Optimize drives	
DeviceAssociati...	DeviceAssociationBroker_b4034	
DeviceAssociati...	Device Association Service	
DeviceInstall	Device Install Service	
DeviceAssociation BrokerSvc_21760a5	DevicePicker_b4034	
DevicesFlowUserSvc_21760a 5	DevicesFlow_b4034	
DevQueryBroker	DevQuery Background Discovery Broker	
Dhcp	DHCP Client	NcaSvc, iphlpsvc, WinHttpAutoProxySvc, NcdAutoSetup
diagnosticshub. standardcollector.service	Microsoft (R) Diagnostics Hub Stand...	
diagsvc	Diagnostic Execution Service	
DiagTrack	Connected User Experiences and Tele...	
DialogBlockingService	DialogBlockingService	
DispBrokerDesktopSvc	Display Policy Service	

Name	DisplayName	Dependencies (Not all Dependencies listed)
DisplayEnhancementService	Display Enhancement Service	
DmEnrollmentSvc	Device Management Enrollment Service	
dmwappushservice	Device Management Wireless Applicat...	
Dnscache	DNS Client	RemoteAccess, RasMan, NcaSvc
DoSvc	Delivery Optimization	
dot3svc	Wired AutoConfig	
DPS	Diagnostic Policy Service	
DsmSvc	Device Setup Manager	
DsSvc	Data Sharing Service	
DusmSvc	Data Usage	
Eaphost	Extensible Authentication Protocol	dot3svc
EFS	Encrypting File System (EFS)	
embeddedmode	Embedded Mode	
EntAppSvc	Enterprise App Management Service	
EventLog	Windows Event Log	Wecsvc, NcdAutoSetup, AppVClient, netprofm
EventSystem	COM+ Event System	igfxCUIService2.0.0.0, COMSysApp, SENS
Fax	Fax	
fdPHost	Function Discovery Provider Host	FDResPub
FDResPub	Function Discovery Resource Publica...	
fhsvc	File History Service	
FontCache	Windows Font Cache Service	
FrameServer	Windows Camera Frame Server	
gpsvc	Group Policy Client	
GraphicsPerfSvc	GraphicsPerfSvc	
hidserv	Human Interface Device Service	
HvHost	HV Host Service	
icssvc	Windows Mobile Hotspot Service	
igfxCUIService2.0.0.0	Intel(R) HD Graphics Control Panel ...	
IKEEXT	IKE and AuthIP IPsec Keying Modules	XboxNetApiSvc
InstallService	Microsoft Store Install Service	
iphlpsvc	IP Helper	NcaSvc
IpxlatCfgSvc	IP Translation Configuration Service	
KeyIso	CNG Key Isolation	XboxNetApiSvc, dot3svc, Eaphost
KtmRm	KtmRm for Distributed Transaction C...	

Name	DisplayName	Dependencies (Not all Dependencies listed)
LanmanServer	Server	
LanmanWorkstation	Workstation	SessionEnv, Netlogon
lfsvc	Geolocation Service	
LicenseManager	Windows License Manager Service	
lltdsvc	Link-Layer Topology Discovery Mapper	
lmhosts	TCP/IP NetBIOS Helper	
LSM	Local Session Manager	
LxpSvc	Language Experience Service	
MapsBroker	Downloaded Maps Manager	
MessagingService_21760a5	MessagingService_b4034	
mpssvc	Windows Defender Firewall	XboxNetApiSvc
MSDTC	Distributed Transaction Coordinator	
MSiSCSI	Microsoft iSCSI Initiator Service	
msiserver	Windows Installer	
MsKeyboardFilter	Microsoft Keyboard Filter	
NaturalAuthentication	Natural Authentication	
NcaSvc	Network Connectivity Assistant	
NcbService	Network Connection Broker	CDPSvc
NcdAutoSetup	Network Connected Devices Auto-Setup	
Netlogon	Netlogon	
Netman	Network Connections	
netprofm	Network List Service	NcdAutoSetup, AppVClient
NetSetupSvc	Network Setup Service	
NetTcpPortSharing	Net.Tcp Port Sharing Service	
NgcCtnrSvc	Microsoft Passport Container	
NgcSvc	Microsoft Passport	
NlaSvc	Network Location Awareness	NcdAutoSetup, AppVClient, netprofm
nsi	Network Store Interface Service	WlanSvc, icssvc, Wcmsvc, upnphost
OneSyncSvc_b4034	Sync Host_b4034	
p2pimsvc	Peer Networking Identity Manager	PNRPAutoReg, p2psvc, PNRPsvc
p2psvc	Peer Networking Grouping	
PcaSvc	Program Compatibility Assistant Ser...	
PeerDistSvc	BranchCache	
perceptionsimul...	Windows Perception Simulation Service	
PerfHost	Performance Counter DLL Host	

Name	DisplayName	Dependencies (Not all Dependencies listed)
PhoneSvc	Phone Service	
PimIndexMaintenanceSvc_21760a5	Contact Data_b4034	
pla	Performance Logs & Alerts	
PlugPlay	Plug and Play	
PNRPAutoReg	PNRP Machine Name Publication Service	
PNRPsvc	Peer Name Resolution Protocol	PNRPAutoReg, p2psvc
PolicyAgent	IPsec Policy Agent	
Power	Power	
PrintNotify	Printer Extensions and Notifications	
PrintWorkflowUserSvc_21760a5	PrintWorkflow_b4034	
ProfSvc	User Profile Service	XblGameSave, TokenBroker, UserManager, shpamsvc
PushToInstall	Windows PushToInstall Service	
QWAVE	Quality Windows Audio Video Experience	
RasAuto	Remote Access Auto Connection Manager	RemoteAccess
RasMan	Remote Access Connection Manager	
RemoteAccess	Routing and Remote Access	
RemoteRegistry	Remote Registry	
RetailDemo	Retail Demo Service	
RmSvc	Radio Management Service	
RpcEptMapper	RPC Endpoint Mapper	NaturalAuthentication, Schedule, SystemEventsBroker, PrintWorkflowUserSvc_b4034
RpcLocator	Remote Procedure Call (RPC) Locator	
RpcSs	Remote Procedure Call (RPC)	PrintWorkflowUserSvc_b4034, DevicesFlowUserSvc_b4034, DevicePickerUserSvc_b4034, DeviceAssociationBrokerSvc_b4034
SamSs	Security Accounts Manager	MSDTC, LanmanServer, KtmRm
SCardSvr	Smart Card	
ScDeviceEnum	Smart Card Device Enumeration Service	
Schedule	Task Scheduler	NaturalAuthentication
SCPolicySvc	Smart Card Removal Policy	
SDRSVC	Windows Backup	
seclogon	Secondary Logon	
SecurityHealthService	Windows Security Service	

Name	DisplayName	Dependencies (Not all Dependencies listed)
SEMgrSvc	Payments and NFC/SE Manager	
SENS	System Event Notification Service	igfxCUIService2.0.0.0, COMSysApp
Sense	Windows Defender Advanced Threat Pr...	
SensorDataService	Sensor Data Service	
SensorService	Sensor Service	
SensrSvc	Sensor Monitoring Service	
SessionEnv	Remote Desktop Configuration	
SgrmBroker	System Guard Runtime Monitor Broker	
SharedAccess	Internet Connection Sharing (ICS)	
SharedRealitySvc	Spatial Data Service	
ShellHWDetection	Shell Hardware Detection	
shpamsvc	Shared PC Account Manager	
smphost	Microsoft Storage Spaces SMP	
SmsRouter	Microsoft Windows SMS Router Service.	
SNMPTRAP	SNMP Trap	
spectrum	Windows Perception Service	
Spooler	Print Spooler	Fax
sppsvc	Software Protection	
SSDPSRV	SSDP Discovery	upnphost
ssh-agent	OpenSSH Authentication Agent	
SstpSvc	Secure Socket Tunneling Protocol Se...	RemoteAccess, RasMan
StateRepository	State Repository Service	AppXSvc
stisvc	Windows Image Acquisition (WIA)	
StorSvc	Storage Service	
svsvc	Spot Verifier	
swprv	Microsoft Software Shadow Copy Prov...	
SysMain	SysMain	
SystemEventsBroker	System Events Broker	NaturalAuthentication, Schedule
TabletInputService	Touch Keyboard and Handwriting Pane...	
TapiSrv	Telephony	Fax
TermService	Remote Desktop Services	UmRdpService
Themes	Themes	
TieringEngineService	Storage Tiers Management	
TimeBrokerSvc	Time Broker	

Name	DisplayName	Dependencies (Not all Dependencies listed)
TokenBroker	Web Account Manager	
TrkWks	Distributed Link Tracking Client	
TroubleshootingSvc	Recommended Troubleshooting Service	
TrustedInstaller	Windows Modules Installer	
tzautoupdate	Auto Time Zone Updater	
UdkUserSvc_b4034	Udk User Service_b4034	
UevAgentService	User Experience Virtualization Service	
UmRdpService	Remote Desktop Services UserMode Po...	
UnistoreSvc_b4034	User Data Storage_b4034	UserDataSvc_b4034, PimIndexMaintenanceSvc_b4034
upnphost	UPnP Device Host	
UserDataSvc_b4034	User Data Access_b4034	
UserManager	User Manager	XblGameSave, TokenBroker
UsoSvc	Update Orchestrator Service	
UwfServicingSvc	Unified Write Filter Servicing Help...	
VacSvc	Volumetric Audio Compositor Service	
VaultSvc	Credential Manager	
vds	Virtual Disk	
vmicguestinterface	Hyper-V Guest Service Interface	
vmicheartbeat	Hyper-V Heartbeat Service	
vmickvpexchange	Hyper-V Data Exchange Service	
vmicrdv	Hyper-V Remote Desktop Virtualizati...	
vmicshutdown	Hyper-V Guest Shutdown Service	
vmictimesync	Hyper-V Time Synchronization Service	
vmicvmsession	Hyper-V PowerShell Direct Service	
vmicvss	Hyper-V Volume Shadow Copy Requestor	
VSS	Volume Shadow Copy	
W32Time	Windows Time	
WaaSMedicSvc	Windows Update Medic Service	
WalletService	WalletService	
WarpJITSvc	WarpJITSvc	
wbengine	Block Level Backup Engine Service	
WbioSrvc	Windows Biometric Service	
Wcmsvc	Windows Connection Manager	WlanSvc, icssvc
wcncsvc	Windows Connect Now - Config Registrar	

Name	DisplayName	Dependencies (Not all Dependencies listed)
WdiServiceHost	Diagnostic Service Host	
WdiSystemHost	Diagnostic System Host	
WdNisSvc	Microsoft Defender Antivirus Networ...	
WebClient	WebClient	
Wecsvc	Windows Event Collector	
WEPHOSTSVC	Windows Encryption Provider Host Se...	
wercplsupport	Problem Reports Control Panel Support	
WerSvc	Windows Error Reporting Service	
WFDSConMgrSvc	Wi-Fi Direct Services Connection Ma...	
WiaRpc	Still Image Acquisition Events	
WinDefend	Microsoft Defender Antivirus Service	
WinHttpAutoProxySvc	WinHTTP Web Proxy Auto-Discovery Se...	NcaSvc, iphlpsvc
Winmgmt	Windows Management Instrumentation	NcaSvc, iphlpsvc
WinRM	Windows Remote Management (WS-Manag...	
wisvc	Windows Insider Service	
WlanSvc	WLAN AutoConfig	
wlidsvc	Microsoft Account Sign-in Assistant	
wlpasvc	Local Profile Assistant Service	
WManSvc	Windows Management Service	
wmiApSrv	WMI Performance Adapter	
WMPNetworkSvc	Windows Media Player Network Sharin...	
workfolderssvc	Work Folders	
WpcMonSvc	Parental Controls	
WPDBusEnum	Portable Device Enumerator Service	
WpnService	Windows Push Notifications System S...	
WpnUserService_21760a5	Windows Push Notifications User Ser...	
wscsvc	Security Center	
WSearch	Windows Search	workfolderssvc, WMPNetworkSvc
wuauserv	Windows Update	
WwanSvc	WWAN AutoConfig	wlpasvc
XblAuthManager	Xbox Live Auth Manager	XblGameSave
XblGameSave	Xbox Live Game Save	
XboxGipSvc	Xbox Accessory Management Service	
XboxNetApiSvc	Xbox Live Networking Service	

One of the great conversations, I had with a client was about the services back in the XP Embedded days.

Comment: "I know everything that is running on a Linux system. Why are all these services running in the Windows XP Embedded? I don't know what they are doing, but I expect you to know."
My Reply: "Well, this is Windows, not Linux. These Microsoft and 3rd party services are needed for your application to run and operate the way you intend. Only the necessary components have been added to the image to run your application, which eliminates a number of services that you had before when building a full XP Embedded image."
Comment: "Well, I expect to know what each and every service does."
My Reply: "There are descriptions of each service in the service control panel applet, but just by looking at the services there isn't much more to change. I can go through all of them with you, but I am getting paid by the hour."
Comment: "This is ridiculous! Linux doesn't operate like this"
My Reply: "Tell me again what the system does?"
Comment: "It is a headless Internet appliance. It takes a stream off the Internet, manipulates the data, and sends a new stream out on the network."
My Reply: "You should be using Linux not Windows".

Needless to say, the client couldn't point me to a service that was causing any problems with the performance of the system. The client couldn't point out any problems with the image that was created. Yes, it can be uncomfortable when something is running in Windows that you are not aware of. Microsoft has included these services to help users when running Windows as a generic host OS. For Embedded/IoT, we have to dig in a little bit to disable items we do not need. Life was simple with XP Embedded. We just didn't include a component. Windows 10 requires a little more work. Some of the services can be disabled by disabling the feature. For example, HyperV can be disabled in the SIM answer file, which will disable the services. Some services have to be disabled directly. You can use sc.exe in a command window or set-service cmdlet in PowerShell to set the state of a service and the startup mode. Here is a list of services that can be safely disabled.

Application Layer Gateway Service
Alljoyn Router Service
AVCTP Service
Bitlocker
Bluetooth Support Service
Connected User Experience and Telemetry
Certificate Propagation
Diagnostic Policy Service
Diagnostic Service Host
Diagnostic System Host
Distributed Link Tracking Client
Download Maps Manager
Enterprise App Management Service
Fax
File History Service
GameDVR and Broadcast
Geolocation Service
IP Helper
Internet Connection Sharing
Netlogon
Offline Files
Parental Control
Payments and NFC/SE Manager
Phone Service
Program Compatibility Assistant Service
Print Spooler
Remote Registry
Retail Demo Service
Secondary Logon
Smartcard
TCP/IP NetBIOS Helper

Touch Keyboard and Handwriting Panel Service
Windows Biometric Service
Windows Error Reporting Service
Windows Insider Service
Windows Image Acquisition
Windows Camera Frame Server
Windows Connect Now
Windows Insider Service
Windows Media Player Network Sharing Service
Windows Mobile Hotspot Service
Windows Search
Windows Update
Xbox Accessory Live Auth Manager
Xbox Live Auth Manager
Xbox Live Networking Services
Xbox Live Game Save

3.6 Scheduled Tasks

If services weren't confusing enough, there is an issue with scheduled tasks. As Windows has become more feature-rich, more and more scheduled tasks have been created to defer certain actions to run later or run-on-trigger. In the book exercises, the Chapter 3 folder has a schtasklist.bat batch file, which disables many of the scheduled tasks using the schtasks.exe utility. For example:

```
schtasks /Change /TN "\Microsoft\Windows\WindowsUpdate\Scheduled Start" /Disable
```

Running the batch file may not permanently disable a scheduled task. Some internal services will re-establishing some scheduled tasks by design. Just be aware that some tasks are required to run in the system.

3.7 Summary: Make the System an Appliance and Tweak Performance

System performance is mainly predicated on the choice of hardware. This chapter looked at some options for improving performance within the operating system. Application development and optimization choices can affect the look and feel to a user. Creating a custom power plan is a simpler solution to setting individual settings using powercfg.exe. Visual effects can also be preset. If you require more deterministic performance, real-time support is discussed in Chapter 4.

4 Real-Time Support

In the last chapter, performance tweaks were discussed that can be done to the operating system to get better performance. Again, the choice of hardware is very important for the overall performance of the system. Some applications require specific timing to perform correctly. For example, a jet fighter's fly-by-wire controls have to respond immediately, a CNC drill press must hit a specific mark, or a passenger train must stop at a precise place in the terminal. These examples use systems that have a specific deterministic or real-time performance. This short chapter will introduce the ideas for providing a real-time or deterministic response from a Windows system.

4.1 What is Real-time?

There are many definitions of real-time. If you search the Internet for the definition of real-time, you will get descriptions that talk about responding to external events, you will get descriptions that talk about timeliness of response, you will get descriptions that talk about predictability, and you will get descriptions that talk about stability. Although most of the definitions are not explicitly correct in the context of real-time OSes and processes, they do point to some of the basic fundamentals of real-timeliness.

For an operation within a larger dynamic system to be considered to be real-time, it must have a deterministic response to some event, no matter when the event occurs. The responses of real-time operations are bounded, that is, they will be completed within a guaranteed time. The constraints of a system being real-time tell us that we can always predict the response of the system to stimuli and events and we can predict how long it will take to complete that response in the worst case. Implicit in this description is the fact that the system remains stable. There can be no series of stimuli or events that will cause the system to no longer function as designed. The explicit real-time constraints can only be determined by analyzing the system design and the environment in which the system operates.

In terms of an operating system, being deterministic and bounded means that the OS never disables interrupts for longer than a given, well-defined time, and any (non-blocking) OS function will always complete within a guaranteed time. Real-time behavior is like a dictatorship. Rather than give all threads a chance to run, we always let some preferred threads have their share. If there is not enough time left, some threads may not get a chance to run at all. In a typical real-time environment, this may not be seen as bad. This is contrary to time-sharing systems, where the OS makes sure that all threads run eventually. .NET Framework CLR is a good example of time-sharing. Priorities provided by the programmer are no more than hints. Although real-time by itself does not say anything about speed, usually there is some performance requirement as well; but note the difference between the two factors:

- When a system provides the required real-time functionality but is not fast enough, usually a faster CPU solves the problem.
- When real-timeliness is lacking, this cannot be corrected by using a faster CPU.

When we speak of real-timeliness, we have to distinguish between the application and the OS:

- An RTOS is a tool that must provide absolute real-time behavior, or else it cannot be used to build real-time applications. An RTOS by itself is not enough to build a real-time system, but it allows the use of deterministic functions to produce an appropriate response time.
- A real-time application is built on top of an RTOS but may or may not show real-time behavior.

In some cases, real-timeliness may cost performance, an example of which might be the algorithm for memory allocation and freeing. A very fast algorithm may not provide the required determinism and can therefore not be used. An application has real-time requirements when it should always react to some event within a bounded time; next to using a proper RTOS, this also requires that the application behaves in a deterministic way. In other words, to get real-time behavior in an application, an RTOS is required but is not enough by itself.

There are good cases for using an RTOS, even though the application does not require real-timeliness. Examples can be found in embedded systems where configurability of the OS may be a reason to choose an RTOS. A reason for choosing an RTOS in a non-RT application could be the improved reliability of the system.

Now that we have described what real-time is in general, we need to examine the commercial concepts of hard real-time and soft real-time.

4.1.1 Hard Real-Time, Soft Real-Time, and Determinism

A bounded response to events is the key to defining a hard real-time system. Real-time systems require determinism to insure the predictable behavior of the system. Without determinism, a system cannot be called real-time; and without bounded determinism, a system cannot be classified as hard real-time.

The specific degree of determinism required is a function of the frequency of the real-time events (length of the time interval between events) and the effect of delays on the dynamic characteristics of that system. That is, how often do events occur, and how quick and repeatable must the system be in responding to those events. Being able to place a finite and acceptable bound on the value of these numbers is what distinguishes a hard real-time system from a soft real-time system.

A system is said to be hard real-time if the correctness of an operation depends not only upon the logical correctness of the operation but also upon the time at which it is performed. An operation performed after the deadline is, by definition, incorrect, and usually has no value. Examples of hard real-time applications are:

- A Full Authority Digital Engine Controller (FADEC) controls the activities of an aircraft jet engine. The FADEC design mandates particular timing requirements. For example, if the FADEC senses that a turbine drive shaft has broken, then the FADEC MUST respond with a damage-mitigating action in a predetermined time.
- Fly-by-wire flight controls use input electronic signals to measure a pilot's yoke or control-stick motions and create output control signals to control the aircraft's servos which position the control surfaces. The fly-by-wire flight control system MUST transmit the pilot's intentions at a predetermined frequency. If the fly-by-wire system cannot communicate information with sufficient frequency, the aircraft can become unstable --resulting in a crash.
- Unmanned Aerial Vehicle (UAV) control systems rely on sophisticated piloting control algorithms to keep the aircraft in flight, on target, and at a required altitude. The embedded control systems on the UAV are given a defined slice of time to execute these piloting control algorithms. If the embedded system falls behind in executing these algorithms, the UAV may become unstable and fall off course, diverge from the desired course, or even crash.

Unlike the binary result possibilities of hard real-time (success or failure), in a soft real-time system the value of an operation declines steadily after the deadline expires. Examples of soft real-time applications are:

- A network router is a real-time device whose purpose is to manage bidirectional network traffic. It must analyze incoming packets by address and readdress these packets as outgoing packets with modified headers but with the data intact. If the router misses an incoming packet, the sender will typically send it again. The failure of the router to respond within the deadline does not generally result in an overall failure but manifests itself as a bit less performance.
- A cellphone is an embedded device whose goal is to operate in real-time. When you browse for an appointment or phone number, browse the Internet, or interact with applications, you expect the device to respond to touchscreen input in a timely manner. However, if a particular tap or swipe requires seconds to respond rather than the fraction of a second normally required, nothing catastrophic will occur.

4.2 Split System

The split system solution is by far the most popular real-time system implementation. Windows runs on a separate computer that interfaces with a controller board that is performing the real-time tasks. The controller board can be running an FPGA, 8-bit microcontroller, or a full real-time operating system like QNX, VxWorks, Azure RTOS, or other real-time kernels. Windows is simply providing the GUI interface, file storage, and network connection. The real benefit of this implementation is that hard real-time performance can be achieved with a separate controller board.

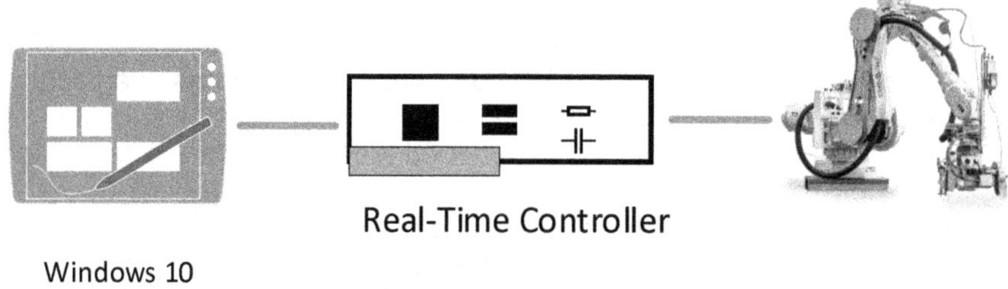

4.3 *Internal Windows Soft Real-time Support- New*

With all the tasks and services that are constantly running, Windows is not a real-time operating system. It has not stopped Microsoft from digging in and seeing if it is possible to create applications with soft real-time performance. Microsoft has been investigating the idea for several years and with the release of Windows 10 21H2, there is a method to get soft real-time with Windows.

The first step is to disable some features and services. Disable idle states using PowerCFG.exe utility. Disable system services for Diagnostic Policy Service, Audio Service, SysMain, and Windows Update (which should always be off in an embedded system, but more on Windows Update in a later chapter). Finally, disable Deferred Procedure Calls (DPC). The following batch script performs these tasks.

```
::Configures the system to support soft-real-time

powercfg.exe /setacvalueindex SCHEME_CURRENT SUB_PROCESSOR IdleDisable 1
powercfg.exe /setactive SCHEME_CURRENT

sc stop dps
sc config dps start=disabled

sc stop Audiosrv
sc config Audiosrv start=disabled

sc stop SysMain
sc config SysMain start=disabled

sc stop wuauserv
sc config wuauserv start=disabled

reg add "HKLM\System\CurrentControlSet\Control\Session Manager\kernel" /v ThreadDpcEnable /t REG_DWORD /f /d 0
```

To guarantee the system will have these items disabled, Microsoft recommends running this script on boot each time. If Unified Write Filter (UWF) is going to be used in the system, it is recommended to run the script once before UWF is enabled, and then run the script on each boot-up.

The second step is to configure the number of cores available for soft real-time applications using the Windows 10 IOT CSP (Configuration service provider). The CSP is a special API that requires system-level access to run. The following PowerShell script is used to configure the Soft Real-Time Cores for the system. This script only needs to be run once:

```
#WindowsIOT CSP is used to set the number of processor cores

$nameSpaceName="root\cimv2\mdm\dmmap"

$className="MDM_WindowsIoT_SoftRealTimeProperties01"

$obj = Get-CimInstance -Namespace $namespaceName -ClassName $className

Add-Type -AssemblyName System.Web

Set-CimInstance -CimInstance $obj

#change the following value to set the number of cores dedicate for
applications
#to use for soft real time

$obj.SetRTCores = 3

Set-CimInstance -CimInstance $obj
```

The script has to be run in the System account. Microsoft calls out the requirement for using PSEXEC.exe from Sysinternals to perform these tasks. There is the alternative Invoke-CommandAs PowerShell cmdlet, which performs the same System account call as PSEXEC.exe. The following PowerShell script installs the cmdlet:

```
Install-PackageProvider -Name NuGet -MinimumVersion 2.8.5.201 -Force
Install-module -Name Invoke-CommandAs -RequiredVersion 3.1.0 -Force
```

Using this new cmdlet, the core setup script can be called as follows:

```
powershell.exe -command "Invoke-CommandAs -ScriptBlock
{c:\setup\SoftRTCoreSetup.ps1} -AsSystem"
```

With the system configured, you can now create applications to take advantage of the soft real-time capability. You can use Win32 Apps to set thread/process priority and CPU core affinity.

To configure a Process for Soft Real-Time:

- SetPriorityClass functions (processthreadsapi.h)
  - ProcessPriorityClass attribute to PROCESS_PRIORITY_CLASS_REALTIME.
  - ProcessBasePriority attribute to LOW_REALTIME_PRIORITY.
- SetProcessAffinityMask function (winbase.h) to set the process to run on the cores reserved for software real-time

To configure a Thread for Soft Real-Time:

- NtSetInformationThread function (ntifs.h) to set the thread's ThreadBasePriority to a value between 16 and 31.
- SetThreadAffinityMask function (winbase.h) to set the thread to run exclusively on the cores which are reserved for the real-time application.

The solution does have drawbacks. If you want to use Audio in your system, then you are out of luck. What happens if a service gets accidentally turned on? The Windows Soft Real-Time solution does provide an alternative to those looking just to scratch out a little more performance.

4.4 TenAsys® INtime® for Windows®

Rather than having to jump through configuration scripts to disable Windows features or having to use external hardware with an RTOS, wouldn't it be nice to run Windows and a real-time operating system on the same hardware? Our final solution does just that. INtime for Windows is a complete real-time operating system that is designed to use real-time embedded virtualization technology to provide real-time services to a Windows Embedded platform. INtime for Windows functions as an add-on kernel to Windows and requires no modification to Windows or additional hardware. INtime for Windows takes advantage of the powerful x64 processor virtualization architecture to allow Windows and INtime to run side-by-side with INtime providing cycle times under 50 microseconds for deterministic, hard real-time response.

INtime for Windows provides shared memory and real-time transport mechanisms that allow Windows applications to share data with INtime real-time applications. The result is a solution that addresses both real-time and non-real-time applications, as diagrammed below.

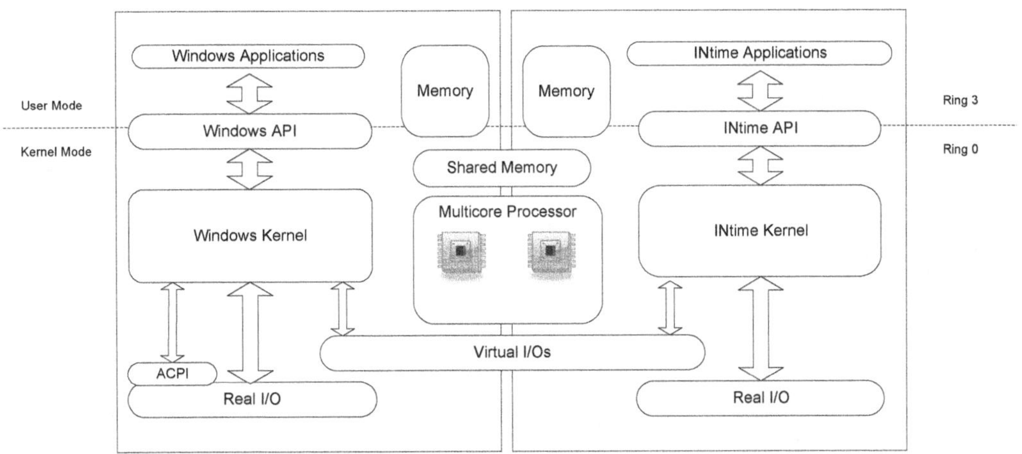

INtime for Windows Architecture

INtime for Windows can also be scaled across one or several processor cores on one or several platforms using the Global Objects network (GOBSnet). The GOBSnet Inter-Process Communication system provides deterministic data exchange across real-time components and Windows as diagrammed below.

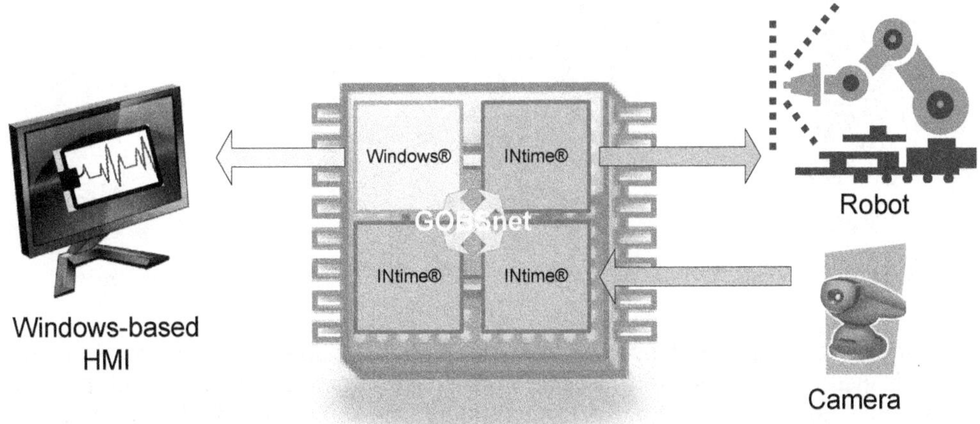

INtime for Windows Scaled Across Multiple Cores ***(Copyright TenAsys)***

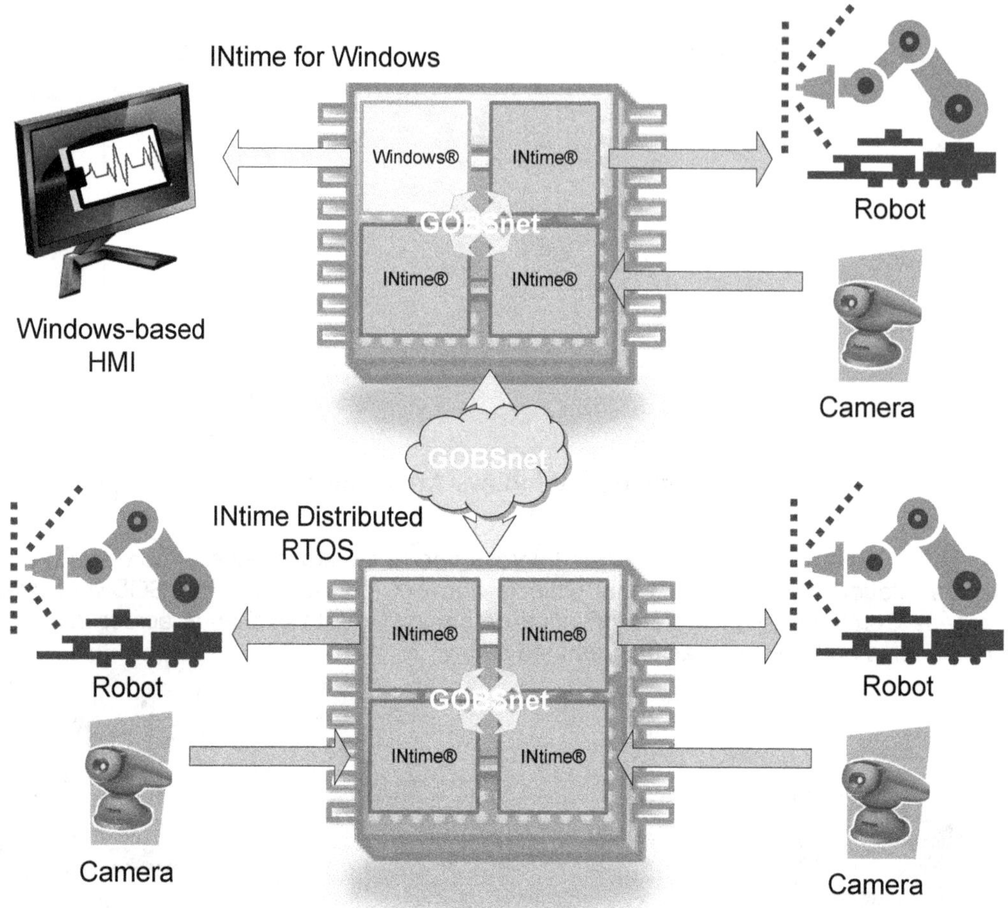

INtime for Windows Scaled Across Multiple Platforms ***(Copyright TenAsys)***

The same development environment that you use for Windows application development, Microsoft Visual Studio, is used to develop real-time INtime applications. INtime comes with an SDK that integrates into Visual Studio. The same Visual Studio development environment tools that you are already familiar with are also used to create, build, and debug INtime applications. In addition to the SDK, there are a number of tools to help manage interrupt threads, latency, jitter, and manage devices between Windows and INtime. One of those tools is INScope, a real-time debugger. INScope, shown below, provides real-time monitoring of processes, threads, and interrupts for both Windows and INtime.

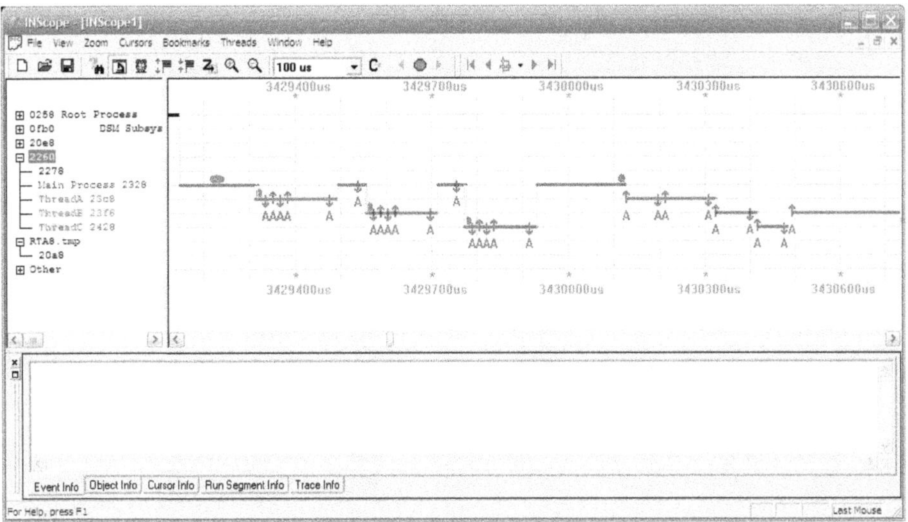

The INtime SDK provides an NT Extensions (NTX) API that was developed to facilitate both communication and synchronization between real-time processes and non-real-time processes. The NTX API uses a shared memory transport mechanism to exchange data between Windows applications and INtime applications. The result is a dual kernel solution that addresses both real-time and non-real-time applications. In a multi-core system, you can assign both operating systems to utilize different cores. The interesting result of the combined architectures is that you can create Windows applications that call real-time threads. The Windows graphical applications and real-time threads can pass information back and forth between each other.

More information can be found on the web: http://www.tenasys.com.

4.5 Summary: Real-Time Applications are Possible

The rich features of Windows are great for general-purpose operating systems, but the architecture doesn't provide the deterministic performance required for hard real-time performance. This chapter explored the options to take advantage of Windows for human interaction, data storage, and communication, but add the real-time support that some systems need.

The details, further definitions, and challenges of developing a real-time solution are a bit beyond the scope of this book. If you want a more detailed discussion of real-time computing, please, take a look at another book: *Real-Time Development from Theory to Practice, Featuring TenAsys®' INtime®*, John R. Malin and Sean D. Liming, Annabooks, 2009.

5 Footprint Reduction

For those migrating from Windows XP Embedded and Windows Embedded Standard 7 to Windows 10 IoT Enterprise, three things stand out from the first 4 chapters:

1. The build process is completely different.
2. The lockdown features have changed significantly.
3. The customization through the selection of components to shrink the operating system image size is no longer available.

The last point about the loss of components has developers trying to wrap their heads around Windows 10's size. Not everyone can afford or needs a 256GB M.2 SATA drive in their systems. Some boards, like the UP Board, have a built-in eMMC flash disk that might be limited to 32 GB. Drive space is a premium for some systems; thus, OS image size is important. This chapter reviews the history of Windows componentization and the new approach for Windows 10 IoT Enterprise LTSC 2021.

5.1 The Value of Componentization

Breaking down Windows into selectable components, allows the OEM to add the features they want in the system, and not include unnecessary features. When it comes to the Windows Services discussed in Chapter 3, if you don't include the component that has the service, you don't have to worry about the service affecting the performance of the system. Componentization allows the OEM to reduce the attack surface, thus making the system a little more secure. Reducing the image size, allows the OEM to use a smaller flash disk that is cheaper. All these points about the value of componentization have been made in the past, and Microsoft delivered componentized versions from Windows NT Embedded through Windows Embedded 8 Standard. Even with componentization, with each successive embedded OS release the size of the image increased.

5.2 Image Size Comparison

As of today, the approximate minimal footprint image sizes for the Windows Embedded/IoT releases are as follows:

Windows OS	**32-Bit Minimal Image Size**	**64-Bit Minimal Image Size**	**Componentizes / Package**
Windows NT Embedded	~9.5MB	N/A	Yes
Windows XP Embedded	~75MB	N/A	Yes

Windows OS	32-Bit Minimal Image Size	64-Bit Minimal Image Size	Componentizes / Package
Windows Embedded Standard 7	550MB	830MB	Yes
Windows Embedded 8 Standard	~2.7GB	~4.4GB	Yes
Windows Embedded 8.1 Industry	~3GB	~5.6GB	No
Windows 10 IoT Enterprise LTSC	~7GB	~13GB	No
Windows 10 IoT Enterprise LTSC 2021	N/A	~14GB	No

These are some big jumps in a minimal footprint from each release of Windows, especially when componentization was no longer implemented.

5.3 The Complexity of Componentization

There is one big problem with components. It is very complex to break down Windows into individual components. Technology keeps changing and the ability to test different combinations is complex. The old Windows Embedded team did all the work to componentize the Windows desktop. They had a big room full of computers from floor to ceiling just for testing, which is why it took several months for a Windows Embedded implementation to be released after the release of the standard Windows desktop. In addition, the old Windows Embedded team was in a different group from the Windows Desktop team. The componentization was impressive work, but there were a few components and features that didn't work quite right. There were workarounds for these problems. The complexity to componentize the OS is not the true reason components were dropped. To better understand, a little context is needed.

5.4 How Did We Get Here?

Please stay with me as this is a long discussion. Let's go all the way back to Microsoft's entry into operating systems. MS-DOS and Windows 3.1 were the top operating systems when I joined Annabooks/Annasoft in 1995. MS-DOS was small enough to be put into a PROM card, DiskOnChip, and there were a couple of MS-DOS ROM versions available. Windows 3.1 added the GUI but was still relatively small in size at the time. Windows 95 was soon released; and even though Windows CE was on the horizon, Windows 95 started to gain momentum for those using embedded PC systems. The only problem was the size of Windows 95. Back then, flash drives were in their infancy and very expensive, so getting the footprint down was a critical design priority. Developing a build tool was not practical back then, so I wrote the paper: *Minimizing the Windows 95 Footprint for Embedded Systems Applications*. It was a manual process to remove unneeded files from a full OS installation. The paper is still floating around the Internet. Using my method, I was able to get the smallest size of Windows 95 size down to 20MB. I don't remember all the functionality that was removed, but the minimal OS was able to run a C++ or VB application.

Windows CE was launched in 1996. As a small 32-bit ROMable OS, Windows CE took off in popularity; but it had a completely different kernel than the Windows desktop. This led to different development processes between Windows CE and Windows desktop. Windows CE was smaller in footprint and designed to be componentized to support onboard flash drives.

Soon after Windows CE's release and the success in getting into the Embedded Market space, Microsoft acquired Component Integrator from VenturCom, which became Windows NT Embedded. NT Embedded was broken into about 230 components. There was no PnP at the time, so building and deploying the image was relatively simple. The image size ranged from 9.5 MB to 40MB, which was large but still fit the flash drives of the time. With the modest success of Windows NT Embedded, Microsoft put a large effort into creating the next offering: Windows XP Embedded.

XP Embedded took componentization to an insane extreme by breaking Windows into 10,000+ components. 9,000 components were for device drivers, and 1000 components were OS components. Many of the OS components were for a single DLL file. Knowing how to build the image became a challenge. Go down the wrong path, and the resulting image would end up with a BSOD Stop 7B error.

Sometimes the biggest problem was trying to figure out what components were needed to get a feature to work. I had a client who wanted the screen saver working, but they also wanted a small image. One would think that dropping in the screen saver component was all that is needed; not even close. I had to build a full OS image to prove that the screen saver was working in XP Embedded, and then compare the component list between the big full-featured image and the smaller desired image. After many OS iterations, the final answer was that the "Windows XP Visual Styles" component was required by the screen saver. I would have never figured that out based on the name. Over time, locating many of the features became tribal knowledge within the Windows Embedded community.

The experience made me create some tools and solutions to speed up the process. First, I created the Full XP Pro-like Solution macro component set. The macro component allowed you to build a full XP Pro image from XP Embedded tools. Great idea at the time, but... well you will see. Second, I created a few tools to help with development. One tool is the SLDXAssistant, which compared SLX and SLD files. SLDXAssistant could compare the build files from the Full XP Pro-like Solution with a smaller build to locate the differences. From there a little sleuth work was needed to find the missing components. Sometimes it took some iterations, but eventually, features were found. Over time I developed a streamlined image development process, which has evolved into the development workflow discussed in Chapter 2. What I found was that all the images I created for customers had the same core OS components. The need to break down Windows into 10,000 components was not really necessary.

Regardless of the design challenges, Windows XP Embedded was popular and successful. One could get an image under 75MB that would simply talk to serial ports. The Full XP Pro-like Solution would become a big problem. Developers started using the Full XP Pro-like solution to create their images and never bothered to shrink the image to remove unneeded features. There were many times I was hired to help a development process that went afoul by developers using the Full XP Pro-like Solution as is. Having programs like Messenger, Outlook Express, IIS, and Games was not desirable in an embedded OS, and the approach to start big and go small wasn't cleaning up the mess. The Full XP Pro-like Solution was only intended as a means to help to track down features, and it was not intended for being the bases for the image. The ramifications of Windows componentization would come later.

XP Embedded's componentization was difficult for some companies, like point-of-sale vendors, who just needed a Windows OS to quickly install onto their devices. Microsoft came out with Windows Embedded for Point of Services (WEPOS). Rather than building an image from components, WEPOS was a simple DVD install with a Wizard that had some selectable features. WEPOS created a fork in the embedded offering, and its success influenced future decisions on componentization. WEPOS became an important part of the story.

The story now turns to Microsoft's legal problems. In the late 1990s. Microsoft was sued by the US Government for predatory practices, which stemmed from the Internet Explorer browser and other software being included in Windows. Looking back the argument over a browser seems small. As a result of this case, Bill Gates turned over the CEO role to Steve Balmer. The EU soon filed a similar antitrust case in 2000. In the EU case, the issue focused on Media Player. RealNetworks, with its RealPlayer®, felt they were at a disadvantage. Microsoft's legal group, including Steve Balmer, argued that Media Player was an integral part of Windows and couldn't be removed from Windows. RealNetworks used Windows XP Embedded to build a Windows image without Media Player. Microsoft was proven wrong using their own product and had to pay over $700 million in fines. Since Windows Embedded sales were very tiny compared to Windows desktop sales, the leadership at Microsoft (i.e. Steve Balmer, Microsoft salesmen extraordinaire) at the time started to look very unfavorably at Windows Embedded. In fact, Steve Balmer would never say the words "Windows Embedded".

Regardless, componentizing Windows continued. After a long wait, WES7, Windows Embedded Standard 7, was released in 2009. This time, Windows was broken down into bigger packages. The Stop 7B issue was resolved with a foundation package that had the core functionality for a successful bootup each time. The image development process was much easier, but the image sizes were bigger. The smallest image size was 550MB and the largest image size was around 3 to 4GB. Developers could build a full Windows 7-like solution, minus games, but this time Microsoft supplied the Application Compatibility macro component, which in essence built a full Windows 7 image. The rationale for the increase in packages and image size was that flash drive sizes were getting bigger and cheaper, so there was no need to break the OS down into smaller components like XP Embedded. There were not too many complaints about the increased image size. Windows XP Embedded only supported 32-bit processors. Now, WES7 supported 64-bit processors. The expectation of 64-bit platforms requiring new hardware, more RAM, and a larger drive size was understood.

Besides WES7, POSReady 7 was released as the successor to WEPOS. You could still install the OS from a DVD as before, but you could also use the same System Image Manager from the ADK that was used for regular Windows Desktop and Server to create a custom OS installer. There was alignment with the desktop team.

Around this time, Apple's iOS and Google's Android for smartphones and tablets started to change the game in the mobile space and how consumers purchased software via application stores. Microsoft scrambled to play catch up. Windows 8 was created to allow app developers to create UWP applications and sell the apps on a Microsoft Store. The Windows 8 tile interface was not a welcome change from the old Start menu of old, and there were other documented problems with Windows 8.

The biggest challenge with Windows Embedded was the 10-year support offering. At this time there were too many Windows Embedded OS products to support. There had been an internal effort for several years to port Windows to an ARM processor. Eventually, Microsoft Phone was moved from Windows CE to Windows 8 on ARM. Since maintaining two operating systems was costly and without a high-volume product to go into, Windows CE's 17-year life came to an end. With Windows CE gone, Microsoft's internal reorganization merged the Windows Embedded team with the Windows Desktop team. Those on the Windows Embedded team faded away as the Windows Desktop team took over. One of the last products from the Windows Embedded team was the ill-fated Windows Embedded 8 Standard, which was more closely aligned with WES7 in package size. Attempts to build the tools and allow developers to create packages were a nice idea, but this was Windows 8, which was dead on arrival. The desktop team's dominant influence came in the form of requiring activation for each of the units shipped, which didn't go well with almost anyone working on Embedded Systems. WES8 was the last componentized Windows OS. Since Windows 8 interface was so bad, Microsoft quickly released Windows 8.1 and Windows 8.1 Embedded industry followed suit. Without a Windows Embedded team, Windows Embedded Industry 8.1 was not componentized, but one could use System Image Manager from the ADK to build images. Since Windows Embedded Industry 8.1 could also be used by Point of Sales OEMs, there was no need for a POSReady 7 follow-up. The number of products to support was getting reduced.

The driving force for Windows 10 was to create one operating system that could support a wide variety of products. With Windows CE gone, there was an effort to create a small version of Windows 10, which ended up being Windows 10 IoT Core. As mentioned already, Windows IoT Core was flawed in concept since UWP applications were mostly rejected by the industry. With so much focus on Azure and getting iOS and Linux connecting to Azure, Windows 10 IoT Enterprise became the only IoT OS product solution from Microsoft. There are some advantages as I already pointed out in Chapter 1. The large image size has been tough to justify. Some of the early interest in Windows 10 were from those OEMs who want to migrate from XP Embedded to Windows 10. The problem was that the hardware was old and the drive sizes were too small to support Windows 10.

At a conference soon after the release of Windows 10 IoT Enterprise, the image size issue was brought up by someone in the room. The question was asked why wasn't Windows 10 IoT Enterprise broken down into selectable components? Microsoft said their marketing research indicated the OEMs were just building full OS images anyway, so there was no need to componentize the OS. My Full XP Pro-like solution came back to haunt me. Microsoft Marketing also incorrectly claimed that development and support complexities, as well as, flash drive sizes and prices are non-factors. I was in the second or third to last row in the conference listening to this rationalization. Two Microsoft minions sat behind me. One stated softly that Microsoft will never componentize Windows ever again, and the other agreed. The statement itself was one thing, but the way they talked with anger, was something I noted. Being minions, they were clearly echoing Steve Balmer and the EU lawsuit. I tilted my head back to glance at them and confirmed that the statement was made for my consumption.

One year later.... A release of Windows 10 included support for Mixed Reality and other new features. At that year's conference, Microsoft put on a very interesting presentation on how Windows 10 is developed internally. There are over 15,000 developers at Microsoft who work on Windows 10. The coordination with such a massive group requires a clear development process with several checks before a release is made. It is an impressive coordination effort to get a release to market. With so many developers, one has to think that there are groups of developers each working on a small piece of the OS. All of these smaller pieces or packages have to be brought together to make a whole OS release.

At the Q & A, I brought up the image size issue: "New features are great, but the image size was increasing. Mixed Reality is a cool technology, but it is not needed in ATMs, cash registers, and most embedded systems." The head of Windows nodded his head and said they have heard the feedback and are looking into the problem. He continued to say that many new features and applications are being put into the Features on Demand (FOD) and the in-box applications disks. They can maintain the core OS and keep the new optional features separate. It doesn't solve the problem, but it slows down image size growth. Eventually, the death of Windows IoT Core brought a change in mindset, and a footprint reduction effort was underway. After a few years of development, the result is a PowerShell script that allows you to remove unwanted packages from the core OS image. For optional FOD packages, you can use DISM to remove them. The concept is that you start with the whole image and remove the things you don't want, thus coming full circle to the similar effort I did for Windows 95. What is old is new again. Between the two approaches: large-to-small and small-to-large, the small-to-large would work best, but this is not how Windows is currently designed nor how the footprint reduction works.

5.5 Reduction PowerShell Script for Core OS

There are two package control solutions, core OS and optional FOD packages. For the Core OS, the RemoveOnIoTEnterpriseS.ps1 script is available on GitHub. The script is located under Windows-IoT-Samples. The script is only for Windows 10 IoT Enterprise LTSC 2021, and it requires the May 24th, 2022 (KB5014023) or later cumulative update package. You can download the package from the Microsoft catalog update site: https://www.catalog.update.microsoft.com/Home.aspx.

Script usage:

```
RemoveOnIoTEnterpriseS.ps1 -List [-suppressPrompts] [-os_variant <string>] [-DismLogFile <string>] [<CommonParameters>]
```

```
RemoveOnIoTEnterpriseS.ps1 -offlineImageFolderPath <DirectoryInfo> -RemoveUnit <string> [-suppressPrompts] [-os_variant <string>] [-DismLogFile <string>] [<CommonParameters>]
```

```
RemoveOnIoTEnterpriseS.ps1 -isOnline -RemoveUnit <string> [-suppressPrompts] [-os_variant <string>] [-DismLogFile <string>] [<CommonParameters>]
```

The script can be run in online and offline modes. Offline implies manipulating the install.wim file, which I don't recommend per my discussion in chapter 1. The chapter exercise will walk through using the script in online mode.

As of this writing, if you run RemoveOnIoTEnterpriseS.ps1 -list, the list of packages that can be removed is shown to be:

Name	Packages
AppManagement_UEV	{Microsoft-Windows-AppManagement-UEV}
BioEnrollment_UX	{Microsoft-Windows-BioEnrollment-UX}
BootEnvironment_Dvd	{Microsoft-Windows-BootEnvironment-Dvd}
Common_RegulatedPackages	{Microsoft-Media-Foundation, Microsoft-Windows-Media-Format, Microsoft-W...
Desktop_SharedPackages	{LanguageFeatures-WordBreaking-Common-legacy, Microsoft-Windows-BioEnrol...
Fonts_DesktopFonts_NonLeanSupplement	{Microsoft-OneCore-Fonts-DesktopFonts-NonLeanSupplement}
LanguageFeatures_WordBreaking_Common_legacy	{LanguageFeatures-WordBreaking-Common-legacy}
Printer_Drivers	{Microsoft-Windows-Printer-Drivers}
Printing_PremiumTools	{Microsoft-Windows-Printing-PremiumTools}
RecoveryDrive	{Microsoft-Windows-RecoveryDrive}

ScreenSavers	{Microsoft-Windows-ScreenSavers-3D}
SensorDataService	{Microsoft-Windows-SensorDataService}
Shell_Wallpaper	{Microsoft-Windows-Shell-Wallpaper-Common}
ShellOptions	{Microsoft-Windows-ShellOptions
SnippingTool	{Microsoft-Windows-SnippingTool}
win32calc	{Microsoft-Windows-win32calc}

The list is small. As future updates of Windows 10 are delivered the packages available to be removed will grow. The real issue with the slow delivery of this feature is how to prevent Windows Update from pulling removed packages back in. No one wants their image on a small disk to run out of room because of Windows Update. The Microsoft teams have to work together to test and verify each package that is to be selectively removed. The benefit will be faster Windows Update as only the packages still in the image will get an update. This feature is going to be evolving over time, and you will have to go back and download the latest RemoveOnIoTEnterpriseS.ps1 script along with the latest cumulative update. The other problem as of this writing is the package's details. One can figure out what some packages do by name, but others not so much. Hopefully, Docs.Microsoft.com will have comprehensive details in the future.

5.6 Remove Optional Packages

For the optional packages, DISM is used to add and remove them. Even though you may not have installed any FOD packages, there are optional packages that get installed. Run DISM /Online /Get-packages to get a list of these optional packages. There will not be many, but use the list to remove any unneeded packages by using DISM /Online /Remove-Package. Here are some examples:

```
DISM.exe /online /Remove-Package
/PackagePath:C:\test\Mypackage.cab

DISM.exe /online /Remove-Package
/PackageName:Microsoft.Windows.Demo~6432b92277ccf1df~x64~en~1.0.0
.0
```

5.7 Other Disk Image Size Tricks

Besides the script, there are a few other tricks that can be done to help reduce the image size or get more drive space:

5.7.1 Disable Features

Using System Image Manager to help create a custom Windows Installer, add the Foundation Package to the answer file. The Foundation Package provides options to enable/disable Windows features. Internet Explorer, Windows Media Player, XPS Print, Hyper-V, etc. can be enabled or disabled via the Foundation Package settings. This will reduce the image size by not installing the feature, but disabling a feature doesn't remove the package from the image, which is buried in the \windows subfolder.

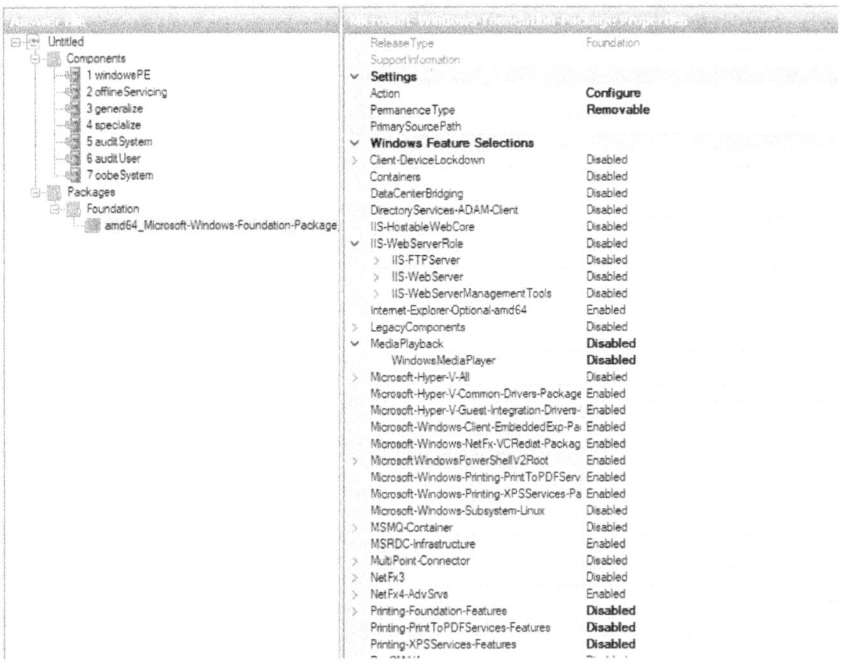

5.7.2 Turn off Hibernation and Disable Virtual Memory

The hiberfil.sys and pagefile.sys files can take up several gigabytes on a disk. If these are not needed, then disabling them can save on space.

5.7.3 Remove a copy of the Windows custom installer

When installing from a USB flash drive, a copy of the installer is put into C:\windows\ConfigSetRoot. You can remove the copy of the installer using the following sync command in the answer file:

cmd.exe /C rd /S /Q c:\Windows\ConfigSetRoot

5.7.4 Compact OS

The compact utility can be used to free up space:

compact /compactos:always

or you can set the Compact option in the answer file.

Component	Configuration Pass	Component Setting	Possible Value / Notes
amd64_Microsoft-Windows-Setup__neutral	1 WindowsPE	Compact	**True**

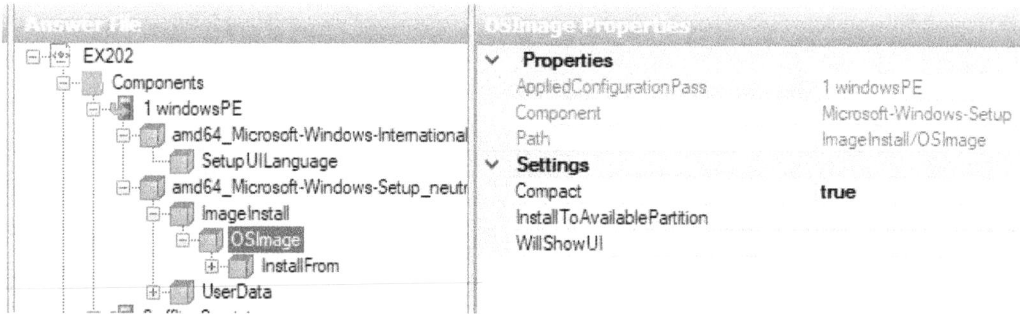

5.7.5 Clean up Windows Update

Running Windows Update to make sure the latest security updates are in the image is important to make sure the OS is secure. The updates will increase the image size. These are some steps to clean up the impact:

- In System Control Panel, you can remove restore points:

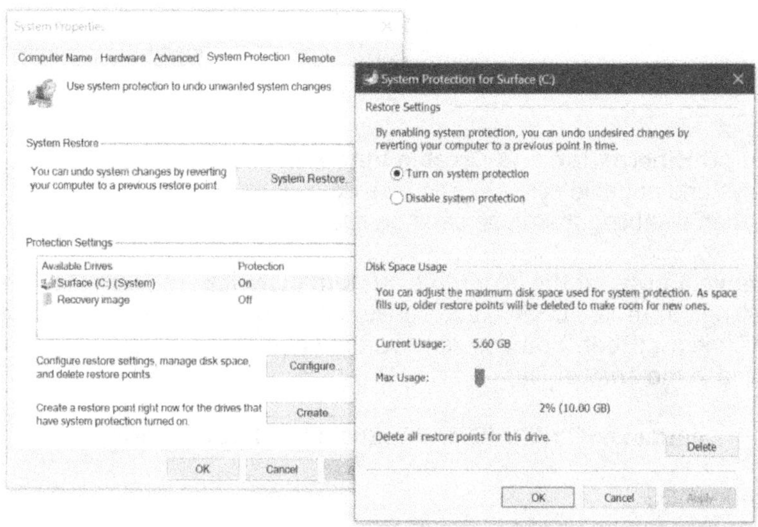

- Run Dism to perform some package cleanup:

Dism.exe /online /Cleanup-Image /StartComponentCleanup /ResetBase

You will want to create a batch file for this command as it will be needed to clean up the image after Windows Update and running the RemoveOnIoTEnterpriseS.ps1 script.

- Run Disk cleanup

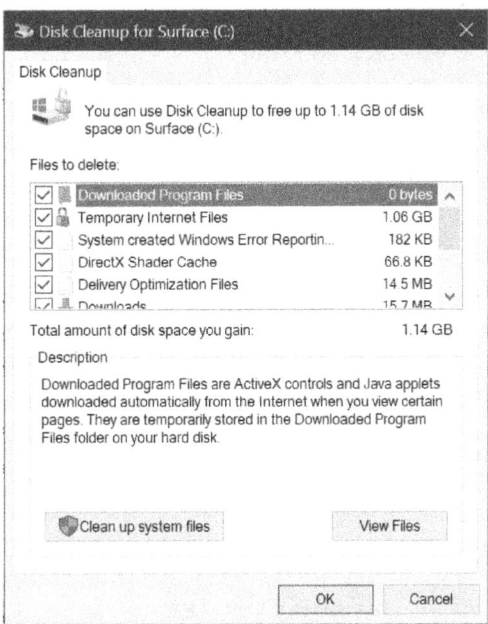

It is a best practice to run the last two clean-up suggestions after running Windows Update and just before running Sysprep. The image will be a bit smaller and faster to capture.

5.7.6 Remove WinRE Partition

Before Windows 10 IoT Enterprise LTSC 2021, the Windows installer would create 3 partitions before the primary: System, Reserved, and Recovery.

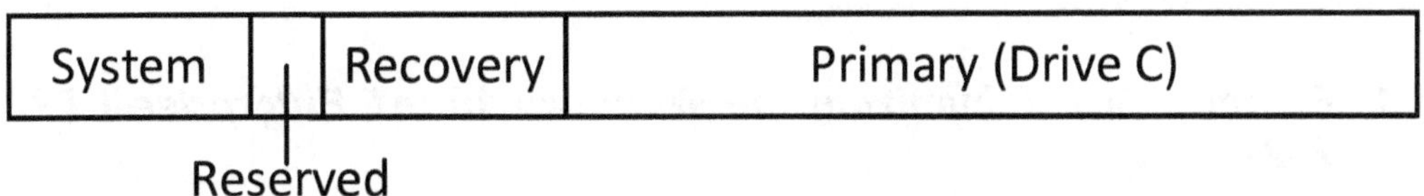

The System and Reserved partitions are needed for boot and UEFI. The recovery partition is for WinRE. WinRE is great for a general-purpose OS, but not so great for an embedded/IoT system when the state of the machine is a concern. This leaves the 500MB recovery partition unused. For those with smaller disks getting this extra space would be very helpful. With the release of Windows 10 IoT Enterprise LTSC 2021, the recovery partition is created after the primary partition. Now, a couple of Pass 7 synchronous commands and the diskpart.exe input file can be used to remove the Recovery partition and to add the 500MB space to the Primary partition.

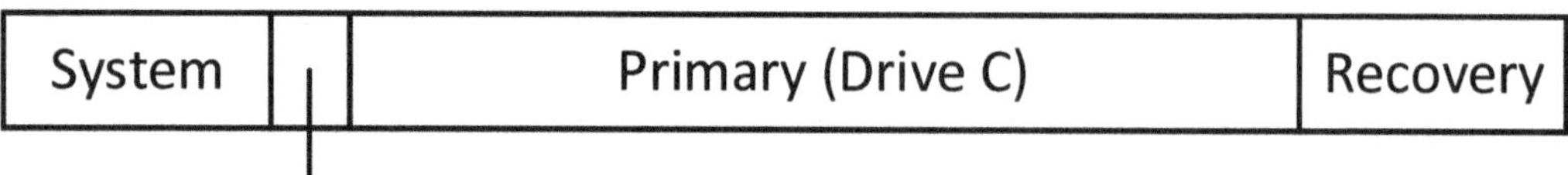

Create a Drive0.txt text file that has the following:

```
select disk 0
select part 4
delete partition override
select part 3
extend
exit
```

The Diskpart commands remove the recovery partition (part 4) and then extend the primary partition (part 3) to fill up the rest of the disk space. One could use the script to create a secondary partition on the drive if needed.

The Pass 7 synchronous commands first disable WinRE and then remove the WinRE partition:

```
reagentc /disable

diskpart.exe /s c:\setup\Drive0.txt
```

After installation of the OS, the WinRE partition will be gone freeing up more space for Drive C.

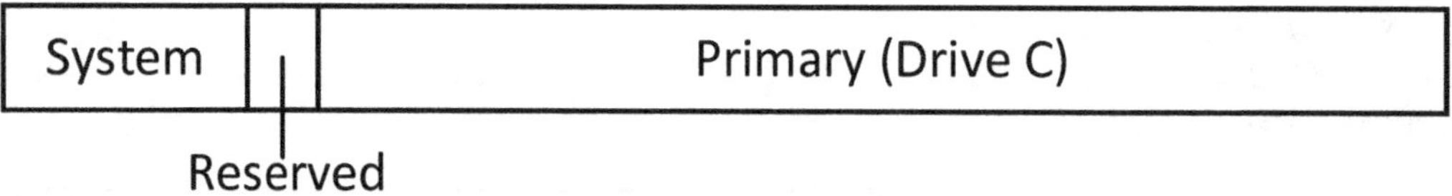

5.8 Exercise 501: Minimizing the Windows 10 IoT Enterprise LTSC 2021 Footprint

I couldn't resist reusing the old title. We are going to build on the EX202 answer file and distribution share to remove the WinRE partition and test the RemoveOnIoTEnterpriseS.ps1 script.

1. Create a text file called Drive0.txt that has the following contents:

```
select disk 0
select part 4
delete partition override
select part 3
extend
exit
```

2. Save the file to the \WinData\DS64\$1\Setup folder.
3. Create another text file called Cleanup-image.bat that has the following contents:

```
Dism.exe /online /Cleanup-Image /StartComponentCleanup /Resetbase
```

4. Save the file to the \WinData\DS64\$1\Setup folder.
5. Chapter 5 Exercise folder has an older RemoveOnIoTEnterpriseS.ps1. You can use this version or download the latest version from GitHub. Copy the RemoveOnIoTEnterpriseS.ps1 to the \WinData\DS64\$1\Setup folder.
6. Open SIM.
7. Open the EX202.xml answer file.
8. Add the following two commands to the Pass 7 Synchronous commands:

```
reagentc /disable

diskpart.exe /s c:\setup\Drive0.txt
```

9. Save the answer file.
10. Build a new configuration set.
11. Copy the configuration set to the USB installation disk.
12. Boot and install the image on the target system.
13. Right-click on Start and click on Disk Management. You should see that the Recovery partition is not present, thus 500MB have been added to drive C.

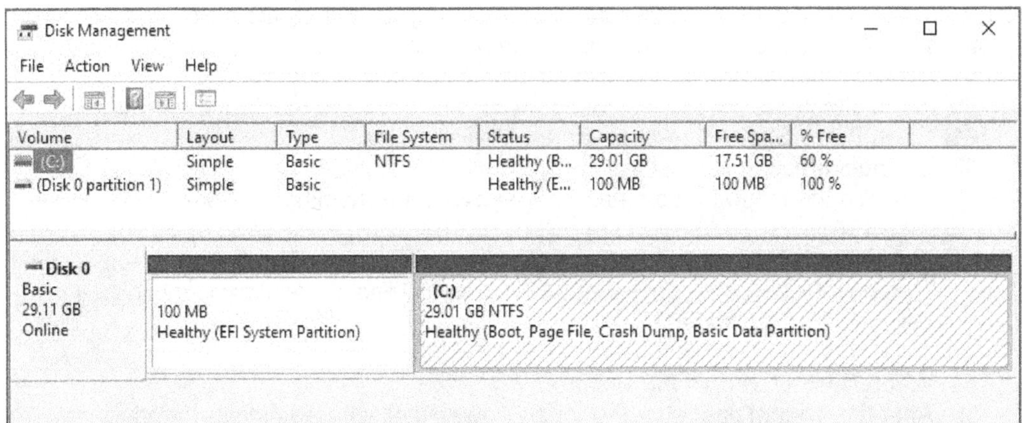

14. After the image has been installed, connect the target system to the Internet.
15. Run Windows Update to download the latest updates. Start->Settings->Update & Security. The latest cumulative update will have the packages that can be removed. The system will require a reboot after the update. Run Windows Update again to check for any of the smaller updates and download any that are available.
16. Open PowerShell with Administrator privileges.
17. Change directory to C:\setup.
18. Run the cleanup-image.bat. This will take a while.
19. Open File Explorer, right-click on drive C and select "Properties" and write down the used space value.
20. Run the calculator application. We will remove the calculator application first.
21. Close the calculator application.
22. Open PowerShell with Administrator privileges.
23. Change directory to C:\setup.
24. Run the following to set the executionpolicy to unrestricted:

    ```
    Set-ExecutionPolicy -ExecutionPolicy Unrestricted
    ```

25. A question will appear about approving the change in execution policy, type A, and hit enter.
26. Run the following to remove calculator application:

    ```
    .\RemoveOnIoTEnterpriseS.ps1 -isOnline -RemoveUnit win32calc
    ```

27. You will be asked twice if you want to remove the package. Type Y and hit enter, and then type remove and hit enter. The package will be removed.
28. Click Y to reboot the system.
29. After the system has rebooted, you can see from the Start menu that the calculator application is gone.

Note: If you run the RemoveOnIoTEnterpriseS.ps1 -list, you will see the calculator package still in the list. The problem is the script is presenting what it can remove irrespective of what has been removed. Hopefully, this will get fixed over time.

30. If you check the drive C disk usage, you might not see much of a difference.
31. Open PowerShell with Administrator privileges.
32. Change directory to C:\setup.
33. Now run the following command to remove the remaining packages:

    ```
    .\RemoveOnIoTEnterpriseS.ps1 -List | foreach { .\RemoveOnIoTEnterpriseS.ps1 -isOnline -suppressPrompts -RemoveUnit $_.Name }
    ```

34. When finished, reboot the system.
35. After the system has rebooted, open PowerShell with Administrator privileges.
36. Change directory to C:\setup.
37. Run the cleanup-image.bat.

38. Check the drive C disk usage, and this time you will notice a small difference of about 0.4GB. Your results will vary.
39. Now let's see what FOD packages are installed in the image. Open PowerShell with Administrator privileges.
40. Run the following command:

```
Dism.exe /Online /Get-Packages
```

You will get a list similar to the following (not exactly) :

```
Package Identity : Microsoft-OneCore-ApplicationModel-Sync-Desktop-FOD-Package~31bf3856ad364e35~amd64~~10.0.19041.1503
State : Installed
Release Type : OnDemand Pack
Install Time : 6/15/2022 10:02 PM

Package Identity : Microsoft-OneCore-DirectX-Database-FOD-Package~31bf3856ad364e35~amd64~~10.0.19041.1
State : Installed
Release Type : OnDemand Pack
Install Time : 12/7/2019 9:50 AM

Package Identity : Microsoft-Windows-Client-LanguagePack-Package~31bf3856ad364e35~amd64~en-US~10.0.19041.1766
State : Installed
Release Type : Language Pack
Install Time : 6/15/2022 10:02 PM

Package Identity : Microsoft-Windows-FodMetadata-Package~31bf3856ad364e35~amd64~~10.0.19041.1
State : Installed
Release Type : Feature Pack
Install Time : 12/7/2019 9:48 AM

Package Identity : Microsoft-Windows-Foundation-Package~31bf3856ad364e35~amd64~~10.0.19041.1
State : Installed
Release Type : Foundation
Install Time : 12/7/2019 9:18 AM

Package Identity : Microsoft-Windows-Hello-Face-Package~31bf3856ad364e35~amd64~~10.0.19041.1348
State : Installed
Release Type : OnDemand Pack
Install Time : 6/15/2022 10:02 PM

Package Identity : Microsoft-Windows-InternetExplorer-Optional-Package~31bf3856ad364e35~amd64~~11.0.19041.1566
State : Installed
Release Type : OnDemand Pack
Install Time : 6/15/2022 10:02 PM

Package Identity : Microsoft-Windows-LanguageFeatures-Basic-en-us-Package~31bf3856ad364e35~amd64~~10.0.19041.1
State : Installed
```

```
Release Type : OnDemand Pack
Install Time : 12/7/2019 9:49 AM

Package Identity : Microsoft-Windows-LanguageFeatures-Handwriting-en-us-
Package~31bf3856ad364e35~amd64~~10.0.19041.1
State : Installed
Release Type : OnDemand Pack
Install Time : 12/7/2019 9:49 AM

Package Identity : Microsoft-Windows-LanguageFeatures-OCR-en-us-
Package~31bf3856ad364e35~amd64~~10.0.19041.1
State : Installed
Release Type : OnDemand Pack
Install Time : 12/7/2019 9:50 AM

Package Identity : Microsoft-Windows-LanguageFeatures-Speech-en-us-
Package~31bf3856ad364e35~amd64~~10.0.19041.1
State : Installed
Release Type : OnDemand Pack
Install Time : 12/7/2019 9:50 AM

Package Identity : Microsoft-Windows-LanguageFeatures-TextToSpeech-en-us-
Package~31bf3856ad364e35~amd64~~10.0.19041.1
State : Installed
Release Type : OnDemand Pack
Install Time : 12/7/2019 9:50 AM

Package Identity : Microsoft-Windows-MediaPlayer-
Package~31bf3856ad364e35~amd64~~10.0.19041.1766
State : Installed
Release Type : OnDemand Pack
Install Time : 6/15/2022 10:02 PM

Package Identity : Microsoft-Windows-MSPaint-FoD-Package~31bf3856ad364e35~amd64~en-
US~10.0.19041.1
State : Installed
Release Type : OnDemand Pack
Install Time : 12/7/2019 9:50 AM

Package Identity : Microsoft-Windows-MSPaint-FoD-
Package~31bf3856ad364e35~amd64~~10.0.19041.746
State : Installed
Release Type : OnDemand Pack
Install Time : 10/6/2021 1:56 PM

Package Identity : Microsoft-Windows-MSPaint-FoD-Package~31bf3856ad364e35~wow64~en-
US~10.0.19041.1
State : Installed
Release Type : OnDemand Pack
Install Time : 12/7/2019 9:50 AM

Package Identity : Microsoft-Windows-MSPaint-FoD-
Package~31bf3856ad364e35~wow64~~10.0.19041.1
State : Installed
Release Type : OnDemand Pack
Install Time : 12/7/2019 9:50 AM
```

```
Package Identity : Microsoft-Windows-Notepad-FoD-Package~31bf3856ad364e35~amd64~en-US~10.0.19041.488
State : Installed
Release Type : OnDemand Pack
Install Time : 10/6/2021 1:56 PM

Package Identity : Microsoft-Windows-Notepad-FoD-Package~31bf3856ad364e35~amd64~~10.0.19041.1741
State : Installed
Release Type : OnDemand Pack
Install Time : 6/15/2022 10:02 PM

Package Identity : Microsoft-Windows-Notepad-FoD-Package~31bf3856ad364e35~wow64~en-US~10.0.19041.1
State : Installed
Release Type : OnDemand Pack
Install Time : 12/7/2019 9:50 AM

Package Identity : Microsoft-Windows-Notepad-FoD-Package~31bf3856ad364e35~wow64~~10.0.19041.1
State : Installed
Release Type : OnDemand Pack
Install Time : 12/7/2019 9:50 AM

Package Identity : Microsoft-Windows-PowerShell-ISE-FOD-Package~31bf3856ad364e35~amd64~en-US~10.0.19041.1
State : Installed
Release Type : OnDemand Pack
Install Time : 12/7/2019 9:50 AM

Package Identity : Microsoft-Windows-PowerShell-ISE-FOD-Package~31bf3856ad364e35~amd64~~10.0.19041.1
State : Installed
Release Type : OnDemand Pack
Install Time : 12/7/2019 9:50 AM

Package Identity : Microsoft-Windows-PowerShell-ISE-FOD-Package~31bf3856ad364e35~wow64~en-US~10.0.19041.1
State : Installed
Release Type : OnDemand Pack
Install Time : 12/7/2019 9:50 AM

Package Identity : Microsoft-Windows-PowerShell-ISE-FOD-Package~31bf3856ad364e35~wow64~~10.0.19041.1
State : Installed
Release Type : OnDemand Pack
Install Time : 12/7/2019 9:50 AM

Package Identity : Microsoft-Windows-Printing-PMCPPC-FoD-Package~31bf3856ad364e35~amd64~en-US~10.0.19041.1
State : Installed
Release Type : OnDemand Pack
Install Time : 12/7/2019 9:51 AM

Package Identity : Microsoft-Windows-Printing-PMCPPC-FoD-Package~31bf3856ad364e35~amd64~~10.0.19041.1741
State : Installed
Release Type : OnDemand Pack
```

```
Install Time : 6/15/2022 10:02 PM

Package Identity : Microsoft-Windows-Printing-WFS-FoD-Package~31bf3856ad364e35~amd64~en-US~10.0.19041.906
State : Installed
Release Type : OnDemand Pack
Install Time : 10/6/2021 1:56 PM

Package Identity : Microsoft-Windows-Printing-WFS-FoD-Package~31bf3856ad364e35~amd64~~10.0.19041.1706
State : Installed
Release Type : OnDemand Pack
Install Time : 6/15/2022 10:02 PM

Package Identity : Microsoft-Windows-QuickAssist-Package~31bf3856ad364e35~amd64~~10.0.19041.1566
State : Installed
Release Type : OnDemand Pack
Install Time : 6/15/2022 10:02 PM

Package Identity : Microsoft-Windows-StepsRecorder-Package~31bf3856ad364e35~amd64~en-US~10.0.19041.1
State : Installed
Release Type : OnDemand Pack
Install Time : 12/7/2019 9:50 AM

Package Identity : Microsoft-Windows-StepsRecorder-Package~31bf3856ad364e35~amd64~~10.0.19041.746
State : Installed
Release Type : OnDemand Pack
Install Time : 10/6/2021 1:56 PM

Package Identity : Microsoft-Windows-StepsRecorder-Package~31bf3856ad364e35~wow64~en-US~10.0.19041.1
State : Installed
Release Type : OnDemand Pack
Install Time : 12/7/2019 9:50 AM

Package Identity : Microsoft-Windows-StepsRecorder-Package~31bf3856ad364e35~wow64~~10.0.19041.1
State : Installed
Release Type : OnDemand Pack
Install Time : 12/7/2019 9:50 AM

Package Identity : Microsoft-Windows-TabletPCMath-Package~31bf3856ad364e35~amd64~~10.0.19041.746
State : Installed
Release Type : OnDemand Pack
Install Time : 10/6/2021 1:56 PM

Package Identity : Microsoft-Windows-UserExperience-Desktop-Package~31bf3856ad364e35~amd64~~10.0.19041.1741
State : Installed
Release Type : OnDemand Pack
Install Time : 6/15/2022 10:02 PM

Package Identity : Microsoft-Windows-WordPad-FoD-Package~31bf3856ad364e35~amd64~en-US~10.0.19041.1
```

```
State : Installed
Release Type : OnDemand Pack
Install Time : 12/7/2019 9:50 AM

Package                Identity                :                Microsoft-Windows-WordPad-FoD-
Package~31bf3856ad364e35~amd64~~10.0.19041.1682
State : Installed
Release Type : OnDemand Pack
Install Time : 6/15/2022 10:02 PM

Package   Identity   :   Microsoft-Windows-WordPad-FoD-Package~31bf3856ad364e35~wow64~en-
US~10.0.19041.1
State : Installed
Release Type : OnDemand Pack
Install Time : 12/7/2019 9:50 AM

Package                Identity                :                Microsoft-Windows-WordPad-FoD-
Package~31bf3856ad364e35~wow64~~10.0.19041.1
State : Installed
Release Type : OnDemand Pack
Install Time : 12/7/2019 9:50 AM

Package Identity : OpenSSH-Client-Package~31bf3856ad364e35~amd64~~10.0.19041.964
State : Installed
Release Type : OnDemand Pack
Install Time : 10/6/2021 1:56 PM

Package Identity : Package_for_DotNetRollup~31bf3856ad364e35~amd64~~10.0.4515.1
State : Installed
Release Type : Update
Install Time : 6/15/2022 10:20 PM

Package Identity : Package_for_KB5003791~31bf3856ad364e35~amd64~~19041.1237.1.3
State : Installed
Release Type : Update
Install Time : 10/6/2021 1:44 PM

Package Identity : Package_for_RollupFix~31bf3856ad364e35~amd64~~19041.1766.1.9
State : Installed
Release Type : Security Update
Install Time : 6/15/2022 10:02 PM

Package Identity : Package_for_ServicingStack_1737~31bf3856ad364e35~amd64~~19041.1737.1.2
State : Installed
Release Type : Update
Install Time : 6/15/2022 10:21 PM

Package Identity : Package_for_ServicingStack~31bf3856ad364e35~amd64~~19041.1220.1.0
State : Installed
Release Type : Security Update
Install Time : 10/6/2021 1:43 PM
```

Amongst the updates and core OS is a number of Feature on Demand (FOD) packages for WordPad, Media Player, PowerShell programs, MS Paint, etc. These can be removed using the DISM /Remove-Package command.

41. Your list will be a little different, so run the following command to capture the list to a text file:

```
Dism.exe /Online /Get-Packages > c:\setup\FOD.txt
```

42. Copy the FOD.txt to a USB flash disk. The information will be used for the next lab.

5.9 Exercises 502: Implementing a Removal Script

A Shrink-Image.bat file will be created and run during a Pass 7 Synchronous command to automate the removal of packages. We will also add the Foundation package to disable some features.

1. Create an internal-shrink.ps1 file that contains the following:

```
c:\setup\RemoveOnIoTEnterpriseS.ps1 -List | foreach { c:\setup\RemoveOnIoTEnterpriseS.ps1 -isOnline -suppressPrompts -RemoveUnit $_.Name }
```

2. Save the file to the \WinData\DS64\$1\Setup folder.
3. Create a shrink-image.bat file in Notepad++ that contains the following to remove all available internal packages that are to be removed and FOD packages for WordPad, OpenSSH, and Steps Recorder:

```
Timeout /t 25

PowerShell.exe -ExecutionPolicy RemoteSigned -File c:\setup\internal-shrink.ps1

DISM /Online /Remove-Package /PackageName:OpenSSH-Client-Package~31bf3856ad364e35~amd64~~10.0.19041.964 /NoRestart

DISM /Online /Remove-Package /PackageName:Microsoft-Windows-WordPad-FoD-Package~31bf3856ad364e35~amd64~~10.0.19041.1682 /NoRestart

DISM /Online /Remove-Package /PackageName:Microsoft-Windows-StepsRecorder-Package~31bf3856ad364e35~amd64~~10.0.19041.746 /NoRestart
```

The timeout is important as we need to delay to allow the cumulative update to install and reboot the system. You will see why in the synchronous commands that are set up. The nested call to internal-shrink.ps1 is the best way to run the next synchronous command. Also, there are a number of FOD packages for the same feature. The batch only includes the latest non-Wow64 package to be removed. Removing only these packages will remove the rest.

Note: The FOD packages' names will be different.

4. Save the file to the \WinData\DS64\$1\Setup folder.
5. If you want to automate the removal of internal packages, you will need to have the latest cumulative update installed in the image along with the latest removal script. As of this writing, the removal of internal packages requires at a minimum the May 24th, 2022 (KB5014023) cumulative update package. We will pre-install this update. Open a browser to https://www.catalog.update.microsoft.com/Home.aspx.

Note: You should always download the latest cumulative update with the latest removal script to give you removal capability of all the latest available packages. This is an additional step to the workflow. This exercise is calling out the older update as a demonstration.

6. Search for kb5014023.
7. From the list, download 2022-06 Cumulative Update for Windows 10 Version 21H2 for x64-based Systems (KB5014699) and place the MSU file in the \WinData\DS64\$1\Setup folder.
8. Open SIM.
9. Open the EX202.xml answer file.
10. Add the amd64_Microsoft-Windows-Foundation-Package to the answer file.
11. In the settings for the amd64_Microsoft-Windows-Foundation-Package, disable the following:

- Internet-Explorer-Optional-amd64
- MediaPlayback
- MicrosoftWindowsPowerShellV2Root

12. Add the following three Pass 7 synchronous commands:

```
Wusa.exe c:\setup\ windows10.0-kb5014023-
x64_5da21689c04afbc2c2f2e902225e31e4176c8ed8.msu /quiet

Shutdown.exe /r /t 0

Cmd.exe /C c:\setup\shrink-image.bat

Shutdown.exe /r /t 0
```

The shutdown command between the installation of the MSU and the running of the batch file is required to complete the installation of the update.

13. Save the answer file.
14. Build a new configuration set.
15. Copy the configuration set to the USB installation disk.
16. Boot and install the image on the target system.

After the system logs in, it will appear that nothing is going on, but the WUSA command is running in the background because of the /quiet switch. You will have to wait for the system to reboot and the shrink-image.bat file to run. If you open up Task Manager, you can see the Windows Modules Installer Worker process is running. The other option is to just run the batch file manually after installing the latest updates.

17. After the second reboot, run the cleanup-image.bat to clean up the image.
18. Open File Explorer, right-click on Drive C, and select Properties. Note the disk usage to get the OS footprint.

5.10 Size Matters

With apologies to Yoda who said that "Size matters not", for IoT, size matters. Most importantly, small size matters to address cost and smaller drive sizes. Componentization used to be the best method to choose what goes into an image and keep the image size as small as possible. Unfortunately, happenstance and a bruised CEO ego diverted the continued progress to break down Windows into components. A light has appeared, and we have two sets of packages that can be removed: Internal Core packages and the optional Feature-on-Demand packages (FOD). The Internal Core packages can be removed using a script, but as of this writing, the list of packages is small. Over time the list of packages will grow as cumulative updates address internal packages. Hopefully, in the future that we go beyond a 0.4GB size reduction. The chapter also looked at a few other tricks to get back more drive space.

These last 4 chapters have walked through creating a custom image and addressing performance and image size. Now, we turn to the next three chapters to look at locking down and securing the image.

6 Lockdown Part 1: User Experience

Many years ago, at a Mobile Embedded Developers Conference (MEDC), a couple of developers approached me to ask some questions. They were from a medical device company. A few years earlier, they had built a medical device using Windows NT Embedded. The device was working perfectly, and they went out to demo the device to various medical customers. At one doctor's office, they set everything up and booted up the system. First came the BIOS screen, then the Windows NT logo, and then the final application was launched. They demonstrated the device's operation, but the doctor was more interested in the OS. The doctor asked if this was running Windows NT. They replied that it was Windows NT Embedded, a special version of Windows NT. The doctor said, "You mean this device is running the same OS that keeps crashing on my office computer?" Needless to say, they walked out of the office without a sale. This little story gave me the idea to develop the "Locking Down Windows XP Embedded" topic for the conference the following year and eventually create a dedicated chapter in my book to cover the topic.

The big design question is what the user sees when the system boots up. Most embedded system developers want to hide the fact that Windows, or any other embedded operating system for that matter, is running underneath. System security and stability are two reasons to hide Windows. If a user sees Explorer Shell with the start bar, they may get the idea to install office programs and games like any generic PC. Making the system look like an appliance changes the perception of what the system really is underneath. I have had a few customers use the Explorer shell with the taskbar as the main shell of their system. These customers learned the hard way about the costs of not locking down a system. If customers are allowed to install whatever they want, there is a good chance that technical support calls will arise for issues that are not related to your actual product. Fighting issues that have nothing to do with your system can really hurt the bottom line and the product's reputation.

This is the first chapter where we begin to look at architecting and locking down the system. This chapter's focus will be on the User Experience, i.e., what the users see on startup, and how the user interacts with the system. The next two chapters cover Embedded Lockdown features and Security respectively. There are some features in these later chapters that will affect the features discussed in this chapter, so it is best to read these three chapters in sequence to get the big picture.

6.1 Device Lockdown Features

The Lockdown Features are split into two areas in the catalog. The first is the package section. Microsoft-Windows-Foundation-Package provides the ability to enable or disable individual Lockdown Features. The second is the component section. There are individual components for each Lockdown Feature. The following sections will cover each feature's component settings. It is possible to add a component and forget to enable the feature in the package. The feature can be enabled in the live image, but the settings will have to be set using WMI or the Embedded Lockdown Manager. This chapter will focus on 3 of these device lockdown features.

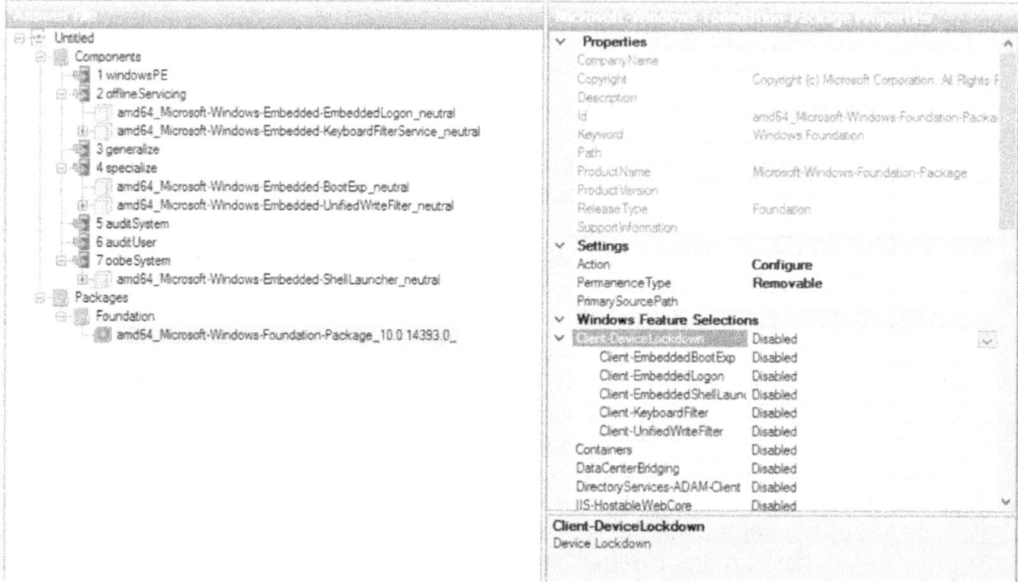

6.2 *Bootup Screens*

Several boot screens appear before the shell is launched.

6.2.1 BIOS Splash Screen

When the computer is first turned on, the BIOS screen appears. For those of you coming from XP Embedded, you might have created a boot.bmp file along with modifications to boot.ini to make your own custom splash screen appear. This feature was removed with WES7; but In Windows 10, Microsoft brought the custom boot splash screen back as follows:

- The boot splash screen is placed in the UEFI firmware.
- The system must boot in UEFI mode and not Legacy mode as discussed in chapter 1.

The BIOS/UEFI screen is not something under Windows' control, and it is not something that we can add to SIM. You will have to ask your board manufacturer to include the splash screen in the firmware. As the operating system loads, this splash screen stays present; and this takes us to the Embedded Boot Experience component.

6.2.2 Microsoft-Windows-Embedded-BootExp Component

The Microsoft-Windows-Embedded-BootExp component controls what is seen when the OS is loading on bootup. The component provides options to either blank the screen or show the logo, or show the logo or status indicator. It can also block the Blue Screen of Death and the bootup trap keys.

Note: If the system takes a little long to boot up and there is nothing on the video screen indicating that the device is alive and well, the user might think that the system crashed, and they might power cycle the system right in the middle of the bootup cycle.

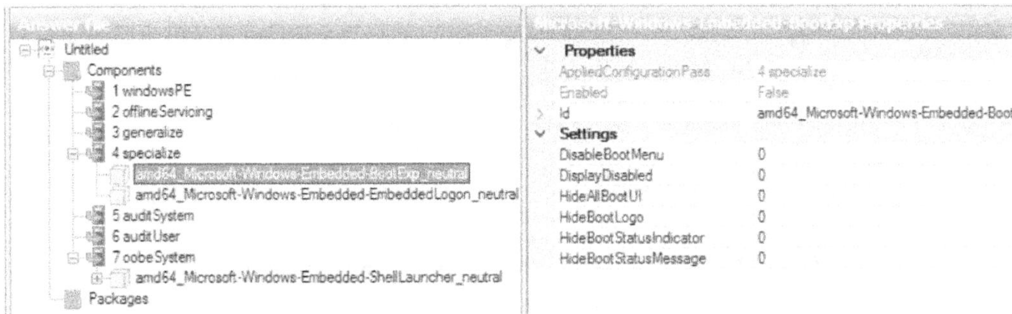

Here are the available settings:

- **DisableBootMenu** – an integer value that disables F8 and F10 during bootup for gaining access to advanced boot options. Possible values are 1 to disable the menu and 0 to enable the menu.

Note: I have found that this feature doesn't really work, and the F8 and F10 keys can be accessed in some systems. The cause is not known nor is their solution.

- **DisplayDisabled** – This hides the Blue Screen of Death (BSOD) from appearing. Possible values are 1 to display a blank screen or 0 to show the error.
- **HideAllBootUI** – an integer value that when set to 1 will suppress all Windows UI elements on startup – logo, status indicator, and status message. A value of 0 will not enable all, but you can suppress individual elements with the following settings.
- **HideBootLogo** – an integer value that can suppress the Windows logo from appearing on startup. Possible values are 1 to suppress the logo, and 0 to not suppress the logo.
- **HideBootStatusIndicator** - an integer value that can suppress the status indicator on startup. Possible values are 1 to suppress the status indicator, or 0 to not suppress the status indicator.

- **HideBootStatusMessage** – an integer value that can suppress status messages from appearing on startup. Possible values are 1 to suppress the status messages, or 0 to not suppress the status messages.

6.3 Login Screen

Once Windows has loaded, the system will come to the logon and lock screens, and there are several components and features that come into play.

6.3.1 Microsoft-Windows-Embedded-EmbeddedLogon Component

The first component is the Microsoft-Windows-Embedded-EmbeddedLogon. This component has settings to suppress Windows UI elements on the logon page, as well as, to hide Microsoft branding badges that appear during bootup and shutdown.

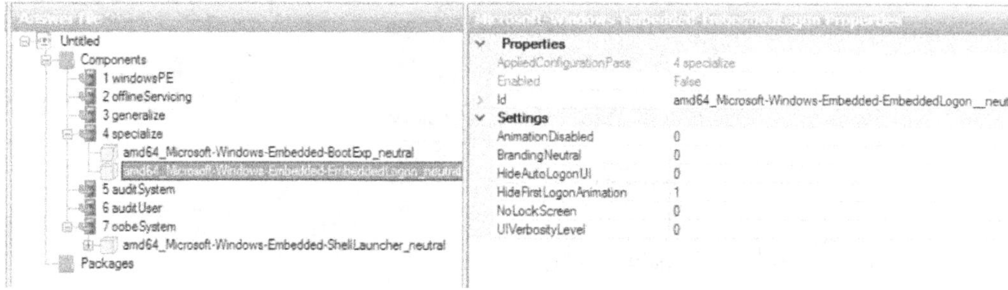

Here are the available settings:

- **AnimationDisabled** - an integer value that enables or disables logon screen transition animation. The possible values are 1 to disable animation, and 0 to enable animation.
- **BrandingNeutral** – an integer value that specifies what logon UI elements appear. There are several values that can be combined using bitwise exclusive-or logic.

  1 - Disables all logon screen UI elements.
  2 - Disables the Shutdown button.
  4 - Disables the Language button.
  8 - Disables the Ease of access button.
  16 - Disables the Switch user button.
  32 - Disables the Blocked Shutdown Resolver (BSDR) screen.

The values are combined in a Bitwise-OR. If you want to block the last 4 elements on the list, but not the shutdown button, the value to enter would be 60. The only UI element that is not covered individually is the network UI. As a security measure, it is wise to disable this button so as not to let someone connect the device to a rogue network. The network UI button can be disabled via Group Policy. Administrative Templates\System\Logon - "Do not display network selection UI". Creating a custom group policy will be discussed in a later chapter. Chapter 8 will discuss how to create a custom Group Policy so we can preconfigure some of these policies.

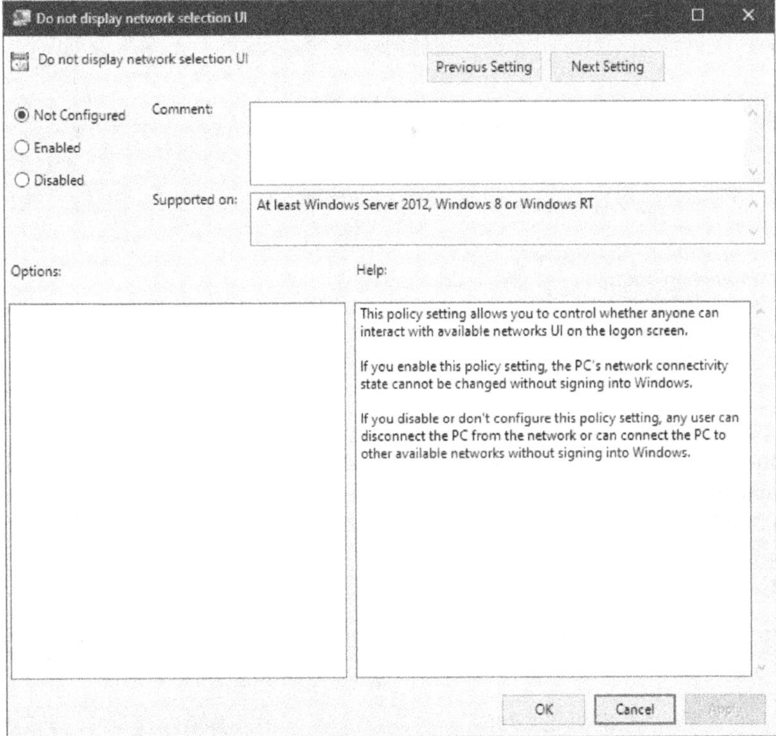

- **HideFirstLogonAnimation** – When set to 1, this will disable the "Hi, We are happy you are here" animation upon first boot of the image. A 0 enables the animation. Sometimes you might want to leave this feature enabled for those in manufacturing who are performing the final configuration. It tells them that the system is alive and working. If the system goes directly to the customer, then it is better to hide this message.
- **HideAutoLogonUI** – an integer value that either shows or hides logon screens when automatic logon is enabled. Possible values are 1 to hide logon screens, or 0 to show logon screens.
- **NoLockScreen** – an integer value that either enables or disables the Lock screen and UI elements. Possible values are 1 to disable the lock screen, or 0 to enable the lock screen.
- **UIVerbosityLevel** – a hexadecimal value that either enables or disables status messages during startup, logon, and shutdown. Possible values are 0x1 to disable the status messages, or 0x4 to enable the status messages.

The settings will be put into the registry (HKLM\SOFTWARE\Microsoft\ Windows Embedded\ EmbeddedLogon) where they can be modified on the fly if necessary. If there are any changes made manually, be sure to change them in the answer file.

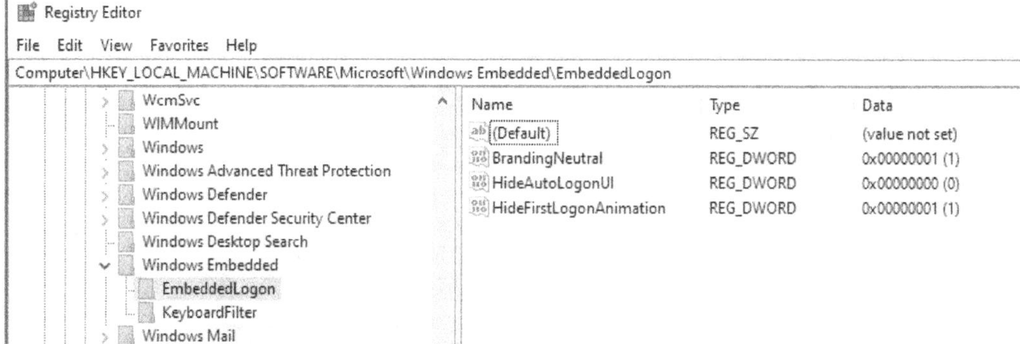

6.3.2 Custom Logon / Lock Screen Background Image

A custom background image for the login and lock screen can be configured via Group Policy. Administrative Templates\Control Panel\Personalization - "Force a specific default lock screen and logon image". You would have to place your jpg or bmp file somewhere in the file system (distribution share). Creating the custom group policy will be discussed in a later chapter.

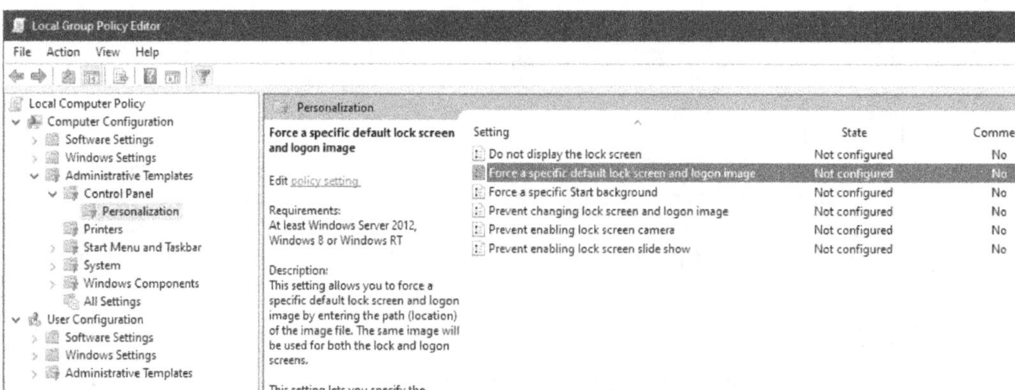

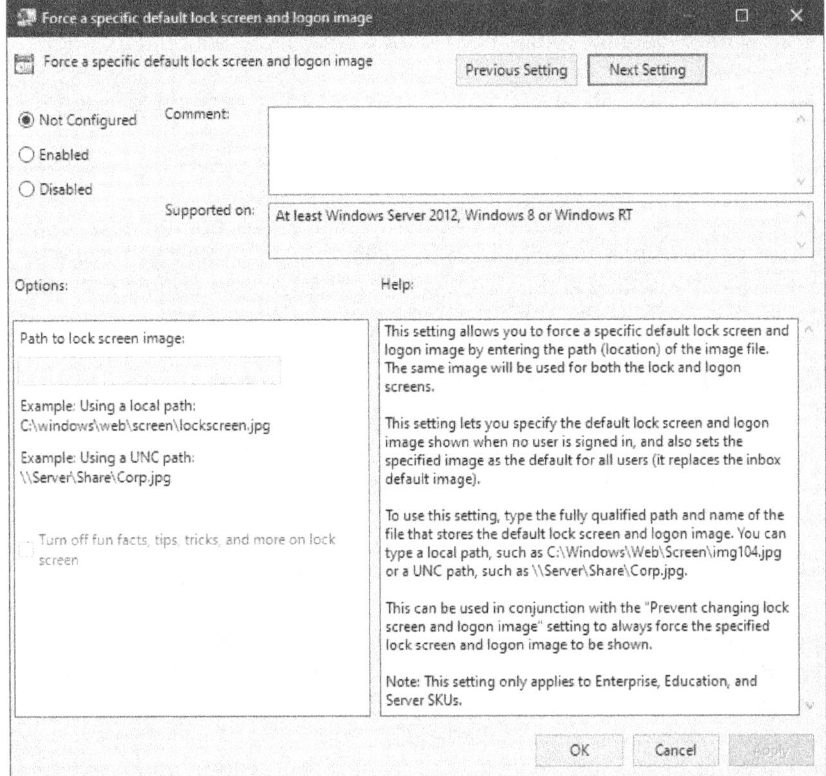

6.3.3 Autologon

Rather than having the system stop at the login screen, the system can autologin to a specific account. If you enable the HideLogonUI settings, then the logon screen never appears when the system is set to auto logon, but there will be a black screen transition from splash screen to shell. The Microsoft-Windows-Shell-Setup component includes the AutoLogon settings that can be placed in the configuration file.

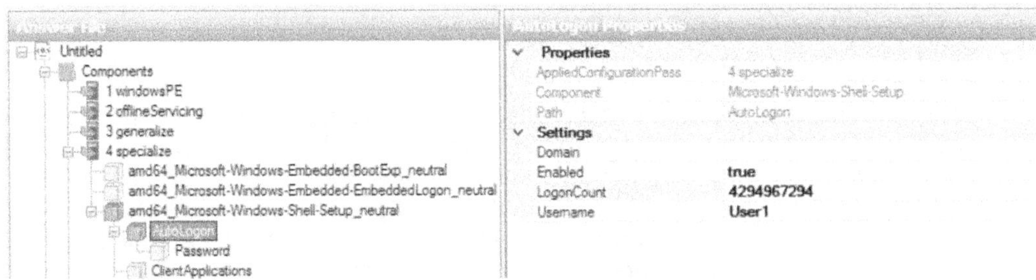

The AutoLogon settings can be accessed via the following registry key:

HKEY_LOCAL_MACHINE\SOFTWARE\Microsoft\Windows NT\CurrentVersion\Winlogon

Value Name: DefaultUserName – User Name of the account to logon

Value Name: DefaultPassword – Password for the account to logon

Value Name: AutoAdminLogon – 0 – disable AutoLogon, 1 – enable AutoLogon.

The LogonCount setting is a security feature. The value decrements each time the autologon user account has been logged into the system. Autologon will stop once the value reaches zero. By setting a very large value, the Autologon should not stop until a few decades have passed depending on usage.

6.4 Shells – Final Application to Run on Startup

Once all of the boot screens have run and the system is logged in, the shell appears. For those coming from the Linux world, the shell in Windows means the final application that runs on bootup and logon. The system must have a shell. Any application can be the shell for the system. There are some fundamental architectural questions to ask at this point:

- With the shell, how does the user interact with the system?
- Does the user see the Windows 10 Shell?
- How does one address system settings like those from the control panel?
- Most developers want the final application to be the shell for the system, but what if the application needs to be upgraded. One cannot replace a running application. How do I upgrade the shell in the field?
- Do I need to have more than one account in the system and does each of these accounts have a different shell?

These are all very important questions for branding, servicing, security, and customer impressions of the device. The primary shell in Windows 10 is Explorer.exe, and it gets launched via the use of the following registry key:

Key: HKEY_LOCAL_MACHINE\Software\Microsoft\Windows NT\CurrentVersion\Winlogon
Value Name: Shell
Type: REG_SZ
Value: Explorer.exe

The “Value” can be changed to any application, but I would not recommend setting up a custom shell this way. Instead, you will want to use the Shell Launcher feature. For those who have read my previous books on Windows XP Embedded, you are familiar with what I have written about different shells for different users. The idea was to set up a shell for each user when they log in. You can have a default shell for users, and an administrator shell when the administrator is logged in. The setup involved changing several registry keys. After writing about shells and different techniques in books and articles, someone at Microsoft finally noticed and took a big step to create an integrated solution, which brings us to the Shell Launcher feature. There are two different Shell Launchers: V1 and V2. You will want to use V1 as V2 is for UWP applications.

6.4.1 Shell Launcher V1

The Shell Launcher V1 allows you to set up different shells for different users. The Microsoft-Windows-Embedded-ShellLauncher_neutral component allows you to define a default shell and/or unique shells for each user account.

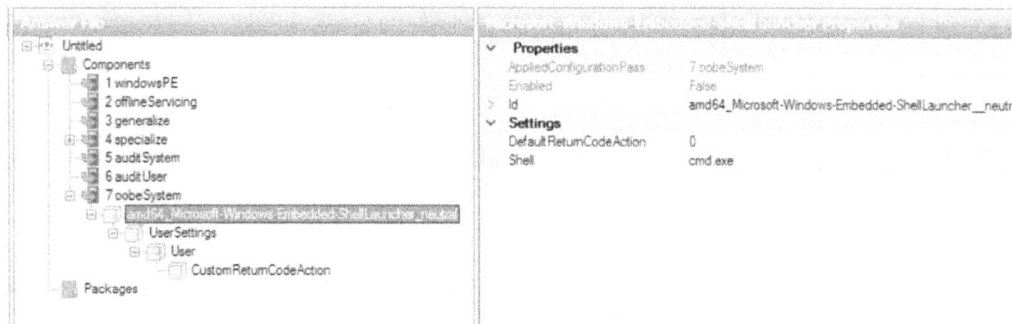

Note: The Shell Launcher component is there, but it still doesn't work.

Here are the settings:

- **Shell** – Points to the application to be launched as the default shell. You can either set the path or call the application by name, if it is already in the execution path. If this is a custom application, you will want to create a module for it. A dependency on Shell Launcher is not a must.
- **DefaultReturnCodeAction** – An integer value that specifies the action to take when the default application exits. Possible Values are 0 – restart shell, 1 – reboot, 2 – shut down, or 3 – do nothing.
- **UserSettings** – Allows you to specify the shell and shell exit action for a specific user account. This shell will be launched over the default shell. You can have different applications launch as the shell for different users.

The following diagram shows the process flow for Shell Launcher. When Shell Launcher is disabled, Explorer.exe is launched as the shell. If Shell Launcher is enabled, then the default shell application is launched if there are no user-defined shell applications. If there is a user-defined shell application, then this shell application launches. If the shell application terminates for any reason the default action will take place.

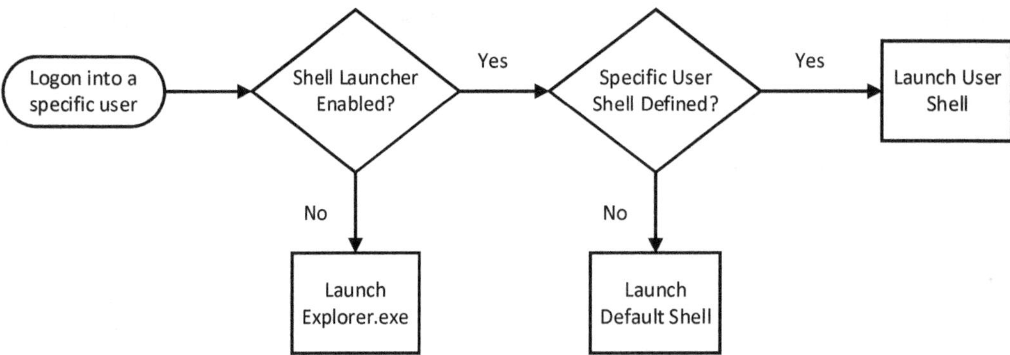

As noted, the shell launcher component doesn't work. Why Microsoft had this working in Windows Embedded 8.1 Industry and cannot make it work in Windows 10 is anyone's guess. This is where the Shell Launcher WMI API set comes to the rescue. (The WMI API details can be found on docs.microsoft.com by searching for "wesl-usersetting"). To address the shortcomings of the component, I created a command line and a GUI utility that are free downloads from annabooks.com. The command line utility can be called with a Pass 7 synchronous command to set up Shell Launcher.

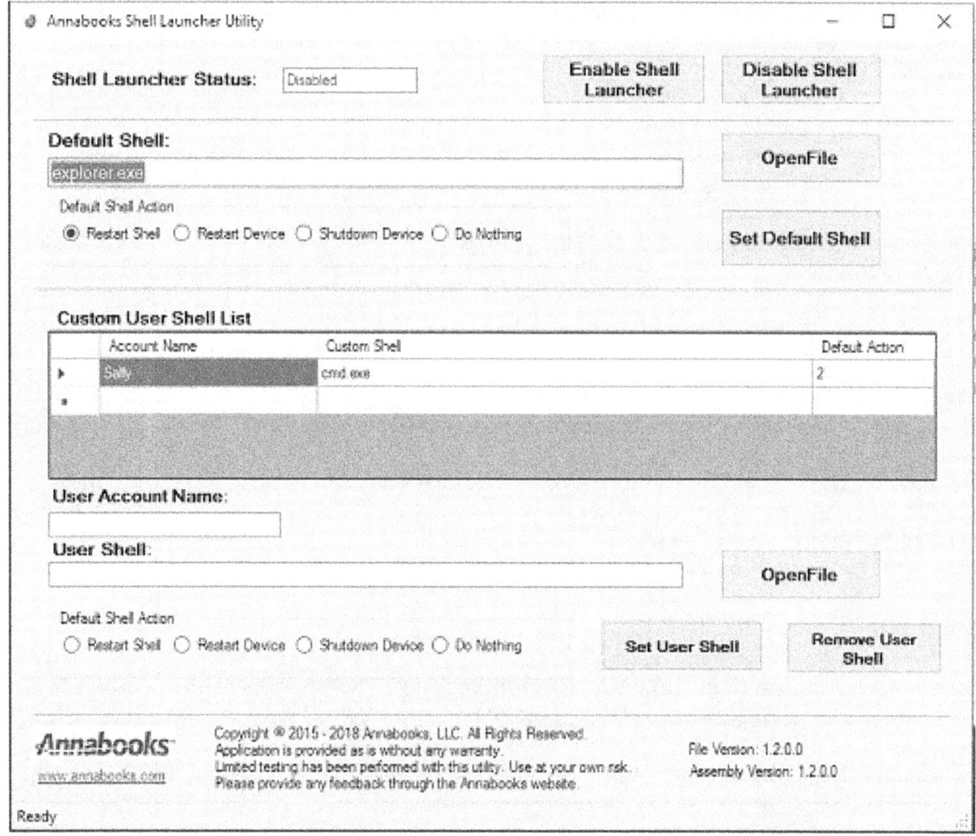

Here is the usage for shlmgr.exe command line utility

```
usage: shlmgr [command] [settings]
Commands:

enable | disable, Enable or Disable Shell Launcher
get-config, List the status and settings of Shell Launcher
set-defaultshell, Sets the default shell
set-usershell, Set up a shell for a specific user
remove-usershell, Remove a custom user shell
Help | ?, This help page

Examples:

shlmgr enable

shlmgr set-defaultshell <path to .exe> <DefaultAction>

where DefaultAcion - 0=Restart Shell, 1=Restart Device, 2=Shutdown Device,
3=Do Nothing
```

```
shlmgr set-usershell <user name> <path to .exe> <DefaultAction>
where DefaultAcion - 0=Restart Shell, 1=Restart Device, 2=Shutdown Device,
3=Do Nothing
User account must exist

shlmgr remove-usershell <user name>
User account must exist
```

If you prefer to integrate some of these controls into your own application, here are some C# code snippets:

Enable Shell Launcher:

```
ManagementScope scope = new ManagementScope(@"root\standardcimv2\embedded");
ManagementClass WESL = new ManagementClass(scope.Path.Path, "WESL_UserSetting",
null);
ManagementBaseObject Enabledparams = WESL.GetMethodParameters("SetEnabled");

Enabledparams["Enabled"] = true;
WESL.InvokeMethod("SetEnabled", Enabledparams, null);
```

Disable Shell Launcher:

```
ManagementScope scope = new ManagementScope(@"root\standardcimv2\embedded");
ManagementClass WESL = new ManagementClass(scope.Path.Path, "WESL_UserSetting",
null);
ManagementBaseObject Enabledparams = WESL.GetMethodParameters("SetEnabled");

Enabledparams["Enabled"] = false;
WESL.InvokeMethod("SetEnabled", Enabledparams, null);
```

Set Default Shell:

```
ManagementScope scope = new ManagementScope(@"root\standardcimv2\embedded");
ManagementClass WESL = new ManagementClass(scope.Path.Path, "WESL_UserSetting",
null);
ManagementBaseObject SetDSParams = WESL.GetMethodParameters("SetDefaultShell");

SetDSParams["Shell"] = txtDefaultShell.Text;
if (rbRestartApp.Checked == true)
{
  SetDSParams["DefaultAction"] = 0;
}
if (rbRestartDevice.Checked == true)
{
  SetDSParams["DefaultAction"] = 1;
}
if (rbShutdownDevice.Checked == true)
{
 SetDSParams["DefaultAction"] = 2;
```

```
}

WESL.InvokeMethod("SetDefaultShell", SetDSParams, null);
```

6.4.2 Shell Launcher V2 (Avoid this version)

Shell Launcher V1 supports .EXE applications such as Win32, .NET Framework, and .NET 6.0. The outlier is UWP applications. As we stated in Chapter 1, UWP is dead, but that didn't stop Microsoft from moving forward and creating Shell Launcher V2 to allow UWP applications to be the shell of the system. Let me be very clear:

!!!!! DO NOT USE SHELL LAUNCHER V2 UNLESS A UWP APPLICATION IS GOING TO BE THE SHELL TO THE SYSTEM. SINCE YOU SHOULDN'T BE CREATING OR RUNNING UWP APPLICATIONS BECAUSE UWP APPLICATIONS ARE DEAD, YOU WILL NEVER USE SHELL LAUNCHER V2!!!!

With all that said, let me provide some coverage. There is no component in SIM for Shell Launcher V2 so you have to use a PowerShell "Bridge WMI Helper" script that calls CSP (configuration service provider) API to set up Shell Launcher V2. The script is listed below and can be found here: https://github.com/microsoft/Windows-iotcore-samples/tree/develop/Samples/ShellLauncherV2. The script has three simple functions, Set-ShellLauncherBridgeWMI, Get-ShellLauncherBridgeWMI, and Clear-ShellLauncherBridgeWMI.

```
$NameSpace = "root\cimv2\mdm\dmmap"
$Class = "MDM_AssignedAccess"

function Get-AssignedAccessCspBridgeWmi
{
   return Get-CimInstance -Namespace $NameSpace -ClassName $Class
}

function Set-ShellLauncherBridgeWMI
{
   param([Parameter(Mandatory=$True)][String] $FilePath)

   $Xml = Get-Content -Path $FilePath
   $EscapedXml = [System.Security.SecurityElement]::Escape($Xml)
   $AssignedAccessCsp = Get-AssignedAccessCspBridgeWmi
   $AssignedAccessCsp.ShellLauncher = $EscapedXml
   Set-CimInstance -CimInstance $AssignedAccessCsp

   # get a new instance and print the value
   (Get-AssignedAccessCspBridgeWmi).ShellLauncher
}

function Clear-ShellLauncherBridgeWMI
```

```
{
   $AssignedAccessCsp = Get-AssignedAccessCspBridgeWmi
   $AssignedAccessCsp.ShellLauncher = $NULL
   Set-CimInstance -CimInstance $AssignedAccessCsp
}

function Get-ShellLauncherBridgeWMI
{
   (Get-AssignedAccessCspBridgeWmi).ShellLauncher
}
```

An XML file is used as input to the PowerShell script. Here is an example:

```
<?xml version="1.0" encoding="utf-8"?>
<ShellLauncherConfiguration
xmlns="http://schemas.microsoft.com/ShellLauncher/2018/Configuration"
xmlns:v2="http://schemas.microsoft.com/ShellLauncher/2019/Configuration">
 <Profiles>
  <DefaultProfile>
   <Shell Shell="%systemroot%\explorer.exe">
    <DefaultAction Action="RestartShell"/>
   </Shell>
  </DefaultProfile>
  <Profile Id="{814B6409-8C51-4EE2-95F8-DB39B70F5F68}">
   <Shell Shell="MyUWPApp" v2:AppType="UWP"
v2:AllAppsFullScreen="true">
    <DefaultAction Action="RestartShell"/>
   </Shell>
  </Profile>
       <Profile Id="{b77fdbba-9a39-4b5e-b381-489d13eb3b6c}">
   <Shell Shell="c:\Program Files\MyApp\myApp.exe"
v2:AllAppsFullScreen="true">
    <DefaultAction Action="RestartShell"/>
   </Shell>
  </Profile>
 </Profiles>
 <Configs>
  <Config>
   <Account Name="user2"/>
   <Profile Id="{814B6409-8C51-4EE2-95F8-DB39B70F5F68}"/>
  </Config>
       <Config>
   <Account Name="user1"/>
   <Profile Id="{b77fdbba-9a39-4b5e-b381-489d13eb3b6c}"/>
  </Config>
 </Configs>
```

```
</ShellLauncherConfiguration>
```

The default shell is set as Explorer.exe, User1 launches myapp.exe, and User2 launches a UWP app. The script has to be run in the System account. Microsoft calls out the requirement for using PSEXEC.exe from Sysinternals to perform this task, but I recommend installing the invoke-commandAs PowerShell cmdlet to avoid leaving the PSEXEC.exe utility in the system. The following PowerShell script installs the cmdlet:

```
Install-PackageProvider -Name NuGet -MinimumVersion 2.8.5.201 -
Force
Install-module -Name invoke-commandas -RequiredVersion 3.1.0 -
Force
```

The ShellLauncherBridgeWmiHelper.ps1 script was modified to simplify the steps by adding the following parameters to the end of the script:

```
#
#Call the WMI Bridge calls based on params
#

if($Get){

   Get-ShellLauncherBridgeWMI
}
if($Clear){
   Clear-ShellLauncherBridgeWMI
}
if($Set){
   Set-ShellLauncherBridgeWMI -FilePath C:\SLV2\mySLV2setup.xml
}
```

This simplifies the calls to the 3 functions. The following is the call to the Set-ShellLauncherBridgeWMI (all one line):

```
powershell.exe -command "Invoke-CommandAs -ScriptBlock
{c:\SLV2\ShellLauncherBridgeWmiHelpers.ps1 -Set} -AsSystem"
```

There is a little wrinkle to this script. If Windows Defender Application Control (WDAC) is enabled and has limits on PowerShell script calls for security, the Set-ShellLauncherBridgeWMI function will fail to run. You have to modify the Set-ShellLauncherBridgeWMI functions with the following:

```
function Set-ShellLauncherBridgeWMI
```

```
{
   param([Parameter(Mandatory=$True)][String] $FilePath)

   $Xml = Get-Content -Path $FilePath
   $EscapedXml = $Xml
   $AssignedAccessCsp = Get-AssignedAccessCspBridgeWmi
   $AssignedAccessCsp.ShellLauncher = $EscapedXml
   Set-CimInstance -CimInstance $AssignedAccessCsp

   # get a new instance and print the value
   (Get-AssignedAccessCspBridgeWmi).ShellLauncher
}
```

Now, you need another script to create an ESC XML file for the XML configuration file.

```
#Create an escaped version of the SLV2 XML file to avoid Device Gaurd issues.

param([Parameter(Mandatory=$True)][String] $FilePath)

$Xml = Get-Content -Path $FilePath
$EscapedXml = [System.Security.SecurityElement]::Escape($Xml)

Set-Content -Path 'C:\SLV2\UWP-LaunchESC.xml' -Value $EscapedXml
```

Once you have converted the XML to an ESC XML file you can call Set-ShellLauncherBridgeWMI with WDAC enabled**. The security hoop-jumping is another reason to avoid UWP applications.**

Note: If you use the Bridge WMI Helper to set up the shell launcher, the Shell Launcher V1 WMI API can still be used to configure the shell launcher for .EXE applications.

6.4.3 Custom Shell Notes – Windows without Explorer.exe as the Shell

Windows was architected so that the shell could easily be replaced, thus giving Microsoft the opportunity to experiment with different shells without having to rebuild the whole operating system. Shell replacement is a great feature. Please, keep in mind that Windows was designed to work with Explorer.exe as the shell. When a custom shell is put into place, you need to be aware of the following:

- Autoplay – Autoplay doesn't work. The little dialog for autoplay is not operational, since this is built into Explorer.exe. Devices can be connected and DVDs placed in the DVD reader, but they will not start automatically unless the shell is programmed to look for these changes in media or hardware state and then launch the appropriate application.
- Boot time – Custom shells can boot faster than Explorer.exe. Services like networking might not be available when the shell is launched. If the application tries to go out to the network, it might fail. You may have to program a wait on

service or set up a delay. If you are programming in C# this would be the System.ServiceProcess namespace. The method WaitForStatus() can check for a service's status.

There is a subculture of developers who like to modify Windows to their own liking. There are many who have created their own shell interface for Windows. Some of these are for multimedia developers and others for gamers. To help those who don't have time to create their own shell we have developed a simple shell application for Embedded/IoT users. The SJJ Shell provides you with a solution for two of the most important challenges in Windows Embedded/IoT system design today: branding and maintenance. The SJJ Shell can be substituted for the standard desktop shell to provide a different and more contemporary look and feel for your device, or the SJJ Shell can be used as a background maintenance shell to launch your main application as the primary shell.

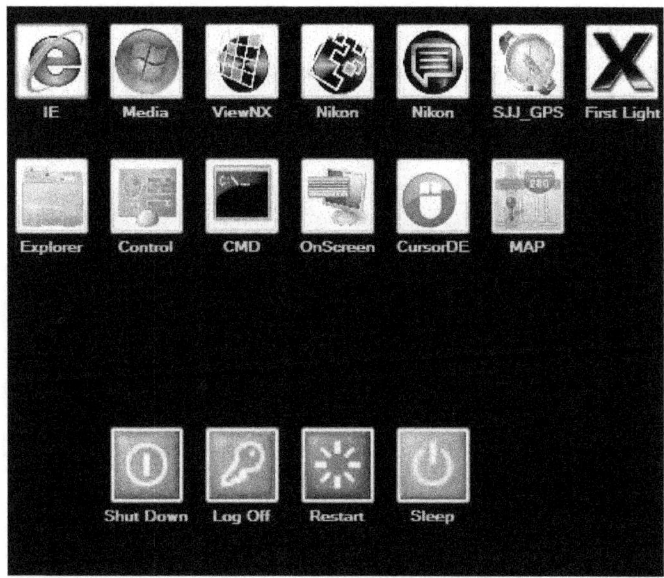

The active controls in the SJJ Shell are graphic buttons that are like shortcut icons on the desktop which launch other applications. Configurability without code modification was the driving design goal for the SJJ Shell; therefore, customization is managed with a single configuration file. Within this configuration file, the number of rows and columns on the screen grid, the button graphics, the location of each graphic button on the screen grid, the button's label text, and the action that each button will take are all customizable. Using the SJJ Shell to launch your main application as the primary shell instead of simply replacing the desktop shell with your main application solves the problem of future maintenance when modifications to, or replacement of, your main application are required. When the SJJ Shell is used to launch your application, it remains in the background and would be configured as an administrative shell, providing access to administrative applications and functions like system restart. Since your main application is a separate process, the application can be closed, dropping you back to the SJJ Shell. Your main application can then be replaced and the system restarted using the SJJ Shell administrative functions that you customized. More information can be found on the website: http://www.annabooks.com/SW_SJJ_SHELL.html.

Whatever shell you put in place will limit what the user can access. The custom shell doubles as a security feature. In some cases, you may want to allow access to service the system. For example, you can set up TCP/IP addresses, check system status, or install device drivers. You may have some of these items built into the shell. There are other tricks that you can implement.

6.5 *Exercise 601 – Creating a Branded Image*

We will employ several different UI concepts in this lab:

- The image will have two user accounts. One will have administrator privileges and the other will be a user account.
- Each account will have a different shell using the Shell Launcher. PowerShell will be the shell for the Administrator account, and AB-test-app.exe will be the shell for the user account.

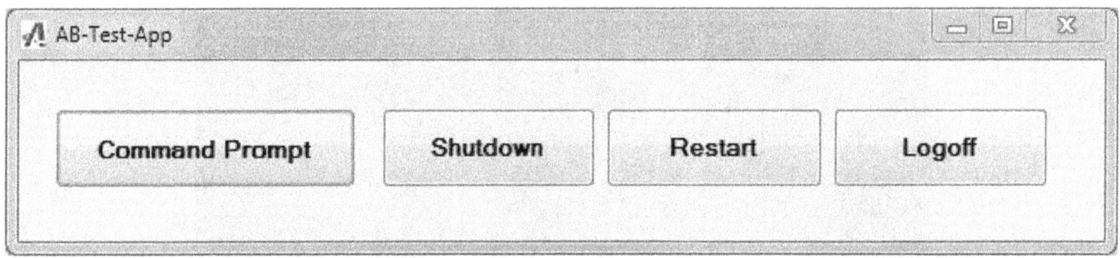

- The image will have the Microsoft branding boot screens removed.
- OOBE screen will be suppressed.

The same basic steps are used to create the answer file and configuration set. Make sure that you create two accounts, not just one.

1. In the C:\WinData\CS folder, delete the AutoUnattend.xml, AutoUnattend_files folder, and the oem folder.
2. Open SIM.
3. Open the catalog file, if it is not opened already.
4. Make sure the C:\WinData\DS64 distribution share is open.
5. Create a new answer file.
6. Following the table below, add the components, and add the corresponding settings.

Component	Configuration Pass	Component Setting	Possible Value / Notes
amd64_Microsoft-Windows-	1 WindowsPE	InputLocale	en-US
	1 WindowsPE	SystemLocale	en-US

International-Core-WinPE__neutral	1 WindowsPE	SetupUILanguage: UILanguage	en-US
	1 WindowsPE	UILanguage	en-US
	1 WindowsPE	UserLocale	en-US
amd64_Microsoft-Windows-Setup__neutral	1 WindowsPE	UserData: AcceptEULA	True
	1 WindowsPE	UserData : ProductKey : Key	Enter the license key
	1 WindowsPE	UserData : ProductKey: WillShowUI	OnError
	1 WindowsPE	ImageInstall: OSInstall : InstallFrom: MetaData: Key	/IMAGE/NAME
	1 WindowsPE	ImageInstall: OSImage : InstallFrom: MetaData: Value	Windows 10 Enterprise 2016 LTSB
amd64_Microsoft-Windows-Shell-Setup__neutral	4 Specialize	ComputerName	ACME
	4 Specialize	TimeZone	Pacific Standard Time
	4 Specialize	AutoLogon: Username	WinGUEST
	4 Specialize	AutoLogon: Enabled	True
	4 Specialize	AutoLogon: LogonCount	4294967294
	4 Specialize	AutoLogon: Password: Value	password
amd64_Microsoft-Windows-International-Core__neutral	7 OOBE System	InputLocale	en-US
	7 OOBE System	SystemLocale	en-US
	7 OOBE System	UILanguage	en-US
	7 OOBE System	UserLocale	en-US
amd64_Microsoft-Windows-Shell-Setup__neutral	7 OOBE System	UserAccounts : LocalAccounts : LocalAccount : Name	WinADMIN
	7 OOBE System	UserAccounts : LocalAccounts : LocalAccount : DisplayName	WinADMIN
	7 OOBE System	UserAccounts : LocalAccounts : LocalAccount :Group	Administrators
	7 OOBE System	UserAccounts : LocalAccounts : LocalAccount : Password : Value	password
	7 OOBE System	UserAccounts : LocalAccounts : LocalAccount : Name	WinGUEST
	7 OOBE System	UserAccounts : LocalAccounts : LocalAccount : DisplayName	WinGUEST
	7 OOBE System	UserAccounts : LocalAccounts : LocalAccount :Group	Users
	7 OOBE System	UserAccounts : LocalAccounts : LocalAccount : Password : Value	password

	7 OOBE System	OOBE : ProtectYourPC	3
	7 OOBE System	OOBE : HideEULAPage	True
	7 OOBE System	OOBE : HideWirelessSetupInOOBE	True
	7 OOBE System	OOBE : HideOEMRegistrationScreen	True
	7 OOBE System	OOBE : HideLocalAccountScreen	True
	7 OOBE System	OOBE : HideOnlineAccountScreen	True

7. Add the amd64_Microsoft-Windows-Embedded-EmbeddedLogon component to Pass 2.
8. In the settings, change the following settings to 1: AnimationDisabled, BrandingNeutral, and NoLockScreen

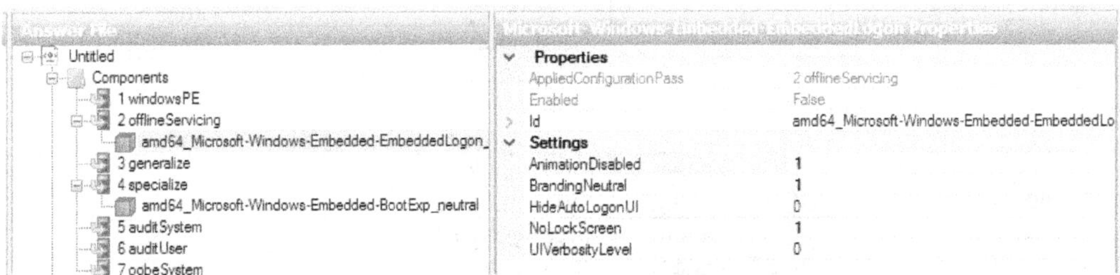

9. Add amd64_Microsoft-Windows-Embedded-BootExp component to Pass 4.
10. In the settings, change the following settings to 1: DisableBootMenu, HideBootLogo, and HideBootStatusMessage

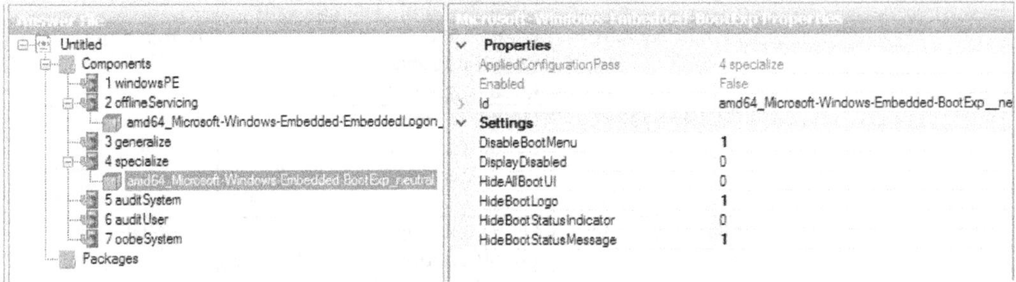

For laughs, we will add items to the Shell Launcher component, but these settings will not be applied to the image.

11. Add the amd64_Microsoft-Windows-Embedded-ShellLauncher to Pass7.
12. For the Shell setting add the following C:\Program Files\Annabooks\AB-Test-App.exe.

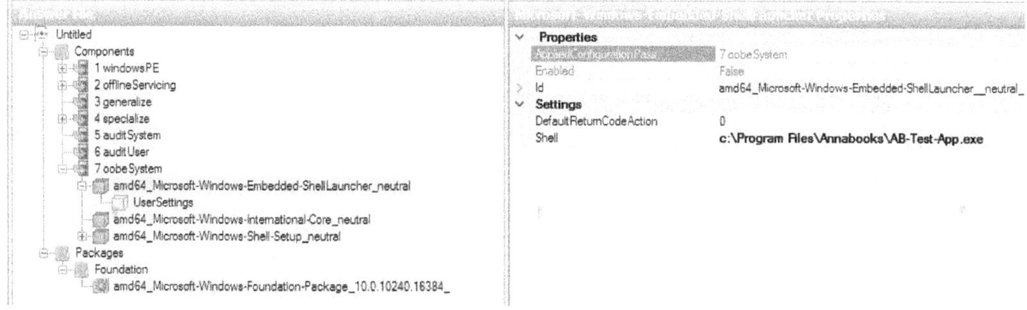

13. Under UserSettings, add a new User.
14. For the new User change the setting as follows:

- AccountName: WinADMIN
- Key: 1
- Shell: C:\Windows\system32\Windowspowershell\v1.0\powershell.exe

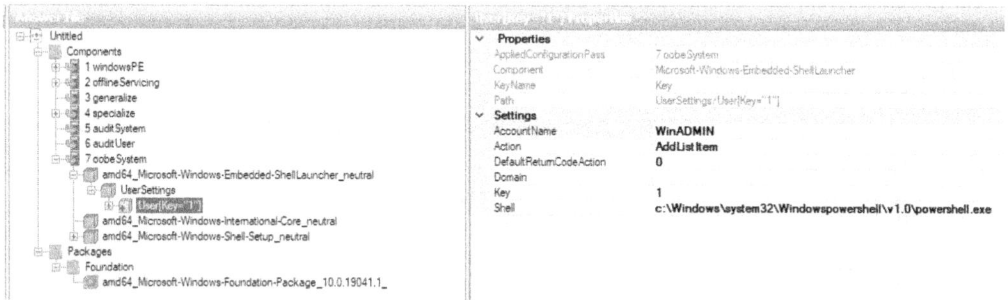

15. Download the Shell Launcher utilities from Annabooks.com and place them in the same folder as the AB-Test-App.exe \$OEM$ Folders\$1\Program Files\Annabooks folder.
16. Create another folder under \$OEM$ Folders\$1 called setup.
17. Using Notepad or Notepadd++ create a batch file called shell-setup.bat.
18. Add the following to the shell-setup.bat file:

```
"c:\Program Files\Annabooks\shlmgr.exe" set-defaultshell "c:\Program Files\Annabooks\AB-Test-App.exe" 0
"c:\Program Files\Annabooks\shlmgr.exe" set-usershell WinADMIN "c:\Windows\system32\Windowspowershell\v1.0\powershell.exe" 0
"c:\Program Files\Annabooks\shlmgr.exe" enable
```

19. Save the file to the C:\WinData \$OEM$ Folders\$1\setup folder.
20. The last step is to enable the lockdown features in the foundation package. Add the amd64_Microsoft-Windows-Foundation-Package to the answer file.
21. Under the foundation Package, enable the following features:

a. Client-DeviceLockdown
b. Client-EmbedddBootExp
c. Client-EmbeddedLogon
d. Client-EmbeddedShell-Launcher

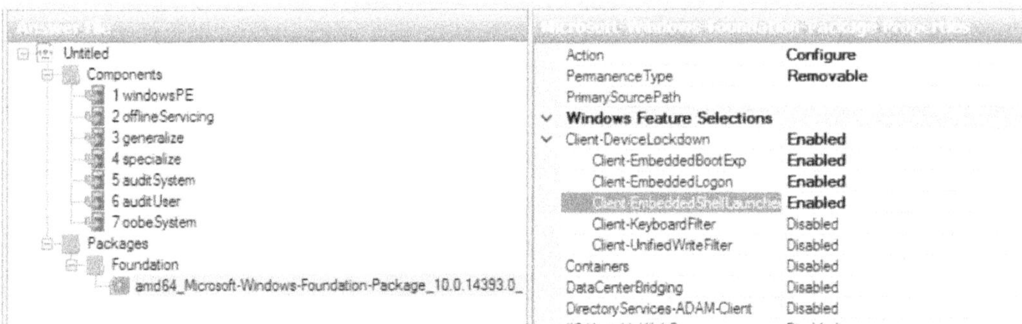

Although Shell Launcher is in the image, it is not enabled by default, thus the batch file created earlier will enable Shell Launcher.

22. Now we are going to add two Pass 7 Sync Commands. From the menu, select Insert->Synchronous Command->Pass 7 oobeSystem…
23. The Create Synchronous Command dialog appears. Enter the following to enable Shell Launcher:

    cmd.exe /C c:\setup\shell-setup.bat

24. Click Ok.
25. Repeat steps 20 through 22 to create another Synchronous Command under Pass 7 oobeSystem… that will reboot the system for the Shell Launcher changes to take effect:

    Shutdown.exe /r /t 0

26. Validate the answer file.
27. Save the answer file as EX601.
28. Deploy the OS image to the target system. Be sure to delete all partitions and recreate the default partition before installing the image. The image will boot into the WinGUEST account.
29. To complete the setup, log off the WinGUEST account.
30. Log on to the WinADMIN account.

Important: Since the Pass 7 Synchronous Commands will only run in an administrator account, they run when you first log in to WinADMIN. The first Sync Command sets up and enables Shell Launcher. The second command reboots the system for the changes to take effect. The exercise was set up this way to demonstrate this concept.

31. The system will boot into the WinGUEST account, and AB-Test-App.exe is the shell.
32. Click the Logoff button.
33. Log into the WinADMIN account, and you will see that PowerShell is the shell.
34. Shut down the target system when finished by entering the following at the PowerShell prompt and hitting enter:

    shutdown /s /t 0

6.6 *Multi-monitor and Screen Rotation*

Now and again, there are questions on how to preset screen resolutions, configure multiple monitors, or rotate the screen. Video resolution can be configured in the answer file, but for screen rotation or support for multiple monitors, there is a utility developed by Nir Sofer called MultiMonitorTool. The utility is a combination of GUI and command line tools. The details of the tool can be found on the website: http://www.nirsoft.net/utils/multi_monitor_tool.html.

6.7 *Manufacturing – When to Enable Shell Launcher in the Image*

One final thought on Shell Launcher has to do with when Shell Launcher gets enabled. If the plan is to install the final application during production, then it is a good idea to keep Shell Launcher disabled. Only after installing the final application in manufacturing should Shell Launcher be enabled. If the application is already in the image, then enable Shell Launcher using the Sysprep unattended file. Enabling later allows you some time to make any manual changes to the image using Explorer.exe before creating the master image. In either case, the GUI and command line utilities will continue to be helpful.

6.8 *Summary: First Impressions*

The customer's impression of an embedded device can change based on the system's look and feel. There are different components to hide the boot and logon screen. Setting up custom shells is much easier, and don't forget to Sysprep an image before cloning it to other devices. A unique interface provides one level of locking down the system. There are three more chapters to go for the architecture and lockdown discussion. The next chapter looks at some unique Windows Embedded/IoT lockdown features.

7 Lockdown Part 2: UWF and Keyboard Filter

The previous chapter began the discussion of architecture and lockdown. Three of the device lockdown features that cover the user experience were discussed. This chapter will cover the last two lockdown features: the Unified Write Filter (UWF) to block permanent write access to a drive and the keyboard filter to restrict keyboard entry. The chapter will touch on a few other features to disable via Group Policy.

7.1 Unified Write Filter (UWF)

For those who are familiar with Windows XP Embedded and WES7, you will remember the different available write filters: Enhanced Write Filter (EWF), File Based Write Filter (FBWF), and the Registry filter. Starting with Windows Embedded 8 Standard, all three were replaced with the Unified Write Filter (UWF).

UWF is the most important feature for embedded/IoT systems. As the name implies, any writes to the disk are blocked and sent to an overlay. The overlay can be a RAM cache or an on-disk page file cache. When the system reboots, the information in the overlay is purged. UWF can be set up to block all writes, or it can be set up to allow some items to be written to the disk. UWF provides some level of protection from viruses that could get into the system. The real benefit is to help preserve the life of a flash disk due to all the constant disk reads and writes Windows is making to the disk and to help prevent disk corruption from a sudden power loss. The next few sections dig into the UWF features and architecture.

7.1.1 UWF Architecture

Detailed information about the internals of UWF is not well documented. UWF is conceptually based on previous write-filters (Enhanced Write Filter, File Based Write Filter, and Registry Filter) that were first developed with Windows NT Embedded and updated in Windows XP Embedded. Unlike the previous filters, UWF is a sector-based filter driver rather than a file-based driver. UWF protects each sector on the disk. When you write to protected sectors, the sectors are stored in the overlay. Instead of protecting each file and folder, the goal of the filter is to protect each sector. When a write-through file or folder is written to, the data is written directly to the disk; and as we have later learned, the information is duplicated in the overlay.

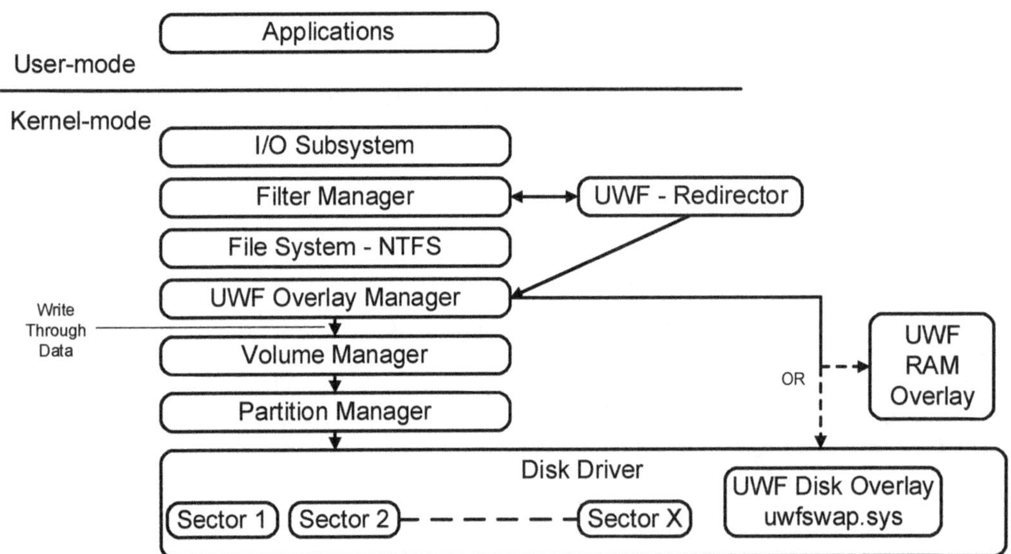

When an application writes to the disk, the UWF Redirector sitting in the Filter Manager checks to see if the data is in a write-through section. If the data is not in a write-thought section, the UWF Overlay Manager sends the data to the overlay (either disk or RAM). If the data is in a write-through section, the UWF Overlay Manager sends the data to the disk and to the overlay (either disk or RAM).

The overlay can exist in RAM or on disk via a swap file (uwfswap.sys). For those familiar with EWF Disk Overlay, this is not the same Disk Overlay since both overlays lose their data on reboot. Microsoft has made some improvements to the UWF. One of these improvements was a new experimental feature that looks to persist Disk Overlay data during a reboot. UWF now supports drives up to 16TB.

The overlay size is 1GB by default, but you can set it larger. The RAM overlay takes RAM away from the OS and applications. Keep in mind pagefile.sys is disabled when UWF is enabled. You will have to experiment with your application and UWF overlay size to find the optimal performance solution. UWF is able to conserve and recycle memory in the overlay cache. When files are deleted, the overlay cache is reduced in size, giving more space back to applications. If RAM is limited, the Disk overlay uwfswap.sys file is the better overlay option.

7.1.2 Application File I/O Interaction with UWF

Applications don't have to be modified, since the disk looks like a read-write medium. All writes, no matter if data is set up to write-through to disk, are sent to the overlay. The little quirk of writing everything to the overlay is something that needs to be taken into consideration when architecting an image. Writing small files to a protected disk is fine, but large files or database files should be on a second unprotected partition. Please analyze the impact that UWF will have on your system and design accordingly. Let's look at the read-only and write-through scenarios. For the read-only example, the diagram below shows data being accessed in a UWF-protected region.

1. A protected file is accessed, modified, and written back to the disk.
2. The modified file is stored in the overlay.
3. When it is accessed again, the file is read out of the overlay.

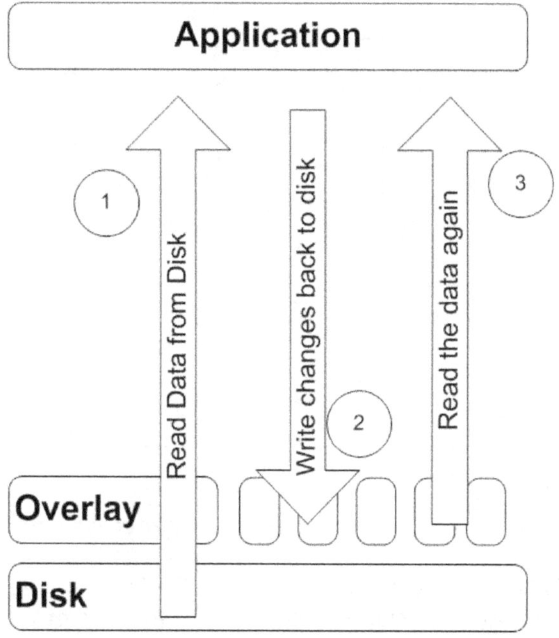

For the write-through example, the diagram below shows data being accessed via a write-through region.

1. An unprotected file is accessed, modified, and written back to the disk.
2. When written back, the file is written directly to the disk since it is unprotected, but the information is also written back to the overlay.
3. When the data is read back again, it is read from the disk.

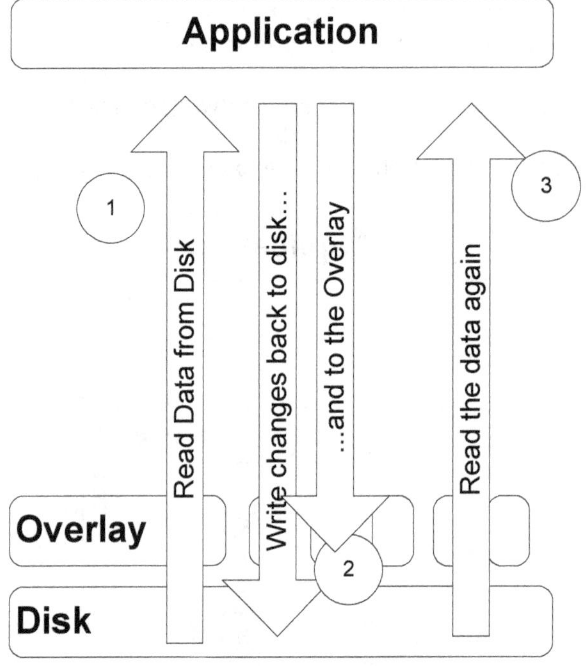

7.1.3 Registry Filtering

UWF also incorporated the ability to preserve registry keys via a registry filter. The Registry Filter was originally created to help resolve an issue with Thin Clients. The problem with the write-filter's RAM overlay was addressing the domain secret key and TSCAL preservation. For example, domain servers update the secret key every month. With a RAM overlay in place, the domain secret registry key would be stored in the overlay and lost during a reboot. The result was a failure to connect to the domain once the next month came around. The Registry Filter was originally developed to preserve these two registry changes across reboots, and it was upgraded to support your own custom registry keys as well. The custom keys that you can preserve are limited to those under HKLM. You should be aware that some keys in the HKLM\System can change on boot-up when the registry filter driver is not loaded. The list of registry keys for the registry filter can be found in the registry:

HKEY_LOCAL_MACHINE\SYSTEM\CurrentControlSet\services\RegFilter\Parameters\MonitoredKeys

7.1.4 Hibernate Once, Resume Many (HORM) – Not Worth It

Boot time has been a top subject for most Windows Embedded developers. Hibernate Once, Resume Many (HORM) was introduced in Windows XP Embedded as a solution to speed up the boot time. HORM is a combination of hibernation and the overlay. The idea is that the system boots from the hiberfil.sys each time. Normally, when the system resumes from hibernation, the first page of the hiberfil.sys is cleared so that you don't reload the same hiberfil.sys on the next reboot. With the write-filter enabled, the page is not lost.

There is a problem if you want to store data on the system. Hiberfil.sys contains the file system tables for all disks in the system. When the system resumes, the file system tables are also restored. Any changes that were made to the file system after the hiberfil.sys file was created and before the system resumes would cause a loss of data. What if you want to preserve data in the system? Since the hiberfil.sys file contains the file system table information for every drive, you will need to implement a dismount/mount solution for any read-write volumes in the system. If you don't implement this solution, any data written to a drive will be lost on resume. There is an article on MSDN titled "Dismounting Volumes in a Hibernate Once/Resume Many Configuration" that provides a sample application for dismounting volumes before calling hibernation. Once the system resumes, the same thread of execution continues and the unmounted drives are re-mounted.

UWF cannot have any write-through files and folders when HORM is enabled. HORM is complex to set up. Since Windows 10 has a better overall boot performance than any of its predecessors, if you are really concerned about boot time, before you decide to use HORM, do the following test:

1. Boot the system normally and record how long it takes to boot.
2. Resume from hibernation and record how long it takes to resume.
3. Resume from standby and record how long it takes to resume. Standby is only good if the system will also be powered.

With M.2 SATA drives and pure UEFI/GPT boot, a cold boot has Windows up and running within seconds. The value of HORM is not worth the time to implement.

7.1.5 Enable UWF in SIM and UWF Settings

The UWF feature can be enabled in SIM under the Microsoft-Windows-Foundation-Package Client-DeviceLockdown section. Remember, both the section, Client-DeviceLockDown, and the Client-UnifiedWriteFitler must be enabled to enable the feature.

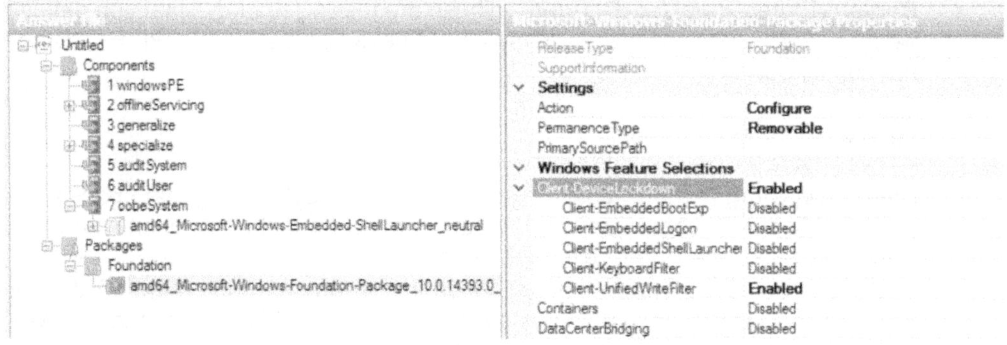

The Microsoft-Windows-Embedded-UnifiedWriteFilter component has a combination of settings to protect the disk and registry.

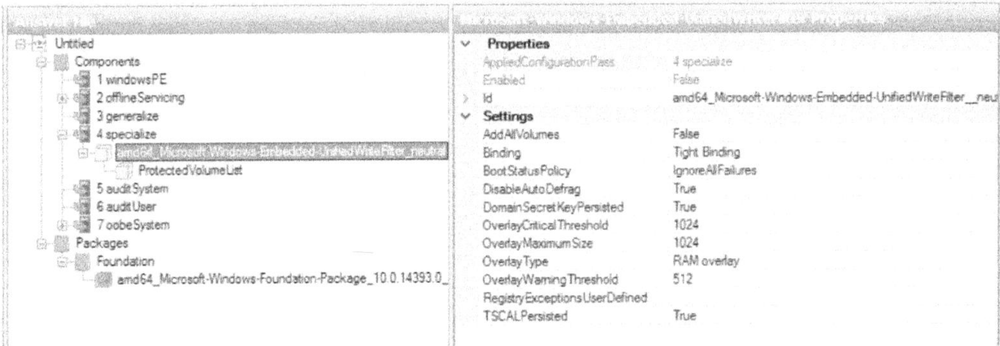

UWF settings can be broken down into 3 different groups. The first group is the generic settings:

- **AddAllVolume** – True or False – Specifies whether all volumes on the device are write-protected. The default is false.
- **Binding** – Provides two options: 1. Loose Binding to enable specifying a volume by using a drive letter. 2. Tight Binding to specify a volume by using the volume device identifier. Tight Binding is the default.
- **BootStatus Policy** – Allows you to display different boot failures. The default is to IgnoreAllFailures.
- **DisableAutoDefrag** – True or False – The default is set to True so automatic disk defragmentation will not run.

The second group is for the Registry Filter:

- **DomainSecretKeyPersisted** – True or False – The default is True, so the Domain Secret Key will be preserved between reboots.
- **TSCALPersisted** – True or False – The default is True, so the TSCAL will be preserved between reboots.
- **RegistryExceptionsUserDefined** – These are the registry keys that you define to be preserved between reboots. Only HKLM keys can be preserved. HKCU keys are not supported.

The third group is for the write-filter:

- **OverlayWarningThreshold** – Integer value in megabytes (MB) that specifies the overlay warning threshold and sends out a warning event notification when UWF overlay size has reached or exceeded this value.
- **OverlayCriticalThreshold** - Integer value in megabytes (MB) that specifies the overlay critical threshold and sends out a critical threshold notification event when UWF overlay size has reached or exceeded this value.
- **OverlayMaximumSize** – Integer value in megabytes (MB) that specifies the maximum overlay size. The default setting is 1024 MB

- **OverlayType** – There are two options: RAM overlay and Disk Overlay. The default setting is RAM.
- **ProtectedVolumeList** – Allows you to define the volumes to be protected by UWF and any write-through files and folders. You must right-click on the sub-component to add a new protected volume and any associated write-through sections. The write-through list must contain absolute paths (i.e. C:\data). The diagram below shows an example.

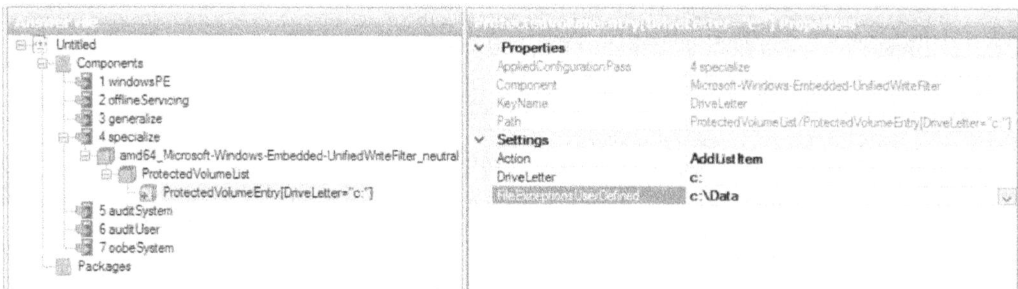

DOES NOT WORK! There is a big problem with all these settings: they don't get applied when you install the image. This was not a problem for Windows Embedded 8.1 Industry. You can set the UWF setting in SIM and the settings would be applied to the installed image. Why this is not working in Windows 10 is a mystery. The workaround solution is to use UWFMGR.EXE or WMI in a Pass 7 sync command to configure and set up UWF.

7.1.6 Managing UWF – UWFMGR and WMI

There are two options for managing UWF. The first is a command line utility called UWFMGR.EXE. The utility is part of the UWF module. The utility's command set is broken down into simple parameters like filter and file. You can enable and disable the filter, add/remove file and registry exclusion, and change the overlay parameters. The command windows must be running as administrator with elevated privileges.

Usage:

Uwfmgr.exe <parameter> [commands] [arguments]

Parameter List:

get-config - Displays all configuration information for both the current and next sessions.
filter - Configures and displays UWF settings, such as filtering state.
overlay - Configures and displays overlay settings.
volume - Configures and displays volume filtering settings.
file - Configures and displays file exclusion settings.
registry - Configures and displays registry key exclusion settings, and commits registry changes.

servicing - Configures and displays servicing mode settings.
help or **?** Displays help for basic parameters.

Filter Commands:

enable - Enables UWF for the next session after the system reboots.
disable - Disables the filter for the next session after the system reboots.
enable-HORM - Enables Hibernate Once, Resume Many for the current session.
disable-HORM - Disables Hibernate Once, Resume Many for the current session.
reset-settings - Reset UWF settings.
help or **?** - Displays usage and help for commands.

Overlay Commands:

set-size - Sets the overlay size for a protected system to the specified value in MB for the next session after the system reboots, enabling the driver to pre-allocate all overlay memory upon system start. This setting takes effect in the next session after the system reboots.
set-type - Sets the overlay type to either RAM or Disk.
set-passthrough - Sets the freespace passthrough (on/off).
set-persistent - Sets the overlay as persistent (on/off).
set-rom-mode - Sets the Read Only Media mode (on/off).
reset-persistentstate- Sets what to do with a persistent overlay on next boot (none/rollback).
set-warningthreshold - Sets the overlay usage size in MB at which the driver issues warning notifications for the current session.
set-criticalthreshold - Sets the overlay usage size in MB at which the driver issues critical notifications for the current session.
get-config - Displays overlay configuration information for both the current and next sessions.
get-availablespace - Displays the remaining available overlay space in the current session.
get-consumption - Displays the amount of the overlay currently used.

Volume Commands:

protect - Protects a volume by adding it to the list of protected volumes for the next session after the system reboots.
unprotect - Removes protection from a volume for the next session after the system reboots.
create-swapfile - Creates swapfile on the volume and sets overlay type to Disk.
get-config - Displays specific volume(s) configuration information for both the current and next sessions.

Volume Arguments:

volume name - Qualifying volume name such as:

- drive letter (e.g. C:)
- device name (e.g. \\?\GLOBALROOT\Device\HarddiskVolume1)
- GUID (e.g. \\?\Volume{4c1b02c1-d990-11dc-99ae-806e6f6e6963})

all - All volumes in the protection list

File Commands:

add-exclusion - Adds a file or directory to the list of excluded files or directories of a protected volume for the next session after the system reboots.
remove-exclusion - Removes exclusion from a file or directory for the next session after the system reboots.
get-exclusions - Displays specific file exclusion configuration information for both the current and next sessions.
commit - Commit all changes to the specified file.
commit-delete - Commit deletion of the specified file. It's allowed to commit a folder deletion, but the folder needs to be empty since the latest reboot.

File Arguments:

Volume name - Qualifying volume name, such as drive letter, device name, or volume GUID.
Path - Directory path for exclusion directory or file.
Filename - Exclusion file name.
all - All volumes in the protection list (applies only to get-exclusions).

Registry Commands:

add-exclusion - Adds a registry key to the list of excluded registry keys of a protected system for the next session after the system reboots.
remove-exclusion - Removes exclusion from a registry key for the next session after the system reboots.
get-exclusions - Displays registry keys excluded for both the current and next sessions.
commit - Commits changes to specified registry value.
commit-delete - Commit deletion of specified registry key or value.

Registry Arguments:

key - Fully qualified registry key name to be excluded or committed.
value - Value name to be committed (only useful in commit command).

Servicing Commands:

enable - Enables UWF Servicing Mode for the next session after the system reboots.

disable - Disables UWF Servicing Mode for the next session after the system reboots.
update-windows - Update the Windows system.
get-config - Displays servicing status of the current session and next session.
help or **?** - Displays usage and help for commands.

The second management option is the programming support using WMI. You can create PowerShell scripts or use any programming language that supports WMI APIs. UWFMGR.EXE looks to have been built on the UWF WMI classes. For scripting, use the namespace root\standardcimv2\embedded. Here is a PowerShell script example to enable UWF:

```
#ps1 Enables UWF
$filter1 = Get-WmiObject -Class "UWF_Filter" -Namespace "root\standardcimv2\embedded"
$HResult = $filter1.Enable()
if($HResult.ReturnValue -ne 0) {
   write-host "Error: $HResult.ReturnValue"
   exit}
Write-Host "Reboot the system for change to take effect"
```

Note: You will want to use the WMI API to get the total amount of overlay space used. There is a good script implementation found on learn.microsoft.com under UWF_Overlay.

WMI classes can be integrated into a custom application. The free UWFUtility is available on Annabooks.com. It is a multi-tab application that covers most of the items in the command line utility. It also can list items in the overlay, which can be helpful for debugging purposes.

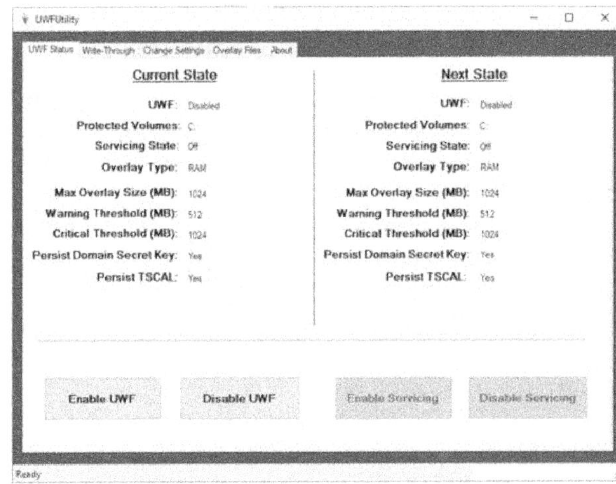

Here are some C# code snippets based on a traditional Windows form application shown below.

Enabled UWF

```
ManagementScope scope = new
ManagementScope(@"root\standardcimv2\embedded");
ManagementClass UWFFilter = new ManagementClass(scope.Path.Path,
"UWF_Filter", null);

foreach (ManagementObject mo in UWFFilter.GetInstances())
{
   ManagementBaseObject UWFEnable = mo.InvokeMethod("Enable", null, null);
}
```

Disable UWF

```
ManagementScope scope = new
ManagementScope(@"root\standardcimv2\embedded");
ManagementClass UWFFilter = new ManagementClass(scope.Path.Path,
"UWF_Filter", null);

foreach (ManagementObject mo in UWFFilter.GetInstances())
{
   ManagementBaseObject UWFEnable = mo.InvokeMethod("Disable", null, null);
}
```

7.1.7 Common Write-Through Section

Some items should never be set up as write-through, such as all of drive C, C:\Windows, C:\Windows\system32, C:\Windows\System32\config, or the roots of all registry hives. These would defeat the purpose of UWF. There are some recommended write-throughs to set up for Background Intelligent Transfer Service (BITS), Networks, and Daylight-saving time (DST).

- Background Intelligent Transfer Service (BITS)
    - % ALLUSERSPROFILE%\Microsoft\Network\Downloader
    - HKEY_LOCAL_MACHINE\Software\Microsoft\Windows\CurrentVersion\BITS\StateIndex
- Network Wired:
    - C:\Windows\dot2svc\Policies
    - C:\ProgramData\Microsoft\dot3svc\Profiles\Interfaces\{<Interface GUID>}\{<Profile GUID>}.xml
    - HKEY_LOCAL_MACHINE\SOFTWARE\Policies\Microsoft\Windows\WiredL2\GP_Policy
    - HKEY_LOCAL_MACHINE\SOFTWARE\Microsoft\dot3svc
    - HKEY_LOCAL_MACHINE\SYSTEM\CurrentControlSet\services\dot3svc

- Network Wireless:
  - C:\Windows\wlansvc\Policies
  - C:\ProgramData\Microsoft\wlansvc\Profiles\Interfaces\{<Interface GUID>}\{<Profile GUID>}.xml
  - HKEY_LOCAL_MACHINE\SOFTWARE\Policies\Microsoft\Windows\Wireless\GPTWirelessPolicy
  - HKEY_LOCAL_MACHINE\SOFTWARE\Microsoft\wlansvc
  - HKEY_LOCAL_MACHINE\SYSTEM\CurrentControlSet\services\WwanSvc
  - HKEY_LOCAL_MACHINE\SYSTEM\CurrentControlSet\services\Wlansvc
- Daylight Savings Time (DST)
  - HKEY_LOCAL_MACHINE\SOFTWARE\Microsoft\Windows NT\CurrentVersion\Time Zones
  - HKEY_LOCAL_MACHINE\SYSTEM\CurrentControlSet\Control\TimeZoneInformation

In addition to the above common write-through sections, I also include the following folder exclusions for event logs and assembly files. The exclusion of the event log folders is for diagnostic purposes so you can read the event logs. The assembly folder addresses .NET assemblies that get optimized in the background. These optimized assembly files can fill up the overlay, and the write-through section relieves the problem.

- C:\Windows\System32\winevt\Logs
- C:\Windows\assembly

7.1.8 UWF Servicing

UWF introduces a servicing mode to support Windows Updates. The intent of this mode is to support Thin Client systems that use Windows Update for servicing the system. The idea is to reboot the system into a special UWF-Servicing account where Windows Updates can be performed. Servicing can be initiated via any three of the UWF management options. The system must be rebooted for the servicing mode to start. Once the system reboots, Windows Update will download and install updates from Windows Update

There is a master servicing script, UwfServicingMasterScript.cmd, found under C:\windows\system32 that you can modify to address custom updates.

Once the servicing has been completed, you can then log back into the regular user accounts. This is an interesting feature for Thin Clients, but treating the embedded system as an appliance is recommended so that you don't have systems in the field in various stages of updates. We will cover managing systems in the field in Chapter 9.

7.2 Mitigating Sudden Power-Off Issues

Now we need to discuss one of the biggest concerns with embedded/IoT systems: sudden power-off. Windows doesn't like it when the power is suddenly cut. Disk and file system corruption can occur. It may not happen right away; but over time with a few sudden power cycles, corruption may pop up. Most modern flash file systems are using NAND flash devices. When data is written to a NAND device, it is written a page at a time; and the page must first be erased before the data is written. A small data write can cause the erasure and rewrite of a much larger area of the flash device than just the cells that are holding the written data. It is during this erase/write cycle when the device is most vulnerable to data loss or corruption if a sudden power-off event occurs. You can certainly try to use a battery backup solution, but battery backups are cost-prohibitive for most systems. Some clients have used supercapacitors to keep the system alive long enough to do a safe shutdown. This is where UWF, along with a few other recommendations, can help mitigate corruption caused by sudden power-off. Working with many clients since the release of Windows NT Embedded, we have developed some best practices to help mitigate disk corruption due to sudden power-off:

- Choose industrial-grade flash – if you are going to use a flash disk as the boot medium, you might want to look for industrial-grade flash devices. It has been claimed by one flash manufacturer that as much as 1/3 of the flash devices on the general market are counterfeit, so know which manufacturers and models of devices work for you, and know your flash device distributor. Also, check for devices that have power sensing technology to latch up address lines or provide power sustain circuitry to allow completion of outstanding writes as power is going down. There are some differences in wear-leveling implementations from device model to device model from the same manufacturer, as well as, from manufacturer to manufacturer. Most SSD and mSATA devices use a dynamic wear leveling scheme. CompactFlash, SD, and USB flash disks use a static wear leveling scheme. Dynamic wear leveling has proven to be better for booting and running an OS, because data that is only being read, like the boot track and core OS code that is not changing, does not get moved and rewritten. Flash life is also longer when dynamic wear leveling is used. There are more details on flash disk technology that cover the internal device's working details, such as the Flash Translation Layer, which maps the physical flash blocks to the OS and manages wear leveling, bad block management, and garbage collection, but this is beyond the scope of this book.
- For small flash disks, keep the number of partitions to a minimum. Some flash manufacturers will not support more than 4 partitions. Again, wear leveling can be taxing for small drives, since Windows and specifically NTFS is constantly reading from and writing to the drive. Since all systems are booting UEFI now, only a drive C partition and the support partitions are recommended. If you need to store data, a second drive is recommended. Empirical testing of the system will determine the best direction.
- Format the disk with NTFS – since Windows 10 will only boot from an NTFS partition, this is really no longer a choice. The journaling that NTFS uses provides some help with recovery after a sudden power-off.

- Protect the boot partition with a write filter. The Unified Write Filter (UWF) is featured in Windows 10 Enterprise.
- Page File turned off – when UWF is enabled, the page file is off by default.
- Disable disk caching – it is better to have everything flushing to the disk rather than get lost in RAM as the power is going down. This section is focused on disk corruption and not data corruption or loss. Data corruption or loss can still occur if data isn't written when the power goes off. Turning off disk caching will help prevent data corruption, but it might not be 100% effective. The dskcache.exe utility was available in XP Embedded to disable the disk cache feature. If you try to turn off disk caching in Windows 10, the OS will turn it on during the next reboot.
- Flash tools – some newer SSD and mSATA devices are coming with software to help tune the flash disk to the drive. These utilities can help make the flash live longer and be more resistant to sudden power-off.

We cannot guarantee that corruption will not occur; but by taking these tips into account, you can mitigate the disk corruption due to sudden power-off. We strongly suggest that you add a power cycle test to your QA process, so you can get a good idea of how well your system holds up to sudden power-off. I have had a number of clients who have rigged up a power cycling solution. Most clients don't see issues for 5000 cycles of constant power on, hold for 3 minutes, and kill power, but your results may be different.

7.3 Keyboard Filter

Limiting user keyboard access is important for the robustness and security of an embedded system. Back in XP Embedded days, I demonstrated the key trap service introduced in MSDN Magazine in 2002. The Keyboard Filter was introduced as an extra download for WES 7 Service Pack 1 (SP1). The Keyboard Filter provides the ability to specify key combinations to block, such as Windows hot keys. Once a key combination has been configured to be blocked, any time that key combination is entered at the keyboard, it will be discarded before being passed on to the operating system or any applications. The Keyboard Filter provides predefined key combinations for commonly used key combinations that can be activated for blocking. The Keyboard Filter also provides the ability to define custom hot key combinations or scan code combinations for blocking, as well. One key on the keyboard can be used as the breakout key to log off of a session and return to the logon screen. The breakout key is useful for management operations when a second account is in the system. The Keyboard Filter supports physical and onscreen keyboards. The Microsoft-Windows-Embedded-KeyboardFilterService component does work and you can set the hot keys that can be blocked or allowed in the answer file.

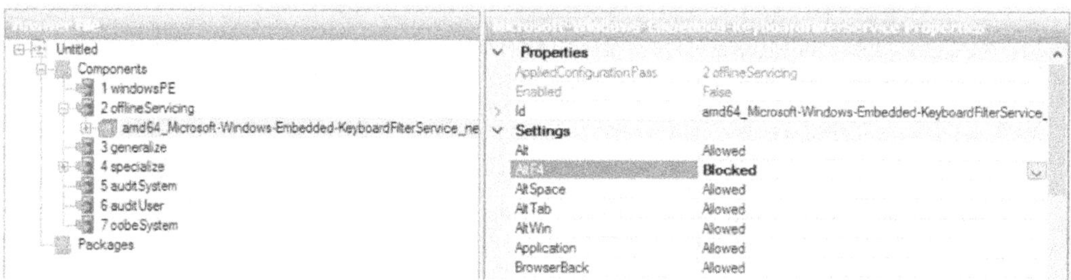

Besides the predefined hot keys, there are three other optional settings:

- **DisableKeyboardFitlerForAdminisrators** – as the name implies, the keyboard filter will be disabled when logged into Administrator accounts.
- **ForceOffAccessbility** – Disables Windows Ease of Access Features, which can be used to backdoor into a system.
- **BreakoutKeyScanCode** – Defines a single key that, when hit 5 times in succession, will log out of a system. This setting is not part of the component and must be set in the registry or using one of the utilities that will be discussed in a few moments.

Important: As a security measure, you should change the BreakoutKeyScanCode to something completely benign. There is no way to set this in the answer file unless you use the registry or one of the keyboard filter utilities. The break-out key when hit 5 times in a row will log out of the current session and the logon screen will appear. The default breakout key is the Windows key (91). Change the value to 0 or something not obvious if you want this hidden trick available for your system.

The keyboard filter service is disabled by default. If you want the service enabled during OS installation, add the following commands as a Pass 7 sync command to the answer file:

- Sc.exe config MsKeyboardFilter start= auto
- Sc.exe start MsKeyboardFilter

There are two ways that the Keyboard Filter can be modified in the target image. There is a WMI API that allows you to write scripts that you can integrate into your application (https://docs.microsoft.com/en-us/windows-hardware/customize/enterprise/keyboardfilter-wmi-provider-reference). The following PowerShell script demonstrates unblocking Alt+F4 predefined key:

```
#PS1 Keyboard Filter Unblock PredefinedKey
$KBfilter = Get-WmiObject -Class "WEKF_PredefinedKey" -Namespace "root\standardcimv2\embedded" | where {$_.Id -
eq "Alt+F4"};
if($KBfilter){
   $KBfilter.Enabled = 0;
   $KBfilter.Put() | Out-Null;
   write-host "Alt+F4 is enabled";
}
```

You can also go into the registry and change the various hot keys:

HKLM\SOFTWARE\Microsoft\Windows Embedded\KeyboardFilter

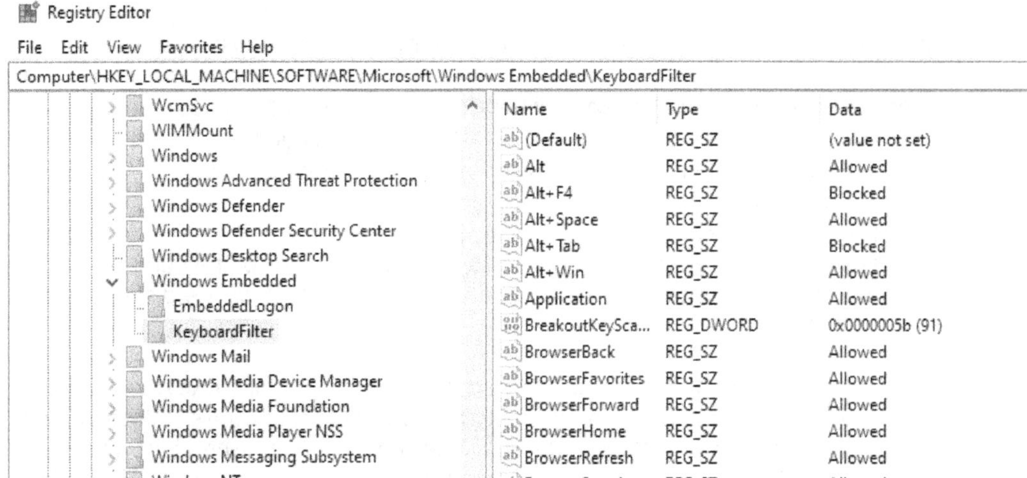

To provide setup and management of the keyboard filter, there is a free command line and GUI utility available on Annabooks.com.

Annabooks Keyboard Filter Utility
Service Status:
Start Keyboard Filter
Stop Keyboard Filter
DisableKeyboardFilterForAdministrators
ForceOffAccessibility
91 BreakoutKeyScanCode (Decimal)
Alt, Alt+F4, Alt+Spacebar, Alt+Tab, Alt+Win, Ctrl+Alt+Delete, Ctrl+Esc, Ctrl+Tab, Ctrl+Windows+F, Ctrl, Ctrl+F4, Ctrl+Windows, Escape, F21, Left Alt+Left Shift+Print Screen, Left Alt+Left Shift+Num Lock, MediaNext, MediaPlayPause, MediaPrev, MediaStop
Shift, Shift+Ctrl+Esc, Shift+Win, Application, LaunchApp1, LaunchApp2, LaunchMail, LaunchMediaSelect, BrowserBack, BrowserForward, BrowserRefresh, BrowserStop, BrowserSearch, BrowserFavorites, BrowserHome, VolumeMute, VolumeDown, VolumeUp
Windows, Windows+B, Windows+Break, Windows+C, Windows+Comma, Windows+D, Windows+Down Arrow, Windows+E, Windows+Enter, Windows+Esc, Windows+F, Windows+F1, Windows+H, Windows+Home, Windows+I, Windows+J, Windows+K, Windows+L, Windows+Left Arrow, Windows+M
Windows+Minus Sign, Windows+O, Windows+P, Windows+Page Down, Windows+Page Up, Windows+Period, Windows+Plus Sign, Windows+Q, Windows+R, Windows+Right Arrow, Windows+Shift+Down Arrow, Windows+Shift+Left Arrow, Windows+Shift+Right Arrow, Windows+Shift+Up Arrow, Windows+Slash (/), Windows+Spacebar, Windows+T, Windows+Tab, Windows+U, Windows+Up Arrow
Windows+V, Windows+W, Windows+Z
Save Changes
Annabooks
www.annabooks.com
Copyright © 2015 - 2018 Annabooks, LLC. All Rights Reserved.
Application is provided as is without any warranty.
Limited testing has been performed with this utility. Use at your own risk.
Please provide any feedback through the Annabooks website.
File Version: 2.3.0.0
Assembly Version: 2.3.0.0
Ready

Here is the internal help for the kbfmgr64.exe command line utility:

```
usage: kbfmgr64 [command] [settings]

Commands:

     Filter On | Off           Start or Stop Keyboard Filter Service
     get-config                   List the settings and pre-defined
key status
     set                           set one of the 3 Keyboard filter
settings:

DisableKeyboardFilterForAdministrators (Admin) On | off
                                  ForceOffAccessibility On | Off
                                  BreakoutKeyScanCode    <decimal
scan code>
     Enable <KeyID>             Sets a predefined key to be blocked
     Enable All               Sets all predefined keys to be blocked
     Disable <KeyID>            Sets a predefined key to be allowed
     Disable All              Sets all predefined keys to be allowed
     Help | ?                   This help page

Examples:

kbfmgr64 filter on

kbfmgr64 set Admin on

kbfmgr64 set BreakoutKeyScanCode 59

kbfmgr64 Enable Alt+F4
```

7.4 Edge Gestures Disable

Windows 8.x introduced several edge-swipe features, but these have been reduced down to right-edge only for Windows 10. The gesture filter isn't so much a filter as it is a group policy setting that can disable edge gestures. Open Gpedit.msc and go to Computer Configuration-> Administrative Templates-> Windows Components -> Edge UI. Change the "Allow edge swipe" to Disabled to turn off the Edge Gesture.

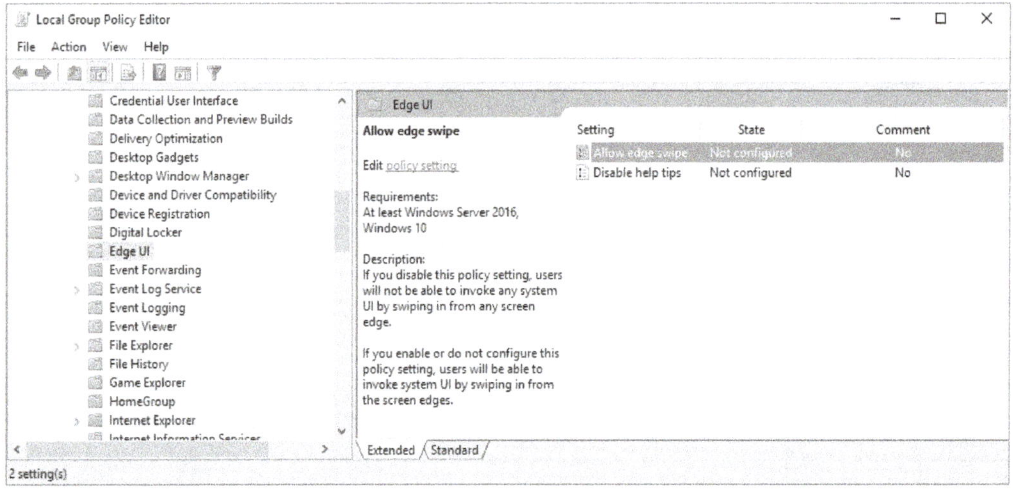

7.5 *Toast Message Disable*

Windows 8.x also introduced the toast filter. The toast filter isn't so much a filter as it is a group policy setting that can disable toast messages from appearing. Open Gpedit.msc and go to User Configuration-> Administrative Templates-> Start Menu and Taskbar->Notifications to locating the different notification settings.

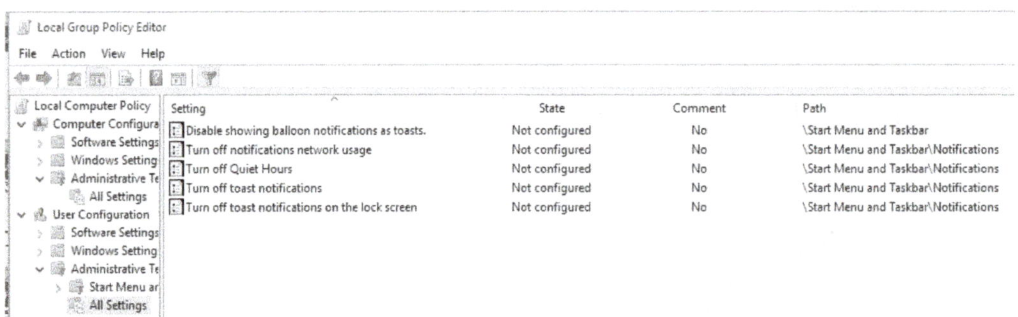

7.6 *Exercise 701: Unified Write Filter and Keyboard Filter*

Let's see how the filters work in a real image. UWF will protect the Operating System files and leave one directory open for read-write access, and it will allow read-write access to a specific registry key. The Dialog Box Filter will block a process, and the Keyboard Filter will block two hot key combinations. You will need Windows Embedded 8.x Industry installation DVD to complete this exercise.

7.6.1 Part 1: Create the Answer File and Build the Configuration Set

The first part is to create the answer file and then create the configuration set. The AB-test-app.exe will be used here again.

1. Open File Explorer.

2. Download the UWFUtility.exe from Annabooks.com and place the file into the C:\WinData\DS1\$OEM$ Folders\$1\Program Files\Annabooks folder.
3. Using Notepad or Notepad++, create a batch file titled uwf.bat, and put the following into the batch file:

```
uwfmgr.exe volume protect c:
uwfmgr.exe overlay set-type disk
uwfmgr.exe file add-exclusion c:\Windows\System32\winevt\Logs
uwfmgr.exe file add-exclusion c:\Windows\assembly
uwfmgr.exe file add-exclusion c:\data
uwfmgr.exe registry add-exclusion HKLM\Software\WinIoT
```

4. Save the file to the C:\WinData\DS1\$OEM$ Folders\$1\setup folder.
5. Open SIM.
6. Open the catalog file, if it is not opened already.
7. Make sure the distribution share under C:\WinData is also open.
8. Create a new answer file with the following settings:

Component	Configuration Pass	Component Setting	Possible Value / Notes
amd64_Microsoft-Windows-International-Core-WinPE__neutral	1 WindowsPE	InputLocale	en-US
	1 WindowsPE	SystemLocale	en-US
	1 WindowsPE	UILanguage	en-US
	1 WindowsPE	UILanguageFallback	en-US
	1 WindowsPE	UserLocale	en-US
amd64_Microsoft-Windows-Setup__neutral	1 WindowsPE	UserData: AcceptEULA	True
	1 WindowsPE	UserData : ProductKey : Key	<Enter the license key>
	1 WindowsPE	UserData : ProductKey: WillShowUI	OnError
	1 WindowsPE	ImageInstall: OSImage : InstallFrom: MetaData: Key *(right-click on InstallFrom to create option)*	/IMAGE/INDEX
	1 WindowsPE	ImageInstall: OSImage : InstallFrom: MetaData: Value	2
amd64_Microsoft-Windows-Shell-Setup__neutral	4 Specialize	ComputerName	ACME
	4 Specialize	TimeZone	Pacific Standard Time
	4 Specialize	AutoLogon: Username	User1
	4 Specialize	AutoLogon: Enabled	True
	4 Specialize	AutoLogon: LogonCount	4294967294
	4 Specialize	AutoLogon: Password: Value	password
amd64_Microsoft-Windows-International-Core__neutral	7 OOBE System	InputLocale	en-US
	7 OOBE System	SystemLocale	en-US
	7 OOBE System	UILanguage	en-US
	7 OOBE System	UserLocale	en-US

Component	Configuration Pass	Component Setting	Possible Value / Notes
amd64_Microsoft-Windows-Shell-Setup__neutral	7 OOBE System	UserAccounts : LocalAccounts : LocalAccount : Name (right-click to insert new local account)	User1
	7 OOBE System	UserAccounts : LocalAccounts : LocalAccount : DisplayName	User1
	7 OOBE System	UserAccounts : LocalAccounts : LocalAccount :Group	Administrators
	7 OOBE System	UserAccounts : LocalAccounts : LocalAccount : Password : Value	password
	7 OOBE System	OOBE : ProtectYourPC	3
	7 OOBE System	OOBE : HideEULAPage	True
	7 OOBE System	OOBE : HideWirelessSetupInOOBE	True
	7 OOBE System	OOBE : HideOEMRegistrationScreen	True
	7 OOBE System	OOBE : HideLocalAccountScreen	True
	7 OOBE System	OOBE : HideOnlineAccountScreen	True

9. Next, we need to enable the UWF and Keyboard filter features. In the Windows Image pane, under Packages->Foundation, Add the Microsoft-Windows-Foundation-Package to the answer file in Pass 2, offline Servicing.
10. In the settings for the amd64_Microsoft-Windows-Foundation-Package, enable the following items:

- Client-DeviceLockdown
- Client-UnifiedWriteFilter
- Client-KeyboardFilter

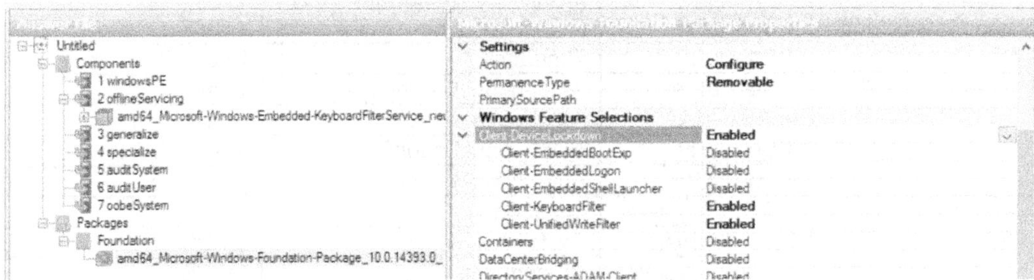

11. Now add the following component to the answer file:

    - Microsoft-Windows-Embedded-KeyboardFilterService to Pass 2

12. Click on the Microsoft-Windows-Embedded-KeyboardFilterService.
13. In the settings, Set the AltF4 and AltTab to Blocked.

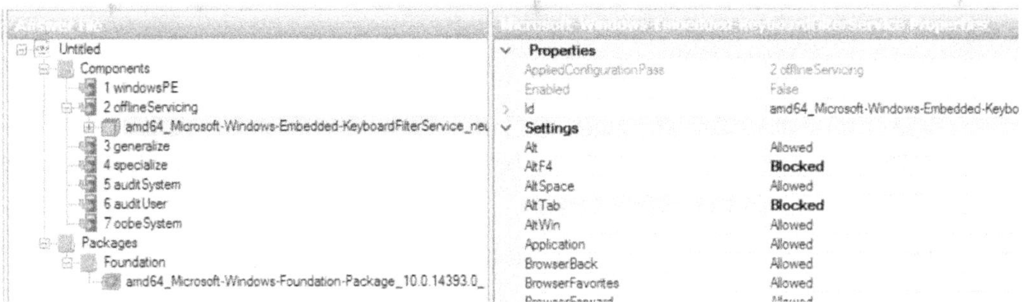

14. Now, we are going to add Synchronous Commands to Pass 7. From the SIM menu, select Insert->Synchronous Command->Pass 7 oobeSystem...
15. The Create Synchronous Command dialog appears. Enter the following to create a directory during OS installation:

    cmd.exe /c md c:\data

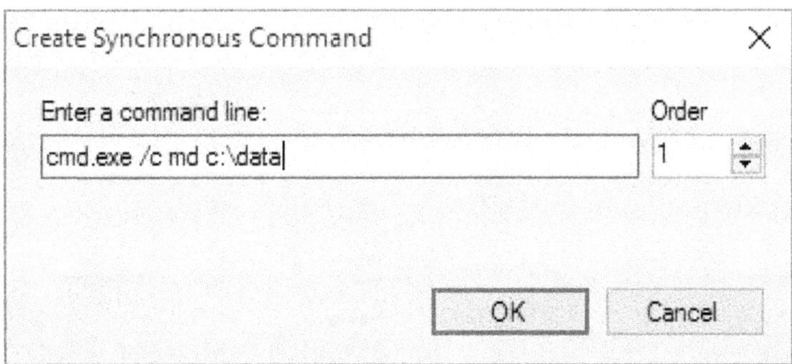

16. Click OK.
17. Repeat the steps above, and enter the command to add a registry key:

    reg.exe ADD HKLM\Software\WinIoT

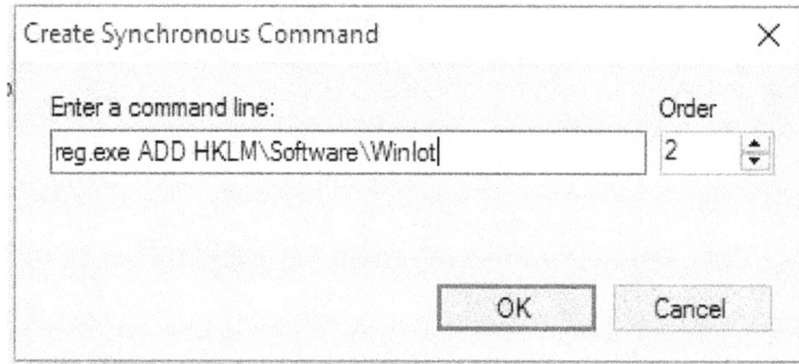

18. Repeat the same steps and add the following command to auto-start the keyboard filter:

    sc.exe config MsKeyboardFilter start= auto

19. Repeat the steps one more time and add the final command:

    sc.exe start MsKeyboardFilter

20. Repeat the steps one last time to add the command to run the uwf.bat file

    Cmd.exe /c c:\setup\uwf.bat

The commands will be placed under the amd64_Microsoft-Windows-Shell-Setupcomponent's FirstLogonCommands settings.

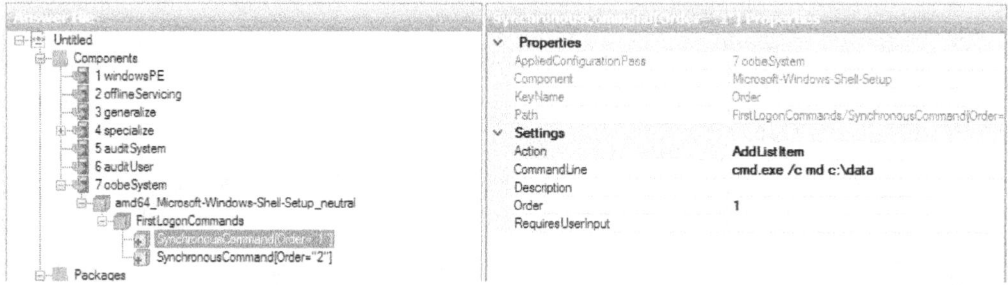

21. Run a validation check.
22. Save the answer file to C:\WinData as EX701.xml.
23. In the \CS folder, delete the AutoUnattend.xml, AutoUnattend_files folder, and the oem folder.

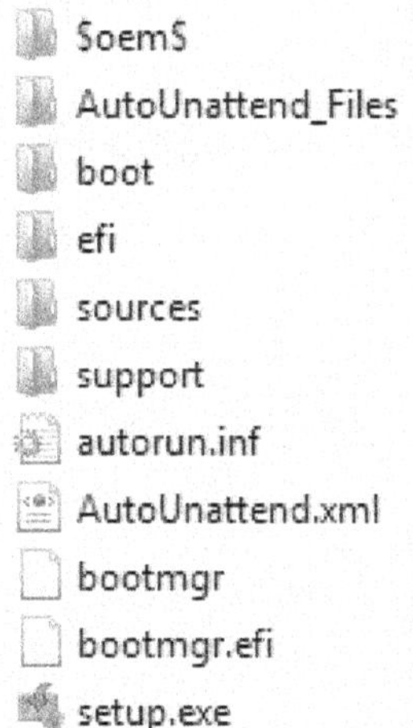

24. Add any Out-of-Box Drivers for your platform to the answer file.
25. In SIM, from the menu, select Tools-> Create Configuration Set.
26. A dialog will appear asking for the location for the configuration set to be created and the location of any OEM files. Set C:\image for the location of the configuration set. For the OEM folder, point to the \$OEM$ Folders under the distribution share: C:\WinData\DS1\$OEM$ Folders.

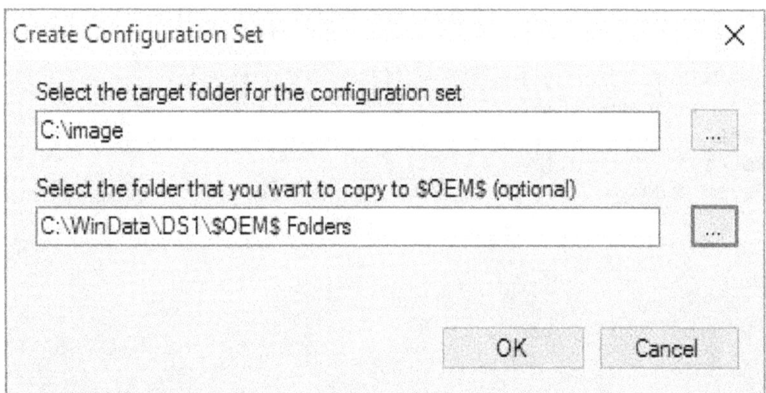

27. Copy the configuration set to the UWB boot disk.
28. Deploy the OS image to the target system. Be sure to delete all partitions and recreate the default partition before installing the image. The image will boot into the User1 account.

7.6.2 Part 2: Testing UWF Registry Filtering

Let's test to see if UWF really works. We will use the UWFMGR.EXE utility to control the state of UWF.

1. Open a Command Prompt with elevated privileges (Run as Administrator) or PowerShell with elevated privileges. If you right-click on the Windows icon, you can select Command Prompt (Admin),
2. Type the following at the command prompt to see the status:

   UWFMGR get-config

```
uwfmgr get-config
Unified Write Filter Configuration Utility version 10.0.19044
Copyright (C) Microsoft Corporation. All rights reserved.

Current Session Settings


FILTER SETTINGS
    Filter state:     OFF
    Commit pending:   N/A
    Shutdown pending: N/A
    HORM mode:        N/A

SERVICING SETTINGS
    Servicing State: OFF

OVERLAY SETTINGS
    Type:                    RAM
    Maximum size:            1024 MB
    Warning Threshold:       512 MB
    Critical Threshold:      1024 MB
    Read Only Media:         OFF
    Freespace Passthrough: OFF
    Persistent:              OFF
    Reset Mode:              N/A
    Reset Saved Mode:        N/A



VOLUME SETTINGS
    *** No volumes configured


REGISTRY EXCLUSIONS
    *** No exclusions

Next Session Settings


FILTER SETTINGS
    Filter state:     OFF
    Commit pending:   N/A
    Shutdown pending: N/A
    HORM mode:        N/A
```

```
SERVICING SETTINGS
    Servicing State: OFF

OVERLAY SETTINGS
    Type:                   Disk
    Maximum size:           1024 MB
    Warning Threshold:      512 MB
    Critical Threshold:     1024 MB
    Read Only Media:        OFF
    Freespace Passthrough: ON
    Persistent:             OFF
    Reset Mode:             N/A
    Reset Saved Mode:       N/A



VOLUME SETTINGS
Volume ef668426-cb56-443f-a27b-ccf54b575f4c [C:]
    Volume state:      Protected
    Volume ID:         ef668426-cb56-443f-a27b-ccf54b575f4c
    Swapfile:          0 MB

    File Exclusions:
Next Session Exclusions for Volume ef668426-cb56-443f-a27b-ccf54b575f4c [C:]
    C:\Windows\System32\winevt\Logs
    C:\Windows\assembly
    C:\data



REGISTRY EXCLUSIONS
    HKLM\Software\WinIoT
```

Note: Your output will look different.

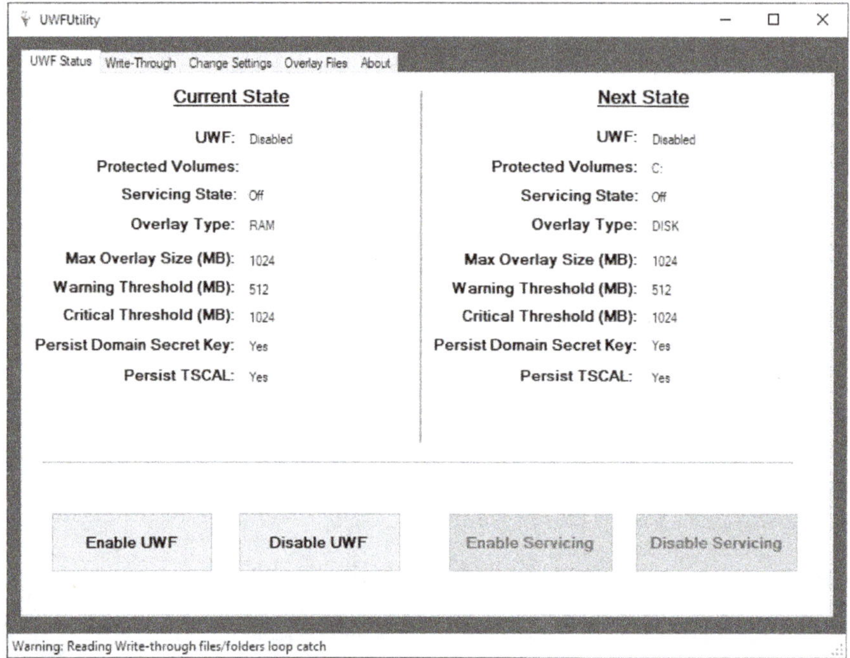

3. Open Registry Editor – open a command prompt with elevated privileges and type regedit and hit Enter.
4. Go to the excluded registry key: HKLM\Software\WinIoT.
5. Under WinIoT, create a new string value called TEST.
6. Add string data to the Test value: "This is a test".

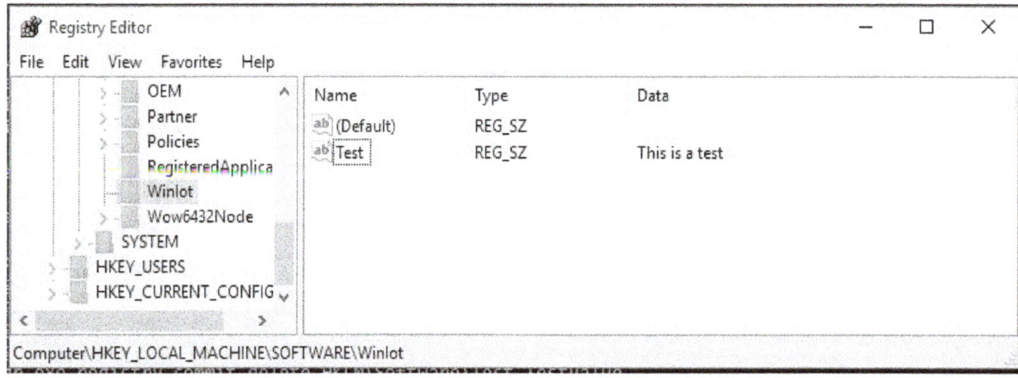

7. UWF is disabled by default. Let's enable UWF. Type the following at the command prompt and hit enter:

```
UWFMGR filter enable
```

8. To double-check that UWF will be enabled for the next session, Type the following at the command prompt and hit enter:

```
UWFMGR get-config
```

You should see UWF being enabled for the next session. You could also use UWFUtility.exe to see the status of UWF.

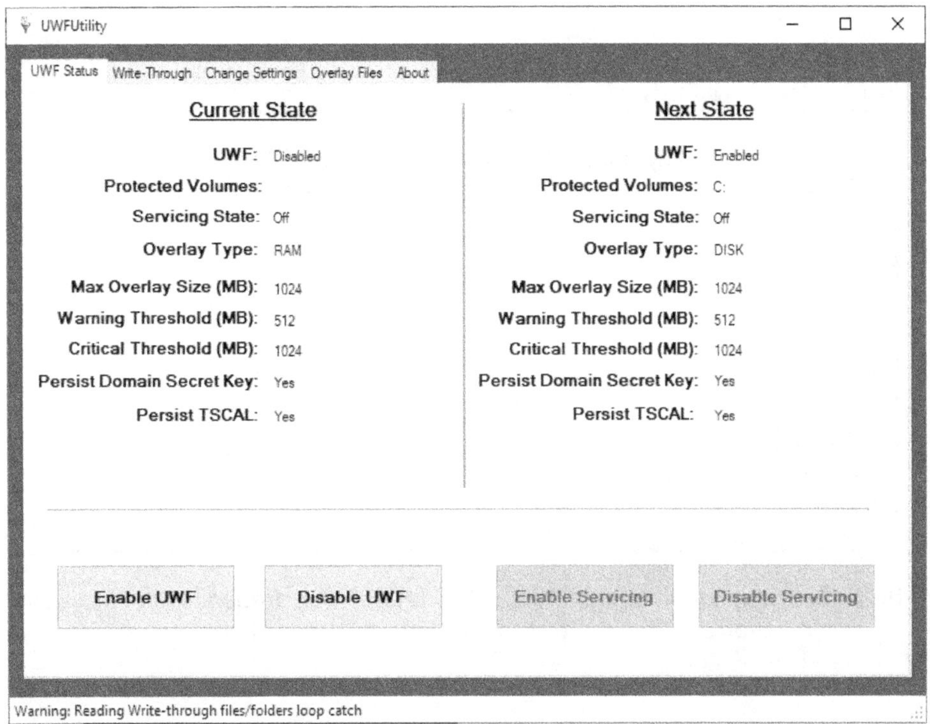

9. Reboot the target system to enable UWF.
10. Open Registry editor.
11. Go to HKLM\Software\WinIoT.
12. Create another string under WinIoT called Test2, and set the string data to “Registry Filter Works”.

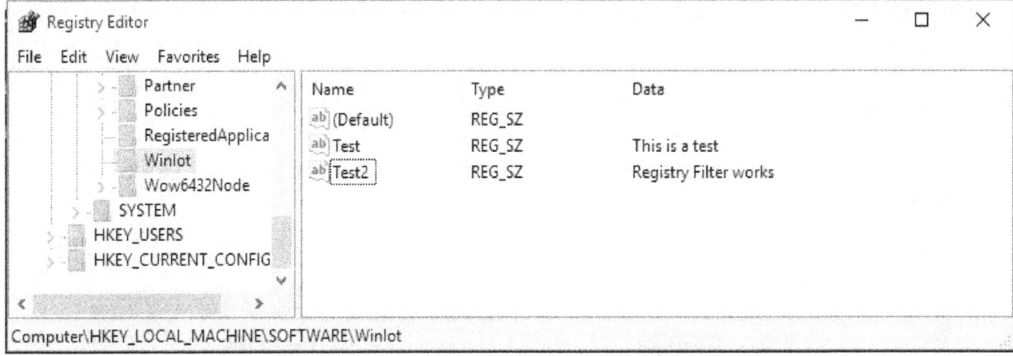

13. Create another key under HKLM\Software called Filtered.
14. Create a string value called Temp and set the data to "I am going away".

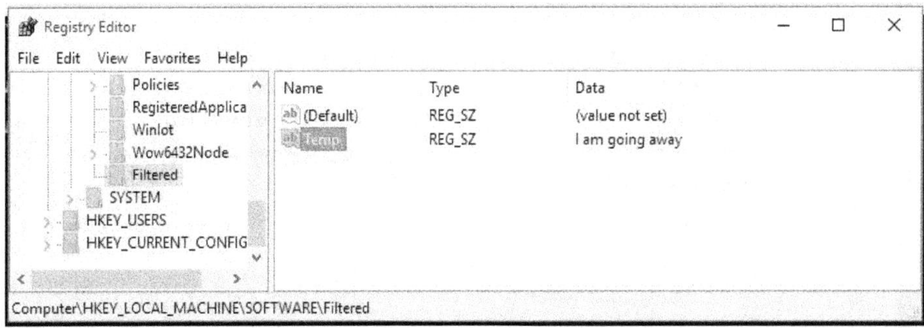

15. Reboot the target system. After the reboot, run Regedit. The two keys under WinIoT should still be there, and the "Filtered" key will be gone.

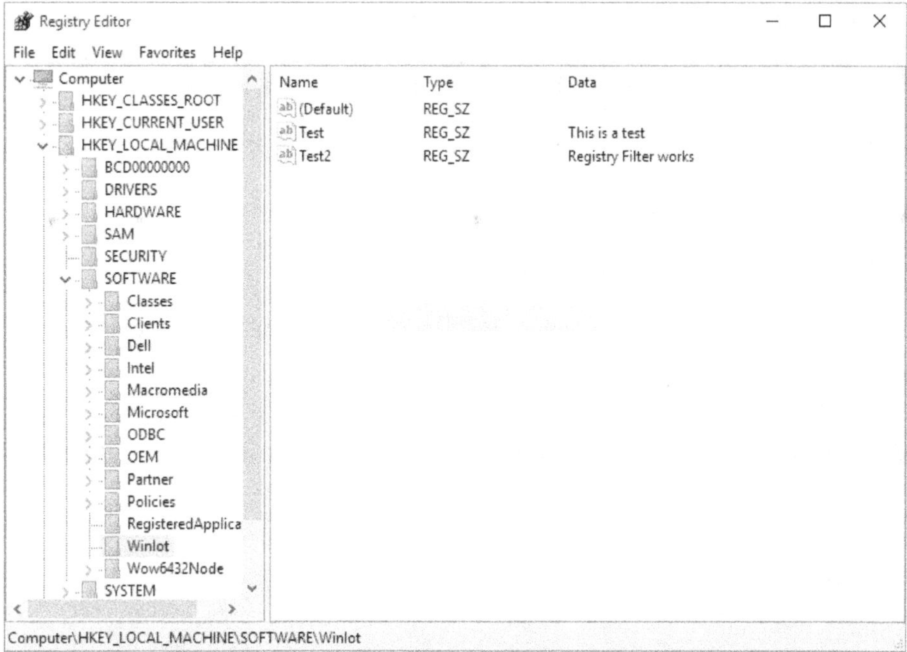

When registry keys are changed or added, the information is put into the regkey file on the system disk. The registry filter preserves keys added to the filter on a reboot, and any registry keys not included in the filter will be lost on a reboot.

7.6.3 Part 3 Testing UWF File/Folder Filtering

Now let's see what happens to files and folders. UWF should still be enabled.

1. Open File Explorer.
2. Create a new file called test1.txt under C:\data.
3. Create another file called test2.txt under the C:\data folder, but then cut and paste the file to C:\. You will be asked to acknowledge this move, since C:\ is protected.
4. Reboot the virtual machine. After the system reboots, the test1.txt file should still exist and test2.txt should be gone. Test2 file disappeared since UWF was enabled and the folder existed in the RAM overlay.
5. Disable UWF either by running "uwfmgr.exe filter disable" from a command prompt or by using the UWFUtility.
6. Reboot the target system.
7. Create a new file called test2.txt, and place it in the C:\ root folder.
8. Reboot the target system. Test2.txt should still be there. Test2 was not lost this time because UWF was disabled, and it was written directly to the disk.
9. Enabled UWF either by running "uwfmgr.exe filter enable" from a command prompt or by using the UWFUtility.
10. Reboot the system
11. After the system reboots, open File Explorer.

12. Right-click on the "C:\Test2.txt" file, and select delete from the context menu. Click OK when asked to send it to the recycle bin. Test2.txt should disappear.
13. Reboot the target. The Test2.txt will remain because it is protected.
14. Now we are going to test the new persistent overlay feature. Disable UWF either by running "uwfmgr.exe filter disable" from a command prompt or by using the UWFUtility.
15. Run the following command to persist the overlay:

```
Uwgmgr overlay set-persistent on
```

16. Enabled UWF either by running "uwfmgr.exe filter enable" from a command prompt or by using the UWFUtility.
17. Reboot the system
18. Create a new file in C:\data called test3.txt and move the file to C:\ root folder.
19. Reboot the system. With UWF enable and persisted overlay enabled, test3.txt will not disappear.

7.6.4 Part 4 Testing the Keyboard Filter

The final test is for the keyboard filter.

1. Check the Keyboard filter settings and status using either kbfmgr64.exe or KBFUtility64.exe utilities.

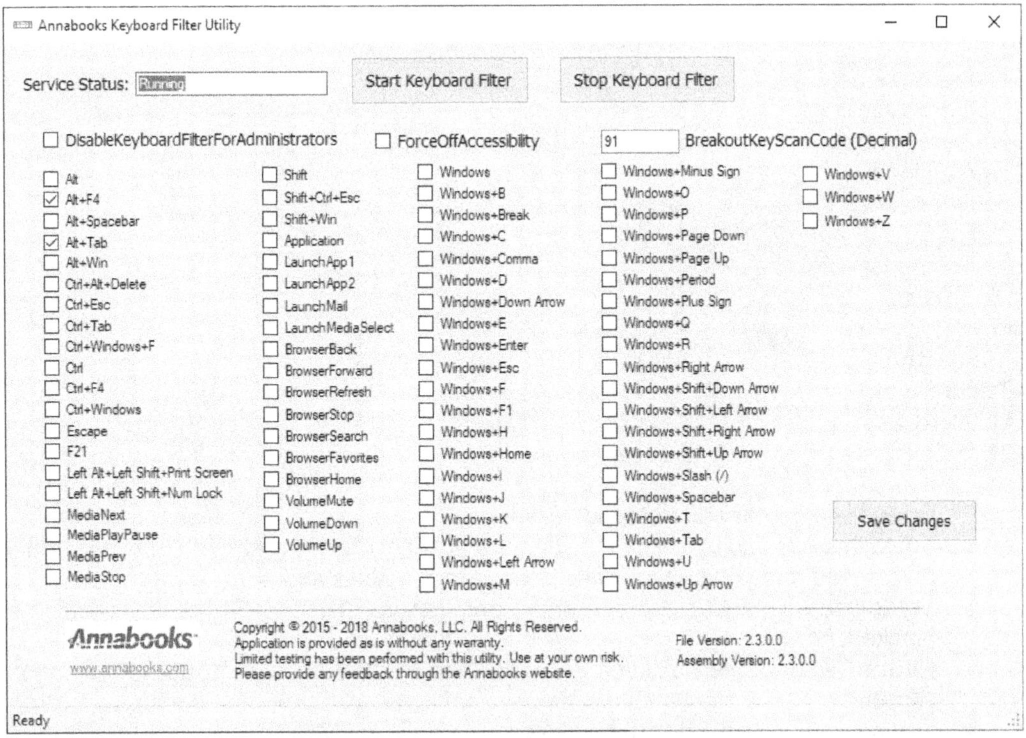

Annabooks Keyboard Filter Utility

Service Status: Running | Start Keyboard Filter | Stop Keyboard Filter

☐ DisableKeyboardFilterForAdministrators ☐ ForceOffAccessibility 91 BreakoutKeyScanCode (Decimal)

☐ Alt
☑ Alt+F4
☐ Alt+Spacebar
☑ Alt+Tab
☐ Alt+Win
☐ Ctrl+Alt+Delete
☐ Ctrl+Esc
☐ Ctrl+Tab
☐ Ctrl+Windows+F
☐ Ctrl
☐ Ctrl+F4
☐ Ctrl+Windows
☐ Escape
☐ F21
☐ Left Alt+Left Shift+Print Screen
☐ Left Alt+Left Shift+Num Lock
☐ MediaNext
☐ MediaPlayPause
☐ MediaPrev
☐ MediaStop
☐ Shift
☐ Shift+Ctrl+Esc
☐ Shift+Win
☐ Application
☐ LaunchApp1
☐ LaunchApp2
☐ LaunchMail
☐ LaunchMediaSelect
☐ BrowserBack
☐ BrowserForward
☐ BrowserRefresh
☐ BrowserStop
☐ BrowserSearch
☐ BrowserFavorites
☐ BrowserHome
☐ VolumeMute
☐ VolumeDown
☐ VolumeUp
☐ Windows
☐ Windows+B
☐ Windows+Break
☐ Windows+C
☐ Windows+Comma
☐ Windows+D
☐ Windows+Down Arrow
☐ Windows+E
☐ Windows+Enter
☐ Windows+Esc
☐ Windows+F
☐ Windows+F1
☐ Windows+H
☐ Windows+Home
☐ Windows+I
☐ Windows+J
☐ Windows+K
☐ Windows+L
☐ Windows+Left Arrow
☐ Windows+M
☐ Windows+Minus Sign
☐ Windows+O
☐ Windows+P
☐ Windows+Page Down
☐ Windows+Page Up
☐ Windows+Period
☐ Windows+Plus Sign
☐ Windows+Q
☐ Windows+R
☐ Windows+Right Arrow
☐ Windows+Shift+Down Arrow
☐ Windows+Shift+Left Arrow
☐ Windows+Shift+Right Arrow
☐ Windows+Shift+Up Arrow
☐ Windows+Slash (/)
☐ Windows+Spacebar
☐ Windows+T
☐ Windows+Tab
☐ Windows+U
☐ Windows+Up Arrow
☐ Windows+V
☐ Windows+W
☐ Windows+Z

Save Changes

Annabooks
www.annabooks.com

Copyright © 2015 - 2018 Annabooks, LLC. All Rights Reserved.
Application is provided as is without any warranty.
Limited testing has been performed with this utility. Use at your own risk.
Please provide any feedback through the Annabooks website.

File Version: 2.3.0.0
Assembly Version: 2.3.0.0

Ready

C:\Program Files\Annabooks> .\kbfmgr64.exe get-config

```
KBFMGR64.EXE - Keyboard Filter Manager
Copyright (c) 2017-2018 Annabooks, LLC. All Rights Reserved
File Version: 1.0.0.0
Provided as is without warranty.

Keyboard Filter Service is Running

DisableKeyboardFilterForAdministrators   Settings:   false
ForceOffAccessibility                    Settings:   false
BreakoutKeyScanCode                      Settings:      91

Key combinations:
Alt                      Settings: Allowed
Application              Settings: Allowed
Ctrl                     Settings: Allowed
Escape                   Settings: Allowed
Shift                    Settings: Allowed
Windows                  Settings: Allowed
Alt+Esc                  Settings: Allowed
Alt+F4                   Settings: Blocked
```

```
Alt+Space                Settings: Allowed
Alt+Tab                  Settings: Blocked
BrowserBack              Settings: Allowed
BrowserFavorites         Settings: Allowed
BrowserForward           Settings: Allowed
BrowserHome              Settings: Allowed
BrowserRefresh           Settings: Allowed:
:
:
:
Win+Z                    Settings: Allowed
Shift+Win                Settings: Allowed
Alt+Win                  Settings: Allowed
Ctrl+Win                 Settings: Allowed
F21                      Settings: Allowed
```

2. Open file explorer and notepad.
3. Try to use Alt+Tab to switch between the applications. The Alt+Tab hot key should be blocked and you cannot switch between the applications.
4. Try to use Alt+F4 to close one of the applications. The Alt+F4 hot key should be blocked.
5. Hit the Windows key 5 times in a row. The system should log out to the logon screen.
6. Log back in and shut down the system.

7.7 Architecture: When to Enable These Features

The Toast Messages and Gestures can be disabled early in the Group Policy. Keyboard Filter can be set up, but if you don't need hot keys while performing manual tasks before running Sysprep, then enable the Keyboard Filter service in the main answer file. As a good habit, always enable the Keyboard Filter in the Sysprep unattended file. UWF should be enabled in the Sysprep unattend file or sometime after mini-setup. UWF cannot be enabled before you perform Sysprep.

7.8 Summary: Drive C and Keyboard Hot Keys

This second chapter on the lockdown features covered the major features of UWF and the keyboard filter. UWF can help with some security protection but most important sudden power loss. The choice of overlay can affect system performance so your application should be tested with UWF, so you know how the system performs. We have not talked about updating the system, which is a very important topic that is covered in Chapter 9. The keyboard filter provides another important security feature to block users from hot keys and getting backdoor access to the system. This brings us to the final lockdown chapter covering security.

8 Lockdown Part 3: Security

The last two chapters have covered the traditional Windows Embedded Lockdown features. In my past books, the topic of security has been a little light. Much has changed in 23 years since Windows NT Embedded was released. Security is now a major topic with each new client. Microsoft has made major changes to Windows to address malware, and they are continuing to make improvements to make Windows more secure and reliable. Windows Security could be a standalone book. This chapter is going to look at many of the different security features at a high level and how and when to set them up in the image.

8.1 Windows Security Evolution

Because Windows was becoming the most popular operating system, it became a big target for attacks. Windows XP SP2 was the first major effort to focus on security. Every Windows release since then has some new security feature or fix that has addressed some security holes that attackers have exploited. Along the way, there has been a mishmash of terminology, products, and direction changes that keep everyone including the attackers guessing. Microsoft marketing has pushed some ideas as the next great thing of the next security brand or product. Device Guard was one of the last branding attempts. The Device Guard name was dropped, but the words "Device Guard" still appear in various settings and in the registry. The big caution here is, that since the launch of Windows 10, Microsoft has presented ideas as if they are available now. The concept versus reality has created confusion and we have to wait to see what reality brings. As of this writing, Microsoft is discussing three levels for device security with Secure-Core as the top level. We will see how all this gets fleshed out over the next few years. For this chapter, the known security features that have been implemented will be covered.

8.2 Hardware and Firmware

As discussed in Chapter 1, choosing the hardware is an important first step to creating a secure device. Many of the low-level security items are in the firmware and not in the operating system. Microsoft is working with chip vendors, board manufacturers, and device driver developers to address the low level to make sure the basics are in place to build up the security model. When looking for a hardware platform, you will want a system that has:

- TPM 1.2 as a minimum. TMP 2.0 is ideal.
- The SecureBoot feature in the firmware.
- A processor that supports hyperthreading and virtual extensions: Intel VT-x, Intel VT-d, AMD-v, and AMD-vi.

Windows security is interlocking with the hardware so the system is protected from power-on to launching the operating system. Once the operating system has launched, further security features can be put in place. The next 3 sections cover some of the traditional security features.

8.3 *Windows Firewall Settings and Policy File*

You can preset some firewall settings in the answer file using the Networking-MPSSVC-Svc component. A better approach is to set up the firewall on the target system and then export a firewall policy file (.wfw). The firewall policy file can then be imported using a Pass 7 Synchronous command during OS installation:

```
netsh advfirewall import c:\setup\Custom-Firewall.wfw
```

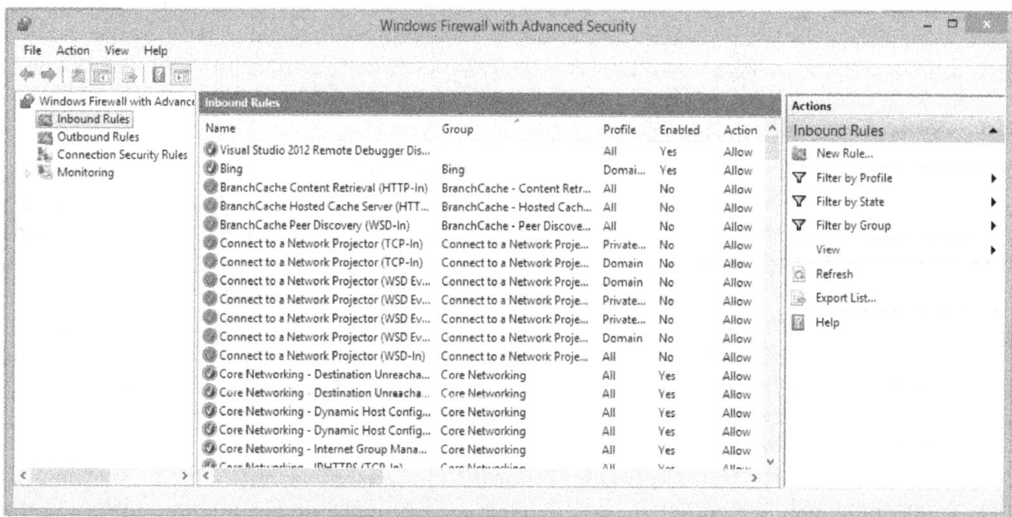

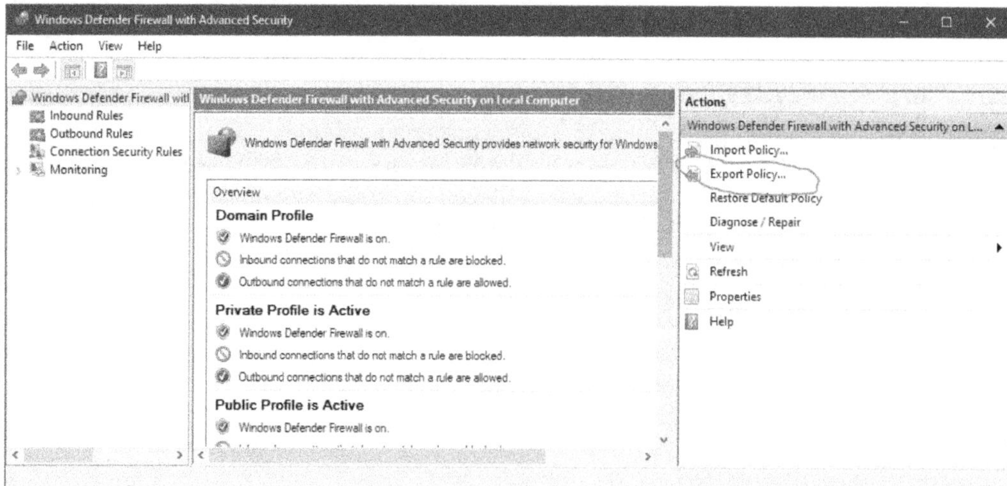

8.4 Antivirus Software

Microsoft Defender Antivirus is the built-in anti-malware solution that provides a basic virus protection solution. There are monthly updates to Windows Defender. We will cover updates in the next chapter. Microsoft Defender provides a basic level of protection. Even if UWF is enabled, it is good to have basic protection. There are several 3rd-party antivirus software products available that can also be installed. Just be aware of their update schemes and how they integrate into Windows. You will have to architect around any files and registry keys that require updating by these products.

8.5 Custom Security Template

By default, the security settings are defined in the "\windows\inf\Defltwk.inf" file. On your desktop, you can access the local security policies using the Local Security Policies found under the Administrative Tools in Control Panel. You can create your own custom security template to set who has disk drive access, folder access, what services are running, password strength, how old a password can be, network access options, etc. MMC.exe is used to create a custom security template. Exercise 801 Part 1 demonstrates a custom security template implementation. It is best to create a security template within the OS you're going to deploy, which is why it is one of the first steps in the development workflow. The custom security template can later be installed using the command line utility Secedit.exe.

```
Secedit /configure /db temp.sdb /cfg c:\customtemp.inf /overwrite
```

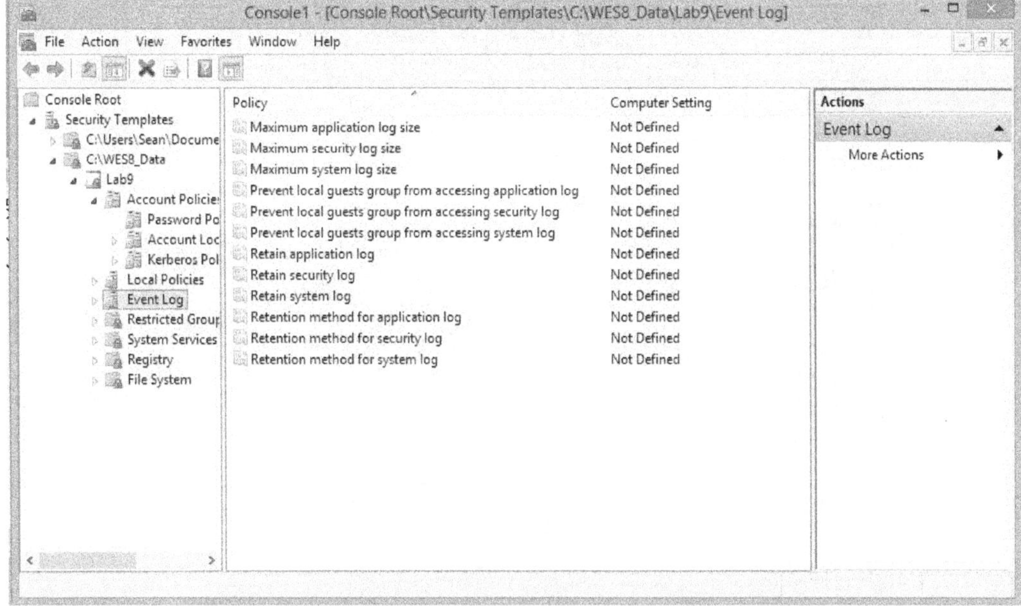

8.6 Custom Group Policies

Group Policies allow you to set up specific Windows components and features. For example, disable autorun, disable OneDrive, set the lock screen background, etc. These policies are set using the Local Group Policy Editor (gpedit.msc). These policy settings correspond to registry keys in the registry, but Gpedit makes changes to the policy files found in "C:\Windows\System32\GroupPolicy" where two different registry.pol files reside. When you make a change to a policy, you have to restart the system for the change to take effect. The registry.pol files are then imported into the registry. You can take advantage of this feature to preset some Group Policy settings. As part of the process outlined in Chapter 2, you would install Windows 10 on the target system, create the custom Group Policies using gpedit.msc, capture the "C:\Windows\System32\GroupPolicy" folder, and place it in the distribution share in \DS64\$$\System32.

Warning: Be aware that some policies like hardware blocking (discussed in the next section) cannot be preset since the operating system has to be installed first.

Sometimes it is easier to set policies directly in the registry. A good example will be in the next section when turning on device blocking. If policy changes are made in the registry, the changes will not be seen in gpedit.msc since the registry.pol files will not reflect the change.

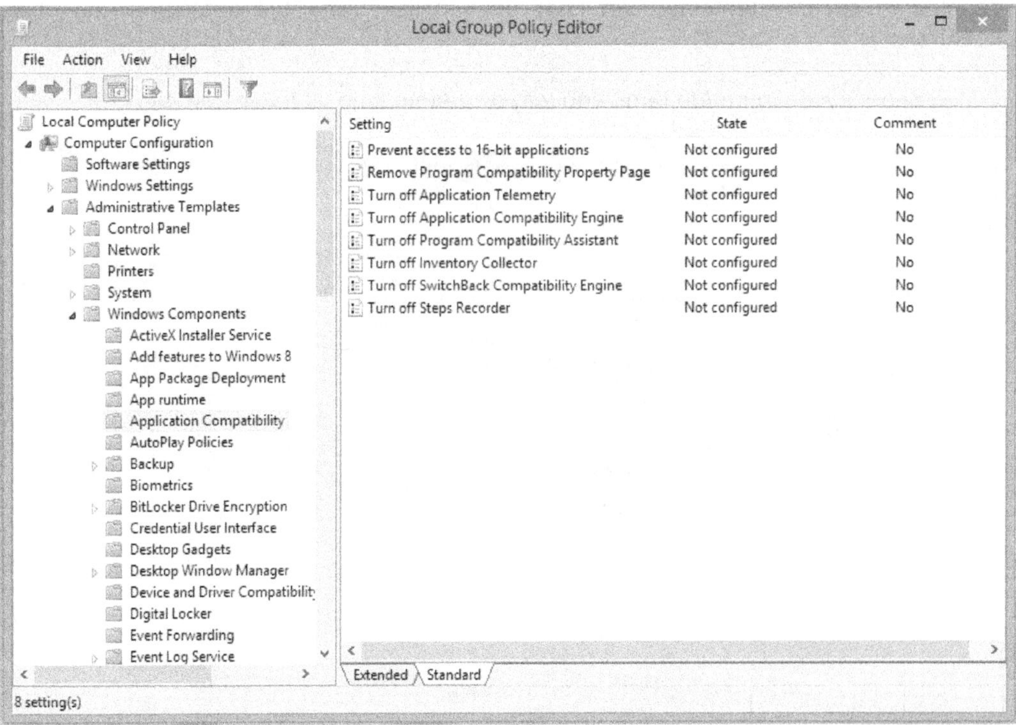

Here are some of the typical group policy settings that I set for most projects:

Computer Configuration

- Microsoft OneDrive for Business 2013 – Disabled
- Microsoft OneDrive for Business 2016 – Disabled
- Require a password when a computer wakes (on-battery) - Disabled
- Require a password when a computer wakes (plugged-in) – Disabled
- Save documents to OneDrive by default – Disabled
- Set the default behavior for AutoRun – Disabled
- Turn on Software Notifications – Disabled
- Disable Windows Error Reporting – Enabled
- Prevent the OneDrive files from syncing over a metered connection – Enabled
- Prevent the usage of OneDrive for file storage – Enabled
- Prevent the usage of OneDrive for file storage on Windows 8.1 – Enabled
- Turn off Autoplay – Enabled
- Turn off reminder balloons - Enabled
- Turn off System Restore - Enabled
- Turn off Windows Error Reporting – Enabled

User Configuration

- Enable screen saver – Disabled
- Microsoft OneDrive for Business 2013 – Disabled
- Microsoft OneDrive for Business 2016 – Disabled
- Password protect the screen saver – Disabled
- Screen saver timeout – Disabled
- Set the default behavior for AutoRun – Disabled
- Desktop Wallpaper – Enabled
    - Wallpaper Name: <path to wallpaper bitmap >
    - Wallpaper Style – <option>
- Disable showing balloon notification toasts – Enabled
- Disable Windows Error Reporting – Enabled
- Load specific theme - Enabled
    - Specific Theme: <path to theme>
- Remove Balloon Tips on Start Menu items – Enabled
- Turn off all balloon notifications – Enabled
- Turn off Autoplay – Enabled
- Turn off feature advertisement balloon notifications – Enabled
- Turn off reminder balloons
- Turn off toast notifications – Enabled
- Turn off toast notifications on the lock screen - Enabled

For documentation and QA script development, there is a nice utility called Registry.POL Viewer. The utility reads the Registry.pol files to see where the settings are configured in the registry. This is only a viewer and not an editor. The utility is available from SDM Software (https://sdmsoftware.com).

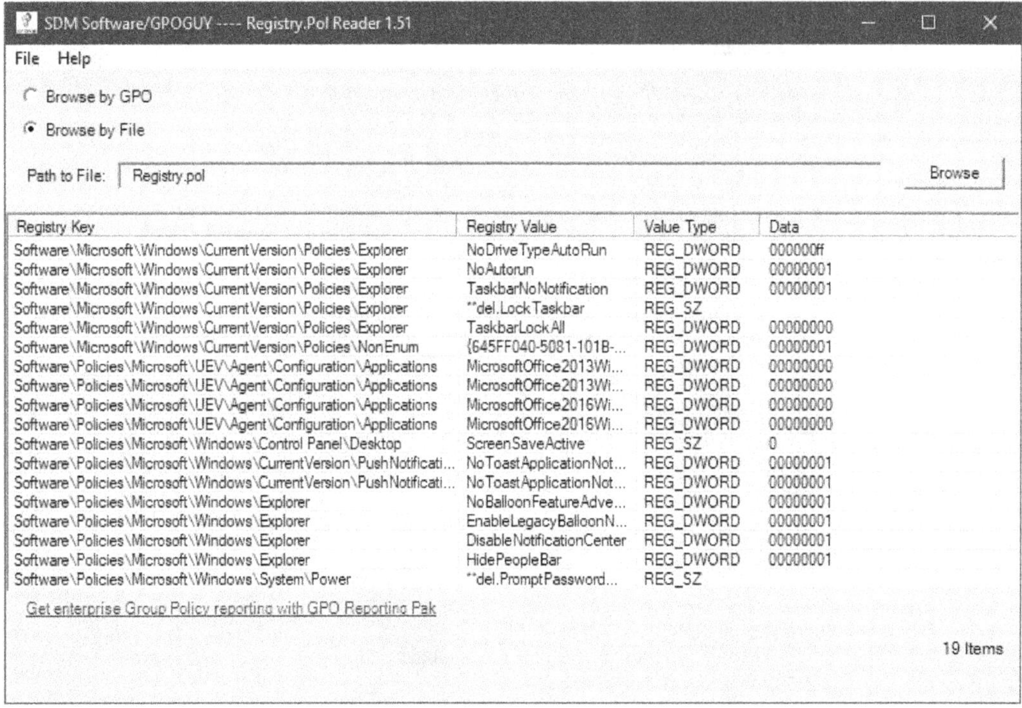

Preconfiguring Group Policies becomes an integral part of the image architecture. The security features discussed in the next few sections can be set up using the Group Policies.

8.7 Exercise 801 – Creating and Implementing Custom Security Solutions

In this lab, we will walk through the basic steps that are needed to create a custom security template, and then we will build this custom security template into a system and test it. We will add the security template to the distribution share.

8.7.1 Part 1: Creating a Custom Security Template

We will create a security template that locks regular user accounts out of the "C:\data" folder. Make sure you have the target OS installed. It is best practice to create the security template using the OS you are going to deploy.

1. Open File Explorer.
2. Edit your distribution share and create the following path to the %OEM% Folders\$$\security\templates folder.
3. Open Microsoft Management Console, MMC.exe.
4. Add a snap-in by choosing it from the dropdown menu File->Add/Remove Snap-in.
5. Scroll down the list of available snap-ins, and select Security Templates.
6. Click on the Add button.

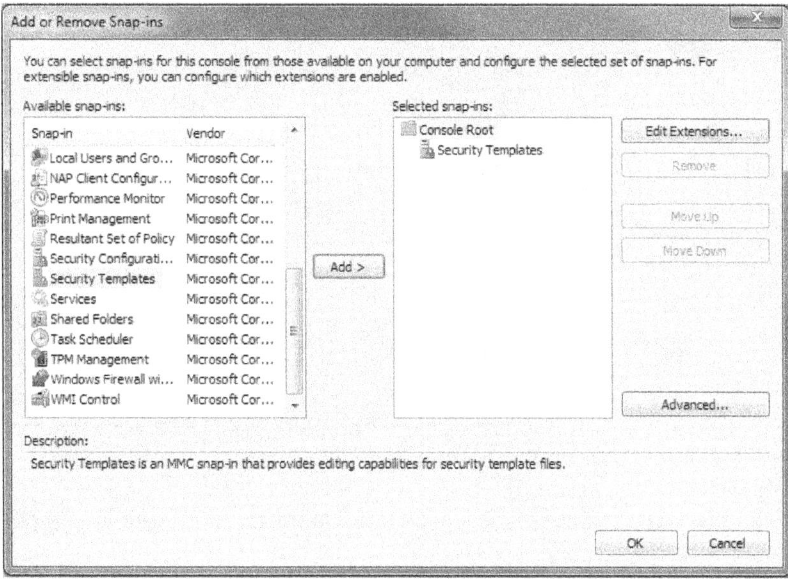

7. Click OK.
8. Expand the Security Templates node, right-click on the "C:\Users\<User_Name>\documents\security\templates" branch, and select New Template from the context menu.
9. Name the new template EX801, and click OK.

10. Expand the EX801 node so that you can see all of the branches.
11. Navigate down the branch EX801->Account Policies->Password Policy.
12. Change the Maximum password age to 0. The passwords will never expire. The Minimum password age will also be set.

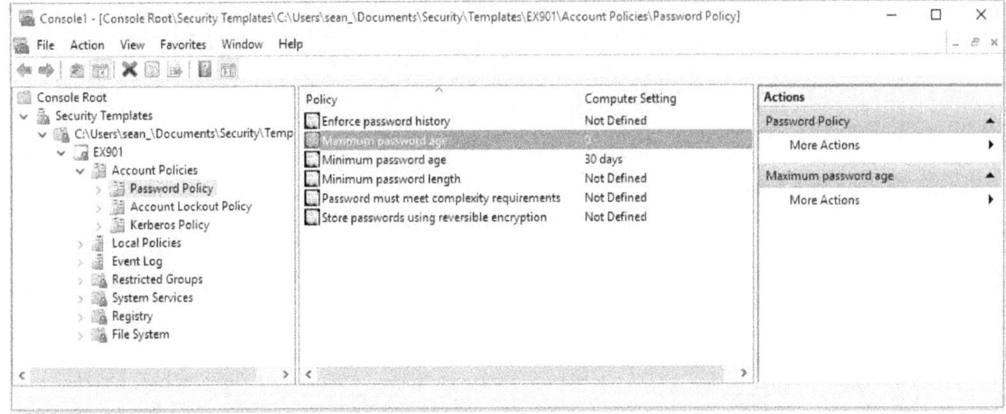

13. Right-click on the File System branch, and select Add File from the context menu.
14. In the folder text box on the bottom, type: C:\data.
15. Click OK.
16. A Security Dialog appears; click on the Users account and uncheck all access permissions.

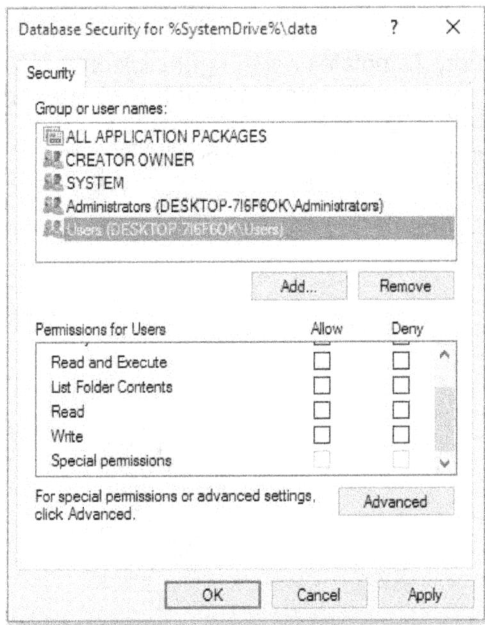

17. Click OK.
18. Keep the defaults for the Add Object dialog. Click OK.
19. Right-click on EX801, select Save As... from the context menu and save the file as EX801.inf to the ...\%OEM% Folders\$$\security\templates folder.
20. Close the MMC console and don't save the console when asked.

8.7.2 Part 2: Group Policy Settings

The goal of SIM is to help you automate the build process, but there is no support in SIM to pre-set Local Group Policies. It would be a nice feature. There is a solution to pre-configured local group policies that has been scattered in the forums and on the Internet. The idea is to create a Windows image, install Windows to a target system, configure the local group policies, capture the GroupPolicy folder, and build the final image with the captured custom local group policies. For this exercise, we will disable change password and logoff options from the CTRL-ALT-DEL screen, thus we can do this on the host system.

1. Normally these steps would be performed on a target system and the files brought over. On the host machine run the Group Policy Editor, gpedit.msc.
2. Go to User Configuration->Administrative Templates->System->CTRL+ALT+DEL Options and set the policies:

    - Remove Change Password – set to Enabled.
    - Remove Logoff –set to Enabled.

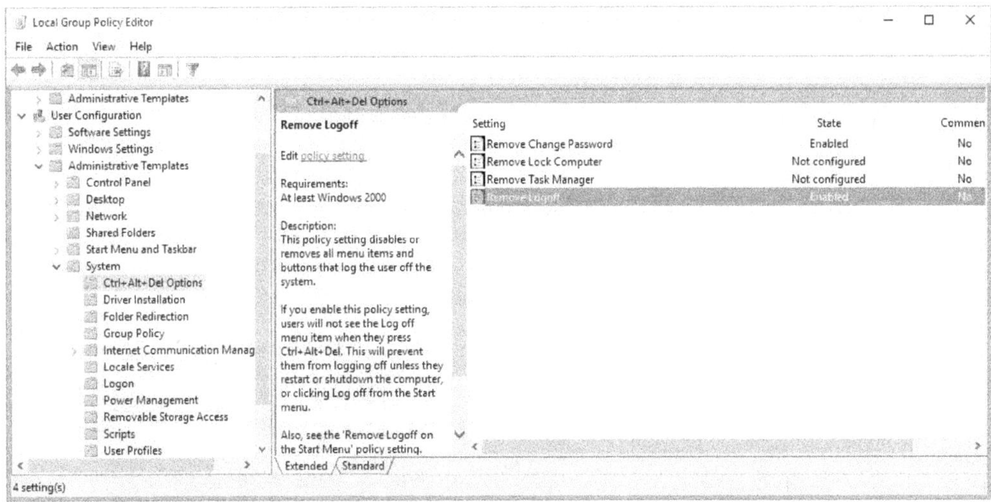

3. Close gpedit.msc.
4. Open File Explorer.
5. Edit your distribution share and set up a folder %OEM% Folders\$$\System32\GroupPolicy.
6. Hit the Alt key; this will pop up the menu if the menu is not visible.
7. From the menu, select View->Options… This will open the Folder Options dialog.
8. Click on the View tab, and change the folder options so that you can see all files, system files, and hidden files.
9. Go to the “C:\Windows\System32\GroupPolicy” folder.
10. Copy the contents in the GroupPolicy folder and place them in the %OEM% Folders\$$\System32\GroupPolicy.

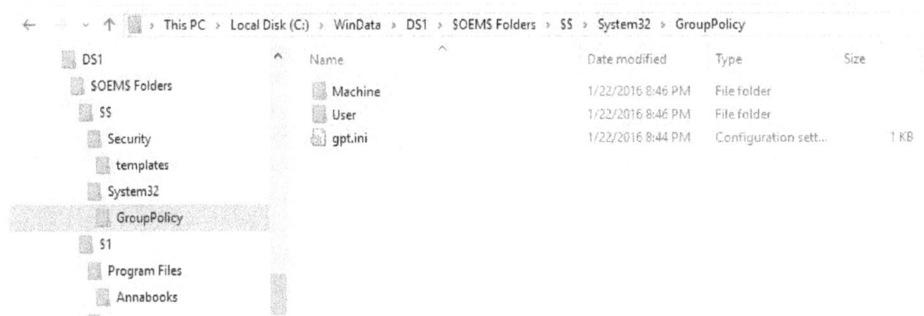

11. Once the copy has been completed, right-click on the GroupPolicy folder, and select properties.
12. Remove the read-only attribute and click Ok,

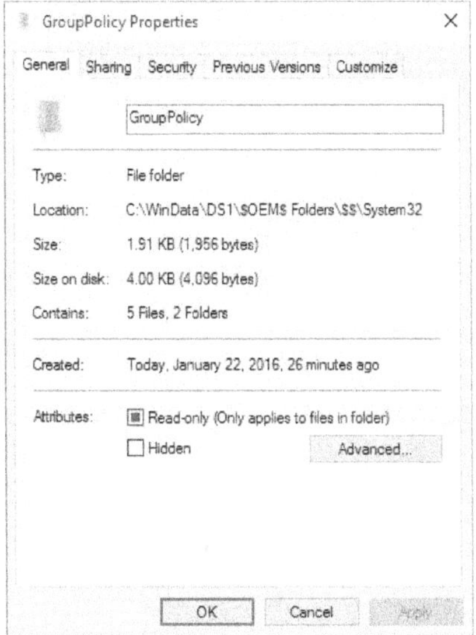

13. Click yes to the propagation dialog.

Note: Once you have copied the group policy over, you will want to change the policy back since this was performed on the host development system.

8.7.3 Part 3: Create Answer File and Deploy and Test the Image with the Security Policy

The steps below assume that you have created a catalog for the target OS. The image will boot to the WADMIN account first.

1. In the \image folder, delete the AutoUnattend.xml, AutoUnattend_files folder, Win10IOT.ISO, and the oem folder.
2. Open SIM.
3. Open the catalog file if it is not opened already.
4. Make sure the distribution share is also opened.
5. Open the EX701 Answer file.
6. Save the answer file as EX801.
7. Change the AutoLogon account from WinGuest to WinAdmin.
8. We now need to remove Shell Launcher from the previous lab. Right-click on the Shell Launcher component and select delete.
9. Disable the Shell Launcher feature in the amd64_Microsoft-Windows-Foundation-Package.
10. Remove the two Pass 7 Synchronous commands that are under amd64_Microsoft-Windows-Shell-Setup__neutral->First Logon Commands.
11. Add three Pass 7 OOBE Synchronous Commands:

    - Cmd.exe /c md c:\data

- Secedit.exe /configure /db temp.sdb /cfg c:\windows\security\templates\EX801.inf
- Attrib.exe –r –h –s /S /D c:\Windows\System32\GroupPolicy

12. Perform a validation check.
13. Save the answer file.
14. Create the configuration set, integrate the configuration set with the installation files, and install the OS on the target system. The image will boot into the WinADMIN account.
15. Log out of the WinADMIN account.
16. Log into the WinGUEST account.
17. Open the command prompt and try to access the "c:\data" folder. You will get an access is denied error, since we disabled access for Users' accounts.

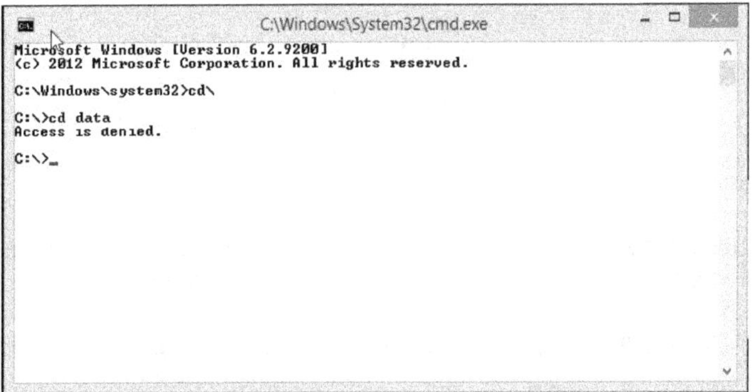

18. Log out.
19. Log back into the WinADMIN account.
20. Open the Command Prompt with elevated privileges. You may use File Explorer to locate cmd.exe, right-click on cmd.exe, and select Run as Administrator.
21. Try accessing the "c:\data" folder. Since this is an administrator account, you have full access.

Since Users don't have access and Administrators have access, the command prompt window must run with elevated privileges to access the directory. Now let's check the group policy

22. On the target system, once the OS has finished installing, open the Group Policy Editor, gpedit.msc. The final image will have the custom local policy settings. If you fail to get access because of user permissions, check the properties of the GroupPolicy folder. The folder and all of the files in it must be full read-write access. Uncheck read-only if checked.
23. Open Control Panel and change the View by to Large Icons view.
24. Open Administrative Tools->Local Security Policy.
25. Under Account Policy -> Password Policy check that the password Max and Min password settings are set correctly.

26. Try a CTRL-ALT-DEL. You should see the two options missing.

27. Shut down the target system.

8.8 *Driver Blocking: Group Policy: Device Installation Restrictions (DIR)*

USB ports have become the de-facto standard to plug in external devices to a PC. Keyboard, mouse, flash drives, cameras, and headphones make use of this flexible port. USB ports can be a security vulnerability. Disabling Auto-run and Auto plan in Group Policy is one gate to block that causes infiltration. Keyboard filter and blocking hotkeys is another gate. There are hybrid devices that can show up as more than one device and could expose a hole. Controlling what gets plugged into the USB ports becomes an important task to address. In 2013, Windows 8.1 Embedded Industry was released. The new OS introduced a new lockdown feature called the USB Filter. One problem with this new feature was the lack of documentation on how to use it. When Windows 10 Enterprise LTSB 2015 was released, the USB filter feature was gone. In its place was a set of Group Policies: "Device Installation Restrictions" (DIR) that controlled device installation. Enabling these policies and the Unified Write Filter (UWF) at the same time could result in a blue screen of death (BSOD). It appears the UWF filter driver was not getting excluded from the list of devices. With the release of Windows 10 Enterprise LTSC 2019, the BSOD issue appears to have been fixed.

The DIRs are for all devices, not just USB. If the system has a PCIe slot, the DIRs can prevent a PCI driver from loading for any random PCIe devices plugged into the slot. The goal is to block devices from installing. Someone can plug in a USB device, and if the device installation restrictions are enabled, the driver for the device will not be installed.

Once device installation restrictions have been disabled, any devices plugged into the system will load a driver if a driver is in the driver store.

There are 10 Device Installation Restrictions policies, and using gpedit.msc, they can be found in the following path:

Computer Configuration : Administrative Templates : System : Device Installation : Device Installation Restrictions

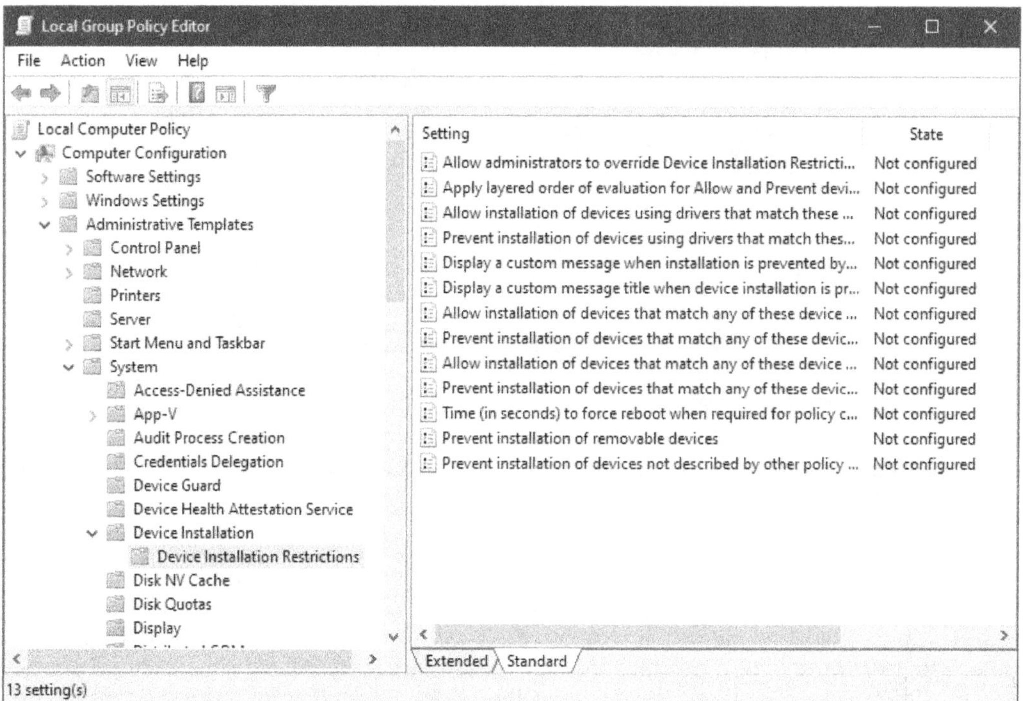

The root registry for these policies is:

HKEY_LOCAL_MACHINE\SOFTWARE\Policies\Microsoft\Windows\DeviceInstall\Restrictions

The next four sections will go over these policies and show the registry keys that go with the policy. The fifth section discussed creates a group policy to preset them during OS installation, but some group policies cannot be preset. We have grouped the policies to help provide a discussion on different setup scenarios. The following lists the policy, the corresponding registry key, and the explanation:

8.8.1 Top Level Policies

These policies control the basic on and off of the Device Installation Restrictions.

- Allow administrators to override Device Installation Restriction policies - By enabling this setting all Administrator accounts can install devices. Disabling the setting will make Administrator accounts adhere to the other policy settings.

Key: HKEY_LOCAL_MACHINE\SOFTWARE\Policies\Microsoft\Windows\DeviceInstall\Restrictions
Value Name: AllowAdminInstall
Type: REG_DWORD
Value Data: 0 - Disable, 1 – Enable

- Prevent installation of removable devices - When enabled, all removable devices are blocked. Disabling the setting removes the restriction.

Key: HKEY_LOCAL_MACHINE\SOFTWARE\Policies\Microsoft\Windows\DeviceInstall\Restrictions
Value Name: DenyRemovableDevices
Type: REG_DWORD
Value Data: 0 - Disable, 1 – Enable

- Prevent installation of devices not described by other policy settings - You can think of this last setting as the master on/off for the Device Installation Restriction. Enabled this setting will block any device from being installed that is not allowed by other settings. It will also prevent device drivers from being updated. This is one setting that should NOT be preset in your custom Group Policy. Two settings allow devices to be installed either by Device ID or by Device Class. The next two groups discuss these settings.

Key: HKEY_LOCAL_MACHINE\SOFTWARE\Policies\Microsoft\Windows\DeviceInstall\Restrictions
Value Name: DenyUnspecified
Type: REG_DWORD
Value Data: 0 - Disable, 1 – Enable

8.8.2 Control by Device ID

There are two policies that either allow or prevent a device from being installed by Device ID. The Device ID isn't the PnP ID but a Hardware ID that you can find listed in the device properties.

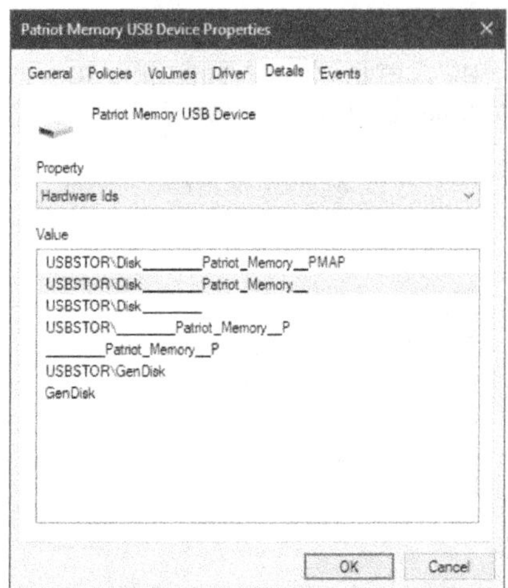

- Allow installation of devices that match any of these device IDs - When enabled, you can list all the devices that are allowed to be connected to the system using the Device ID. You can think of this as the guest list of devices that can be connected to the system when the master policy to Deny Removable Drives is enabled. The list is a numbered item under the AllowDeviceIDs path. The Value Names start with 1 and continue upward in integer values.

Key: HKEY_LOCAL_MACHINE\SOFTWARE\Policies\Microsoft\Windows\DeviceInstall\Restrictions
Value Name: AllowDeviceIDs
Type: REG_DWORD
Value Data: 0 - Disable, 1 – Enable

Key:
HKEY_LOCAL_MACHINE\SOFTWARE\Policies\Microsoft\Windows\DeviceInstall\Restrictions\AllowDeviceIDs
Value Name: 1
Type: REG_SZ
Value Data: *"Hardware ID of the Device"*

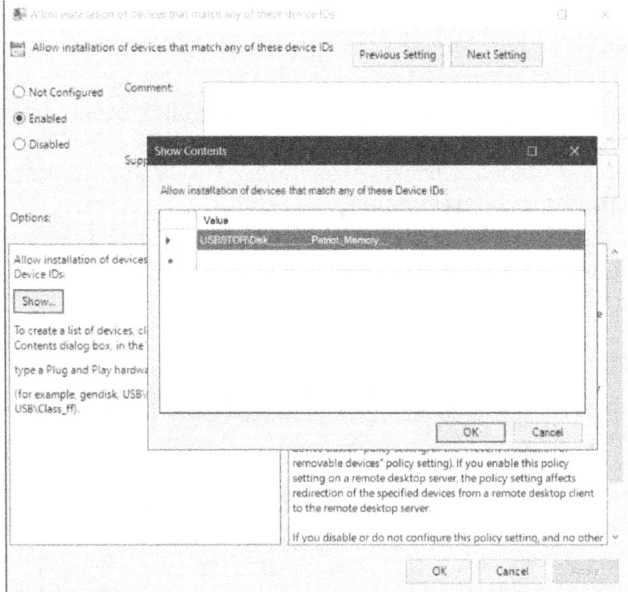

- Prevent installation of devices that match any of these device IDs - This setting is the opposite of the previous settings. When enabled, any listed devices with the matching device ID in the list will be blocked from installing. There is an additional checkbox to retroactively disable devices of the same device ID if already installed. This might come in handy when blocking a hybrid device like a cell modem. You might want to block the CD-ROM device but allow the modem device.

Key: HKEY_LOCAL_MACHINE\SOFTWARE\Policies\Microsoft\Windows\DeviceInstall\Restrictions
Value Name: DenyDeviceIDs
Type: REG_DWORD
Value Data: 0 - Disable, 1 – Enable

Key: HKEY_LOCAL_MACHINE\SOFTWARE\Policies\Microsoft\Windows\DeviceInstall\Restrictions
Value Name: DenyDeviceIDsRetroactive
Type: REG_DWORD
Value Data: 0 - Disable, 1 – Enable

Key:
HKEY_LOCAL_MACHINE\SOFTWARE\Policies\Microsoft\Windows\DeviceInstall\Restrictions\DenyDeviceIDs
Value Name: 1
Type: REG_SZ
Value Data: *"Hardware ID of the Device"*

8.8.3 Control by Device Class

There are two policies that either allow or prevent a device from being installed by Device Class. The Device Class is the high-level grouping of devices like a keyboard or mouse. Microsoft defines the class types with GUIDs. There are two tables of Class GUIDs on

Microsoft Docs: System-Defined Device Setup Classes Available to Vendors and System-Defined Device Setup Classes Reserved for System Use.

- Allow installation of devices using drivers that match these device setup classes - When enabled, you can add a list of device class GUIDs. The list is a numbered item under the AllowDeviceClasses path. The Value Names start with 1 and continue upward in integer values.

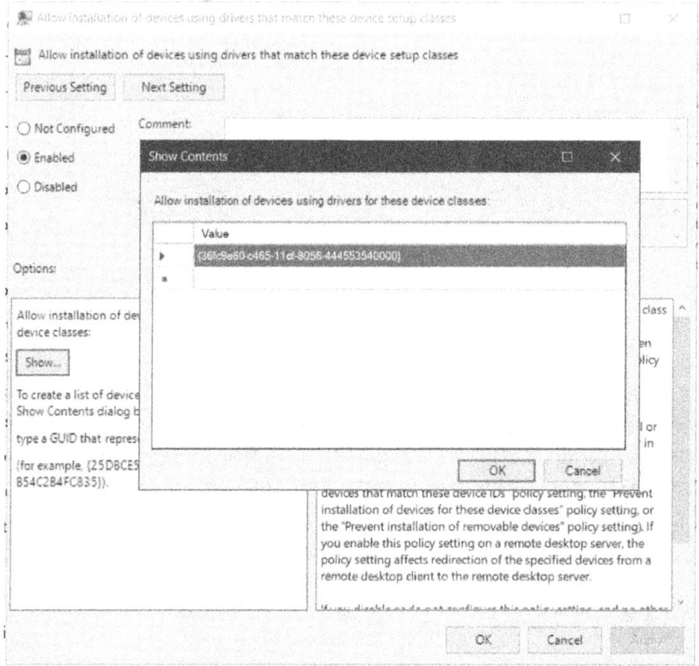

Some classes are dependent on others. For example, enabling a USB keyboard will require adding two classes to the list: Keyboard {4d36e96b-e325-11ce-bfc1-08002be10318} and USB Bus Devices (hubs and host controllers) {36fc9e60-c465-11cf-8056-444553540000}. Allowing a Device Class to be enabled might create a hole in security, as enabling a class will allow any device of that class to be connected to the system. Device ID provides more granular control.

Key: HKEY_LOCAL_MACHINE\SOFTWARE\Policies\Microsoft\Windows\DeviceInstall\Restrictions
Value Name: AllowDeviceClasses
Type: REG_DWORD
Value Data: 0 - Disable, 1 – Enable

Key:
HKEY_LOCAL_MACHINE\SOFTWARE\Policies\Microsoft\Windows\DeviceInstall\Restrictions\AllowDeviceClasses
Value Name: 1
Type: REG_SZ
Value Data: *"Device Class"*

- Prevent installation of devices using drivers that match these device setup classes - This setting is the opposite of the previous setting. When enabled, any listed devices with the matching device class in the list will be blocked from installing. There is an additional checkbox to retroactively disable devices of the same device class if already installed.

Key: HKEY_LOCAL_MACHINE\SOFTWARE\Policies\Microsoft\Windows\DeviceInstall\Restrictions
Value Name: DenyDeviceClasses
Type: REG_DWORD
Value Data: 0 - Disable, 1 – Enable

Key: HKEY_LOCAL_MACHINE\SOFTWARE\Policies\Microsoft\Windows\DeviceInstall\Restrictions
Value Name: DenyDeviceClassesRetroactive
Type: REG_DWORD
Value Data: 0 - Disable, 1 – Enable

Key:
HKEY_LOCAL_MACHINE\SOFTWARE\Policies\Microsoft\Windows\DeviceInstall\Restrictions\DenyDeviceClasses
Value Name: 1
Type: REG_SZ
Value Data: *"Device Class"*

8.8.4 Other Policy Settings

The last three policy settings provide user messaging and auto-restart if a driver has been installed.

- Display a custom message when the installation is prevented by a policy setting - When enabled, the setting will enable a message to be displayed when a device is blocked. This may or may not be useful, as most companies want to hide any messages that might indicate Windows is running in the system.

Key:
HKEY_LOCAL_MACHINE\SOFTWARE\Policies\Microsoft\Windows\DeviceInstall\Restrictions\DeniedPolicy
Value Name: DetailText
Type: REG_SZ
Value Data: *"Message to the user"*

- Display a custom message title when device installation is prevented by a policy setting - When enabled, the setting adds a title to the message defined in the previous setting.

Key:
HKEY_LOCAL_MACHINE\SOFTWARE\Policies\Microsoft\Windows\DeviceInstall\Restrictions\DeniedPolicy
Value Name: SimpleText
Type: REG_SZ
Value Data: *"Title of the Message"*

- Time (in seconds) to force reboot when required for policy changes to take effect - When enabled, the system will force a reboot when a device driver change takes effect.

Key: HKEY_LOCAL_MACHINE\SOFTWARE\Policies\Microsoft\Windows\DeviceInstall\Restrictions
Value Name: ForceReboot
Type: REG_DWORD
Value Data: 0 - Disable, 1 – Enable

Key: HKEY_LOCAL_MACHINE\SOFTWARE\Policies\Microsoft\Windows\DeviceInstall\Restrictions
Value Name: RebootTime
Type: REG_DWORD
Value Data: "*Time in seconds*"

8.8.5 Scenarios and Setup

Since drivers need to be installed during installation, DIR cannot be enabled right away. You can present individual PnP IDs or categories to be allowed or prevented from installing. The full enable must be set on each clone after Sysprep. There are a few scenarios to help with your setup:

Note: The settings will not appear in gpedit.msc if you used reg.exe to add the setting directly. It would be better to set up some of these in a custom Group Policy first and then control the master enable and disable registry key using reg.exe. A note will be made at the end of the policy in the following scenarios.

- Scenario 1: The system has a single Administrator account with a defined USB device to be connected.

In this scenario, the Administrator account needs to be blocked from adding devices so the following settings are configured:

  - Allow administrators to override Device Installation Restriction policies – Disabled (Preset in Group Policy)
  - Allow installation of devices that match any of these device IDs – Enabled and the device ID of the USB device is added to the list. (Preset in Group Policy)
  - Prevent installation of devices not described by other policy settings – Disable (Present in Group Policy and later controlled by a registry key value)

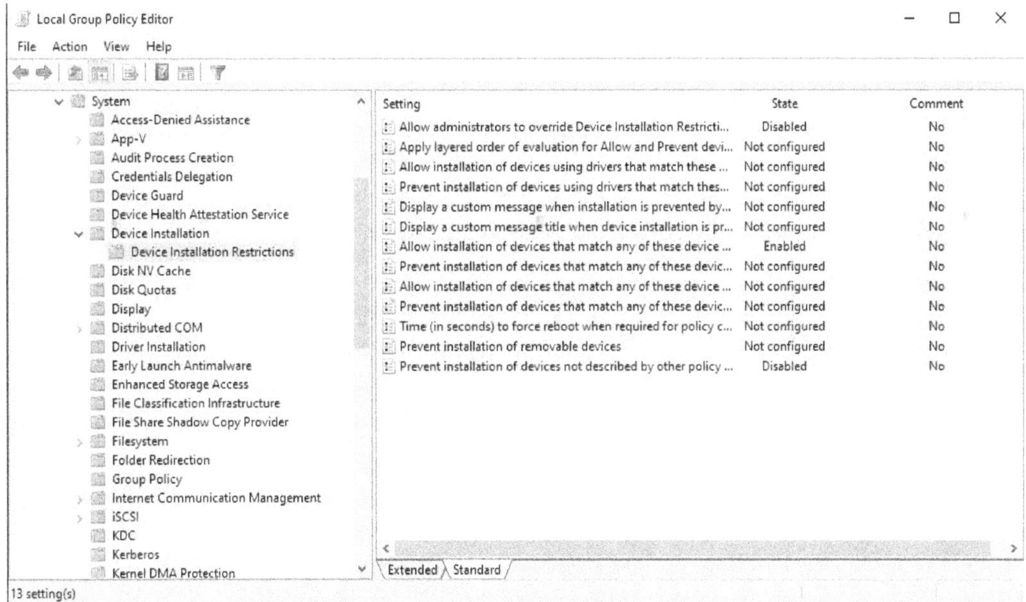

The above screenshot shows the Group Policy settings. Device PnP IDs can be copied from Device Manager and pasted into the Group Policy: “Allow installation of devices that match any of these device IDs.”

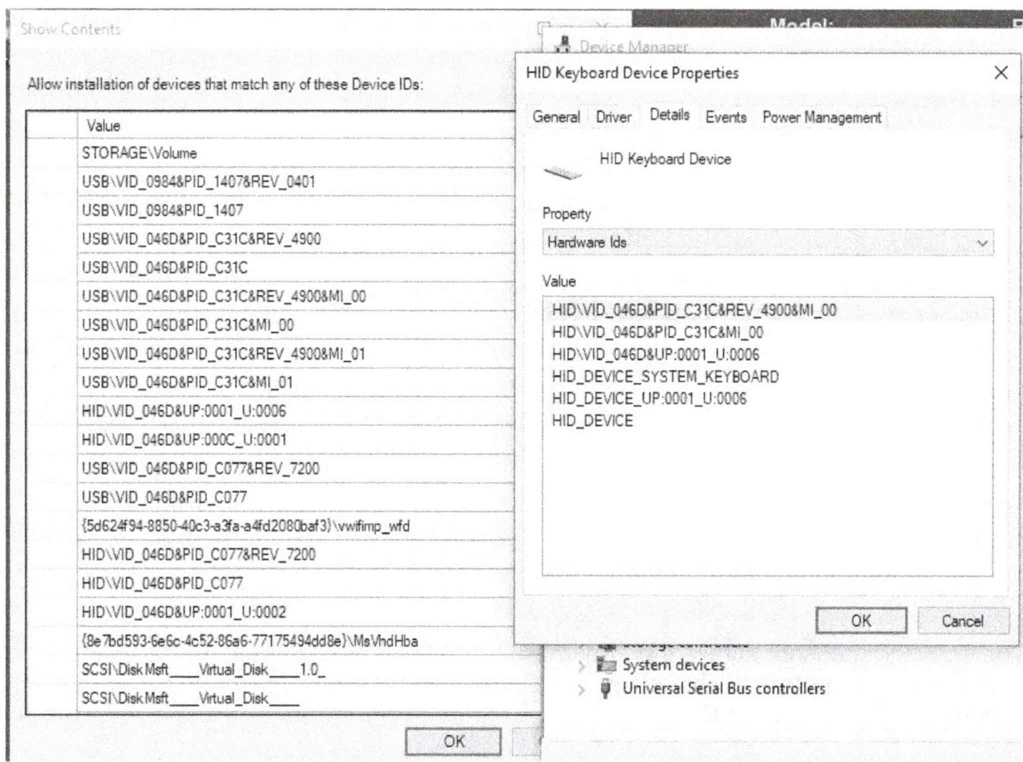

Each clone of the master image can run the following sync command to set the policy “Prevent installation of devices not described by other policy settings“ to 1 to enable device block.

```
Reg.exe add
"HKLM\SOFTWARE\Policies\Microsoft\Windows\DeviceInstall\Restrictions" /v
"DenyUnspecified" /t REG_DWORD /d 1 /f
```

To turn off the device block, make the same call, but change the value from 1 to 0.

```
Reg.exe add
"HKLM\SOFTWARE\Policies\Microsoft\Windows\DeviceInstall\Restrictions" /v
"DenyUnspecified" /t REG_DWORD /d 0 /f
```

- Scenario 2: The system has an Administrator account and User account. The User account is the main account in the system. The User is denied installation of devices. The Administrator can install devices.

This simple scenario has the following settings:

- Allow administrators to override Device Installation Restriction policies – Enabled (Preset in Group Policy)
- Prevent installation of devices not described by other policy settings – Enabled/Disable (controlled by a registry key value)
- (Optional) Prevent installation of removable devices – Enabled (Preset in Group Policy)

- Scenario 3: The system has a single Administrator account. Only mouse and keyboards can be connected to the system.

This is a case where the device class fits.

- Allow administrators to override Device Installation Restriction policies – Disabled (Preset in Group Policy)
- Prevent installation of devices not described by other policy settings – Enabled/Disable (controlled by a registry key value)
- Allow installation of devices using drivers that match these device setup classes – Enabled with the following classes in the list for keyboard, mouse, and USB Bus Device: (Preset in Group Policy)

    - {4d36e96b-e325-11ce-bfc1-08002be10318}
    - {4d36e96f-e325-11ce-bfc1-08002be10318}
    - {36fc9e60-c465-11cf-8056-444553540000}

8.9 TPM Chip

A TPM chip is used to help encrypt data, protect credentials, etc. A TPM chip used to be an optional feature from many board vendors. Those days are long gone. The TPM can be a physical chip on the board or a firmware TPM built into the processor. The Trusted Computing Group defines the TPM specification. For Windows, the minimum version is TPM 1.2, but the best version is TPM 2.0, which Windows 11 requires. For the most part, you will not have to interact with the TPM chip. Windows takes over the TPM so features like BitLocker, Credential Guard, and SecureBoot (Measured Boot) can take advantage of the unique private key in the TPM. There is a management console interface (TPM.msc) that provides status and the ability to clear the TPM to a default factory state, but TPM.msc will go away in the future. There are PowerShell CMDLETs that can be used to interact with the TPM. The only thing you have to do is make sure a TPM is on the board and that you know the version that is being supported to provide for a future upgrade to Windows 11.

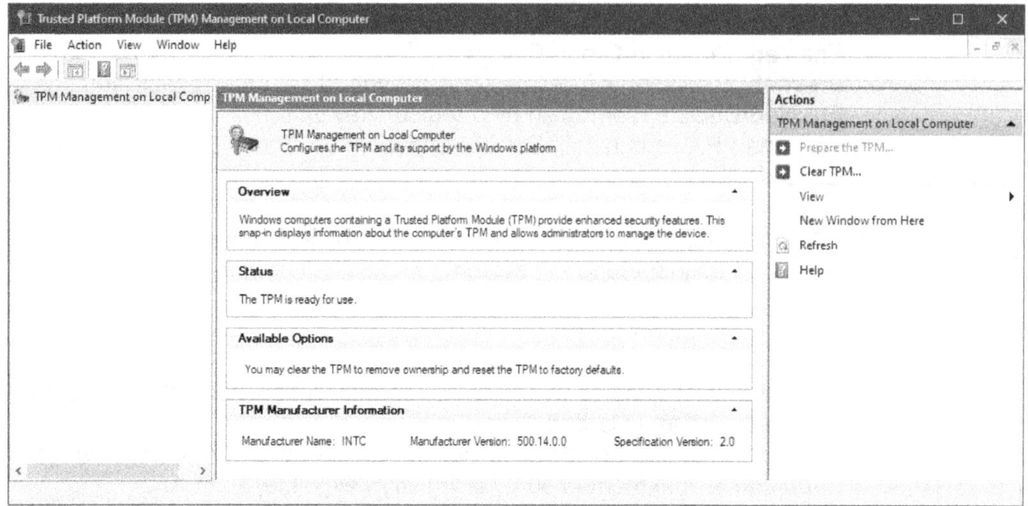

There is a set of 24 Platform Configuration Registers (PCR) banks in TPM. The firmware configures which banks are accessible. These banks store SHA hash values. Windows will check which PCRs are available and use the available PCRs at different points in the boot process. The measured-on-boot feature is part of making a hardware root-of-trust and forcing the bootup process to take the secure path on startup. You can see which bank is being used and what TCG Algorithm identifier is currently in use.

Key: HKEY_LOCAL_MACHINE\SYSTEM\CurrentControlSet\Control\IntegrityServices
Value: TPMActivePCRBanks

Key: HKEY_LOCAL_MACHINE\SYSTEM\CurrentControlSet\Control\IntegrityServices
Value: TPMDigestAlgID - Use the bit field value to look up the algorithm used in the Hash Algorithms Bit Field table in the TCG Algorithm Registry documentation on the TCG website.

8.10 BitLocker

BitLocker provides data encryption capability and protection from stolen data. BitLocker uses the unique key of the TPM chip to encrypt the data on a drive. The goal is to prevent someone from casually removing the drive from the system and accessing the data. If the drive is encrypted, then the only way to access the data on the drive outside of the system is with the recovery key. Since each TPM has a unique security key built in and Sysprep will not run with BitLocker enabled, BitLocker will have to be enabled in manufacturing on each system after Sysprep. In the Sysprep unattended file, a Pass 7 Synchronous command to run the BitLocker manage-bde.exe utility to enable BitLocker can be added:

```
manage-bde -on c: -skiphardwaretest
```

When each clone boots for the first time, it will run the command and start the encryption process. To get the status of BitLocker, you can check the BitLocker control panel using manage-bde.exe

```
manage-bde.exe -status
```

Some off-the-shelf systems have been known to kick off BitLocker during initial Windows installation. A Pass 7 Synchronous command in the main answer file can be added to disable BitLocker:

```
manage-bde -off c:
```

If you want to generate a recovery key, then you will have to run something like the following to save the file to a USB flash disk.

```
manage-bde -protectors -add c: -RecoveryPassword > <path to USB
flash disk>\MyBitlockerKey.txt
```

This brings up a challenge. If you want to provide service for recovering data on a system that has crashed and if you are selling hundreds to thousands of systems, a procedure will have to be put into place to catalog each recovery key with a system's serial number. How the recovery keys are managed is up to you. You need to assess internal company capabilities and costs to find the optimal solution.

Windows is a general-purpose operating system and there are Group Policy settings and PowerShell modules to manage BitLocker. Manage-bde.exe has several other command line options. The basic options presented here are the ones typically used for building a Windows Embedded/IoT system.

8.11 SecureBoot, UEFI, SecureLaunch

The chapter has covered many security features when Windows is up and running. Most of us have seen old diagrams where firmware runs first and looks to the boot sector to launch the operating system. Systems are vulnerable before the Windows kernel has launched. Windows XP used the boot.ini file to point to NTLoader and load the kernel. Boot.ini was a text file that malware could easily modify and load anything before loading the Windows kernel. Windows 7 changed the boot process. The boot.ini information was moved into a binary file (Boot Manager) that could only be managed with utilities running with elevated privileges. Winload replaced NTLoader to load the kernel. The new boot solution only lasted as long as it took malware developers to get more sophisticated with new types of attacks using rootkits: firmware rootkits, bootkits, kernel rootkits, and driver rootkits. Microsoft, along with all of its hardware partners, has been working on protecting the bootup process.

Intel developed new firmware to replace the old BIOS called the Extended Framework Interface (EFI), which is now a specification called Unified Extended Framework Interface UEFI, managed by the UEFI Forum. UEFI allows a PC to boot into 64-bit mode directly, thus opening the possibility for low-level board testing, GPT boot drives, and advanced low-level security. When a system boots, the firmware can check itself to make sure that it is good before proceeding on, thus addressing the firmware rootkits. Once the firmware has completed its setup, the next step is to load the operating system. Microsoft has created what is called a Trusted Boot sequence. SecureBoot with a key in the firmware checks to verify that the Windows loader is the correct one before proceeding on. The Kernel loads along with the various system drivers. An Early Launch Anti-Malware (ELAM) is the last to load in the Trusted Boot sequence. The purpose of ELAM is to verify that the 3rd-party device drivers are safe before loading them. From power-on to ELAM loading, there are measured checks that work in concert with the TPM to verify that the whole boot process is free of rootkits.

So, that was a very high-level summary of the boot process. What does all of this mean for securing a Windows image? You are either 1 of 2 OEM types. Most OEMs buy a PC board off-the-shelf. As mentioned before, you will want a system that has UEFI and SecureBoot in the firmware, and TPM 1.2 or 2.0 support. Most boards, today, support UEFI. It must be made clear to the board vendor that the SecureBoot and TPM options are needed. You have to make sure that SecureBoot is enabled in the firmware, but there is a little more that needs to be done:

- You could create your own signed key for the OS loader so that only your custom image boots. I am going to leave this to Microsoft Docs to cover this process, as this is a very rare request. Just enabling SecureBoot is good enough.
- If the system supports PCI hot-plug technology like Thunderbolt™, the system could be exposed to DMA attacks. To prevent this from happening, you will have to enable SecureBoot with DMA protection. This will be covered a little later.
- The measured boot data is stored and checked on each boot to verify that the system is clean of rootkits. The information is stored in the C:\Windows\Logs\MeasuredBoot folder. If there are suspected problems such as BitLocker recover mode, there is a tool in the Windows Hardware Lab Kit (TBSLogGenerator) and another tool in the TPM Platform Crypto-Provider Toolkit (PCPTool) to help decode these log files.
- If your system is going to be connected to a domain, the generated measured boot information could be stored in a local server or cloud server attestation. This acts as another check level that the system has booted properly. The use of Measured Boot and remote attestation process is more for IT departments that monitor computers on their network. More information on Measured Boot can be found in the online article: Secure the Windows boot process: https://docs.microsoft.com/en-us/windows/security/information-protection/secure-the-windows-10-boot-process

The other type of OEM is the one building a custom board. In this case, you will have to develop the firmware yourself, which means creating the SecureBoot database in the firmware. Make sure that any option ROMs (aka UEFI drivers) from add-on board vendors are signed and included in the SecureBoot database. The tasks required to create your own firmware are beyond the scope of this book, but the Microsoft Docs site covers the details for OEMs who choose to build their own hardware.

With many OEMs creating different versions of UEFI firmware, there is a risk an exploit or flaw could occur during the launch of Windows. Since Boot Manager and Winload are still interacting with the UEFI firmware, a gate or boundary between UEFI and Windows Kernel launching is needed. SecureLaunch adds a measured trusted boundary that splits the boot process from an untrusted UEFI boot process to loading Windows. For completeness, SecureLaunch used to be known as SystemGuard. The UEFI code can still run, but any information needed to load the kernel is passed through a Dynamic Root of Trust (DRTM) event and a RAM disk. The TPM is used in the DRTM event process to measure any changes during the transition from UEFI to launching the Windows kernel. A different loader called Trusted Computing Base (TCB) performs the launching of the Windows Kernel. There is also the System Management Mode (SMM) CPU that handles power management, thermal monitoring, and other hardware items. Attackers could exploit the SMM to gain access to other functions in the system such as memory, I/O, and the CPU registers. When enabled SecureLaunch protects the SMM bus as well. SecureLaunch can be set up by Group Policy or using registry keys. We will cover the setup a little later.

8.12 Hypervisor-protected Code Integrity (HVCI)

To protect against malware attacking the kernel, Hypervisor-protected Code Integrity (HVCI) is a virtualization-based security (VBS) solution that isolates critical functions from the rest of the operating system. For example, an exploit could attack the kernel and gain access to sensitive memory and I/O. Local Security Authority (LSA) can be optionally protected by VBS.

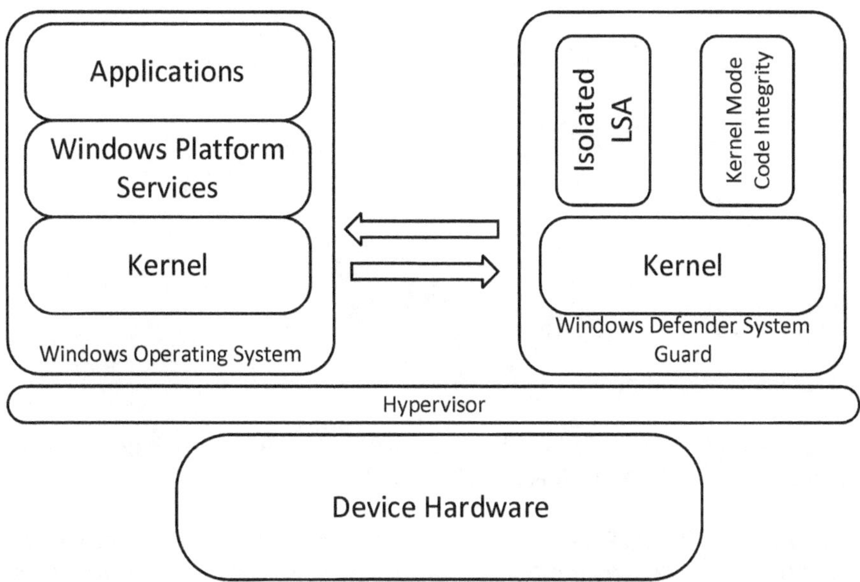

HVCI runs at a higher trusted level than the kernel. HVCI monitors the kernel code and only allows the code to run if it is legitimate. Optionally, HVCI can protect the Local Security

Authority (LSA). The option is known as Credential Guard. Device drivers have to be signed with an EV certificate to be able to use HVCI. Microsoft has been working with hardware vendors to make sure drivers are signed. The hardware must support booting UEFI and have hypervisor capability. HVCI is enabled by Group Policy, registry keys, or a PowerShell script, which leads us to the next section.

8.13 Device Guard (SecureBoot, Secure Launch, HVCI/DG/CG) and the Credential Guard Readiness Tool

How do we enable SecureBoot, SecureLaunch, and HVCI/DG/CG? SecureBoot gets set up and enabled in the firmware. HVCI/DG/CG and Secure Launch can be enabled in three different ways.

8.13.1 Enable with Group Policy

First, is the Group Policy in Computer Configuration->Administrative Templates->System->Device Guard->Turn on Virtualization Based Security.

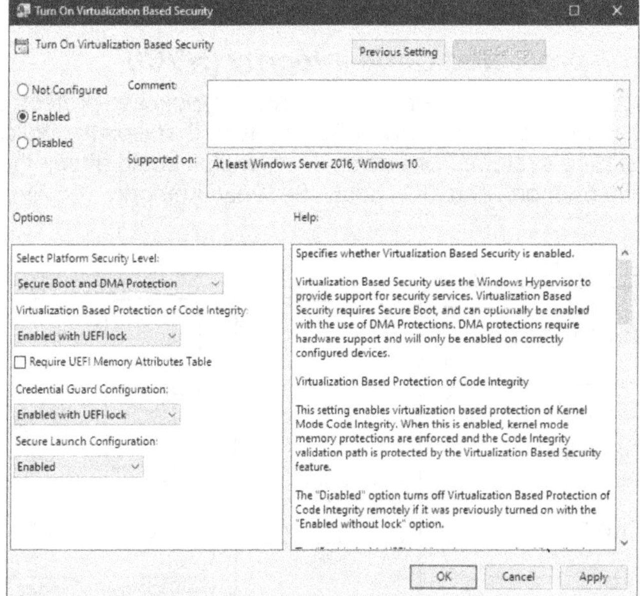

Here are the different options:

- Select Platform Security Level – SecureBoot has to be enabled in the firmware. The selection is to add DMA protection or not.

- Virtualization-Based Protection of Code Integrity – This enables Kernel Mode Code Integrity. There are two enable options. The first is "Enabled with UEFI lock", which blocks remote users from disabling the feature. A physical user must be preset to disable the feature, which requires a reboot. “Enabled without lock” allows the feature to be disabled remotely.

To enable Virtualization-Based Protection of Code Integrity, the firmware must support the UEFI Memory Attributes Table. This is part of what goes into working with the board vendor to make sure that the UEFI firmware has internal signed drivers. All Windows drivers in the system must be compatible with the feature or the system may crash. The Device Guard Readiness tool that we will talk about can check for compatibility.

- Credential Guard Configuration – This option enables the protection of the system credentials. There are two enable options. The first is “Enabled with UEFI lock”, which blocks remote users from disabling the feature. A physical user must be preset to disable the feature, which requires a reboot. “Enabled without lock” allows the feature to be disabled remotely.

- Secure Launch – Enabling this option adds Secure Launch to the boot chain.

8.13.2 Enable with Registry Keys

The second method to enable the different features and options is using registry keys. The actual key and a reg.exe command are listed below.

- To enable VBS “Turn on Virtual Based Security”

```
Key: "HKLM\SYSTEM\CurrentControlSet\Control\DeviceGuard"
Name: “EnableVirtualizationBasedSecurity"
Type: REG_DWORD
Date: 1
```

```
reg add "HKLM\SYSTEM\CurrentControlSet\Control\DeviceGuard" /v "EnableVirtualizationBasedSecurity" /t REG_DWORD /d 1 /f
```

- Select Platform Security Level

  - To enable VBS and require Secure boot only (value 1)

```
Key: "HKLM\SYSTEM\CurrentControlSet\Control\DeviceGuard"
Name: “RequirePlatformSecurityFeatures"
Type: REG_DWORD
Date: 1
```

```
reg add "HKLM\SYSTEM\CurrentControlSet\Control\DeviceGuard" /v "RequirePlatformSecurityFeatures" /t REG_DWORD /d 1 /f
```

  - To enable VBS with Secure Boot and DMA (value 3)

```
Key: "HKLM\SYSTEM\CurrentControlSet\Control\DeviceGuard"
Name: “RequirePlatformSecurityFeatures"
Type: REG_DWORD
```

```
Date: 1

reg add "HKLM\SYSTEM\CurrentControlSet\Control\DeviceGuard" /v "RequirePlatformSecurityFeatures" /t REG_DWORD /d 3 /f
```

- Virtualization-Based Protection of Code Integrity
  - To enable HVCI

```
Key:
"HKLM\SYSTEM\CurrentControlSet\Control\DeviceGuard\Scenarios\HypervisorEnforcedCodeIntegrity"
Name: "Enabled"
Type: REG_DWORD
Date: 1

reg add "HKLM\SYSTEM\CurrentControlSet\Control\DeviceGuard\Scenarios\HypervisorEnforcedCodeIntegrity" /v "Enabled" /t REG_DWORD /d 1 /f
```

  - To enable virtualization-based protection of Code Integrity policies without UEFI lock (value 0).

```
Key:
"HKLM\SYSTEM\CurrentControlSet\Control\DeviceGuard\Scenarios\HypervisorEnforcedCodeIntegrity"
Name: "Locked"
Type: REG_DWORD
Date: 0

reg add "HKLM\SYSTEM\CurrentControlSet\Control\DeviceGuard\Scenarios\HypervisorEnforcedCodeIntegrity" /v "Locked" /t REG_DWORD /d 0 /f
```

  - To enable virtualization-based protection of Code Integrity policies with UEFI lock (value 1). There are two keys to set:

```
Key:
"HKLM\SYSTEM\CurrentControlSet\Control\DeviceGuard\Scenarios\HypervisorEnforcedCodeIntegrity"
Name: "Locked"
Type: REG_DWORD
Date: 0

reg add "HKLM\SYSTEM\CurrentControlSet\Control\DeviceGuard\Scenarios\HypervisorEnforcedCodeIntegrity" /v "Locked" /t REG_DWORD /d 1 /f

Key: "HKLM\SYSTEM\CurrentControlSet\Control\DeviceGuard"
Name: "Locked"
Type: REG_DWORD
```

```
Date: 1

reg add "HKLM\SYSTEM\CurrentControlSet\Control\DeviceGuard" /v "Locked" /t REG_DWORD /d 0 /f
```

- Credential Guard Configuration
    - To Enable Credential Guard

```
Key: "HKLM\SYSTEM\CurrentControlSet\Control\DeviceGuard\
Scenarios\CredentialGuard"
Name: "Enabled"
Type: REG_DWORD
Date: 1

reg add " HKLM\SYSTEM\CurrentControlSet\Control\DeviceGuard\
Scenarios\CredentialGuard " /v "Enabled" /t REG_DWORD /d 1 /f
```

- To enable Credential Guard without UEFI lock (value 0)

```
Key: "HKLM\SYSTEM\CurrentControlSet\Control\DeviceGuard"
Name: "Locked"
Type: REG_DWORD
Date: 1

reg add "HKLM\SYSTEM\CurrentControlSet\Control\DeviceGuard" /v "Locked" /t REG_DWORD /d 0 /f
```

- To enable Credential Guard with UEFI lock (value 1)

```
Key: "HKLM\SYSTEM\CurrentControlSet\Control\DeviceGuard"
Name: "Locked"
Type: REG_DWORD
Date: 1

reg add "HKLM\SYSTEM\CurrentControlSet\Control\DeviceGuard" /v "Locked" /t REG_DWORD /d 1 /f
```

Note: if HVCI (VBS) has UEFI Locked, then the Locked value needs to be 1.

- To Enabled Secure Launch

```
Key: "HKLM\SYSTEM\CurrentControlSet\Control\DeviceGuard\Scenarios\"
Name: "Enabled"
Type: REG_DWORD
Date: 1

reg add "HKLM\SYSTEM\CurrentControlSet\Control\DeviceGuard\Scenarios\
SystemGuard" /v "Enabled" /t REG_DWORD /d 1 /f
```

8.13.3 Check and Enable with Windows Defender Device Guard and Windows Defender Credential Guard Readiness Tool

The third method to enable HVCI, Device Guard, and Credential Guard is to use the Windows Defender Device and Windows Defender Credential Guard Readiness Tool PowerShell script (aka DGreadiness tool). The script performs two functions. The first is to check to see if the system supports HVCI and Device Guard, and the second is to enable/disable HVCI. As of this writing, there are two versions of the DGreadiness script available Version 3.6.x. and Version 3.7.x. Version 3.6 is part of a download, and Version 3.7 is found on a docs.microsoft.com page: Windows Defender Device Guard and Windows Defender Credential Guard hardware readiness tool - Windows security | Microsoft Docs. I recommend that you use the latest version 3.7.x available.

```
Usage:  DG_Readiness.ps1  -[Capable/Ready/Enable/Disable/Clear]  -
[DG/CG/HVCI] -[AutoReboot] -Path <Path to the SIPolicy file>

DG_Readiness.ps1 /? Will bring up the help
```

Here are examples of the usage:

```
To Enable only HVCI
Usage: DG_Readiness.ps1 -Enable -HVCI

To Enable only CG
Usage: DG_Readiness.ps1 -Enable -CG

To Verify if DG/CG is enabled
Usage: DG_Readiness.ps1 -Ready

To Disable DG/CG.
Usage: DG_Readiness.ps1 -Disable

To Verify if DG/CG is disabled
Usage: DG_Readiness.ps1 -Ready

To Verify if this device is DG/CG Capable
Usage: DG_Readiness.ps1 -Capable

To Verify if this device is HVCI Capable
Usage: DG_Readiness.ps1 -Capable -HVCI
```

There are separate options to enable HVCI, Device Guard, and Credential Guard; but to enable all of them, just perform the following:

```
DG_Readiness.ps1 -Enable
```

To check if the system is capable of supporting HVCI and Device Guard, you would run the following: DG_Readiness.ps1 -Capable. The system will have to be rebooted. As the system boots, a log file is generated: C:\DGLogs\DeviceGuardCheckLog.txt. The same call to the script needs to be run again to generate the final report. The check performs 10 steps:

- Step 1: Driver compatibility – all drivers must be EV signed. The step checks to see if the drivers will work with HVCI.
- Step 2: Secure boot present – checks to see if SecureBoot is enabled in the firmware.
- Step 3: Microsoft UEFI HSTI Tests – Hardware Security Test Interface (HSTI) is something that can be added to the firmware to provide Windows with a method to check the low-level security.
- Step 4: OS Architecture – Just verifies the system is 64-Bit.
- Step 5: Supported OS SKU: Only Windows Enterprise and Server SKUs are supported.
- Step 6: Virtualization Firmware – A check is made to see if the firmware has the processor virtualization enabled: Intel VT-x, Intel VT-d, AMD-v, and AMD-vi.
- Step 7: TPM version – Checks the TPM version.
- Step 8: Secure MOR – Checks to see if the MemoryOverwriteRequestControlLock (MOR) is in the UEFI firmware. MOR is to aid in protecting against low-level attacks on the system.
- Step 9: NX Protector- also known as Data Execution Prevention (DEP). Protects against buffer overflow attacks.
- Step 10: SMM Mitigation – Protection for the System Management Mode (SMM) CPU.

The final report will list detailed results for each step, provide a summary, and state whether HVCI or Device Guard can be enabled on the machine. If everything checks out, you can simply enable HVCI/DG: DG_Readiness.ps1 -Enable and reboot the system. If you need to disable HVCI/DG/CG, the call to DG_Readiness.ps1 -Disable requires a reboot. Once rebooted, there will be a screen that appears asking you to hit the Windows key to disable HVCI/DG/CG. This is the human interaction check that we discussed earlier if someone tries to disable HVCI/DG/CG remotely. Exercise 802 will cover using a script.

8.14 Exercise 802 – Device Guard Readiness Tool

We will re-use Exercise 801 to develop a test for the Device Guard Readiness tool. The exercise is best used with an image that is running on real hardware.

8.14.1 Check the System

1. Make sure the image from Exercise 801 is running on your target.
2. Make sure you are in the WinAdmin account.
3. Either download or get the latest DGReadiness script from Microsoft.com.
4. Put the DGReadiness.PS1 script in the C:\setup folder of the target.
5. Open Windows PowerShell with Administrative privileges.

6. Change to the c:\setup folder
7. Run the following:

```
Set-ExecutionPolicy -ExecutionPolicy RemoteSigned
```

8. A question will appear. Hit the 'A' key and hit enter.
9. Run the script as follows:

```
DGReadiness.PS1 -capable
```

The output will be similar to the following:

```
###########################################################################

Readiness Tool Version 3.7.2 Release.
Tool to check if your device is capable to run Device Guard and Credential Guard.

###########################################################################

###########################################################################
OS and Hardware requirements for enabling Device Guard and Credential Guard
 1. OS SKUs: Available only on these OS Skus - Enterprise, Server, Education and
Enterprise IoT
 2. Hardware: Recent hardware that supports virtualization extension with SLAT
To learn more please visit: https://aka.ms/dgwhcr
###########################################################################

Checking if the device is DG/CG Capable
 ===================== Step 1 Driver Compat =====================
Enabling Driver verifier

Verifier Flags: 0x02001000

  Standard Flags:

    [ ] 0x00000001 Special pool.
    [ ] 0x00000002 Force IRQL checking.
    [ ] 0x00000008 Pool tracking.
    [ ] 0x00000010 I/O verification.
    [ ] 0x00000020 Deadlock detection.
    [ ] 0x00000080 DMA checking.
    [ ] 0x00000100 Security checks.
    [ ] 0x00000800 Miscellaneous checks.
    [ ] 0x00020000 DDI compliance checking.

  Additional Flags:

    [ ] 0x00000004 Randomized low resources simulation.
    [ ] 0x00000200 Force pending I/O requests.
    [ ] 0x00000400 IRP logging.
    [ ] 0x00002000 Invariant MDL checking for stack.
    [ ] 0x00004000 Invariant MDL checking for driver.
    [ ] 0x00008000 Power framework delay fuzzing.
    [ ] 0x00010000 Port/miniport interface checking.
    [ ] 0x00040000 Systematic low resources simulation.
    [ ] 0x00080000 DDI compliance checking (additional).
    [ ] 0x00200000 NDIS/WIFI verification.
```

```
    [ ] 0x00800000 Kernel synchronization delay fuzzing.
    [ ] 0x01000000 VM switch verification.
    [X] 0x02000000 Code integrity checks.

  Internal Flags:

    [X] 0x00001000 Additional debug information.

    [X] Indicates flag is enabled.

  Advanced Options:

    Log Only Code Integrity Statistics

  Boot Mode:

    Oneboot

  Rules:

    All rules are using default settings

  Verified Drivers:

    All Drivers

The system reboot is required for the changes to take effect.
Enabling Driver Verifier and Rebooting system
Please re-execute this script after reboot....
Please reboot manually and run the script again....
```

10. Reboot the system.
11. After the system has been booted, open Windows PowerShell with Administrative privileges.
12. Change to the C:\setup folder
13. Run the following:

```
DGReadiness.PS1 -capable
```

The script will process the results from the reboot and generate a report listing the results from the 10 steps and a summary if HVCI can be enabled.

Failure result:

```
====================== Summary ======================
Machine is not Device Guard / Credential Guard compatible because of the following:
Secure boot validation failed.

Incompatible HVCI Kernel Driver Modules found
NX Protector is absent
SMM Mitigation is absent
```

Successful result:

```
====================== Summary ======================
```

```
Device Guard / Credential Guard can be enabled on this machine.

The following additional qualifications, if present, can enhance the security of
Device Guard / Credential Guard on this system:
HSTI is absent

To learn more about required hardware and software please visit:
https://aka.ms/dgwhcr
```

8.14.2 Enable Disabled HVCI/DG/CG

If the script shows that HVCI/DG/CG can be enabled perform the following:

1. Boot into the BIOS and make sure that SecureBoot is enabled.
2. Let the system boot.
3. Open Windows PowerShell with Administrative privileges.
4. Change to the C:\setup folder.
5. Run the following:

```
DGReadiness.PS1 -Enable
```

6. Reboot the system.
7. After the system reboots, you can check the status. Open Windows PowerShell with Administrative privileges.
8. Change to the c:\setup folder
9. Run the following:

```
DGReadiness.PS1 -Ready
```

10. HVCI/DG/CG should show that they are enabled.

```
########################################################################
##

Readiness Tool Version 3.7.2 Release.
Tool to check if your device is capable to run Device Guard and Credential
Guard.

########################################################################
##

########################################################################
##
OS and Hardware requirements for enabling Device Guard and Credential Guard
 1. OS SKUs: Available only on these OS Skus - Enterprise, Server, Education
and Enterprise IoT
 2. Hardware: Recent hardware that supports virtualization extension with
SLAT
To learn more please visit: https://aka.ms/dgwhcr
########################################################################
##
```

```
Credential-Guard is enabled and running.
HVCI is enabled and running.
Config-CI is enabled and running. (Enforced mode)
HVCI, Credential Guard, and Config CI are enabled and running.
```

11. To disable HVCI/DG/CG run the following:

```
DGReadiness.PS1 -Disable
```

12. Reboot the system.
13. As the system reboots, you will be asked to hit the Windows key to confirm disabling HVCI/DG/CG. Hit the Windows key and let the system boot.
14. You can check to see that HVCI/DG/CG is disabled by running the script again with the -Ready option.

8.15 Complete Windows Boot Process

Now that we have covered all the firmware for virtual-based security, the diagram below is my attempt to show the whole boot process with all the new security measures in place. Showing the whole boot process on a printed page is difficult because you have an image of a long train of connected boxes that make up the whole sequence. Much thought and development have gone into securing Windows from power-on. With more hooks being made into the firmware, I wouldn't be surprised if someday installing trusted UEFI firmware is part of installing Windows.

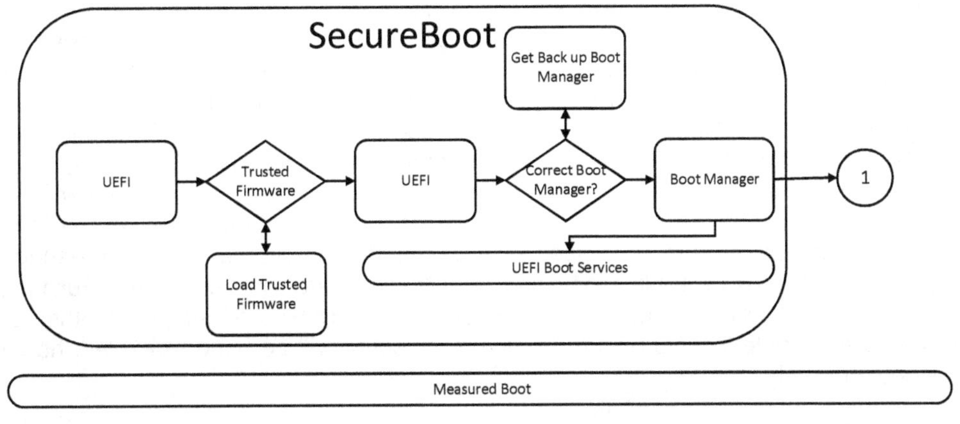

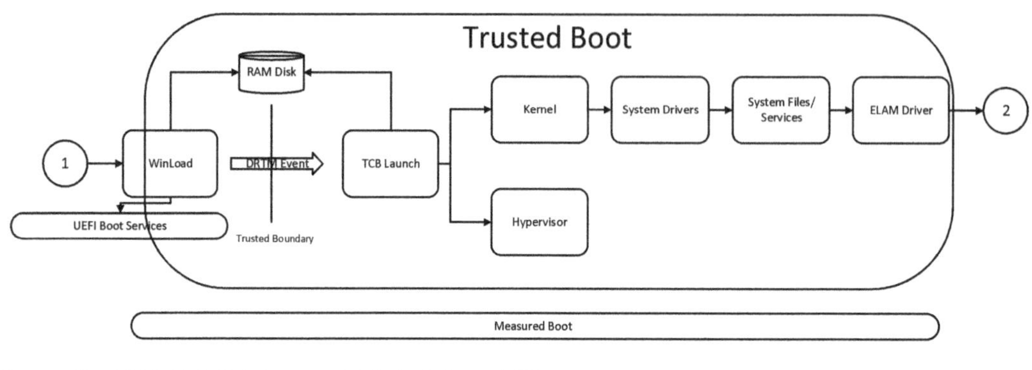

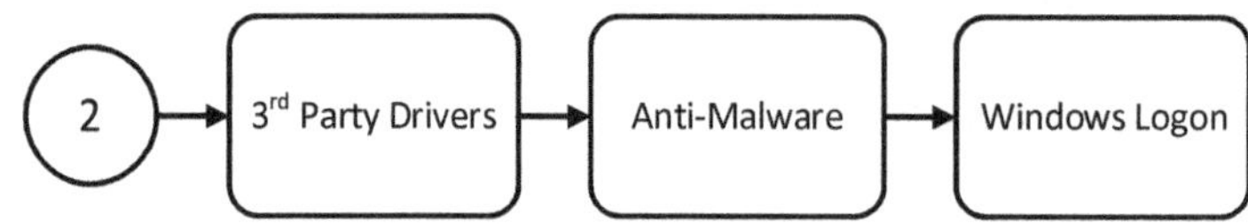

8.16 Windows Defender Application Control (WDAC)

Last, but not least, is Windows Defender Application Control. WDAC is the replacement for the old AppLocker feature. Like a bouncer at a bar, WDAC reviews what is on the guest list to run in the system. If an application is on the guest list, the application will run. If the application is not on the guest list, the application is blocked and a block event is sent to the Event Log. WDAC doesn't have any hardware requirements. Regardless of whether HVCI/DG/CG can be implemented or not, WDAC is an important security feature to implement. WDAC's only relationship to HVCI/DG/CG is the previously mentioned Device Guard Readiness script that can enable and disable WDAC as well. Like all the other security features, the WDAC documentation has been all over the place. As of this writing, the WDAC documentation has been pulled together on the Microsoft Docs site, but it is lengthy in its explanation. The documentation is trying to reach a wide audience that includes IT departments running multiple generic computers on a network. Different scenarios are presented and addressed. The key to all the documentation is creating the WDAC Policy, the list of applications and features that are allowed to run. For single-purposed devices, like Embedded/IoT systems, the process is simple. Rather than interpreting the whole WDAC document, a simple script will be used to explain how the policy gets created.

8.16.1 WDAC Policy File

A WDAC policy file is an XML file that gets converted to a binary file (.p7b file). The binary file gets placed in a specific directory of Windows. Two methods can be used to create the WDAC Policy file. The first is a PowerShell script that uses WDAC CMDLETs and the second is a WDAC Policy Wizard. The PowerShell script is the best way to understand how the WDAC Policy is created, so we will focus on this one first.

There are two key elements to a WDAC policy file: File Rules and Policy Rules. The best page on docs.microsoft.com for WDAC information is here: Understand Windows

Defender Application Control (WDAC) policy rules and file rule: https://docs.microsoft.com/en-us/windows/security/threat-protection/windows-defender-application-control/select-types-of-rules-to-create

Here is an example of a PowerShell script that creates a policy file based on common file and policy rules

```
1   #Generates the Windows Defender Application Control policy
2
3   #Create audit policy first
4   New-CIPolicy -Level PcaCertificate -Fallback Hash -FilePath "c:\setup\AuditPolicy.xml" -UserPEs 3> CIPolicylog.txt
5
6   #Add Policy Option
7   Set-RuleOption -FilePath "c:\setup\AuditPolicy.xml" -Option 10
8
9   #Create Separate Policy XML file for enforcement
10  copy "c:\setup\AuditPolicy.xml" "c:\setup\EnforcedCIPolicy.xml"
11
12  #Remove Audit mode
13  Set-RuleOption -FilePath "c:\setup\EnforcedCIPolicy.xml" -Option 3 -Delete
14
15  #Create the SIPolicy.p7b file
16  ConvertFrom-CIPolicy -XmlFilePath "c:\setup\EnforcedCIPolicy.xml" -BinaryFilePath "c:\setup\SIPolicy.p7b"
```

Line 4 is the most important line:

```
New-CIPolicy -Level PcaCertificate -Fallback Hash -FilePath "c:\setup\AuditPolicy.xml" -UserPEs 3> CIPolicylog.txt
```

The New-CIPolicy CMDLET creates the new policy file. The -Level and -Fallback options are for setting the file rules. You can have a primary rule -Level and a secondary rule -Fallback. Microsoft Docs lists 11 file rule levels:

- Hash
- FileName
- FilePath
- SignedVersion
- Publisher
- FilePublisher
- LearCertificate
- PcaCertificate
- RootCertificate, WHQL
- WHQLPublisher
- WHQLFilePublisher.

Note: RootCertificate is listed but not supported. The WHQL is for creating a driver policy, and Windows includes a driver policy by default. The rest are for applications.

The script uses PcaCertificate as the primary rule and Hash as the secondary rule, which I recommend for Embedded/IoT systems. Any file that doesn't have a code signing certificate that is picked up by the PcaCertificate rule will have a hash code in the final policy file. You may choose a different level of certificate to support. The choice is yours.

Hash is the strictest level. Could you hash all the files in the policy? The problem with that approach is that when an application needs to be updated, so does the policy file with the new hash. It takes time for the script to run to generate the new policy file. The PcaCertificate as the primary rule is the best option to allow for application updates without having to create a new WDAC policy file each time an application is updated. You will want a code signing certificate for all your applications. There is a very important note about certificate signing keys in Microsoft Docs:

Note: WDAC only supports signer rules for RSA certificate signing keys with a maximum of 4096 bits.

Where Azure and device driver development require high-level certificates, WDAC is at a lower level. This may change in the future, so please keep an eye on the Microsoft Docs site for any updates. You will have to work with your certificate authority to get the right certificate. Once you have the certificate, you can install the public key into the certificate store by calling the following Pass 7 synchronous command:

```
certutil.exe -addstore -f root "<path>mycertificate.cer"
```

Next on the command line is –FilePath, which is for the full path to the XML file. -UserPEs tells the command to include all user applications. Without the -UserPEs, all user applications will be blocked regardless of the file rules. 3>CIPolicylog.txt will log any issues during the generation of the policy file to the CIPolicylog.txt file.

There are 21 policy rules that can be set in the WDAC Policy file. On the Microsoft Docs webpage mentioned earlier, there is a nice table that lists the details of each rule. New-CIPolicy will generate a policy with 4 of the 21 rules by default:

- Enabled:Unsigned System Integrity Policy
- Enabled:Audit Mode
- Enabled:Advanced Boot Options Menu
- Required:Enforce Store Applications

The -UserPEs option adds Enabled:UMCI. Line 7 from the script above demonstrates adding a Policy Rule by adding Enabled:Boot Audit On Failure. A couple of the defaults are interesting to note. The first is Enable: Audit Mode. The Policy XML file that gets generated is for Audit mode, which is helpful to test the policy without enforcing the policy. Any potential blocks will be recorded in the Event Log. Audit Mode allows you to modify the XML file to test different File and Policy rules or merge different WDAC Policy files. The second is the Enabled:Advanced Boot Options Menu, which is the F8 key on boot. The option will override the Microsoft-Windows-Embedded-BootExp component's DisableBootMenu option. If you want to remove the option and block the F8 key, add the following to the script after line 7:

```
Set-RuleOption -FilePath "c:\setup\AuditPolicy.xml" -Option 9 -Delete
```

Line 10 creates a copy of the XML file that will turn into the enforced policy. Line 13 removes the Enable:Audit Mode options from the new EnforcedCIPolicy XML file. Line 16 creates the final .p7b binary file that Windows uses to enforce the WDAC policy. Once you have a working policy file, a best-known practice is to save the XML files as these can be used for future editing or be merged with other policy files.

Inside the WDAC policy XML files, you can see a specific layout that covers the Rules (Policy Rules), FileRules, and Signatures (Certificates). The resulting XML file is a couple of thousand lines long. To show the different sections, the XML listing below is a “reduced” version of an original XML. The XML was generated on a system that didn't pass the Device Guard Readiness tool, thus the device driver that shows up needed a hash. There is a SigningScenerios section, which split the FileRules IDs between drivers and Windows. The Certificates are also linked with signer IDs under the AllowedSigners section. Normally, you wouldn't have to worry about understanding the details of the XML file, but there is always an odd case that needs to be addressed manually.

```
<?xml version="1.0" encoding="utf-8"?>
<SiPolicy xmlns="urn:schemas-microsoft-com:sipolicy">
  <VersionEx>10.0.0.0</VersionEx>
  <PlatformID>{2E07F7E4-194C-4D20-B7C9-6F44A6C5A234}</PlatformID>
  <Rules>
    <Rule>
      <Option>Enabled:Unsigned System Integrity Policy</Option>
    </Rule>
  </Rules>
  <!--EKUS-->
  <EKUs />
  <!--File Rules-->
  <FileRules>
    <Allow ID="ID_ALLOW_A_24B"
FriendlyName="C:\Windows\System32\drivers\BthA2dp.sys Hash Sha1"
Hash="D4D6C3A45A3EFD02E77057638E185E6F99BE91F4" />
    <Allow ID="ID_ALLOW_A_1"
FriendlyName="C:\Windows\WinSxS\x86_windows-defender-management-
powershell_31bf3856ad364e35_10.0.19041.1_none_3d95cd0a88523a81\Defe
nder.psd1 Hash Sha1"
Hash="572D3185360AED0F9E099795B19F274AE38516A3" />
  </FileRules>
  <!--Signers-->
  <Signers>
    <Signer ID="ID_SIGNER_S_1" Name="Microsoft Windows Production
PCA 2011">
```

```
      <CertRoot Type="TBS" Value="4E80BE107C860DE896384B3EFF50504DC2D76AC7151DF3102A4450637A032146" />
    </Signer>
    <Signer ID="ID_SIGNER_S_4D" Name="Microsoft Code Signing PCA 2011">
      <CertRoot Type="TBS" Value="F6F717A43AD9ABDDC8CEFDDE1C505462535E7D1307E630F9544A2D14FE8BF26E" />
    </Signer>
  </Signers>
  <!--Driver Signing Scenarios-->
  <SigningScenarios>
    <SigningScenario Value="131" ID="ID_SIGNINGSCENARIO_DRIVERS_1" FriendlyName="Auto generated policy on 02-17-2022">
      <ProductSigners>
        <FileRulesRef>
          <FileRuleRef RuleID="ID_ALLOW_A_24B" />
        </FileRulesRef>
        <AllowedSigners>
            <AllowedSigner SignerId="ID_SIGNER_S_4D" />
        </AllowedSigners>
      </ProductSigners>
    </SigningScenario>
    <SigningScenario Value="12" ID="ID_SIGNINGSCENARIO_WINDOWS" FriendlyName="Auto generated policy on 02-17-2022">
      <ProductSigners>
        <FileRulesRef>
          <FileRuleRef RuleID="ID_ALLOW_A_1" />
        </FileRulesRef>
        <AllowedSigners>
          <AllowedSigner SignerId="ID_SIGNER_S_1" />
        </AllowedSigners>
      </ProductSigners>
    </SigningScenario>
  </SigningScenarios>
  <UpdatePolicySigners />
  <CiSigners>
    <CiSigner SignerId="ID_SIGNER_S_1" />
  </CiSigners>
  <HvciOptions>0</HvciOptions>
  <PolicyTypeID>{A244370E-44C9-4C06-B551-F6016E563076}</PolicyTypeID>
</SiPolicy>
```

The script has generated a policy for allowable applications and drivers. For applications and drivers that you want to block or deny, you will have to modify the XML file to include a file rule. For example, if you wanted to deny Notepad.exe from running you have to add a FileRule:

```
<Deny ID="ID_DENY_NOTEPAD" FriendlyName="Notepad.exe"
FileName="c:\Windows\System32\notepad.exe"
MinimumFileVersion="10.0.19041.1566"/>
```

And add a reference in the SigningScenerios section:

```
<FileRuleRef RuleID="ID_DENY_NOTEPAD"/>
```

Here is an update to the example XML that includes the rule to deny notepad.exe.

```
<?xml version="1.0" encoding="utf-8"?>
<SiPolicy xmlns="urn:schemas-microsoft-com:sipolicy">
  <VersionEx>10.0.0.0</VersionEx>
  <PlatformID>{2E07F7E4-194C-4D20-B7C9-6F44A6C5A234}</PlatformID>
  <Rules>
    <Rule>
      <Option>Enabled:Unsigned System Integrity Policy</Option>
    </Rule>
  </Rules>
  <!--EKUS-->
  <EKUs />
  <!--File Rules-->
  <FileRules>
    <Allow ID="ID_ALLOW_A_24B"
FriendlyName="C:\Windows\System32\drivers\BthA2dp.sys Hash Sha1"
Hash="D4D6C3A45A3EFD02E77057638E185E6F99BE91F4" />
    <Allow ID="ID_ALLOW_A_1"
FriendlyName="C:\Windows\WinSxS\x86_windows-defender-management-
powershell_31bf3856ad364e35_10.0.19041.1_none_3d95cd0a88523a81\Defe
nder.psd1 Hash Sha1"
Hash="572D3185360AED0F9E099795B19F274AE38516A3" />
    <Deny ID="ID_DENY_NOTEPAD" FriendlyName="Notepad.exe"
FileName="c:\Windows\System32\notepad.exe"
MinimumFileVersion="10.0.19041.1566"/>
  </FileRules>
  <!--Signers-->
  <Signers>
    <Signer ID="ID_SIGNER_S_1" Name="Microsoft Windows Production
PCA 2011">
      <CertRoot Type="TBS"
Value="4E80BE107C860DE896384B3EFF50504DC2D76AC7151DF3102A4450637A03
2146" />
    </Signer>
    <Signer ID="ID_SIGNER_S_4D" Name="Microsoft Code Signing PCA
2011">
      <CertRoot Type="TBS"
Value="F6F717A43AD9ABDDC8CEFDDE1C505462535E7D1307E630F9544A2D14FE8B
F26E" />
    </Signer>
  </Signers>
  <!--Driver Signing Scenarios-->
  <SigningScenarios>
```

```
    <SigningScenario Value="131" ID="ID_SIGNINGSCENARIO_DRIVERS_1" FriendlyName="Auto generated policy on 02-17-2022">
      <ProductSigners>
        <FileRulesRef>
          <FileRuleRef RuleID="ID_ALLOW_A_24B" />
        </FileRulesRef>
        <AllowedSigners>
            <AllowedSigner SignerId="ID_SIGNER_S_4D" />
        </AllowedSigners>
      </ProductSigners>
    </SigningScenario>
    <SigningScenario Value="12" ID="ID_SIGNINGSCENARIO_WINDOWS" FriendlyName="Auto generated policy on 02-17-2022">
      <ProductSigners>
        <FileRulesRef>
          <FileRuleRef RuleID="ID_ALLOW_A_1" />
        </FileRulesRef>
        <FileRulesRef>
           <FileRuleRef RuleID="ID_DENY_NOTEPAD"/>
        </FileRulesRef>
        <AllowedSigners>
          <AllowedSigner SignerId="ID_SIGNER_S_1" />
        </AllowedSigners>
      </ProductSigners>
    </SigningScenario>
  </SigningScenarios>
  <UpdatePolicySigners />
  <CiSigners>
    <CiSigner SignerId="ID_SIGNER_S_1" />
  </CiSigners>
  <HvciOptions>0</HvciOptions>
  <PolicyTypeID>{A244370E-44C9-4C06-B551-F6016E563076}</PolicyTypeID>
</SiPolicy>
```

Once the policy file is created, WDAC can be enabled in three different ways:

1. Group Policy – Computer Configuration->Administrative Templates->System->Device Guard->Deploy Windows Defender Application Control. The policy allows you to point to the present location of the policy file. The file will be copied to the C:\Windows\System32\CodeIntegrity folder. A reboot must take place for the policy to be enabled.

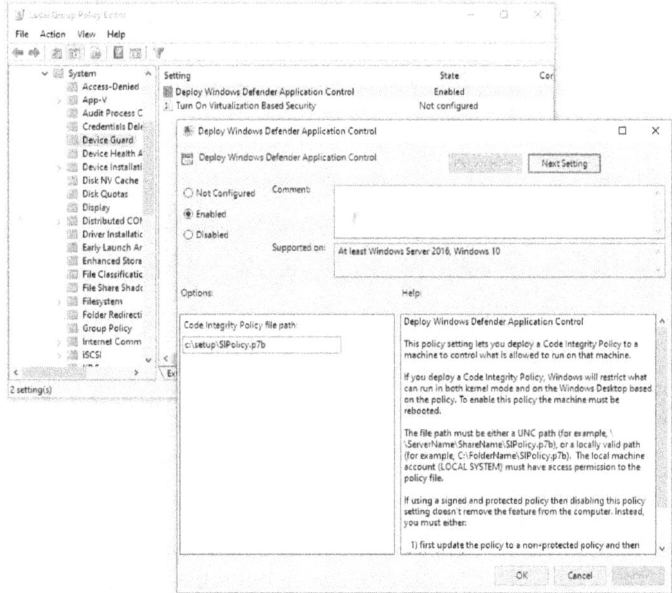

2. Copy the SIPolicy.p7b file to the C:\Windows\System32\CodeIntegrity folder. A reboot must take place for the policy to be enabled.
3. Use the Device Guard Readiness to import the WDAC policy file when enabling HVCI:

```
DG_Readiness.ps1 -Enable -SIPolicyPath c:\<path>\SIPolicy.p7b
```

To disable the WDAC policy file, delete the SIPolicy.p7b file from the C:\Windows\System32\CodIntegrity folder and reboot the system.

The second method to create a policy file is to use the WDAC Policy Wizard. The WDAC Policy Wizard provides some nice functions to create, edit, and merge policy files.

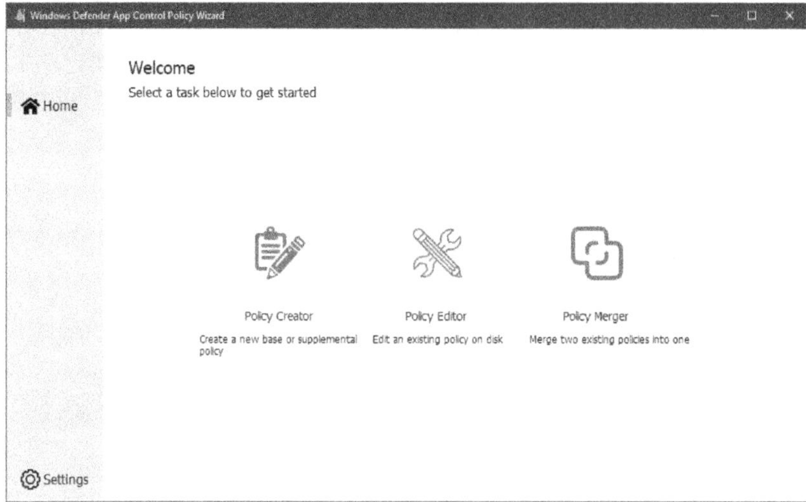

From my experience, the PowerShell script is the best way to generate the policy file on the target system, but WDAC Policy Wizard is very helpful with the other two functions. For example, you may need to add a file to your list of applications that are allowed or denied, the wizard simplifies editing the current policy so you can generate a new policy for your system.

8.16.2 Warning! PowerShell Language Modes, UWP, and Shell Launcher V2 Bridge Script Issues

Staying away from UWP applications has been mentioned in previous chapters. There is an important reason for this other than UWP is going away. When it comes to managing a system in the field and controlling the state of Shell Launcher. WDAC is a good security measure to implement regardless of the other security features. By default, WDAC sets PowerShell scripts to run in Constrained Language Mode. PowerShell Language modes determine what language elements can run during a given session. There are four language modes: Full Language, Restricted Language, No Language, and Constrained Language. Constrained Language mode blocks certain cmdlets from running. In the context of Shell Launcher V2, the cmdlets that are part of the Shell Launcher V2 Bridge script are blocked. Chapter 6 discusses the modifications required to pre-escape the XML file. Since signing UWP applications results in a different name every time you updated the application, Shell Launcher V2 has to be updated with the new name to address the application's update.

If you stick to .NET or .NET Framework applications (.EXE), you can simply use Shell Launcher V1 WMI APIs to manage Shell Launcher. An update to a .NET or .NET Framework application (.EXE) that is signed with a code signing certificate will not force any changes to Shell Launcher or WDAC policy. To finish this soap box warning, don't create or use UWP applications, and don't make UWP the shell of the system. Instead, create .NET or .NET Framework applications (.EXE) and use Shell Launcher V1 WMI to control the state of Shell Launcher.

8.17 Exercise 803: WDAC Policy Creation and Test

We will reuse the image from Exercises 801 and 802 to test WDAC. The AB-Test-App.exe will be used to test that the policy is working.

1. Make sure the image from Exercise 801 is running on your target.
2. Make sure you are in the WinAdmin account.
3. On the target system, if the AB-Test-App.exe application is in C:\Program Files\Annabooks folder, delete the application.
4. Create the WDAC-Policy.ps1 script on the target system:

```
#Generates the Windows Defender Application Control policy

#Create audit policy first
New-CIPolicy -Level PcaCertificate -Fallback Hash -FilePath "c:\setup\AuditPolicy.xml" -UserPEs 3> CIPolicylog.txt

#Add Policy Option
Set-RuleOption -FilePath "c:\setup\AuditPolicy.xml" -Option 10

#Create Separate Policy XML file for enforcement
copy "c:\setup\AuditPolicy.xml" "c:\setup\EnforcedCIPolicy.xml"

#Remove Audit mode
Set-RuleOption -FilePath "c:\setup\EnforcedCIPolicy.xml" -Option 3 -Delete

#Create the SIPolicy.p7b file
ConvertFrom-CIPolicy -XmlFilePath "c:\setup\EnforcedCIPolicy.xml" -BinaryFilePath "c:\setup\SIPolicy.p7b"
```

5. Open PowerShell with Administrative privileges, and run the WDAC-Policy.ps1. Since the script is generating the policy based on certificate and hash, the process will take some time.
6. Once finished, copy the SIPolicy.p7b file to the C:\Windows\System32\CodeIntegrity folder, and reboot the system.
7. Once the system has rebooted, you should be able to run programs that were present in the system when the policy file was created. For example, run notepad.
8. Copy the AB-Test-App.exe to C:\Program files\Annabooks folder, and try to run the application. A pop-up will appear to indicate the application has been blocked.
9. Open Event log, Applications and Services Logs->Microsoft->Windows->CodeIntegrity. You should see Errors.

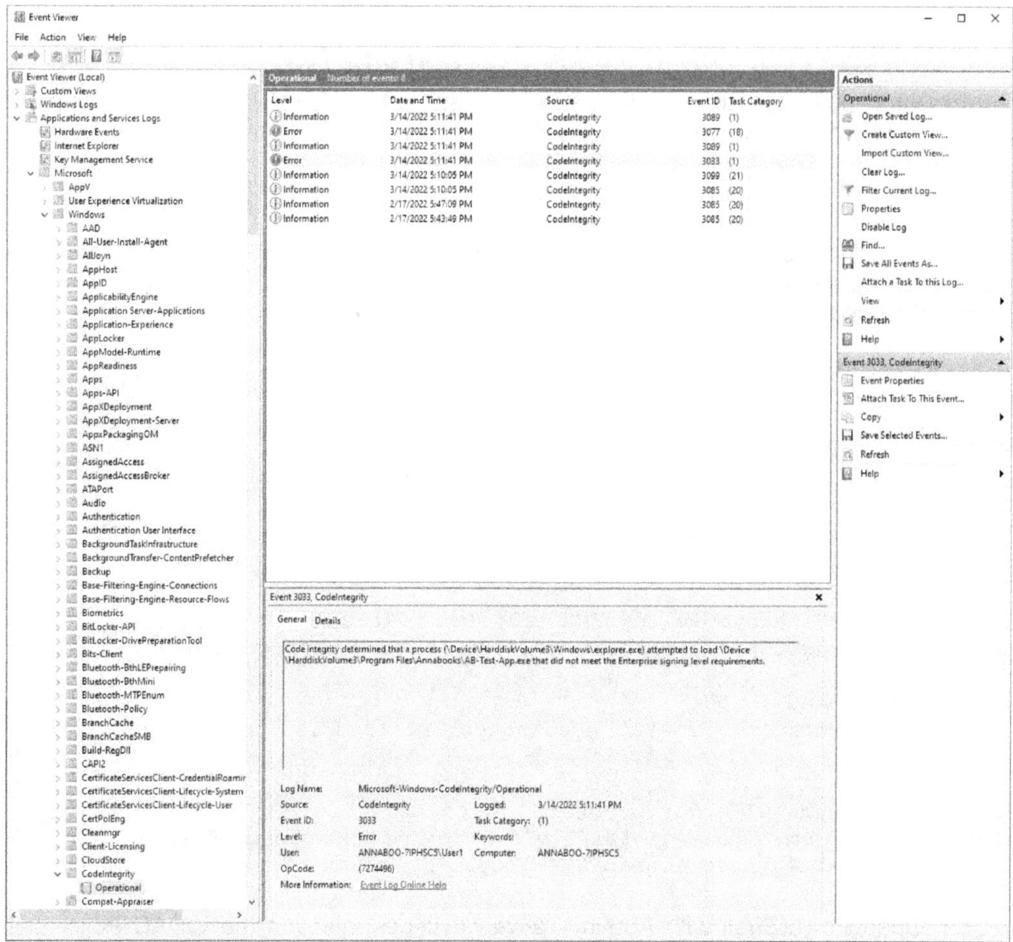

10. Click on the error and you will see that AB-Test-App.exe was blocked since the application is not part of the policy file.

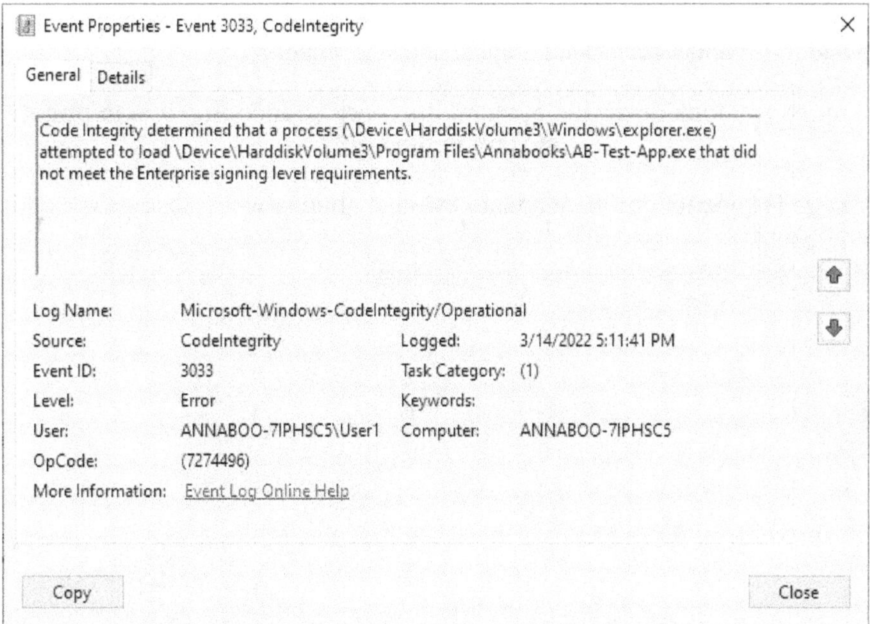

8.18 *Biosecurity Access*

The previous sections have covered the internal security features available in Windows 10. The only thing not covered is biosecurity access, which involves a bigger architecture plan to store and save biometric identities. Windows Hello is a feature to implement, but where the accounts are housed is something that needs to be determined. There hasn't been much interest in this feature, currently, but I may cover this in a future paper.

8.19 *Security from the Cloud for the End Customer*

With Microsoft focusing on the cloud, it makes sense they would have a cloud security solution. Microsoft Defender for Endpoint is a security cloud service where the devices are registered with the service. Microsoft Defender for Endpoint is an end customer solution so the end customer can monitor devices on their network. How an OEM sells Microsoft Defender for Endpoint as a solution is the greater question and something to explore in a future paper.

8.20 *Summary: How Much Do You Lock Down?*

The number of Windows security features has expanded greatly since Windows XP Service Pack 2. A constant and vigilant effort has been made to provide protection from power-on to shut down. All the security features discussed here are for the OEM to implement in the device. The biggest expansion is the hooks that have been made into the firmware. Maybe in the future when you install Windows, the firmware will also be part of the installation.

This chapter is the last of the lockdown chapters. There is one thing I mention in my training courses and the clients I assist with architecting their images:

"The more you lock down the system, the more challenging it is to update the system in the field."

The message is important as we lead into the next chapter which discusses updating the system.

9 Updates and Image Servicing

The last 3 chapters have focused on locking down the system. This chapter will discuss updating the system in the field, which brings me to my words of caution:

"The more you lock down the system, the more challenging it is to update the system in the field."

9.1 Servicing Plan: Architecture, Architecture, ... Architecture!

As you architect how the system is going to be locked down, you should keep in mind how the system will be upgraded or serviced in the field. Even though you are using the LTSC version, every month there are new security updates and hotfixes available. Microsoft has made Windows updates easier with cumulative updates every month so you don't have to apply past updates to make the system current. This is a big improvement for those who remember Windows XP Embedded. Some systems never get updated. For example, slot machines are never updated. The security is so strict that a CRC check is done on boot to make sure that the OS image has not changed, thus patching updates is not possible. For everyone else, if your system is connected to a network, it is a good idea to provide security updates. There are a number of questions to address when thinking about the servicing plan:

- What gets updated? applications, drivers, patches, etc.?
- When do updates go out? Most companies provide updates once or twice a year?
- How is the update delivered to the device: remotely, via a field technician, or mailed to the customer?
- Who performs the update: Remote, field technician, or client?
- What is the best cost-effective way to support systems in the field?
- Do you add a second account to handle the updates?
- Do you create a custom update application to keep users from seeing that Windows is in the system?
- What about UWF?
- Does the WDAC Policy have to be updated?
- Are there any changes to Shell Launcher configuration?

All of these questions and more need to be addressed while you are architecting the image.

9.2 Update Solutions

There are a plethora of Windows Embedded\IoT systems, which means there is no single solution that fits all systems. You are on your own to develop an update solution for your system. These are some common solutions that I see clients implementing:

- Update on a USB stick or a DVD – An update is placed on a USB disk. The update includes a script to apply the update. The system boots up and the custom shell or applications see the update on the USB drive. The shell or applications will then perform any actions to address UWF and other security items and then run the script. Once completed, any actions to enable UWF or other security items will be addressed.

- Full image replacement – Simplest update is to wipe out the image and replace it with a new one. Boot from a WinPE USB disk, and use DISM to apply an FFU just like installing the image during development. If data has to be preserved, the data is copied to a safe location first. Once the image has been applied, the data is put back onto the system.

- WinPE on a separate partition – This solution can be done, but I have only implemented it in practice 3 times. A second bootable partition can boot to WinPE and replace the C drive partition with a WIM file. The solution can be used for system recovery or updating the OS image.

What about remote updates from the cloud? There have been some 3rd-party remote update solutions, but these are very rare. You could create your own cloud solution. With the Azure push from Microsoft, you would think that they would have a solution for remote cloud connection and update. Microsoft has been pushing the updates from the cloud idea since 2014. We will have to see if they will actually deliver a solution. Regardless of the mechanism you choose for the updates, the solution needs to be architected at design-time of the image.

9.3 UWF Servicing Mode

If you are using Unified Write Filter (UWF) to protect the operating system, UWF will have to be disabled before any updates are applied. From the above solutions, many clients have implemented a solution to disable UWF, set a servicing flag, and then reboot the system. After the system has rebooted, the update can be processed, the servicing flag can be reset, UWF can then be enabled, and finally, the system can be rebooted. There is the UWF Service Mode that can be set using the uwfmgr.exe or the WMI API. With UWF Servicing Mode on after a reboot, the system will show a UWF screen saver (UwfServicingScr.scr) and run UwfServicingMasterScript.cmd that is found in the C:\Windows\System32 folder. This will trigger Windows Update to run and download the latest updates. You can modify the script to add your own custom updates or even skip Windows Updates from running. If you prefer not to use the UwfServicingScr.scr, there is a registry key that can be set to create a custom message on the screen.

```
[HKEY_LOCAL_MACHINE\Software\Microsoft\Windows Embedded\ServicingScreenSaver]
```

```
"ColorBackground"=dword:000000ff
"ColorText"=dword:0000ff00
"ColorProgress"=dword:00ff0000
"ScreenSaverTitle"=" System Update"
"ScreenSaverSubTitle"="System updates are being installed… Please wait"
"HideScreenSaverText"=dword:00000000
"HideScreenSaverProgress"=dword:00000000
"Font"="Arial"
```

Warning: UWF Servicing Mode is ideal for thin clients. I have seen posts from other folks that have run into problems where the system gets stuck in the UWF servicing mode or the custom screen saver doesn't appear.

9.4 Disable Windows Update: Control Thy System

Disabling Windows Update may sound counter to supporting the system in the field, but you will want to control the updates that get put on the system and when they get applied. There have been times when an update has broken something in the system. If this happens to systems in the field, your company will take a hit in support calls. My suggestion is to disable Windows Update so you don't have little grenades going off. From the workflow discussion in Chapter 2, after the initial installation of the image and all the custom setup that has to be performed, run Windows Update so the master image gets all the latest updates and patches. You will have to reboot and re-run Windows Update to get all the updates. Once finished, you will want to clean up the system by performing the following:

1. Open PowerShell as Administrator, and run the following:

   Dism.exe /online /Cleanup-Image /StartComponentCleanup /Resetbase

2. Run Disk clean-up to remove all excess items. Open Control Panel ->Administrative Tools->Disk Cleanup:
   a. Select drive C.
   b. Click on the Cleanup System Files button.
   c. Select drive C.
   d. Select all items in the list.
   e. Click OK and Click Delete Files.
3. Reboot the system.

At this point, you can run Sysprep and capture the master image. In your Sysprep unattended file, Windows Update should be disabled by running the following commands:

```
reg.exe add HKLM\SOFTWARE\Policies\Microsoft\Windows\WindowsUpdate /v
DoNotConnectToWindowsUpdateInternetLocations /t REG_DWORD /d 1 /f
reg.exe add HKLM\SOFTWARE\Policies\Microsoft\Windows\WindowsUpdate /v
ExcludeWUDriversInQualityUpdate /t REG_DWORD /d 1 /f
reg.exe add HKLM\SOFTWARE\Policies\Microsoft\Windows\WindowsUpdate /v
SetDisableUXWUAccess /t REG_DWORD /d 1 /f
reg.exe add HKLM\SOFTWARE\Policies\Microsoft\Windows\WindowsUpdate\AU /v
NoAutoUpdate /t REG_DWORD /d 1 /f
Sc.exe stop wuauserv
```

```
Sc.exe config wuauserv start=disabled
schtasks /Change /TN "\Microsoft\Windows\WindowsUpdate\Scheduled Start"
/Disable
```

When each system boots the first time, Windows Update will be disabled. Microsoft tries very hard to enable Windows Update in a variety of ways. The commands above are the currently known solution, but there could be other systems or tasks that need to be set. Later in the chapter, we will walk through creating a patch.

9.5 Getting Windows Updates to Create a System Patch

Since you want to control what updates get put into the system, you will need a process to get the latest updates. The good news is that the cumulative update scheme means that all you need is the latest updates for the given month to get all the past updates. Typically, there are 3 to 4 updates that get applied monthly. To find out which updates are needed for your system, follow these steps:

1. Take the master image and install it on a target system.
2. Enable Windows Update, which means undoing the commands discussed in section 9.4. You may want to create a script for this.
3. Run Windows update to download the latest updates.
4. Use Program and Features->view installed updates to get a list of the latest updates.
5. With the list, you can go to the Microsoft Update Catalog site (http://www.catalog.update.microsoft.com/Home.aspx) and download each KB update.

At this point, you should test the system to make sure that nothing has been broken. If everything works fine, the MSU files that you have downloaded can be put into a script to patch the system in the field. The WUSA.exe utility can be used to install the MSU file:

```
wusa.exe d:\winemb6.0-KB1111-x86.msu /quiet
```

A different approach to installing updates is to create a Configuration Set with updates only. DISM is used to install the updates based on the Configuration Set. Using a Configuration Set is ideal when there are multiple MSU files that need to be applied.

1. Extract the CAB file from each MSU by running the following command:

   expand –f:* Windows-KBXXXXX.msu <destination folder>

2. Once all the cab files have been extracted, open SIM.
3. Create a new distribution share.
4. Import all the extracted CAB files into the distribution share.
5. Create a new answer file.
6. Add all the updates to the answer file.

7. Create a Configuration Set. The resulting Configuration Set will consist of an AutoUnattend.xml file and AutoUnattend folder containing all of the CAB update files. This is the patch for Windows Updates.
8. The AutoUnattend.xml file and the AutoUnattend folder need to be copied to the target system's "C:\Windows\ConfigSetRoot" folder. You will need to create the folder called ConfigSetRoot if it doesn't exist.
9. Once copied over, you can run the following command to install the patch:

```
DISM /Online /Apply-
Unattend:c:\Windows\ConfigSetRoot\AutoUnattend.xml
```

10. The system will have to be rebooted to complete the update process.

9.6 *WinPE*

Windows Preinstallation Environment (WinPE) is a lightweight version of the Windows OS. WinPE plays an important part in the installation and manufacturing processes, but it can also be used for servicing images in the field. For example, WinPE can be used to install a patch from a bootable CD/DVD or USB flash drive. WinPE supports DISM to capture and apply FFU and WIM files and PowerShell so you can run scripts to apply custom updates. You can customize WinPE to have a custom interface and extended features. There are optional WinPE Components (cab files) located in the "C:\Program Files (x86)\Windows Kits\10\Assessment and Deployment Kit\Windows Preinstallation Environment" folder that can add more capability to a standard WinPE image like .NET Framework support, for example. There is a set for x86 and amd64. The cab files are applied to the boot.wim file found in the WinPE images "\sources" folder.

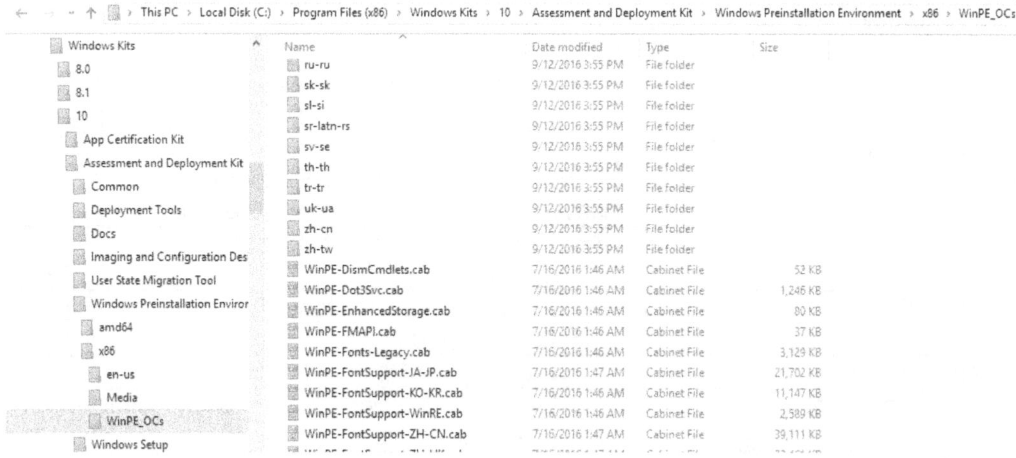

There is no shutdown.exe utility, but WinPE includes Wpeutil.exe, which is a multifunction command line utility that provides options for shutdown and reboot. The utility supports enabling and disabling the firewall, initializing the network, and setting the language.

9.6.1 WinPE Optional Components

The following table lists some of the optional components that can be added to the boot.wim file using DISM.EXE:

Package	Description
WinPE-EnhancedStorage	Adds the ability to discover additional functionality for storage devices such as encrypted drives.
WinPE-FMAPI	Provides support for Windows PE File Management API for discovering and restoring deleted files from unencrypted volumes. Password or recovery key can be used to discover and restore files from Bitlocker encrypted volumes.
WinPE-FONTSupport-<region>	Font support for the following languages: Japanese [ja-JP], Korean [ko-KR], Chinese (PRC) [zh-CN], Chinese (Hong Kong SAR) [zh-HK], Chinese (Taiwan) [zh-TW].
WinPE-Fonts-Legacy	Supports legacy fonts that are no longer supported by Windows.
WinPE-HTA	Adds HTML support for applications created with an HTML interface.
WinPE-MDAC	Adds Microsoft Data Access Component (MDAC) support.
WinPE-NetFX	Adds support for a subset of .NET Framework 4.5 APIs. Not all APIs are available. Please review the online help for more information.
WinPE-PowerShell	Adds PowerShell version 3. Remoting, ISE, and PowerShell 2.0 are not supported.
WinPE-DismCmdlets	Adds DISM cmdlets for managing images, servicing, and applying Unattend.xml settings. Image management cmdlets enable DISM to access Windows images for offline servicing.
WinPE-SecureBootCmdlets	Adds the Secure Boot cmdlets for managing the UEFI (Unified Extensible Firmware Interface) environment variables for Secure Boot.
WinPE-StorageWMI	Adds PowerShell cmdlets for storage management.
WinPE-PPPoE	Adds Point-to-Point Protocol over Ethernet (PPPoE) support.
WinPE-RNDIS	Adds support for Remote NDIS.
WinPE-LegacySetup	Contains all of the files from the \sources folder on the Windows Media.
WinPE-Setup	Parent to Client and Server optional components.
WinPE-Setup-Client	Contains the client branding files.
WinPE-Setup-Server	Contains the server branding files.

WinPE-SecureStartup	Enables Provisioning and Management for Bitlocker and TPM.
WinPE-Scripting	Adds support for Windows Script Host (WSH).
WinPE-WinReCfg	Add the Winrecfg.exe tool for Windows Recovery Environment.
WinPE-WMI	Provides a subset of WMI providers for system diagnostics.
WinPE-WDS-Tools	Adds support for Windows Deployment Services tools.

Since these optional components are language-neutral, you will have to add their associated language-specific component as well. For example, WinPE-HTA.cab will require the WinPE-HTA_en_us.cab file to be included.

Note: If you create an application to run in WinPE, you must compile for the correct bitness: 32-bit or 64-bit. .NET Framework applications have a 32-Bit preferred check box that has to be unchecked for 64-bit support.

9.6.2 Dual boot with Windows and WinPE

Some of our clients have asked for a second recovery partition that allows for a factory restore. You can create a custom WinPE image that can perform the restore using DISM to restore from a WIM file. The WinPE image along with the WIM file can be placed in a second partition, but to boot the partition requires modification of the BCD store. The following calls to bcdedit.exe set up the second partition.

```
bcdedit -store c:\boot\bcd /create {ramdiskoptions} /d "Factory Restore"
bcdedit /set {ramdiskoptions} ramdisksdidevice partition=d:
bcdedit /set {ramdiskoptions} ramdisksdipath \boot\boot.sdi
bcdedit -create {e7352fbf-1d0f-11e4-a76a-e03f4914f1dd} /d "Factory
Restore Image" /application OSLOADER
bcdedit /set {e7352fbf-1d0f-11e4-a76a-e03f4914f1dd} device
ramdisk=[d:]\sources\boot.wim,{ramdiskoptions}
bcdedit /set {e7352fbf-1d0f-11e4-a76a-e03f4914f1dd} osdevice
ramdisk=[d:]\sources\boot.wim,{ramdiskoptions}

REM For MBR Only:
bcdedit /set {e7352fbf-1d0f-11e4-a76a-e03f4914f1dd} path
\windows\system32\boot\winload.exe

REM For UEFI Only:
(bcdedit /set {e7352fbf-1d0f-11e4-a76a-e03f4914f1dd} path
\windows\system32\winload.efi)

bcdedit /set {e7352fbf-1d0f-11e4-a76a-e03f4914f1dd} systemroot \windows
bcdedit /set {e7352fbf-1d0f-11e4-a76a-e03f4914f1dd} detecthal yes
bcdedit /set {e7352fbf-1d0f-11e4-a76a-e03f4914f1dd} winpe yes
bcdedit /displayorder {current} {e7352fbf-1d0f-11e4-a76a-e03f4914f1dd}
bcdedit /timeout 10
```

There is a call to set the path to the Windows Loader. There is a call to winload.exe, if you are booting from a legacy boot partition and a call to winload.efi, if you are booting from UEFI. Choose one command or the other but not both.

Note: The same GUID can be used for all systems, so it is safe to create a master image with the same BCD information. It is recommended that you create your own GUID using a GUID generator tool.

Note: Recovery from a second partition is a quick-fix solution. If the hard drive fails completely, there will be no way to boot to the second partition, thus it is a good idea to have another means to update the system.

9.7 *Exercise 901: Custom WinPE*

The WinPE image can be modified to add some support components and boot to a custom shell. Normally, WinPE launches a specific set of applications during startup. Winpeshl.exe (WinPE Shell) launches Startnet.cmd. Startnet.cmd is a command file that launches Wpeinit.exe. Wpeinit.exe runs the background tasks, such as installing PnP devices, starting up network resources, and processing settings in an Unattend.xml file. If you want to launch a custom shell, you can add a Winpeshl.ini file. The INI file directs Winpeshl.exe to launch an application instead of processing startnet.cmd. For example:

```
[LaunchApp]
AppPath = %SYSTEMROOT%\System32\foo.exe
```

If you need to access network resources, you will have to run wpeinit.exe when the custom shell is launched. Also, you could modify the startnet.cmd to run other scripts and applications. This exercise provides a walk-through to create a custom WinPE 64-bit disk that will have a custom shell. The custom shell is a .NET Framework 4.5, 64-bit application. The ADK comes with several tools to create and deploy WinPE disks, starting with the shortcut link to open the environment.

1. Using File Explorer, copy WinPE-NetFx.cab found in the "C:\Program Files (x86)\Windows Kits\10\Assessment and Deployment Kit\Windows Preinstallation Environment\amd64\WinPE_OCs\" folder to the C:\WinData folder.

2. Using File Explorer, copy WinPE-NetFx_en-us.cab found in the "C:\Program Files (x86)\Windows Kits\10\Assessment and Deployment Kit\Windows Preinstallation Environment\ amd64\WinPE_OCs\en-us" folder to the C:\WinData folder:

3. From the start menu under Windows Kits, right-click on the "Deployment and Imaging Tools Environment" shortcut and select Run as Administrator. This will open a command prompt with environment settings for WinPE builds.

4. To create an amd64 WinPE image in the C:\WinPE folder, type the following command and hit Enter:

copype amd64 c:\winpe

5. Now mount the boot.wim file from the WinPE image you created to the "C:\WinPE\mount" folder using DISM.

dism /Mount-Image /ImageFile:c:\winpe\media\sources\boot.wim /index:1 /MountDir:c:\winpe\mount

```
C:\Program Files (x86)\Windows Kits\10\Assessment and Deployment Kit\Deployment Tools>dism /mount-image /imagefile:c:\Wi
nPE\media\sources\boot.wim /index:1 /MountDir:c:\WinPE\mount

Deployment Image Servicing and Management tool
Version: 10.0.10240.16384

Mounting image
[==========================100.0%==========================]
The operation completed successfully.

C:\Program Files (x86)\Windows Kits\10\Assessment and Deployment Kit\Deployment Tools>
```

6. Once the image has been mounted, use DISM to add the new packages in this order:

   Dism /image:c:\winpe\mount /Add-Package /PackagePath:c:\windata\winpe-NetFx.cab
   Dism /image:c:\winpe\mount /Add-Package /PackagePath:c:\windata\winpe-NetFx_en-us.cab

```
C:\Program Files (x86)\Windows Kits\10\Assessment and Deployment Kit\Deployment Tools>dism /image:c:\Winpe\mount /Add-Pa
ckage /PackagePath:c:\WinData\WinPE-NetFx.cab

Deployment Image Servicing and Management tool
Version: 10.0.10240.16384

Image Version: 10.0.10240.16384

Processing 1 of 1 - Adding package WinPE-NetFx-Package~31bf3856ad364e35~x86~~10.0.10240.16384
[==========================100.0%==========================]
The operation completed successfully.

C:\Program Files (x86)\Windows Kits\10\Assessment and Deployment Kit\Deployment Tools>dism /image:c:\Winpe\mount /Add-Pa
ckage /PackagePath:c:\WinData\WinPE-NetFx_en-us.cab

Deployment Image Servicing and Management tool
Version: 10.0.10240.16384

Image Version: 10.0.10240.16384

Processing 1 of 1 - Adding package WinPE-NetFx-Package~31bf3856ad364e35~x86~en-US~10.0.10240.16384
[==========================100.0%==========================]
The operation completed successfully.

C:\Program Files (x86)\Windows Kits\10\Assessment and Deployment Kit\Deployment Tools>
```

7. Under C:\Winpe\mount\Program Files, create a directory called Annabooks.
8. Copy the AB-WinPE-App.exe from the Chapter 9 book exercises folder to the "C:\winpe\mount\program files\annabooks" folder.

Note: AB-WinPE-App.exe is for WinPE since shutdown.exe is not present in WinPE. The utility makes calls to Wpeutil.exe instead.

9. Open Notepad, and enter the following:

```
[LaunchApp]
AppPath="x:\Program Files\Annabooks\AB-WinPEShell.exe"
```

10. Save the file as Winpeshl.ini to the \WinData folder. When saving, select the Save as type to All Files to keep Notepad from applying the default ".txt" extension to the save file name. Check to be sure that Notepad did not append the ".txt" extension to the file name. Rename it back to "Winpeshl.ini" if it did.
11. Copy the file to the "C:\winpe\mount\Windows\System32" folder.
12. Close all File Explorer Windows and make sure that nothing is accessing the C:\winpe\mount folder, and unmount the boot.wim file:

```
DISM /Unmount-Image /MountDir:c:\winpe\mount /commit
```

```
C:\Program Files (x86)\Windows Kits\10\Assessment and Deployment Kit\Deployment Tools>dism /UNmount-image /MountDir:c:\W
inPE\mount /commit

Deployment Image Servicing and Management tool
Version: 10.0.10240.16384

Saving image
[==========================100.0%==========================]
Unmounting image
[==========================100.0%==========================]
The operation completed successfully.

C:\Program Files (x86)\Windows Kits\10\Assessment and Deployment Kit\Deployment Tools>
```

13. The final step is to deploy the image to boot media. You can either simply copy the image to a USB flash disk or use MakeWinPEMedia.cmd to create an ISO file. If you copy to a USB flash disk, make sure to follow the steps for UEFI boot using Rufus.

To make an ISO, type the following and hit Enter:

MakeWinPEMedia /ISO c:\winpe c:\winpe\Winpe-x86.iso

```
C:\Program Files (x86)\Windows Kits\10\Assessment and Deployment Kit\Windows Preinstallation Environment>MakeWinPEMedia.
cmd /ISO c:\WinPE c:\Winpe\Winpe-x86.iso
Creating c:\Winpe\Winpe-x86.iso...

100% complete

Success

C:\Program Files (x86)\Windows Kits\10\Assessment and Deployment Kit\Windows Preinstallation Environment>
```

Once completed, you can burn the ISO to a DVD.

14. Boot the target to the WinPE image.
15. Click on the Command Prompt button to open a command window.
16. Click on the shutdown button to shut down the system.

9.8 *Summary: Don't Forget Servicing*

Although servicing is usually the last thing to be implemented, it must be included in the design process from the beginning. The previous 3 chapters focused on locking down the system. A lot of time can be spent during development on the subject of locking down the system; but as was warned at the beginning of this chapter, "The more you lock down the system, the more challenging it is to update the system in the field.". How the system is serviced in the field must be addressed at design time and especially during the design of the methods used to lock down the system. Since every system is unique, it is up to you to develop the update process that will work the best for your system. This chapter provided some common update options, as well as, the tools and methods available to assist with the update process. These will guide you in the design of your servicing methodology.

We have come to the end of the Windows 10 IoT Enterprise integration instructions. The next chapters focus on accessing low-speed bus I/O such as GPIO, SPI, I2C, and UART.

10 RHPROXY and Low Power I/O

The Windows 10 evolution has introduced several new technologies such as Cortana, Mixed Reality, containers, improved Linux subsystem, and Device Guard. Some of these topics are covered in depth in other chapters. In this section, we will look at old microcontroller I/O technology that was added to Windows 10 in 2018.

GPIO, I2C, SPI, PWM, ADC, and UART have been I/O standards on microcontrollers for decades. Many microcontrollers have these I/O features multiplexed on pins, which gives the developer flexibility to configure the microcontroller for a specific application. SoC processors integrated different microcontroller I/O to support mobile applications. Support for microcontroller I/O was absent from Intel Architecture processors until the release of the Intel Atom® processor family. Each new generation of Intel Atom has expanded the microcontroller I/O support. Intel calls this the Low Power Sub System (LPSS). Industrial PC board manufacturers have exposed these I/O differently. As a result, Windows Embedded (Desktop) didn't provide microcontroller I/O API support until the effort to create one Windows operating system. Today, there is Windows Runtime API support for GPIO, I2C, SPI, PWM, ADC, and UART, which will be covered in the following chapters. Before we dive into each I/O class, there is the underlying architecture to discuss.

10.1 The Back Story

Historically, support for microcontroller I/O in Windows has been made available in a variety of formats. Windows CE and the short-lived .Net Micro Framework had API support for these I/O built in, but support in the Windows desktop was only available through custom hardware, device drivers, and API sets. As the focus to create one Windows operating system, the microcontroller I/O API set was added in stages:

- First, Windows CE mobile was dropped as the mobile operating system in favor of Windows 8 running on ARM processors. Mobile hardware developers needed a solution to interface to peripherals attached to microcontroller I/O. New driver frameworks were created so custom drivers could easily be written for dedicated devices connected to GPIO, I2C, SPI, and UART. OEMs could then access the data through standard C/C++ DLL API calls.

- Next, Windows 8.1 took the next step with the "Windows for Devices" side project, which had a cut-down version of Windows 8.1 running on the Intel Galileo board. Since UWP applications run in a sandbox with limited access to outside resources, access through a DLL was not possible. Also, many platforms exposed the I/O on headers so applications could easily be programmed to access different peripherals. A solution was needed to allow user-mode applications to access the microcontroller I/O directly. A resource hub and API set were created as a bridge between UWP applications and device drivers for GPIO, I2C, SPI, and UART ports.

- Windows 10 was launched as the single operating system solution that reaches a wide range of devices from simple IoT platforms to virtual/augmented reality platforms. There are different SKUs of Windows 10 from IoT Core, the smallest footprint, to Windows 10 Enterprise on the desktop. User mode application access to GPIO, I2C, SPI, and UART was only made available for Windows 10 IoT Core. The Raspberry Pi 2/3 and the MinnowBoard Max were the first platforms to support Windows 10 IoT Core and the API to access microcontroller I/O. This allowed time to flush out any errors in the API and resource hub solution. For Windows desktop, user-mode application support for GPIO, I2C, SPI, and UART was not made available until the release of Windows 10 version 16299, build 1709.

Now that there is a set of Windows Runtime microcontroller I/O API classes, we can just start writing programs to access the I/O for any platform that runs Windows, well, not exactly. It all depends on the I/O support provided with the hardware. There are two key pieces to check with your hardware vendor before moving forward with application development. The first piece comes from the Industrial PC board vendor with additional support being made in the firmware. The second piece comes with installing the correct device drivers.

10.2 Resource Hub Proxy (RHPROXY)

In Windows 8, three driver frameworks were created to support the different microcontroller I/O. Mobile OEMs could write device drivers for dedicated devices attached to the I/O.

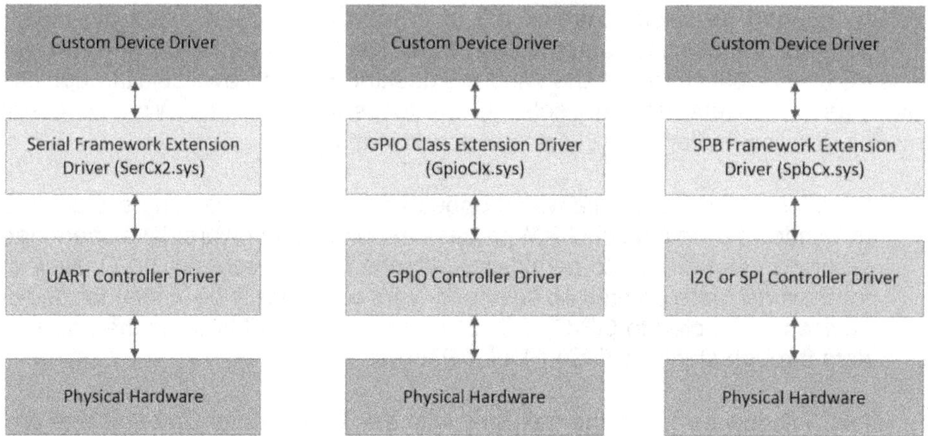

The extension drivers were designed to make device driver development easier, but device driver development is tricky. Writing applications is much easier, thus using a cut-down Windows 8.1, the Windows for Devices program looked into providing a solution to access microcontroller I/O from user-mode applications. The Resource Hub Proxy (RHPROXY) was developed to interact directly with the Framework Extension drivers to provide access to the microcontroller I/O. Since the different I/O can be wired to different devices, i.e. the SPI port is used to program firmware chips rather than to be exposed to I/O headers for general access. RHPROXY lets the board manufacturers define in the firmware what I/O is available to the programmers. Microsoft provides a guide for the independent hardware vendor, IHV, to integrate RHPROXY support into their firmware: "Enable user mode access to GPIO, I2C, and SPI" (https://docs.microsoft.com/en-us/windows/uwp/devices-sensors/enable-usermode-access).

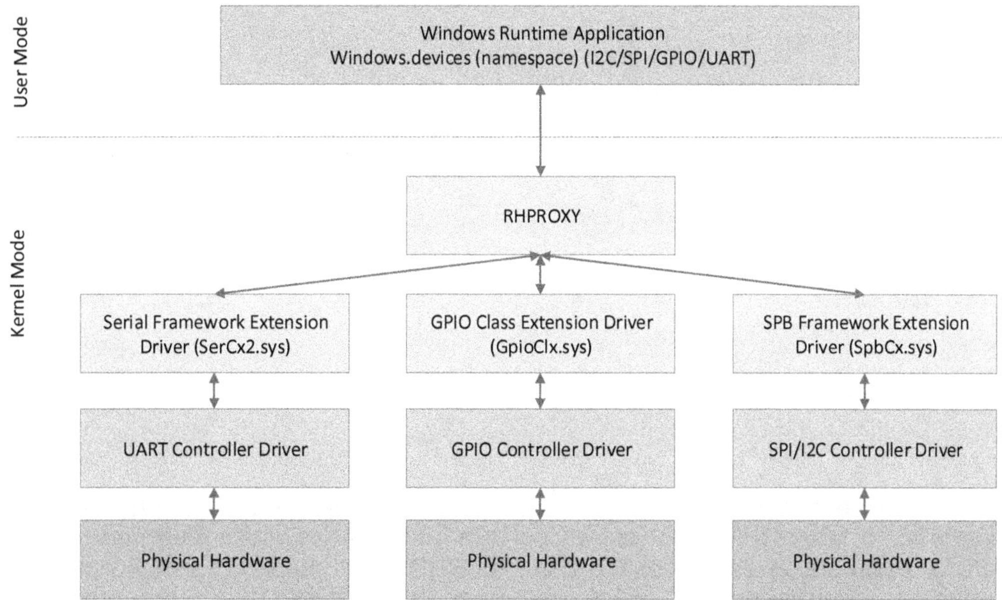

RHPROXY is a driver that shows up under the System Devices in Device Manager.

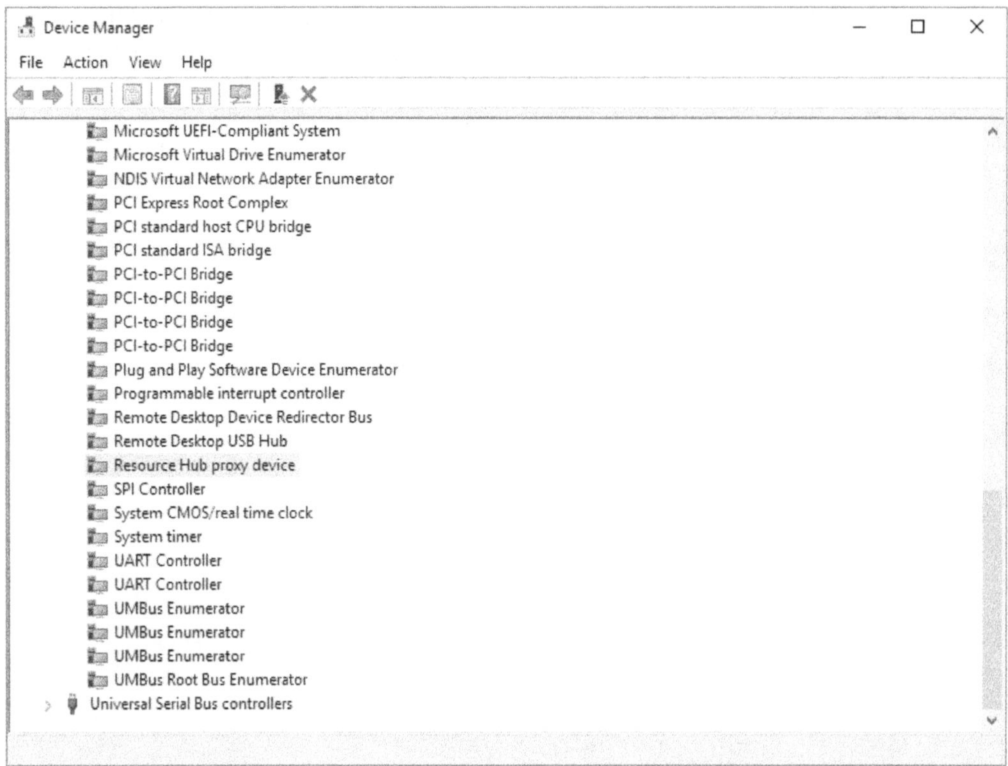

For the driver to load, the firmware must list "ACPI\MSFT8000" in the ACPI tables. In the MinnowBoard Max, RHPROXY shows up in a Secondary System Description Table (SSDT). There are several options to check for RHPROXY support in your PC platform, the first is to install Windows 10 16299 or newer and see if RHPROXY shows up in Device Manager or the registry under HKLM\HARDWARE\APCI\.

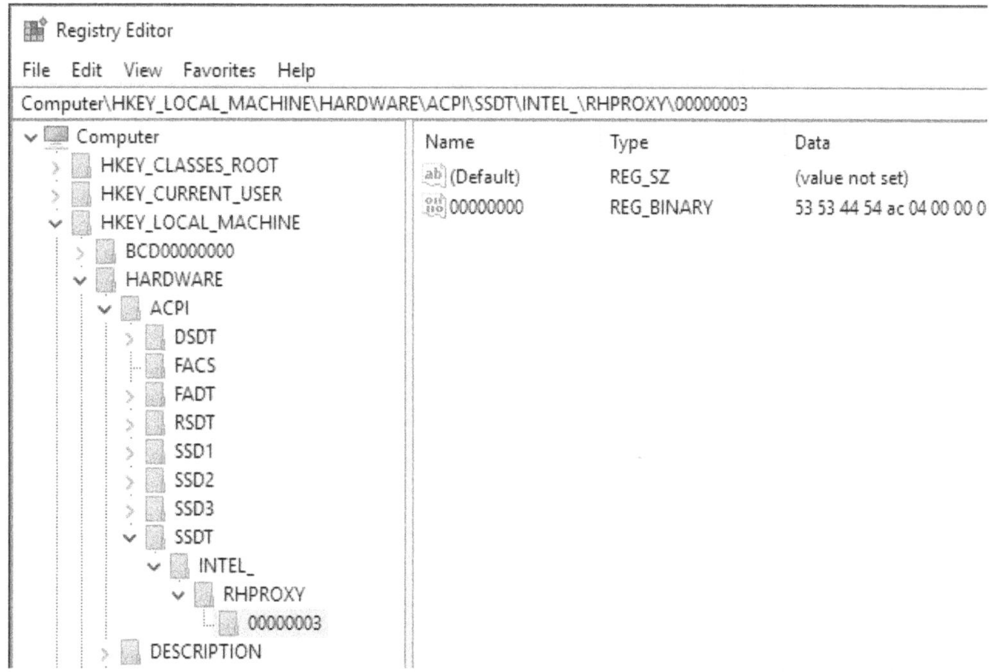

Following the aforementioned Microsoft guidelines, one could add the support to the registry; but intimate knowledge of the hardware is required, which might not be possible in most cases. If you want to access microcontroller I/O from a Windows Runtime application, you will have to work with your hardware vendor to get support in the firmware.

10.3 Correct Device Driver Support is Required

The second piece is installing the correct device drivers. After installing Windows Enterprise 16299 or higher, you might see that RHPROXY shows up with errors. Device drivers for GPIO, I2C, SPI, and UART are needed for RHPROXY to run correctly.

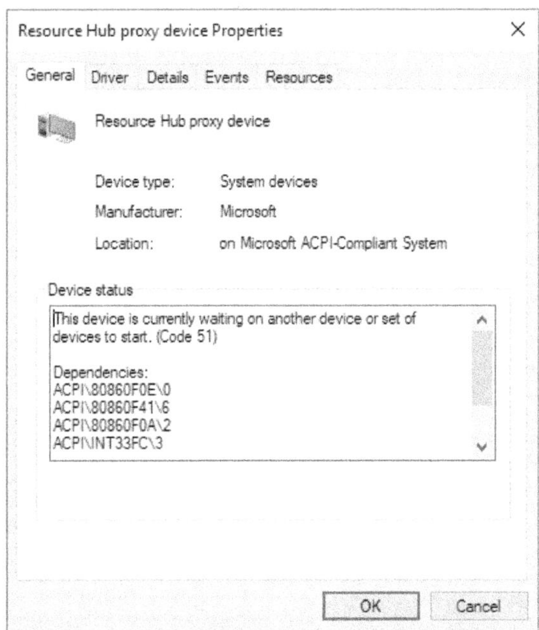

The Hardware IDs are defined in the firmware in the Differentiated System Description Table (DSDT). Every platform will have different Hardware IDs for the microcontroller I/O. For the MinnowBoard Max, the Hardware IDs for the I/O are as follows:

Hardware IDs	Driver Name
ACPI\80860F0E\0	SPI Controller
ACPI\80860F41\6	I2C Controller
ACPI\80860F0A\2	UART Controller
ACPI\80860F0A\1	UART Controller
ACPI\INT33FC\3	GPIO Controller
ACPI\INT33FC\1	GPIO Controller

The GPIO, I2C, SPI, and UART drivers that loaded with Windows 10 Enterprise 16299 or higher desktop had the correct Hardware IDs, but they were not the correct versions for use with RHPROXY. For example, the SPI controller showed up as the "Intel(R) Atom/Celeron/Pentium Processor SPI Controller", and there wasn't a driver file associated with that listing. Checking the INF files for other I/O drivers showed they were built with the framework extension, but they still didn't work.

```
:
:
; -------------- Driver install section
[i2c.AddService]
DisplayName    = %Driver_Service.Desc%
ServiceType    = 1                    ; SERVICE_KERNEL_DRIVER
StartType      = 3                    ; SERVICE_DEMAND_START
```

```
ErrorControl    = 1                ; SERVICE_ERROR_NORMAL
ServiceBinary   = %12%\iaioi2c.sys
Dependencies    = SpbCx
AddReg          = i2c_Service_addReg
 :
 :
```

Intel released a BSP for the E3800 family called the Intel® Embedded Drivers for Microsoft Windows* 10 IoT Core. Once these drivers were loaded, RHPROXY ran as expected. The table below lists the processor and Intel Atom BSPs for Windows 10 IoT Core.

Intel Atom® Processor	Windows 10 IoT Core BSP Website
E3900 (Apollo Lake)	https://www.intel.com/content/www/us/en/embedded/products/apollo-lake/technical-library.html
N3000, x5-E8000 and x5-Z8350 (Braswell / Cherry Trail)	https://www.intel.com/content/www/us/en/embedded/products/braswell/software-and-drivers.html
Intel Atom® E3800 (Bay Trail)	https://downloadcenter.intel.com/download/25618/Intel-Embedded-Drivers-for-Microsoft-Windows-10-IoT-Core-32-bit-and-64-bit-MR1

For the NXP's IMXP8P ARM processor, firmware support with RHPROXY and the device drivers are already provided with the Windows 10 kit and on the NXP website. If you purchase hardware off-the-shelf, just make sure that the IHV has support for Windows 10 IoT. If you roll your own hardware, then you will have to customize the firmware and device drivers using NXP's firmware source file and BSP source files.

10.4 Hardware Platforms

The following chapters demonstrate different microcontroller I/O applications. These were developed and tested on different platforms.

Board	Processor	GPIO	UART	SPI	I2C	PWM	ADC
AAEON UP Board	Intel® Atom x5-Z8350	X	X	X	X		
AAEON UP² Board	Intel® Celeron™ N3350	X	X	X	X		
ASUS IMX8P-IM-A	NXP ARM IMX8M	X	X	X	X	X	
WinSystems SBC35-427	Intel® Atom E3900	X		X	X		

Note: Some boards list support for ADC, and there is an ADC API class. There is no ADC device driver available at the time of this writing to provide an example.

Note: The exercises have been tested with ASUS IMX8P-IM-A, but this is an ARM64 platform that is not covered in this book.

The implementation of the I/O on each board will be different. Some use level shifters to change voltages to standard 3.3V or 5V. Some processors will have starting values for specific ports. Please check with your board manufacturer to get these details. Many boards have fixed I/O pin assignments for exposed header pins, however, the UP Board and UP^2 Board have BIOS settings to customize the exposed I/O header pins. The following two sections cover the BIOS settings for the UP Board and UP^2 Board.

10.4.1 UP Board BIOS Settings

To enable RHPROXY support, you have to set the operating system that is running in the BIOS settings. In the BIOS setup, set the following:

Boot -> OS Image ID: Windows 10 IoT Core

Since Windows 10 IoT Core and Windows 10 Enterprise LTSC (aka Windows 10 IoT Enterprise) are the same operating system, the setting applies to both. With the OS Image ID set, RHPROXY is enabled in the firmware. According to the UP Board specification, the I/O from the Intel Atom goes through a CPLD to the 40-pin HAT connector. The CPLD acts as a voltage level shifter so the 40-pin HAT connector has 3.3V tolerant pins. The HAT connector has two 3.3v out pins, two 5v out pins, and 8 ground (GND) pins. The rest of the 28 pins are for GPIO, I2C, UART, SPI, ADC, PWM, and SDIO.

There is UWP API support for I2C, UART, SPI, ADC, and PWM, but there is driver support only for I2C, UART, and SPI on the UP Board. What the firmware calls out for pin numbering and I/O names is different from what Windows will indicate. The differences can cause some confusion for the developers. Here is the explanation of the differences:

- The firmware lists the GPIO as 1-28, whereas Windows lists the GPIO as 0-27.
  - The GPIO must be configured for input or output, and one still needs to set the input or output drive mode for the corresponding pin in the Windows application. A mismatch between the firmware settings and the Windows application settings or the omission of either the firmware settings or the Windows application settings will result in an error.
- The firmware has I2C0 and I2C1, but Windows only supports the firmware's I2C0, which is called I2C1 in Windows.
- The UP Board specification calls pin 26 as SPI2_CS1N, but the firmware only shows this pin as GPIO23 rather than SPI2 chip select. This has been confirmed with Windows that pin 24 SPI2_CS0N is the only SPI chip select available.

In the **Advanced-> HAT Configuration** section of the firmware, there are two steps to set up the I/O. The first is to enable the serial I/O, so the shared GPIO on the pin is disabled. The table below lists the firmware options and the settings to enable the Serial I/O.

Firmware Option	Setting	Notes
LPSS I2C #1 Support	**ACPI**	I2C0
I2C #1 Speed	**400K**	I2C0 max speed
LPSS I2C #2 Support	**Disabled**	I2C1 – Not supported in Windows
LPSS PWM #1 Support	**Disabled**	Pin 32 No driver available
LPSS PWM #2 Support	**Disabled**	Pin 33 No driver available
LPSS SPI Support	**ACPI**	Enables SP2
LPSS HSUART Support	**ACPI**	Enables UART1
SCC SDIO Support	**Disabled**	Not supported
I2C0/GPIO Selection	**ISC0**	Need to set this so I2C is enabled
I2S/GPIO Selection	**GPIO**	There is no I2S support in Windows
HAT Output Enabled	**Enabled**	This is the master switch for the CPLD to enable the HAT I/O
LED2	**Off**	Unknown
LED3	**Off**	Unknown
LED4	**Off**	Unknown
ADC	**Disabled**	Pin 7 No driver available

If SPI, UART, I2C along with ADC, SDIO, I2S, and PWM were disabled, all 28 of the GPIO pins will be GPIO pins in Windows. Once SPI, UART, and I2C are enabled, the pins for these I/O are dedicated to the serial devices and cannot be used for GPIO.

The second step is to configure the GPIO. In the **Advanced-> HAT, Configuration-> GPIO Configuration In Pin Order**, you can set any enabled GPIO for input or output. If set to output the initial state of Low (Logic 0 / 0V) or High (Logic 1 / 3.3v) can also be set.

If the above table has the settings to enable I2C0, SPI, and UART1, the following table for the 40-pin HAT header shows the I/O in **bold** that is available for Windows UWP applications.

				HAT Header					
OS-Serial I/O	**OS-GPIO**	**BIOS**	**UP Board Documentation**	**Odd Pin**	**Even Pin**	**UP Board Documentation**	**BIOS**	**OS-GPIO**	**OS-Serial I/O**
			3.3V	1	2	5V			
	GPIO0	GPIO1	GPIO1/~~I2C1_SDA~~	3	4	5V			
	GPIO1	GPIO2	GPIO2/~~I2C1_SCL~~	5	6	GND			
	GPIO2	GPIO3	GPIO3/ ~~ADC~~	7	8	GPIO16/UART1-TX	GPIO16	GPIO15	**UART1-TX**
			GND	9	10	GPIO17/UART1-RX	GPIO17	GPIO16	**UART1-RX**
UART1-RTS	GPIO3	GPIO4	GPIO4/UART1_RTS	11	12	GPIO18	GPIO18	**GPIO17**	

	GPIO4	GPIO5	GPIO5/~~SDIO~~	13	14	GND			
	GPIO5	GPIO6	GPIO6/~~SDIO~~	15	16	GPIO19 /~~SDIO~~	GPIO19	**GPIO18**	
			3.3V	17	18	GPIO20/~~SDIO~~	GPIO20	**GPIO19**	
SPI2-MOSI	GPIO6	GPIO7	GPIO7/SPI2-MOSI	19	20	GND			
SPI2-MISO	GPIO7	GPIO8	GPIO8/SPI2-MISO	21	22	GPIO21 /~~SDIO~~	GPIO21	**GPIO20**	
SPI2-CLK	GPIO8	GPIO9	GPIO9/SP2-CLK	23	24	GPIO22/SPI2-CSON	GPIO22	GPIO21	**SPI2-CS0**
			GND	25	26	GPIO23	GPIO23	**GPIO22**	
I2C1_SDA	GPIO9	GPIO10	GPIO10/I2C0_SDA	27	28	GPIO24/I2C0_SCL	GPIO24	GPIO23	**I2C1_SCL**
	GPIO10	GPIO11	GPIO11	29	30	GND			
	GPIO11	GPIO12	GPIO12	31	32	GPIO25/~~PWM0~~	GPIO25	**GPIO24**	
	GPIO12	GPIO13	GPIO13/~~PWM1~~	33	34	GND			
	GPIO13	GPIO14	GPIO14	35	36	GPIO26/UART1_CTS	GPIO26	GPIO25	**UART1-CTS**
	GPIO14	GPIO15	GPIO15/~~SDIO~~	37	38	GPIO27 / ~~I2S-DI~~	GPIO27	**GPIO26**	
			GND	39	40	GPIO28 / ~~I2S-DO~~	GPIO28	**GPIO27**	

Note: The I/O that is crossed out is not available for Windows at the time of this writing. Once you save the changes and boot into Windows, Device Manager will show RHPROXY support, and UWP applications can be developed to access the I/O.

10.4.2 UP² Board BIOS Settings for HAT Connector

To enable RHPROXY support, you have to set which operating system is running. In the BIOS setup, set the following:

Boot -> OS Selection: Windows 10 IoT Core

Since Windows 10 IoT Core and Windows 10 Enterprise LTSC (aka Windows 10 IoT Enterprise) are the same operating system, the setting applies to both. With the OS Image ID set, RHPROXY is enabled in the firmware. According to the UP² Board specification, the I/O from the Intel Atom goes through a CPLD to the 40-pin HAT connector. The CPLD acts as a voltage level shifter so the 40-pin HAT connector has 3.3V tolerant pins. The HAT connector has two 3.3v out pins, two 5v out pins, and 8 ground (GND) pins. The rest of the 28 pins are for GPIO, I2C, UART, SPI, ADC, PWM, and SDIO.
There is UWP API support for I2C, UART, SPI, ADC, and PWM, but there is driver support only for I2C, UART, and SPI on the UP² Board. The UP² Board documentation on the HAT connector is a little different from what the firmware is showing and what Windows is supporting. The differences can cause some confusion for the developers. Here is what we have found in our lab testing:

- The firmware has a list of GPIO and their pin assignments. Lab testing shows that these don't match. The pinout table shows what we have found with the current version of the firmware.

- The firmware has I2C1, I2C2, I2C6, and I2C7, but Windows only supports the firmware's I2C1, and Windows sees this as I2C0.
- There is the ability to enable SP1 and SPI3, but SPI3 pin assignments are unknown. There is also no mention of SPI3 in any documentation on the forum at the time of this writing.

In the **Advanced-> HAT Configuration** section of the firmware, there are two steps to set up the I/O. The first is to enable the serial I/O, so the shared GPIO on the pin is disabled. The table below lists the firmware options and the settings to enable the Serial I/O.

Firmware Option	Setting	Notes
LPSS HSUART#2 Support	**ACPI Mode**	UART2 in Windows
LPSS SPI #1 Support	**ACPI Mode**	SPI1 in Windows
LPSS SPI #2 Support	**Disabled**	
LPSS SPI #3 Support	**Disabled**	SPI3 shows up for Pins 7, 13, 15, and 29, but function assignments are unknown
LPSS I2C #1 Support	**ACPI**	I2C0 in Windows
LPSS I2C #2 Support	**Disabled**	
LPSS I2C #6 Support	**Disabled**	Shows up on EX-HAT as I2C5
LPSS I2C #7 Support	**Disabled**	Shows up on EX-HAT as I2C6
GPIO / PWM #0 Selection	**GPIO**	
GPIO / PWM #1 Selection	**GPIO**	
GPIO / PWM #3 Selection	**GPIO**	
GPIO / I2S5 Selection	**GPIO**	
HD-Audio / I2S6 Selection	**Disabled**	
GPIO / I2S2 Selection	**GPIO**	
GPIO / Speaker Selection	**GPIO**	
GPIO / SP1 Selection	**GPIO**	Enabled SPI1 on EX HAT Pins 37,39,41,43,45 – But are not functional.
GPIO / DMIC / I2S4 Selection	**GPIO**	

If SPI, UART, I2C along with ADC, SDIO, I2S, and PWM were disabled, in theory, the pins all become GPIO pins, but this is not the case. Several pins are tied to the output of GPIO 48 but are inverted. Once SPI, UART, and I2C are enabled, the pins for these I/O are dedicated to the serial devices and cannot be used for GPIO.

The second step is to configure the GPIO, which is below the settings for the serial setup. Scroll down to set any enabled GPIO for input or output. If set to output the initial state of Low (Logic 0 / 0V) or High (Logic 1 / 3.3v) can also be set.

If the above table has the settings to enable I2C0, SPI, and UART1, the following table for the 40-pin HAT header shows the I/O in **bold** that is available for Windows UWP applications.

OS-Serial I/O	OS-GPIO	BIOS	UP^2 Board Documentation	HAT Header		UP^2 Board Documentation	BIOS	OS-GPIO	OS-Serial I/O
				Odd Pin	Even Pin				
			3.3V	1	2	5V			
		GPIO1	GPIO0/~~I2C1_SDA~~	3	4	5V			
		GPIO2	GPIO1/~~I2C1_SCL~~	5	6	GND			
		GPIO3	GPIO2/ ~~ADC~~	7	8	GPIO15/UART1-TX	GPIO16		**UART2-TX**
			GND	9	10	GPIO16/UART1-RX	GPIO17		**UART2-RX**
UART2-RTS	GPIO2	GPIO4	GPIO3/UART1_RTS	11	12	GPIO17	GPIO18	**GPIO41**	
	GPIO5	GPIO5	GPIO4/~~ADC~~	13	14	GND			
	GPIO6	GPIO6	GPIO5/~~ADC~~	15	16	GPIO18	GPIO19	**GPIO48**	
			3.3V	17	18	GPIO19	GPIO20	**GPIO11**	
SPI1-MOSI	/GPIO48	GPIO7	GPIO6/SPI1-MOSI	19	20	GND			
SPI1-MISO	/GPIO48	GPIO8	GPIO7/SPI1-MISO	21	22	GPIO20	GPIO21	**GPIO10**	
SPI1-CLK	/GPIO48	GPIO9	GPIO8/SP1-CLK	23	24	GPIO21/SPI1-CSON	GPIO22	/GPIO48	**SPI1-CS0**
			GND	25	26	GPIO22/SP1-CS1N	GPIO23	/GPIO48	**SPI1-CS0**
I2C0_SDA	/GPIO48	GPIO10	GPIO9/I2C0_SDA	27	28	GPIO23/I2C0_SCL	GPIO24	/GPIO48	**I2C0_SCL**
	GPIO7	GPIO11	GPIO10	29	30	GND			
	GPIO14	GPIO12	GPIO11	31	32	GPIO24/~~PWM0~~	GPIO25	**/GPIO48**	
	GPIO24	GPIO13	GPIO12/~~PWM1~~	33	34	GND			
	GPIO40	GPIO14	GPIO13	35	36	GPIO25/UART1_CTS	GPIO26		**UART2-CTS**
	GPIO13	GPIO15	GPIO14	37	38	GPIO26 / ~~I2S-DI~~	GPIO27	**/GPIO48**	
			GND	39	40	GPIO27 / ~~I2S-DO~~	GPIO28	**/GPIO48**	

Note: The I/O that is crossed out is not available for Windows at the time of this writing.
Note: Pins 3, 5, and 7 are not tied to any I/O. Future BIOS versions might change this support.

Once you save the changes and boot into Windows, Device Manager will show RHPROXY support, and UWP applications can be developed to access the I/O.

There is a 60-pin Panasonic P5K header (Part No. AXK6S60547YG) on the board that is called the EX HAT connector. It exposes LVDS, SPI, 2 I2C ports, DMIC, and ADC. If none of these options are selected, the pins become GPIO. Although the BIOS settings appear to configure the EX HAT pins, nothing appears to be functioning as expected, and Windows doesn't have driver support for the EX HAT connector at the time of this writing.

If support becomes available, there is a solution to expose the pins for the tiny header. The socket for the EX HAT connector is Panasonic Part No. AXK5S60047YG. Proto Advantage (www.proto-advantage.com) offers a surface-mount adapter that can accommodate the socket connector: "Dual Row 0.5mm Pitch 60-Pin Connector to DIP-60 Adapter" (Part No. DR050D254P060) (Proto Advantage - Dual Row 0.5mm Pitch 60-Pin Connector to DIP-60 Adapter (proto-advantage.com). A DIP Pin can be added to create headers for each pin.

10.5 *Exercise 1001: SDK Bus Tools*

A set of C++ Bus test application projects are part of the Windows IoT Core samples on Git hub. Even though Windows IoT Core is at end-of-life, these sample I/O applications still apply to Windows 10 Enterprise. These command-line test tools provide some basic diagnostic support for GPIO, UART, SPI, I2C, and PWM. The Bus Tools are essential tools for debugging devices that get attached to the I/O. Basic tests can be performed using these command-line tools before writing code. This exercise looks at setting up, building, and deploying the applications to a target system. For this project, you will need the following:

- Visual Studio 2022
- Windows IoT Core Samples from Git hub: GitHub - microsoft/Windows-iotcore-samples: Official code samples repository for Windows 10 Internet of Things (IoT).
- Visual Studio 2022 Remote Debug tools that are appropriate for your processor architecture (AMD64): Download Visual Studio 2022 for Windows & Mac (microsoft.com). The Remote tools will be installed on the target platform.
- A platform running Windows 10 and supporting RHPOXY and the I/O drivers.
- Ethernet connectivity is required for the host development system to remotely download to the target system.

10.5.1 On the Target System

1. Install Windows 10 on a target platform that has the low-power I/O pins available. Make sure that RHPROXY is found in Device Manager.
2. Set the computer name to X64-APPTEST, or something that you like. The computer will be used for remote connections.
3. Run the installer for the Visual Studio 2022 Remote Debug Tools.

4. After installation, run the Remote Debugger, a screen will appear asking to make changes to the firewall for the remote debugger, click "Configure remote Debugging".

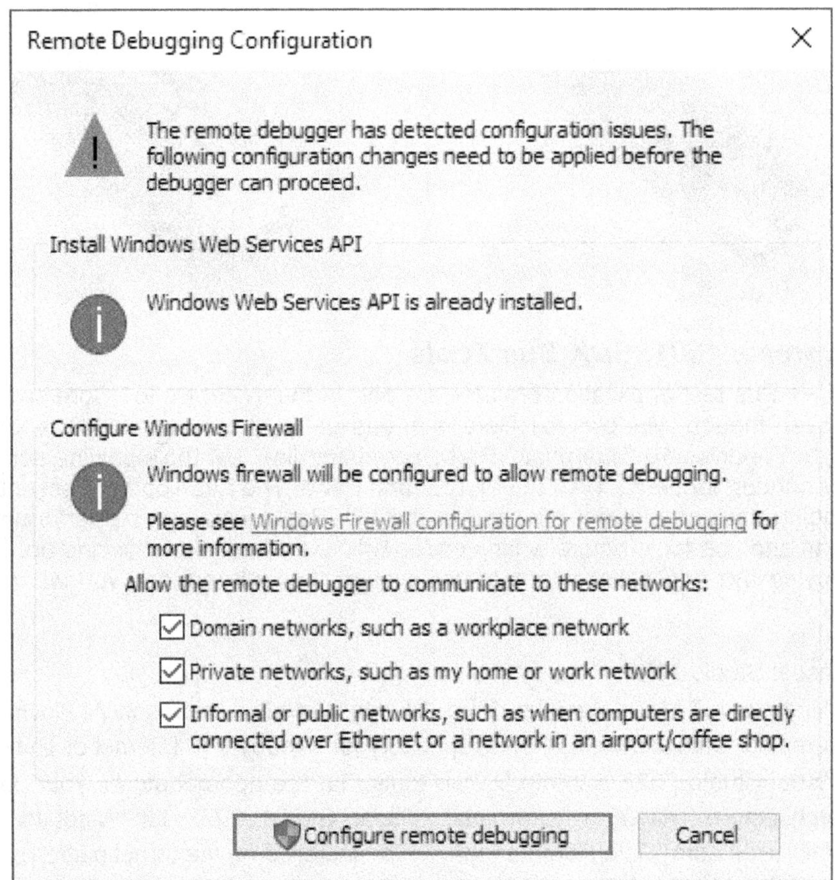

5. Create a folder called "test" in the root of the C drive

10.5.2 On the host system

These steps are for those who are building for an AMD64 64-bit processor. You will have to adjust for other processor types.

1. Install Visual Studio 2022.
2. Download and extract the complete Windows IoT Core Sample applications from GitHub.

3. Open Visual Studio and then open the windows-iot-bus-tools.sln file under the Windows-iotcore-samples-develop\BusTools folder.
4. You will be asked to upgrade the project. Click Ok

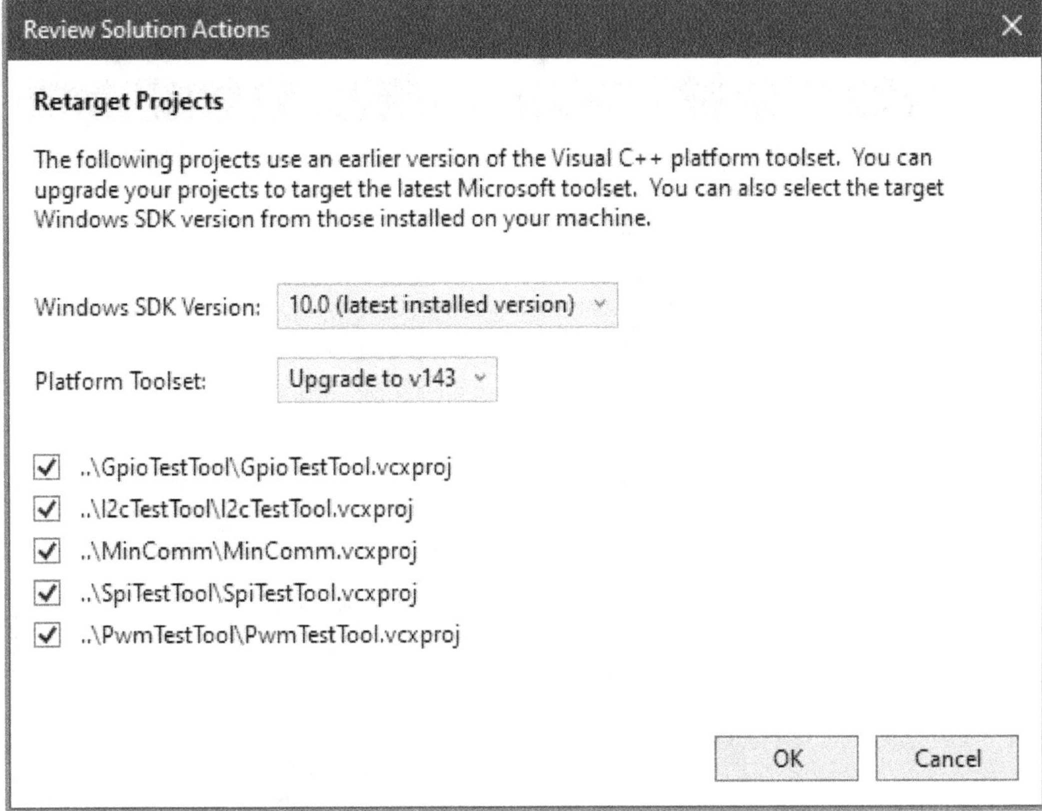

5. For each project, you need to set up the remote debugger settings. Right-click on the GpioTestTool in Solution Explorer and select "Properties" from the context menu.
6. Make sure the Configuration drop-down is set for "All Configurations" and the Platform is set for the x64 processor.
7. On the left side, click on Debugging.
8. Set the "Debugger to launch:" to Remote Windows Debugger, and then set the following:

- Remote Command: c:\test\GpioTestTool.exe
- Working Directory c:\test

- Remote Server Name: <the computer name of the remote computer>:4026
- Connection: Remote with Windows authentication
- Deployment Directory: c:\test
- Deploy Visual C++ Debug Runtime Libraries: Yes
- Deploy Visual C++ Runtime Libraries: Yes

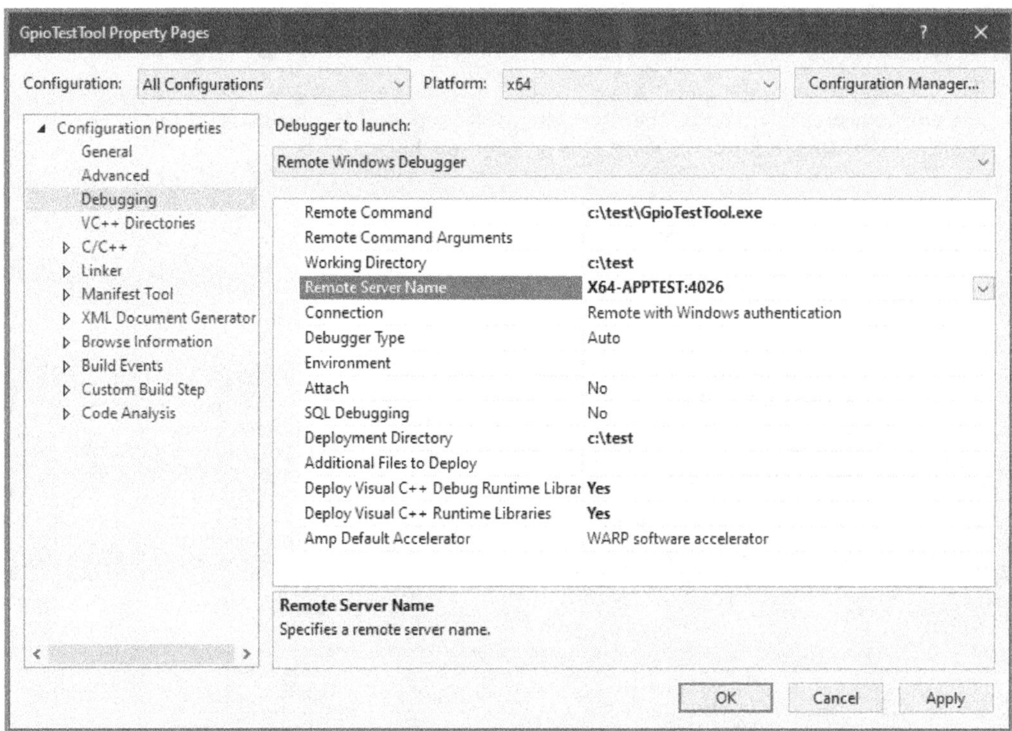

9. Click the Apply button and then click the OK button.
10. Repeat steps 7 through 11 for the remaining applications: i2cTestTool.exe, MinComm.exe, PwmTestTool.exe, and SPiTestTool.exe.
11. In Solution Explorer, click on the “windows-iot-bus-tools”.
12. From the menu, click on Build->Configuration Manager and check Deploy for all projects.

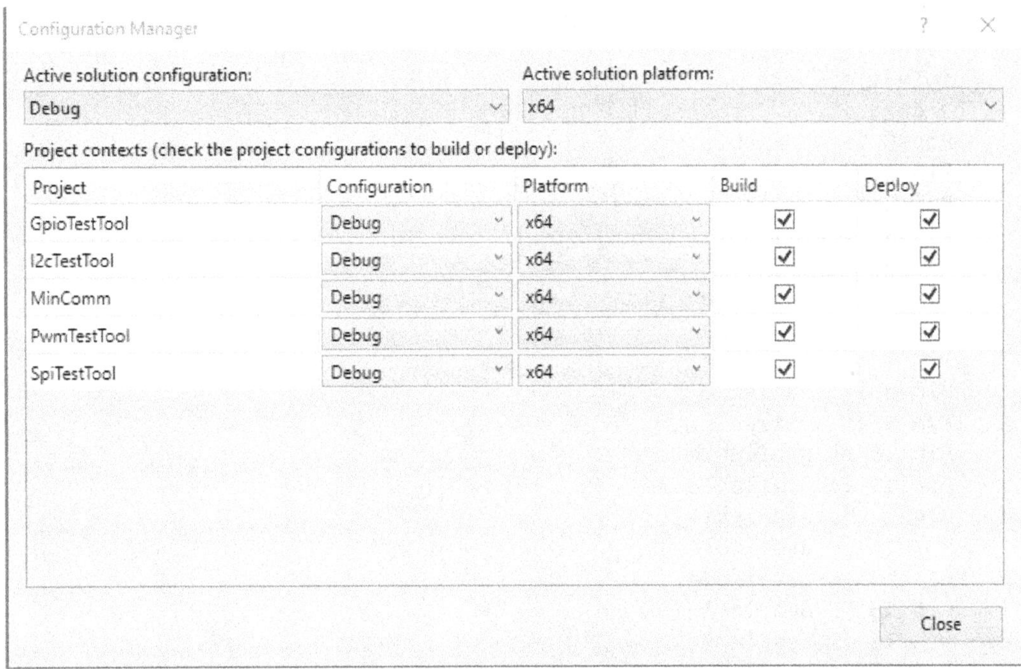

13. With the target up and running with the remote debugger, from the menu, select Build-> Build Solution to build the whole project.
14. Now let's deploy to the target system, from the menu select Build->Deploy Solution.
15. Enter the remote machine's credentials when it appears on the screen. All 5 applications should download to the remote system in the c:\test folder.

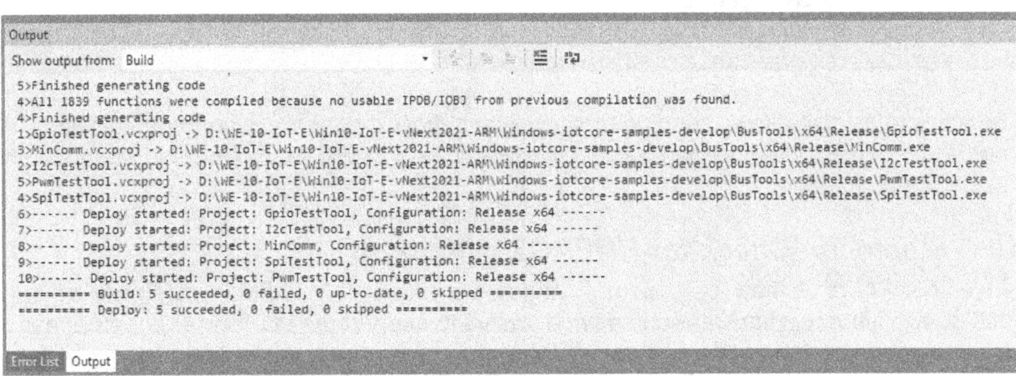

10.5.3 Running the Bus Tools

With the bus tools on the target system, let's test them out to see what is available.

1. Open a command prompt on the target machine

2. Change the directory to the c:\test folder and run the following:

```
GpioTestTool.exe -list
The default GPIO controller has 28 pins:
  Pin 0 is available
  Pin 1 is available
  Pin 2 is available
  Pin 3 is available
  Pin 4 is available
  Pin 5 is available
  Pin 6 is available
  Pin 7 is available
  Pin 8 is available
  Pin 9 is available
  Pin 10 is available
  Pin 11 is available
  Pin 12 is available
  Pin 13 is available
  Pin 14 is available
  Pin 15 is available
  Pin 16 is available
  Pin 17 is available
  Pin 18 is available
  Pin 19 is available
  Pin 20 is available
  Pin 21 is available
  Pin 22 is available
  Pin 23 is available
  Pin 24 is available
  Pin 25 is available
  Pin 26 is available
  Pin 27 is available
```

The application also allows sending a ping, setting drive mode, and writing and reading 1s and 0s. The other bus tools perform similar functions. We will exercise these bus tools in the following chapters.

10.6 Summary: Check for RHPROXY Support

Since RHPROXY is now part of the Windows desktop, IHV OEMs are slowly adding RHPROXY support in firmware and device drivers to support the I/O. Earlier chapters have stressed the importance of UEFI and TPM support for performance and security. If you want to write applications that will access the Low-Power I/O, then you will have to either ask your IHV to see if they support RHPROXY and have the appropriate device driver support available. The techniques and tools called out can help remove any doubt regarding whether the hardware can support the low power I/O. If you have the supported hardware, the next chapter looks into the GPIO class.

11 GPIO

The simplest I/O is the general-purpose input-output (GPIO) pin, which, depending on the direction, either outputs a logical 1 or 0 or inputs a logical 1 or 0. GPIO can be used to turn on and off an LED, take input from a switch, or drive current through a relay. With a wide variety of uses, the actual drive mode can vary depending on the implementation and application. When choosing hardware, some key items to ask a board vendor about the GPIO are the voltage level tolerances, how much current the pins can source in output mode, are the pins bi-direction, and what is the drive mode. The most important information to look for is the starting state of the GPIO pin and whether it is an open-collector output or has internal pull-up resistors. You don't want to design a circuit that gets triggered by a logic 1 from a GPIO output that initially starts with a logic 1 on boot up. A good user manual will list the GPIO pins and their starting states and physical properties. If the GPIO pins are coming from the processor, you can refer to the processor's datasheets for more information. The boards listed in the previous chapter have input and output drive modes as there are no internal and external pull-up or pull-down resistors. The implementation direction, voltage tolerances, and starting state will be different for each board.

With that brief introduction, the focus of this chapter is to implement some of the key features of the Windows Runtime GPIO Namespace.

11.1 Windows Runtime GPIO Namespace

The GPIO namespace consists of 5 Classes with various methods, properties, and events, 2 Structures for diagnostics, and 6 Enumerations for various values. The following table provides a usage guideline for the namespace:

Type : Name	Basic Function	Event	Diagnostic
Class : GpioChangeCounter			X
Class : GpioChangeReader			X
Class : GpioController	X		
Class : GpioPin	X		
Class : GpioPinValueChangedEventArgs		X	
Struct : GpioChangeCount			X
Struct : GpioChangeRecord			X
Enum : GpioChangePolarity			X
Enum : GpioOpenStatus	X		X
Enum : GpioPinDriveMode	X		

Type : Name	Basic Function	Event	Diagnostic
Enum : GpioPinEdge		X	
Enum : GpioPinValue	X		
Enum : GpioSharingMode	X		

The GPIO diagnostic features allow you to count the level changes of a GPIO pin over a given period of time. This is a very helpful tool to find out if an application is missing events.

11.2 GpioTestTool

The last chapter covered the Bus Tools sample applications. The GpioTestTool can be used to list all the available GPIO pins in a system, as well as, perform basic I/O operations on a specific GPIO Pin. The list of available GPIO pins doesn't mean they are accessible. Some systems will report a few internal GPIOs that are not accessible. The GpioTestTool can be used to further test each GPIO pin.

To access a specific pin, run GpioTestTool with the GPIO number. Once you do, you type "help" to get the list of commands available.

```
C:\test>GpioTestTool.exe
Missing required command line parameter PinNumber

GpioTestTool: Command line GPIO testing utility
Usage: GpioTestTool.exe [-list] PinNumber

  -list        List the available pins on the default GPIO controller.
  PinNumber    The pin number with which you wish to interact. This
               parameter is required.

Example:
  GpioTestTool.exe -list
  GpioTestTool.exe 47

C:\test>GpioTestTool.exe 0
Type 'help' for a list of commands
> help
Commands:
 > write 0|1                        Write pin low (0) or high (1)
 > high                             Alias for 'write 1'
 > low                              Alias for 'write 0'
 > toggle                          Toggle the pin from its current state
 > read                             Read pin
 > setdrivemode drive_mode          Set the pins's drive mode
    where drive_mode = input|output|
                       inputPullUp|inputPullDown
 > interrupt on|off                 Register or unregister for pin value
```

```
                                    change events.
 > info                             Dump information about the pin
 > help                             Display this help message
 > quit                             Quit
```

You can get the basic setup of the pin:

```
> info
        Pin Number: 0
      Sharing Mode: Exclusive
  Debounce Timeout: 0 ms
        Drive Mode: input
             Value: High
```

You can change the setup and toggle the pin.

```
> setdrivemode output
> read
High
> low
> read
Low
```

You can attach something to a pin and perform basic commands to test the attached device. Now, let's take a look at a few programming examples.

11.3 Exercise 1101 Basic Output – The Flashing LED

The first program is the hello world for GPIO programs, the toggling LED. You will need a resistor-LED circuit as follows that is connected to a GPIO used for output.

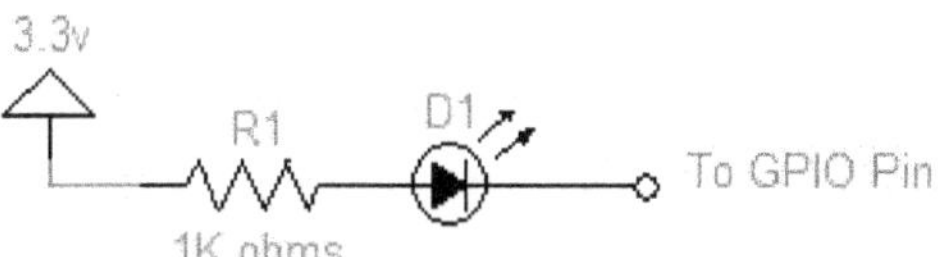

We will use the target system setup in Exercise 1001 to test the circuit and the application.

11.3.1 Basic Setup and Notes on Remote Debugging

Let's create the basic program. If you have Visual Studio installed on your target machine that is fine, but most people will want to do a remote debugging.

1. Open Visual Studio 2022.
2. Create a new "WPF Application" project. Make sure you select the correct WPF Application template for .NET.

Note: The project is a .NET application, not a .NET Framework application. If you see .NET Framework in the project description, it is the wrong project.

3. Click Next.
4. Name the project "GPIO-ToggleLED" and set the folder location to C:\VS-Apps on your development machine. To do remote debugging with .NET, the remote machine folder architecture must match the development machine. Visual Studio Remote Debugging documentation describes the setup as well.
5. Click Next.
6. Select .NET 6.0 (Long-term support) from the drop-down box.
7. Click the Create Button.
8. Once the application opens, we need to do a little more set up to support the Windows Runtime Namespaces. There is a little trick that has to be performed by selecting the Target Windows OS and Target Framework. We already selected the Target Framework so the next step here is to select the target OS. From the menu, select Project->GPIO-ToggleLED Properties.
9. Under Application->General set the following for the targeted Windows OS:
    a. Target OS version: 10.0.19041.0
    b. Supported OS version: 10.0.19041.0

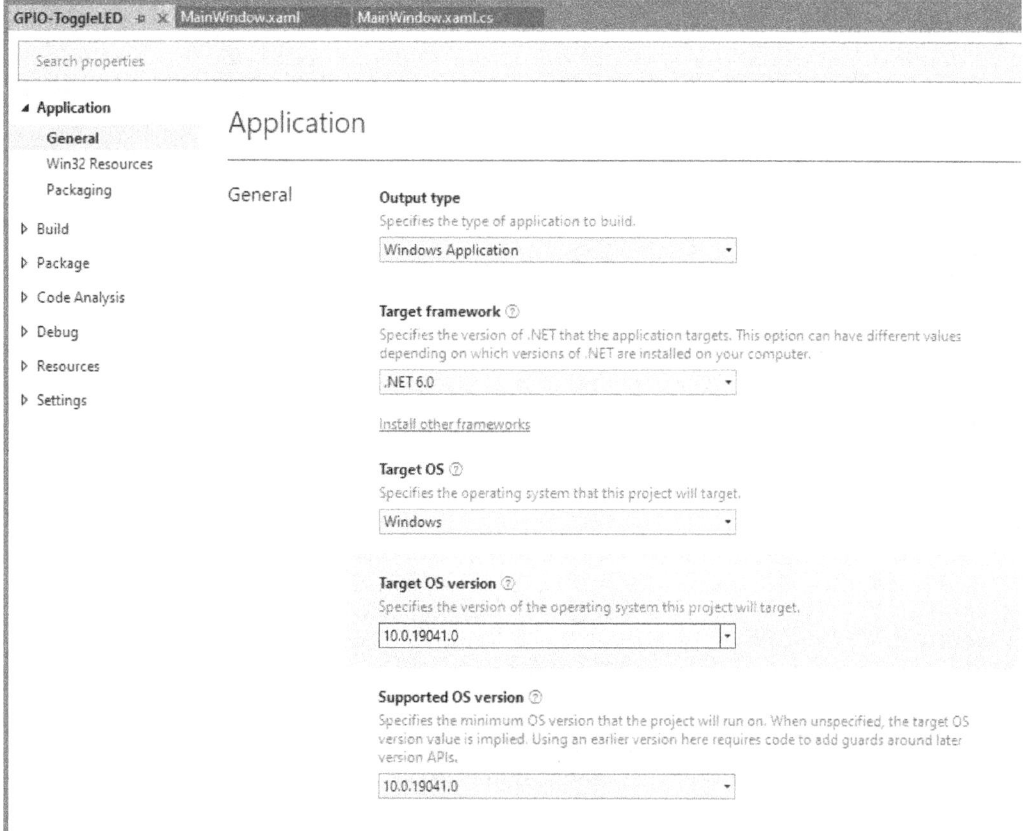

10. Scroll down the Build, and set the following:
    a. Platform target: x64

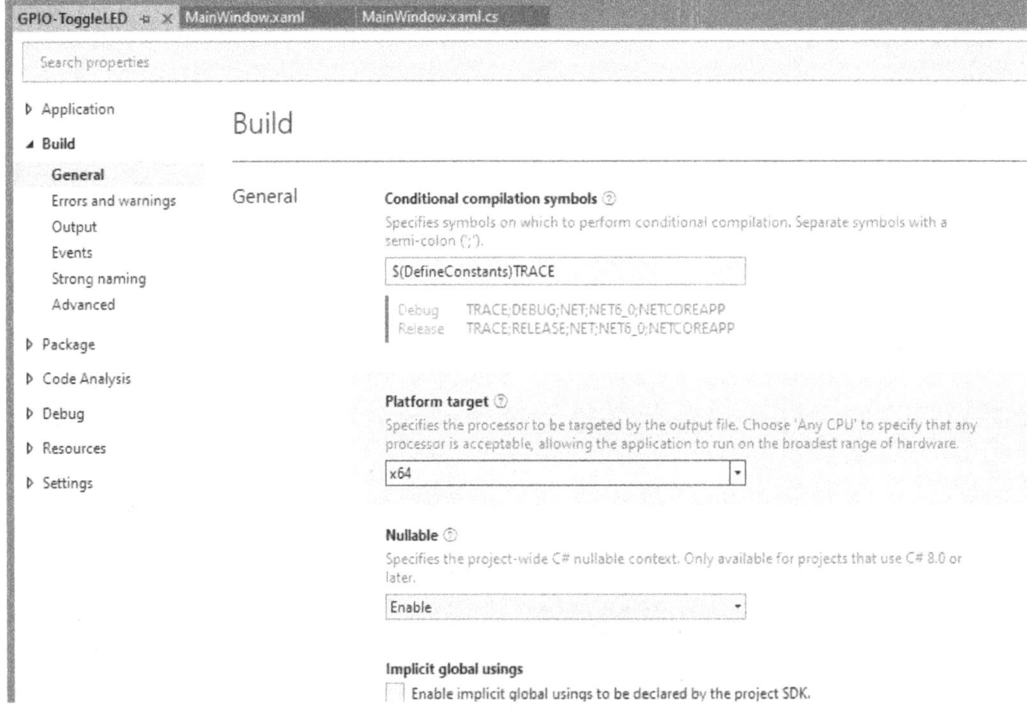

Note: If you forget to set the correct Target Framework and Target OS, Visual Studio will not let you reference the Windows.Devices namespace.

11. Save the project.

11.3.2 Set Up the XAML Controls

A single button on the page will be used to toggle the external LED. A text box will hold status messages from the code.

1. In Solution Explorer, open the MainWindow.xaml.
2. The designer and XAML editor will appear. At the top, left of the Designer, set the orientation that fits your target's display.
3. Set the Background to black. Click on the application in designer, in Properties->Brush select Solid Color Brush, and leave the default black color.
4. Add a Button to the middle of the grid.
    a. Name: btnToggle
    b. Common->Content: Toggle LED
5. Add a TextBox Control below the button near the bottom of the application.
    a. Name: txtStatus
    b. Common->Text: Status

6. Save the MainWindow.xaml file.

Here is the XAML Code:

```
<Window x:Class="GPIO_ToggleLED.MainWindow"
     xmlns="http://schemas.microsoft.com/winfx/2006/xaml/presentation"
     xmlns:x="http://schemas.microsoft.com/winfx/2006/xaml"
     xmlns:d="http://schemas.microsoft.com/expression/blend/2008"
     xmlns:mc="http://schemas.openxmlformats.org/markup-compatibility/2006"
     xmlns:local="clr-namespace:GPIO_ToggleLED"
     mc:Ignorable="d"
     Title="MainWindow" Height="450" Width="800">
  <Grid Background="Black">
     <Button x:Name="btnToggle" Content="Toggle LED"
HorizontalAlignment="Left" Height="57" Margin="257,135,0,0"
VerticalAlignment="Top" Width="263"/>
     <TextBox x:Name="txtStatus" HorizontalAlignment="Left" Height="65"
Margin="200,257,0,0" TextWrapping="Wrap" Text="Status" VerticalAlignment="Top"
Width="433"/>

  </Grid>
</Window>
```

11.3.3 Write the Code

Now let's write the code behind the GUI.

1. Open MainWindow.xaml.cs
2. Add the following using statement to enable the GPIO namespace:

```
using Windows.Devices.Gpio;
```

3. Just inside the MainWindow class add the following private variables and constant:

```
private GpioPin myPin;
private const int GPIO_LED_PIN = 0;
```

The GPIO_LED_PIN holds the pin number for the GPIO connected to the circuit. GPIO 0 is being used for the UP board in this case. Change the number to match your hardware. You will also notice that MainWindow() has a warning about a non-nullable field for myPin. Since myPin is used in different methods in the program, it has to be accessible. You can follow the Visual Studio recommendation to suppress the warning.

Note: You must set GPIO 0 to output in the BIOS for the UP Boards. Please see the previous chapter for the HAT pinout.

4. After the MainWindows() method, create a new public GPIOSetUp() method to initialize the GPIO pin:

```
public void GPIOSetUp()
{
    GpioController myGPIOController = GpioController.GetDefault();
    if (myGPIOController == null)
    {
  txtStatus.Text = "GPIO controller NOT found";
    }
    else
    {
        try
        {
            myPin = myGPIOController.OpenPin(GPIO_LED_PIN);
        }
        catch(Exception ex)
        {
            txtStatus.Text = "Error!: " + ex.ToString();
        }
        if(myPin == null)
        {
            txtStatus.Text = "GPIO " + GPIO_LED_PIN.ToString() + " not
found";
        }
        else
        {
            try
            {
                myPin.SetDriveMode(GpioPinDriveMode.Output);
                myPin.Write(GpioPinValue.High);
                txtStatus.Text = "GPIO is ready";
            }
            catch(Exception ex)
            {
                txtStatus.Text = "Error!: " + ex.ToString();
            }
        }
    }
}
```

The code has several steps to set up the GPIO pin. The first step is to get access to the default controller. There is typically one and only one GPIO controller available. The next step is to open the GPIO_LED_PIN and report any errors. As mentioned before, there can be multiple GPIO pins in a system that are listed but not accessible, so a check is put in place to see if myPin is null. The final step is to set the drive mode and report back the status.

5. In MainWindow.xaml, double-click on the button to generate the click event behind the button.
6. Add the following code in the btnToggle_Click handler:

```
private void btnToggle_Click(object sender, RoutedEventArgs e)
{
    if (myPin.Read() == GpioPinValue.High)
    {
        myPin.Write(GpioPinValue.Low);
    }
    else
    {
        myPin.Write(GpioPinValue.High);
    }
}
```

The code performs a basic toggle each time the button is pressed to send a high or low to the GPIO pin. When Low, the LED turns on, and when High, the LED turns off.

7. Save the project.
8. Build a debug version of the project and correct any errors.

11.3.4 Test the Application

The application is ready to be tested in the target system. To do remote debugging, we have to make a few more changes to the project settings:

1. In the C:\VS-Apps folder of your development machine, determine where the GPIO-ToggleLED.exe file is located: C:\VS-Apps\GPIO-ToggleLED\GPIO-ToggleLED\bin\Debug\net6.0-windows10.0.19041.0.
2. On the target machine, create an exact folder structure under c:\VS-apps - C:\VS-Apps\GPIO-ToggleLED\GPIO-ToggleLED\bin\Debug\net6.0-windows10.0.19041.0 that matches the development machine.
3. Run Visual Studio Remote Debug, and make a note of the computer name and port number listed in the Visual Studio Remote Debug output.
4. In Visual Studio running on the development machine, open the GPIO-ToggleLED Properties page.
5. Click on Debug, on the left side, and click Open debug launch profile UI.
6. Check the check box for Use remote machine and enter the Target systems computer name with the port number e.g. “X64-APPTEST:4026”.

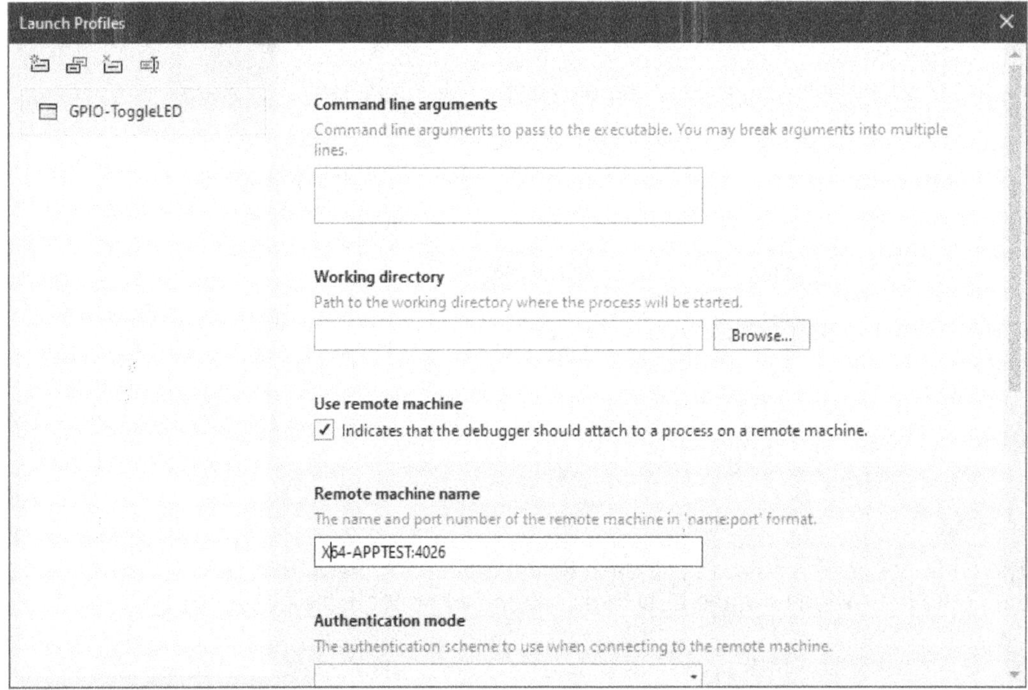

7. Close the Window.
8. In the properties, scroll up to Build Events.
9. In the Post-build event, enter the following to do a copy of the output to the remote system (this is all one line):

xcopy C:\VS-Apps\GPIO-ToggleLED\GPIO-ToggleLED\bin\Debug\net6.0-windows10.0.19041.0 \\X64-APPTEST\VS-Apps\GPIO-ToggleLED\GPIO-ToggleLED\bin\Debug\net6.0-windows10.0.19041.0 /Y

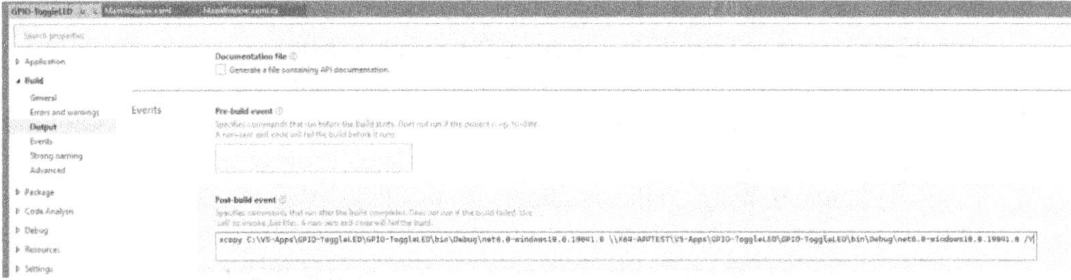

10. Save the project.
11. Build the debug version of the application again. The output files should be copied to the remote system.
12. Start the debug session.

13. You will be asked for the target system's login credentials. Enter the user's name and password and click OK.
14. Once the application has loaded on the target system, click on the Toggle Button and watch the LED turn on and off.
15. Stop debugging when finished.

11.4 Exercise 1102 Input Interrupt

Building on the last exercise, this exercise will add an RC-inverter circuit as a one-shot pulse generator to act as an interrupt source to a GPIO pin. On each rising edge of the interrupt, the application will toggle the state of the LED connected to another GPIO to transition either from on to off or from off to on.

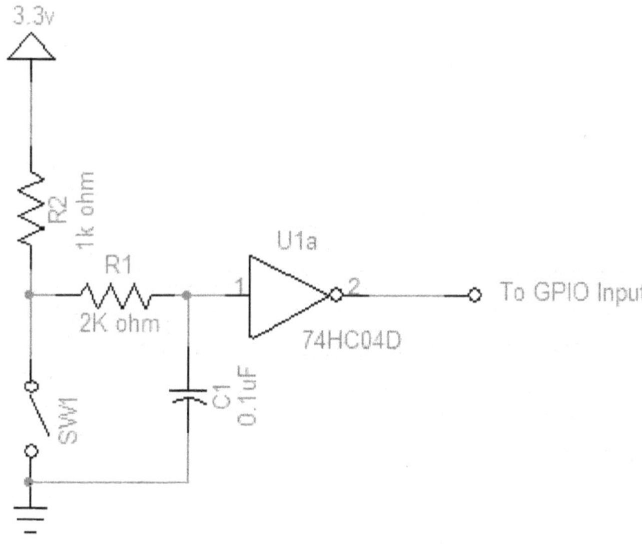

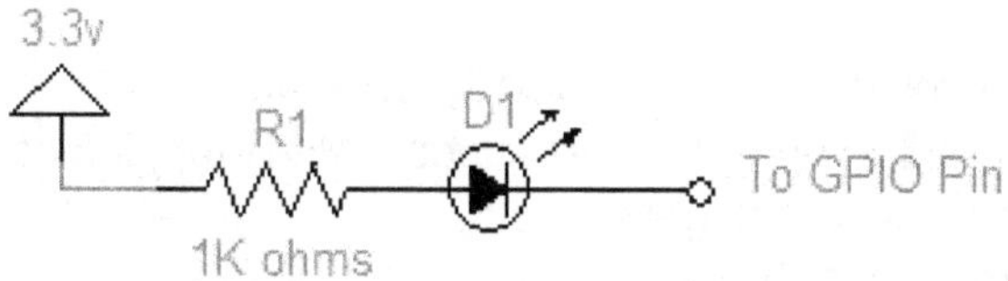

11.4.1 Basic Setup

First, let's create the project.

1. Open Visual Studio 2022

2. Create a new "WPF Application" project. Make sure you select the correct WPF Application template for .NET.

Note: The project is a .NET application, not a .NET Framework application. If you see .NET Framework in the project description, it is the wrong project.

3. Click Next.
4. Name the project "GPIO-InputInterrupt" and set the folder location to C:\VS-Apps on your development machine.
5. Click Next.
6. Select .NET 6.0 (Long-term support) from the drop-down box.
7. Click the "Create" button.
8. Once the application opens, we need to do a little more set up to support the Windows Runtime Namespaces. There is a little trick that has to be performed by selecting the Target Windows OS and Target Framework. We already selected the Target Framework so the next step here is to select the target OS. From the menu, select Project->GPIO-ToggleLED Properties.
9. Under Application->General set the following for the targeted Windows OS:
    a. Target OS version: 10.0.19041.0
    b. Supported OS version: 10.0.19041.0
10. Scroll down the Build, and set the following:
    a. Platform target: x64
11. Click on Debug on the left side, and click Open debug launch profile UI.
12. Check the check box for Use remote machine and enter the Target system's computer name with the port number e.g. "X64-APPTEST:4026".
13. Close the Window.
14. Save the project.

11.4.2 Set Up the XAML Controls

Since an external button is being used to perform the toggle, the GUI will only contain a text box for any status messages from the code.

1. In Solution Explorer, open the MainWindow.xaml.
2. The designer and XAML editor will appear. At the top, left of the Designer, set the orientation that fits your target's display.
3. Set the Background to black.
4. Add a TextBox Control toward the bottom of the application.
    a. Name: txtStatus
    b. Common->Text: Status
5. Save the MainPage.xaml file.

Here is the XAML Code:

```
<Window x:Class="GPIO_InputInterrupt.MainWindow"
      xmlns="http://schemas.microsoft.com/winfx/2006/xaml/presentation"
      xmlns:x="http://schemas.microsoft.com/winfx/2006/xaml"
      xmlns:d="http://schemas.microsoft.com/expression/blend/2008"
      xmlns:mc="http://schemas.openxmlformats.org/markup-compatibility/2006"
      xmlns:local="clr-namespace:GPIO_InputInterrupt"
      mc:Ignorable="d"
      Title="MainWindow" Height="450" Width="800">
   <Grid Background="Black">
      <TextBox x:Name="txtStatus" HorizontalAlignment="Left" Height="76"
Margin="242,188,0,0" TextWrapping="Wrap" Text="Status" VerticalAlignment="Top"
Width="290"/>
   </Grid>
</Window>
```

11.4.3 Write the Code

The code is similar to the previous application. The difference will be a value-change event handler instead of a button event handler.

1. Open MainWindow.xaml.cs
2. Add the following using statement to enable GPIO namespace:

```
using Windows.Devices.Gpio;
```

3. Just inside the MainWindow class add the following private variables and constant:

```
private GpioPin myLedPin;
private const int GPIO_LED_PIN = 0;
private GpioPin myInterrupt;
private const int GPIO_INT_PIN = 1;
```

The GPIO_LED_PIN and GPIO_INT_PIN hold the pin numbers for the GPIO's connected to the circuits. Change the numbers to match your hardware. You will also notice that MainWindows() has a warning about a non-nullable field for myPin. Since myPin is used in different methods in the program, it has to be accessible. You can follow the Visual Studio recommendation to suppress the warning.

4. After the MainWindow() method, create a new public GPIOSetUp() method to initialize the GPIO pins and event handler:

```
public void GPIOSetUp()
{
    GpioController myGPIOController = GpioController.GetDefault();
```

```
    if (myGPIOController == null)
    {
        txtStatus.Text = "GPIO controller NOT found";
    }
    else
    {
        try
        {
            myLedPin = myGPIOController.OpenPin(GPIO_LED_PIN);
            myInterrupt = myGPIOController.OpenPin(GPIO_INT_PIN);
        }
        catch (Exception ex)
        {
            txtStatus.Text = "Error!: " + ex.ToString();
        }
        if (myLedPin == null)
        {
            txtStatus.Text = "GPIO " + GPIO_LED_PIN.ToString() + " not
found";

        }else if (myInterrupt == null)
        {
            txtStatus.Text = "GPIO " + GPIO_INT_PIN.ToString() + " not
found";
        }
        else
        {
            try
        {
                myLedPin.SetDriveMode(GpioPinDriveMode.Output);
                myLedPin.Write(GpioPinValue.High);

                myInterrupt.SetDriveMode(GpioPinDriveMode.Input);
                myInterrupt.ValueChanged += MyInterrupt_ValueChanged;

                txtStatus.Text = "GPIO is ready";
            }
            catch (Exception ex)
            {
                txtStatus.Text = "Error!: " + ex.ToString();
            }
        }
    }
}
```

The code checks on both GPIO pins to make sure they are not null. Once the GPIO is set up, the myLedPin's drive mode is set to output, and myInterrupt's drive mode is set to input. A value change event is set up for myInterrupt.

5. Fill in the following code of the value change event:

```
private void MyInterrupt_ValueChanged(GpioPin sender,
GpioPinValueChangedEventArgs args)
{
   if(GpioPinEdge.RisingEdge == args.Edge)
   {
      if (myLedPin.Read() == GpioPinValue.High)
      {
     myLedPin.Write(GpioPinValue.Low);
      }
      else
      {
           myLedPin.Write(GpioPinValue.High);
      }
   }
}
```

When the switch is open the inverter is outputting a 0 or Low. As soon as the button is pressed the Low becomes a high for a few seconds until the button is released to drop back to a Low. A check is made to verify that a rising edge (Low to High) was detected before turning the LED on or off. If this rising edge check was not made, then the code needs to be tested for a level interrupt.

6. Save the project.
7. Build a debug version of the project and correct any errors.

11.4.4 Test the Application

The application is ready to be tested in the target system. To do remote, debugging we have to make a few more changes to the project settings:

1. In the C:\VS-Apps folder of you development machine, determine where the GPIO-ToggleLED.exe file is located: C:\VS-Apps\GPIO-InputInterrupt\GPIO-InputInterrupt\bin\Debug\net6.0-windows10.0.19041.0
2. On the target machine, create an exact folder structure under c:\VS-apps - C:\VS-Apps\GPIO-InputInterrupt\GPIO-InputInterrupt\bin\Debug\net6.0-windows10.0.19041.0 that matches the development machine.
3. Run Visual Studio Remote Debug, and make a note of the computer name and port number listed in the Visual Studio Remote Debug output.
4. In Visual Studio running on the development machine, open the GPIO-ToggleLED Properties page.
5. In the properties, scroll up to Build Events.

6. In the Post-build event, enter the following to do a copy of the output to the remote system (this is all one line):

xcopy C:\VS-Apps\\GPIO-InputInterrupt\GPIO-InputInterrupt\bin\Debug\net6.0-windows10.0.19041.0 \\X64-APPTEST\VS-Apps\GPIO-InputInterrupt\GPIO-InputInterrupt\bin\Debug\net6.0-windows10.0.19041.0 /Y

7. Save the project.
8. Build the debug version of the application again. The output files should be copied to the remote system.
9. Start the debug session. The project will be deployed to the target system.
10. You will be asked for the target system's login credentials. Enter the user's name and password and click OK.
11. Once the application has loaded on the target system, push the switch on the one-shot RC-inverter circuit to trigger an interrupt. The LED should turn on or off. Hit the switch a few times to see the LED toggle on and off.
12. Stop debugging when finished.

11.4.5 Interrupt Latency Test

As stated in an earlier chapter, Windows is not a deterministic operating system. With all the services and processes that are running, there will be delays to any event response. Using an O-Scope, you get can see the latency change with each push of the button.

1. Start the debugger to download and run the application on the target platform.
2. Connect two O-scope probes to the 2 GPIO pins.
3. Set up the O-Scope for a single trigger set on the rising edge of the interrupt signal (GPIO input).
4. Hit the one-shot switch and you should see two signals. You may have to adjust the sec/dev to see the delta time between the two signals. You may have to reset the trigger and try again to get a good picture. In the figure below, the upper trace is the interrupt and the lower trace is the output.
5. Using the cursors, the time delta (latency) between the rising edge of the one-shot circuit, and the transition of the output GPIO can be measured.
6. Reset the O-scope trigger and hit the one-shot switch. The latency will be different.

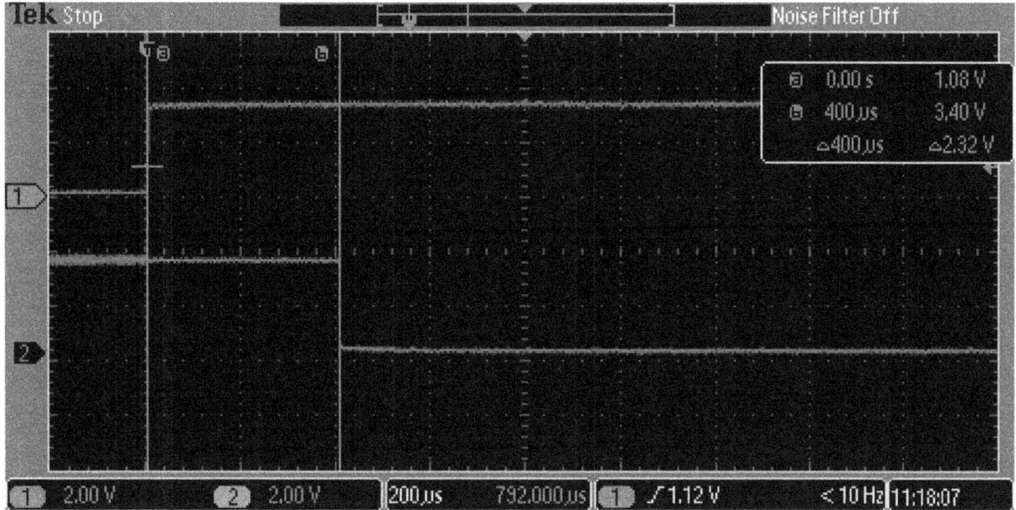

11.5 Exercise 1103 – Diagnostics

The GPIO namespace includes some diagnostic APIs to get the change event counts and time stamps. The last exercises will be modified to provide a count of the rise edge interrupt and a record for changes on the LED pin.

1. Add a Button to the middle of the grid and above the status text box control.
   a. Name: btnGetCount
   b. Common->Content: Get Count
2. Add another button next to the Get Count button
   a. Name: btnReadData
   b. Common->Content: Get Reader Data
3. Add two more private variables for the counter.

```
private GpioChangeCounter myCounter;
private GpioChangeReader myReader;
```

4. In GPIOSetup() method, add a couple of lines to instantiate the new GpioChangeCounter to myInterrupt and start the counter.

```
public void GPIOSetUp()
{
    GpioController myGPIOController = GpioController.GetDefault();
    if (myGPIOController == null)
    {
        txtStatus.Text = "GPIO controller NOT found";
    }
    else
```

```
    {
        try
        {
            myLedPin = myGPIOController.OpenPin(GPIO_LED_PIN);
            myInterrupt = myGPIOController.OpenPin(GPIO_INT_PIN);
            myCounter = new GpioChangeCounter(myInterrupt);
            myCounter.Polarity = GpioChangePolarity.Rising;
            myReader = new GpioChangeReader(myLedPin);
            myReader.Polarity = GpioChangePolarity.Both;

        }
        catch (Exception ex)
        {
            txtStatus.Text = "Error!: " + ex.ToString();
        }
        if (myLedPin == null)
        {
            txtStatus.Text = "GPIO " + GPIO_LED_PIN.ToString() + " not
found";

        }else if (myInterrupt == null)
        {
            txtStatus.Text = "GPIO " + GPIO_INT_PIN.ToString() + " not
found";
        }
        else
        {
            try
            {
                myLedPin.SetDriveMode(GpioPinDriveMode.Output);
                myLedPin.Write(GpioPinValue.High);

                myInterrupt.SetDriveMode(GpioPinDriveMode.Input);
                myInterrupt.ValueChanged += MyInterrupt_ValueChanged;

                myCounter.Start();
                myReader.Start();
                txtStatus.Text = "GPIO is ready";
            }
            catch (Exception ex)
            {
                txtStatus.Text = "Error!: " + ex.ToString();
            }
        }
    }
}
```

5. Double-click on the Get Count button to generate a button handler, and fill in the following code:

```
private void btnGetCount_Click(object sender,
Windows.UI.Xaml.RoutedEventArgs e)
{
   txtStatus.Text = "Interrupt Count: " +
myCounter.Read().Count.ToString() + " Relative time:  " +
myCounter.Read().RelativeTime.ToString();
}
```

6. Double-click on the Read Data button to generate a button handler, and fill in the following code:

```
private void btnReadData_Click(object sender,
Windows.UI.Xaml.RoutedEventArgs e)
{

    var myRecords = myReader.GetAllItems();

    txtStatus.Text = "";

    foreach(GpioChangeRecord aRecord in myRecords)
    {
      txtStatus.Text += "Time: " + aRecord.RelativeTime.ToString() + "
Edge Type: " + aRecord.Edge.ToString() + "\n";
    }
}
```

7. Save, build, and debug the project.
8. Hit the one-shot button a few times, and then click on the Get Count button to see how many times the button was pressed.
9. Click on the Read Data button to get a list of times and types of edge changes to the LED button.
10. Stop debugging when finished.

The GPIOChangeCounter and GPIOChangeReader can help diagnose issues or track when values changed on a given interrupt pin.

11.6 Summary: 1 and 0

GPIOs are very common hardware interconnect mechanisms in control systems. The chapter showed what to look for in hardware and provided basic application examples for the usage of the Windows Runtime GPIO namespace. Other I/O like SPI and I2C sometimes take advantage of a GPIO to handle an interrupt signal.

12 UART

Serial ports have been mainstays in computing since the 1960s. Serial ports have been used to connect computers to devices like terminals, modems, printers, chip-to-chip communication, and other equipment. In this chapter, we will be discussing the UART or universal asynchronous receiver/transmitter serial port. Most microcontrollers include UART ports that are TTL or 3.3V compatible to connect to other chips. For longer transmissions between systems, converter chips are used for a more robust longer-distance electrical connection. RS-232 is the most popular serial port, but there are also other standards like RS-422, RS-423, RS-449, and RS-485 that have had wide use.

12.1 Serial Port Standards

The following table covers the different serial port standards

Serial Port Standard	Description
UART	The basic UART port is available on most microprocessors. UARTs are typically used to communicate with local UART devices on the same board. The 3 main UART signals are RX, TX, and GND, and they are typically TTL 0 to 5V or 0 to 3.3V depending on the processor. The UART signals can be buffered for longer transmissions with level-shifting transceivers like RS-232.
RS-232	RS-232 is one of the oldest and most popular serial communication standards. Personal computers have used RS-232 ports since the first IBM PCs were introduced in August of 1981. Speed is a limiting factor for RS-232 topping out at 256K baud. Regardless of the limitation of today's hyper-fast PCs, many embedded systems still use RS-232. Signal-wise, RS-232 defines voltage levels and the conditions for logic ones and zeroes. Unlike SPI, voltage levels are within +/- 15 volts. A positive voltage is a logic zero and a negative voltage is logic one. Ground is at zero volts and voltages near zero volts are not valid RS-232 logic levels. The voltage levels themselves will be dependent on the power supply available. Some transceiver chips include special charge pump circuitry to produce the RS-232 signal voltages from a single, low voltage DC power source. These chips take the 0 and 1 logic levels and translate them to RS-232 signal levels. The iPac-9302 makes use of these transceiver chips so additional power supply inputs to support the RS-232 voltage levels are not needed. Depending on the transmitter drivers, the bit rate, and the capacitance of the cable, RS-232 cable lengths are

Serial Port Standard	Description
	typically a few feet long: 25 to 50 feet (6 to 15 meters). Low capacitance RS-232 cables can extend that range to up to 100 feet (30.5 meters).
RS-422	RS-422 offers a different signal scheme using balanced or differential signaling. The advantage of RS-422 over RS-232 is the potential for higher baud rates and longer cable lengths. The cabling defined by the standard is usually a twisted pair with a maximum cable length of 3900 feet (1200 meters). RS-422 has been used to extend the transmission length between devices. RS-422 also supports multi-drop connections, where one driver can signal up to 10 receivers.
RS-485	RS-485 is another differential signal standard that supports cable lengths up to 4000 feet (1200m). Unlike RS-422, RS-485 supports multipoint serial communication, where up to 32 transceivers and 32 receivers can be connected to the same 2 wires. Communication is half-duplex. Signaling is based on voltage transmission with signals ranging from -7 to +12V. RS-485 has no data protocol defined, so it is up to the developer to define the protocol. This means careful designing must go into interfacing systems with RS-485 to avoid communication collisions.

12.2 Windows Runtime SerialCommunication Namespace and Other Namespaces

The SerialCommunication Namespace can access serial devices that are exposed as discussed in Chapter 10. UART serial devices can be accessed through the SerCx2.sys driver or Serial-to-USB usber.sys, as well as popular USB serial devices from FTDI, Prolific, and Silicon-Labs. The classic built-in PC serial COM ports are not supported.

The SerialCommunication Namespace consists of 3 classes and several Enumerators, but the main class is the SerialDevice class which contains the core properties, events, and methods used to enumerate access to the serial device. Notice that the read, write, or data receive event was mentioned since data to and from a serial port is a stream. The Windows Storage Stream classes DataReader and DataWriter are used to read and write to the serial port. Tasks are used in place of events to send and receive the data stream.

Type : Name	Basic Function	Event	Diagnostic
Class : ErrorReceivedEventArgs		X	
Class : PinChangedEventArgs		X	
Class : SeriealDevice	X		
Enum: Serial Error	X		
Enum: SerialHandshake	X		
Enum: SeralParity	X		
Enum: SerialPinChange	X		
Enum: SerialStopBitCount	X		

12.3 PC Serial Ports – SerialPort Class

In contrast to the SerialCommunication Namespace, is the old reliable SerialPort Class for Windows Form applications and PC serial and USB to serial COM ports. The SerialPort class has been covered extensively, so the following exercises will focus on the SerialCommunication Namespace. As we go through the exercises, the reason will be self-evident.

	UART Ports (ARM, x86, x64)	USB to Serial (ARM, x86, x64)	PC Serial Ports (x86, x64)
Windows Runtime SerialCommunication Namespace	X	X	
SerialPort Class		X	X

12.4 MinComm.exe

Chapter 10 covered the Bus Tools sample applications. The Mincomm.exe test tool can be used to list all the available UARTS in a system. The list of available UARTs doesn't mean they are accessible. Some systems will report a few internal UARTSs that are not accessible.

```
C:\test>MinComm.exe -help
MinComm: Serial Terminal for OneCore
Usage: MinComm.exe [-list] device_path [baud=<B>] [parity=<P>] [data=<D>]
[stop=<S>]      [xon={on|off}]      [odsr={on|off}]      [octs={on|off}]
[dtr={on|off|hs}] [rts={on|off|hs|tg}] [idsr={on|off}]
  -list                List all available serial ports on the system and
exit.
  device_path          Device path or COM port to open (e.g. COM1)
  baud=<B>            Specifies the transmission rate in bits per second.
  parity={n|e|o|m|s}   Specifies how the system uses the parity bit to
check
                       for transmission errors. The abbreviations stand
for
                       none, even, odd, mark, and space.
  data={5|6|7|8}       Specifies the number of data bits in a character.
  stop={1|1.5|2}       Specifies the number of stop bits that define the
end of
                       a character.
  xon={on|off}           Specifies whether the xon or xoff protocol for
data-flow
                       control is on or off.
  odsr={on|off}       Specifies whether output handshaking that uses the
                       Data Set Ready (DSR) circuit is on or off.
  octs={on|off}       Specifies whether output handshaking that uses the
```

```
                      Clear To Send (CTS) circuit is on or off.
  dtr={on|off|hs}      Specifies whether the Data Terminal Ready (DTR)
circuit
                      is on or off or set to handshake.
  rts={on|off|hs|tg}  Specifies whether the Request To Send (RTS) circuit
is
                      set to on, off, handshake, or toggle.
  idsr={on|off}        Specifies whether the DSR circuit sensitivity is
on
                      or off.
Parameters that are not specified will default to the port's current
configuration. For more information on the connection parameters, see the
Technet documentation for the Mode command:
  https://technet.microsoft.com/en-us/library/cc732236.aspx
Examples:
  Connect to the first serial port found in the port's current
configuration:
    MinComm.exe
  List all serial ports on the system:
    MinComm.exe -list
  Open COM1 in 115200 8N1 configuration:
    MinComm.exe COM1 baud=115200 parity=n data=8 stop=1

  Open COM1 in 115200 8N1 configuration:
    MinComm.exe \\.\COM1 baud=115200 parity=n data=8 stop=1
  Open device interface in 115200 8N1 configuration:
    MinComm.exe      \\?\USB#VID_FFFF&PID_0005#{86e0d1e0-8089-11d0-9ce4-
08003e301f73} baud=115200 parity=n data=8 stop=1
```

12.5 Exercise 1201: Serial Transmit with SparkFun™ SerLCD

SparkFun.com has a number of electronic hobby builder products. This exercise will use a SparkFun 16 x 2 matrix Serial LCD. SparkFun has a number of these devices that have different output colors. As of this writing, the latest LCDs support SPI, I2C, and Serial interfaces. The application will have an interface allowing the user to enter some text and send it to the display.

Note: The following exercise is based on an older Serial LCD model (4/15/2015) that has a different 3.3v powered controller, so the command set will be different.

Note: Make sure that you have completed Exercise 1001 to set up a target system.

12.5.1 Basic Setup

Here is the basic setup of the application.

1. Open Visual Studio 2022.

2. Create a new "WPF Application" project. Make sure you select the correct WPF Application template for .NET.

Note: The project is a .NET application, not a .NET Framework application. If you see .NET Framework in the project description it is the wrong project.

3. Name the project "UART-SerLCD" and set the folder location to C:\VS-Apps on your development machine. To do remote debugging with .NET, the remote machine folder architecture must match the development machine. Visual Studio Remote Debugging documentation describes the setup as well.
4. Click the "Next" button.
5. Select .NET 6.0 (Long-term support) from the drop-down box.
6. Click the "Create" button.
7. Once the application opens, we need to do a little more set up to support the Windows Runtime Namespaces. From the menu, select Project->UART-SerLCD Properties.
8. Under Application->General set the following for the targeted Windows OS:
    a. Target OS version: 10.0.19041.0
    b. Supported OS version: 10.0.19041.0
9. Scroll down the Build, and set the following:
    a. Platform target: x64

Note: If you forget to set the correct Target Framework and Target OS, Visual Studio will not let you reference the Windows.Devices namespace.

10. Save the project.

12.5.2 Set Up the XAML Controls

The UI will have a text box and a button. The text box will allow the user to enter a message, and a button control will then send the message to the LCD.

1. In Solution Explorer, open the MainWindow.xaml.
2. The designer and XAML editor will appear. At the top, left of the Designer set the orientation that fits your target's display.
3. Set the Background to black. Click on the application in designer, in Properties->Brush select Solid Color Brush, and leave the default black color.
4. Add a TextBox Control.
    a. Name: txtMessage
    b. Common->Text: Write Message Here
5. Add a Button control below the text box
    c. Name: btnSend

    d. Common->Content: Send Message to LCD

6. Save the project.

Here is the XAML Code:

```
<Window x:Class="UART_SerLCD.MainWindow"
      xmlns="http://schemas.microsoft.com/winfx/2006/xaml/presentation"
      xmlns:x="http://schemas.microsoft.com/winfx/2006/xaml"
      xmlns:d="http://schemas.microsoft.com/expression/blend/2008"
      xmlns:mc="http://schemas.openxmlformats.org/markup-compatibility/2006"
      xmlns:local="clr-namespace:UART_SerLCD"
      mc:Ignorable="d"
      Title="MainWindow" Height="450" Width="800">
   <Grid Background="Black">
      <TextBox x:Name="txtMessage" HorizontalAlignment="Left" Height="74"
Margin="83,94,0,0" TextWrapping="Wrap" Text="Write Message Here"
VerticalAlignment="Top" Width="614"/>
      <Button x:Name="btnSend" Content="Send Message to LCD"
HorizontalAlignment="Left" Height="51" Margin="101,236,0,0"
VerticalAlignment="Top" Width="230"/>
   </Grid>
</Window>
```

12.5.3 Write the Code

Now let's write the code behind the GUI.

1. Open MainWindow.xaml.cs.
2. Add the following using statements to enable SerialCommunication, Enumeration, and Storage.Streams namespaces:

```
using Windows.Devices.SerialCommunication;
using Windows.Devices.Enumeration;
using Windows.Storage.Streams;
```

3. In the MainWindow.xaml double-click on the button to generate the event handler.

The button click is going to be the core part of the application. The text in the text box control will be sent to the LCD. The button event will enumerate the UART port, send some commands to the LCD including the message and a built-in message, and then close the UART port.

4. Since serial communication is asynchronous, modify the event handler declaration by adding an "async" between "private" and "void".
5. Fill in the following code:

```
private async void btnSend_Click(object sender, RoutedEventArgs e)
{
    string aqs = SerialDevice.GetDeviceSelector("UART1");
    DeviceInformationCollection deviceInfo = await
DeviceInformation.FindAllAsync(aqs);
    SerialDevice myCom1 = await
SerialDevice.FromIdAsync(deviceInfo[0].Id);

    byte[] LCDCLEAR = new byte[] { 0xFE, 0x01 };
    byte[] LCDLINE1 = new byte[] { 0xFE, 0x80 };
    byte[] LCDLINE2 = new byte[] { 0xFE, 0xC0 };
    byte[] LCDMOVECURR1 = new byte[] { 0xFE, 0x14 };
    byte[] LCDMOVECURL1 = new byte[] { 0xFE, 0x10 };
    byte[] LCDSCROLLRIGHT = new byte[] { 0xFE, 0x1C };
    byte[] LCDSCROLLLEFT = new byte[] { 0xFE, 0x18 };
    byte[] LCDVISUALON = new byte[] { 0xFE, 0x0C };
    byte[] LCDVISUALOFF = new byte[] { 0xFE, 0x08 };
    byte[] LCDCURON = new byte[] { 0xFE, 0x0E };
    byte[] LCDCUROFF = new byte[] { 0xFE, 0x0C };
    byte[] LCDBLINKON = new byte[] { 0xFE, 0x0D };
    byte[] LCDBLINKOFF = new byte[] { 0xFE, 0x0C };


   if (myCom1 == null)
    {
        txtMessage.Text += "Error1";
    }
    else
    {
        myCom1.BaudRate = 9600;
        myCom1.DataBits = 8;
        myCom1.Parity = SerialParity.None;
        myCom1.StopBits = SerialStopBitCount.One;
        myCom1.Handshake = SerialHandshake.None;

        DataWriter dataWriter = new DataWriter(myCom1.OutputStream);
        dataWriter.WriteBytes(LCDCLEAR);
        await dataWriter.StoreAsync();
        dataWriter.WriteBytes(LCDCURON);
        await dataWriter.StoreAsync();
        dataWriter.WriteBytes(LCDBLINKON);
        await dataWriter.StoreAsync();
        dataWriter.WriteString(txtMessage.Text.ToString());
        await dataWriter.StoreAsync();
        dataWriter.WriteBytes(LCDLINE2);
        await dataWriter.StoreAsync();
        dataWriter.WriteString("Win10 IoT E");
```

```
        await dataWriter.StoreAsync();
        dataWriter.DetachStream();
        myCom1.Dispose();
    }
}
```

The first 3 lines enumerate the UART1. If your target is using a different UART port number, please change the value for your target. From the SerLCD datasheet, we have taken all the LCD controller commands and created byte array variables for each one. If the UART is instantiated correctly, the COM port settings such as baud rate, data bits, etc. are configured to match the SerLCD communication settings. The Datawriter is instantiated with the serial port as the output stream. Each command and message is sent to the Datawriter, and then the StroreAsync() method is called to transmit the data to the UART port. Once all the messages have been sent, the UART port is disposed of.

6. Save the project.
7. Build a debug version of the project and correct any errors.

12.5.4 Test the Application

The application is ready to be tested in the target system. Make sure that the SparkFun SerLCD is connect to the target board:

- Rx pin connected to the Tx of the UART on the target board
- VCC 3.3V is connect to the 3.3V pin on the target board
- GND is connect to a gnd pin on the target board.

1. In the C:\VS-Apps folder of your development machine, determine where the UART-SerLCD.exe file is located: C:\VS-Apps\UART-SerLCD\UART-SerLCD\bin\Debug\net6.0-windows10.0.19041.0
2. On the target machine, create an exact folder structure under C:\VS-apps - C:\VS-Apps\UART-SerLCD\UART-SerLCD\bin\Debug\net6.0-windows10.0.19041.0
3. Run Visual Studio Remote Debug, and make a note of the computer name and port number listed in the Visual Studio Remote Debug output.
4. In Visual Studio running on the development machine, open the UART-SerLCD Properties page.
5. Click on Debug on the left side, and click Open debug launch profile UI.
6. Check the check box for Use remote machine and enter the Target systems computer name with the port number: X64-APPTEST:4026
7. Close the Window.
8. In the properties, scroll up to Build Events.
9. In the Post-build event enter the following to do a copy of the output to the remote system (this is all one line):

xcopy C:\VS-Apps\UART-SerLCD\UART-SerLCD\bin\Debug\net6.0-windows10.0.19041.0 \\X64-APPTEST\VS-Apps\UART-SerLCD\UART-SerLCD\bin\Debug\net6.0-windows10.0.19041.0 /Y

10. Save the project.
11. Build the debug version of the application again. The output files should be copied to the remote system.
12. Start the debug session.
13. You will be asked for the target system's login credentials. Enter the user's name and password and click OK.
14. Once the application has loaded on the target system, enter a message in the text box control and hit the send message to LCD button. The LCD will show the message on line 1 and the message "Win10 IoT E" on line 2.
15. Stop debugging when finished.

You can modify the output commands to try different command options and debug the application again to see the results.

12.6 Exercise 1202 – SerLCD Assembly Library

Entering all the byte arrays for the Serial LCD commands, as well as, enumerating the UART port each time is tedious. A Class library can be created with methods for all the SerLCD commands, as well as, UART enumeration.

12.6.1 Create the Assembly Library

1. Open Visual Studio 2022, if not already open
2. Create a new project and select WPF Class Library – "A project for creating a class library that targets a .NET WPF Application".
3. Name the project SparkFunSerLCD and set the folder location to C:\VS-Apps.
4. Click Next
5. Select .NET 6.0 (Long-term support) from the drop-down box.
6. Click the "Create" button.
7. Once the application opens, we need to do a little more set up to support the Windows Runtime Namespaces. From the menu, select Project-> SparkFunSerLCD Properties.
8. Under Application->General set the following for the targeted Windows OS:
    a. Target OS version: 10.0.19041.0
    b. Supported OS version: 10.0.19041.0
9. Scroll down the Build, and set the following:
    a. Platform target: x64
10. Save the project.
11. Rename Class.cs to SparkFunSerLCD.cs and save the project.

12. Change the namespace to Annabooks.SparkFunSerLCD
13. Fill in the following code:

```
using System;
using Windows.Devices.SerialCommunication;
using Windows.Devices.Enumeration;
using Windows.Storage.Streams;
namespace Annabooks.SparkFunSerLCD
{
    public class SparkFunSerLCD
    {
        private byte[] LCDCLEAR = new byte[] { 0xFE, 0x01 };
        private byte[] LCDLINE1 = new byte[] { 0xFE, 0x80 };
        private byte[] LCDLINE2 = new byte[] { 0xFE, 0xC0 };
        private byte[] LCDMOVECURR1 = new byte[] { 0xFE, 0x14 };
        private byte[] LCDMOVECURL1 = new byte[] { 0xFE, 0x10 };
        private byte[] LCDSCROLLRIGHT = new byte[] { 0xFE, 0x1C };
        private byte[] LCDSCROLLLEFT = new byte[] { 0xFE, 0x18 };
        private byte[] LCDVISUALON = new byte[] { 0xFE, 0x0C };
        private byte[] LCDVISUALOFF = new byte[] { 0xFE, 0x08 };
        private byte[] LCDCURON = new byte[] { 0xFE, 0x0E };
        private byte[] LCDCUROFF = new byte[] { 0xFE, 0x0C };
        private byte[] LCDBLINKON = new byte[] { 0xFE, 0x0D };
        private byte[] LCDBLINKOFF = new byte[] { 0xFE, 0x0C };
        public SerialDevice UartPort;
        private DataWriter lcdUARTDataWriter;
        private bool lcdReady = false;
        public string connectionError = "";
        public SparkFunSerLCD(String uart)
        {
            LCDUARTInitialize(uart);
        }
        public async void LCDUARTInitialize(String uartPort)
        {
            try
            {
                string aqs =
SerialDevice.GetDeviceSelector(uartPort);
```

```
                DeviceInformationCollection deviceInfo = await DeviceInformation.FindAllAsync(aqs);
                UartPort = await SerialDevice.FromIdAsync(deviceInfo[0].Id);
            }
            catch (Exception ex)
            {
                connectionError = ex.Message;
            }
            if (UartPort != null)
            {
                UartPort.BaudRate = 9600;
                UartPort.DataBits = 8;
                UartPort.Parity = SerialParity.None;
                UartPort.StopBits = SerialStopBitCount.One;
                UartPort.Handshake = SerialHandshake.None;

                lcdUARTDataWriter = new DataWriter(UartPort.OutputStream);
                lcdUARTDataWriter.WriteBytes(LCDCLEAR);
                await lcdUARTDataWriter.StoreAsync();
                lcdUARTDataWriter.WriteBytes(LCDCUROFF);
                await lcdUARTDataWriter.StoreAsync();
                lcdReady = true;
            }

        }

        public async void ClearLCD()
        {
            lcdUARTDataWriter.WriteBytes(LCDCLEAR);
            await lcdUARTDataWriter.StoreAsync();
        }

        public async void LCDCursorOn()
        {
            lcdUARTDataWriter.WriteBytes(LCDCURON);
            await lcdUARTDataWriter.StoreAsync();
        }

        public async void LCDCursorOff()
        {

            lcdUARTDataWriter.WriteBytes(LCDCUROFF);
            await lcdUARTDataWriter.StoreAsync();

        }

```

```
        public async void LCDBlinkOn()
        {

            lcdUARTDataWriter.WriteBytes(LCDBLINKON);
            await lcdUARTDataWriter.StoreAsync();

        }

        public async void LCDBlinkOff()
        {

            lcdUARTDataWriter.WriteBytes(LCDBLINKOFF);
            await lcdUARTDataWriter.StoreAsync();

        }

        public async void LCDOn()
        {

            lcdUARTDataWriter.WriteBytes(LCDVISUALON);
            await lcdUARTDataWriter.StoreAsync();

        }

        public async void LCDOff()
        {

            lcdUARTDataWriter.WriteBytes(LCDVISUALOFF);
            await lcdUARTDataWriter.StoreAsync();

        }

        public async void LCDScrollRight()
        {

            lcdUARTDataWriter.WriteBytes(LCDSCROLLRIGHT);
            await lcdUARTDataWriter.StoreAsync();

        }

        public async void LCDScrollLeft()
        {

            lcdUARTDataWriter.WriteBytes(LCDSCROLLLEFT);
            await lcdUARTDataWriter.StoreAsync();

        }

```

```
        public async void LCDMoveCursorRight1()
        {

            lcdUARTDataWriter.WriteBytes(LCDMOVECURR1);
            await lcdUARTDataWriter.StoreAsync();

        }

        public async void LCDMoveCursotLeft1()
        {

            lcdUARTDataWriter.WriteBytes(LCDMOVECURL1);
            await lcdUARTDataWriter.StoreAsync();

        }

        public async void LCDWriteString(string outputString)
        {

            lcdUARTDataWriter.WriteString(outputString);
            await lcdUARTDataWriter.StoreAsync();
        }

        public async void LCDWriteStringLine1(string outputString)
        {

            lcdUARTDataWriter.WriteBytes(LCDLINE1);
            await lcdUARTDataWriter.StoreAsync();
            lcdUARTDataWriter.WriteString(outputString);
            await lcdUARTDataWriter.StoreAsync();

        }

        public async void LCDWriteStringLine2(string outputString)
        {

            lcdUARTDataWriter.WriteBytes(LCDLINE2);
            await lcdUARTDataWriter.StoreAsync();
            lcdUARTDataWriter.WriteString(outputString);
            await lcdUARTDataWriter.StoreAsync();
        }

        public bool LCDstatus()
        {
            return lcdReady;
        }
    }
}
```

Lines 12-24 set up the byte array SerLCD commands. The constructor method has to call a different method when an instance of the class is enumerated. Constructors cannot be asynchronous. The UART is passed in from the application to the constructor method and passed to the LCDUARTInitialize() method which attempts to open the serial port. The rest of the methods in the library exercise the different commands available, and each is an asynchronous command. There is an additional method to get the LCD status. You will also notice that SparkFunSerLCD() has a warning about a non-nullable field for UartPort and lcdUARTDataWriter. These are used in different methods in the program, it has to be accessible. You can follow the Visual Studio recommendation to suppress the warning.

14. Save the project.
15. Build a debug version of the project and correct any errors.

12.6.2 Create the UART-SerLCD2 Application that uses the new Assembly

The class library is ready to use in an application.

1. Open Visual Studio 2022.
2. Create a new "WPF Application" project. Make sure you select the correct WPF Application template for .NET.

Note: The project is a .NET application, not a .NET Framework application. If you see .NET Framework in the project description it is the wrong project.

3. Name the project "UART-SerLCD2" and set the folder location to C:\VS-Apps on your development machine. To do remote debugging with .NET, the remote machine folder architecture must match the development machine. Visual Studio Remote Debugging documentation describes the setup as well.
4. Click the "Next" button.
5. Select .NET 6.0 (Long-term support) from the drop-down box.
6. Click the "Create" button.
7. Once the application opens, we need to do a little more set up to support the Windows Runtime Namespaces. From the menu, select Project->UART-SerLCD2 Properties.
8. Under Application->General set the following for the targeted Windows OS:
    a. Target OS version: 10.0.19041.0
    b. Supported OS version: 10.0.19041.0
9. Scroll down the Build, and set the following:
    a. Platform target: x64

Note: If you forget to set the correct Target Framework and Target OS, Visual Studio will not let you reference the Windows.Devices namespace.

10. Save the project.

12.6.3 Set Up the XAML Controls

1. In Solution Explorer, open the MainWindow.xaml.
2. The designer and XAML editor will appear. At the top, left of the Designer set the orientation that fits your target's display.
3. Set the Background to black. Click on the application in designer, in Properties->Brush select Solid Color Brush, and leave the default black color.
4. Add a TextBox Control.
    a. Name: txtMessage
    b. Common->Text: Write Message Here
5. Add a Button control below the text box
    a. Name: btnSend
    b. Common->Content: Send Message to LCD
6. Add a TextBox Control.
    a. Name: txtStatus
    b. Common->Text: Ready
7. Save the project.

Here is the XAML code:

```
<Window x:Class="UART_SerLCD2.MainWindow"
      xmlns="http://schemas.microsoft.com/winfx/2006/xaml/presentation"
      xmlns:x="http://schemas.microsoft.com/winfx/2006/xaml"
      xmlns:d="http://schemas.microsoft.com/expression/blend/2008"
      xmlns:mc="http://schemas.openxmlformats.org/markup-compatibility/2006"
      xmlns:local="clr-namespace:UART_SerLCD2"
      mc:Ignorable="d"
      Title="MainWindow" Height="450" Width="800">
   <Grid Background="Black">
      <TextBox x:Name="txtMessage" HorizontalAlignment="Left" Height="87"
Margin="81,75,0,0" TextWrapping="Wrap" Text="Write Message Here"
VerticalAlignment="Top" Width="619"/>
      <Button x:Name="btnSend" Content="Send Message to LCD"
HorizontalAlignment="Left" Height="51" Margin="81,188,0,0"
VerticalAlignment="Top" Width="191"/>
      <TextBox x:Name="txtStatus" HorizontalAlignment="Left" Height="60"
Margin="81,298,0,0" TextWrapping="Wrap" Text="Ready" VerticalAlignment="Top"
Width="605"/>
   </Grid>
</Window>
```

12.6.1 Write the Code

1. Now we need to add the class library. Click Project->Add Project Reference.
2. Browse to the location of the SparkFunSerLCD.dll that is in the SparkFunSerLCD Class Library Project output.

3. Select the dll and click "Add" and then click "OK". The namespace for the library can be added to the using directives.
4. Open MainWindow.xaml.cs
5. Add the following using statements to add Annabooks.SparkFunSerLCD and System Threading namespaces

```
using Annabooks.SparkFunSerLCD;
using System.Threading;
```

6. Just within the MainWindow class, add the following to create a new instance of the SparkFunSerLCD.

```
private SparkFunSerLCD mySerLCD;
```

7. Below the MainWindow() method, create a new LCDSetup() method and fill in the following:

```
private void LCDSetup()
{
   mySerLCD = new SparkFunSerLCD("UART1");
   Thread.Sleep(2000);
   if (mySerLCD.LCDstatus())
   {
     Application.Current.Dispatcher.Invoke((Action)(()=> txtStatus.Text = "LCD is
Ready"));
   }
   else
   {
```

```
        Application.Current.Dispatcher.Invoke((Action)(() => txtStatus.Text = "LCD is
Not ready: " + mySerLCD.connectionError));
    }
}
```

The method instantiates mySerlLCD as a new instance of SparkFunSerLCD using UART1. Since it is a good idea to check the status of the UART connection attempt, LCDSetup() has to be run as a separate thread since we need it to finish to have access to the LCDStatus() method. Since LCDSetup() is running as a separate thread, Lambda expressions are used to send the message to the UI thread.

8. In the MainWindow() method, create a Thread that calls LCDSetup() method and start the thread.

```
public MainWindow()
{
    InitializeComponent();
    Thread lcdStart = new Thread(new ThreadStart(LCDSetup));
    lcdStart.Start();
}
```

9. In the MainWindow.xaml, double-click on the button to generate the event handler.
10. Fill in the code:

```
private void btnSend_Click(object sender, RoutedEventArgs e)
{
    if (mySerLCD.LCDstatus())
    {
        mySerLCD.ClearLCD();
        mySerLCD.LCDBlinkOn();
        mySerLCD.LCDWriteString(txtMessage.Text);
        txtStatus.Text = "Message Sent to LCD";
    }
}
```

A check is made again that the LCD is ready and then proceeds to send the message to the LCD.

11. Save the project.
12. Build a debug version of the project and correct any errors.

12.6.2 Test the Application

1. In the C:\VS-Apps folder of your development machine, determine where the UART-SerLCD2.exe file is located: C:\VS-Apps\UART-SerLCD2\UART-SerLCD2\bin\Debug\net6.0-windows10.0.19041.0

2. On the target machine, create an exact folder structure under C:\VS-apps - C:\VS-Apps\UART-SerLCD2\UART-SerLCD2\bin\Debug\net6.0-windows10.0.19041.0
3. Run Visual Studio Remote Debug, and make a note of the computer name and port number listed in the Visual Studio Remote Debug output.
4. In Visual Studio running on the development machine, open the UART-SerLCD2 Properties page.
5. Click on Debug on the left side, and click Open debug launch profile UI.
6. Tick the check box for Use remote machine and enter the Target systems computer name with the port number: X64-APPTEST:4026
7. Close the Window.
8. In the properties, scroll up to Build Events.
9. In the Post-build event enter the following to do a copy of the output to the remote system (this is all one line):

```
xcopy C:\VS-Apps\UART-SerLCD2\UART-SerLCD2\bin\Debug\net6.0-
windows10.0.19041.0 \\X64-APPTEST\VS-Apps\UART-SerLCD2\UART-
SerLCD2\bin\Debug\net6.0-windows10.0.19041.0 /Y
```

10. Save the project.
11. Build the debug version of the application again. The output files should be copied to the remote system.
12. Start the debug session.
13. You will be asked for the target system's login credentials. Enter the user's name and password and click OK.
14. Once the application has loaded on the target system, enter a message in the text box control and hit the send message to LCD button. The LCD will show the message on line 1 and the message "Win10 IoT E" on line 2.
15. Stop debugging when finished.

The application performs the same as before and has fewer lines of code sans the checking on the LCD status. Class Libraries help to break down the project into smaller chunks.

12.7 Exercise 1203 – GPS

Serial Communication transmit is straightforward, but serial receive is a different story. In this exercise, a GPS will send data to be received and processed. The Parallax SIM33EAU GPS Module will be used for this exercise. The SIM33EAU supports 3.3V to 5V power, but we will use 3.3V for the UP Board. The only connections to the module that you need are power, ground, and SIM33EAU TXD to the Target's UART RX.

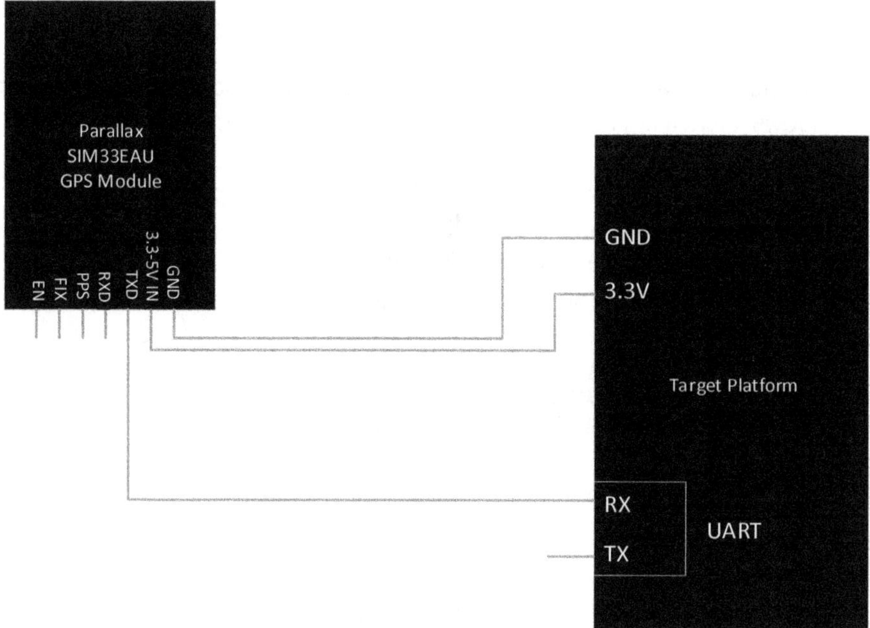

There is just one catch. If you look closely at the SerialCommunication namespace and the SerialPort class, you will notice a difference in the events that can be triggered. Specifically, there is no receive interrupt event in the SerialCommunication namespace like there is in the SerialPort class. Windows Runtime implemented the architecture a little differently. All the interrupt handling is performed by the driver. The code loops on a DataReader with a serial port time out. The loop is run in a task and controlled by the Windows task scheduled. Running as a task is preferred to running in a thread, as a thread will consume too many resources compared to a task.

12.7.1 Basic Setup

The first step is to set up the basic project.

1. Open Visual Studio 2022.
2. Create a new "WPF Application" project. Make sure you select the correct WPF Application template for .NET.

Note: The project is a .NET application, not a .NET Framework application. If you see .NET Framework in the project description it is the wrong project.

3. Name the project "UART-GPS" and set the folder location to C:\VS-Apps on your development machine. To do remote debugging with .NET, the remote machine folder architecture must match the development machine. Visual Studio Remote Debugging documentation describes the setup as well.
4. Click the "Next" button.

5. Select .NET 6.0 (Long-term support) from the drop-down box.
6. Click the “Create” button.
7. Once the application opens, we need to do a little more set up to support the Windows Runtime Namespaces. From the menu, select Project->UART-GPS Properties.
8. Under Application->General set the following for the targeted Windows OS:
    a. Target OS version: 10.0.19041.0
    b. Supported OS version: 10.0.19041.0
9. Scroll down the Build, and set the following:
    a. Platform target: x64

Note: If you forget to set the correct Target Framework and Target OS, Visual Studio will not let you reference the Windows.Devices namespace.

10. Save the project.

12.7.2 Set Up the Controls in the Form

The UI will have a text box showing the raw data coming from the serial port. There will be several other text boxes that break down the serial string into readable data groups: Longitude, Latitude, UTC time, and the number of satellites that are connected. There is a text box to display the count of the number of UART port reads, and a status text box to display any errors.

1. In Solution Explorer, open the MainWindow.xaml.
2. The designer and XAML editor will appear. At the top, left of the Designer set the orientation that fits your target’s display.
3. Add a Label Control.
    a. Name: txtbTitle
    b. Common->Content: GPS Output
    c. Text: Font Size 18 px
4. Add a TextBox Control.
    a. Name: txtGPSOutput
    b. Common->Text: <blank>
    c. In the XAML code add the following property: VerticalScrollBarVisibility="Visible"
5. Add a StatusBar Control to the bottom of the window.
    a. Add a Status Label item to the StatusBar control
    b. Name: txtStatus
    c. Common->Content: Ready
6. Add a Label Control.
    a. Name: txtbTime
    b. Common->Content: Time (UTC):

    c. Text: Font Size 18 px
7. Add a TextBox Control.
    a. Name: txtTime
8. Add a Label Control.
    a. Name: txtbLatitude
    b. Common->Content: : Latitude:
    c. Text: Font Size 18 px
9. Add a TextBox Control.
    a. Name: txtLatitude
10. Add a TextBox Control.
    a. Name: txtNSLatitude
11. Add a Label Control.
    a. Name: txtbLogitude
    b. Common->Content: Longitude
    c. Text: Font Size 18 px
12. Add a TextBox Control.
    a. Name: txtLogitude
13. Add a TextBox Control.
    a. Name: txtEWLongitude
14. Add a Label Control.
    a. Name: txtbSats
    b. Common->Content: Satellites Used:
    c. Text: Font Size 18 px
15. Add a TextBox Control.
    a. Name: txtSats
16. Add a Label Control.
    a. Name: txtbCount
    b. Common->Content: Read Count:
    c. Text: Font Size 18 px
17. Add a TextBox Control.
    a. Name: txtCount
18. Save the project file.

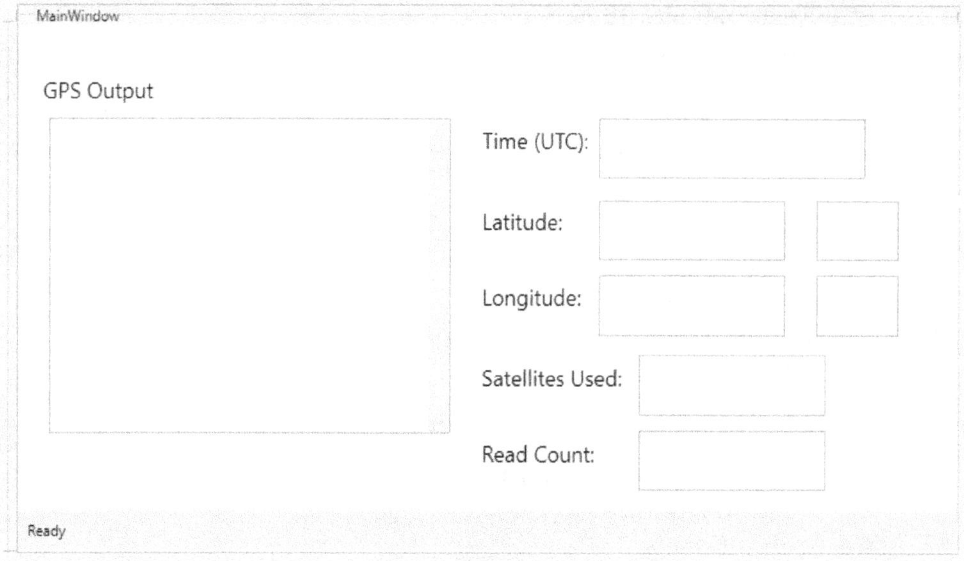

Here is the XAML code:

```
<Window x:Class="UART_GPS.MainWindow"
      xmlns="http://schemas.microsoft.com/winfx/2006/xaml/presentation"
      xmlns:x="http://schemas.microsoft.com/winfx/2006/xaml"
      xmlns:d="http://schemas.microsoft.com/expression/blend/2008"
      xmlns:mc="http://schemas.openxmlformats.org/markup-compatibility/2006"
      xmlns:local="clr-namespace:UART_GPS"
      mc:Ignorable="d"
      Title="MainWindow" Height="450" Width="800">
   <Grid>
      <Label x:Name="txtbTitle" Content="GPS Output" HorizontalAlignment="Left"
Height="36" Margin="16,36,0,0" VerticalAlignment="Top" Width="118"
FontSize="18"/>
      <TextBox x:Name="txtGPSOutput" HorizontalAlignment="Left" Height="259"
Margin="26,77,0,0" TextWrapping="Wrap" VerticalAlignment="Top" Width="343"
VerticalScrollBarVisibility="Visible"/>
      <StatusBar x:Name="txt" HorizontalAlignment="Center" Height="32"
Margin="0,400,0,0" VerticalAlignment="Top" Width="800">
         <Label x:Name="txtStatus" Content="Ready" Height="29" Width="619"/>
      </StatusBar>
      <Label x:Name="txtbTime" Content="Time (UTC):" HorizontalAlignment="Left"
Height="40" Margin="391,77,0,0" VerticalAlignment="Top" Width="99"
FontSize="18"/>
      <TextBox x:Name="txtTime" HorizontalAlignment="Left" Height="49"
Margin="495,77,0,0" TextWrapping="Wrap" VerticalAlignment="Top" Width="226"/>
      <Label x:Name="txtbLatitude" Content="Latitude:" HorizontalAlignment="Left"
Height="40" Margin="391,144,0,0" VerticalAlignment="Top" Width="99"
FontSize="18"/>
```

```
    <TextBox x:Name="txtLatitude" HorizontalAlignment="Left" Height="49"
Margin="495,144,0,0" TextWrapping="Wrap" VerticalAlignment="Top" Width="158"/>
    <TextBox x:Name="txtNSLatitude" HorizontalAlignment="Left" Height="49"
Margin="680,144,0,0" TextWrapping="Wrap" VerticalAlignment="Top" Width="69"/>
    <Label x:Name="txtbLongitude" Content="Longitude:"
HorizontalAlignment="Left" Height="40" Margin="391,206,0,0"
VerticalAlignment="Top" Width="99" FontSize="18"/>
    <TextBox x:Name="txtLongitude" HorizontalAlignment="Left" Height="50"
Margin="495,206,0,0" TextWrapping="Wrap" VerticalAlignment="Top" Width="158"/>
    <TextBox x:Name="txtEWLongitude" HorizontalAlignment="Left" Height="50"
Margin="680,206,0,0" TextWrapping="Wrap" VerticalAlignment="Top" Width="69"/>
    <Label x:Name="txtbSats" Content="Satellites Used:"
HorizontalAlignment="Left" Height="40" Margin="391,273,0,0"
VerticalAlignment="Top" Width="136" FontSize="18"/>
    <TextBox x:Name="txtSats" HorizontalAlignment="Left" Height="50"
Margin="530,271,0,0" TextWrapping="Wrap" VerticalAlignment="Top" Width="158"/>
    <Label x:Name="txtbCount" Content="Read Count:" HorizontalAlignment="Left"
Height="40" Margin="391,335,0,0" VerticalAlignment="Top" Width="136"
FontSize="18"/>
    <TextBox x:Name="txtCount" HorizontalAlignment="Left" Height="50"
Margin="530,333,0,0" TextWrapping="Wrap" VerticalAlignment="Top" Width="158"/>
  </Grid>
</Window>
```

12.7.3 Write the Code

Now let's write the code behind the GUI.

1. Open MainWindow.xaml.cs.
2. Add the following using statements to enable SerialCommunication, Enumeration, and Storage.Streams namespaces:

```
using Windows.Devices.SerialCommunication;
using Windows.Devices.Enumeration;
using Windows.Storage.Streams;
```

3. Inside the MainWindow class and before the MainWindow() method add the following global variables:

```
SerialDevice myUART1;
DataReader myDataReader;
private int count = 0;
```

4. After the MainWindows() method, create a new method called UartSetup() and fill in the following code:

```
public async void UartSetup()
{
    string aqs = SerialDevice.GetDeviceSelector("UART1");
    DeviceInformationCollection deviceInfo = await
DeviceInformation.FindAllAsync(aqs);
    myUART1 = await SerialDevice.FromIdAsync(deviceInfo[0].Id);
    if (myUART1 == null)
    {
        txtStatus.Content = "Error - Serial Port not found";
    }
    else
    {
        txtStatus. Content = "UART1 Found";
        myUART1.BaudRate = 9600;
        myUART1.DataBits = 8;
        myUART1.Parity = SerialParity.None;
        myUART1.StopBits = SerialStopBitCount.One;
        myUART1.Handshake = SerialHandshake.None;
        myUART1.ReadTimeout = TimeSpan.FromMilliseconds(100);
        myUART1.WriteTimeout = TimeSpan.FromMilliseconds(100);

        UartListener();
    }
}
```

The method enumerates the UART, and if successful, configures the UART settings for baud rate, data bits, etc. In addition, two key settings are also added: ReadTimeout and WriteTimeout. Since there is no data receive event, a read from the UART will read any data that is available from the device driver buffer. Without the ReadTimeout timing out, the read never completes and the application never receives any data. The WriteTimeout is not needed for this application, but it could have been added to the previous exercise.

5. Add a call to UartSetup() after this.InitializeComponent(); in the MainWindow () method.

```
public MainWindow()
{
    InitializeComponent();
    UartSetup();
}
```

6. To handle the read and parsing of the GPS data, create three methods UartListener(), UartReader(), and GPSParser().
7. Fill in the code for the UartListener():

```
private async void UartListener()
```

```
{
    try
    {
        myDataReader = new DataReader(myUART1.InputStream);
        txtStatus.Content = "Awaiting messages";
        while (true)
        {
            await UartReader();
        }
    }
    catch (TaskCanceledException exTCE)
    {
        txtStatus. Content = "Receive Error " + exTCE.Message;
    }
    catch (Exception ex)
    {
        txtStatus. Content = "Error!: " + ex.ToString();
    }
    finally
    {
        if (myDataReader != null)
        {
            myDataReader.DetachStream();
            myDataReader = null;
        }
    }
}
```

The DataReader is instantiated and a call to read data continuously from the serial port is started. Break on any errors.

8. Fill in the code for the UartReader():

```
private async Task UartReader()
{
    Task<UInt32> loadAsyncTask;
    uint ReadBufferLength = 1024;
    string GPSOutput;
    myDataReader.InputStreamOptions = InputStreamOptions.Partial;

    loadAsyncTask = myDataReader.LoadAsync(ReadBufferLength).AsTask();
    UInt32 bytesRead = await loadAsyncTask;
    if (bytesRead > 0)
    {

        GPSOutput = myDataReader.ReadString(bytesRead) + "\n";
        txtGPSOutput.Text = GPSOutput.ToString();
```

```
            txtStatus.Content = bytesRead.ToString() + " bytes read
successfully!";
            GPSParser(GPSOutput);
            count++;
            txtCount.Text = count.ToString();
        }
    }
```

The GPS outputs data once a second. A task is used to assist in reading data from the UART. When the Read Timeout is exhausted, the task completes. The DataReader has the string and the string gets put on txtGPSOutput. The number of bytes read is listed in the Status box, and the read counter is incremented. To break the string up into something readable, a call is made to the GPSParser(). The SIM33EAU outputs National Marine Electronics Association (NMEA) strings. There are different strings for the current position, speed and heading, and satellite and channel information. Please check the manual for details on the NMEA strings that are produced. The parser will simply look at the current position. The strings begin with a header followed by a comma-delimited set of data. Between each comma is a piece of data. Please see the documentation on the breakdown of each string.

$GPGGA,091926.000,3113.3166,N,12121.2682,E,1,09,0.9,36.9,M,7.9,M,,0000*56<CR>
<LF>

9. Fill in the code for the GPSParser();

```
private void GPSParser(string GPS)
{
    string[] gpsValues = GPS.Split(',');
    if (gpsValues.Length != 0)
    {
        if (gpsValues[0].Equals("$GNGGA") && (gpsValues.Length > 1))
        {
            txtTime.Text = gpsValues[1].ToString();
            txtLatitude.Text = gpsValues[2].ToString();
            txtNSLatitude.Text = gpsValues[3].ToString();
            txtLongitude.Text = gpsValues[4].ToString();
            txtEWLongitude.Text = gpsValues[5].ToString();
            txtSats.Text = gpsValues[7].ToString();
        }
    }
}
```

The string method Split(), breaks up the GPS string into several string arrays. Selected strings are then displayed in specific text boxes, which makes the strings a little easier to read.

10. Save the project.

11. Build a debug version of the project and correct any errors.

12.7.4 Test the Application

The application is ready to be tested in the target system. For best results, the test should be performed outside with a clear view of the sky.

1. In the C:\VS-Apps folder of your development machine, determine where the UART-GPS.exe file is located: C:\VS-Apps\UART-GPS\UART-GPS\bin\Debug\net6.0-windows10.0.19041.0
2. On the target machine, create an exact folder structure under C:\VS-apps - C:\VS-Apps\UART-GPS\UART-GPS\bin\Debug\net6.0-windows10.0.19041.0
3. Run Visual Studio Remote Debug, and make a note of the computer name and port number listed in the Visual Studio Remote Debug output.
4. In Visual Studio running on the development machine, open the UART-GPS Properties page.
5. Click on Debug on the left side, and click Open debug launch profile UI.
6. Tick the check box for Use remote machine and enter the Target systems computer name with the port number: X64-APPTEST:4026
7. Close the Window.
8. In the properties, scroll up to Build Events.
9. In the Post-build event enter the following to do a copy of the output to the remote system (this is all one line):

```
xcopy C:\VS-Apps\UART-GPS\UART-GPS\bin\Debug\net6.0-windows10.0.19041.0
\\X64-APPTEST\VS-Apps\UART-GPS\UART-GPS\bin\Debug\net6.0-
windows10.0.19041.0 /Y
```

10. Save the project.
11. Build the debug version of the application again. The output files should be copied to the remote system.
12. Start the debug session.
13. You will be asked for the target system's login credentials. Enter the user's name and password and click OK.
14. The system will start to pull data from the GPS and appear in the different text boxes.
15. Stop debugging when finished.

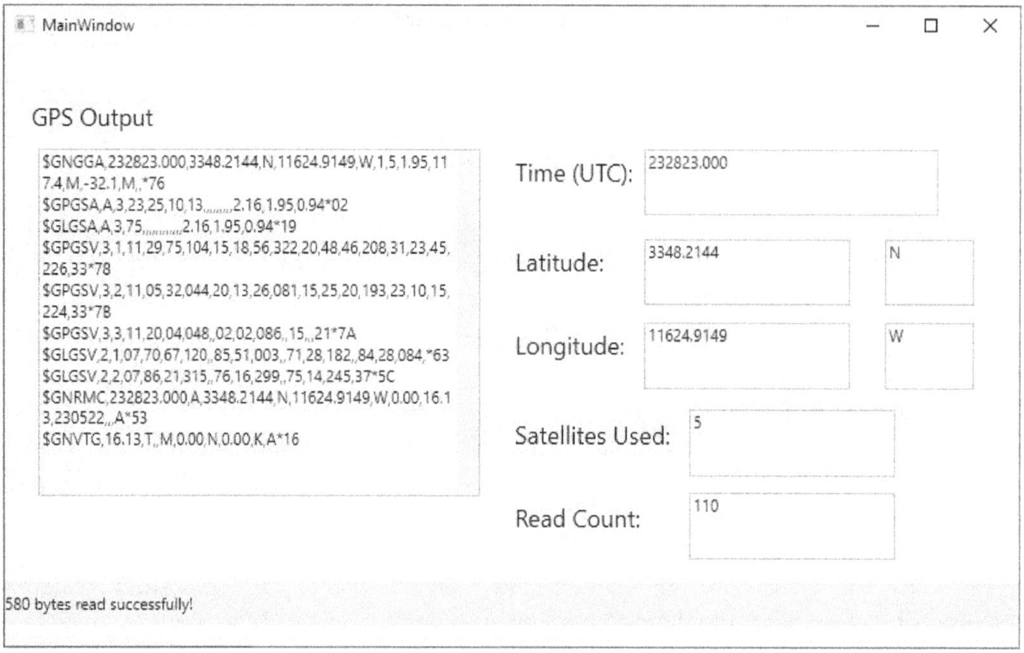

MainWindow

GPS Output

```
$GNGGA,232823.000,3348.2144,N,11624.9149,W,1,5,1.95,11
7.4,M,-32.1,M,,*76
$GPGSA,A,3,23,25,10,13,,,,,,,,,2.16,1.95,0.94*02
$GLGSA,A,3,75,,,,,,,,,,,,2.16,1.95,0.94*19
$GPGSV,3,1,11,29,75,104,15,18,56,322,20,48,46,208,31,23,45,
226,33*78
$GPGSV,3,2,11,05,32,044,20,13,26,081,15,25,20,193,23,10,15,
224,33*78
$GPGSV,3,3,11,20,04,048,,02,02,086,,15,,,21*7A
$GLGSV,2,1,07,70,67,120,,85,51,003,,71,28,182,,84,28,084,*63
$GLGSV,2,2,07,86,21,315,,76,16,299,,75,14,245,37*5C
$GNRMC,232823.000,A,3348.2144,N,11624.9149,W,0.00,16.1
3,230522,,,A*53
$GNVTG,16.13,T,,M,0.00,N,0.00,K,A*16
```

Time (UTC): 232823.000

Latitude: 3348.2144 N

Longitude: 11624.9149 W

Satellites Used: 5

Read Count: 110

580 bytes read successfully!

12.8 Exercise 1204: Simple Serial Terminal

The previous exercises have looked at transmit and receive operations separately. This exercise will create a simple serial terminal application that performs both transmit and receive operations. It is simple since there is a sample Windows Runtime Serial Terminal application on Github. The application is modeled after other serial port applications like HyperTerminal and Putty. The sample on Github uses a task for both transmit and receive operations, a connection and disconnection button, and a token to signal the read task to shut down. The application in this exercise is down to the nuts-and-bolts so it can be applied to communicate with other devices. Since this is a terminal application, another device is needed to communicate with the target systems. Here are the hardware setup options:

- Loop-Back: A wire connecting Tx and Rx of the targets UART is all that is needed to test the application. The target talks to itself.
- Optional: If you want to talk to your host machine over a null modem cable you will need the following:
    - Schmart Board RS232 to UART board: RS232 I/O Module | Schmartboard. An RS-232 transceiver chip is needed to translate the RX and TX digital signals to the expected RS232 signal levels.
    - Serial null modem cable.
    - RS232 to USB adapter.

  - Terminal program such as ABCOMTerm (www.annabooks.com), HyperTerminal or Tera Term.

- Machine-to-machine communication over RS-232: a separate PC with a terminal application is needed for the application to interact with. A NULL modem serial cable will connect the serial ports of the target and the PC with the terminal software. For the target system, a USB-to-Serial adapter can be used or a UART-to-RS232 adapter like SchmartBoard's RS-232 Module (PN: 710-0001-01) connected to the UART.

12.8.1 Basic Setup

Here is the basic setup of the application.

1. Open Visual Studio 2022.
2. Create a new "WPF Application" project. Make sure you select the correct WPF Application template for .NET.

Note: The project is a .NET application, not a .NET Framework application. If you see .NET Framework in the project description it is the wrong project.

3. Name the project "UART-Terminal" and set the folder location to C:\VS-Apps on your development machine. To do remote debugging with .NET, the remote machine folder architecture must match the development machine. Visual Studio Remote Debugging documentation describes the setup as well.
4. Click the "Next" button.
5. Select .NET 6.0 (Long-term support) from the drop-down box.
6. Click the "Create" button.
7. Once the application opens, we need to do a little more set up to support the Windows Runtime Namespaces. From the menu, select Project->UART-Terminal Properties.
8. Under Application->General set the following for the targeted Windows OS:
    a. Target OS version: 10.0.19041.0
    b. Supported OS version: 10.0.19041.0
9. Scroll down the Build, and set the following:
    a. Platform target: x64

Note: If you forget to set the correct Target Framework and Target OS, Visual Studio will not let you reference the Windows.Devices namespace.

10. Save the project.

12.8.2 Set Up the XAML Controls

There will be a text box for the user to enter a message, and a button to send the message out the UART port. Another text box will pick up messages received from the UART, and a label will display status messages.

1. The designer and XAML editor will appear. At the top, left of the Designer set the orientation that fits your target's display.
2. Add a TextBox Control.
    a. Name: txtMessage
    b. Common->Text: Write Message Here
3. Add a Button control below the text box.
    a. Name: btnSend
    b. Common->Content: Send Message
4. Add a TextBox Control.
    a. Name: txtReceive
    b. Common->Text:
5. Add a TextBox Control.
    a. Name: txtStatus
    b. Common->Content: Ready
6. Save the project.

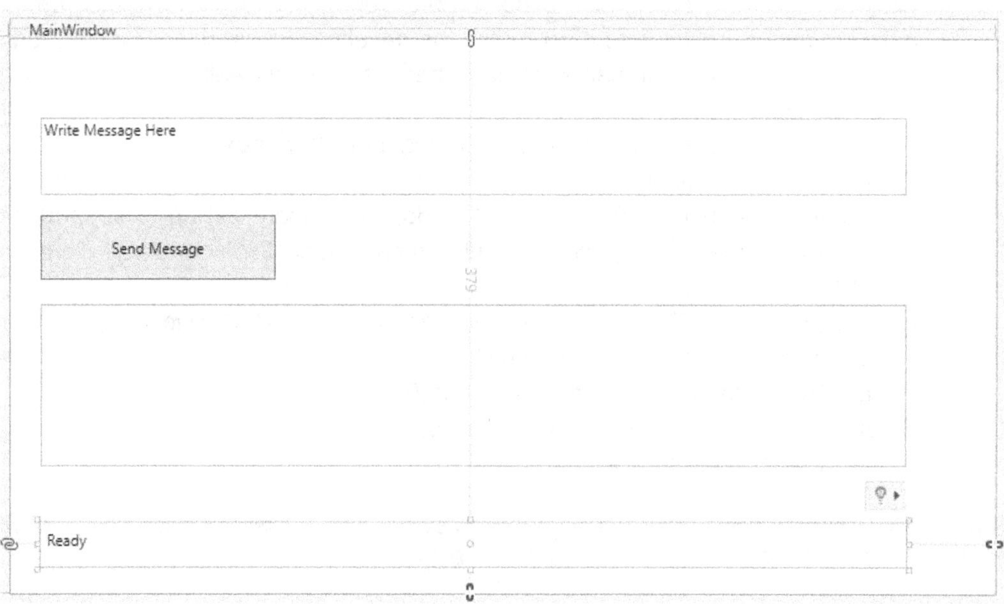

Here is the XAML code:

```
<Window x:Class="UART_Terminal.MainWindow"
    xmlns="http://schemas.microsoft.com/winfx/2006/xaml/presentation"
    xmlns:x="http://schemas.microsoft.com/winfx/2006/xaml"
    xmlns:d="http://schemas.microsoft.com/expression/blend/2008"
    xmlns:mc="http://schemas.openxmlformats.org/markup-compatibility/2006"
    xmlns:local="clr-namespace:UART_Terminal"
    mc:Ignorable="d"
    Title="MainWindow" Height="450" Width="800">
  <Grid>
    <TextBox x:Name="txtMessage" HorizontalAlignment="Left" Height="60"
Margin="24,62,0,0" TextWrapping="Wrap" Text="Write Message Here"
VerticalAlignment="Top" Width="703"/>
    <Button x:Name="btnSend" Content="Send Message"
HorizontalAlignment="Left" Height="50" Margin="24,138,0,0"
VerticalAlignment="Top" Width="192"/>
    <TextBox x:Name="txtReceive" HorizontalAlignment="Left" Height="126"
Margin="24,208,0,0" TextWrapping="Wrap" VerticalAlignment="Top" Width="703"/>
    <Label x:Name="txtStatus" Content="Ready" HorizontalAlignment="Left"
Height="34" Margin="24,379,0,0" VerticalAlignment="Top" Width="703"/>
  </Grid>
</Window>
```

12.8.3 Write the Code

Now let's write the code behind the GUI.

1. Open MainWindow.xaml.cs.
2. Add the following using statements to enable SerialCommunication, Enumeration, and Storage.Streams namespaces:

```
using Windows.Devices.SerialCommunication;
using Windows.Devices.Enumeration;
using Windows.Storage.Streams;
```

3. From within the MainWindow Class, add the enumeration for the UART, DataReader, and DataWriter:

```
SerialDevice myUART1;
DataReader myDataReader;
DataWriter myDataWriter;
```

4. Below the MainWindow() method, create a new method called UartSetup() and fill in the following code:

```
public async void UartSetup()
{
    string aqs = SerialDevice.GetDeviceSelector("UART1");
```

```
    DeviceInformationCollection deviceInfo = await
DeviceInformation.FindAllAsync(aqs);
    myUART1 = await SerialDevice.FromIdAsync(deviceInfo[0].Id);
    if (myUART1 == null)
    {
        txtStatus.Text = "Error - Serial Port not found";
    }
    else
    {
        txtStatus.Text = "UART1 Found";
        myUART1.BaudRate = 115200;
        myUART1.DataBits = 8;
        myUART1.Parity = SerialParity.None;
        myUART1.StopBits = SerialStopBitCount.One;
        myUART1.Handshake = SerialHandshake.None;
        myUART1.ReadTimeout = TimeSpan.FromMilliseconds(100);
        myUART1.WriteTimeout = TimeSpan.FromMilliseconds(100);

        myDataWriter = new DataWriter(myUART1.OutputStream);
    }
}
```

5. Add a call to the UartSetup() method in the MainPage() method:

```
public MainWindow()
{
    this.InitializeComponent();
    UartSetup();
}
```

6. In the MainWindow. xaml double-click on the button to generate the event handler.
7. After btnSend_Click handler, create a method called UartTalker() and fill in the following code:

```
private async void UartTalker()
{
    myDataWriter.WriteString(txtMessage.Text.ToString());
    UInt32 bytesWritten = await myDataWriter.StoreAsync();
    if (bytesWritten > 0)
    {
        txtStatus.Text = bytesWritten.ToString() + " bytes written
successfully";
    }
}
```

8. In the btnSend_Click handler, add the call to the UartTalker() method:

```
private void btnSend_Click(object sender, RoutedEventArgs e)
{
    if (txtMessage.Text.Length != 0)
    {
        UartTalker();
        txtMessage.Text = "";
    }
    else
    {
        txtStatus.Text = "Enter text you want to send";
    }
}
```

The goal of the exercise is to understand the nuts and bolts of serial communication. The code has been written this way so the UartTalker() method can be reused to support chip-to-chip communication over a serial port.

9. Next comes the creation of the UartListener() and UartReader() methods:

```
private async void UartListener()
{
    try
    {
        myDataReader = new DataReader(myUART1.InputStream);
        txtStatus.Text = "Awaiting messages";
        while (true)
        {
            await UartReader();
         }
    }
    catch(TaskCanceledException exTCE)
    {
        txtStatus.Text = "Receive Error " + exTCE.Message;
    }
    catch (Exception ex)
    {
        txtStatus.Text = "Error!: " + ex.ToString();
    }
    finally
    {
       if (myDataReader != null)
       {
            myDataReader.DetachStream();
            myDataReader = null;
        }
    }
}
```

```
private async Task UartReader()
{
    Task<UInt32> loadAsyncTask;
    uint ReadBufferLength = 1024;

    myDataReader.InputStreamOptions = InputStreamOptions.Partial;

    loadAsyncTask = myDataReader.LoadAsync(ReadBufferLength).AsTask();
    UInt32 bytesRead = await loadAsyncTask;
    if (bytesRead > 0)
    {
        txtReceive.Text += myDataReader.ReadString(bytesRead) + "\n";
        txtStatus.Text = bytesRead.ToString() + " bytes read
successfully!";
    }
}
```

10. Add the call to UartListner() after `myDataWriter = new DataWriter(myUART1.OutputStream);` in the UartSetup() method.
11. Save the project.
12. Perform a build and fix any errors.

12.8.4 Test the Application

With the application created, it can be tested on the target system. You can use a simple wire to loop Tx to Rx for loop-back testing. Make sure the wire is connected before debugging the application.

1. In the C:\VS-Apps folder of your development machine, determine where the UART-Terminal.exe file is located: C:\VS-Apps\UART- Terminal\UART-Terminal\bin\Debug\net6.0-windows10.0.19041.0
2. On the target machine, create an exact folder structure under C:\VS-apps - C:\VS-Apps\UART- Terminal\UART- Terminal\bin\Debug\net6.0-windows10.0.19041.0
3. Run Visual Studio Remote Debug, and make a note of the computer name and port number listed in the Visual Studio Remote Debug output.
4. In Visual Studio running on the development machine, open the UART-Terminal Properties page.
5. Click on Debug on the left side, and click Open debug launch profile UI.
6. Check the check box for Use remote machine and enter the Target system's computer name with the port number: X64-APPTEST:4026
7. Close the Window.
8. In the properties, scroll up to Build Events.

9. In the Post-build event enter the following to do a copy of the output to the remote system (this is all one line):

```
xcopy C:\VS-Apps\UART-Terminal\UART-Terminal\bin\Debug\net6.0-windows10.0.19041.0 \\X64-APPTEST\VS-Apps\UART-Terminal\UART-Terminal\bin\Debug\net6.0-windows10.0.19041.0 /Y
```

10. Save the project.
11. Build the debug version of the application again. The output files should be copied to the remote system.
12. Start the debug session.
13. You will be asked for the target system's login credentials. Enter the user's name and password and click OK.
14. Once the application has loaded on the target system, enter a message in the text box control and hit the send message. The message should appear in the receive text box.
15. Stop debugging when finished.

12.9 Summary: UART

UARTs are fundamental to any microprocessor and are a versatile, low-cost data connection mechanism. There can be any number of ports available on any particular chip or board combination. UARTs allow for chip-to-chip communication on a board, and standards like RS-232, RS-422, and RS-485 allow for longer-range serial transmission and in some cases connection to multiple devices on a common serial connection.

The exercises here provide basic examples that can be reused for other applications. The implementation of Windows Runtime takes a little getting used to compared to the old SerialPort class, but once you get used to the asynchronous commands and hidden serial interrupt, creating an application becomes second nature.

13 Serial Peripheral Interface (SPI)

The last chapter covered serial ports. Now, we will look at a special serial port solution called Serial Peripheral Interface or SPI. Microcontrollers have used the SPI and I2C, which we will cover in the next chapter, as a way to act as an expansion bus for different peripherals. Intel processors started using the SPI bus to program flash and interface with TPM chips, and they have expanded to support other peripheral chips with the Intel Atom® family of processors. What appears to be a very simple bus has quite a bit of complexity. We will spend some time on the background of this communication bus before implementing an example. This chapter will cover the following:

- SPI bus technical details.
- SPI Namespace.
- Developing libraries for the SPI peripherals for code re-use.

13.1 The Serial Peripheral Interface (SPI) Bus, Not for Bit Banging!

The SPI bus is a versatile, synchronous data bus. Motorola was the originator of the SPI bus in 1979, and it is a full-duplex, multi-drop, master/slave bus architecture. The physical bus consists of the following 4 signal lines and is sometimes known as a "four-wire" bus because of this:

SCLK: the serial clock line (controlled by the master device).
MOSI: Master Output, Slave Input data line (data transferring from the master device to the slave device).
MISO: Master Input, Slave Output data line (data transferring from the slave device to the master device).
SS or CS: Slave Select or Chip Select line (active low control line controlled by the master device which activates the selected slave device).

One of the nice things about the SPI interface, unlike the UART interface, is that it can have multiple devices attached and simply use the Chip Select line to initiate communication with a specific device. The master device always initiates the communication by activating the slave device it wishes to communicate with by driving the slave device's CS line low and then while holding the device's CS line low, clocking data to the slave device, using the SCLK and MOSI lines while simultaneously clocking data from the slave device, using the SCLK and MISO lines. The slave device cannot spontaneously send data on the bus to the master device. Since the data from the master to the slave and the data from the slave to the master are clocked simultaneously by the clock signal, there is a cause-and-effect issue for data transfer. Typically, at the start of a data exchange, the master will send a command and possibly some data in the initial frame and ignores the data that it gets back from the slave. If a response from the slave is required, the master typically sends one or more dummy data frames for the sole purpose of reading back the response data from the slave device. The slave ignores the data being sent by the master device and uses each dummy write to send back its response data. There is no specific protocol definition for command and response data defined by the SPI bus. It is completely up to the slave device to define the command and data framing structure, and for the master device to accommodate this. The number of bits that comprise a unit of transfer in each frame can also vary. The unit of transfer is typically, as small as, 4 bits to as many as 16 bits or more, and odd-number bit fields are allowed but not typically supported.

There are two types of data transfer defined for the SPI bus: single-transfer mode and continuous-transfer or burst mode. In the single-transfer modes, the Chip Select, CS, is used to delineate the start and end of each data unit being transferred. In the continuous, or burst, mode, CS delineates the start and end of each complete transfer sequence. An example of the timing of each transfer mode can be seen in the following figures:

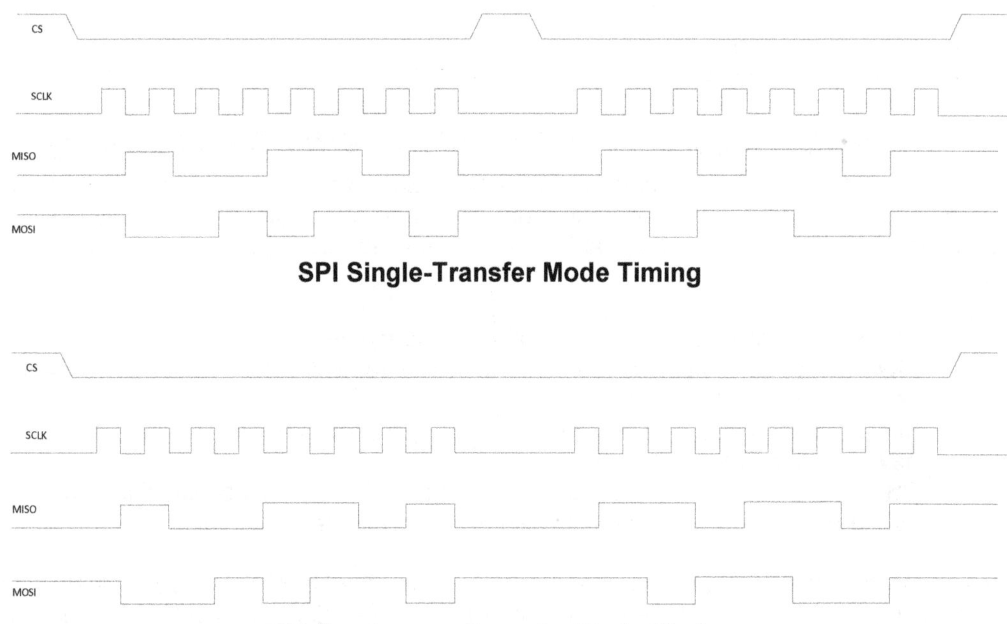

SPI Single-Transfer Mode Timing

SPI Continuous-Transfer Mode Timing

It can be seen that the difference between the single and continuous-transfer modes is the activity of the Chip Select signal and the resulting timing between each unit of data transfer. In the single-transfer mode, the Chip Select always goes active before data is transferred and always returns to the inactive state after all the bits in the unit of transfer have been successfully transferred. When multiple transfers are performed in the single-transfer mode, time is consumed each time the Chip Select has to transition from active to inactive and back to active, again. There is also a delay from the time when the Chip Select goes active until the first data clock transition occurs. This contributes to the data exchange overhead. When the continuous or burst mode is used for multiple transfers, the Chip Select goes active at the beginning of the transfer series and remains active until all transfers have been completed. There is no overhead from the Chip Select toggling between each unit of data transfer, thus there is less overhead.

You might then ask "why would we use the single-transfer mode?" When the SPI bus was created, most of the slave devices were small inexpensive devices that did not even contain a microprocessor. These devices were, and still are, typically constructed out of FPGAs, PALs, etc. They lack complex logic to do clock pulse counting and interval timing. The devices are designed to run across a wide variety of clock frequencies and can tolerate a lot of clock jitter (variability of the clock pulse interval from clock pulse to clock pulse). All of this contributes to very low-cost devices that can easily be interfaced with a variety of master devices and transfer data reliably at high speed. Consequently, most of these low-cost slave devices do not support continuous or burst mode data transfer. Over time, with the constant lowering of the price of small microprocessor systems, slave devices have become more complex, and their data requirements have become more demanding as well. Therefore, slave devices that support the continuous-transfer mode have become more available.

The SPI bus was intended to accommodate a variety of devices with a wide variety of data transfer speeds. It also is accommodating to different clocking methods. These clocking methods are defined by the clock polarity and phase. The clock polarity is the steady state of the clock line when no data is being transferred. Hence, the clock polarity is 1 if the unclocked, steady state of the clock line is logic 1, and the clock polarity is 0 if the unclocked steady state of the clock line is logic 0. The phase dictates which clock edge is used to validate data bits. A phase of 0 determines that data bits are validated on the first clock edge transition, and a phase of 1 determines that data bits are validated on the second clock edge transition. Each different combination of polarity and phase defines a mode, and therefore there are 4 modes numbered Mode 0 through Mode 3. The table below shows the 4 SPI modes:

Mode Number	**Clock Polarity**	**Clock Phase**	**Bit Validation Clock Edges**
0	0	0	Positive
1	0	1	Negative
2	1	0	Negative
3	1	1	Positive

Chip manufacturers don't call out the mode numbers directly. They will provide a timing diagram to help you figure out the correct mode. Here is Mode 0 timing diagram:

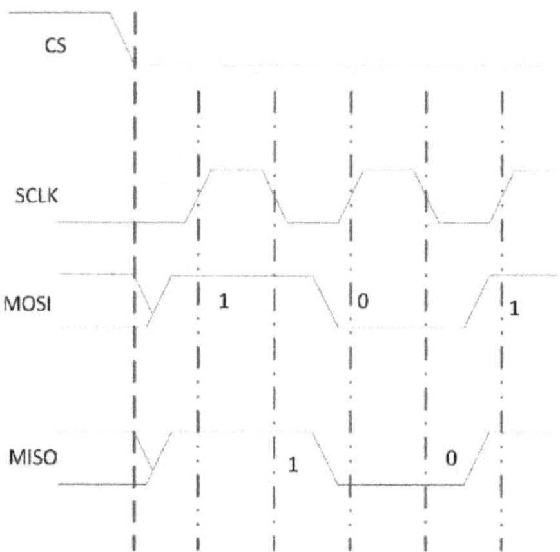

MOSI data is latched on the rising edge of the clock, while MISO is latched on the falling edge. Here is Mode 1 timing diagram:

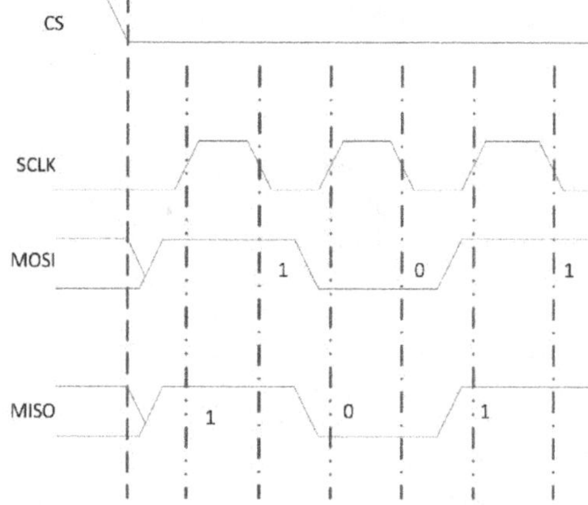

MOSI data is latched on the falling edge while MISO is on the rising edge. Here is Mode 2 timing diagram:

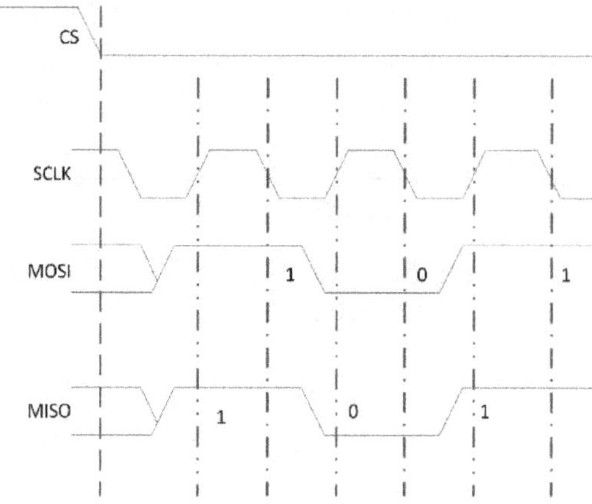

The clock phase has changed relative to the Chip Select going low. MOSI data is latched on the falling edge while MISO is on the rising edge. Here is Mode 3 timing diagram

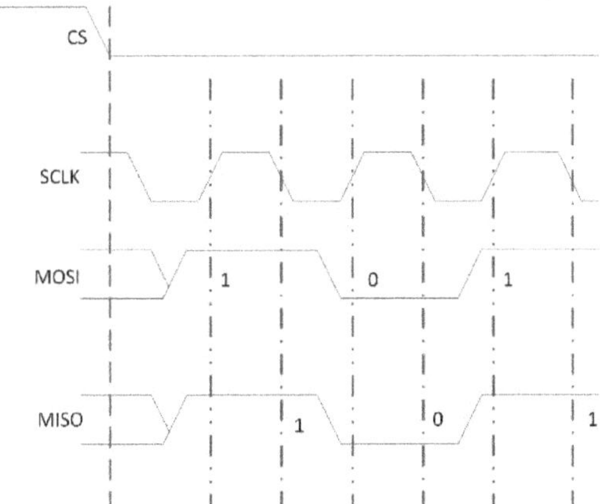

The clock phase has changed relative to the Chip Select going low. MOSI data is latched on the rising edge of the clock, while MISO is latched on the falling edge.

There are some subtleties in the clock timing when it comes to clocking the first data bit of a transfer series. Modes 0 & 2 are straightforward. In Mode 0 the steady state of the clock is logic 0 and the first bit of the transfer series is validated with the first transit of the clock from logic 0 to logic 1 (positive clock edge). Similarly, in Mode 2 the steady state of the clock is logic 1 and the first bit of the transfer series is validated with the first transit of the clock from logic 1 to logic 0 (negative clock edge). The subtlety lies with Modes 1 & 3. In Mode 1, the steady state of the clock is logic 0, but the first bit of the transfer series is not validated until the second clock edge. Therefore, the clock must first transit from the steady state logic 0 to logic 1, and then when it transits back to logic 0 (negative clock edge), the first bit of the transfer series is validated. In Mode 3, the steady state of the clock is logic 1, but the first bit of the transfer series is not validated until the second clock edge. Therefore, the clock must first transit from the steady state logic 1 to logic 0, and then when it transits back to logic 1 (positive clock edge), the first bit of the transfer series is validated. The clock edge that is used to validate the first data bit is the same clock edge that is used to validate each successive data bit in the transfer sequence, however, the starting time of the transfer can vary ½ of the clock period depending on the mode.

The concept of master and slave in SPI is rather ironic if you think about it. The slave device actually dictates the timing of the data transfer. It is up to the master device to configure itself appropriately and accommodate the slave device's requirements. Determining the mode is an important parameter to determine the mode setting when setting up the SPI port.

13.2 SPI Connectivity Basics

Unlike UART and RS-232 communications, SPI allows more than one slave device to be connected to the SPI bus. All the target platforms mentioned in Chapter 13 have a master SPI port, but only a couple have more than one Chip Select line to support multiple devices. Even with the ability to connect more than one SPI device to a master SPI port, the master can only talk to one slave device at a time. To facilitate this and to eliminate data signal conflictions on the bus, all SPI devices are tri-stated when not selected. The master must only select one slave device at a time.

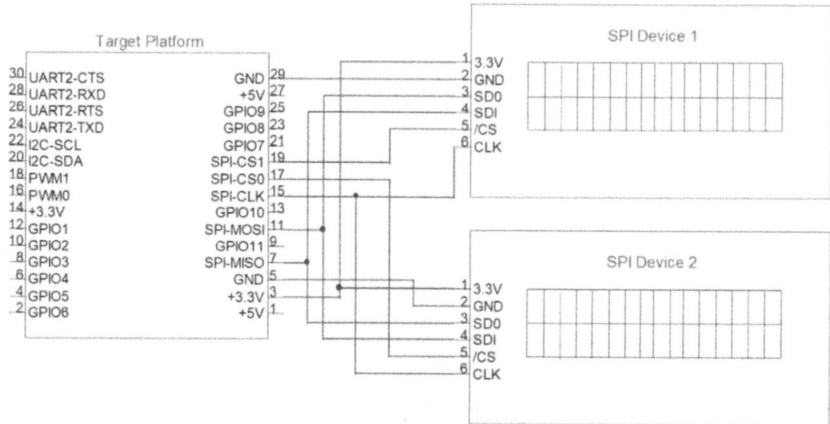

Other than the physical layer, there is no protocol associated with SPI communications, thus there is no overhead that would be required to support some kind of communication stack. Data can be transmitted at very high rates; clock rates. The flip side is that the management of commands and data between the application on the SPI-Host and each SPI slave device must be managed on an individual device-by-device basis. Each device will have a different command and data exchange protocol which the managed code application must understand and implement. Each device may even have a different maximum clock rate and phasing between the Chip Select, the clock, and the data signals, which must be set up properly when each SPI object is created. The key to this is understanding the SPI device datasheet, which requires some interpretation.

13.3 Windows Runtime SPI Namespace

The SPI Namespace consists of 4 classes, 1 Interface, and 2 Enumerations. Most of the Namespace elements provide info, settings, and statistics. The SpiDevice Class provides the core functionality to connect, transfer data, and get settings, which will be the focus of the exercises. The SPI device's datasheet contains the critical information to set up communication and the protocol to communicate with the device. Once the connection to the SPI port is made with the SPI settings of SPI port, Frequency, Chip Select, and mode, there are four methods to communicate with the device:

Method	Description
Read(Byte[])	Reads bytes from the device and places the results into a Byte[] array.

Write(Byte[])	Writes all the bytes in the Byte[] array to the device.
TransferFullDuplex(Byte[], Byte[])	Writes all the bytes in the Byte[] array to the devices, and then Reads bytes from the device and places the results into a Byte[] array.
TransferSequential(Byte[], Byte[])	Half duplex of byte write-read.

Byte[] arrays are used to communicate with the SPI device. The SPI device's datasheet contains the byte codes to send commands and retrieve information. The following exercises demonstrate the use of the SPI namespace.

13.4 SpiTestTool.exe

Chapter 10 covered the Bus Tools sample applications. The SpiTestTool.exe test tool can be used to list all the available SPI bus ports in a system, as well as, perform some basic tests on a device connected to the SPI bus. The list of available SPI bus ports doesn't mean they are accessible. Some systems will report a few internal SPI ports that are not accessible.

```
C:\test>SpiTestTool.exe
  Type 'help' for a list of commands
> help
Commands:
 > write { 00 11 22 .. FF }          Write bytes to device
 > read N                            Read N bytes
 > writeread { 00 11 .. FF } N       Write bytes then read N bytes
 > fullduplex { 00 11 .. FF }        Perform full duplex transfer
 > info                              Display device information
 > help                              Display this help message
 > quit                              Quit

> info
        DeviceId:           \\?\ACPI#MSFT8000#1#{dcde6af9-6610-4285-828f-
caaf78c424cc}\SPI2
  ChipSelectLine: 0
            Mode: 0
   DataBitLength: 8
  ClockFrequency: 4000000 Hz
```

13.5 Exercise 1301: SPI Pressure Sensor

This exercise will use the Sparkfun MPL115A1 Pressure Sensor breakout board to read pressure (50 to 115kPa). The application will have a button that performs the action of reading the pressure from the reader and posting the pressure results to two text boxes (kPa and inHg). A status box will report any status messages.

Note: The Sparkfun MPL115A1 breakout board went end-of-life during the writing of the book, but the MPL115A1 part itself is still available. The Sparkfun MS5803-14BA is another

SPI Pressure sensor part, but not a drop-in replacement. The MPL115A1 project has been kept in to discuss datasheet-to-code for the pressure conversion process and demonstrate SPI connectivity.

The key to reading and calculating the pressure is in the interpretation of the datasheet. The first items we need are the SPI mode, operating frequency, and transfer mode. The datasheet has a timing diagram and table that shows the SPI mode is 0, the operating frequency is 8 MHz, and a full-duplex transfer mode is used. The next piece of information is how to read the data from the sensor. The datasheet provides a nice flow diagram of the tasks to be performed. The resulting pressure and temperature readings are calculated from formulas from different registers within the sensor. A combination of coefficients programmed in at the factory and the output readings from an internal Analog to Digital converter (ADC) for both readings.

Pressure = (a0 * (b1+c12*Tadc)*Padc+b2*Tadc)*((115-50)/1023) + 50

The coefficients a0, b1, b2, and c12 consist of multiple bits that have an integer and fractional part. Much of the work in the program is calculating the coefficients before performing the final calculation.

13.5.1 Basic Setup

Here is the basic setup of the application.

1. Open Visual Studio 2022.
2. Create a new "WPF Application" project. Make sure you select the correct WPF Application template for .NET.
3. Name the project "SPIPressure", and set the folder location to C:\VS-Apps on your development machine. To do remote debugging with .NET, the remote machine folder architecture must match the development machine. Visual Studio Remote Debugging documentation describes the setup as well.
4. Click the "Next" button.
5. Select .NET 6.0 (Long-term support) from the drop-down box.
6. Click the "Create" button.
7. Once the application opens, we need to do a little more set up to support the Windows Runtime Namespaces. From the menu, select Project-> SPIPressure Properties.
8. Under Application->General set the following for the targeted Windows OS:
    a. Target OS version: 10.0.19041.0
    b. Supported OS version: 10.0.19041.0
9. Scroll down the Build, and set the following:
    a. Platform target: x64
10. Save the project.

13.5.2 Set Up the XAML Controls

The UI will have three text boxes and a button. Two of the text boxes will show the pressure readings, and the last test box will display the status messages. The button handler will perform most of the work.

1. In Solution Explorer, open the MainWindow.xaml.
2. The designer and XAML editor will appear. At the top, left of the Designer set the orientation that fits your target's display.
3. Add a TextBox Control.
    a. Name: txtPressure
    b. Common->Text: <empty>
4. Add a Label next to the TextBox
    a. Common->Text: kPa
5. Add a TextBox Control
    a. Name: txtPressureinHg
    b. Common->Text: <empty>
6. Add a Label next to the TextBox
    a. Common->Text: inHg
7. Add a TextBox Control
    a. Name: txtStatus
    b. Common->Text: Ready
8. Add a Button control below the text box
    a. Name: btnGetPressure
    b. Common->Content: Get Pressure
9. Save the project.

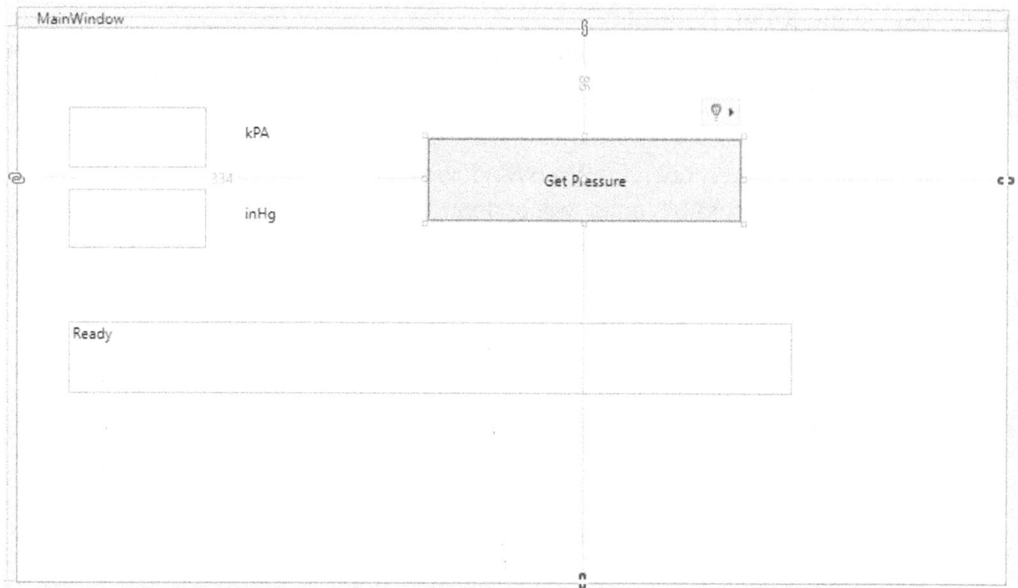

Here is the XAML Code:

```
<Window x:Class="SPIPressure.MainWindow"
        xmlns="http://schemas.microsoft.com/winfx/2006/xaml/presentation"
        xmlns:x="http://schemas.microsoft.com/winfx/2006/xaml"
        xmlns:d="http://schemas.microsoft.com/expression/blend/2008"
        xmlns:mc="http://schemas.openxmlformats.org/markup-compatibility/2006"
        xmlns:local="clr-namespace:SPIPressure"
        mc:Ignorable="d"
        Title="MainWindow" Height="450" Width="800">
    <Grid>
        <TextBox x:Name="txtPressure" HorizontalAlignment="Left" Height="47"
Margin="41,62,0,0" TextWrapping="Wrap" VerticalAlignment="Top" Width="112"/>
        <Label Content="kPA" HorizontalAlignment="Left" Height="37"
Margin="180,68,0,0" VerticalAlignment="Top" Width="67"/>
        <TextBox x:Name="txtPressureinHg" HorizontalAlignment="Left" Height="47"
Margin="41,126,0,0" TextWrapping="Wrap" VerticalAlignment="Top" Width="112"/>
        <Label Content="inHg" HorizontalAlignment="Left" Height="37"
Margin="180,131,0,0" VerticalAlignment="Top" Width="67"/>
        <TextBox x:Name="txtStatus" HorizontalAlignment="Left" Height="56"
Margin="41,230,0,0" TextWrapping="Wrap" Text="Ready" VerticalAlignment="Top"
Width="587"/>
        <Button x:Name="btnGetPressure" Content="Get Pressure"
HorizontalAlignment="Left" Height="64" Margin="334,86,0,0"
VerticalAlignment="Top" Width="252"/>
    </Grid>
</Window>
```

13.5.3 Write the Code

Now let's write the code behind the GUI.

1. Open MainWindow.xaml.cs.
2. Add the following using statements to enable SPI, Enumeration, and Threading namespaces:

```
using Windows.Devices.Enumeration;
using Windows.Devices.Spi;
using System.Threading;
```

3. Above the MainWindow() method add the following:

```
private SpiDevice myPressureSensor;
private const byte SPI_CHIP_SELECT_LINE = 0;
```

4. After the MainWindow() method, create a new method, SPISetup(), and add the following code.

Note: If you are not sure of the SPI device for your hardware, use the SpiTestTool.exe tool discussed in section 13.4.

```
private async void SPISetup()
{

    try
    {
        SpiConnectionSettings spiSettings = new
SpiConnectionSettings(SPI_CHIP_SELECT_LINE);
        spiSettings.ClockFrequency = 8000000;
        spiSettings.Mode = SpiMode.Mode0;

        string aqs = SpiDevice.GetDeviceSelector("SPI2");
        DeviceInformationCollection spiDeviceInfo = await
DeviceInformation.FindAllAsync(aqs);
        myPressureSensor = await
SpiDevice.FromIdAsync(spiDeviceInfo[0].Id, spiSettings);
        if (myPressureSensor != null)
        {
            txtStatus.Text = "Pressure sensor ready";
        }
        else
        {
            txtStatus.Text = "Pressure NOT sensor ready";
        }
    }
```

```
    catch (Exception ex)
    {
        txtStatus.Text = ex.Message;
    }
}
```

The code sets up the SPI Mode and frequency and then attempts to connect to the SPI device. A new instance of the SpiDevice is instantiated with settings from the MPL115A1. The txtStatus is updated with the result.

5. In the MainPage() method add the code to call the SPISetup().

```
public MainWindow()
{
    InitializeComponent();
    SPISetup();
}
```

6. In MainPage.xaml, double-click on the button to generate the event handler in MainPage.xaml.cs, and then add the following code:

```
private void btnGetPreassure_Click(object sender, RoutedEventArgs e)
{
    byte[] coeffData = { 0x88, 0x0, 0x8A, 0x0, 0x8C, 0x0, 0x8E, 0x0,
0x90, 0x0, 0x92, 0x0, 0x94, 0x0, 0x96, 0x0, 0x0 };
    byte[] readCOEFF = new byte[17];

    byte[] starPTconversion = { 0x24, 0x0 };
    byte[] readPTConversionStart = new byte[2];
    byte[] getPT = { 0x80, 0x0, 0x82, 0x0, 0x84, 0x0, 0x86, 0x0, 0x0 };
    byte[] readPT = new byte[9];

  //Read from the SPI port
    myPressureSensor.TransferFullDuplex(coeffData, readCOEFF);
    myPressureSensor.TransferFullDuplex(starPTconversion,
readPTConversionStart); // data is always zero
    Thread.Sleep(50);
    myPressureSensor.TransferFullDuplex(getPT, readPT);

    var coefA = readCOEFF[1] << 8 | readCOEFF[3];
    var coefB1 = readCOEFF[5] << 8 | readCOEFF[7];
    var coefB2 = readCOEFF[9] << 8 | readCOEFF[11];
    var coefC12 = readCOEFF[13] << 8 | readCOEFF[15];

    var Padc = (readPT[1] << 8 | readPT[3]) >> 6;
    var Tadc = (readPT[5] << 8 | readPT[7]) >> 6;
```

```
//convert coeffs
bool coefAneg = false;
if ((coefA & 0x8000) == 0x8000)
{
    coefA = (coefA ^ 0xFFFF) + 1; //twos complimnet
    coefAneg = true;
}

var coefAInt = coefA >> 3;
var coefAfrac = coefA & 0x7;
if (coefAneg)
{
    coefAInt = -coefAInt;
    coefAfrac = -coefAfrac;
}
double a0 = (double)coefAInt + (double)coefAfrac / 8;

bool coefB1neg = false;
if ((coefB1 & 0x8000) == 0x8000)
{
    coefB1 = (coefB1 ^ 0xFFFF) + 1;
    coefB1neg = true;
}

var coefB1Int = coefB1 >> 13;
var coefB1Frac = coefB1 & 0x1FFF;
if (coefB1neg)
{
    coefB1Int = -coefB1Int;
    coefB1Frac = -coefB1Frac;
}
double b1 = (double)coefB1Int + (double)coefB1Frac / 8192;

bool coefB2neg = false;
if ((coefB2 & 0x8000) == 0x8000)
{
    coefB2 = (coefB2 ^ 0xFFFF) + 1;
    coefB2neg = true;
}

var coefB2Int = coefB2 >> 14;
var coefB2Frac = coefB2 & 0x3FFF;
if (coefB2neg)
{
    coefB2Int = -coefB2Int;
    coefB2Frac = -coefB2Frac;
}
```

```
    double b2 = (double)coefB2Int + (double)coefB2Frac / 16384;

    bool coefC12neg = false;
    if ((coefC12 & 0x8000) == 0x8000)
    {
        coefC12 = (coefC12 ^ 0xFFFF) + 1;
        coefC12neg = true;
    }

    var coefC12Frac = coefC12 >> 2;
    if (coefC12neg)
    {
        coefC12Frac = -coefC12Frac;
    }
    double c12 = (double)coefC12Frac / 4194303;

  //Final calculations
    double Pcomp = a0 + ((b1 + (c12 * Tadc)) * Padc) + (b2 * Tadc);
    double PressureResult = (Pcomp * 65 / 1023) + 50;
    txtPressure.Text = Math.Round(PressureResult, 2).ToString();

    double PressureinHg = PressureResult * .02953 / 0.1;
    txtPressureinHg.Text = Math.Round(PressureinHg, 2).ToString();
}
```

The button event handler first sets up the byte arrays that will be used to get the sensor data from the chip. The first full-duplex transfer gets the coefficients and puts them in the readCOEFF[] byte array. The second full-duplex transfer starts the conversion process. Any data returned in the readPTConversionStart[] array is ignored. The thread sleeps for 50 ms, which is more than enough time for the conversion to be completed per the datasheet. The final full-duplex transfer retrieves the resulting pressure and temperature readings. The results are placed into the readPT[] byte array. As far as the SPI access is concerned, that is it. The rest of the code works on the calculation. Each coefficient is extracted from the readCOEFF[] byte array. The coefficients consist of a sign bit, a number of integer bits, and some fraction bits. Keep in mind that the first byte returned from the SPI transfer must be ignored. In this case, the value of 0. The second byte in readCOEFF[] is put into coefA and the bits are bitwise shifted left 8 to accommodate the remaining byte from readCOEFF[3]. This is repeated for coefB1, coefB2, and coefC12. The ADC results for pressure and temperature are put into their respective variables in a similar manner. The next step is to go through each coefficient and determine the sign and fractional part. The results are put into double types. The final calculations are made and the results appear in the text boxes.

7. Save the project.
8. Build a debug version of the project and correct any errors.

13.5.4 Test the Application

The application is ready to be tested in the target system.

1. Connect the MPL115A1 to your target platform's SPI port.

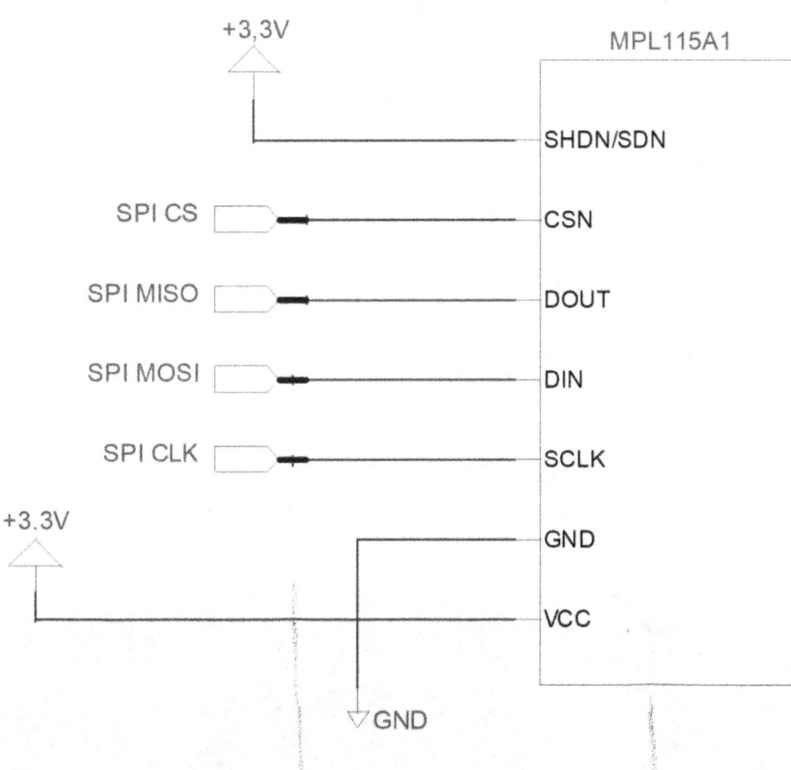

2. In the C:\VS-Apps folder of your development machine, determine where the SPIPressure.exe file is located: C:\VS-Apps\SPIPressure\SPIPressure\bin\Debug\net6.0-windows10.0.19041.0.
3. On the target machine, create an exact folder structure under C:\VS-apps - C:\VS-Apps\ SPIPressure\SPIPressure\bin\Debug\net6.0-windows10.0.19041.0.
4. Run Visual Studio Remote Debug, and make a note of the computer name and port number listed in the Visual Studio Remote Debug output.
5. In Visual Studio running on the development machine, open the SPIPressure Properties page.
6. Click on Debug on the left side, and click Open debug launch profile UI.
7. Check the checkbox for Use remote machine and enter the Target system's computer name with the port number: X64-APPTEST:4026
8. Close the Window.

9. In the properties, scroll up to Build Events.
10. In the Post-build event, enter the following to do a copy of the output to the remote system (this is all one line):

```
xcopy C:\VS-Apps\SPIPressure\SPIPressure\bin\Debug\net6.0-windows10.0.19041.0
\\X64-APPTEST\VS-Apps\SPIPressure\SPIPressure\bin\Debug\net6.0-
windows10.0.19041.0 /Y
```

11. Save the project.
12. Build the debug version of the application again. The output files should be copied to the remote system.
13. Start the debug session.
14. You will be asked for the target system's login credentials. Enter the user's name and password and click OK.
15. Once the application has loaded on the target system, the status should show connection has been successful. Click the Get Pressure button, and the pressure reading from the sensor will be displayed.
16. Stop debugging when finished.

If you have an O-scope that can read the SPI bus, connect the scope probes to the SPI lines. When you push the button, you can see the full-duplex transfer taking place. The first picture below shows the coefficients being read.

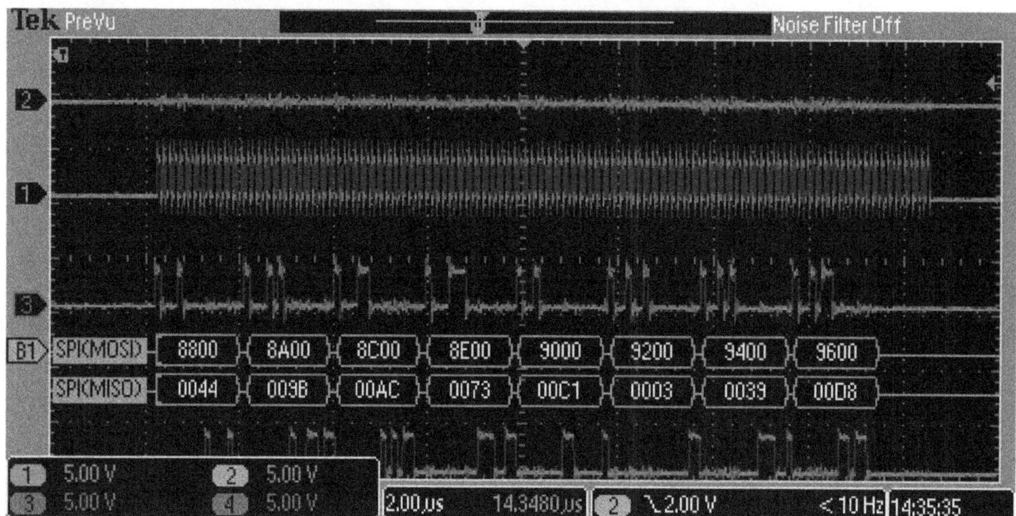

Adjusting the trigger to trigger on the read pressure bytes, you can see the data read for the pressure and temperature as shown in the following picture.

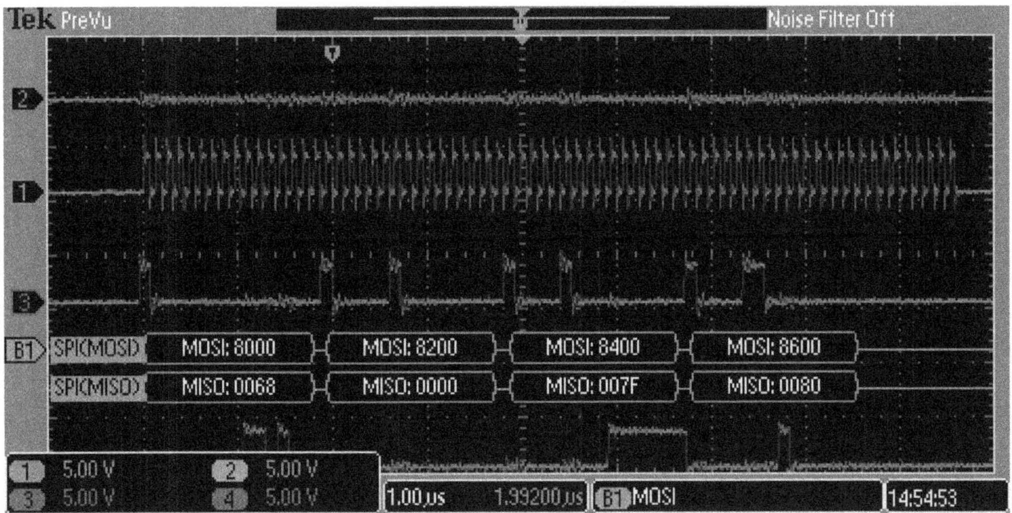

13.6 *Exercise 1302: SPI Pressure Sensor Assembly Library*

Let's create a library for the MPL115A1 that addresses the common operations that have to be made.

13.6.1 Create the Assembly Library

Here are the basic setup steps:

1. Open Visual Studio 2022, if not already open.
2. Create a new project and select WPF Class Library – "A project for creating a class library that targets a .NET WPF Application".
3. Name the project MPL115A1 and set the folder location to C:\VS-Apps.
4. Click Next.
5. Select .NET 6.0 (Long-term support) from the drop-down box.
6. Click the "Create" button.
7. Once the application opens, we need to do a little more set up to support the Windows Runtime Namespaces. From the menu, select Project->MPL115A1 Properties.
8. Under Application->General set the following for the targeted Windows OS:
   a. Target OS version: 10.0.19041.0
   b. Supported OS version: 10.0.19041.0
9. Scroll down the Build, and set the following:
   a. Platform target: x64.
10. Save the project.
11. Rename Class.cs to MPL115A1.cs and save the project.
12. Change the namespace to Annabooks.MPL115A1.
13. Fill in the following code:

```
using System;
using System.Threading;
using Windows.Devices.Enumeration;
using Windows.Devices.Spi;

namespace Annabooks.MPL115A1
{
    public class MPL115A1
    {
        private SpiDevice sensorMPL115A1;
        private double a0;
        private double b1;
        private double b2;
        private double c12;

        private bool MPL115A1Ready = false;
        public string connectionError = "";

        public MPL115A1(string SPI_Port, int frequency, int SPI_Chip_Select, bool SPI_Bus_Shared)
        {
            MPL115A1SPISetup(SPI_Port, frequency, SPI_Chip_Select, SPI_Bus_Shared);
        }

        private async void MPL115A1SPISetup(string SPI_Port, int frequency, int SPI_Chip_Select, bool SPI_Bus_Shared)
        {

            try
            {
                SpiConnectionSettings spiSettings = new SpiConnectionSettings(SPI_Chip_Select);
                spiSettings.ClockFrequency = frequency;
                if (SPI_Bus_Shared)
                {
                    spiSettings.SharingMode = SpiSharingMode.Shared;
                }
                else
                {
                    spiSettings.SharingMode = SpiSharingMode.Exclusive;
                }
                spiSettings.Mode = SpiMode.Mode0;

                string aqs = SpiDevice.GetDeviceSelector(SPI_Port);
```

```
                DeviceInformationCollection spiDeviceInfo = await DeviceInformation.FindAllAsync(aqs);
                sensorMPL115A1 = await SpiDevice.FromIdAsync(spiDeviceInfo[0].Id, spiSettings);
            }
            catch(Exception ex)
            {
                connectionError = ex.Message;
            }

            if (sensorMPL115A1 != null)
            {
                MPL115A1Ready = true;
                //we will get the coefficients now since they never change.
                byte[] coeffData = { 0x88, 0x0, 0x8A, 0x0, 0x8C, 0x0, 0x8E, 0x0, 0x90, 0x0, 0x92, 0x0, 0x94, 0x0, 0x96, 0x0, 0x0 };
                byte[] readCOEFF = new byte[17];

                sensorMPL115A1.TransferFullDuplex(coeffData, readCOEFF);

                var coefA = readCOEFF[1] << 8 | readCOEFF[3];
                var coefB1 = readCOEFF[5] << 8 | readCOEFF[7];
                var coefB2 = readCOEFF[9] << 8 | readCOEFF[11];
                var coefC12 = readCOEFF[13] << 8 | readCOEFF[15];

                //convert coeffs
                bool coefAneg = false;
                if ((coefA & 0x8000) == 0x8000)
                {
                    coefA = (coefA ^ 0xFFFF) + 1; //twos complimnet
                    coefAneg = true;
                }

                var coefAInt = coefA >> 3;
                var coefAfrac = coefA & 0x7;
                if (coefAneg)
                {
                    coefAInt = -coefAInt;
                    coefAfrac = -coefAfrac;
                }
                a0 = (double)coefAInt + (double)coefAfrac / 8;

                bool coefB1neg = false;
                if ((coefB1 & 0x8000) == 0x8000)
                {
                    coefB1 = (coefB1 ^ 0xFFFF) + 1;
```

```
                    coefB1neg = true;
                }

                var coefB1Int = coefB1 >> 13;
                var coefB1Frac = coefB1 & 0x1FFF;
                if (coefB1neg)
                {
                    coefB1Int = -coefB1Int;
                    coefB1Frac = -coefB1Frac;
                }
                b1 = (double)coefB1Int + (double)coefB1Frac / 8192;

                bool coefB2neg = false;
                if ((coefB2 & 0x8000) == 0x8000)
                {
                    coefB2 = (coefB2 ^ 0xFFFF) + 1;
                    coefB2neg = true;
                }

                var coefB2Int = coefB2 >> 14;
                var coefB2Frac = coefB2 & 0x3FFF;
                if (coefB2neg)
                {
                    coefB2Int = -coefB2Int;
                    coefB2Frac = -coefB2Frac;
                }
                b2 = (double)coefB2Int + (double)coefB2Frac / 16384;

                bool coefC12neg = false;
                if ((coefC12 & 0x8000) == 0x8000)
                {
                    coefC12 = (coefC12 ^ 0xFFFF) + 1;
                    coefC12neg = true;
                }

                var coefC12Frac = coefC12 >> 2;
                if (coefC12neg)
                {
                    coefC12Frac = -coefC12Frac;
                }
                c12 = (double)coefC12Frac / 4194303;
            }
        }

        public double ReadPressure_kPa()
        {
            byte[] starPTconversion = { 0x24, 0x0 };
            byte[] readPTConversionStart = new byte[2];
```

```
            byte[] getPT = { 0x80, 0x0, 0x82, 0x0, 0x84, 0x0, 0x86, 0x0, 0x0 };
            byte[] readPT = new byte[9];
            sensorMPL115A1.TransferFullDuplex(starPTconversion, readPTConversionStart); // data returned is always zero
            Thread.Sleep(50);
            sensorMPL115A1.TransferFullDuplex(getPT, readPT);

            var Padc = (readPT[1] << 8 | readPT[3]) >> 6;
            var Tadc = (readPT[5] << 8 | readPT[7]) >> 6;

            double Pcomp = a0 + ((b1 + (c12 * Tadc)) * Padc) + (b2 * Tadc);
            double PressureResult = (Pcomp * 65 / 1023) + 50;
            return Math.Round(PressureResult, 2);
        }

        public double ReadPressure_inHg()
        {
            double PressureinHg = ReadPressure_kPa() * .02953 / 0.1;
            return Math.Round(PressureinHg, 2);
        }

        public bool MPL115A1Status()
        {
            return MPL115A1Ready;
        }

    }
}
```

The constructor for the class takes in the SPI bus port number, frequency, Chip Select value, and whether the bus is shared or not. The constructor makes a call to set up the SPI port. Since the coefficients are static values, once the connection to the SPI devices is made, the coefficients are extracted and placed in private member variables. The only other public methods are to read the pressure and check the status of the connection.

14. Save the project.
15. Build a debug version of the project. Correct any errors and rebuild again if necessary.

13.6.2 Create the SPIPressure2 Application that uses the new Assembly

The class library is ready to use in an application.

1. Open Visual Studio 2022.
2. Create a new "WPF Application" project. Make sure you select the correct WPF Application template for .NET.

Note: The project is a .NET application, not a .NET Framework application. If you see .NET Framework in the project description, it is the wrong project.

3. Name the project "SPIPressure2" and set the folder location to C:\VS-Apps on your development machine. To do remote debugging with .NET, the remote machine folder architecture must match the development machine. Visual Studio Remote Debugging documentation describes the setup as well.
4. Click the "Next" button.
5. Select .NET 6.0 (Long-term support) from the drop-down box.
6. Click the "Create" button.
7. Once the application opens, we need to do a little more set up to support the Windows Runtime Namespaces. From the menu, select Project->SPIPressure2 Properties.
8. Under Application->General set the following for the targeted Windows OS:
    a. Target OS version: 10.0.19041.0
    b. Supported OS version: 10.0.19041.0
9. Scroll down the Build, and set the following:
    a. Platform target: x64

Note: If you forget to set the correct Target Framework and Target OS, Visual Studio will not let you reference the Windows.Devices namespace.

10. Save the project.

13.6.3 Set up the XAML Controls

1. In Solution Explorer, open the MainWindow.xaml.
2. The designer and XAML editor will appear. At the top, left of the Designer set the orientation that fits your target's display.
3. Add a TextBox Control.
    a. Name: txtPressure
    b. Common->Text: <empty>
4. Add a Label next to the TextBox
    a. Common->Content: kPa
5. Add a TextBox Control
    a. Name: txtPressureinHg
    b. Common->Text: <empty>
6. Add a Label next to the TextBox
    a. Common->Content: inHg
7. Add A TextBox Control
    a. Name: txtStatus

   b. Common->Text: Ready
8. Add a Button control below the text box
   a. Name: btnGetPreassure
   b. Common->Content: Get Pressure
9. Save the project.

Here is the XAML Code:

```
<Window x:Class="SPIPressure2.MainWindow"
      xmlns="http://schemas.microsoft.com/winfx/2006/xaml/presentation"
      xmlns:x="http://schemas.microsoft.com/winfx/2006/xaml"
      xmlns:d="http://schemas.microsoft.com/expression/blend/2008"
      xmlns:mc="http://schemas.openxmlformats.org/markup-compatibility/2006"
      xmlns:local="clr-namespace:SPIPressure2"
      mc:Ignorable="d"
      Title="MainWindow" Height="450" Width="800">
   <Grid>
      <TextBox x:Name="txtPressure" HorizontalAlignment="Left" Height="47"
Margin="41,62,0,0" TextWrapping="Wrap" VerticalAlignment="Top" Width="112"/>
      <Label Content="kPA" HorizontalAlignment="Left" Height="37"
Margin="180,68,0,0" VerticalAlignment="Top" Width="67"/>
      <TextBox x:Name="txtPressureinHg" HorizontalAlignment="Left" Height="47"
Margin="41,126,0,0" TextWrapping="Wrap" VerticalAlignment="Top" Width="112"/>
      <Label Content="inHg" HorizontalAlignment="Left" Height="37"
Margin="180,131,0,0" VerticalAlignment="Top" Width="67"/>
      <TextBox x:Name="txtStatus" HorizontalAlignment="Left" Height="56"
Margin="41,230,0,0" TextWrapping="Wrap" Text="Ready" VerticalAlignment="Top"
Width="587"/>
      <Button x:Name="btnGetPressure" Content="Get Pressure"
HorizontalAlignment="Left" Height="64" Margin="334,86,0,0"
VerticalAlignment="Top" Width="252" Click="btnGetPressure_Click"/>
   </Grid>
</Window>
```

13.6.4 Write the Code

1. Now we need to add the class library. Click Project->Add Reference.
2. Browse to the location of the MPL115A1.dll that is in the Class Library Project.
3. Select the dll and click "Add" and then click "OK". The namespace for the library can be added to the using directives.
4. Open MainWindows.xaml.cs
5. Add the following using statements to add Annabooks.MPL115A1 and System Threading namespaces.

```
using Annabooks.MPL115A1;
```

```
using System.Threading;
```

6. Just within the MainWindow class, add the following to create a new instance of the MPL115A1.

```
MPL115A1 myPressureSensor = null;
```

7. Below the MainWindow() method, create a new PressureSensorSetup() method and fill in the following:

```
private void PressureSensorSetup()
{
    myPressureSensor = new MPL115A1("SPI2", 8000000, 0, false);
    Thread.Sleep(1000);
    if (myPressureSensor.MPL115A1Status())
    {
      Application.Current.Dispatcher.Invoke((Action)(() => txtStatus.Text = "Preasure
Sensor is Ready"));
    }
    else
    {
      Application.Current.Dispatcher.Invoke((Action)(() => txtStatus.Text = "Preasure
Sensor is NOT Ready: " + myPressureSensor.connectionError));
    }
}
```

The method instantiates myPressureSensor as a new instance of MPL115A1 using SP2 as the port, 80000 as the frequency, Chip Select 0, and bus not shared. The thread is put to sleep for about a second and then the status of the connection is made and reported.

8. In the MainWindow() method, create a thread that calls the PressureSensorSetup() method and start the thread.

```
public MainWindow()
{
    InitializeComponent();
    Thread setupPressureSensor = new Thread(new
ThreadStart(PressureSensorSetup));
    setupPressureSensor.Start();
}
```

9. In the MainWindow.xaml, double-click on the button to generate the event handler.
10. Fill in the code:

```
private void btnGetPreassure_Click(object sender, RoutedEventArgs e)
{
```

```
        if (myPressureSensor.MPL115A1Status())
        {
            txtPressure.Text =
myPressureSensor.ReadPressure_kPa().ToString();
            txtPressureinHg.Text =
myPressureSensor.ReadPressure_inHg().ToString();
        }
    }
```

A check is made that the sensor is ready and then proceeds to read the sensor.

11. Save the project.

13.6.5 Test the Application

1. In the C:\VS-Apps folder of your development machine, determine where the SPIPressure2.exe file is located: C:\VS-Apps\SPIPressure2\SPIPressure2\bin\Debug\net6.0-windows10.0.19041.0
2. On the target machine, create an exact folder structure under C:\VS-apps - C:\VS-Apps\ SPIPressure2\SPIPressure2\bin\Debug\net6.0-windows10.0.19041.0
3. Run Visual Studio Remote Debug, and make a note of the computer name and port number listed in the Visual Studio Remote Debug output.
4. In Visual Studio running on the development machine, open the SPIPressure2 Properties page.
5. Click on Debug on the left side, and click Open debug launch profile UI.
6. Check the checkbox for Use remote machine and enter the Target system's computer name with the port number: X64-APPTEST:4026
7. Close the Window.
8. In the properties, scroll up to Build Events.
9. In the Post-build event enter the following to do a copy of the output to the remote system (this is all one line):

xcopy C:\VS-Apps\SPIPressure2\SPIPressure2\bin\Debug\net6.0-windows10.0.19041.0 \\X64-APPTEST\VS-Apps\SPIPressure2\SPIPressure2\bin\Debug\net6.0-windows10.0.19041.0 /Y

10. Save the project.
11. Build the debug version of the application again. The output files should be copied to the remote system.
12. Start the debug session.
13. You will be asked for the target system's login credentials. Enter the user's name and password and click OK.

14. Once the application has loaded on the target system, the status should show that the connection has been successful. Click the Get Pressure button, and the pressure reading from the sensor will be displayed.
15. Stop debugging when finished.

The application performs the same as before and has fewer lines of code sans the checking on the MPL115A1 status. Class Libraries help to break down the project into smaller chunks.

13.7 Exercise 1303: SPI ADC

Since none of the reference boards support ADC, this exercise will use the Microchip MCP3002 10-Bit ADC with a SPI interface. The MCP3002 has two input channels and a reference voltage of 2.7v to 5v. A differential reading between the two channels can be obtained from the device. The clock frequency is dependent on the reference voltage, but the SPI mode is 0. Since the ADCs are a 10-Bit, two bytes will be read, but only the lower 10 bits of the 16 bits are used to calculate the result. This solution might come in handy when one is trying to measure a DC supply voltage.

13.7.1 Basic Setup

Here is the basic setup of the application.

1. Open Visual Studio 2022
2. Create a new "WPF Application" project. Make sure you select the correct WPF Application template for .NET.
3. Name the project "SPIADC", and set the folder location to C:\VS-Apps on your development machine. To do remote debugging with .NET, the remote machine folder architecture must match the development machine. Visual Studio Remote Debugging documentation describes the setup as well.
4. Click the "Next" button.
5. Select .NET 6.0 (Long-term support) from the drop-down box.
6. Click the "Create" button.
7. Once the application opens, we need to do a little more set up to support the Windows Runtime Namespaces. From the menu, select Project-> SPIADC Properties.
8. Under Application->General set the following for the targeted Windows OS:
    a. Target OS version: 10.0.19041.0
    b. Supported OS version: 10.0.19041.0
9. Scroll down the Build, and set the following:
    a. Platform target: x64
10. Save the project.

13.7.2 Set Up the XAML Controls

The UI will have outputs for Channels 0 and 1, as well as, differential output for the differences between the two channels. Radio buttons will be used to set the reference voltage of 3.3V or 5V.

1. In Solution Explorer, open the MainWindow.xaml.
2. The designer and XAML editor will appear. At the top, left of the Designer set the orientation that fits your target's display.
3. Add a Label Control.
    a. Common->Text: Reference Voltage
4. Add a Radio button
    a. Name: rb3v
    b. Common->Content: 3.3V
5. Add a Radio button
    a. Name: rb5v
    b. Common->Content: 5V
6. Add a Label Control.
    a. Common->Content: Channel 0 Reading
7. Add a Label Control.
    a. Common->Text: Channel 1 Reading
8. Add a TextBox Control
    a. Name: txtChannel0Result
    b. Common->Text: <empty>
9. Add a Label next to the TextBox
    a. Common->Content: V
10. Add a TextBox Control
    a. Name: txtChannel1Result
    b. Common->Text: <empty>
11. Add a Label next to the TextBox
    a. Common->Content: V
12. Add a Button control
    a. Name: btnReadChannel0
    b. Common->Content: Read Channel 0
13. Add a Button control
    a. Name: btnReadChannel1
    b. Common->Content: Read Channel 1
14. Add a TextBox Control
    a. Name: txtChannelDiff
    b. Common->Text: <empty>
15. Add a Label next to the TextBox
    a. Common->Content: V

16. Add a Button control
    a. Name: btnCh0PCh1N
    b. Common->Content: Read Diff Ch0+ Ch1-
17. Add a TextBox Control
    a. Name: txtStatus
    b. Common->Text: <empty>
18. Save the project.

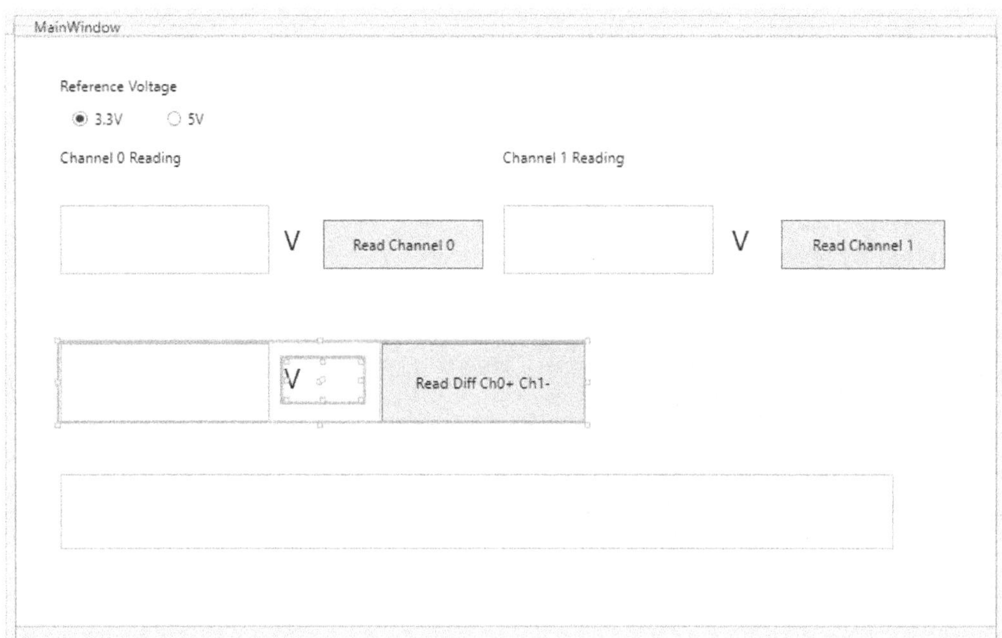

Here is the XAML code:

```
<Window x:Class="SPIADC.MainWindow"
        xmlns="http://schemas.microsoft.com/winfx/2006/xaml/presentation"
        xmlns:x="http://schemas.microsoft.com/winfx/2006/xaml"
        xmlns:d="http://schemas.microsoft.com/expression/blend/2008"
        xmlns:mc="http://schemas.openxmlformats.org/markup-compatibility/2006"
        xmlns:local="clr-namespace:SPIADC"
        mc:Ignorable="d"
        Title="MainWindow" Height="480" Width="800">
    <Grid Margin="0,0,0,-6">
        <TextBox x:Name="txtChannel0Result" HorizontalAlignment="Left" Height="54"
Margin="36,133,0,0" Text="" TextWrapping="Wrap" VerticalAlignment="Top"
Width="172" IsReadOnly="True"/>
```

```
        <TextBlock HorizontalAlignment="Left" Height="40" Margin="36,30,0,0"
Text="Reference Voltage" TextWrapping="Wrap" VerticalAlignment="Top"
Width="172"/>
        <TextBlock HorizontalAlignment="Left" Height="40" Margin="36,87,0,0"
Text="Channel 0 Reading" TextWrapping="Wrap" VerticalAlignment="Top"
Width="172"/>
        <TextBox x:Name="txtChannel1Result" HorizontalAlignment="Left" Height="54"
Margin="408,133,0,0" Text="" TextWrapping="Wrap" VerticalAlignment="Top"
Width="172" IsReadOnly="True"/>
        <TextBlock HorizontalAlignment="Left" Height="40" Margin="408,87,0,0"
Text="Channel 1 Reading" TextWrapping="Wrap" VerticalAlignment="Top"
Width="172"/>
        <Button x:Name="btnReadChannel0" Content="Read Channel 0" Height="39"
Margin="254,144,416,0" VerticalAlignment="Top" Width="130"
Click="btnReadChannel0_Click"/>
        <TextBlock HorizontalAlignment="Left" Height="35" Margin="220,145,0,0"
Text="V" TextWrapping="Wrap" VerticalAlignment="Top" Width="28"
FontSize="22"/>
        <TextBlock HorizontalAlignment="Left" Height="35" Margin="594,145,0,0"
Text="V" TextWrapping="Wrap" VerticalAlignment="Top" Width="26"
FontSize="22"/>
        <Button x:Name="btnReadChannel1" Content="Read Channel 1" Height="39"
Margin="628,144,39,0" VerticalAlignment="Top" Width="133"
Click="btnReadChannel1_Click"/>
        <TextBox x:Name="txtChannelDiff" HorizontalAlignment="Left" Height="62"
Margin="36,242,0,0" Text="" TextWrapping="Wrap" VerticalAlignment="Top"
Width="172" IsReadOnly="True"/>
        <Button x:Name="btnCh0PCh1N" Content="Read Diff Ch0+ Ch1-" Height="62"
Margin="300,242,334,0" VerticalAlignment="Top" Width="165"
Click="btnCh0PCh1N_Click" />
        <TextBox x:Name="txtStatus" HorizontalAlignment="Left" Height="59"
Margin="36,345,0,0" Text="" TextWrapping="Wrap" VerticalAlignment="Top"
Width="680" IsReadOnly="True"/>
        <RadioButton x:Name="rb3v" Content="3.3V" Height="32" Margin="45,58,699,0"
VerticalAlignment="Top" Width="56" IsChecked="True"/>
        <RadioButton x:Name="rb5v" Content="5V" Height="32" Margin="122,58,622,0"
VerticalAlignment="Top" Width="56"/>
        <TextBlock HorizontalAlignment="Left" Height="35" Margin="220,254,0,0"
Text="V" TextWrapping="Wrap" VerticalAlignment="Top" Width="66"
FontSize="22"/>

    </Grid>
</Window>
```

13.7.3 Write the Code

Now, let's write the code behind the GUI.

1. Open MainWindow.xaml.cs

2. Add the following using statements to enable the SPI and the Enumeration namespaces:

```
using Windows.Devices.Enumeration;
using Windows.Devices.Spi;
```

3. Above the MainWindow() method add the following:

```
private SpiDevice myADC;
private const byte SPI_CHIP_SELECT_LINE = 0;
private byte[] Channel0 = { 0x68, 0x00 };
private byte[] Channel1 = { 0x78, 0x00 };
private byte[] DiffCh0PCh1N = { 0x48, 0x0 };
private byte[] DiffCh0NCh1P = { 0x58, 0x0 };
```

The private members define the SPI port instance, the Chip Select, and the commands to retrieve data from the ADC.

4. After the MainWindow() method create a new method SPISetup() and add the following code. The code sets up the SPI Mode and frequency and then attempts to connect to the SPI device.

```
private async void SPISetup()
{
    try
    {
        SpiConnectionSettings spiSettings = new
SpiConnectionSettings(SPI_CHIP_SELECT_LINE);
        spiSettings.ClockFrequency = 8000000;
        spiSettings.Mode = SpiMode.Mode0;

        string aqs = SpiDevice.GetDeviceSelector("SPI2");
        DeviceInformationCollection spiDeviceInfo = await
DeviceInformation.FindAllAsync(aqs);
        myADC = await SpiDevice.FromIdAsync(spiDeviceInfo[0].Id,
spiSettings);

        if (myADC != null)
        {
            txtStatus.Text = "ADC is ready";
        }
        else
        {
            txtStatus.Text = "ADC is NOT ready";
        }
```

```
        }
        catch (Exception ex)
        {
            txtStatus.Text = ex.Message;
        }
    }
```

The frequency is set lower to accommodate both reference voltages. The status of the attempt to connect to the SPI device is reported in the txtStatus.

5. In the MainWindow() method add the code to call the SPISetup() method.

```
public MainWindow()
{
    InitializeComponent();
    SPISetup();
}
```

6. In MainWindow.xaml, double-click on the btnReadChannel0 to generate the event handler in MainWindow.xaml.cs, and then add the following code:

```
private void btnReadChannel0_Click(object sender, RoutedEventArgs e)
{

    byte[] adcCh0Out = new byte[2];
    myADC.TransferFullDuplex(Channel0, adcCh0Out);
    var adcCh0OutInt = (adcCh0Out[0] << 8 | adcCh0Out[1]) & 0x3FF;


    if (rb3v.IsChecked == true)
    {
        txtChannel0Result.Text = Math.Round((double)adcCh0OutInt / 1024 *
3.3, 2).ToString();

    }
    if (rb5v.IsChecked == true)
    {
        txtChannel0Result.Text = Math.Round((double)adcCh0OutInt / 1024 *
5, 2).ToString();
    }
}
```

A single full-duplex transfer is used to retrieve the current results from the ADC Channel0. Based on the reference voltage, the result is calculated using the formula from the datasheet.

7. In MainWindow.xaml, double-click on the btnReadChannel1 to generate the event handler in MainWindow.xaml.cs, and then add the following code:

```
private void btnReadChannel1_Click(object sender, RoutedEventArgs e)
{
    byte[] adcCh1Out = new byte[2];
    myADC.TransferFullDuplex(Channel1, adcCh1Out);

    var adcCh1OutInt = (adcCh1Out[0] << 8 | adcCh1Out[1]) & 0x3ff;


    if (rb3v.IsChecked == true)
    {
        txtChannel1Result.Text = Math.Round((double)adcCh1OutInt / 1024 *
3.3, 2).ToString();

    }
    if (rb5v.IsChecked == true)
    {
        txtChannel1Result.Text = Math.Round((double)adcCh1OutInt / 1024 *
5, 2).ToString();
    }
}
```

8. In MainWindow.xaml, double-click on the `btnCh0PCh1N` to generate the event handler in MainWindow.xaml.cs, and then add the following code:

```
private void btnCh0PCh1N_Click(object sender, RoutedEventArgs e)
{

    byte[] adcDiffOut = new byte[2];
    myADC.TransferFullDuplex(DiffCh0PCh1N, adcDiffOut);

    var adcDiffOutInt = (adcDiffOut[0] << 8 | adcDiffOut[1]) & 0x3ff;

    if (adcDiffOutInt > 0) //if IN+ is equal to or bloew IN- the result
is 0x00 so we test for 0
    {
        if (rb3v.IsChecked == true)
        {
            txtChannelDiff.Text = Math.Round((double)adcDiffOutInt / 1024
* 3.3,2).ToString();
        }
        if (rb5v.IsChecked == true)
        {
            txtChannelDiff.Text = Math.Round((double)adcDiffOutInt / 1024
* 5,2).ToString();
```

```
        }
    }
    else
    {
        myADC.TransferFullDuplex(DiffCh0NCh1P, adcDiffOut); //Flip the
differential input to test for negative
        adcDiffOutInt = (adcDiffOut[0] << 8 | adcDiffOut[1]) & 0x3ff;
        if (rb3v.IsChecked == true)
        {
            txtChannelDiff.Text = (-Math.Round((double)adcDiffOutInt /
1024 * 3.3,2)).ToString();
        }
        if (rb5v.IsChecked == true)
        {
            txtChannelDiff.Text = (-Math.Round((double)adcDiffOutInt /
1024 * 5,2)).ToString();
        }
    }
}
```

11. Save the project.
12. Build a debug version of the project and correct any errors.

13.7.4 Test the Application

The application is ready to be tested in the target system.

1. Connect the MCP3002 to your target platform's SPI port.

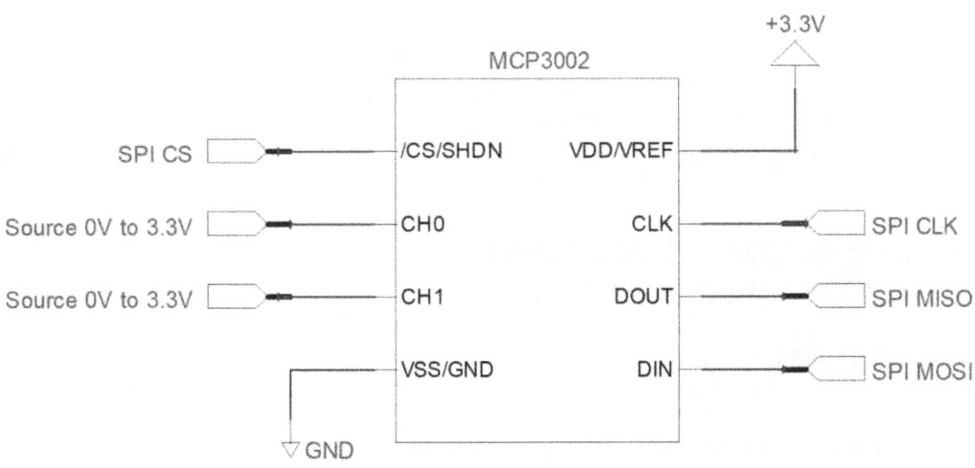

2. Connect a 0v to 3.3V DC power source to Ch0 and another to Ch1 of the MCP3002. The power sources can be batteries or a bench supply.
3. In the C:\VS-Apps folder of your development machine, determine where the SPIADC.exe file is located: C:\VS-Apps\SPIADC\SPIADC\bin\Debug\net6.0-windows10.0.19041.0
4. On the target machine, create an exact folder structure under C:\VS-apps - C:\VS-Apps\SPIADC\SPIADC\bin\Debug\net6.0-windows10.0.19041.0
5. Run Visual Studio Remote Debug, and make a note of the computer name and port number listed in the Visual Studio Remote Debug output.
6. In Visual Studio running on the development machine, open the SPIADC Properties page.
7. Click on Debug on the left side, and click Open debug launch profile UI.
8. Check the checkbox for Use remote machine and enter the Target systems computer name with the port number: X64-APPTEST:4026
9. Close the Window.
10. In the properties, scroll up to Build Events.
11. In the Post-build event enter the following to do a copy of the output to the remote system (this is all one line):

```
xcopy C:\VS-Apps\SPIADC\SPIADC\bin\Debug\net6.0-windows10.0.19041.0 \\X64-APPTEST\VS-Apps\SPIADC\SPIADC\bin\Debug\net6.0-windows10.0.19041.0 /Y
```

12. Save the project.
13. Build the debug version of the application again. The output files should be copied to the remote system.
14. Start the debug session.
15. You will be asked for the target system's login credentials. Enter the user's name and password and click OK.
16. Once the application has loaded on the target system, hit the different buttons to get the readings from the ADC. If you can, adjust the input voltage to Ch0 or Ch1 and verify that the readings changed appropriately.
17. Stop debugging when finished.

13.8 Exercise 1304: SPI ADC Library

Now, let's create a library for the MCP3002.

13.8.1 Create the Library

Here are the basic setup steps:

1. Open Visual Studio 2022, if not already open.

2. Create a new project and select WPF Class Library – "A project for creating a class library that targets a .NET WPF Application".
3. Name the project MCP3002 and set the folder location to C:\VS-Apps.
4. Click Next.
5. Select .NET 6.0 (Long-term support) from the drop-down box.
6. Click the "Create" button.
7. Once the application opens, we need to do a little more set up to support the Windows Runtime Namespaces. From the menu, select Project->MCP3002 Properties.
8. Under Application->General set the following for the targeted Windows OS:
    a. Target OS version: 10.0.19041.0
    b. Supported OS version: 10.0.19041.0
9. Scroll down the Build, and set the following:
    a. Platform target: x64
10. Save the project.
11. Rename Class.cs to MCP3002.cs and save the project.
12. Change the namespace to Annabooks.MCP3002
13. Fill in the following code:

```
using System;
using Windows.Devices.Enumeration;
using Windows.Devices.Spi;

namespace Annabooks.MCP3002
{
    public class MCP3002
    {

        private SpiDevice adcMCP3002;
        private byte[] Channel0 = { 0x68, 0x00 };
        private byte[] Channel1 = { 0x78, 0x00 };
        private byte[] DiffCh0PCh1N = { 0x48, 0x0 };
        private byte[] DiffCh0NCh1P = { 0x58, 0x0 };

        private bool MPC3002Ready = false;
        public string connectionError = "";

        public MCP3002(string SPI_Port, int frequency, int SPI_Chip_Select, bool SPI_Bus_Shared)
        {
            MPC3002SPISetup(SPI_Port, frequency, SPI_Chip_Select, SPI_Bus_Shared);
        }
```

```
        private async void MPC3002SPISetup(string SPI_Port, int frequency, int SPI_Chip_Select, bool SPI_Bus_Shared)
        {
            try
            {
                SpiConnectionSettings spiSettings = new SpiConnectionSettings(SPI_Chip_Select);
                spiSettings.ClockFrequency = frequency;
                if (SPI_Bus_Shared)
                {
                    spiSettings.SharingMode = SpiSharingMode.Shared;
                }
                else
                {
                    spiSettings.SharingMode = SpiSharingMode.Exclusive;
                }
                spiSettings.Mode = SpiMode.Mode0;

                string aqs = SpiDevice.GetDeviceSelector(SPI_Port);
                DeviceInformationCollection spiDeviceInfo = await DeviceInformation.FindAllAsync(aqs);
                adcMCP3002 = await SpiDevice.FromIdAsync(spiDeviceInfo[0].Id, spiSettings);
            }
            catch (Exception ex)
            {
                connectionError = ex.Message;
            }
            if(adcMCP3002 != null)
            {
                MPC3002Ready = true;
            }
        }

        public int ReadChannel0()
        {
            if(MPC3002Ready == true)
            {
                byte[] adcCh0Out = new byte[2];
                adcMCP3002.TransferFullDuplex(Channel0, adcCh0Out);
                var adcCh0OutInt = (adcCh0Out[0] << 8 | adcCh0Out[1]) & 0x3FF;
                return adcCh0OutInt;
            }
            else
            {
                return 0;
```

```
            }
        }

        public int ReadChannel1()
        {
            if(MPC3002Ready == true)
            {
                byte[] adcCh1Out = new byte[2];
                adcMCP3002.TransferFullDuplex(Channel1, adcCh1Out);
                var adcCh1OutInt = (adcCh1Out[0] << 8 | adcCh1Out[1]) & 0x3FF;
                return adcCh1OutInt;
            }
            else
            {
                return 0;
            }
        }

        public int ReadDiff()
        {
            if(MPC3002Ready == false)
            {
                return 0;
            }
            byte[] adcDiffOut = new byte[2];
            adcMCP3002.TransferFullDuplex(DiffCh0PCh1N, adcDiffOut);

            var adcDiffOutInt = (adcDiffOut[0] << 8 | adcDiffOut[1]) & 0x3ff;

            if (adcDiffOutInt > 0) //The output data doesn't have a sign bit. If IN+ is equal to or below IN- the result is 0x00 so we test for 0
            {
                return adcDiffOutInt;
            }
            else //If 0 then we flip the differential input to test for negative - not a real-time solution
            {
                adcMCP3002.TransferFullDuplex(DiffCh0NCh1P, adcDiffOut);
                adcDiffOutInt = (adcDiffOut[0] << 8 | adcDiffOut[1]) & 0x3ff;
                return -adcDiffOutInt;
            }
        }

```

```
        public bool MCP3002Status()
        {
            return MPC3002Ready;
        }
    }
}
```

The constructor for the class takes in the SPI bus port number, frequency, Chip Select value, and whether the bus is shared or not. The constructor makes a call to set up the SPI port. The public methods provide results for reading channel 0, channel 1, and the difference in voltage between the two. There is a method for getting the status of MCP3002.

6. Save the project.
7. Build a debug version of the project for your processor architecture.

13.8.2 Create the SPIADC2 Application that uses the new Assembly

The class library is ready to use in an application.

1. Open Visual Studio 2022.
2. Create a new "WPF Application" project. Make sure you select the correct WPF Application template for .NET.

Note: The project is a .NET application, not a .NET Framework application. If you see .NET Framework in the project description it is the wrong project.

3. Name the project "SPIADC2" and set the folder location to C:\VS-Apps on your development machine. To do remote debugging with .NET, the remote machine folder architecture must match the development machine. Visual Studio Remote Debugging documentation describes the setup as well.
4. Click the "Next" button.
5. Select .NET 6.0 (Long-term support) from the drop-down box.
6. Click the "Create" button.
7. Once the application opens, we need to do a little more set up to support the Windows Runtime Namespaces. From the menu, select Project->SPIADC2 Properties.
8. Under Application->General set the following for the targeted Windows OS:
    a. Target OS version: 10.0.19041.0
    b. Supported OS version: 10.0.19041.0
9. Scroll down the Build, and set the following:
    a. Platform target: x64

Note: If you forget to set the correct Target Framework and Target OS, Visual Studio will not let you reference the Windows.Devices namespace.

10. Save the project.

13.8.3 Setup the XAML Controls

1. In Solution Explorer, open the MainWindows.xaml.
2. The designer and XAML editor will appear. At the top, left of the Designer set the orientation that fits your target's display.
3. Add a Label Control.
    a. Common->Content: Reference Voltage
4. Add a Radio button
    a. Name: rb3v
    b. Common->Content: 3.3V
5. Add a Radio button
    a. Name: rb5v
    b. Common->Content: 5V
6. Add a Label Control.
    a. Common->Content: Channel 0 Reading
7. Add a Label Control.
    a. Common->Content: Channel 1 Reading
8. Add a TextBox Control
    a. Name: txtChannel0Result
    b. Common->Text: <empty>
9. Add a Label next to the TextBox
    a. Common->Content: V
10. Add a TextBox Control
    a. Name: txtChannel1Result
    b. Common->Text: <empty>
11. Add a Label next to the TextBox
    a. Common->Content: V
12. Add a Button control below the text box
    a. Name: btnReadChannel0
    b. Common->Content: Read Channel 0
13. Add a Button control below the text box
    a. Name: btnReadChannel1
    b. Common->Content: Read Channel 1
14. Add a TextBox Control
    a. Name: txtChannelDiff

   b. Common->Text: <empty>
15. Add a Label next to the TextBox
   a. Common->Content: V
16. Add a Button control below the text box
   a. Name: btnCh0PCh1N
   b. Common->Content: Read Diff Ch0+ Ch1-
17. Add a TextBox Control
   a. Name: txtStatus
   b. Common->Text: <empty>
18. Save the project.

Here is the XAML code:

```
<Window x:Class="SPIADC.MainWindow"
      xmlns="http://schemas.microsoft.com/winfx/2006/xaml/presentation"
      xmlns:x="http://schemas.microsoft.com/winfx/2006/xaml"
      xmlns:d="http://schemas.microsoft.com/expression/blend/2008"
      xmlns:mc="http://schemas.openxmlformats.org/markup-compatibility/2006"
      xmlns:local="clr-namespace:SPIADC"
      mc:Ignorable="d"
      Title="MainWindow" Height="480" Width="800">
   <Grid Margin="0,0,0,-6">
      <TextBox x:Name="txtChannel0Result" HorizontalAlignment="Left" Height="54"
Margin="36,133,0,0" Text="" TextWrapping="Wrap" VerticalAlignment="Top"
Width="172" IsReadOnly="True"/>
      <TextBlock HorizontalAlignment="Left" Height="40" Margin="36,30,0,0"
Text="Reference Voltage" TextWrapping="Wrap" VerticalAlignment="Top"
Width="172"/>
      <TextBlock HorizontalAlignment="Left" Height="40" Margin="36,87,0,0"
Text="Channel 0 Reading" TextWrapping="Wrap" VerticalAlignment="Top"
Width="172"/>
      <TextBox x:Name="txtChannel1Result" HorizontalAlignment="Left" Height="54"
Margin="408,133,0,0" Text="" TextWrapping="Wrap" VerticalAlignment="Top"
Width="172" IsReadOnly="True"/>
      <TextBlock HorizontalAlignment="Left" Height="40" Margin="408,87,0,0"
Text="Channel 1 Reading" TextWrapping="Wrap" VerticalAlignment="Top"
Width="172"/>
      <Button x:Name="btnReadChannel0" Content="Read Channel 0" Height="39"
Margin="254,144,416,0" VerticalAlignment="Top" Width="130"
Click="btnReadChannel0_Click"/>
      <TextBlock HorizontalAlignment="Left" Height="35" Margin="220,145,0,0"
Text="V" TextWrapping="Wrap" VerticalAlignment="Top" Width="28"
FontSize="22"/>
      <TextBlock HorizontalAlignment="Left" Height="35" Margin="594,145,0,0"
Text="V" TextWrapping="Wrap" VerticalAlignment="Top" Width="26"
FontSize="22"/>
```

```
    <Button x:Name="btnReadChannel1" Content="Read Channel 1" Height="39"
Margin="628,144,39,0" VerticalAlignment="Top" Width="133"
Click="btnReadChannel1_Click"/>
    <TextBox x:Name="txtChannelDiff" HorizontalAlignment="Left" Height="62"
Margin="36,242,0,0" Text="" TextWrapping="Wrap" VerticalAlignment="Top"
Width="172" IsReadOnly="True"/>
    <Button x:Name="btnCh0PCh1N" Content="Read Diff Ch0+ Ch1-" Height="62"
Margin="300,242,334,0" VerticalAlignment="Top" Width="165"
Click="btnCh0PCh1N_Click" />
    <TextBox x:Name="txtStatus" HorizontalAlignment="Left" Height="59"
Margin="36,345,0,0" Text="" TextWrapping="Wrap" VerticalAlignment="Top"
Width="680" IsReadOnly="True"/>
    <RadioButton x:Name="rb3v" Content="3.3V" Height="32" Margin="45,58,699,0"
VerticalAlignment="Top" Width="56" IsChecked="True"/>
    <RadioButton x:Name="rb5v" Content="5V" Height="32" Margin="122,58,622,0"
VerticalAlignment="Top" Width="56"/>
    <TextBlock HorizontalAlignment="Left" Height="35" Margin="220,254,0,0"
Text="V" TextWrapping="Wrap" VerticalAlignment="Top" Width="66"
FontSize="22"/>

  </Grid>
</Window>
```

13.8.4 Write the Code

1. Now we need to add the class library. Click Project->Add Reference.
2. Browse to the location of the MCP3002.dll that is in the Class Library Project.
3. Select the dll and click “Add” and then click “OK”. The namespace for the library can be added to the using directives.
4. Open MainWindow.xaml.cs.
5. Add the following using statements to add the Annabooks.MCP3002 and the System Threading namespaces.

```
using Annabooks.MCP3002;
using System.Threading;
```

6. Just within the MainWindows class and before the MainWindows() method, add the following to create a new instance of the MPL115A1.

```
MCP3002 myADC;
```

7. Below the MainWindow() method, create a new ADCSetup() method and fill in the following:

```
private void ADCSetup()
```

```
{
    myADC = new MCP3002("SPI2", 8000000, 0, false);
    Thread.Sleep(1000);
    if (myADC.MCP3002Status())
    {
        Application.Current.Dispatcher.Invoke((Action)(() => txtStatus.Text = "ADC is
Ready"));
    }
    else
    {
        Application.Current.Dispatcher.Invoke((Action)(() => txtStatus.Text = "ADC is
NOT Ready: " + myADC.connectionError));
    }
}
```

The method instantiates myADC as a new instance of MCP3002 using SP2 as the port, 80000 as the frequency, Chip Select 0, and bus not shared. The thread is put to sleep for about a second and then the status of the connection is made and reported.

8. In the MainWindow() method, create a Thread that calls ADCSetup() method and starts the thread.

```
public MainWindow()
{
    InitializeComponent();
    Thread adcStartup = new Thread(new ThreadStart(ADCSetup));
    adcStartup.Start();
}
```

9. In the MainWindow.xaml, double-click on all three buttons to generate the event handlers.
10. Fill in the code for each event handler:

```
private void btnReadChannel0_Click(object sender, RoutedEventArgs e)
{
    if (myADC.MCP3002Status())
    {
        txtChannel0Result.Text = Math.Round((double)myADC.ReadChannel0()
/ 1024 * 3.3, 2).ToString();
    }
}

private void btnReadChannel1_Click(object sender, RoutedEventArgs e)
{
    if (myADC.MCP3002Status())
    {
        txtChannel1Result.Text = Math.Round((double)myADC.ReadChannel1()
/ 1024 * 3.3, 2).ToString();
```

```
        }
    }

    private void btnReadDIFF_Click(object sender, RoutedEventArgs e)
    {
        if (myADC.MCP3002Status())
        {
            txtChannelDiff.Text = Math.Round((double)myADC.ReadDiff() / 1024
    * 3.3, 2).ToString();
        }
    }
```

11. Save the project.
12. Build a debug version of the project and correct any errors.

13.8.5 Test the Application

1. In the C:\VS-Apps folder of your development machine, determine where the SPIADC2.exe file is located: C:\VS-Apps\SPIADC2\SPIADC2\bin\Debug\net6.0-windows10.0.19041.0
2. On the target machine, create an exact folder structure under C:\VS-apps - C:\VS-Apps\ SPIADC2\SPIADC2\bin\Debug\net6.0-windows10.0.19041.0
3. Run Visual Studio Remote Debug, and make a note of the computer name and port number listed in the Visual Studio Remote Debug output.
4. In Visual Studio running on the development machine, open the SPIADC2 Properties page.
5. Click on Debug on the left side, and click Open debug launch profile UI.
6. Check the checkbox for Use remote machine and enter the Target systems computer name with the port number: X64-APPTEST:4026
7. Close the Window.
8. In the properties, scroll up to Build Events.
9. In the Post-build event enter the following to do a copy of the output to the remote system (this is all one line):

xcopy C:\VS-Apps\SPIADC2\SPIADC2\bin\Debug\net6.0-windows10.0.19041.0 \\X64-APPTEST\VS-Apps\SPIADC2\SPIADC2\bin\Debug\net6.0-windows10.0.19041.0 /Y

10. Save the project.
11. Build the debug version of the application again. The output files should be copied to the remote system.
12. Start the debug session.
13. You will be asked for the target system's login credentials. Enter the user's name and password and click OK.

14. Once the application has loaded on the target system, hit the different buttons to get the readings from the ADC. If you can, adjust the input voltage to Ch0 or Ch1 and verify that the readings changed appropriately.
15. Stop debugging when finished.

The application performs the same as before and has fewer lines of code sans the checking on the MCP3002 status. Class Libraries help to break down the project into smaller chunks.

13.9 The SPI Summary

In this chapter, we learned about the SPI bus and writing managed code applications for SPI devices. SPI can support multiple devices on the SPI bus by using GPIOs and OR-gates to provide Chip Selects for each device. Not having a specific protocol, each SPI device is free to implement its own command and data interchange rules, which frees the implementation from the overhead of a protocol stack for faster operation. Gathering the technical information on the SPI device is important to set up the SPI communication settings correctly and understand the command protocol to transmit to and receive from the SPI device. There are other popular SPI devices available. You can apply the same analysis techniques to write a managed code application for any of these devices.

Creating libraries for devices allow for code reuse and makes your applications simpler to write and debug. This comes in handy when you have multiple devices connected to the SPI bus, each having its own communications rules.

14 Inter-Integrated Circuit (I^2C)

Last but not least is the Inter-Integrated Circuit or I^2C (I2C) special serial port solution. Like the SPI port discussed in the last chapters, I2C provides another expansion capability for microcontrollers to add peripherals. Intel used a special variation of I2C called System Management Bus (SMBus) to address power management in a PC. Unlike SPI, I2C offers a simpler, single-byte communication between the host controller and peripheral. This chapter will cover the following:

- I2C bus technical details.
- I2C Namespace.
- Developing libraries for the I2C peripherals for code re-use.

14.1 The Inter-Integrated Circuit (I2C) Bus

I2C was developed by Phillips Semiconductor (now NXP Semiconductors) in 1982. I2C offers a simple 2-wire interface with the following signals:

SCL - the serial clock line (controlled by the host controller device).

SDA – the serial data line

Both signals are open-collector or open-drain, which requires a pullup resistor. Multiple I2C peripherals can exist on a single I2C bus. Each device has its own built-in 7-bit address so the host controller program can access the device by address. Some I2C peripherals might have additional signals to change the address to another built-in address.

Note: Like the SPI, I2C also uses the anachronistic terms of master and slave.

The clock speed can vary:

- Low-speed mode: 10 kbit/s
- Standard mode: 100 kbit/s
- Fast mode: 400 kbit/s,
- Fast Mode-plus: 1 Mbit/s
- High-Speed Mode: 3.4 Mbit/s
- Ultra-Fast-mode: 5Mbit/s

Signaling is performed when the host controller sends a START condition along with the 7-bit address and a bit indicating write or read operation. The I2C peripheral will then send back an ACK to which the host controller continues with the rest of the transmission to write or read data to/from the device. All data read from the peripheral starts with the most significant bit (MSB). An ACK will follow when the data transition has been completed. A STOP transmission condition is sent to stop the communication. The START signal is when SDA goes from High to Low with the SCL High. The end transmission is SDA going from Low to High with SCL High. Transmission between the host controller and peripheral can be single read, single write, or a combination of write-reads.

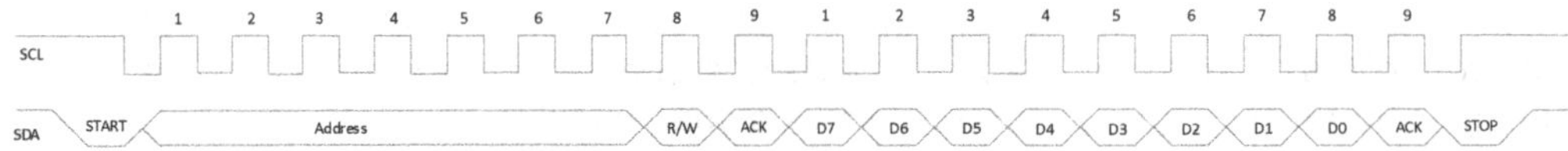

Multiple I2C devices can connect to the same bus. Pull-up resistors are needed for SCL and SDL lines. The SparkFun breakout boards have these pull-up resistors in the design. These boards provide a means to break the connection to the resistors so that only one set of pull-up resistors is used in the circuit.

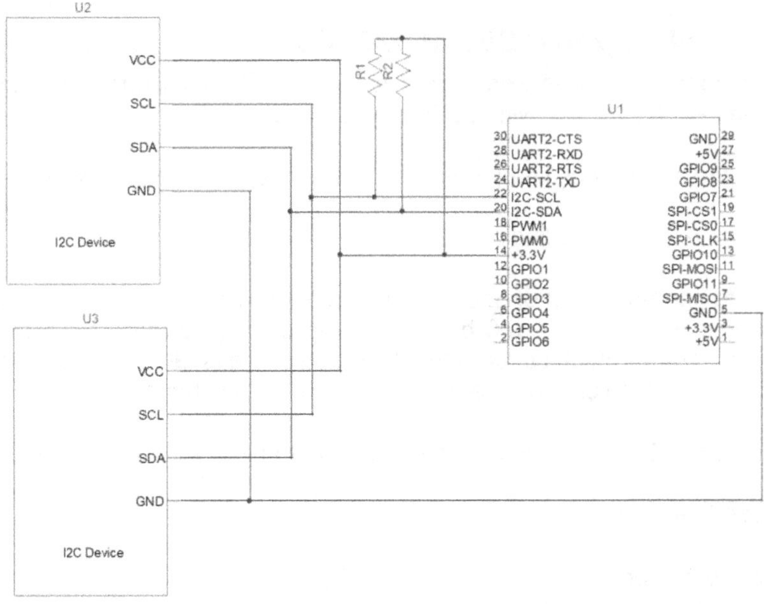

14.2 Windows Runtime I2C Namespace

The I2C Namespace consists of 3 classes, 1 structure for partial read/write information, 3 enumerators, and 1 interface for device statistics. The I2cDevice class contains the core functionality to connect and perform read/write operations over the I2C bus. The I2C peripheral's datasheet contains critical information about clock speed, mode, address, and data transfer methods to use. Once a connection is made, there are six different methods to communicate with the device:

Method	Description
Read(Byte[])	Reads bytes from the device and places the results into a Byte[] array.
Write(Byte[])	Writes all the bytes in the Byte[] array to the devices.
WriteRead(Byte[], Byte[])	Writes all the bytes in the Byte[] array to the devices, and then Reads bytes from the device and places the results into a Byte[] array.
ReadPartial(Byte[])	Reads bytes from the device and places the results into a Byte[] array. Provides additional data such as ByteTransferred and Status on the transfer.
WritePartial(Byte[])	Writes all the bytes in the Byte[] array to the devices. Provides additional data such as ByteTransferred and Status on the transfer.
WriteReadPartial(Byte[], Byte[])	Writes all the bytes in the Byte[] array to the devices, and then Reads bytes from the device and places the results into a Byte[] array. Provides additional data such as ByteTransferred and Status on the transfer.

Byte[] arrays are used to communicate with the I2C device. The I2C device's datasheet contains the byte codes to send commands and retrieve information. The following exercises demonstrate the use of the I2C namespace.

14.3 I2cTestTool.exe

Chapter 10 covered the Bus Tools sample applications. The I2cTestTool.exe test tool can be used to list all the available I2C bus ports in a system, as well as, perform some basic tests on a device connected to the I2C bus. The list of available I2C bus ports doesn't mean they are accessible. Some systems will report a few internal I2C ports that are not accessible.

```
C:\test>I2cTestTool.exe
Missing required command line parameter SlaveAddress

I2cTestTool: Command line I2C testing utility
Usage: I2cTestTool.exe [-list] SlaveAddress [FriendlyName]

  -list          List available I2C controllers and exit.
  SlaveAddress   The slave address of the device with which you
                 wish to communicate. This is a required parameter.
  FriendlyName   The friendly name of the I2C controller over
                 which you wish to communicate. This parameter is
                 optional and defaults to the first enumerated
                 I2C controller.
```

```
Examples:
  List available I2C controllers and exit:
    I2cTestTool.exe -list

  Open connection on the first enumerated controller to slave address
0x57:
    I2cTestTool.exe 0x57

  Open connection on I2C1 to slave address 0x57:
    I2cTestTool.exe 0x57 I2C1

C:\test>I2cTestTool.exe 0x48
  Type 'help' for a list of commands
> help
Commands:
 > write { 00 11 22 .. FF }         Write bytes to device
 > read N                           Read N bytes
 > writeread { 00 11 .. FF } N      Write bytes, restart, read N bytes
 > info                             Display device information
 > help                             Display this help message
 > quit                             Quit

> info
       DeviceId:          \\?\ACPI#MSFT8000#4#{a11ee3c6-8421-4202-a3e7-
b91ff90188e4}\I2C1
  Slave address: 0x48
      Bus Speed: StandardMode (100Khz)
>
```

14.4 Exercise 1401: I2C Temperature Sensor – TMP102

This exercise will use the SparkFun TMP102 Temperature Sensor breakout board to read the ambient temperature (-25 °C to + 85 °C). The breakout board has the 4.7KΩ pull-up resistors on SDA and SCL so there is no need to add them. Pin A0 is pulled to ground via a 10KΩ resistor so the address will be 0x48. The application will have a single button that gets the data from the sensor and reports back the temperature in Celsius and Fahrenheit. A status box will report any status messages.

The TMP102 datasheet provides the key information:

- Address: 0x48 – Pin A0 is pulled to ground, but can be changed to support 3 other addresses.
- Clock speed – The chip supports 100kbit/s to 3.4Mbit/s
- The temperature register has 13 bits. On boot, the chip is configured with extended mode disabled (EM=0) so only the upper 12 bits of the temperature register are needed to calculate the temperature.

- From the timing diagram, the WriteRead() method will be used to read the temperature data from the chip.
- The final formula to calculate temperature in Celsius:

tempC = (temperature register value) * 0.0625.

14.4.1 Basic Setup

Here is the basic setup of the application.

1. Open Visual Studio 2022
2. Create a new "WPF Application" project. Make sure you select the correct WPF Application template for .NET.
3. Name the project "I2CTempSensor" and set the folder location to C:\VS-Apps on your development machine. To do remote debugging with .NET, the remote machine folder architecture must match the development machine. Visual Studio Remote Debugging documentation describes the setup as well.
4. Click the "Next" button.
5. Select .NET 6.0 (Long-term support) from the drop-down box.
6. Click the "Create" button.
7. Once the application opens, we need to do a little more set up to support the Windows Runtime Namespaces. From the menu, select Project-> I2CTempSensor Properties.
8. Under Application->General set the following for the targeted Windows OS:
    a. Target OS version: 10.0.19041.0
    b. Supported OS version: 10.0.19041.0
9. Scroll down the Build, and set the following:
    a. Platform target: x64
10. Save the project.

14.4.2 Set Up the XAML Controls

The UI will have three text boxes and a button. Two of the text boxes will show the temperature readings, and the last text box will display the status messages. The button will perform most of the work.

1. In Solution Explorer, open the MainWindow.xaml.
2. The designer and XAML editor will appear. At the top, left of the Designer set the orientation that fits your target's display.
3. Add a Label
    a. Common->Text: Temperature in Celsius
4. Add a TextBox Control.
    a. Name: txtTempCReading
    b. Common->Text: temp C

5. Add a Label
   a. Common->Text: Temperature in Fahrenheit
6. Add a TextBox Control
   a. Name: txtTempFReading
   b. Common->Text: temp F
7. Add A TextBox Control
   a. Name: txtStatus
   b. Common->Text: Ready
8. Add a Button control
   a. Name: btnReadTemp
   b. Common->Content: Read Temp
9. Save the project.

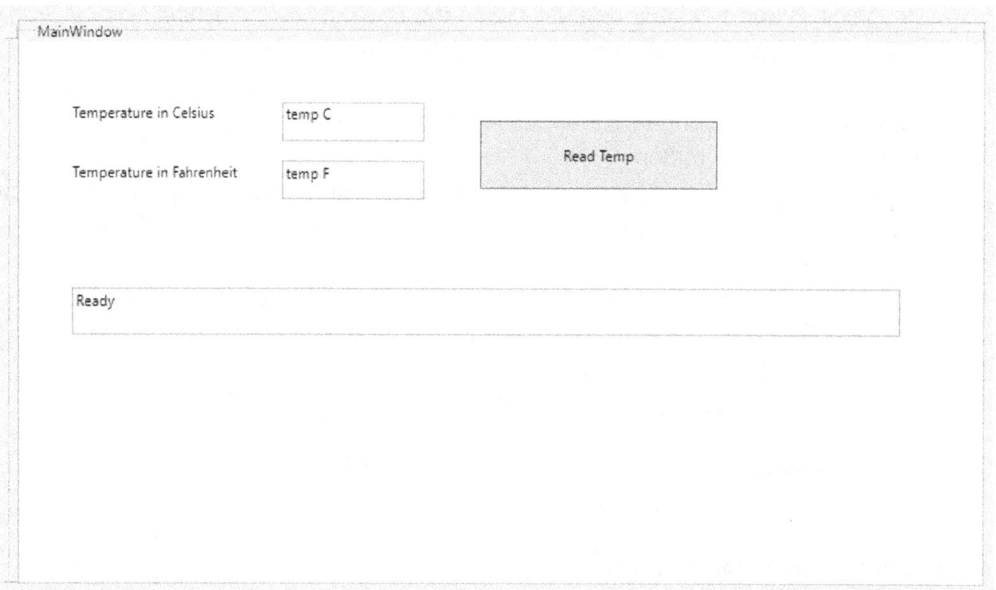

Here is the XAML Code:

```
<Window x:Class="I2CTempSensor.MainWindow"
      xmlns="http://schemas.microsoft.com/winfx/2006/xaml/presentation"
      xmlns:x="http://schemas.microsoft.com/winfx/2006/xaml"
      xmlns:d="http://schemas.microsoft.com/expression/blend/2008"
      xmlns:mc="http://schemas.openxmlformats.org/markup-compatibility/2006"
      xmlns:local="clr-namespace:I2CTempSensor"
      mc:Ignorable="d"
      Title="MainWindow" Height="450" Width="800">
   <Grid>
```

```
        <TextBox x:Name="txtTempCReading" HorizontalAlignment="Left" Height="31"
Margin="220,49,0,0" Text="temp C" TextWrapping="Wrap" VerticalAlignment="Top"
Width="118"/>
        <Button x:Name="btnReadTemp" Content="Read Temp" Margin="384,64,220,0"
VerticalAlignment="Top" Height="54" Width="196" Click="btnReadTemp_Click"/>
        <TextBox x:Name="txtStatus" HorizontalAlignment="Left" Height="38"
Margin="44,0,0,0" Text="Ready" TextWrapping="Wrap" VerticalAlignment="Center"
Width="687"/>
        <TextBlock x:Name="txtBCelcius" HorizontalAlignment="Left" Height="31"
Margin="44,49,0,0" Text="Temperature in Celsius" TextWrapping="Wrap"
VerticalAlignment="Top" Width="256"/>
        <TextBox x:Name="txtTempFReading" HorizontalAlignment="Left" Height="31"
Margin="220,96,0,0" Text="temp F" TextWrapping="Wrap" VerticalAlignment="Top"
Width="118"/>
        <TextBlock x:Name="txtBFahrenheit" HorizontalAlignment="Left" Height="31"
Margin="44,96,0,0" Text="Temperature in Fahrenheit" TextWrapping="Wrap"
VerticalAlignment="Top" Width="256"/>

    </Grid>
</Window>
```

14.4.3 Write the Code

Now let's write the code behind the GUI.

1. Open MainWindow.xaml.cs.
2. Add the following using statements to enable the SPI, and the Enumeration namespaces:

```
using Windows.Devices.Enumeration;
using Windows.Devices.I2c;
```

3. Above the MainWindow() method add the following:

```
private const byte TEMP_TMP102_ADDR = 0x48;
private I2cDevice I2CTemp;
private const byte TempRegisterAddr = 0x00;
private const byte ConfigRegisterAddr = 0x01;
private const byte TlowRegisterAddr = 0x02;
private const byte ThighRegisterAddr = 0x03;
```

Note: The last three constants will not be used in the program, but are provided so one can play with the other registers.

4. After the MainWindow() method, create a new method, TempSetup(), and add the following code.

Note: If you are not sure of the I2C device for your hardware, use the I2C bus tool discussed in Chapter 13.

```
private async void TempSetup()
{
    I2cConnectionSettings i2cSettings = new
I2cConnectionSettings(TEMP_TMP102_ADDR);
    i2cSettings.BusSpeed = I2cBusSpeed.FastMode;

    string aqs = I2cDevice.GetDeviceSelector("I2C1");
    DeviceInformationCollection i2cDevInfo = await
DeviceInformation.FindAllAsync(aqs);
    I2CTemp = await I2cDevice.FromIdAsync(i2cDevInfo[0].Id, i2cSettings);
    if (I2CTemp == null)
    {
        txtStatus.Text = "Error getting I2C connection";
    }
    else
    {
        txtStatus.Text = "Ready to Read Temp";
    }
}
```

The code sets up the I2cBusSpeed and connection settings with the address. A new instance of the I2cDevice is instantiated with the connection settings. The txtStatus is updated with the results.

5. In the MainWindow() method, add the code to call the `TempSetup()`.

```
public MainWindow()
{
    InitializeComponent();
    TempSetup();
}
```

6. In MainWindow.xaml, double-click on the button to generate the event handler in MainPage.xaml.cs, and then add the following code:

```
private void btnReadTemp_Click(object sender, RoutedEventArgs e)
{
    byte[] Readbuf = new byte[2];
    byte[] RegAddrBuf = new byte[] { TempRegisterAddr };
    I2CTemp.WriteRead(RegAddrBuf, Readbuf);


    byte tempMSB = Readbuf[0];
    var tempMSBs = tempMSB << 4;
    byte tempLSB = Readbuf[1];
    var tempLSBs = tempLSB >> 4;
```

```
    var tempFinal = tempMSBs + tempLSBs;

    if((tempFinal & 0x800) == 0x800) //detect if negative
    {
        tempFinal = (tempFinal ^ 0xFFF) + 1; //twos compliment
        tempFinal = -tempFinal;
    }

    double tempC = Convert.ToDouble(tempFinal) * 0.0625;
    double tempF = (tempC * 1.8) + 32.0;

    txtTempCReading.Text = tempC.ToString() + " C";
    txtTempFReading.Text = tempF.ToString() + " F";
}
```

The byte[] arrays are set up to perform the WriteRead() method. The WriteRead() method is called to get the temperature from the temperature register (0x00). Since we need the upper 12 of the 16 bits. The first byte is put into a variable and bitwise shifted 4 left. The second byte is put into another variable and bitwise shifted 4 right. The two variables are added together to get the full 12-bit value. A check for negative temperature is made before the final conversion and output to the two text boxes.

7. Save the project.
8. Build a debug version of the project and correct any errors.

14.4.4 Test the Application

The application is ready to be tested in the target system.

1. Connect the TMP102 to your target platform's I2C port.

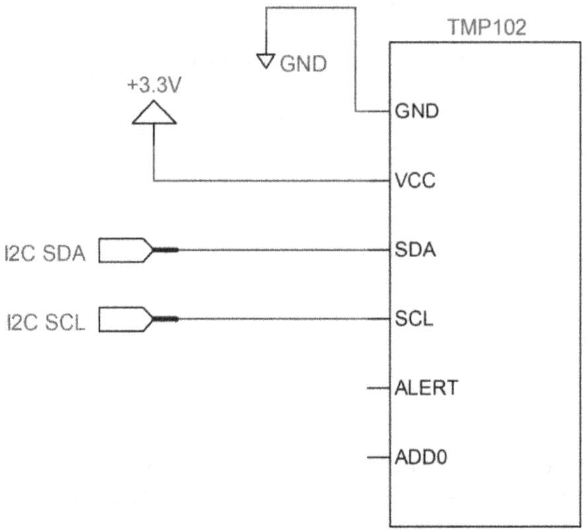

2. Make sure that the firmware has the I2C Bus speed set to 400Khz.
3. In the C:\VS-Apps folder of your development machine, determine where the I2CTempSensor.exe file is located: C:\VS-Apps\I2CTempSensor\I2CTempSensor\bin\Debug\net6.0-windows10.0.19041.0
4. On the target machine, create an exact folder structure under C:\VS-apps - C:\VS-Apps\I2CTempSensor\I2CTempSensor \bin\Debug\net6.0-windows10.0.19041.0
5. Run Visual Studio Remote Debug, and make a note of the computer name and port number listed in the Visual Studio Remote Debug output.
6. In Visual Studio running on the development machine, open the I2CTempSensor Properties page.
7. Click on Debug on the left side, and click Open debug launch profile UI.
8. Check the checkbox for Use remote machine and enter the Target system's computer name with the port number: X64-APPTEST:4026
9. Close the Window.
10. In the properties, scroll up to Build Events.
11. In the Post-build event enter the following to do a copy of the output to the remote system (this is all one line):

xcopy C:\VS-Apps\I2CTempSensor\I2CTempSensor\bin\Debug\net6.0-windows10.0.19041.0 \\X64-APPTEST\VS-Apps\I2CTempSensor\I2CTempSensor\bin\Debug\net6.0-windows10.0.19041.0 /Y

12. Save the project.
13. Build the debug version of the application again. The output files should be copied to the remote system.

14. Start the debug session.
15. You will be asked for the target system's login credentials. Enter the user's name and password and click "OK".
16. Once the application has loaded on the target system, hit the button to get the reading from the sensor.
17. Stop debugging when finished.

If you have an O-scope that can read the I2C bus, connect the scope probes to the I2C lines. When you push the button, you can see the WriteRead transfer taking place. The Write used the I2C address (0x48) and the register (0x00) to retrieve the data. The Read uses the I2C address (0x48) to retrieve the two bytes.

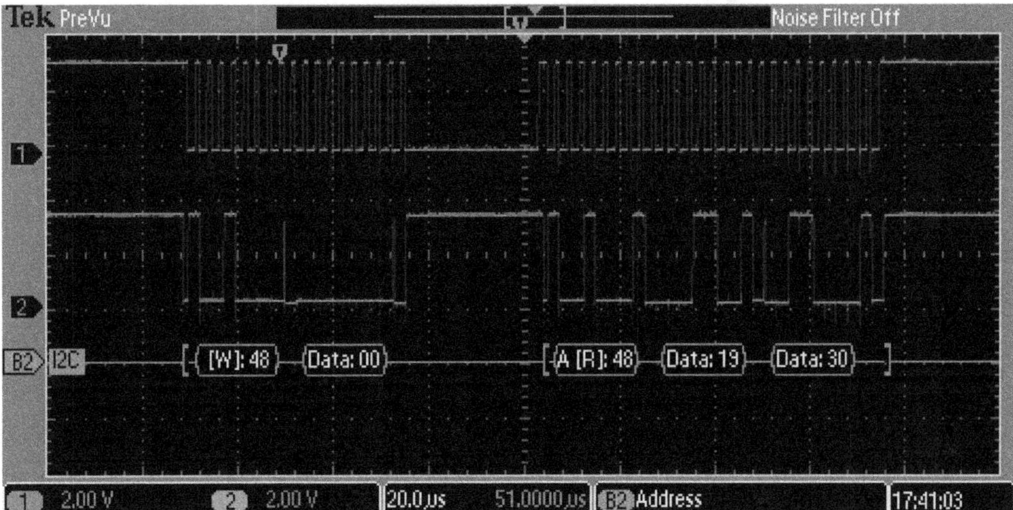

14.5 Exercise 1402: I2C Temperature Sensor Assembly Library with .NET Core 2.1 Application

Let's create a library for the TMP102 that addresses the common operations that have to be made when using this device.

14.5.1 Create the Assembly Library

1. Open Visual Studio 2022, if not already open
2. Create a new project and select WPF Class Library – "A project for creating a class library that targets a .NET WPF Application".
3. Name the project TMP102 and set the folder location to C:\VS-Apps.
4. Click Next.
5. Select .NET 6.0 (Long-term support) from the drop-down box.
6. Click the "Create" button.

7. Once the application opens, we need to do a little more set up to support the Windows Runtime Namespaces. From the menu, select Project->TMP102 Properties.
8. Under Application->General set the following for the targeted Windows OS:
    a. Target OS version: 10.0.19041.0
    b. Supported OS version: 10.0.19041.0
9. Scroll down the Build, and set the following:
    a. Platform target: x64
10. Save the project.
11. Rename Class.cs to TMP102.cs and save the project.
12. Change the namespace to Annabooks.TMP102
13. Fill in the following code:

```
using System;
using Windows.Devices.Enumeration;
using Windows.Devices.I2c;

namespace Annabooks.TMP102
{
    public class TMP102
    {

        private I2cDevice sensorTMP102;
        private const byte TempRegisterAddr = 0x00;
        private const byte ConfigRegisterAddr = 0x01;
        private const byte TlowRegisterAddr = 0x02;
        private const byte ThighRegisterAddr = 0x03;

        private bool tempReady = false;
        public string connectionError = "";

        public TMP102(string I2Cport, bool I2CBusShared, byte addr)
        {
            switch (addr)
            {
                case 0x48:
                    I2CInitialize(I2Cport, I2CBusShared, 0x48);
                    break;
                case 0x49:
                    I2CInitialize(I2Cport, I2CBusShared, 0x49);
                    break;
                case 0x4A:
                    I2CInitialize(I2Cport, I2CBusShared, 0x4A);
                    break;
                case 0x4B:
```

```
                    I2CInitialize(I2Cport, I2CBusShared, 0x4B);
                    break;
                default:
                    tempReady = false;
                    break;
            }
        }
        private async void I2CInitialize(string I2Cport, bool I2CBusShared, byte addr)
        {
            try
            {
                I2cConnectionSettings i2cSettings = new I2cConnectionSettings(addr);
                i2cSettings.BusSpeed = I2cBusSpeed.FastMode;
                if (I2CBusShared)//True
                {
                    i2cSettings.SharingMode = I2cSharingMode.Shared;
                }
                else//false
                {
                    i2cSettings.SharingMode = I2cSharingMode.Exclusive;
                }
                string aqs = I2cDevice.GetDeviceSelector(I2Cport);
                DeviceInformationCollection i2cDevInfo = await DeviceInformation.FindAllAsync(aqs);
                sensorTMP102 = await I2cDevice.FromIdAsync(i2cDevInfo[0].Id, i2cSettings);
            }
            catch(Exception ex)
            {
                connectionError = ex.Message;
            }

            if (sensorTMP102 != null)
            {
                tempReady = true;
            }
        }

        public double ReadTempC()
        {
            byte[] Readbuf = new byte[2];
            byte[] RegAddrBuf = new byte[] { TempRegisterAddr };
            sensorTMP102.WriteRead(RegAddrBuf, Readbuf);

            byte tempMSB = Readbuf[0];
```

```
            var tempMSBs = tempMSB << 4;
            byte tempLSB = Readbuf[1];
            var tempLSBs = tempLSB >> 4;
            var tempFinal = tempMSBs + tempLSBs;
            if ((tempFinal & 0x800) == 0x800) //detect if negative
            {
                tempFinal = (tempFinal ^ 0xFFF) + 1; //twos compliment
                tempFinal = -tempFinal;
            }
            double tempC = Convert.ToDouble(tempFinal) * 0.0625;
            return tempC;
        }

        public double ReadTempF()
        {
            byte[] Readbuf = new byte[2];
            byte[] RegAddrBuf = new byte[] { TempRegisterAddr };
            sensorTMP102.WriteRead(RegAddrBuf, Readbuf);

            byte tempMSB = Readbuf[0];
            var tempMSBs = tempMSB << 4;
            byte tempLSB = Readbuf[1];
            var tempLSBs = tempLSB >> 4;
            var tempFinal = tempMSBs + tempLSBs;
            if ((tempFinal & 0x800) == 0x800) //detect if negative
            {
                tempFinal ^= 0xFFF; //twos compliment
                tempFinal = -tempFinal;
            }
            double tempC = Convert.ToDouble(tempFinal) * 0.0625;
            double tempF = (tempC * 1.8) + 32.0;
            return tempF;

        }

        public bool TMP102Status()
        {
            return tempReady;
        }

    }
}
```

The constructor takes in the I2C port, I2C peripheral address, and the bus share mode to set up the I2C connection. Since the address can be 1 of 4 values a switch case statement is used to call the private method to make the connection. The remaining 3 public methods read the temperature for Celsius and Fahrenheit and get the sensor status.

6. Save the project.
7. Build a debug version project for your processor architecture.

14.5.2 Create the I2CTempSensor2 Application that uses the new Assembly

The class library is ready to use in an application.

1. Open Visual Studio 2022.
2. Create a new "WPF Application" project. Make sure you select the correct WPF Application template for .NET.
3. Name the project "I2CTempSensor2", and set the folder location to C:\VS-Apps on your development machine. To do remote debugging with .NET, the remote machine folder architecture must match the development machine. Visual Studio Remote Debugging documentation describes the setup as well.
4. Click the "Next" button.
5. Select .NET 6.0 (Long-term support) from the drop-down box.
6. Click the "Create" button.
7. Once the application opens, we need to do a little more set up to support the Windows Runtime Namespaces. From the menu, select Project-> I2CTempSensor2 Properties.
8. Under Application->General set the following for the targeted Windows OS:
    a. Target OS version: 10.0.19041.0
    b. Supported OS version: 10.0.19041.0
9. Scroll down the Build, and set the following:
    a. Platform target: x64
10. Save the project.

14.5.3 Set Up the XAML Controls

The UI will have three text boxes and a button. Two of the text boxes will show the temperature readings, and the last text box will display the status messages. The button will perform most of the work.

1. In Solution Explorer, open the MainWindow.xaml.
2. The designer and XAML editor will appear. At the top, left of the Designer set the orientation that fits your target's display.
3. Add a Label.
    a. Common->Text: Temperature in Celsius
4. Add a TextBox Control.
    a. Name: txtTempCReading
    b. Common->Text: temp C
5. Add a Label.

   a. Common->Text: Temperature in Fahrenheit
6. Add a TextBox Control.
   a. Name: txtTempFReading
   b. Common->Text: temp F
7. Add A TextBox Control.
   a. Name: txtStatus
   b. Common->Text: Ready
8. Add a Button control.
   a. Name: btnReadTemp
   b. Common->Content: Read Temp
9. Save the project.

14.5.4 Write the Code

Now, let's write the code behind the GUI.

1. We need to add the class library. Click Project->Add Reference.
2. Browse to the location of the TMP102.dll that is in the Class Library Project.
3. Select the dll and click "Add" and then click "OK". The namespace for the library can be added to the using directives.
4. Open Form1.cs in code view.
5. Add the following using statements to add the Annabooks.TMP102 and the System Threading namespaces.

```
using Annabooks.TMP102;
using System.Threading;
```

6. Just within the MainWindow class and before the MainWindow() method, add the following to create a new instance of the TMP102.

```
TMP102 myTemp;
```

7. Below the MainWindow() method, create a new TempSetup() method and fill in the following:

```
private void TempSetup()
{
   myTemp = new TMP102("I2C1", false, 0x48);
   Thread.Sleep(2000);
   if (myTemp.TMP102Status())
   {
      Application.Current.Dispatcher.Invoke((Action)(() => txtStatus.Text = "Temp
Sensor is Ready"));
   }
```

```
  else
  {
     Application.Current.Dispatcher.Invoke((Action)(() => txtStatus.Text = "Temp
Sensor is NOT Ready: " + myTemp.connectionError));
  }
}
```

The method instantiates myTMP as a new instance of TMP102 using I2C2 as the port, bus not shared, and address of 0x48. The thread is put to sleep for about two seconds and then the status of the connection is made and reported.

8. In the MainWindow() method, create the Thread that calls TempSetup() method and start the thread.

```
public MainWindow()
{
   InitializeComponent();
   Thread temptStatus = new Thread(new ThreadStart(TempSetup));
   temptStatus.Start();
}
```

9. In the designer, double-click on the button to generate the event handler.
10. Fill in the code for the handler:

```
private void btnReadTemp_Click(object sender, RoutedEventArgs e)
{
    if (myTemp.TMP102Status())
    {
        txtTempCReading.Text = myTemp.ReadTempC().ToString();
        txtTempFReading.Text = myTemp.ReadTempF().ToString();
    }
}
```

11. Save the project.
12. Build a debug version of the project and correct any errors.

14.5.5 Test the Application

The application is ready to be tested in the target system.

1. Connect the TMP102 to your target platform's I2C port.
2. Make sure that the firmware has the I2C Bus speed set to 400Khz.
3. In the C:\VS-Apps folder of your development machine, determine where the I2CTempSensor2.exe file is located: C:\VS-

Apps\I2CTempSensor2\I2CTempSensor2\bin\Debug\net6.0-windows10.0.19041.0

4. On the target machine, create an exact folder structure under C:\VS-apps - C:\VS-Apps\I2CTempSensor2\I2CTempSensor2\bin\Debug\net6.0-windows10.0.19041.0
5. Run Visual Studio Remote Debug, and make a note of the computer name and port number listed in the Visual Studio Remote Debug output.
6. In Visual Studio running on the development machine, open the I2CTempSensor2 Properties page.
7. Click on Debug on the left side, and click Open debug launch profile UI.
8. Check the checkbox for Use remote machine and enter the Target system's computer name with the port number: X64-APPTEST:4026
9. Close the Window.
10. In the properties, scroll up to Build Events.
11. In the Post-build event enter the following to do a copy of the output to the remote system (this is all one line):

xcopy C:\VS-Apps\I2CTempSensor2\I2CTempSensor2\bin\Debug\net6.0-windows10.0.19041.0 \\X64-APPTEST\VS-Apps\I2CTempSensor2\I2CTempSensor2\bin\Debug\net6.0-windows10.0.19041.0 /Y

12. Save the project.
13. Build the debug version of the application again. The output files should be copied to the remote system.
14. Start the debug session.
15. You will be asked for the target system's login credentials. Enter the user's name and password and click "OK".
16. Once the application has loaded on the target system, hit the button to get the reading from the sensor.
17. Stop debugging when finished.

14.6 Exercise 1403: I2C Humidity Sensor Assembly Library

For this last example, the SparkFun SHTC3 humidity sensor (0 to 100 %RH) will be used to demonstrate the I2C Write() and Read() methods. The sensor also supports temperature readings (-40°C to 125°C). Rather than going through the application and converting it to an assembly, the project will simply create the Class Library and an application to test the assembly.

The SHTC3 sensor's datasheet provides some basic information:

- Address: 0x70

- Standard Mode clock frequency for 100 kbit/s.
- Wakeup command 0x3517.
- Commands to read Humidity and Temperature data are determined by Clock stretching and power mode. On startup, clock stretching is disabled and the chip runs in Normal power mode. These commands will be used.
- Both Humidity and Temperature consist of 16-bits of data each along with a CRC checksum. The most significant byte is read in first.
- There is a delay of about 12.1mS in Normal Mode between the issuance of the command to take the measurement and when the measurement is ready to be read.

14.6.1 Create the Assembly Library

1. Open Visual Studio 2022, if not already open
2. Create a new project and select WPF Class Library – "A project for creating a class library that targets a .NET WPF Application".
3. Name the project SHTC3 and set the folder location to C:\VS-Apps.
4. Click Next.
5. Select .NET 6.0 (Long-term support) from the drop-down box.
6. Click the "Create" button.
7. Once the application opens, we need to do a little more set up to support the Windows Runtime Namespaces. From the menu, select Project-> SHTC3 Properties.
8. Under Application->General set the following for the targeted Windows OS:
    a. Target OS version: 10.0.19041.0
    b. Supported OS version: 10.0.19041.0
9. Scroll down the Build, and set the following:
    a. Platform target: x64
10. Save the project.
11. Rename Class.cs to SHTC3.cs and save the project.
12. Change the namespace to Annabooks. SHTC3.
13. Fill in the following code:

```
using System;
using System.Threading;
using Windows.Devices.Enumeration;
using Windows.Devices.I2c;

namespace Annabooks.SHTC3
{
    public class SHTC3
    {
```

```
        private const byte SHTC3_ADDR = 0x70;
        private byte[] TEMPERATURE_CSD = { 0x78, 0x66 };
        private byte[] HUMIDITYMESSURE_CSD = { 0x58, 0xE0 };
        private byte[] WAKESENSOR = { 0x35, 0x17 };
        private byte[] SLEEPSENSOR = { 0xB0, 0x98 };
        private byte[] SOFTRESET = { 0x80, 0x5D };

        private I2cDevice SHTC3Sensor;

        private double tempResult = 0.0;
        private double humidityResult = 0.0;

        private bool SHTC3Ready = false;
        public string connectionError = "";

        public SHTC3(string I2Cport, bool I2CBusShared)
        {
            I2CInitialize(I2Cport, I2CBusShared);
        }

        private async void I2CInitialize(string I2Cport, bool
I2CBusShared)
        {
            try
            {
                I2cConnectionSettings i2cSettings = new
I2cConnectionSettings(SHTC3_ADDR);
                i2cSettings.BusSpeed = I2cBusSpeed.StandardMode;
                if (I2CBusShared)//True
                {
                    i2cSettings.SharingMode = I2cSharingMode.Shared;
                }
                else//false
                {
                    i2cSettings.SharingMode = I2cSharingMode.Exclusive;
// The device gets exclusive hold for hold master calls
                }
                string aqs = I2cDevice.GetDeviceSelector(I2Cport);
                DeviceInformationCollection i2cDevInfo = await
DeviceInformation.FindAllAsync(aqs);
                SHTC3Sensor = await
I2cDevice.FromIdAsync(i2cDevInfo[0].Id, i2cSettings);
            }
            catch (Exception ex)
            {
                connectionError = ex.Message;
            }
            if (SHTC3Sensor != null)
```

```
            {
                SHTC3Ready = true;
            }
        }

        public double ReadTempC()
        {

            if (SHTC3Ready == false)
            {
                connectionError = "SHTC3 Not ready";
                return 0;
            }

            SHTC3Sensor.Write(WAKESENSOR); //wake the sensor
            Thread.Sleep(10);
            SHTC3Sensor.Write(TEMPERATURE_CSD); //take the messurment
            Thread.Sleep(500);

            byte[] tempBuf = new byte[3]; //get all three bytes, but we
will focus on the first two
            SHTC3Sensor.Read(tempBuf);

            var tempBufFinal = tempBuf[0] << 8;
            tempBufFinal += tempBuf[1];
            tempResult = ((Convert.ToDouble(tempBufFinal) * 175) /
Math.Pow(2, 16)) - 45;

            SHTC3Sensor.Write(SLEEPSENSOR); // Put the sensor back to
sleep
            return Math.Round(tempResult, 2);

        }

        public double ReadHumidity()
        {
            if (SHTC3Ready == false)
            {
                connectionError = "SHTC3 Not ready";
                return 0;
            }
            SHTC3Sensor.Write(WAKESENSOR); //wake the sensor
            Thread.Sleep(10);
            SHTC3Sensor.Write(HUMIDITYMESSURE_CSD); //take the measurment
            Thread.Sleep(500);

            byte[] humidityBuf = new byte[3];
            SHTC3Sensor.Read(humidityBuf);
```

```
            var humidityFinal = humidityBuf[0] << 8;
            humidityFinal += humidityBuf[1];
            humidityResult = ((Convert.ToDouble(humidityFinal) * 100) /
Math.Pow(2, 16));

            SHTC3Sensor.Write(SLEEPSENSOR); // Put the sensor back to
sleep
            return Math.Round(humidityResult, 2);
        }

        public void HumiditySensorSoftReset()
        {
            SHTC3Sensor.Write(SOFTRESET);
        }

        public double GetLastTemp()
        {
            return Math.Round(tempResult, 2);
        }

        public double GetLastHumidity()
        {
            return Math.Round(humidityResult, 2);
        }

        public bool HTU21DStatus()
        {
            return SHTC3Ready;
        }

    }
}
```

The class starts by setting up the constants and the byte[] arrays for the address and the commands to be used in this example. The assembly doesn't support all the commands that the chip supports. For this exercise, we are only focusing on the startup state of the device. The constructor takes in the I2C port value and the I2C bus share mode, and then it makes the call to connect to the device. The SHTC3Ready is set to True if successful. The ReadTempC() and ReadHumidity() methods perform the same operations as follows:

- Wake the sensor
- Take the measurement
- Delay .5 seconds for the measurement to complete
- Read the temperature/humidity from the sensor
- Calculate the temperature/humidity result and store it in the member variable
- Put the sensor to sleep

- Return the result

The CRC checksum is not used. The remaining public methods retrieve the last measurement readings, reset the I2C, and provide connection status.

14. Save the project.
15. Build a debug version of the project and correct any errors.

14.6.2 Create the I2C Humidity Application that uses the new Assembly

The class library is ready to use in an application.

1. Open Visual Studio 2022.
2. Create a new "WPF Application" project. Make sure you select the correct WPF Application template for .NET.
3. Name the project "I2CHumiditySensor" and set the folder location to C:\VS-Apps on your development machine. To do remote debugging with .NET, the remote machine folder architecture must match the development machine. Visual Studio Remote Debugging documentation describes the setup as well.
4. Click the "Next" button.
5. Select .NET 6.0 (Long-term support) from the drop-down box.
6. Click the "Create" button.
7. Once the application opens, we need to do a little more set up to support the Windows Runtime Namespaces. From the menu, select Project-> I2CHumiditySensor Properties.
8. Under Application->General set the following for the targeted Windows OS:
    a. Target OS version: 10.0.19041.0
    b. Supported OS version: 10.0.19041.0
9. Scroll down the Build, and set the following:
    a. Platform target: x64
10. Save the project.

14.6.3 Set Up the XAML Controls

1. In Solution Explorer, open the MainWindow.xaml.
2. The designer and XAML editor will appear. At the top, left of the Designer set the orientation that fits your target's display.
3. Add a TextBox Control.
    a. Name: txtHumidity
    b. Common->Text: Humidity
4. Add a Label next to the TextBox.
    a. Common->Text: %RH

5. Add a TextBox Control.
    a. Name: txtTemp
    b. Common->Text: Temp
6. Add a Label next to the TextBox.
    a. Common->Text: °C
7. Add a Button control.
    a. Name: btnReadTemp
    b. Common->Content: Read Temp
8. Add A TextBox Control.
    a. Name: txtStatus
    b. Common->Text: Ready
9. Save the project.

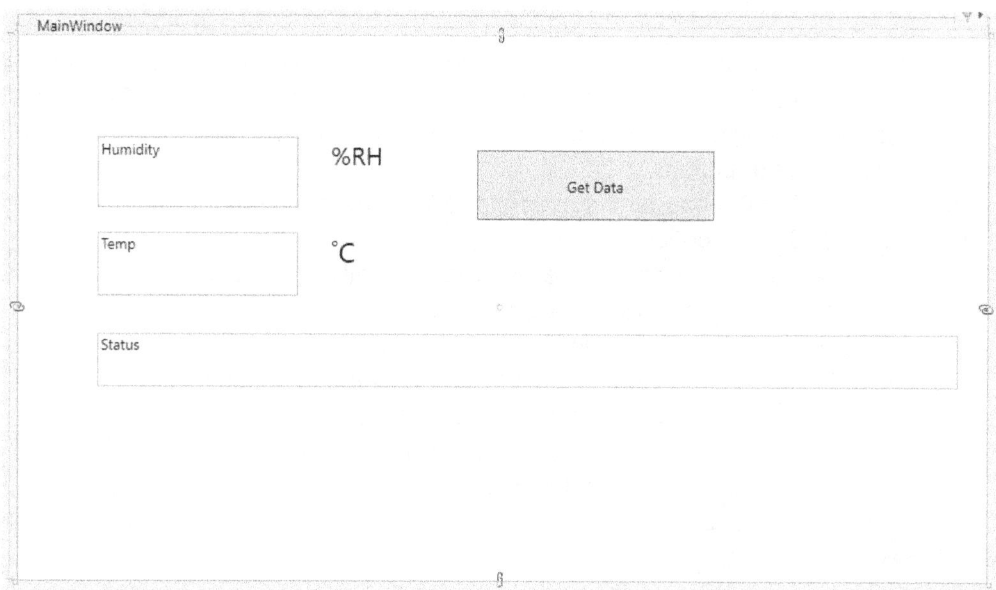

Here is the XAML Code:

```
<Window x:Class="I2CHumiditySensor.MainWindow"
        xmlns="http://schemas.microsoft.com/winfx/2006/xaml/presentation"
        xmlns:x="http://schemas.microsoft.com/winfx/2006/xaml"
        xmlns:d="http://schemas.microsoft.com/expression/blend/2008"
        xmlns:mc="http://schemas.openxmlformats.org/markup-compatibility/2006"
        xmlns:local="clr-namespace:I2CHumiditySensor"
        mc:Ignorable="d"
        Title="MainWindow" Height="450" Width="800">
    <Grid>
```

```
    <TextBox x:Name="txtHumidity" HorizontalAlignment="Left" Height="56"
Margin="65,81,0,0" Text="Humidity" TextWrapping="Wrap" VerticalAlignment="Top"
Width="168"/>
    <TextBox x:Name="txtTemp" HorizontalAlignment="Left" Height="50"
Margin="65,157,0,0" Text="Temp" TextWrapping="Wrap" VerticalAlignment="Top"
Width="168"/>
    <TextBox x:Name="txtStatus" HorizontalAlignment="Left" Height="43"
Margin="65,237,0,0" Text="Status" TextWrapping="Wrap" VerticalAlignment="Top"
Width="711"/>
    <Button x:Name="btnGetData" Content="Get Data" Height="56"
Margin="380,91,225,0" VerticalAlignment="Top" Width="195"
Click="btnGetData_Click"/>
    <TextBlock HorizontalAlignment="Left" Height="56" Margin="260,81,0,0"
Text="%RH" TextWrapping="Wrap" VerticalAlignment="Top" Width="85"
FontSize="20"/>
    <TextBlock HorizontalAlignment="Left" Height="50" Margin="260,157,0,0"
Text="°C" TextWrapping="Wrap" VerticalAlignment="Top" Width="91"
FontSize="22"/>

  </Grid>
</Window>
```

14.6.4 Write the Code

Now, let's write the code behind the GUI.

1. We need to add the class library. Click Project->Add Reference.
2. Browse to the location of the SHTC3.dll that is in the Class Library Project.
3. Select the dll and click "Add" and then click "OK". The namespace for the library can be added to the using directives.
4. Open MainWindow.xaml.cs
5. Add the following using statements to add the Annabooks.SHTC3 and the System Threading namespaces.

```
using Annabooks.SHTC3;
using System.Threading;
```

6. Just within the MainWindows class and before the MainWindow() method, add the following to create a new instance of the SHTC3.

```
SHTC3 mySHTC3;
```

7. Below the MainWindow() method, create a new HumidtySetup() method and fill in the following:

```
private void HumiditySensorSetup()
```

```
{
   mySHTC3 = new SHTC3("I2C1", false);
   Thread.Sleep(1100);
   if (mySHTC3.HTU21DStatus())
   {
      Application.Current.Dispatcher.Invoke((Action)(() => txtStatus.Text = "Humidity
Sensor is Ready"));
   }
   else
   {
      Application.Current.Dispatcher.Invoke((Action)(() => txtStatus.Text = "Humidity
Sensor is NOT Ready: " + mySHTC3.connectionError));
   }
}
```

The method instantiates mySHTC3 as a new instance of SHTC3 using I2C2 as the port and bus not shared. The thread is put to sleep for about 1.1 seconds and then the connection is made and the status reported.

8. In the MainWindow() method, create the Thread that calls the HumidtySetup() method and starts the thread.

```
public MainWindow()
{
    InitializeComponent();
    Thread setupHumiditySensor = new Thread(new
ThreadStart(HumiditySensorSetup));
    setupHumiditySensor.Start();
}
```

9. In the MainWindow.xaml, double-click on the button to generate the event handler.
10. Fill in the code for the handler:

```
private void btnGetData_Click(object sender, RoutedEventArgs e)
{
    if (mySHTC3.HTU21DStatus())
    {
        txtHumidity.Text = mySHTC3.ReadHumidity().ToString();
        txtTemp.Text = mySHTC3.ReadTempC().ToString();
    }
}
```

11. Save the project.
12. Build a debug version of the project and correct any errors.

14.6.5 Test the Application

The application is ready to be tested in the target system.

1. Connect the SHTC3 to your target platform's I2C port.

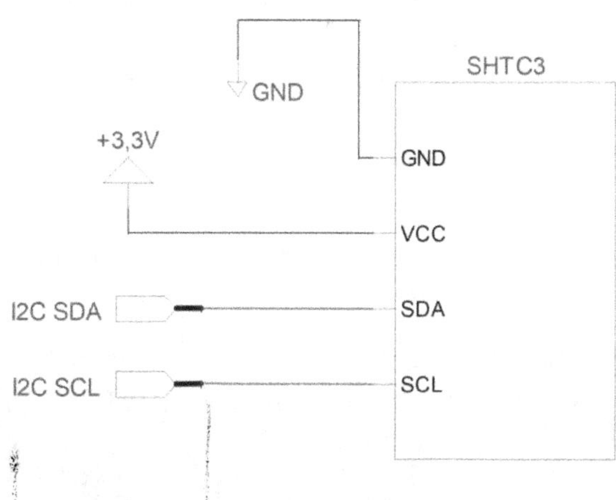

2. Make sure that the firmware has the I2C Bus speed set to 400Khz.
3. In the C:\VS-Apps folder of your development machine, determine where the I2CHumiditySensor.exe file is located: C:\VS-Apps\I2CHumiditySensor\I2CHumiditySensor\bin\Debug\net6.0-windows10.0.19041.0
4. On the target machine, create an exact folder structure under C:\VS-apps - C:\VS-Apps\I2CHumiditySensor\I2CHumiditySensor\bin\Debug\net6.0-windows10.0.19041.0
5. Run Visual Studio Remote Debug, and make a note of the computer name and port number listed in the Visual Studio Remote Debug output.
6. In Visual Studio running on the development machine, open the I2CHumiditySensor Properties page.
7. Click on Debug on the left side, and click Open debug launch profile UI.
8. Check the checkbox for Use remote machine and enter the Target system's computer name with the port number: X64-APPTEST:4026
9. Close the Window.
10. In the properties, scroll up to Build Events.
11. In the Post-build event enter the following to do a copy of the output to the remote system (this is all one line):

```
xcopy C:\VS-Apps\I2CHumiditySensor\I2CHumiditySensor\bin\Debug\net6.0-windows10.0.19041.0 \\X64-APPTEST\VS-Apps\I2CHumiditySensor\I2CHumiditySensor\bin\Debug\net6.0-windows10.0.19041.0 /Y
```

12. Save the project.
13. Build the debug version of the application again. The output files should be copied to the remote system.
14. Start the debug session.
15. You will be asked for the target system's login credentials. Enter the user's name and password and click "OK".
16. Once the application has loaded on the target system, hit the button to get the reading from the sensor.
17. Stop debugging when finished.

Using an O-Scope, the Write() and Read() calls can be seen going across the wires. Here is the Write() call to wake the sensors.

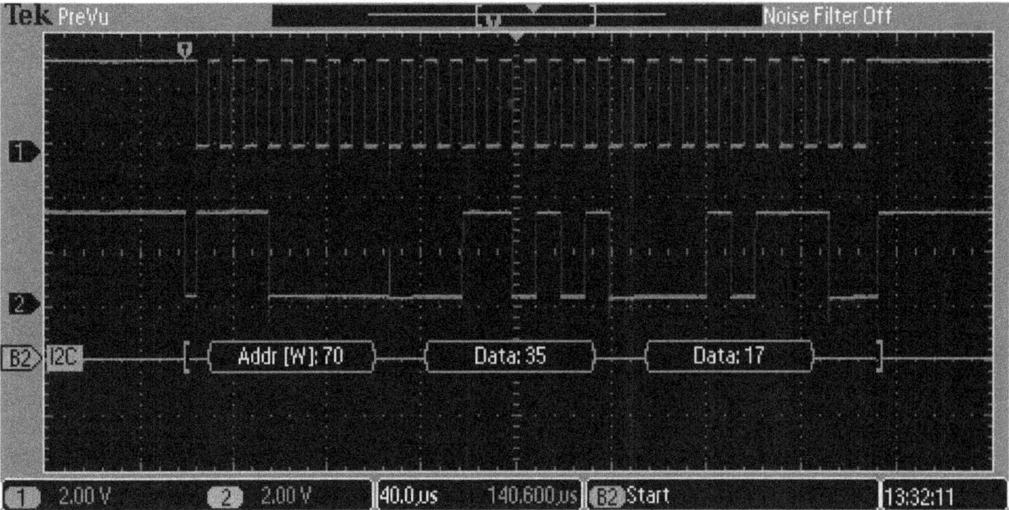

Here is the Write() call to start the humidity measurement:

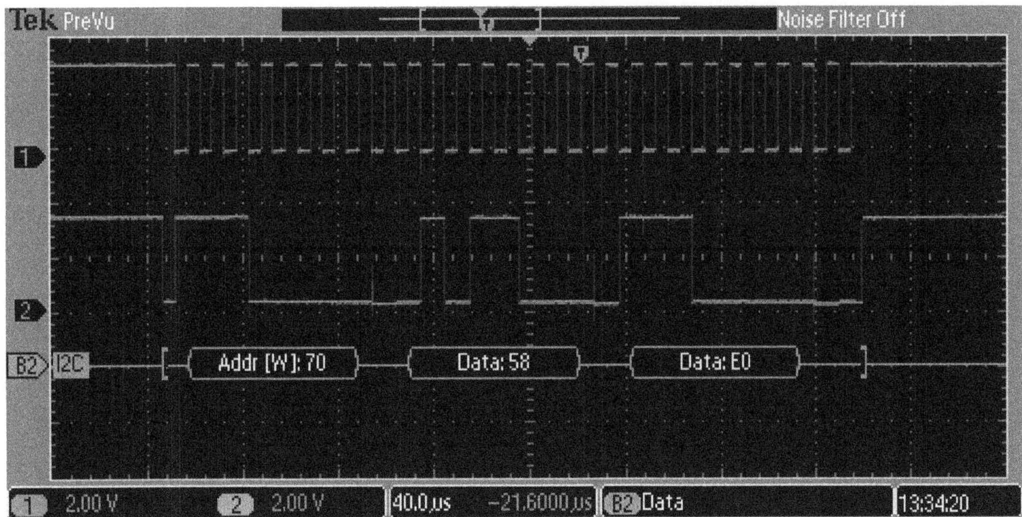

Finally, here is the Read() to read back the 3 bytes.

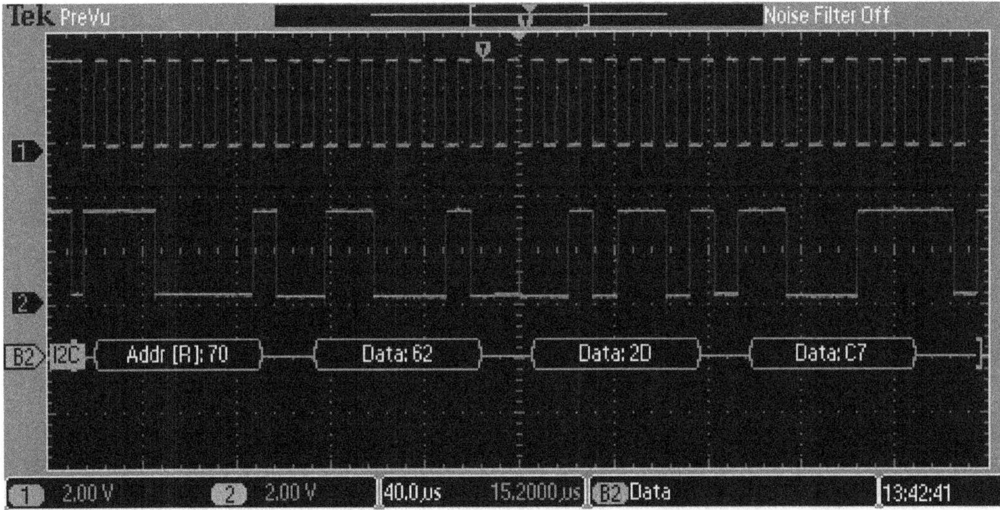

14.7 The I2C Summary

In this chapter, we learned about the I2C bus and writing managed code applications for the I2C devices. The I2C bus simple wire interface is fast becoming a popular solution in the hobbyist and maker markets. The two-wire interface simplifies the design and built-in addressing allows for multiple I2C peripherals to be on the same bus. Not having a specific protocol, each I2C device is free to implement its own command and data interchange rules, which frees the implementation from the overhead of a protocol stack allowing for faster operation. Gathering the technical information on the I2C device is important to set up the I2C communication settings properly and understand the command protocol to transmit to and receive from the I2C device.

We also created assembly libraries for devices, allowing for code reuse and making your applications simpler to write and debug. This comes in handy when you have multiple devices connected to the I2C bus with each having its own communications rules.

15 Pulse Width Modulation

Pulse-width modulation (PWM) is used for controlling backlit displays, motor control, and wireless transmission. PWM is an output-only square wave signal that many microprocessors support. This chapter will cover:

- PWM Overview.
- PWM Namespace.
- The exercise will cover PWM Motor Control.

15.1 Pulse-Width Modulation Overview

Pulse-width modulation is a simple, yet powerful technique for controlling an analog signal with a digital device, like a microprocessor. The simplicity is in the control electronics that switch an analog signal on or off. When an analog signal is switched from off to on and then back to off, a pulse is generated. When the analog signal is switched on and off repeatedly, a pulse train is generated. By controlling the period of time from the start of one pulse to the start of the next pulse in a pulse train, the modulation frequency can be established and controlled. By controlling the period of time that each pulse of a pulse train is on and the period of time that each pulse of a pulse train is off, the duty cycle can be established and controlled. Pulse-width modulation is the creation and control of a pulse train's frequency and duty cycle. Pulse-width modulation can be used to control power to a device or to transmit information. The following picture shows some example pulse trains with different fixed and varying duty cycles, but with the same frequency.

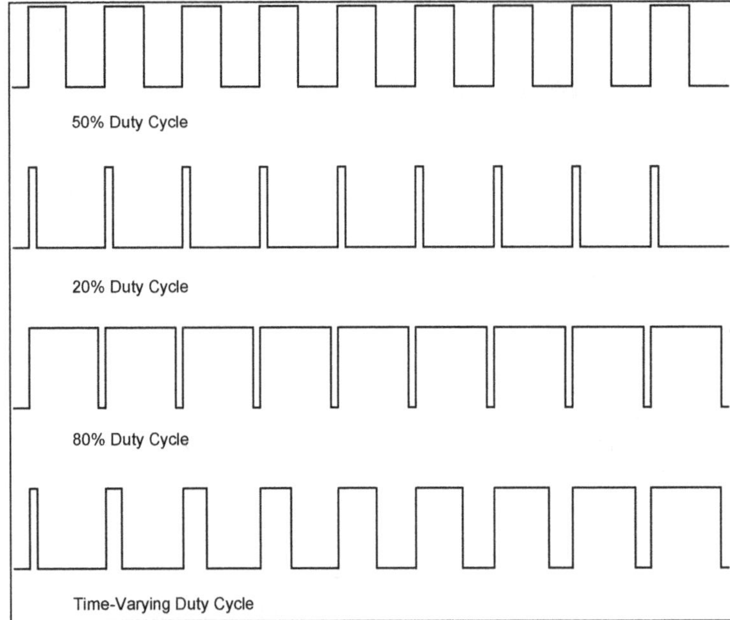

Depending on how a PWM is programmed, it can produce a signal output from a continuous level (100% duty cycle) to a pulse train that can approach a 0% duty cycle. A microprocessor generates the PWM signal using a combination of the internal clock base frequency and internal counters to generate the duty cycle and frequency. Each microcontroller has different internal PWM hardware implementations.

WARNING: Be careful what you connect to your platform!
PWMs are used in a variety of applications, and motor control is one of them. Connecting motors directly to a PWM signal is not recommended since an inductive surge current can damage the chip. An h-bridge or buffer motor controller is recommended as an interface.

You should consult your hardware manufacturer for more information on external hardware support.

15.2 PWM Namespace

The PWM Namespace consists of two classes and one enumerator. The PwmController class makes the connection to the controller, provides controller information, sets the frequency, and opens the PWM output pin. PWMPin class can close the PWM output pin, set the duty cycle, and start/stop the PWM output signal. The Enumerator sets the start polarity active high or active low.

The basic sequence of operations is as follows:

- Enumerate a new PWMController.

- Instantiate a new PwmPin with a PWMContoller opening the pin.
- Start the PWM pin
- Set the duty cycle
- Set the frequency – this will start the output signal.
- Stop the PWM pin when finished.

Intuitively, one may think that setting the frequency and duty cycle should come before starting the pin. If you did this, there would be no output from the PWM.

15.3 PwmTestTool.exe

Chapter 10 covered the Bus Tools sample applications. The PwmTestTool.exe test tool can be used to list all the available PWM controllers in a system, as well as, output a signal with a specific frequency and duty cycle. The list of available PWM controllers doesn't mean they are accessible. Some systems will report a few internal PWM controllers that are not accessible.

```
C:\Test2>PwmTestTool.exe
Missing required command line parameter

pwmTestTool: Command line PWM testing utility
Usage: PwmTestTool.exe [-list] [FriendlyName]

  -list          List available PWM controllers and exit.
  FriendlyName   The friendly name of the PWM controller over
                 which you wish to communicate. This parameter is
                 optional and defaults to the first enumerated
                 PWM controller.

Examples:
  List available PWM controllers and exit:
    PwmTestTool.exe -list

  Open connection to PWM1:
    PwmTestTool.exe PWM1

C:\Test2>PwmTestTool.exe pwm3
  Type 'help' for a list of commands
> help
Commands:
 > freq <f>                         Set controller frequency (Hz)
 > open <pin>                       Open pin
 > start                            start PWM
 > stop                             stop PWM
 > dutycycle <percentage>           set duty cycle percentage
 > polarity                         toggle polarity
```

```
  > info                              Display device information
  > help                              Display this help message
  > quit                              Quit

> info
 ActualFrequency: 16109.3
    MaxFrequency: 16109.3
    MinFrequency: 3.93295
        PinCount: 1
>
```

15.4 Exercise 1501: PWM Motor Control

Of all the boards discussed in Chapter 10, the ASUS IMX80-IM-A is the only platform with support for PWM. There is no PWM device driver for the UP boards. This exercise is provided as a reference until support becomes available. This exercise was developed using the ASUS IMX80-IM-A to output a PWM signal. The PWM signal was connected to a motor control circuit to control a motor. The following schematic shows the SparkFun TB6612FNG motor controller and the Micro Gearmotor – 90RPM (6-12V).

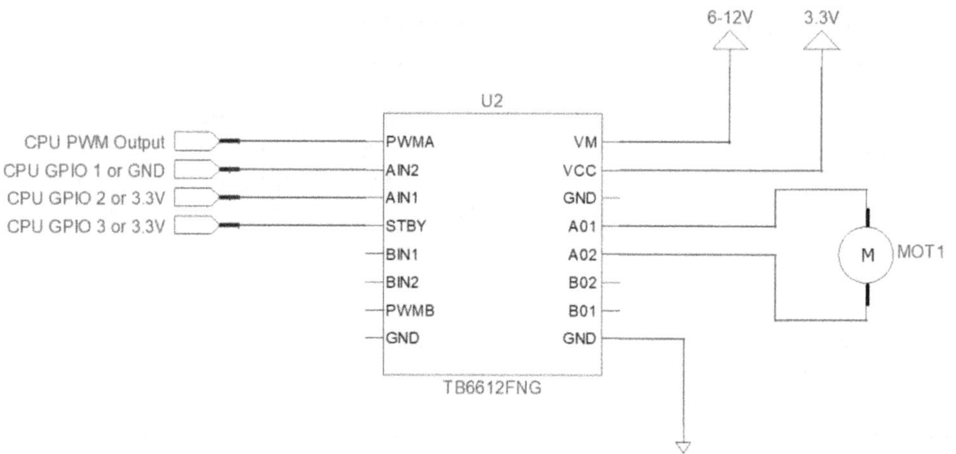

Note: At the time of this writing, the GPIO pins on the ASUS IMX80-IM-A were not functional. The schematic provides alternating high and low signals so the motor controller can cause the motor drive shaft to rotate when the PWM signal is applied. The exercise will not include the GPIO controls for the direction and standby functions.

If you don't have a motor controller, you can use an O-scope to see the PWM signal. You will have to add a resistive load to the PWM output signal to sample it with the O-scope.

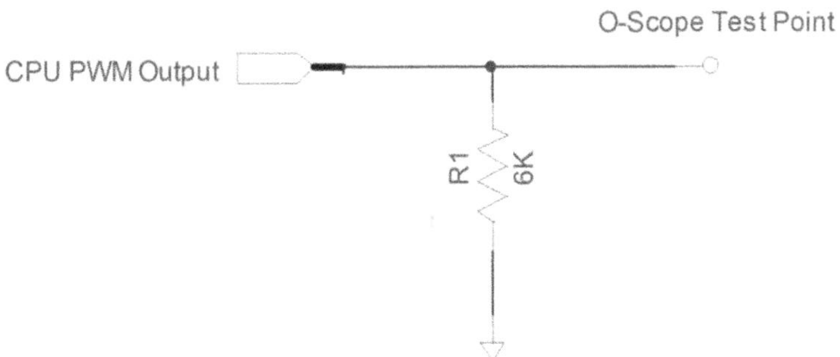

15.4.1 Basic Setup

Here is the basic setup of the application.

1. Open Visual Studio 2022
2. Create a new "WPF Application" project. Make sure you select the correct WPF Application template for .NET.
3. Name the project "PWMMotor", and set the folder location to C:\VS-Apps on your development machine. To do remote debugging with .NET, the remote machine folder architecture must match the development machine. Visual Studio Remote Debugging documentation describes the setup as well.
4. Click the "Next" button.
5. Select .NET 6.0 (Long-term support) from the drop-down box.
6. Click the "Create" button.
7. Once the application opens, we need to do a little more set up to support the Windows Runtime Namespaces. From the menu, select Project-> PWMMotor Properties.
8. Under Application->General set the following for the targeted Windows OS:
    a. Target OS version: 10.0.19041.0
    b. Supported OS version: 10.0.19041.0
9. Save the project.

15.4.2 Set Up the XAML Controls

The UI will have six text boxes and two buttons. One text box will show the pin count, two of the text boxes will show the minimum frequency and the maximum frequency, one text box will show the running frequency, one text box will show the duty cycle, and the last test box will display the status messages. One of the buttons will start the PWM, and the other button will stop the PWM.

1. In Solution Explorer, open the MainWindow.xaml.

2. The designer and XAML editor will appear. At the top, left of the Designer set the orientation that fits your target's display.
3. Add a Label.
    a. Common->Content: PinCount
4. Add a TextBox Control.
    a. Name: txtPinCount
    b. Common->Text: <empty>
5. Add a Label.
    a. Common->Content: Min Frequency
6. Add a TextBox Control.
    a. Name: txtMinFreq
    a. Common->Text: <empty>
7. Add a Label.
    a. Common->Content: Max Frequency
8. Add a TextBox Control.
    a. Name: txtMaxFreq
    b. Common->Text: <empty>
9. Add A TextBox Control.
    a. Name: txtStatus
    b. Common->Text: Ready
10. Add a Button control.
    a. Name: btnStart
    b. Common->Content: Start PWM
11. Add a Button control.
    a. Name: btnStop
    b. Common->Content: Stop PWM
12. Add a Label.
    a. Common->Content: Duty Cycle
13. Add a TextBox Control.
    a. Name: txtDutyCycle
    b. Common->Text: <empty>
14. Add a Label.
    a. Common->Text: Running Freq
15. Add a TextBox Control.
    a. Name: txtFreq
    b. Common->Text: <empty>
16. Save the project.

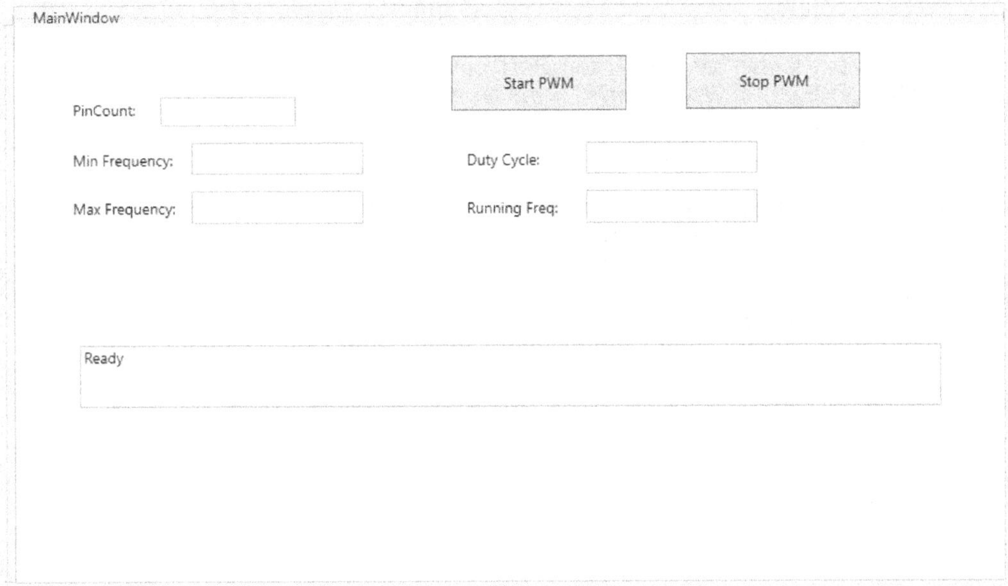

Here is the XAML Code:

```
<Window x:Class="PWMMotor.MainWindow"
      xmlns="http://schemas.microsoft.com/winfx/2006/xaml/presentation"
      xmlns:x="http://schemas.microsoft.com/winfx/2006/xaml"
      xmlns:d="http://schemas.microsoft.com/expression/blend/2008"
      xmlns:mc="http://schemas.openxmlformats.org/markup-compatibility/2006"
      xmlns:local="clr-namespace:PWMMotor"
      mc:Ignorable="d"
      Title="MainWindow" Height="450" Width="800">
   <Grid>
      <Label Content="PinCount:" HorizontalAlignment="Left" Margin="42,52,0,0"
VerticalAlignment="Top" Width="61" Height="26"/>
      <TextBox x:Name="txtPinCount" HorizontalAlignment="Left" Height="23"
Margin="118,55,0,0" TextWrapping="Wrap" VerticalAlignment="Top" Width="109"/>
      <Label Content="Min Frequency:" HorizontalAlignment="Left"
Margin="42,91,0,0" VerticalAlignment="Top"/>
      <TextBox x:Name="txtMinFreq" HorizontalAlignment="Left" Height="25"
Margin="143,91,0,0" TextWrapping="Wrap" VerticalAlignment="Top" Width="138"/>
      <Label Content="Max Frequency:" HorizontalAlignment="Left"
Margin="42,129,0,0" VerticalAlignment="Top"/>
      <TextBox x:Name="txtMaxFreq" HorizontalAlignment="Left" Height="25"
Margin="143,129,0,0" TextWrapping="Wrap" VerticalAlignment="Top" Width="138"/>
      <TextBox x:Name="txtStatus" HorizontalAlignment="Center" Height="49"
Margin="0,249,0,0" TextWrapping="Wrap" Text="Ready" VerticalAlignment="Top"
Width="695"/>
```

```
        <Label Content="Duty Cycle:" HorizontalAlignment="Left" Margin="359,91,0,0"
VerticalAlignment="Top"/>
        <TextBox x:Name="txtDutyCycle" HorizontalAlignment="Left" Height="25"
Margin="460,91,0,0" TextWrapping="Wrap" VerticalAlignment="Top" Width="138"/>
        <Label Content="Running Freq:" HorizontalAlignment="Left"
Margin="359,129,0,0" VerticalAlignment="Top"/>
        <TextBox x:Name="txtFeq" HorizontalAlignment="Left" Height="25"
Margin="460,129,0,0" TextWrapping="Wrap" VerticalAlignment="Top" Width="138"/>
        <Button x:Name="btnStart" Content="Start PWM" HorizontalAlignment="Left"
Height="43" Margin="352,23,0,0" VerticalAlignment="Top" Width="141"/>
        <Button x:Name="btnStop" Content="Stop PWM" HorizontalAlignment="Left"
Height="43" Margin="541,22,0,0" VerticalAlignment="Top" Width="141"/>

    </Grid>
</Window>
```

15.4.3 Write the Code

Now let's write the code behind the GUI.

1. Open MainWindow.xaml.cs.
2. Add the following using statements to enable the PWM, and the Enumeration namespaces:

```
using Windows.Devices.Enumeration;
using Windows.Devices.Pwm;
```

3. Above the MainWindow() method add the following:

```
private PwmController myPWMController;
private PwmPin myPWM;
```

4. After the MainWindow() method, create a new method, InitPWM(), and add the following code.

Note: If you are not sure of the PWM device for your hardware, use the PWM bus tool discussed in Chapter 10.

```
public async void InitPWM()
{
    try
    {
        string aqs = PwmController.GetDeviceSelector("PWM3");
        DeviceInformationCollection deviceInfoPWM = await
DeviceInformation.FindAllAsync(aqs);
        myPWMController = await
PwmController.FromIdAsync(deviceInfoPWM[0].Id);
        txtPinCount.Text = myPWMController.PinCount.ToString();
```

```
        txtMinFreq.Text = myPWMController.MinFrequency.ToString();
        txtMaxFreq.Text = myPWMController.MaxFrequency.ToString();
        myPWM = myPWMController.OpenPin(0);
    }
    catch (Exception ex)
    {
        txtStatus.Text = ex.ToString();
    }
}
```

The code enumerates the PWM and opens the Pin. The properties for the enumerator controller are output to the different text boxes. The frequency values could be put into a slider control to change the frequency from min to max. The duty cycle, from 0 to 100%, could also be controlled by a slider control. This exercise will stick to a fixed frequency and duty cycle.

5. In the MainWindow() method add the code to call the SPISetup().

```
public MainWindow()
{
    InitializeComponent();
    InitPWM();
}
```

6. In MainWindow.xaml, double-click on the buttons to generate the event handlers in MainWindow.xaml.cs, and then add the following code to both event handlers:

```
private void btnStart_Click(object sender, RoutedEventArgs e)
{
    try
    {
        myPWM.Start();
        myPWM.SetActiveDutyCyclePercentage(0.4);
        myPWMController.SetDesiredFrequency(30.0);
        txtDutyCycle.Text =
myPWM.GetActiveDutyCyclePercentage().ToString();
        txtFreq.Text = myPWMController.ActualFrequency.ToString();
    }
    catch (Exception ex)
    {
        txtStatus.Text = ex.ToString();
    }
}
```

The PWM Start button event handler starts the PwmPin and then sets the duty cycle and frequency. Once the frequency has been set, the PWM output signal starts. The current duty cycle and frequency are displayed.

```
private void btnStop_Click(object sender, RoutedEventArgs e)
{
    try
    {
        myPWM.Stop();
        txtDutyCycle.Text = "0";
        txtFreq.Text = "0";
    }
    catch (Exception ex)
    {
        txtStatus.Text = ex.ToString();
    }
}
```

The PWM Stop button event handler stops the PWM output signal and then sets the duty cycle and frequency text box results to zero.

7. Save the project.
8. Build a debug version of the project and correct any errors.

The application is missing the controls for the three GPIO pins to control the direction of the motor, as well as, stop the motor with the standby signal. Since this book focuses on Intel Architecture processors and there is no platform as of this writing that is available for PWM implementation, there are no further steps to test the application. When a system becomes available, just perform the same steps as outlined in previous chapters to set up a remote download and debug session to test the application.

15.5 SUMMARY: Pulse Width Modulation (PWM)

PWM is used in different applications such as LCD backlight and motor control. The PWM Namespace is simple to use. The exercise demonstrated how to use the PWM methods and properties to control the PWM output signal. The key is the proper sequence of steps to produce the desired output signal.

16 Analog-to-Digital Converter (ADC)

As the name implies, an analog-to-digital converter, or ADC, is an electronic device that is used to convert an analog voltage signal, sampled at a particular instance in time, into a digital value. Analog voltage signals, that most electronic devices process, are typically a voltage representation of a physical parameter like light, sound, pressure, temperature, etc. that is converted to a corresponding analog voltage using a transducer. This chapter will cover the following:

- ADC Overview
- ADC Namespaces

16.1 Analog-To-Digital Converter Overview

An analog-to-digital converter, or ADC, is an electronic device that takes discrete measurements of an analog voltage and converts it to a digital value that can be used for display or further digital processing. Each ADC conversion of an analog voltage signal is essentially a snapshot of the analog signal, which could be time-varying. An analog voltage signal may assume any value within a continuous range, as opposed to a digital voltage signal, which will be one of two values: logical 0 or logical 1. Many of the inputs that we sense as humans are in analog form, i.e., sound, light, pressure, or temperature to name a few. The analog voltage signals that most electronic devices process are typically a voltage representation of a physical input source like those just mentioned. Analog signals of light, sound, pressure, temperature, etc. are converted to corresponding analog voltage signals using a transducer. To process these analog voltage signals with digital electronics, like microprocessors, it is necessary to convert the time-varying analog voltage from a transducer or other source into a time-varying series of digital measurements, snapshots. The ADC accomplishes just that. The ADC is the camera, so to speak. The ADC periodically samples one or more analog voltage signals and converts each sample of each signal into a digitally coded representation of each analog signal at the time it was sampled. The digital coding format and the range of digital values will vary depending on the design of the ADC.

Typical encoding schemes are single-ended binary or bipolar binary. Single-ended binary conversion produces a positive binary value that is typically linearly related to the analog signal and ranges from some minimum value to some maximum value. Bipolar binary conversion produces a signed binary value that is typically linearly related to the analog signal ranging from some maximum negative value to some maximum positive value. ADC digital encoding is by no means limited to these basic examples. BCD encoding, Gray code, or other digital encoding schemes can be used and the digital conversion does not have to be linear. Logarithmic, parabolic, or other non-linear conversion schemes can be implemented as well.

A typical ADC linear transfer function is shown in the following picture:

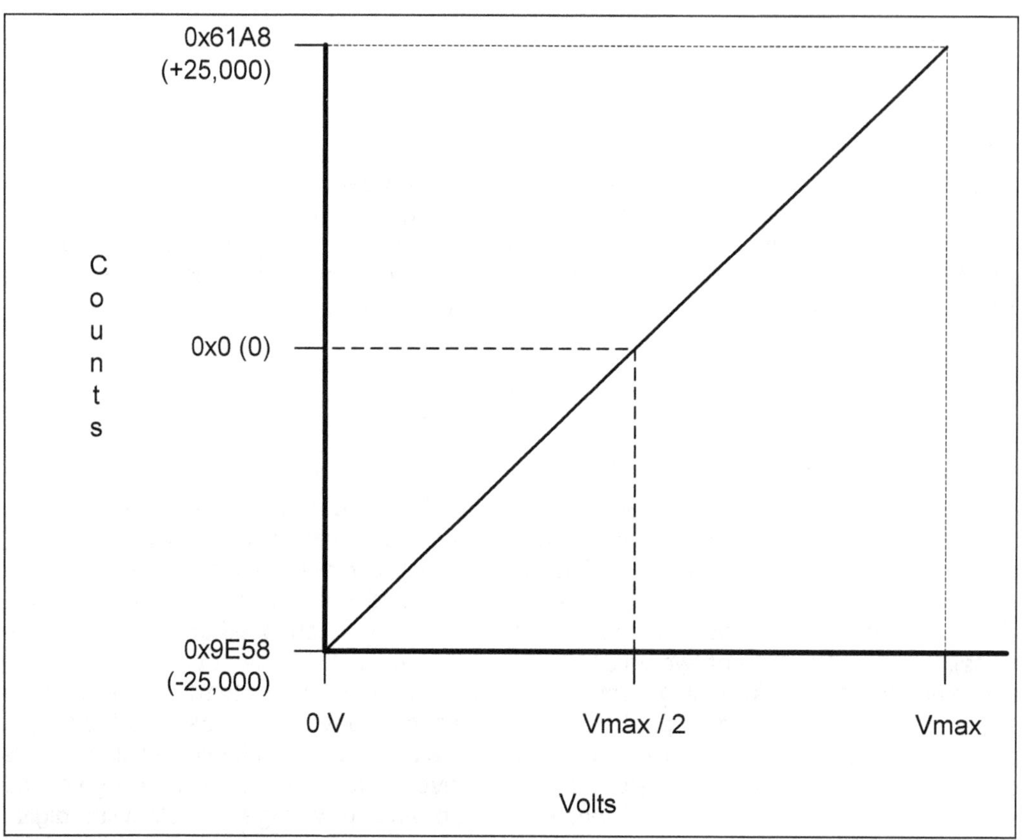

16.2 ADC Channels and Bits

Every ADC chip has unique characteristics. The MCP3002 used in Chapter 13 Exercises 1303 and 1304 is a dual-channel 10-Bit ADC Converter. The maximum sampling rate is 200 kHz at V_{dd} = 5.5 V and 75 kHz at V_{dd} = 2.7 V. Chapter 13 exercises used the ADC to measure a fixed DC voltage. For a time-varying signal, a little more effort needs to be taken so that the sampled results are not distorted by the sampling process itself. The sampling rate and the frequency components of the sampled time-varying signal need to be compared, and the amplitude variation of the time-varying signal that needs to be resolved needs to be known. Nyquist sampling theory and Fourier analysis are beyond the scope of this book; but put simply, the sampling frequency determines the frequency range that can be resolved and the bit-width of the ADC converter determines the amplitude variation of the time-varying signal that can be resolved. The MCP3002 uses the power supply voltage of the chip, as the reference voltage. The converter is 10 bits, so the converter can resolve a voltage of V_{dd}/1024 or 5.37 mV at 5.5 V_{dd} or 2.6 mV at 2.7 V_{dd}.

Based on the Nyquist sample rate, if the maximum frequency component of the time-varying signal coming in is more than half the sample rate, the signal will not be sampled without distortion. Therefore, at a V_{dd} of 5.5 V, a time-varying signal with a maximum frequency component of more than 100 kHz, and at a V_{dd} of 2.7 V a time-varying signal with a maximum frequency component of more than 37.5 kHz cannot be sampled correctly by the MPC3002.

16.3 Windows Runtime ADC and ADC.Provider Namespaces

The Windows.Devices.Adc Namespace consists of two classes and one enumerator. The AdcController class makes the connection to the controller, provides controller information and opens the ADC channel input pin. The AdcChannel class can close the ADC channel input pin, read the value, or read the value as a percentage of the maximum possible value. The Enumerator sets whether the input is differential, measuring between two pins or single-ended, measuring the simple value of a particular pin. The Windows.Devices.Adc.Provider Namespace exposes a Provider interface for a user to implement a specific ADC controller driver. An ADC provider is needed for the Windows.Devices.Adc to talk to the controller.

16.4 No ADC Exercises

As of this writing, none of the platforms support ADC input. There is not even a bus tool available to check out the ADC controllers. There are ADC chips with SPI and I2C interfaces, which make up for what the system might be missing. The Chapter 13 SPI ADC exercises cover one device. For an I2C ADC, there is the Adafruit ADS1115 breakout board.

16.5 SUMMARY: Analog-To-Digital Converter (ADC)

Devices that produce an electronic analog signal can be captured and processed using an ADC. Light, sound, temperature, etc. sensor devices can be captured by an ADC. Robotics, image recognition, AI systems, etc., use ADCs to collect and process data from various sensor inputs.

17 Putting It All Together: Sensors to Cloud

The last few chapters have covered accessing different I/O via Windows Runtime APIs. Now, we will put all of the book's concepts together to build a project. The application will be a Weather Station built with WPF .NET 6. The application will use the SHTC3 Temperature-Humidity sensor (I2C) and the MPL115A1 Pressure sensor (SPI) from earlier chapters. Shell Launcher will launch the application as the shell, UWF will protect drive C, and Device Guard will be enabled to protect the system. The application will display Temperature, Humidity, and Pressure on the display, as well as, send data to an Azure IoT Central application. Before doing this final exercise, you should have read all the previous chapters and gone through all of the previous exercises.

Note: we are going to create an application in the middle of the image development workflow. Typically, application development and Windows image development are separate tasks. This exercise is just a microcosm of the full development process.

Hardware Requirements:

- Intel Architecture 64-bit platform that has SPI, I2C, TPM support, and Ethernet or WIFI.
- SHTC3 humidity sensor breakout board available from SparkFun https://www.sparkfun.com/products/16467.
- MPL115A1 barometric pressure sensor breakout board available from SparkFun https://www.sparkfun.com/products/9721.

Note: The Sparkfun MPL115A1 breakout board went end-of-life during the writing of the book, but the MPL115A1 part itself is still available. There is also the MPL115A2 breakout board, which has an I2C interface.

Software Requirements:

1. Visual Studio 2022.
2. .NET 6.X Desktop Runtime Installer.
3. Remote Tools for Visual Studio 2022.
4. Azure account, which is needed for Azure IoT Central.
5. SHTC3 and MPL115A1 assemblies from earlier chapters.
6. Azure CLI (https://docs.microsoft.com/en-us/cli/azure/install-azure-cli-windows?tabs=azure-cli).

The workflow discussed in Chapter 2 will be the guide for the operating system development process. This project expands on the workflow to include the application development.

17.1 Target System Setup and Starting the Workflow

Let's get started setting up the target system. We will gather the device drivers, group policy, custom power plan, and custom security template. Then we will set up the system for application development. The details for some of the steps, like creating a power plan, are discussed in previous chapters and will not be duplicated here. Where call-outs are made without supporting details, refer back to the earlier chapters for the detailed steps.

1. Wire the SHTC3 to the I2C port and the MPL115A1 to the SPI port of your platform.
    a. Perform any changes to the firmware setup to enable SPI and I2C support.
    b. For the MPL115A1 the /SHLD pin can be attached to a GPIO, and the GPIO can be set to high to enable the device. For the UP Boards, the firmware can automatically set the GPIO high on boot.
2. Install Windows 10 Enterprise 2021 LTSC
    a. Create a simple domain account with a simple password. This Windows installation is only for development and will be wiped out eventually.
    b. Install all device drivers and extract the drivers using the appropriate DISM commands.
    c. Create a custom "Balanced" power plan that never sleeps or goes to hibernate.
    d. Create a custom security template that disables the password timeout.
    e. Open gpedit.msc and set the following:

<u>Computer Configuration</u>

- Configure Offer Remote Assistance – Disabled
- Configure Solicited Remote Assistance – Disabled
- Microsoft OneDrive for Business 2013 – Disabled
- Microsoft OneDrive for Business 2016 – Disabled
- Require a password when a computer wakes (on-battery) - Disabled
- Require a password when a computer wakes (plugged-in) – Disabled
- Save documents to OneDrive by default – Disabled
- Set the default behavior for AutoRun – Disabled
- Turn on Software Notifications – Disabled
- Disable Windows Error Reporting – Enabled
- Prevent the display of the user interface for critical errors – Enabled
- Prevent the OneDrive files from syncing over a metered connection – Enabled
- Prevent the usage of OneDrive for file storage – Enabled
- Prevent the usage of OneDrive for file storage on Windows 8.1 – Enabled

- Turn off Autoplay – Enabled
- Turn off reminder balloons - Enabled
- Turn off System Restore - Enabled
- Turn off Windows Error Reporting – Enabled

User Configuration

- Enable screen saver – Disabled
- Microsoft OneDrive for Business 2013 – Disabled
- Microsoft OneDrive for Business 2016 – Disabled
- Set the default behavior for AutoRun – Disabled
- Disable showing balloon notification toasts – Enabled
- Disable Windows Error Reporting – Enabled
- Remove Balloon Tips on Start Menu items – Enabled
- Turn off all balloon notifications – Enabled
- Turn off Autoplay – Enabled
- Turn off feature advertisement balloon notifications – Enabled
- Turn off reminder balloons – Enabled
- Turn off toast notifications – Enabled
- Turn off toast notifications on the lock screen – Enabled

3. Copy the Drivers, Power Plan POW file, Security Template INF file, and the Group Policy folder created in step 2 to a USB flash disk.
4. Install .NET 6.X Desktop Runtime.
5. Install Remote Tools for Visual Studio 2022.
6. Create a folder in the root of the C: drive called VS-Apps. This will be the location to place the binaries for remote debugging.
7. Share the C:\VS-Apps folder, and add the local user account to have full access to the shared folder. The folder will be remotely accessed via the development machine for developing the application.
8. On the development machine, create a Project1 folder under \WinData
9. Copy all the items created in 2 to a USB flash disk and put them in the \WinData\Project1 folder.

17.2 Create Azure IoT Central Application

Azure IoT Central is a SaaS solution that provides a simple implementation of Azure IoT. The Azure IoT Central allows a developer to create cloud applications quickly. We will walk through the process to create an application and a device template. Three key pieces of information will be collected to make the connection between the remote application running on the device and the Azure IoT Central applications.

1. If you have to sign up for Azure to get access to Azure IoT Central, the pay-as-you-go plan will keep the cost down. Azure IoT Central allows for 2 free devices to

connect with a limited number of messages a month. We will take advantage of the free 7-day plan to implement the application.

2. Log into your Azure IoT Central account: https://apps.azureiotcentral.com/
3. On the left side, click Build.
4. Azure IoT Central comes with several pre-built application templates for different industries. We will create a custom application. Click on the Create button in the Custom App tile.

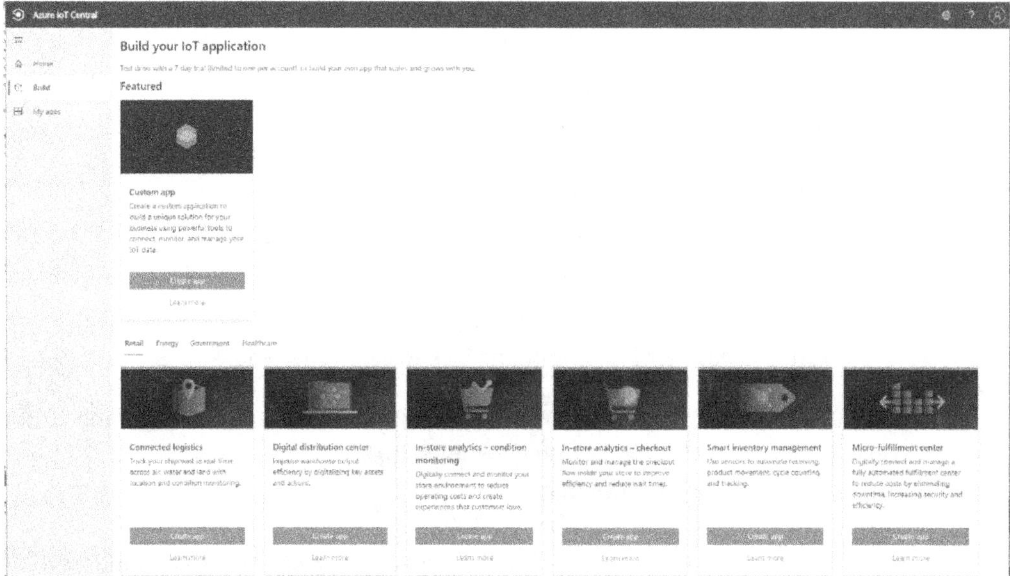

5. Set the application name to Weather.
6. Select Free under the pricing plan.
7. Click the Create button.

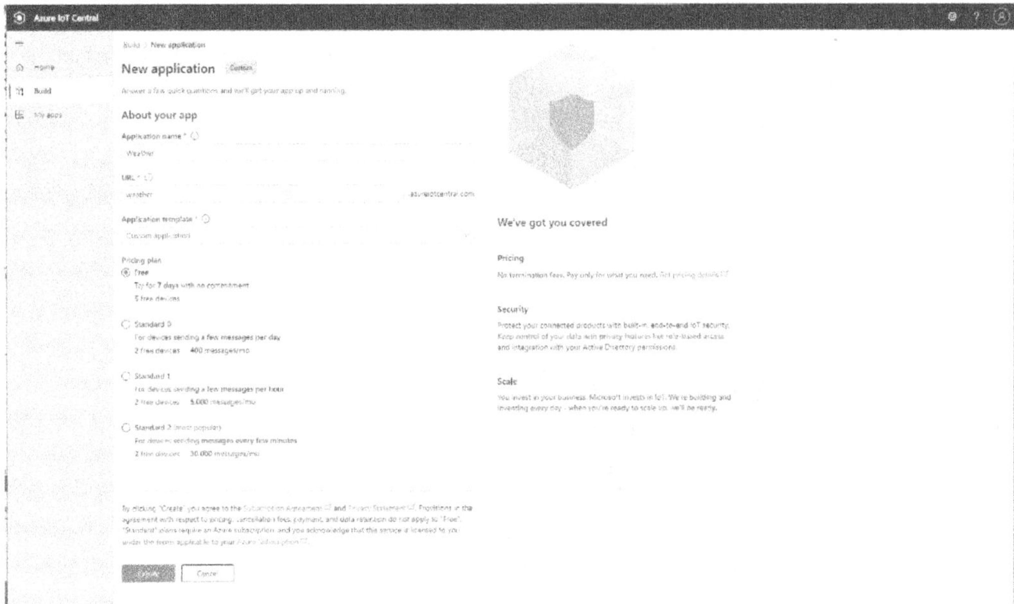

8. The application is generated and the Dashboard appears. On the left side click on the "Device templates".
9. Click on the "Create a device template" button.

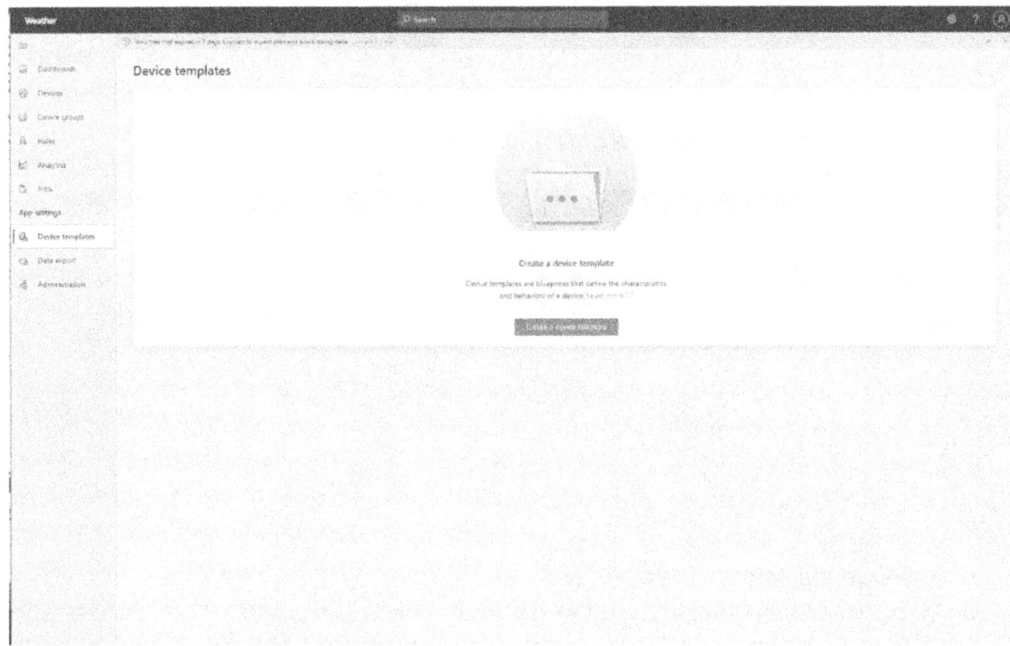

10. In addition to pre-build applications, Azure IoT Central comes with several pre-built device templates to build on. We will create a custom template. Click on the "IoT device" tile.
11. Click "Next: Customize" on the bottom of the screen.

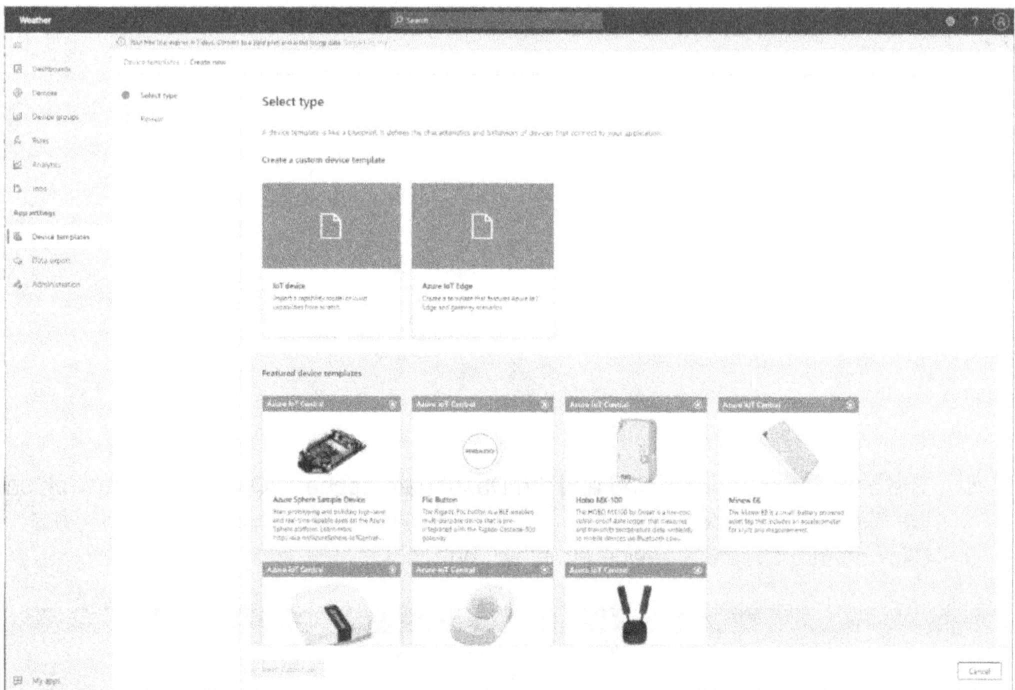

12. Name the template "WeatherStation" and click "Next: Review".

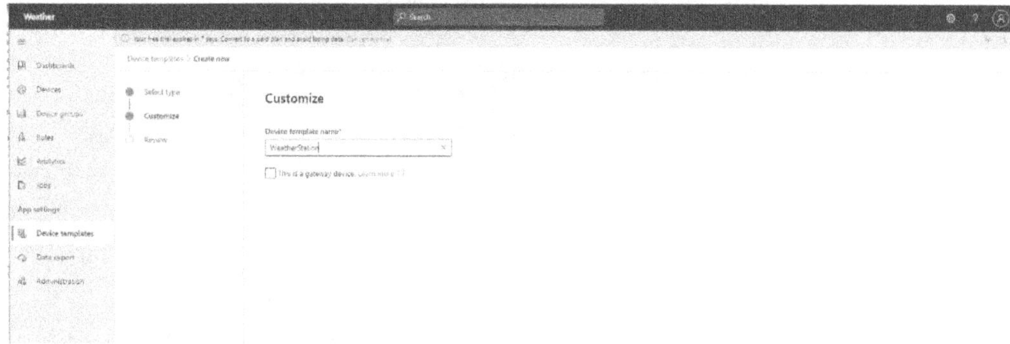

13. Click Create on the review page.
14. Now, we will add the model to the template. The model is a JSON implementation of the information and commands that the application will be using. You can create

a JSON file and import it. Here we will use the graphical tools to create the model. Click on the "Custom Model" tile.

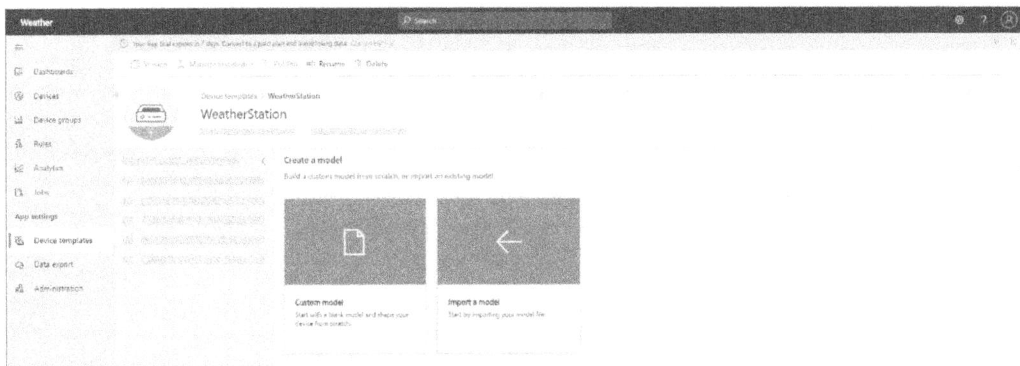

15. On the Model page, we will add three telemetry Capabilities, click the "Add capability" and add the following capabilities

Display Name	Capability Type	Schema	Units	Display Unit
Temperature	telemetry	Double	Degree Celsius	C
Humidity	telemetry	Double	Percent	RH
Barometric Pressure	telemetry	Double	Kilopascal	kPa

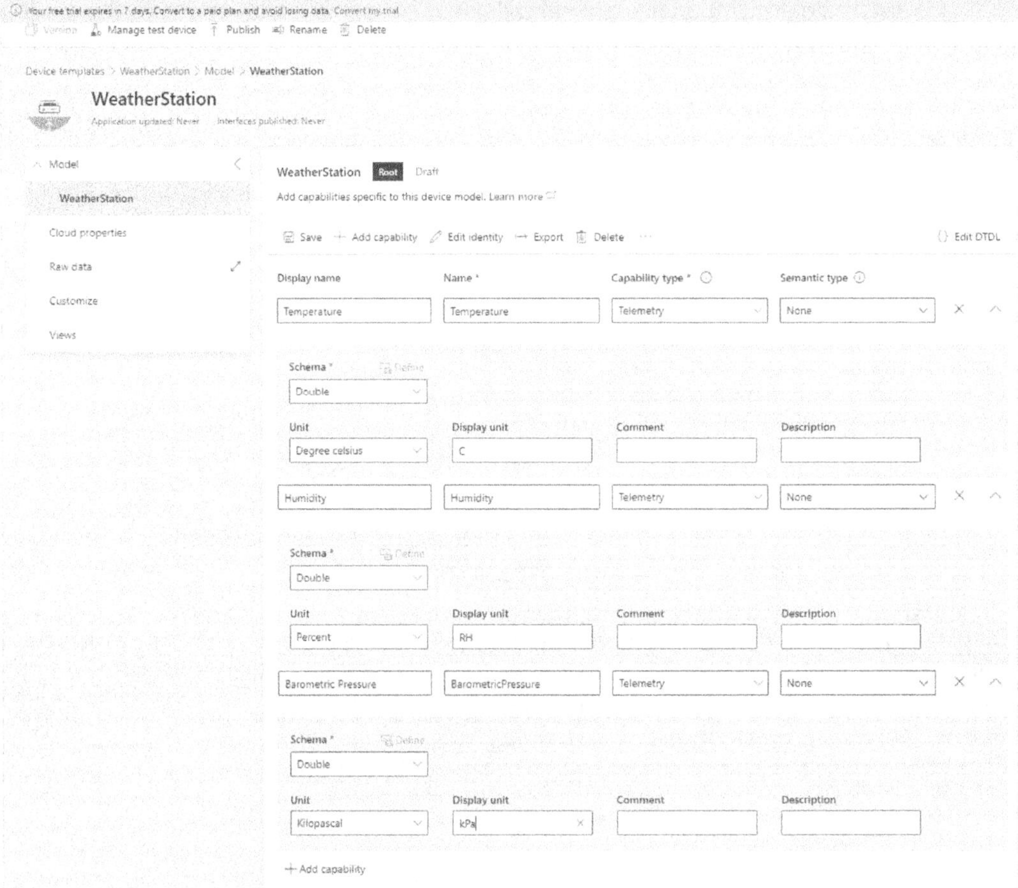

16. Click Save to save the changes.
17. Now, we need to create the Dashboard view to display the data. Click on Views.
18. There are three options. Click on “Visualizing the device”.

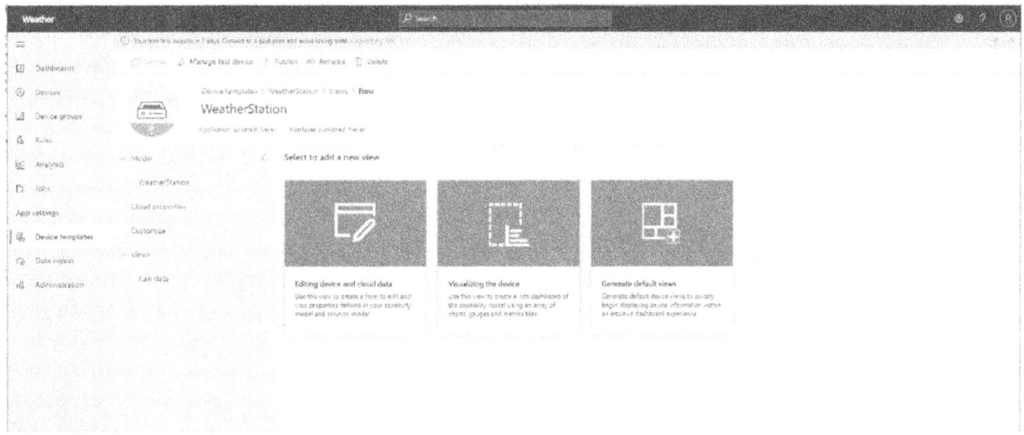

19. Change the View Name to “Overview”.
20. Click on “Start with devices”.
21. Under telemetry, select Temperature from the drop-down and click “Add tile”. A Line chart tile is created for temperature.
22. Repeat steps 21-22 for Humidity and Pressure capabilities.
23. Click Save.
24. We will create another view that will need a line chart for all three capabilities. Under telemetry add all three capabilities, and click “Add tile”.
25. Rename the tile “Weather History” and click Update.
26. Click Save.

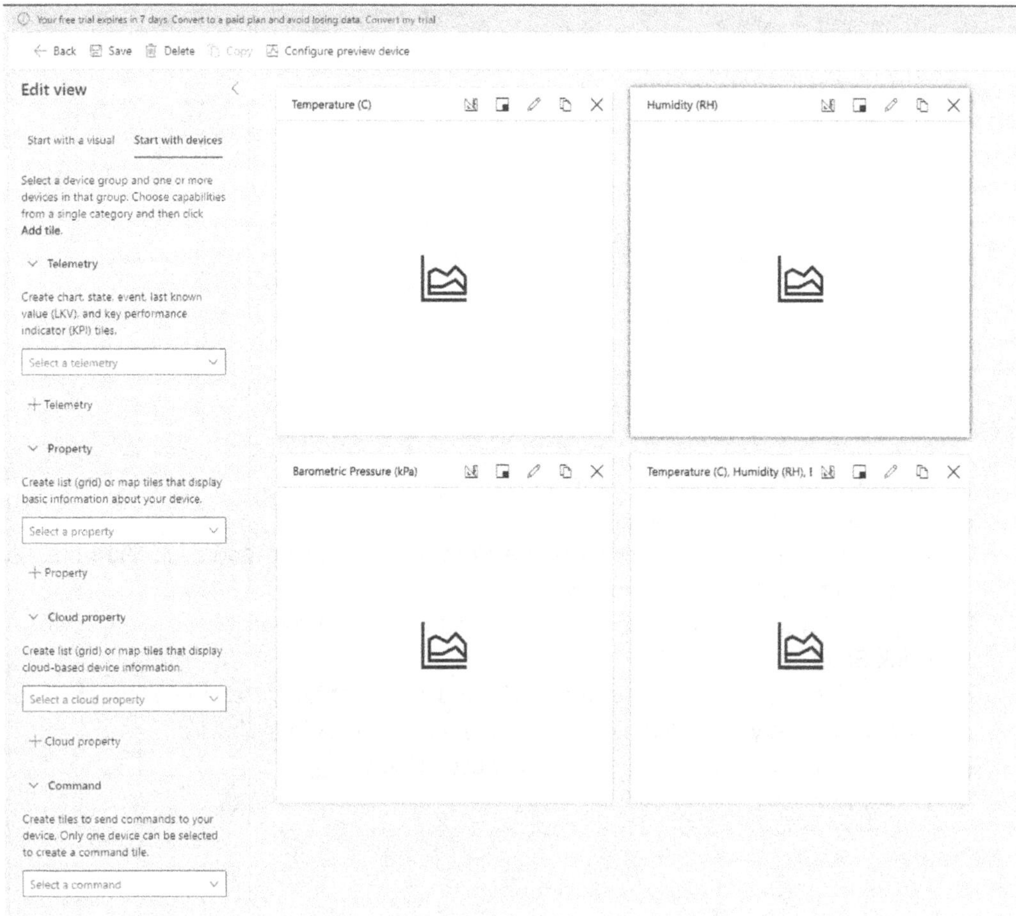

27. Go back to the root Overview view.
28. Change the Visualization for each to “Last Known Value”.
29. Change the size for each tile to 1x1.

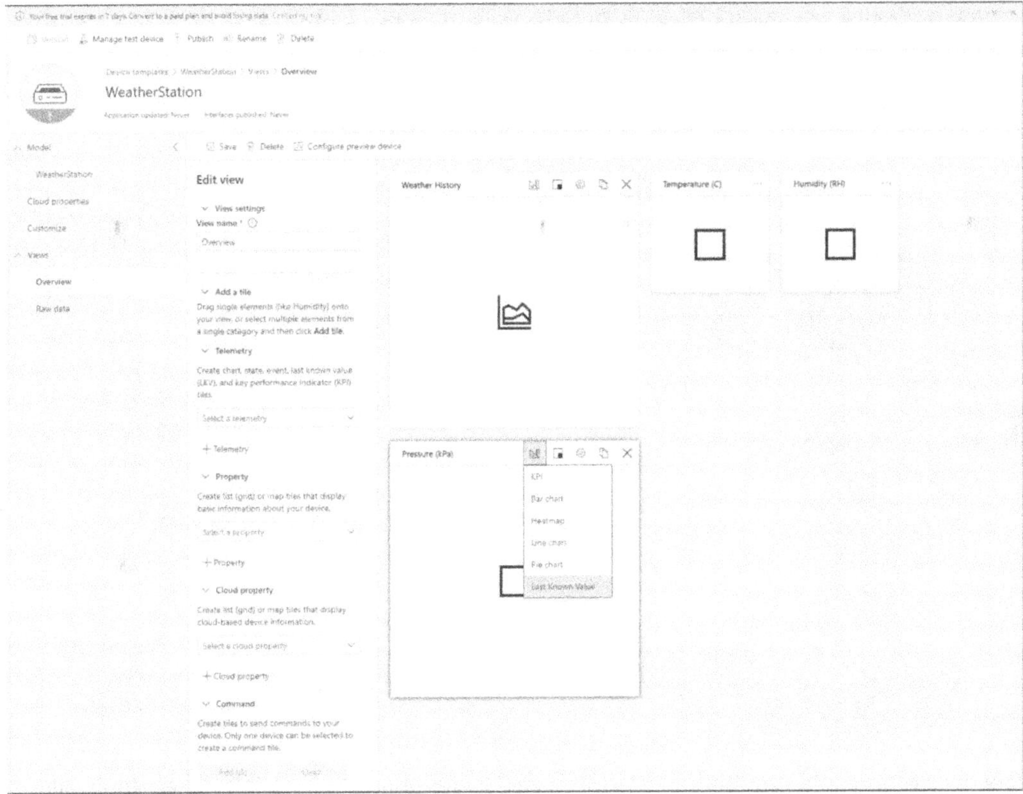

30. Arrange the tiles per the picture below.
31. Save the changes.

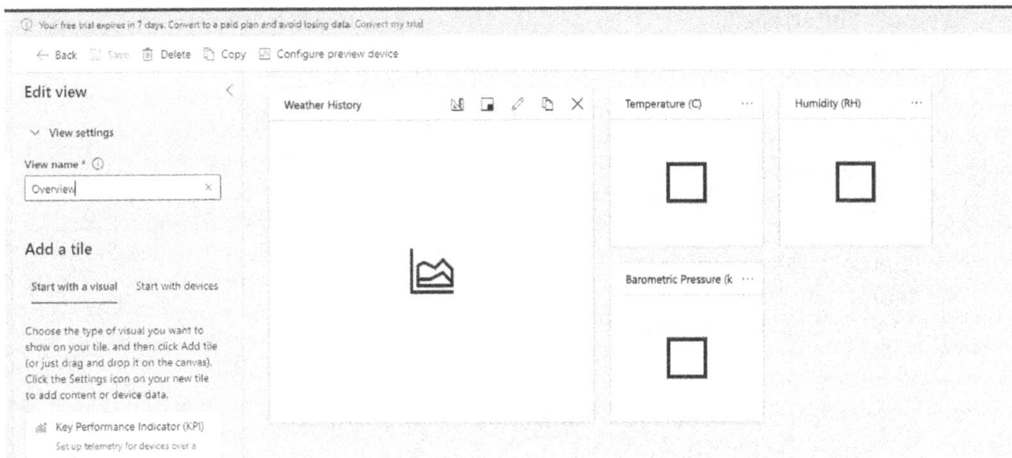

32. Click "Back" to go back to the WeatherStation template.

33. From the top menu, click on Publish to publish the template.
34. A dialog appears, click on the Publish button to publish the template.

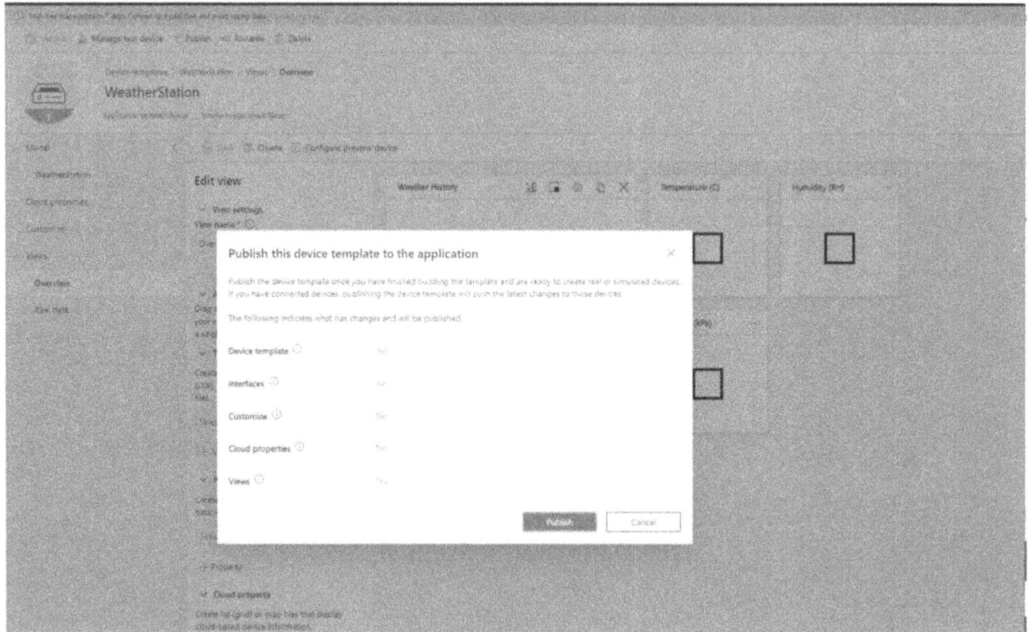

The device template can be exported to a JSON file and imported into other applications in the future. Here is a look at the exported JSON file for the Weather Station template.

```
{
  "@id": "dtmi:weather:WeatherStation_5yd;1",
  "@type": "Interface",
  "contents": [
    {
      "@id": "dtmi:weather:WeatherStation_5yd:Temperature;1",
      "@type": "Telemetry",
      "displayName": {
        "en": "Temperature"
      },
      "name": "Temperature",
      "schema": "double",
      "unit": "degreeCelsius"
    },
    {
      "@id": "dtmi:weather:WeatherStation_5yd:Humidity;1",
      "@type": "Telemetry",
      "displayName": {
        "en": "Humidity"
```

```
        },
        "name": "Humidity",
        "schema": "double",
        "unit": "percent"
      },
      {
        "@id": "dtmi:weather:WeatherStation_5yd:BarometricPressure;1",
        "@type": "Telemetry",
        "displayName": {
          "en": "Barometric Pressure"
        },
        "name": "BarometricPressure",
        "schema": "double",
        "unit": "kilopascal"
      }
    ],
    "displayName": {
      "en": "WeatherStation"
    },
    "@context": [
      "dtmi:iotcentral:context;2",
      "dtmi:dtdl:context;2"
    ]
  }
```

Now, we need 3 pieces of information for our application to connect to Azure IoT Central and exchange data with the application. These items were created as we created the application and the template.

35. In the WeatherStation device template, click on “Edit Identity”.
36. A sidebar will appear on the right. Click on the copy button for the Interface @id. This will link the template to the device when the device connects to Azure IoT Central.
37. Open Notepad, and paste the result.
38. Click Cancel to close the template.

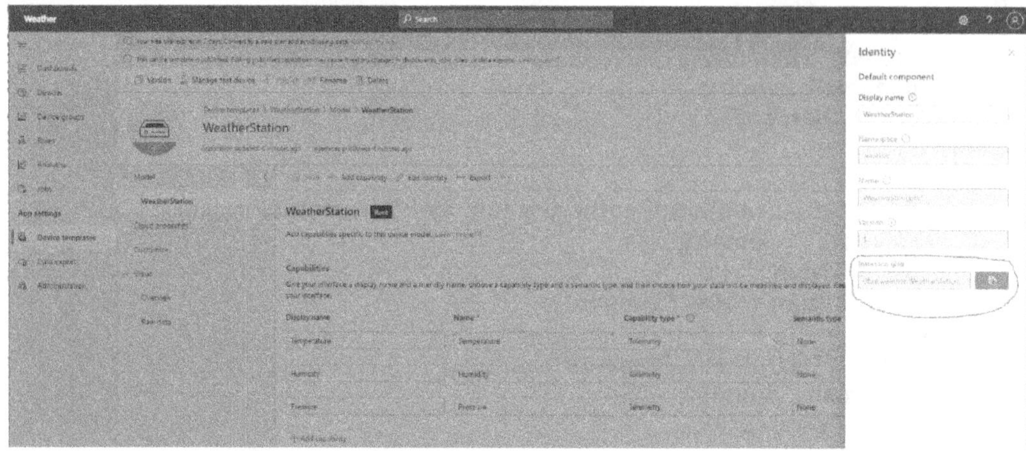

39. On the left side, click on Security->Permissions.
40. Click on “Device connection groups”.
41. Click on “SAS-IoT-Devices”.
42. Click on the copy button next to “ID scope”.
43. Paste the result to the notepad file.
44. Click on the copy button next to the “Primary key”.
45. Past the result to the notepad file.

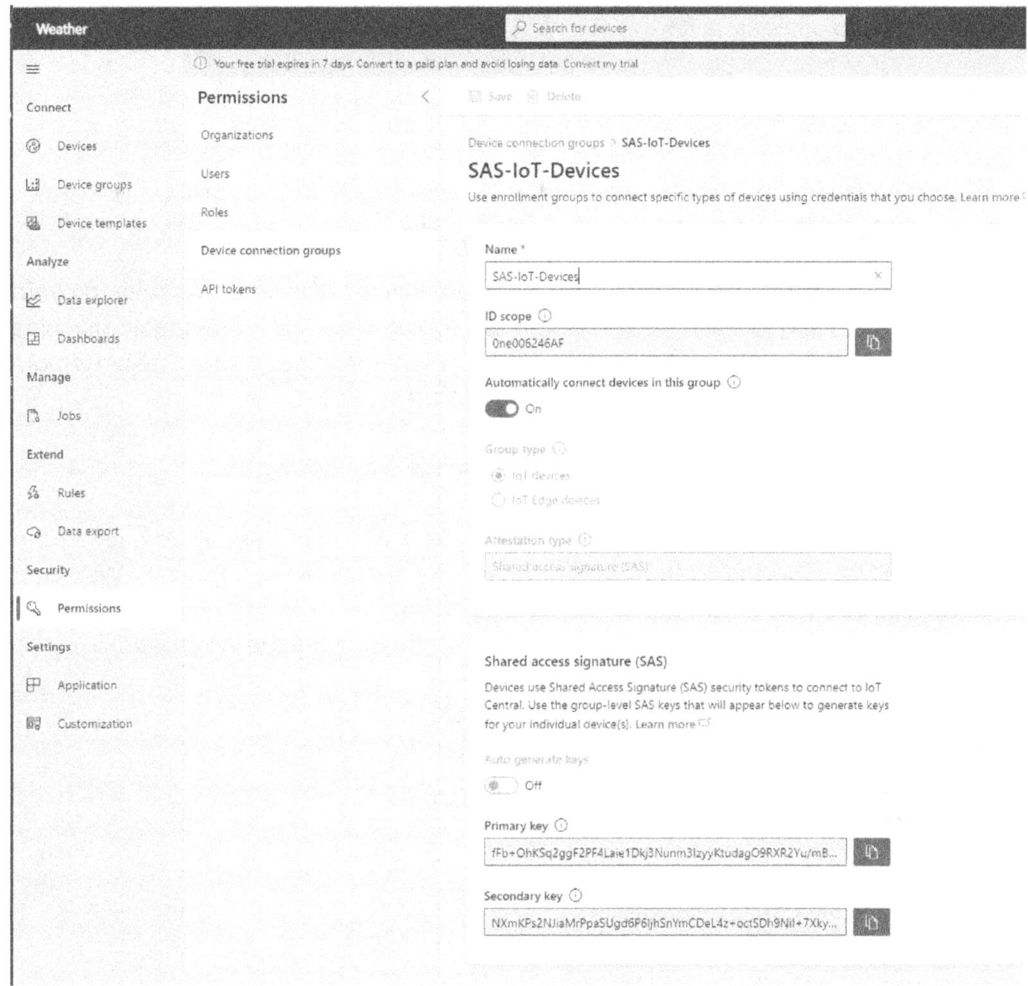

46. Save the notepad file with the three copied items (Interface @id, ID scope, and primary key) as Weather-connect.txt. We will use the information in our application to make the connection to Azure IoT Central.

17.3 Create the Weather Application in Visual Studio

With the Azure IoT Central application created and the connection information gathered, we can create the application.

17.3.1 Install Azure CLI

We will need to generate a key to allow the application to connect to the WeatherStation application in the cloud.

1. On your development machine, install Azure CLI, which will be used in the next section to generate a key.

17.3.1 Create the Visual Studio Project

The first step is to create the project and perform the basic setup tasks.

1. Open Visual Studio 2022.
2. Create a new "WPF Application" project. Make sure you select the correct WPF Application template for .NET.
3. Name the project "Weather1", and set the folder location to C:\VS-Apps on your development machine. To do remote debugging with .NET, the remote machine folder architecture must match the development machine. Visual Studio Remote Debugging documentation describes the setup as well.
4. Click the Next button.
5. Select ".NET 6.0 (Long-term support)" from the drop-down box.
6. Click the Create button.
7. Once the application opens, we need to do a little more set up to support the Windows Runtime Namespaces. From the menu, select Project->Weather1 Properties.
8. Under Application->General set the following for the targeted Windows OS:
    a. Target OS version: 10.0.19041.0
    b. Supported OS version: 10.0.19041.0
9. Scroll down the Build, and set the following:
    a. Platform target: x64
10. Save the project.

17.3.2 Set Up the XAML Controls

Now we will set up the UI.

1. In Solution Explorer, open the MainPage.xaml.
2. Add a Label.
    a. Common->Content: Weather Station1
    b. Text->Bold Checked
    c. Text->Font Size: 16px
3. Add a TextBox below the label.
    a. Name: txtTemp
    b. Common->Text <empty>
4. Add a Label next to the TextBox.
    a. Content: °C
    b. Text->Bold Checked
    c. Text->Font Size: 16px

5. Add a TextBox below the temperature TextBox and Label.
    a. Name: txtHumidity
    b. Common->Text <empty>
6. Add a Label next to the TextBox.
    a. Content: %RH
    b. Text->Bold Checked
    c. Text->Font Size: 16px
7. Add a TextBox below the humidity TextBox and Label.
    a. Name: txtPressure
    b. Common->Text <empty>
8. Add a Label next to the TextBox.
    a. Content: kPa
    b. Text->Bold Checked
    c. Text->Font Size: 16px
9. Add a StatusStrip to the bottom of the frame.
10. Add a Label to the StatusStrip.
    a. Name: txtStatus
    b. Content: Ready
11. Save the project.

Here is the XAML code:

```
<Window x:Class="Weather1.MainWindow"
    xmlns="http://schemas.microsoft.com/winfx/2006/xaml/presentation"
    xmlns:x="http://schemas.microsoft.com/winfx/2006/xaml"
    xmlns:d="http://schemas.microsoft.com/expression/blend/2008"
    xmlns:mc="http://schemas.openxmlformats.org/markup-compatibility/2006"
    xmlns:local="clr-namespace:Weather1"
    mc:Ignorable="d"
    Title="MainWindow" Height="450" Width="800">
  <Grid>
    <Label Content="WeatherStation1" HorizontalAlignment="Left" Height="52"
Margin="85,31,0,0" VerticalAlignment="Top" Width="219" FontWeight="Bold"
FontSize="16"/>
    <TextBox x:Name="txtTempt" HorizontalAlignment="Left" Height="52"
Margin="85,88,0,0" TextWrapping="Wrap" VerticalAlignment="Top" Width="183"/>
    <Label Content="°C" HorizontalAlignment="Left" Height="45"
Margin="290,95,0,0" VerticalAlignment="Top" Width="102" FontWeight="Bold"
FontSize="16"/>
    <TextBox x:Name="txtHumidity" HorizontalAlignment="Left" Height="52"
Margin="85,152,0,0" TextWrapping="Wrap" VerticalAlignment="Top" Width="183"/>
    <Label Content="%RH" HorizontalAlignment="Left" Height="45"
Margin="290,159,0,0" VerticalAlignment="Top" Width="102" FontWeight="Bold"
FontSize="16"/>
```

```
        <TextBox x:Name="txtPressure" HorizontalAlignment="Left" Height="52"
Margin="85,219,0,0" TextWrapping="Wrap" VerticalAlignment="Top" Width="183"/>
        <Label Content="kPa" HorizontalAlignment="Left" Height="45"
Margin="290,226,0,0" VerticalAlignment="Top" Width="102" FontWeight="Bold"
FontSize="16"/>
        <StatusBar Margin="0,394,0,0">
            <Label x:Name="txtStatus" Content="Ready" Height="30" Width="408"/>
        </StatusBar>
    </Grid>
</Window>
```

The designer should show the following:

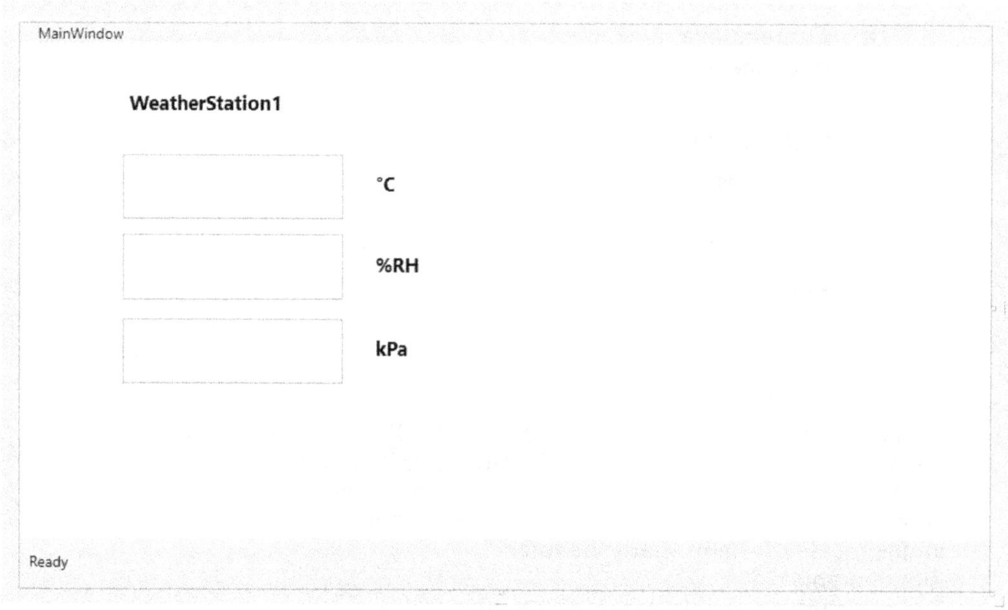

MainWindow

WeatherStation1

°C

%RH

kPa

Ready

17.3.3 Write the code

Now, we will create the code behind the interface.

1. The first step is to add the assemblies and Packages needed to write the code. In Solution Explorer, right-click on "Dependencies" and select "Add Project References".
2. Click on "Browse", and click on the "Browse" button, locate and add the SHTC3.dll. This adds support for the SHTC3 Humidity-Temperature sensor.
3. Click on the "Browse" button, locate and add the MPL115A1.dll. This adds support for the MPL115A1 Pressure sensor.

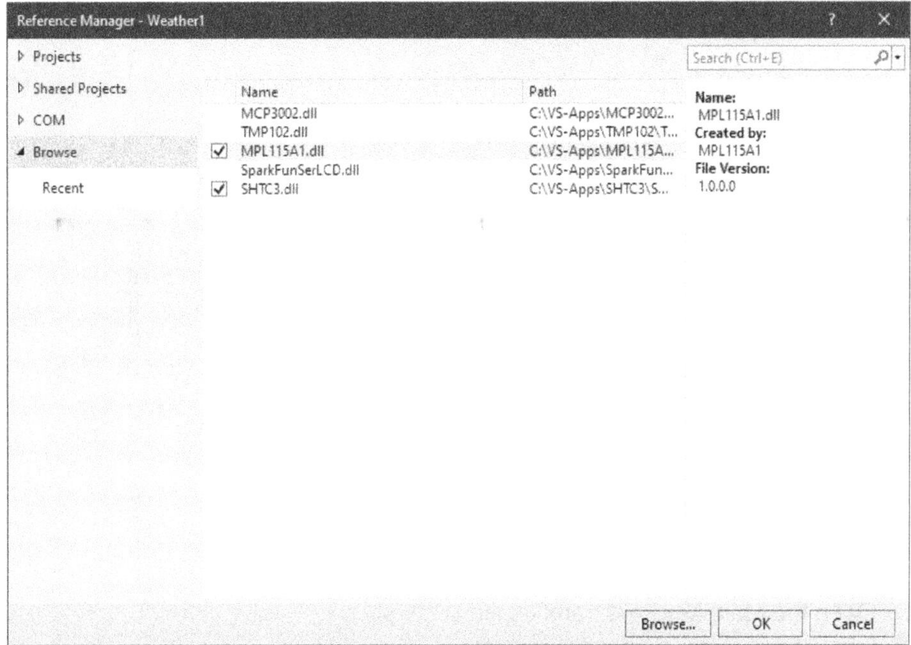

4. Make sure both assemblies are checked and click OK.
5. Right-click on Dependencies and select “Manage NuGet Package”.
6. Click on Browse, and search for “Microsoft.Azure.Devices.Client”.
7. Install Microsoft.Azure.Devices.Client and accept all the dialogs that appear afterward.
8. Repeat the search and install the following Azure packages:
    a. Microsoft.Azure.Devices.Provisioning.Client
    b. Microsoft.Azure.Devices.Provisioning.Transport.Mqtt

The three packages are for accessing Azure. The following picture shows all the assemblies.

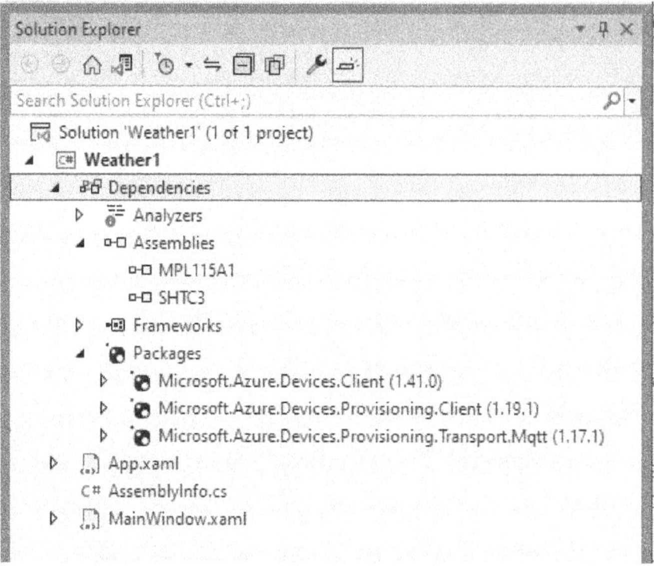

9. Open the MainWindows.xaml.cs file.
10. Add the following, using statements:

```
using Annabooks.MPL115A1;
using Annabooks.SHTC3;
using System.Threading;
using Microsoft.Azure.Devices.Provisioning.Client;
using Microsoft.Azure.Devices.Provisioning.Client.Transport;
using Microsoft.Azure.Devices.Shared;
using Microsoft.Azure.Devices.Client;
using System.Text.Json;
```

11. Above the MainWindow() method, add the following:

```
private MPL115A1 myPressureSensor;
private SHTC3 myTempHumidity;
private string IOTHUB_DEVICE_DPS_ENDPOINT = "global.azure-devices-
provisioning.net";
private string IOTHUB_DEVICE_DPS_ID_SCOPE = ""; //Application Device
Connectivity
private string IOTHUB_DEVICE_DPS_DEVICE_ID = "WeatherStation1";
private string IOTHUB_DEVICE_DPS_DEVICE_KEY = ""; //Generated via Azure
CLI
private const string ModelId = ""; //Comes from Template Identity
private DeviceClient deviceClient;
```

Now, we will fill in the information in the empty quotes from the Weather-connect.txt file.

12. Copy and paste the ID scope value to the IOTHUB_DEVICE_DPS_ID_SCOPE.
13. Copy and paste the Interface @Id value to the ModelId.
14. The IOTHUB_DEVICE_DPS_DEVICE_KEY must be generated using the Primary key. Open a command prompt window.
15. Run the following to add an extension:

```
az extension add --name azure-iot
```

16. Now run the following using the Primary key:

```
az iot central device compute-device-key --device-id WeatherStation1 --
pk <primary key value from Azure IoT Central application>
```

Note: If you have more than one device, you would run the command for each device with a different device-id making sure it matches the value of the private string IOTHUB_DEVICE_DPS_DEVICE_ID. Each device will have its own device key to connect to the Azure IoT Central application.

17. An alphanumeric value will appear. Copy and paste the alphanumeric result to the IOTHUB_DEVICE_DPS_DEVICE_KEY.
18. Save the project. These three items make the connection to Azure, the Weather Application, and the WeatherStation Template.
19. After the MainWindow() method, create the SensorSetup() method and add the following code:

```
private async void SensorSetup()
{
    //Get an instance of the PressureSensor
    myPressureSensor = new MPL115A1("SPI2", 8000000, 0, false);
    Thread.Sleep(1000);
    if (myPressureSensor.MPL115A1Status())
    {
        Application.Current.Dispatcher.Invoke((Action)(() =>
txtStatus.Content = "Preasure Sensor is Ready"));
    }
    else
    {
        Application.Current.Dispatcher.Invoke((Action)(() =>
txtStatus.Content = "Preasure Sensor is NOT Ready: " +
myPressureSensor.connectionError));
    }

    //Get an instance of the Temperature / Humidity Sensor
    myTempHumidity = new SHTC3("I2C1", false);
    Thread.Sleep(1100);
    if (myTempHumidity.HTU21DStatus())
    {
```

```
        Application.Current.Dispatcher.Invoke((Action)(() =>
txtStatus.Content += " and Humidity Sensor is Ready"));
    }
    else
    {
        Application.Current.Dispatcher.Invoke((Action)(() =>
txtStatus.Content += " and Humidity Sensor is NOT Ready: " +
myTempHumidity.connectionError));
    }

    //PnP Connect to the Azure IoT Central Application
    //Provision the Device assigned to the Weather Station template using
the connection information from the app
    SecurityProvider symmetricKeyProvider = new
SecurityProviderSymmetricKey(IOTHUB_DEVICE_DPS_DEVICE_ID,
IOTHUB_DEVICE_DPS_DEVICE_KEY, null);
    ProvisioningTransportHandler mqttTransportHandler = new
ProvisioningTransportHandlerMqtt();
    ProvisioningDeviceClient pdc =
ProvisioningDeviceClient.Create(IOTHUB_DEVICE_DPS_ENDPOINT,
IOTHUB_DEVICE_DPS_ID_SCOPE, symmetricKeyProvider, mqttTransportHandler);
    var pnpPayload = new ProvisioningRegistrationAdditionalData
    {
        JsonData = $"{{ \"modelId\": \"{ModelId}\" }}",
    };

    DeviceRegistrationResult dpsRegistrationResult = await
pdc.RegisterAsync(pnpPayload);

    var authMethod = new
DeviceAuthenticationWithRegistrySymmetricKey(dpsRegistrationResult.Device
Id, IOTHUB_DEVICE_DPS_DEVICE_KEY);

    var options = new ClientOptions
    {
        ModelId = ModelId,
    };
    deviceClient = DeviceClient.Create(dpsRegistrationResult.AssignedHub,
authMethod, TransportType.Mqtt, options);


    while (true)
    {
        double _temprature = myTempHumidity.ReadTempC();
        double _humidity = myTempHumidity.ReadHumidity();
        double _pressure = myPressureSensor.ReadPressure_kPa();
```

```
        Application.Current.Dispatcher.Invoke((Action)(() => txtTemp.Text
= _temprature.ToString()));
        Application.Current.Dispatcher.Invoke((Action)(() =>
txtHumidity.Text = _humidity.ToString()));
        Application.Current.Dispatcher.Invoke((Action)(() =>
txtPressure.Text = _pressure.ToString()));

        //Create a Json message
        //The following will group each telemetry item into a single
message. The Telemetry names must match the telemetry names set up in the
template.
        var weatherTelemetry = new
        {
            Temperature = _temprature,
            Humidity = _humidity,
            BarometricPressure = _pressure,
        };

        var telemetryMessageString =
JsonSerializer.Serialize(weatherTelemetry);
        var telemetryMessage = new
Message(Encoding.ASCII.GetBytes(telemetryMessageString));

        await deviceClient.SendEventAsync(telemetryMessage);

        Thread.Sleep(5000);
    }
}
```

The first several lines create an instance for the sensors. Next comes the connection to Azure using the keys and ID generated from creating the application and template. The final result is the creation of the deviceClient instance, which will be used to send data to the Azure IoT Central application. Finally, there is the big while-loop, which does all the processing. The sensors are read and the data is displayed in the GUI. Since the SensorSetup() method is running in a separate thread, the dispatcher.invoke() method is used with a Lambda Expression to display the results. The measurements are then wrapped into a JSON message string and sent to the Azure Weather application. A delay of 5 seconds is performed before the loop runs again.

20. Modify the MainWindow() method with the following:

```
public MainWindow()
{
    InitializeComponent();
    Thread setupSensors = new Thread(new ThreadStart(SensorSetup));
    setupSensors.Start();
}
```

21. Save the project.
22. Build a debug version of the project and correct any errors.

17.3.4 Test the Application

Now, we are ready to test the application.

1. In the C:\VS-Apps folder of your development machine, determine where the Weather1.exe file is located: C:\VS-Apps\Weather1\Weather1\bin\Debug\net6.0-windows10.0.19041.0
2. On the target machine, create an exact matching folder structure under C:\VS-apps - C:\VS-Apps\Weather1\Weather1\bin\Debug\net6.0-windows10.0.19041.0
3. Run Visual Studio Remote Debug, and make a note of the computer's name and port number listed in the Visual Studio Remote Debug output.
4. In Visual Studio running on the development machine, open the Weather1 Properties page.
5. Click on Debug on the left side, and click "Open debug launch profile UI".
6. Check the checkbox for Use remote machine and enter the Target systems computer name with the port number: X64-APPTEST:4026
7. Close the Window.
8. In the properties, scroll up to Build Events.
9. In the Post-build event enter the following to do a copy of the output to the remote system (this is all one line):

xcopy C:\VS-Apps\Weather1\Weather1\bin\Debug\net6.0-windows10.0.19041.0 \\X64-APPTEST\VS-Apps\Weather1\Weather1\bin\Debug\net6.0-windows10.0.19041.0 /Y

10. Save the project.
11. Build the debug version of the application again. The output files should be copied to the remote system.
12. Start the debug session.
13. You will be asked for the target system's login credentials. Enter the user's name and password and click OK.
14. Run the debugger. The application will start and eventually, the sensor readings will appear in the GUI.
15. In Azure IoT Central, click on the Devices, and eventually, the WeatherStation1 device will appear.

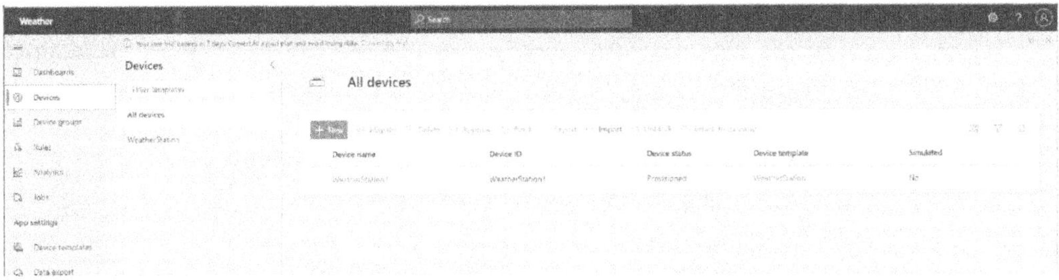

16. Click on the "WeatherStation1" device to open the Dashboard. Sensor data will start appearing. You can let the system run for a while, and maybe blow on the sensors to generate different values.

17. Click on "Raw data" to see the JSON messages coming through.

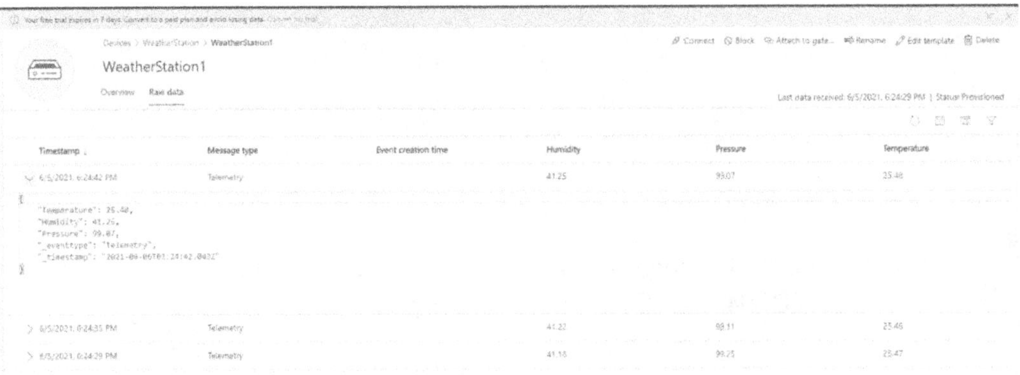

18. Stop debugging when finished.
19. Rebuild a Release version of the application. The release version will be used in building the image.

17.4 Set Up the Distribution Share and Create the Answer File

The application is ready and all the other pieces from the image have been collected. We can now build the custom image.

17.4.1 Set Up the Distribution Share

First, create the distribution share.

1. Create a folder under WinData called “DS64P1”.
2. Open SIM and create a new distribution share under DS64P1.
3. Create a folder with the name of the platform under C:\WinData\DS64P1\Out-of-Box Drivers and copy the device drivers captured in Section 17.1 to the folder.
4. Create folders $1 and $$ under C:\WinData\DS64P1\$OEM$ Folders.
5. Create a Setup folder, a Setup2 folder, and a “Program Files” folder under C:\WinData\DS64P1\$OEM$ Folders\$1.

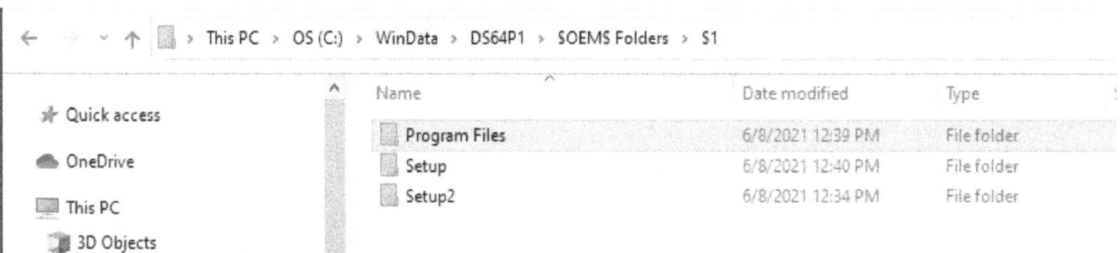

6. Copy the custom power plan, security template, WDAC-Policy.ps1 (from exercise 803), and the .NET 6.X installer to C:\WinData\DS64P1\$OEM$ Folders\$1\Setup.
7. Copy the Device Guard readiness folder containing the PowerShell script to C:\WinData\DS64P1\$OEM$ Folders\$1\Setup2

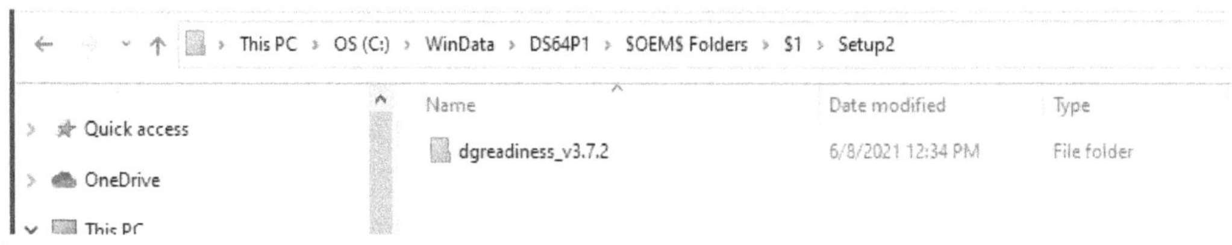

8. Create an Annabooks folder and a Weather folder under C:\WinData\DS64P1\$OEM$ Folders\$1\Program Files

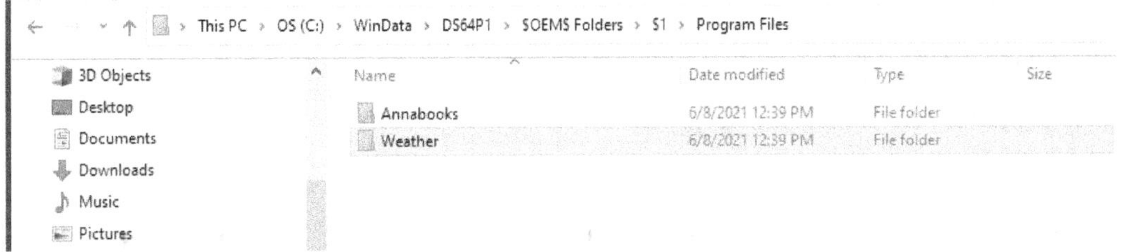

9. Copy the files for the Weather1 applications to the C:\WinData\DS64P1\$OEM$ Folders\$1\Program Files\Weather folder.

› WinData › DS64P1 › OEM Folders › $1 › Program Files › Weather

Name	Date modified	Type	Size
DotNetty.Buffers.dll	10/8/2018 10:15 AM	Application exten...	172 KB
DotNetty.Codecs.dll	10/8/2018 10:14 AM	Application exten...	137 KB
DotNetty.Codecs.Mqtt.dll	10/8/2018 10:14 AM	Application exten...	35 KB
DotNetty.Common.dll	10/8/2018 10:14 AM	Application exten...	150 KB
DotNetty.Handlers.dll	10/8/2018 10:14 AM	Application exten...	51 KB
DotNetty.Transport.dll	10/8/2018 10:14 AM	Application exten...	177 KB
Microsoft.Azure.Amqp.dll	9/19/2020 6:45 PM	Application exten...	384 KB
Microsoft.Azure.Devices.Client.dll	5/14/2021 9:50 PM	Application exten...	682 KB
Microsoft.Azure.Devices.Provisioning.Cli...	5/6/2021 12:41 AM	Application exten...	38 KB
Microsoft.Azure.Devices.Provisioning.Tra...	5/6/2021 12:46 AM	Application exten...	84 KB
Microsoft.Azure.Devices.Shared.dll	5/6/2021 12:33 AM	Application exten...	38 KB
Microsoft.Extensions.DependencyInjecti...	11/14/2016 8:41 PM	Application exten...	35 KB
Microsoft.Extensions.Logging.Abstractio...	2/17/2017 5:01 PM	Application exten...	43 KB
Microsoft.Extensions.Logging.dll	2/17/2017 5:01 PM	Application exten...	18 KB
Microsoft.WindowsAzure.Storage.dll	9/15/2018 1:06 AM	Application exten...	760 KB
MPL115A1.dll	6/4/2021 1:52 PM	Application exten...	10 KB
MPL115A1.pdb	6/4/2021 1:52 PM	Program Debug D...	18 KB
MPL115A1.pri	6/4/2021 1:52 PM	PRI File	1 KB
Newtonsoft.Json.dll	11/9/2019 12:56 AM	Application exten...	678 KB
SHTC3.dll	6/4/2021 1:52 PM	Application exten...	9 KB
SHTC3.pdb	6/4/2021 1:52 PM	Program Debug D...	16 KB
SHTC3.pri	6/4/2021 1:52 PM	PRI File	1 KB
Weather1.deps.json	6/7/2021 3:37 PM	JSON File	85 KB
Weather1.dll	6/7/2021 3:37 PM	Application exten...	15 KB
Weather1.exe	6/7/2021 3:37 PM	Application	171 KB
Weather1.pdb	6/7/2021 3:37 PM	Program Debug D...	22 KB
Weather1.runtimeconfig.dev.json	6/7/2021 3:37 PM	JSON File	1 KB
Weather1.runtimeconfig.json	6/7/2021 3:37 PM	JSON File	1 KB

10. Copy the keyboard filter, Shell Launcher, and UWF utilities from Annabooks.com to the C:\WinData\DS64P1\$OEM$ Folders\$1\Program Files\Annabooks folder.

This PC › OS (C:) › WinData › DS64P1 › OEM Folders › $1 › Program Files › Annabooks

Name	Date modified	Type	Size
kbfmgr64.exe	9/25/2018 6:42 PM	Application	12 KB
KBFUtility64.exe	9/25/2018 6:49 PM	Application	198 KB
shlmgr.exe	3/7/2018 10:42 PM	Application	279 KB
SLUtility.exe	3/6/2018 11:28 AM	Application	555 KB
UWFUtility.exe	10/14/2019 3:42 PM	Application	583 KB

11. Create a System32 folder under C:\WinData\DS64P1\$OEM$ Folders\$$.
12. Copy the custom Group Policy folder to C:\WinData\DS64P1\$OEM$ Folders\$$.

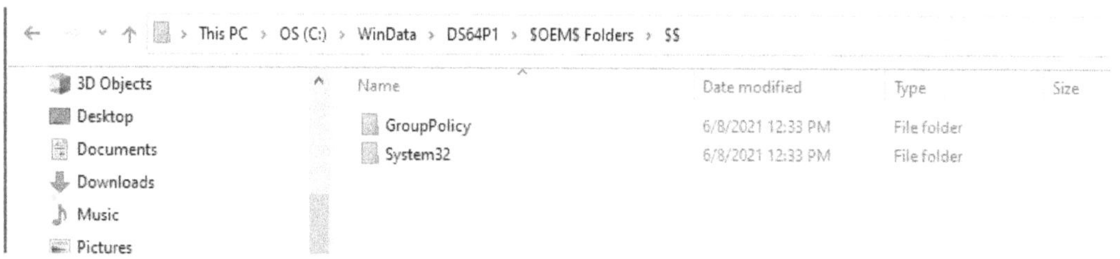

13. Create a Sysprep folder under C:\WinData\DS64P1\$OEM$ Folders\$$\System32.

17.4.2 Create the Answer File

Now, let's create the answer file.

1. With the Windows 10 Enterprise LTSC 2021 catalog and newly created distribution share open, create a new answer file in SIM.
2. In the distribution share, right-click on the folder containing the drivers and select "Insert Pass 2 offlineServicing".
3. Using the following table, add the components and settings to the answer file.

Component	Configuration Pass	Component Setting	Possible Value / Notes
amd64_Microsoft-Windows-International-Core-WinPE__neutral	1 WindowsPE	InputLocale	en-US
	1 WindowsPE	SystemLocale	en-US
	1 WindowsPE	UILanguage	en-US
	1 WindowsPE	UILanguageFallback	en-US
	1 WindowsPE	UserLocale	en-US
	1 WindowsPE	SetupUILanguage : UILanguage	En-US
amd64_Microsoft-Windows-Setup__neutral	1 WindowsPE	UserData: AcceptEULA	True
	1 WindowsPE	UserData : ProductKey : Key	<Enter the license key>
	1 WindowsPE	UserData : ProductKey: WillShowUI	OnError

Component	Configuration Pass	Component Setting	Possible Value / Notes
	1 WindowsPE	ImageInstall: OSImage : InstallFrom: MetaData: Key *(right-click to create option)*	/IMAGE/NAME
	1 WindowsPE	ImageInstall: OSImage : InstallFrom: MetaData: Value	Windows 10 Enterprise LTSC 2021
amd64_Microsoft-Windows-Embedded-BootExp__neutral	4 Specialize	DisableBootMenu	1
	4 Specialize	HideBootLogo	1
	4 Specialize	HideBootStatusMessage	1
amd64_Microsoft-Windows-Embedded-EmbeddedLogon__neutral	4 Specialize	AnimationDisabled	1
	4 Specialize	BrandingNeutral	1
	4 Specialize	HideAutoLogonUI	1
	4 Specialize	NoLockScreen	1
amd64_Microsoft-Windows-Shell-Setup__neutral	4 Specialize	ComputerName	*
	4 Specialize	RegisteredOwner	ACME
	4 Specialize	TimeZone	Pacific Standard Time
amd64_Microsoft-Windows-International-Core__neutral	7 OOBE System	InputLocale	en-US
	7 OOBE System	SystemLocale	en-US
	7 OOBE System	UILanguage	en-US
	7 OOBE System	UserLocale	en-US
amd64_Microsoft-Windows-Shell-Setup__neutral	7 OOBE System	AutoLogon: Username	User1
	7 OOBE System	AutoLogon: Enabled	True
	7 OOBE System	AutoLogon: LogonCount	4294967294
	7 OOBE System	AutoLogon: Password: Value	password
	7 OOBE System	OOBE : HideEULAPage	True
	7 OOBE System	OOBE : HideLocalAccountScreen	True
	7 OOBE System	OOBE : HideOEMRegistrationScreen	True
	7 OOBE System	OOBE : HideOnlineAccountScreen	True
	7 OOBE System	OOBE : HideWirelessSetupInOOBE	True
	7 OOBE System	OOBE : ProtectYourPC	3
	7 OOBE System	UserAccounts : LocalAccounts : LocalAccount : Description	WeatherAdmin
	7 OOBE System	UserAccounts : LocalAccounts : LocalAccount : DisplayName	WeatherAdmin
	7 OOBE System	UserAccounts : LocalAccounts : LocalAccount :Group	Administrators
	7 OOBE System	UserAccounts : LocalAccounts : LocalAccount : Name	WeatherAdmin

Component	Configuration Pass	Component Setting	Possible Value / Notes
	7 OOBE System	UserAccounts : LocalAccounts : LocalAccount : Password : Value	password

4. Add the amd64_Microsoft-Windows-Foundation-Package and set the following items.

Package	Windows Feature Selection	Possible Value / Notes
amd64_Microsoft-Windows-Foundation-Package	Client-DeviceLockdown	Enabled
	Client-EmbeddedBootExp	Enabled
	Client-Embedded-Logon	Enabled
	Client-EmbeddedShellLauncher	Enabled
	Client-KeyboardFilter	Disable
	Client-UnifiedWriteFilter	Enabled

Note: The keyboard filter is disabled, but could be enabled if required.

5. Add the following Pass 7 Synchronous commands:

Order	Synchronous Command
1	powercfg.exe /IMPORT C:\Setup\weatherplan.pow 571FFEB9-38E3-4EAA-9DF0-972D8C6323FB
2	powercfg.exe /S 571FFEB9-38E3-4EAA-9DF0-972D8C6323FB
3	powercfg.exe /H OFF
4	Secedit.exe /configure /db temp.sdb /cfg C:\setup\Project1.inf
5	C:\setup\windowsdesktop-runtime-6.0.5-win-x64.exe /install /quiet /norestart
6	cmd.exe /C rd /S /Q c:\Windows\ConfigSetRoo
7	bcdedit /set {current} bootstatuspolicy ignoreallfailures

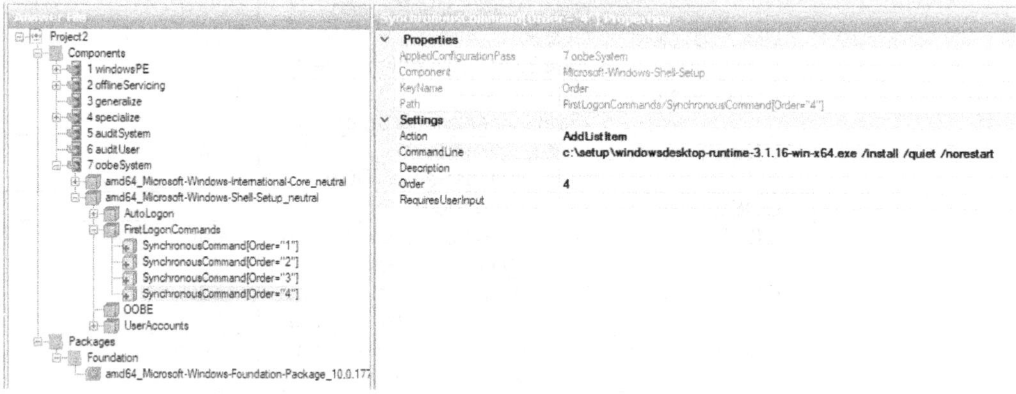

6. Save the answer file to C:\WinData as "Project1.xml".
7. Close the Answer file.

17.4.3 Create the Sysprep unattended file

1. In SIM, create a new Answer file.
2. Use the following table to fill in the components and settings for the answer file

Component	Configuration Pass	Component Setting	Possible Value / Notes
amd64_Microsoft-Windows-PnpSysprep__neutral	3 generalize	PersistAllDeviceInstalls	true
amd64_Microsoft-Windows-Embedded-BootExp__neutral	4 Specialize	DisableBootMenu	1
	4 Specialize	HideBootLogo	1
	4 Specialize	HideBootStatusMessage	1
amd64_Microsoft-Windows-Embedded-EmbeddedLogon__neutral	4 Specialize	AnimationDisabled	1
	4 Specialize	BrandingNeutral	1
	4 Specialize	HideAutoLogonUI	1
	4 Specialize	NoLockScreen	1
amd64_Microsoft-Windows-Shell-Setup__neutral	4 Specialize	ComputerName	*
	4 Specialize	ProductKey	<Enter the license key>
	4 Specialize	RegisteredOwner	ACME
	4 Specialize	TimeZone	Pacific Standard Time
amd64_Microsoft-Windows-International-Core__neutral	7 OOBE System	InputLocale	en-US
	7 OOBE System	SystemLocale	en-US
	7 OOBE System	UILanguage	en-US
	7 OOBE System	UserLocale	en-US
amd64_Microsoft-Windows-Shell-Setup__neutral	7 OOBE System	AutoLogon: Username	User1
	7 OOBE System	AutoLogon: Enabled	True
	7 OOBE System	AutoLogon: LogonCount	4294967294
	7 OOBE System	AutoLogon: Password: Value	password
	7 OOBE System	OOBE : HideEULAPage	True
	7 OOBE System	OOBE : HideLocalAccountScreen	True
	7 OOBE System	OOBE : HideOEMRegistrationScreen	True
	7 OOBE System	OOBE : HideOnlineAccountScreen	True
	7 OOBE System	OOBE : HideWirelessSetupInOOBE	True
	7 OOBE System	OOBE : ProtectYourPC	3
	7 OOBE System	OOBE : SkipMachineOOBE	True
	7 OOBE System	OOBE : SkipUserOOBE	True

Component	Configuration Pass	Component Setting	Possible Value / Notes
	7 OOBE System	UserAccounts : LocalAccounts : LocalAccount : Description	WeatherAdmin
	7 OOBE System	UserAccounts : LocalAccounts : LocalAccount : DisplayName	WeatherAdmin
	7 OOBE System	UserAccounts : LocalAccounts : LocalAccount :Group	Administrators
	7 OOBE System	UserAccounts : LocalAccounts : LocalAccount : Name	WeatherAdmin
	7 OOBE System	UserAccounts : LocalAccounts : LocalAccount : Password : Value	password

3. Add the following Pass 7 Synchronous commands:

Order	Synchronous Command
1	reg.exe add HKLM\SOFTWARE\Policies\Microsoft\Windows\WindowsUpdate /v DoNotConnectToWindowsUpdateInternetLocations /t REG_DWORD /d 1 /f
2	reg.exe add HKLM\SOFTWARE\Policies\Microsoft\Windows\WindowsUpdate /v ExcludeWUDriversInQualityUpdate /t REG_DWORD /d 1 /f
3	reg.exe add HKLM\SOFTWARE\Policies\Microsoft\Windows\WindowsUpdate /v SetDisableUXWUAccess /t REG_DWORD /d 1 /f
4	reg.exe add HKLM\SOFTWARE\Policies\Microsoft\Windows\WindowsUpdate\AU /v NoAutoUpdate /t REG_DWORD /d 1 /f
5	Sc.exe stop wuauserv
6	Sc.exe config wuauserv start= disabled
7	schtasks /Change /TN "\Microsoft\Windows\WindowsUpdate\Scheduled Start" /Disable
8	powershell -ExecutionPolicy RemoteSigned -File C:\setup2\dgreadiness_v3.6\DG_Readiness_Tool_v3.6.ps1 -Enable -SIPolicyPath C:\setup2\SIPolicy.p7b
9	"C:\Program Files\Annabooks\shlmgr.exe" enable
10	uwfmgr.exe filter enable
90	shutdown.exe /r /t 5

4. Save the Answer file to C:\WinData\DS64P1\$OEM$ Folders\$$\System32\Sysprep as: Project1-un.xml".

17.5 Build, Deploy, and Run Sysprep

With both answer files created, it is time to test the image.

17.5.1 Build and Deploy

1. If there is a "CS" folder under C:\WinData make sure it is cleared out. If you don't have a "CS" folder under C:\WinData, create one.

2. In SIM, open the Project1.xml file.
3. From the menu, select “Tools->Create Configuration Set”.
4. Set the path for the configuration set to C:\WinData\CS and set the OEM folder path to C:\WinData\DS64P1\OEM Folders

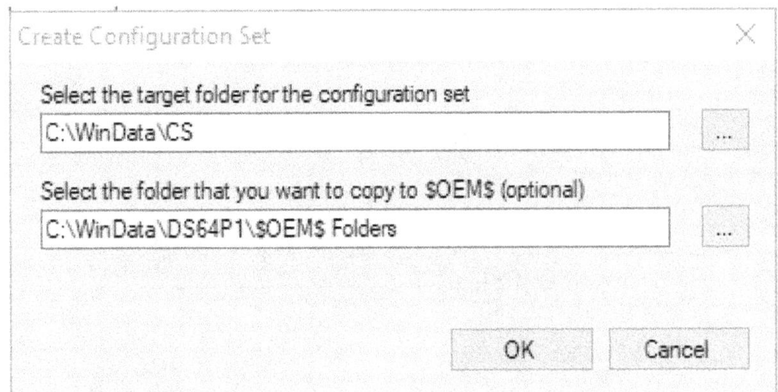

5. Click “OK” to create the configuration set.
6. Plugin a USB flash disk.
7. Open the Rufus utility(https://rufus.ie/).
8. Make sure that your flash disk is the selected “Device”.
9. Set the Boot selection to UEFI:NTFS (Note: you may have to expand the drive properties or show the advanced format option to get this Boot selection option).
10. The File system should be set to NTFS.

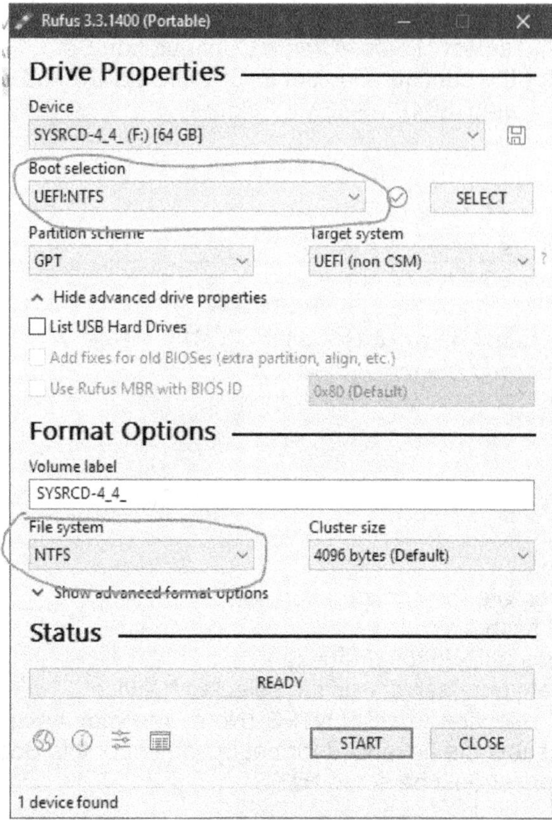

11. Optional: change the volume name to your liking.
12. Click "Start" – The USB flash disk will be split into two partitions: a small boot FAT partition and a larger NTFS partition.
13. Mount the Windows 10 Enterprise LTSC 2021 ISO/IMG file and copy the contents to the NTFS partition of the USB flash disk.
14. Copy the configuration set to the NTFS partition.
15. Safely eject the USB flash disk.
16. Plug the USB flash disk into the target system.
17. Power on the target system, and set the BIOS to boot to the USB flash disk.
18. The setup program will eventually display the partition options. Clear out any partition and click on the unallocated partition and click "Next".

17.5.2 Run WDAC PowerShell Script

The installation process will take some time. The system will eventually come to the Windows Desktop

1. Open PowerShell with Administrative privileges.
2. Run the WDAC-Enforce.ps1 script. This will take some time.

3. When the process is finished, make sure the SiPolicy.p7b file is in the C:\Setup2 folder. The file will be copied to the Windows\System32\CodeIntegrity folder when the DGReadiness script runs during mini-setup.

17.5.3 Run Windows Update, Optional Shrink Image, and Cleanup

Now, we need to run Windows Update to get the latest updates.

1. Click on "Start->Settings".
2. Click on "Updates & Security".
3. Click on "Check for Updates". This will take a while, and you will have to reboot the system. Typically, a new image will have a few extra updates, but future updates should be limited to about 3 – cumulative, security, and Windows Defender.
4. Re-run Check for Updates until there are no more updates found.
5. Now that the updates have been installed, you can run the last Footprint Reduction script and remove items that are not needed for this application.

Note: Since the Footprint Reduction script is a moving target as of this writing, we will not be specific on what to remove.

6. Open a PowerShell command window with administrative privileges, and run the following:

```
Dism.exe /online /Cleanup-Image /StartComponentCleanup /Resetbase
```

The process will take a few minutes.

7. Open Control Panel.
8. Open Administrative Tools.
9. Run Disk Clean Up.
10. Click "OK" to clean up drive C.
11. In the Disk Clean Up dialog, if there is a button to clean up system files, click the button.
12. Select all items and click OK.
13. Click OK to confirm disk clean-up.

17.5.4 Run Sysprep

1. In PowerShell, change the directory to C:\Windows\System32\Sysprep.
2. Run the following command:

Sysprep.exe /generalize /oobe /shutdown /unattend:C:\Windows\System32\Syprep\Project1-un.xml

3. Sysprep will run and shut down the system.
4. Typically, at this point, the image would be captured to an FFU file. We will skip this since this is a test. Boot the target system and let it run through mini-setup.

Once the mini-setup has completed, Weather1 will launch as the shell and start displaying the sensor information. The data will be sent to the Azure IoT Central Weather Application. After observing the operation for a time, you can shut down the system.

17.6 Delete the Weather Application in Azure IoT Central

If you are no longer going to use the Weather application in Azure IoT Central, it can be deleted.

1. Log into your Azure IoT Central Account.
2. Go to My apps->Weather.
3. In the Weather application, go to Administration, and click the "Delete" button to delete the application.
4. Click the "Delete" button in the dialog to confirm the deletion.
5. The request for information dialog can be skipped

17.7 Summary

After 16 chapters, this single chapter demonstrated using the workflow to create a custom image with an application that accesses I/O and sends data to the cloud. Many of the features discussed in this book were implemented in this exercise. The project is just an example and other customization steps can be considered, such as blocking USB ports, disabling Windows Hotkeys, removing unneeded items, and providing for upgrading the system in the field. The exercise covered application and image development together. Typically, these are separate tasks. The goal of the exercise was to give you a good understanding of the process and all the feature setup that has to go into a custom Windows 10 IoT Enterprise LTSC image.

A Bibliography

Besides the online help files, various books, articles, websites, and presentations were used in the development of this book.

a. Books

Starter Guide for Windows® 10 IoT Enterprise, Sean D. Liming and John R. Malin, 2017, ISBN-13: 978-0-9911887-2-7

Starter Guide for Windows® System Image Manager, Sean D. Liming and John R. Malin, 2013, ISBN-13: 978-0-9859461-8-0

Professional's Guide to Windows® Embedded 8 Standard, Sean D. Liming, Annabooks, 2013, ISBN: 978-0-9859461-4-2

Professional's Guide to Windows® Embedded Standard 7, Sean D. Liming, Annabooks, 2010, ISBN: 978-0-9842801-1-7

Real-Time Development from Theory to Practice, John R. Malin and Sean D. Liming, Annabooks, 2009, ISBN-13: 978-0-9842801-0-0

Windows NT Embedded Step-By-Step, Sean D. Liming, Annabooks, 2000, ISBN: 0-929392-68-X

Windows XP Embedded Advanced, Sean D. Liming, RTC Books, 2003, ISBN: 0-929392-77-9

Windows XP Embedded Supplemental Toolkit, Sean D. Liming, Cedar Hill Publishing, 2005, ISBN 1-932373-96-9

Professional's Guide To .NET Micro Framework Application Development, John R. Malin and Sean D. Liming, Annabooks, 2012, ISBN-13: 978-0-9842801-9-3

Windows Internals 5th Edition, Mark E. Russinovich and David A. Solomon, Microsoft press, 2009, ISBN-13: 978-0-7356-2530-3

Inside Windows NT, Helen Custer, Microsoft Press, 1993, ISBN: 1-55615-481-X

b. Articles

"***UP Square (UP2) Board Firmware Settings to Enable SPI/I2C/GPIO/UART for Windows 10 IoT Enterprise***", Sean Liming and John R. Malin, Annabooks.com, January 2021.

"***UP Board Firmware Settings to Enable SPI/I2C/GPIO/UART for Windows 10 IoT Enterprise***", Sean Liming and John R. Malin, Annabooks.com, December 2020.

"***Windows ADK: Checking Run-Time License Key Activations with the Volume Activation Management Tool***", Sean Liming and John R. Malin, Annabooks.com, November 2020.

"***Windows 10 IoT Enterprise: Image Development Workflow***", Sean Liming and John R. Malin, Annabooks.com, September 2020

"***Windows 10 IoT Enterprise: Why No Components Like Previous Windows Embedded Releases?***", Sean Liming and John R. Malin, Annabooks.com, February 2020

"***Windows 10 IoT Enterprise (17763): Block Device Installation***", Sean Liming and John R. Malin, Annabooks.com, September 2019

"***How to Get Started with Windows 10 IoT Licensing***", Sean Liming and John R. Malin, Annabooks.com, August 2019

"***DISM + FFU Capture and Restore an Image***", Sean Liming and John R. Malin, Annabooks.com, February 2019

"***Windows® 10 IoT Enterprise: Multi-Project / Multi-Platform Support in SIM***", Sean Liming and John R. Malin, Annabooks.com, July 2018

"***Windows 10 IoT Enterprise (14393): Turn Off Windows Update and Managing Updates***", Sean Liming and John R. Malin, Annabooks.com, May 2018

"***Industrial PC Requirements to Access GPIO/I2C/SPI/UART from Windows 10 UWP Applications***", Sean Liming and John R. Malin, Annabooks.com, January 2018

"***C++ Q&A: Typename, Disabling Keys in Windows XP with TrapKeys***", Paul DiLascia, MSDN Magazine, September 2002.

"***Different Shells for Different Users***", Sean Liming, MSDN.Microsoft.com. August 2003.

"***Installing FireFox Browser on WES 7***", Sean Liming and John R. Malin, seanliming.com, April 2010.

"***Installing Java on WES 7***", Sean Liming and John R. Malin, seanliming.com, April 2010.

"***Custom Power Settings for WES 7/8 and WEI 8.x***", Sean D. Liming and John R. Malin, www.annabooks.com, May 2014

c. Websites

INtime and eVM information was found at the TenAsys website: http://www.tenasys.com

Force firmware code to be measured and attested by Secure Launch on Windows 10 – Microsoft Blog

Secure the Windows boot process - Windows security – Microsoft Docs

System Guard Secure Launch and SMM protection (Windows 10) - Windows security – Microsoft Docs

Secure boot - Microsoft Docs

Enable virtualization-based protection of code integrity - Microsoft Docs

Windows Defender Device Guard and Windows Defender Credential Guard hardware readiness tool - Microsoft Docs

Windows Defender Application Control and virtualization-based code integrity (Windows 10) - Windows security – Microsoft Docs

Microsoft recommended block rules (Windows) - Windows security - Microsoft Docs

Decode Measured Boot logs to track PCR changes - Windows security - Microsoft Docs

About the Authors

Sean Liming is owner of Annabooks. He has been involved with embedded systems for over two decades and has authored several articles and books, including the popular *Windows XP Embedded Advanced* and *Professional's Guide to Windows® Embedded Standard 7*. Sean has worked at Intel and Annasoft Systems, and had been a Microsoft MVP since 2002. He received his BSEE from California State Polytechnic University in Pomona, California, where he focused on computer architecture and design.

John R. Malin was an early pioneer in using IBM-PC's to develop embedded software for x86-based embedded devices in the mid 80's. Over the past 20 years, John has worked with a number of embedded operating systems starting with VRTX, Nucleus, PharLap, ThreadX, Windows CE, XP Embedded, Windows Embedded Standard, and .NET Micro Framework. He has also co-authored a number of articles, white papers covering embedded development, and the book *Real-Time Development from Theory to Practice*. John is a cofounder of Annabooks, LLC and has a BS and MS in Solid State Physics from Case Western Reserve University.

Index

O

P

R

S

T

U

V

W